ALSO BY SCOTT PETERSON

Me Against My Brother: At War in Somalia, Sudan, and Rwanda

Let the Swords

IRAN—A JOURNEY

Encircle Me

BEHIND THE HEADLINES

SCOTT PETERSON

SIMON & SCHUSTER

New York   London   Toronto   Sydney

Simon & Schuster
1230 Avenue of the Americas
New York, NY 10020

First Simon & Schuster hardcover edition September 2010

SIMON & SCHUSTER and colophon are registered trademarks
of Simon & Schuster, Inc.

For information about special discounts for bulk purchases,
please contact Simon & Schuster Special Sales at
1-866-506-1949 or business@simonandschuster.com.

The Simon & Schuster Speakers Bureau can bring authors
to your live event. For more information or to book an event,
contact the Simon & Schuster Speakers Bureau at
1-866-248-3049 or visit our website at www.simonspeakers.com.

Designed by Ruth Lee-Mui

Manufactured in the United States of America

10 9 8 7 6 5 4 3 2 1

Library of Congress Cataloging-in-Publication Data

Peterson, Scott, date.
    Let the swords encircle me : Iran—a journey behind the headlines /
Scott Peterson.—1st Simon & Schuster hardcover ed.
        p.   cm.
    Includes bibliographical references and index.
    1. Iran—History—1979–1997.   2. Iran—History—1997–   3. Iran—Politics and
government—1979–1997.   4. Iran—Politics and government—1997–   5. Iran—
Social conditions—1979–1997.   6. Iran—Social conditions—1997–   7. Iran—Foreign
relations—United States.   8. United States—Foreign relations—Iran.   I. Title.
    DS318.8.P49   2010
    955.05'4—dc22   2010017761
ISBN 978-1-4165-9728-5
ISBN 978-1-4165-9739-1 (ebook)

For Iranians, with hope that they will one day achieve the freedom they so desire, and so deserve;

and for four hearts that beat with the promise of understanding, as they make their way in this world:

Olivia Rose
Guy Aragorn Grey
Finn Daniel Sirajiddin
Natasha Jade Samarra

Contents

Legend holds that on the desert plains of Karbala in 680 A.D., Imam Hossein saw the insistence of the enemy, tens of thousands strong, to kill him and his small band of Believers. He spoke these defiant words, baring his chest before the blades, and immortalizing himself as the Lord of the Martyrs:

"If the religion of Mohammad will only endure with my death, then *Oh, let the swords encircle me!*"

Let the Swords Encircle Me

Introduction

"Because for us, the war is not over . . ."

Fʀᴏᴍ ʜɪꜱ ꜰɪʀꜱᴛ ʙʀᴇᴀᴛʜ, the bearded Believer invokes divine power, for among the most devout every communication begins: "In the name of God, the Merciful, the Compassionate . . ."

This Iranian holy warrior chooses his words deliberately, speaking to me in 1998 in a cramped office in the mosque at Tehran University, where the threadbare furnishings and plain walls mark a monastic preoccupation with issues of the spirit.

His eyes are fearless. And with the certainty of an evangelist on a mission of conversion, Dr. Alireza Zakani is about to take me back with him to the marshy, trench-laced battlefields of the Iran-Iraq War of the 1980s. He was wounded ten times and survived fifteen major offensives that remain among the bloodiest engagements in modern warfare.

Zakani was just fifteen when he volunteered for the carnage, breaking the age rules to join what he believed to be a "sacred" war. The fight had sparked a spiritual reckoning for Iran, deepened zeal for Iran's 1979 Islamic Revolution, and forged a militant ideology that today forms the bedrock of the Islamic Republic. In their eagerness to get to the war—to prove their faith, their purity of heart—young men would alter the birth date on their identity cards so they could "legally" sign up for combat.

Zakani was as religious as he was eager. His forehead is marked with the indelible dark smudge of a life spent in daily prayer, by the clay disk that Shiite Muslims bend down and press with their heads five times a day, to physically connect with the earth from whence they came.

"We didn't enter the battlefield to become martyrs, only to defend Islam and the Revolution," intones Zakani, his paralyzed right hand resting limply by his side.[1] "But we knew that if we died, we were going to be martyrs, and that was important to us. So we would have victory either way. If we died, we still won—martyrdom is the highest aim."

Still today, that collective war experience is alive, and affects every aspect of Iran's politics and worldview. Iranians call it the "Imposed War," launched in 1980 when Iraqi forces invaded Iran. The turbulent Islamic Revolution ushered in by Ayatollah Ruhollah Khomeini was still young and vulnerable. Then it was beset by a horrific war of attrition and Iraqi chemical weapon attacks that left one million dead and wounded on both sides.

The Revolution survived, but even Saddam Hussein felt obliged to mark the scale of the slaughter. Halfway through the war, in Baghdad, he built the towering crossed-swords monument, its hands larger-than-life metal replicas of those of the Iraqi dictator. When I first saw it in the late 1990s, what struck me most was not the magnificence of the swords, but the nets filled with five thousand Iranian helmets from the battlefield.[2]

The Iranian beliefs forged in that crucible—where the Iraqi enemy drew overt and covert support from the West—are one cause of the still-bitter estrangement between the United States and Iran. The war became a vehicle to enhance hatred for both sides. In Iran throughout those eight years of conflict, anti-American vitriol became more and more a pillar of Iranian policy. And in America, anti-Revolution disdain led the United States to provide Saddam with satellite intelligence, to make Iraq's chemical weapon attacks even more lethal.

Inside Iran, the trauma of the conflict meant that ever afterward,

True Believers like Zakani would seek to impose their grip on the rest of Iran's diverse society. After such wartime sacrifices, these ideologues saw themselves as Iran's self-appointed moral authority, tasked with "defending" the Revolution against all threats, especially those from the West. They wanted to convert their wartime scar tissue into a divine right to rule.

When I first met Dr. Zakani in 1998, that small office was far from the front lines, both in years and miles. At the heart of Tehran University, the mosque is on the edge of a vast asphalted space with a high roof, where carpets are laid down every Friday and prayers attract thousands. Among the revolutionary banners, this saying from Ayatollah Khomeini has long endured: "We will resist America until our last breath." Prayer leaders hold the barrel of an AK-47 assault rifle in one hand while they lead the nation in ritual anti-Western chants.

The rest of the week it is quieter. And so it was when I found Zakani at the mosque office, transported from the present to a past that was very close to his soul. He was back in the reeds, tasting the ingrained dirt of the trenches, breathing the pungent smell of exploding shells, and hearing the air-slicing whistle of blast-hot shrapnel. More than anything, he was reaffirming his conviction that it was God's war, a battle to proselytize, to convert pagan Iraqis to God's way, to prove His transcendent supremacy. Zakani was doing divine work fighting along the southern front, and found inspiration and evidence of it everywhere.

But nearly a decade after the conflict, Zakani's type was no longer the majority. This was because the same war that bonded Iranians with a new national unity—doing so much to solidify the Islamic Revolution—also sowed seeds of deeper division in Iranian society. The spiritual sense with which tens of thousands marched to the front line was not shared by all.

So the war experience magnified the social rift in Iran between those who fought and bled, and those others—most often wealthy residents of north Tehran who had the means to flee the country—who rejected all notions of a "sacred war" and skipped out on its dangers.

Even among war veterans, many were growing disillusioned by the repressive authoritarianism and incompetence of the clerical regime, traits which they thought were undermining the very freedoms they had fought for.

It was all these Iranians, the moderates who sometimes leaned toward the West, and war veterans and other revolutionaries adrift in their fear of permanent social and political stagnation, who had in 1997 voted President Mohammad Khatami to the highest elected position in the country, by a landslide. Those voters wanted to keep their Revolution, but they also wanted to reform it.

The back-and-forth between these hard-line and reformist factions—sometimes taking place brutally on the streets, beyond the ballot box—has defined politics in Iran since the Revolution. The winner determines whether Iran should be more a militarized Islamic theocratic state, issuing orders from on high to a spiritualized and compliant populace—which doesn't really exist so neatly in Iran—or whether Iran's self-declared status as a "republic," dependent for legitimacy on the democratic will of the people, should prevail.

That very contest was at the root of the disputed election of June 2009, when the controversial archconservative President Mahmoud Ahmadinejad was declared the unexpected landslide victor. What is not in dispute is that more than 80 percent of Iranians turned out to vote—the highest level ever in a presidential race—because many thought their vote could dislodge the hard-line incumbent. Iran's Supreme Leader Ayatollah Seyyed Ali Khamenei immediately praised the result as a "divine assessment." But many Iranians called it a coup d'état against democracy. Weeks of violence and bloodshed ensued, searing the legacy of Iran's Revolution with unprecedented division.

Now the regime was creating new martyrs—for democracy. Officially, just thirty-six Iranians died in that first burst, though some reports said there were more than two hundred in Tehran alone. Among the dead was Neda Agha Soltan, a twenty-six-year-old activist shot at close range by a *basiji* militiaman passing on a motorcycle. Cell phone footage of her death, of the blood flooding obscenely out of her mouth and nose and across her face, turned Neda's demise into the iconic image of Iran's tumult.

The mask had slipped.

Thirty years after the Revolution, its innate savagery was exposed again and now raw. Many Iranians were enraged. Many were afraid. Some were murderous. Some burned posters of the Supreme Leader. The streets echoed with the chants of "Death to the Dictator" and "Death to Khamenei." The Islamic Republic—at least down the militarized path where Khamenei had chosen to steer it—had created its own crisis of legitimacy. In the minds of countless Iranians, the regime itself was subverting the Revolution's original founding principle of freedom.

"The Revolution is your legacy," opposition leader Mir Hossein Mousavi declared to rally his supporters.[3] "To protest against lies and fraud is your right. Be hopeful that you will get your right and do not allow others who want to provoke your anger . . . to prevail."

At the peak of the violence in June 2009, Khamenei called the protesters "enemies" who sought to depict Iran's "definitive victory as a doubtful victory."[4] Those enemies would be crushed. There was no fraud. How could there be compromise over "God's blessing"?

The Revolution was no longer about the will of the people, the gold standard that had often been held up by Ayatollah Khomeini as a crucial basis of legitimacy. Instead, in one decisive power play in 2009, the contest was hijacked by the most extreme factions in politics. Iranians had witnessed the culmination of a years-long effort to revitalize hard-line conservative rule and make it permanent. With critical roles played by Iran's elite Revolutionary Guard and Basij militia, religious ideology was morphing into militarism.

"Do not be worried about the events and earthquakes that have occurred. Know that God created this world as a test," the ultraconservative Ayatollah Mohammad Taghi Mesbah-Yazdi told the Revolutionary Guard.[5] "The Supreme Leader holds a great many of the blessings God has given us, and at a time of such uncertainties our eyes must turn to him."

• • •

IN SO MANY WAYS, Iran's revolutionary generation has failed to come to terms with itself. For three decades, powerful forces have stood in tension with each other, the religious hard-liners against the secular moderates; those who demand isolation against those who yearn for contact with the West. The result has been a destructive imbalance in Iran's "sacred" political system—one that I have seen played out during the latter half of Iran's Revolution.

What for some Iranians is a dated, irrelevant governing philosophy holding the country back in political, economic, and cultural seclusion is for True Believers still the only one that counts. And the example of that frontline doctor I met in 1998 helps to understand why. Back then, Dr. Zakani's political and religious certitude could be measured in the lines etched across his face, and the heart he put into the ideals of the Revolution.

"I knew it even then, that this Revolution brought us self-respect, self-understanding. It gave us the gift of freedom," the fighter turned doctor told me. He specialized in pediatrics after the war, before eventually turning to hard-line politics.

Of the three points of the rhyming (in Farsi) revolutionary slogan "Independence, Freedom, Islamic Republic," it was independence from Iran's painful past, the history of constant manipulations by outside powers, that resonated with Zakani. For him, Iraq's 1980 invasion was simply the latest attempt by Western enemies—after imposing sanctions and fomenting internal unrest—to topple the regime. "We went to break the chain of these plots, to defend our holy Revolution," Zakani told me. He predicted that another war would be "imposed upon us" by the West. The conspiracy was a reality for Zakani and his comrades.

A decade later, Iran really *would* be surrounded by the forces of its archenemy, with tens of thousands of U.S. troops east and west, in neighboring Afghanistan and Iraq, and to the south the U.S. Navy's Fifth Fleet, based in Bahrain. The regional tug-of-war was under way, Zakani told me: "I believe, and the revolutionary people believe, that the U.S. will not leave us alone. So they will try to impose problems. The Americans are watching us."

To this day Iran paints the current standoff with the United States and the West the same way it did the war with Iraq in the 1980s: with broad strategic and religious brushstrokes. Zakani's decision to volunteer for the war—like that of so many of his fellow fighters—was in response to the personal charisma of Ayatollah Khomeini, the man they called God's Deputy on Earth.

"Giving us this feeling to fight was one of the miracle arts of Imam Khomeini—he inspired people to religion," Zakani told me. Khomeini's "biggest gift" to Iranian believers was the sense of invincible justice, that the Iraq war was a "jihad to save Islam." Hardships were severe: steaming temperatures in the south, or freezing snows in the mountains of the northwestern front. The ever-present chance of death. And yet there was a worse fate: *only* severe wounding, perhaps from chemical weapons, and so no glory of martyrdom.

"A lot of dust built up on Islam over the centuries. The Imam shook off the dust and showed the realities of this religion to find the real Islam," Zakani told me, growing animated at the significance of the event. The Revolution aimed to create an Islamic government, he said, but also "had a much further extended message for outside Iran—a message of spirituality for the outside world." These views were so dangerous to the West, believes Zakani, that it "was good reason for international oppressors to attack us."

Zakani's moment of epiphany came one night along the front, when Iranian frogmen directed his small boat with flashlights to an Iraqi position on an island. Hours of hand-to-hand combat ensued, and the Iranians prevailed. When it was over, after a meal and prayers of thanks, a rustle of reeds revealed more than twenty Iraqi soldiers in the water, waving white shirts of surrender. Instead of slaughtering them, Dr. Zakani and his unit tended to the three badly wounded Iraqis and shared some of their own "good bread," made from wheat and milk.

One of the treated Iraqi soldiers became very emotional and started to weep, Zakani recalled. "Now I know what is Islam," he said, and he then went back to the marsh to retrieve more and more surrendering Iraqis. For Zakani, it was evidence of how weak the enemy was, how devoid of spiritual motivation. It meant victory was Iran's. A victory that belonged to God.

"They were crying: 'Now I know where is Islam, and which side is atheism,' " Zakani told me. "That's what our real Islam is; see how we even treat our enemies? Yet in your country, the U.S., they introduce us as those who just want to fight. They show a different face."

FROM MY EARLIEST INTERVIEWS in Iran, the significance of such heartfelt ideology began to dawn on me. Over the course of more than thirty reporting visits to Iran since 1996—a depth of recent experience greater than any other American foreign correspondent—I have been able to probe a society that is largely, and often deliberately, hidden from Western eyes. Iran is a nation where the cultural and religious forces of light and darkness are seen to wage war; where every word, image, and sensibility is often, for an American, deliciously unexpected and counterintuitive.

Iran is also the most enigmatic, fascinating, and challenging nation, as drippingly sensuous as it can be violent; with a life-loving people imbued with a 2,500-year history of Persian pride, art, poetry, and passion.

Iran is a bastion of Islamic radicalism and resistance that has inspired militants for a generation and revels in the most sacred and mournful Shiite Muslim rites. It glories in the aspirations of martyrdom and the protest of flag burnings. Iran is also a charter member of President George W. Bush's Axis of Evil.

So getting Iran "right"—for their people, and for ours—should be the highest priority. This book aims to challenge the reader's perception of Iran by providing a revealing and realistic understanding of the Islamic Republic and the voices of its people that will be crucial when choices are made between peace and war.

For beyond a cabal of cantankerous hard-liners and an expanding nuclear program, Iran is a place awash with color and life that many Westerners would recognize. Don't confuse Iran with the monochromatic existences that marked the Taliban's Afghanistan or Saddam Hussein's Iraq, to the east and west of the Persian massif, or indeed either of those societies after the arrival of American troops—all of which I reported upon extensively.

Iran's social landscape could not be more different and more vibrant. It includes nose-job clinics and underground heavy metal bands, and malls jammed with irreverent and "Westoxicated" youth who go to parties sodden with alcohol, drugs, and pursuits of the flesh. It has a vocal population determined to create parallel realities of freedom, to temporarily remove their lives from clerical rule. It is also a nation full of ordinary people, getting by at work and at school, and with their families, who often shudder at the extremes they see around them and wish to remain untouched by any of it.

My journey for so many years has aimed to understand Iran, to discover and describe its human face, to hunt for common ground where it is to be found. I have sought to ease the persistent and dangerous prejudices that grew out of the takeover of the U.S. Embassy in Tehran in 1979. Popular anger in the United States found crass expression in bumper stickers that read I DON'T BRAKE FOR IRANIANS. When I was in high school, my running buddy gleefully wore a "Ban Iran" T-shirt. Crowds of militant Americans in Beverly Hills attacked Iranian students with baseball bats during the hostage crisis; elsewhere an Iranian student was subjected to what police called an "execution."[6]

The persistent prejudice was understood even by elementary school pupils in Tehran. In early 2008, a girl wearing a black chador came up to me and said shyly, "Can I ask you a question?"[7] She was part of a class trip to Khomeini's former place of preaching in an old neighborhood of north Tehran. She asked: "Do Americans think Iranians are riding camels and shooting here, there, and everywhere?"

"The problem is, Americans don't know us," complained Mahmoud Abdollahi, who worked for the government's press department.[8] Before the Revolution he was at film school in New York and told entertaining stories about narrowly escaping a beating by a gang in the Bronx while searching for a mosque. Iranians "have beards, but they are not terrorists," Abdollahi said. "They are human and have families and farms—just a different culture. I lived in your country, and I like your people so much." Holding his thick black beard in both hands, he was more pleading than hopeful: "You journalists have a holy job, more holy than the priest. You should work as a mirror; it's a heavy responsibility."

I often describe Iran as a paradise for journalists, where the tree of knowledge is ripe with counterintuitive succulence and therefore always sweet and unexpected. So I delighted in my early visas, recognizing them as forbidden fruit but realizing only years later how rare they were, and what geostrategic insight they would provide.

I have witnessed a crowd of Iranians spontaneously *prevent* an American flag being burned by militants. I have observed hot tears of sorrow and devotion falling at Iran's many war cemeteries. I have felt the powerful chants of thousands of men shake the ground as they pounded their chests in unison with religious fervor. I have played paintball in Tehran on five hundred tons of sand carried from the Caspian Sea; been to cinemas and vasectomy clinics; talked to female firefighters proud of rescuing women and children; found American NBA players scoring high in Iran's basketball leagues; and mourned with my distraught Iranian colleagues when a 2005 plane crash killed sixty-eight fellow journalists in Tehran.

And I have marveled at the joyful reaction on the street when I carried a large flower arrangement—Iran is a country with a flower shop on nearly every corner, and a history of paying floral tribute to friends and presidents alike. Walking on drab and broken sidewalks, Tehranis would lock eyes on the flowers, and I saw their faces brighten like a blessing as they were swept away from the tough daily grind to a lush Garden of Eden.

But these Persians with such a well-honed affection for flowers come from the same country which repeatedly sent assassination squads to Europe to kill regime opponents in the 1990s. The same country that killed or helped kill hundreds of Americans in attacks from Beirut to Baghdad. The same country full of Believers willing to sacrifice themselves in human wave attacks against Iraq in the 1980s, with pictures of Khomeini sewn crudely onto their uniforms and divine dreams in their minds.

Perhaps most precious of all, I have seen how Iranians cope with their unique regime: by adhering to, loving, and embracing it in the name of God; or attacking, vilifying, and undermining it, sometimes just to spite God. And while many Iranians despise rule by men in turbans, I have learned that few would accept any outsiders toying with that rule on their behalf. They want to grasp freedom for themselves, and wage with their own hands the internal battle that will define what that freedom means.

For just as Americans are so often proud of their nation, Iranians are fiercely proud of their own patriotism, their heritage, and of what it means to be Iranian.

FOR THOSE WHOSE LIVES span both societies, the heady sense of exceptionalism drawn from both Iran and the United States can be as untamable as it is enlightening. Witness the bald irreverence of a good friend of mine—let's call him Reza—and how he successfully shuttles between the iron-willed world of war veteran Zakani and the "corrupted" one of the West.

These two men represent the extremes. If Dr. Zakani sits at one end of Iran's broad social spectrum, then Reza sits at the other. Between them live the majority of Iranians, occupying a most fertile ground of varied voices, aspirations, and daily struggles.

Short and sure, Reza was raised in the United States and grated against authority—a characteristic common to both Americans and Iranians alike. He told me he had a "machine life" in America, of early starts, school, and work. But returning to Iran as a teenager in the mid-1990s was tough, too. He was stopped fourteen times in the first two months, his long hair and cowboy boots drawing the attention of hard-line morality police. A girlfriend at his side often complicated the picture. "I was in shock," Reza tells me. "They said: 'What the hell is this look?' Everybody used to be afraid at that time."[9]

But not Reza. These days he has a receding hairline and a face that can shift in a wink from earnest, attentive sobriety to a very mischievous smile. "Everything is here but freedom, and that can be bought," Reza informs me. He may be an extreme example—very unlike the average working Iranian—but he is also not alone as he pushes the envelope again and again. He had done his military service, for example, among the *basiji* militia, the outfit known for its uncompromising ideologues and rigorous religious training. "I was one of the hard-liners!" Reza says in disbelief.

But he was an impertinent soldier. Reza once humiliated an overbearing commander when ordered to make tea by secretly unzipping his trousers and dripping in three drops of his own urine. "I watched him drink my piss!" Reza exclaims triumphantly, and laughs at the practical joke. On a remote training base near the Caspian Sea, he selectively doled out gifts of marijuana, opium, pornography, and good Marlboro cigarettes, winning well-chosen friends who enabled him to break all the rules, so that he could fish when he wanted to and have campfires in the nearby forest. His homemade still produced alcohol that he carried in plastic Baggies.

For Reza, the God-sanctioned war of the 1980s for which Zakani was ready to die was nothing more than a meaningless illusion, a mythology used as a tool by fanatics to spread their fanaticism. But like many Iranians, Reza is also an operator, a master of deception who understands these competing trends in his own society and knows how to manipulate the system to get whatever he wants. His secret history includes teaching English at a university, where he parlayed his popular American accent into a job. But he was often buzzed from the booze he carried to class disguised in plastic water bottles, a clove of raw garlic ready in his pocket for a quick chew to mask the telltale scent of spirits. Persians, he told me, detest an overpowering odor of garlic on the breath.

Reza has appeared on Iranian television, also partly inebriated, in tearful scenes of devotion meant to encourage greater religiosity—acts he dismisses as "brainwashing." He can't stop chortling about the scene: "I had my little garlic and wore so much cologne, it was like a cloud!"

Reza is an absolute example of how Iranians often lead double lives and get away with it. I joined him one late night at a Tehran pool and sports complex, where he and some friends were sneak-drinking alcohol between sessions in the sauna. I enjoyed a swim, too, then the sauna, the heat made all the hotter by a boy whose job was to wave a towel vigorously as a fan, creating air flow and a furnace effect.

Afterward, when my glassy-eyed host finally got behind the wheel, he surveyed the glittering, empty avenues that stretched out below the north Tehran perch. He revved the engine like the practiced hot-rodder that he is, schooled in racing in Southern California during a very different youth. He turned to me with his hand on the stick shift, and boasted that he had once driven rally cars in the States. It was not an idle boast: Reza shot out of the parking lot, tires squealing, as my fear was swallowed by uncertainty—even marvel—at this flagrant display of fun in the uptight Islamic Republic.

We took flight, the car careening down the avenues, his friends racing alongside in their cars, windows down, music pumping on too-large and expensive speakers. It was a perfect re-creation of the rush of freedom I felt when growing up in America, pedal to the metal, with screaming music on a long stretch of deserted highway in Seattle. Reza gave voice to a fact rarely recognized by outsiders, which applies if you have money. Over the rushing wind, the roaring engine, and the pounding sound system, he slipped me a twisted grin and shouted, "In Iran, anything is possible!"

BUT NOTHING IS EASY, especially if you are an American journalist. To gauge the difficulties of reporting in Iran, and tapping into its complex political currents, consider my nine-year quest to cover a story that emerged in 1998, that day I interviewed Zakani, the front-line doctor. He had told me about the mysterious power that could still be found in the former battlefields along Iran's border with Iraq. The martyrs there spoke wisdom from a soil drenched in blood. Zakani wanted to send me on a quest to join an ideological tour of the front called the Followers of the Light Path.

Twice each year, the *basiji* organized bus trips for students to hear those voices, to see for themselves their spiritual pedigree. Perhaps I would like to visit with them? No Western journalist had ever been on such a tour, which was clearly a mechanism of spreading inspiration for the regime. Normally, such events were off-limits to foreigners, or at least very hard to find.

From his position as the head of the Basij students at Tehran University—the Iranian equivalent of an ideological ivory tower— Zakani acknowledged that not every Iranian believed as he did. But instead of the hostility that emanated from many of his fellow hardliners, he spoke in conciliatory tones about liberal Iranians. "It is natural that not everyone thinks the same way. We are convinced people are for the Revolution, but at the same time some are Westernized and have different views," Zakani told me. He noted that 98.2 percent of Iranians voted in favor of forming an Islamic Republic in 1979, the only time such a referendum was conducted.

"We try to attract them to us. We don't want to refuse them, except those who pull a gun on us," Zakani said. "We as fundamentalists believe we should make the rest aware, we should give them guidance; talk to them." This liberal crowd was only a "minority" and not a threat, he asserted. "But our response is to make sure it doesn't expand . . . this mandate has been given to us by the war."

I must have indicated a sufficient understanding of Zakani's words, for he honored me with a gift of a *basiji* scarf, a *chafiyeh,* its soft white cloth crosshatched with thin black lines in a pattern distinctive from the Palestinian version. It still had flecks of dried blood. It was a genuine relic, the same kind favored by Iran's young warriors as they strode into the fight—worn as a scarf, or used as a prayer rug, or turned into a tourniquet or makeshift bandage.

"We're trying to transfer these feelings and beliefs to the next generations, because for us the war is not over," Zakani told me. "The oppressors are always after us . . . so we must be wary." In many ways, he was right. Iran's "enemies" in the United States were "investing" in minority groups, he said, noting that $20 million had not long before been earmarked by the United States to undermine the regime.

And Zakani was finding success in passing on the message. He had letters of appreciation from students who had made the trip to the border, undergone a Saul-to-Paul conversion, and now embraced the sacred nature of the war. They described, in childish Persian penmanship, how the gritty, otherwise unremarkable battlefield had been transformed by their journey into a symbol for the most heroic legend of Shiite Muslim belief: the seventh-century martyrdom of Imam Hossein ibn Ali on the plains of Karbala, in modern-day Iraq. At the top of each questionnaire was printed this quotation, to put the students in the right mood: "Here is the center of the earth. Love was raised from here; here is also the ladder to the sky [heaven]."[10]

The new converts could not have been more eager. The first was a pharmacy student of modest religious commitment who now never missed her prayers.

"You may not believe that this letter is being written by a nineteen-year-old girl student," she began. "Come and hear my heart! Listen to what I want to say. Understand me that I never believed in the war front, in the fighters. Now would you believe how I think today?"

She explained how she had found her "real self," how she learned that "martyrs are witness and the martyrs would never leave us alone. They are always with us." She acknowledged that the place itself looked like any other. "But I tell you, brother, that's not true. You have to have a deep eye to see the difference . . . the ear to hear [the land] say what it has been witness to. If you don't believe me, wait until judgment day!"

The second testimonial came from the son of a martyr, who did not understand his father's sacrifice until he stood upon the spot. "I was here to find my father. Although I did not see him, I felt him and his comrades, and I truly believe that in all the moments of your life, the martyrs are watching your actions. And if you really don't follow their sacred goals, they would not be happy with us."

After receiving Dr. Zakani's invitation, I wanted to go, too. I was eager to push the limits of what was possible for a foreign journalist to do in Iran, which would enable me to glimpse one of the fundamental seedbeds of the Islamic Republic. As a seeker of revelatory experience—how better to tell human stories?—I could see that such a journey would be rich with emotive power. But it was almost a decade and many frustrating but useful lessons later before I would get close to Iran's former front lines, to feel for myself the revolutionary magic that still grips and inspires Iran's True Believers and sustains the ideology of the regime.

My own saga to get there tells much about Iran today: How steadfast and ideological it can be. How self-defeating its bureaucracy so often is. And how remarkably similar on many levels Iranians and Americans truly are. That unexpected revelation helps explain the rancor of the U.S.-Iran divide all these years—what prideful fighter wants to be the first to give in? Further experience gave me one reason after another to take seriously warnings about the risks of any U.S. conflict with Iran, or of even believing that it is possible to "defeat" the Islamic system until it corrodes further and eventually defeats itself.

Before I got anywhere near the border, I needed permission from the Ministry of Culture and Islamic Guidance, which handles all Western press requests. When in 1998 I first broached my interest in making the trip with students and other pilgrims on the Followers of the Light Path tour, or Rahian-e Nour, these officials were dismissive.

"The border? No, no chance of that," I was told with a shake of the head. Forget it.

When I explained that the Basij chief at Tehran University had made the invitation, eyes widened. "Well, if *they* want you to go, that's different!" But over the years the trip proved impossible to arrange. Or I had just missed one, and they only happen once a year, not twice. Or as the war drums from Washington began to quicken their martial cadence, and accusations flew that the United States was recruiting anti-regime minorities in the border areas, it all just became too sensitive.

The chances of making my journey seemed to dim in 2003 and 2004, as those militant Iranians most paranoid of the West—and most dangerously suspicious of journalists of all types, Iranian and foreign—clawed their way back into power. Finally, the firebrand Mahmoud Ahmadinejad became president in 2005, vowing to restore the roots of the Revolution. Among all the candidates—and there were a host of conservatives running—he alone explicitly disdained improving ties with the United States, saying Iran had "no particular need" of them. These were indeed the revolutionary roots he was seeking. The Islamic Republic, again, was taking on the world. And it was finding enemies everywhere.

Nevertheless, early in 2007 permission was finally granted for me to go to the border region, to the former battlefield where the dead martyrs lived on. Ironically, that green light came at one of the lowest points in U.S.-Iran relations, when the two nations—egged on by their respective noisy neoconservative leaders—were bracing for war.

The United States raised the stakes in January 2007 by detaining five Iranian "diplomats" in the northern Iraqi city of Arbil and accusing them of being Revolutionary Guard operatives working against American troops—though the real target was two of Iran's most senior security officials.[11]

As Washington talked regime change, U.S. forces and agents just across the borders in Iraq and Pakistan had been encouraging Arab, Kurdish, and Baluchi minorities of Iran to mobilize against Tehran.[12] Among them were the Pakistan-based Sunni Jundallah (Soldiers of God) guerrillas, which declared responsibility for, among other operations, bombing a busload of Revolutionary Guard soldiers, an attack that killed eleven in February 2007. Later that year, President Bush signed a presidential finding asking for $400 million to escalate military and CIA covert operations inside Iran to destabilize the regime.

U.S. Special Forces were reported to be already at work within Iran's

borders, clandestinely laying the groundwork for combat and planting radiation sniffer units that could detect any presence of highly
enriched uranium, the key ingredient of a nuclear weapon. Armageddon seemed just around the corner. Iran was responding with shrill
denunciations.

And the permission for my battlefield pilgrimage came at another
low point, too, between me and Tehran. I had received only a single
visa, for just a few days, despite more than a year of trying. When I
finally did get back to Iran, I wanted to understand why I had been
shut out for so long. I had my suspicions and found out how very
closely Iranian officials study the American media. On some levels,
I was caught up in a small-scale version of the same rhetorical battle
poisoning U.S.-Iran relations.

After so many visits to Iran, the files kept in Tehran about me are
certainly very fat, overstuffed with stories—and doubtless very many
intelligence reports about my activities. While sometimes that can
work to your favor, because officials (and security services) may feel
they "know" me, it can also create new obstacles, when those same
people ask, "*Why* do we know Mr. Peterson so well?"

In Iran, such questions are reason enough to delay a visa, or reject
one. But there had been other issues with my newspaper, the *Christian
Science Monitor,* and with me. Tehran grated at some decidedly anti-
regime editorials, and elsewhere on the opinion pages an extraordinary piece that argued for a "timely defensive first strike" against
Iranian nuclear and military targets.[13] It urged "anticipatory self-
defense" attacks against 2,500 aim points in Iran. The writer claimed
that such strikes would be "entirely legal" and rooted in a 1625 "classic" treatise, in which Hugo Grotius "expresses the enduring principle:
'It be lawful to kill him who is preparing to kill.' "

Iranian officials were apoplectic, and complained that the opinion piece supported the neoconservative "agenda of war among
civilizations."

I understood the Iranian outrage and knew that it would extend far beyond official circles, to Iranians themselves. Yet in Iran I was de-termined not to let expectations of any official affect my work. Early on in my visits, I had made a deliberate decision to let the facts and voices that I found speak for themselves. But any Western journal-ist who writes about Iran becomes a "player." Whether you like it or not, Iranian papers and news agencies of all political flavors will quote your work—or misquote it—to suit their purposes.

So praise and searing criticism of my own writing has—and should—come from both sides. My words have sometimes been balm to reformists, who believed I delivered decisive blows to their hide-bound hard-line opponents. Likewise, extreme right-wingers have en-thused that they had never seen such understanding of their beliefs by a foreign journalist—much less by an American.

My hope had always been that, on balance, all sides would respect professional work, and Iranian officialdom would see in my overlarge files a commitment to being a student of Iran. Usually that openness worked, enabling me to prevail in many visa battles. But not always, and less and less, as Iran's conservatives expanded their complaints be-yond the op-ed page.

I felt sure that one problem was a story about my 2005 visit to the Jamkaran mosque.[14] Superstitious Shiite Muslims believe that the el-egant blue- and green-tiled mosque, with its perfect columnar mina-rets, south of Tehran near Iran's religious center of Qom, had been ordered built by the Mahdi and provides a close link to him. This was the mysterious "hidden Imam" who had disappeared twelve centuries before. He was the Shiite Messiah, and legend held that he would one day return and bring perfect justice to the world.

Among those waiting fervently for his arrival was Ahmadinejad, who as mayor of Tehran was rumored to have ordered a reconfigura-tion of city streets to prepare for the Imam's triumphant return. The story required two weeks of the most intense reporting I had ever done in Iran—tracking down source after source, clerical and lay, to understand the resonance of Jamkaran for the new president's rule.

When I explored Ahmadinejad's spiritual mind-set, analysts spoke of how similar it was to that of the evangelical President Bush and American "end of days" believers.

"This kind of mentality makes you very strong," the conservative Iranian columnist Amir Mohebian told me.[15] "Bush said: 'God said to me, attack Afghanistan and attack Iraq.' The mentality of Mr. Bush and Mr. Ahmadinejad is the same here; both think God tells them what to do," he said, adding that such beliefs have similar roots in Christian and Muslim theology. "If you think these are the last days of the world, and Jesus will come [again], this idea will change all your relations. If you think the Mahdi will come in two, three, or four years, why should I be soft? Now is the time to stand strong, to be hard."

My story delved into many issues controversial in Iran but politically ascendant. Comparisons of Ahmadinejad to the most reviled U.S. leader that Iranians can remember also won few favors. Right-wing American writers and Iran bashers quoted the story at length, as proof that Ahmadinejad was an unstable fanatic, detached from reality and prone to spiritual illusions.[16] But the reporting also gave me a detailed understanding of some shadowy religious factions, including the Hojjatiyeh, which had been outlawed by Khomeini and advocated creating chaos in the world to speed the return of the Mahdi.

The fact that my story was an issue for the Iranians became clear when I returned to Iran in March 2007, with high hopes of finally visiting the border area with the Followers of the Light Path. My curiosity was piqued when the new Iranian chief of foreign press asked me to critique a story that had appeared in an English-language magazine about the Middle East. It claimed that Ahmadinejad and many of his crowd were card-carrying members of the Hojjatiyeh, a "radical secret society" determined to sow global crisis.[17] Ahmadinejad's 2005 victory had been a "silent coup" for the Hojjatiyeh, the sources in the story argued, enabling the group to promote a "concept of chaos" that would herald the "dawn of a New Islamic world."

Asking me to critique the piece was like a school quiz, and—struck by the strange request—I swiftly wrote an unsigned, undated eight hundred words about how I understood Ahmadinejad's worldview to be different. Contrary to the Hojjatiyeh's chaos theory, I wrote, Ahmadinejad believed that doing good works and purity of spirit were the best preparation for the return of the Mahdi.

"You wrote that without putting a word wrong," press director Mohsen Moghadaszadeh told me a few days later. "We should call you *hojjatoleslam*," he joked, referring to the mid-rank of cleric just below ayatollah, which means "proof of Islam."

Had I just been rehabilitated? Would visas now be more forthcoming? Was I now back on the list of friends, or still that of enemies? Or had evidence of my reporting diligence reassured the Ministry of Islamic Guidance that I was no more dangerous—and no less dangerous—than an honest observer? All would be clear soon as my years-long bid to reach the border areas finally came to a climax.

Plans looked promising at first. I was to join a bus full of faithful students in Tehran, drive with them to the former war zone, then take in the ideological show in the dusty battlefields. But inexplicably, plans were scaled back, again and again. I waited in Tehran for a week, and was told that only one hurdle remained, the agreement of a top general. Partial approval was finally given, not exactly for the border areas, but for two cities nearby, Ahvaz and Dezful, which had been rocketed during the war and had famously produced legions of martyrs. Full permission might come once I was on the ground.

It would just have to do. And in Iran, when pursuing issues this close to the beating ideological heart of the regime, it was not a bad option. Ahvaz was sensitive in its own right as the center of Iran's ethnic Arab minority, which had recently suffered a series of blasts and anti-regime riots. Tehran blamed the British—even the Canadians— for stirring unrest in the city. Journalists almost never received permission to visit.

So I smiled to myself as my plane touched down in Ahvaz; I was buoyed by an expectant sense of adventure. But even before the IranAir jet stopped taxiing, a text message came from Tehran on the mobile phone. Fars News Agency, tied to the Revolutionary Guard, was quoting a senior Iranian general opposing my visit and specifically naming "Scott Daniel Peterson" of the *Monitor.*

It was the same general who had delayed my permission.

"Until the release of the Iranian diplomats kidnapped in Arbil, Iraq, American journalists are not allowed to visit the sites of the eight-year Sacred Defense," declared Brigadier General Mir-Faisal Baqerza-deh, head of the Foundation for the Preservation and Propagation of the Values of the Sacred Defense.[18] Remarkably, it seemed that one weathered reporter was worth five Iranian diplomat/agents picked up months before in Iraq.

The Fars News report was a serious public censure, and part of a bigger game. I knew that such a high-profile statement like this would not be reversed. The hard-line press quickly picked up the story that I had been refused permission to visit the border, and turned me into a full-blown spy. The newspaper *Siyasat-e Rooz* in Tehran claimed that "when the enemy is expanding the range of its threats and propaganda constantly," dispatching journalists to the border "can only be described as a cover-up." [19]

Naming the "high-circulation" *Monitor* (my editors chuckled gamely at this misperception), *Siyasat-e Rooz* apocryphally reminded its readers of the "history of America dispatching spies to regions under the cover of being correspondents." It called on the Iranian military to deal with "utter sensitivity and neutralize the military plots of America against the Islamic nation."

About me, the newspaper braced for the worst: "There is no doubt that those who have been appointed for this mission by America are among the experienced spies of the CIA, who are responsible for evaluating the potential of our country's military arrangements."

I felt I had no choice but to return to Tehran on the next plane, finally defeated after so many years in my quest to see the battlefield, and to witness the ideological revitalization. But the Islamic Guidance Ministry—still aglow perhaps from my treatise on the Hojjatiyeh— told me to stay put. They promised to back me if any problem arose in the two cities where they had already granted permission to report.

So along with two Iranian policemen, who changed out of their uniforms for this foray and were required as escorts, I began to work.

And what of the result, of all the politicking, fearmongering, and my nine-year effort to witness how Iran passes the revolutionary torch from father to son? I was not able to do the Rahian-e Nour tour itself or get right to the border. The photographs shot by Iranian colleagues showed women in billowing black shrouds climbing on the carcasses of tanks at the former desert front, and rows of colorful flags set up along trench lines that marked the beginning of no-man's-land.

That front was denied me. I had no access to the impressionable pilgrims, as they collected the sacred soil into Ziploc plastic bags to take home in remembrance. I would not hear the hours of war stories and ideological lectures those pilgrims would have heard. In fact, judging by the reaction of one Tehran friend, who made her own private visit, the place itself was a disappointment. "It was riddled with dog turds, plastic bags, and garbage, and no way recognizable as a place for emotion," she told me about one of the most sacred sites, at Shalamche.[20] "I was not even moved to take pictures. You could only see truckloads of shit on the road to sell to Iraq. It was a mess."

Though I missed the show, in fact I gained a much more powerful and authentic understanding of the sacred dynamic from the True Believers and their families, whom I met as they frequented the war graves in Ahvaz and Dezful.

Far from a hindrance, the presence of my two policemen proved useful at reassuring people, once these men heard my questions and saw that I was not out to sabotage the regime. But they were not enough to reassure all of Iran's security services. Very late one night, two bearded men arrived at my Ahvaz hotel, and I was summoned to the lobby. They introduced themselves as Iranian intelligence agents.[21]

One was heavyset with a dark face, short beard, and a daub of gray scar tissue in the middle of his forehead from a lifetime spent kneeling in prayer, head pressed to the ground. He was dressed all in black and gave the name "Hosseini," which was not his real name. He did most of the talking and knew some English. He had volunteered to fight when he was eleven years old, getting his start taking food to soldiers. The other man, spindly, tall, and less certain, pulled out a school copybook and started making detailed notes, his effort dwindling as the night wore on.

They seemed to know plenty about me already, judging by their precise understanding of my program. Someone had gained access to my trip request, someone who meant to undermine it. They asked if they could take photographs of me and videotape our conversation. I well knew that nothing good comes from any videotape in the hands of Iranian intelligence. It could easily be misused, cut and edited, distorted, and broadcast in ways that would jeopardize my professional reputation, inside Iran and out.

And why did Iranian intelligence agents need video of me, if this were just a "friendly chat," as they claimed? They stated that they could have a hidden camera or a microphone anywhere (and of course they would have). I said I understood. And agreed that they could take still photographs—not video. Iranian officialdom had enough of those from my press card and frequent visa requests. But taking pictures was very different from acquiescing to a taped interrogation. Just the act of requesting the video was enough to doubt the Iranians' real intent, to raise the level of menace.

The questioning got under way. In the empty hotel lobby after midnight, we were alone. "Hosseini" settled deeper into his brown leatherette chair. "So . . . ," he began, quite seriously. "When does the bombing start?"

I

Old Glory, Great Satan

Let America be angry with us, and die of this anger.

—Ayatollah Mohammad Hosseini Beheshti, slogan painted
at Tehran's central Haft-e Tir square

BENEATH IRAN'S ANTI-AMERICAN FAÇADE is a nation that has much in common with its stated nemesis—from an ambitious self-image and public reliance on the divine, to a habit of defining itself in terms of its enemies. And hidden behind the mullah's mask is the most unashamedly pro-American population in the Middle East. It was no surprise to me that after September 11, 2001, several thousand Iranians were the first—and among the very few in the region—to hold spontaneous candlelight vigils of mourning and solidarity with the United States.[1]

I have found that Americans and Iranians are, in fact, remarkably similar in mind-set and belief, so much so that in the future, the United States and Iran could well become the most powerful "natural" allies in the region. They share a spiritual thought model, a national arrogance, the frequent need of an "enemy" in political discourse, and a belief in their own exceptionalism and "manifest destiny" that for Iran includes its nuclear ambitions.

It is a provocative concept, considering that these very similarities have also made the United States and Iran proud and uncompromising enemies for a generation. Both nations swear by peace, even cherish it as a sacred motivator. Yet both are also unafraid of war or using violence if they feel threatened, or believe their survival is at stake, or see a greater "defensive" and self-justifying good. Especially if that "good" might yield acts of heroism and sacrifice. Parallels between America and Iran abound. The duel is between two peoples who hold national pride and their own brand of historical entitlement above all else.

Both Americans and Iranians inherently understand this—about themselves. But to better appreciate the often sanctimonious and uncompromising reactions of the other, they should each hold up a mirror.

Americans. Iranians. "They look at the world in just two colors: black and white," Javad Vaeidi, the editor of *Diplomatic Hamshahri* newspaper, told me.[2] "In their [American] mind they think they have a duty from God, and are on a mission. It is very dangerous. We have the same group, with the same mind-set. Both peoples think they are the emperor of the world."

Branded by hard-liners in Washington as an "Islamo-fascist" state that threatens world peace, Iran has in fact not invaded any country since the eighteenth century—in marked contrast to the United States. Iran looks at the American troops gathered along each of its borders and sees blatant menace.

And arrogance? As the author Hooman Majd notes, Iran has "a culture that is, it's true, proud beyond the comprehension of most Westerners."[3] But would not many—if not most—Americans admit to a similar magnitude of arrogance? Only when Americans look at Iranians and see how much of themselves is reflected there—holding up that mirror for an objective view—will they better fathom and judge Iran's actions.

Similarities aside, America's perpetual diplomatic dance with Iran could not be more strategic. Iran today presents itself as the vanguard of an unbending Islamic leadership locked in a battle of wills with the United States and the West. Can such a regional superpower and nascent nuclear nation really be ignored, or safely isolated? For three decades mutual hostility has festered. Demonizing the "Great Satan" remains a pillar of the Revolution, its anti-American stance an "endless religious duty."

Yet despite that history, Iran's hidden pro-American bent is no secret to Iranians themselves. Watching it unfold in public, however, is almost unheard-of . . .

The Flag-Burning Metric

It was the darkest hour of the night in Tehran, the empty streets wet with the kind of cleansing spring rain that always gave off, to my nostrils, a rare sense of regeneration in Iran. In every living room across the Islamic Republic, televisions were lit up to watch a momentous World Cup soccer game. It was a chance pairing in June 1998, an unprecedented face-to-face challenge of two archenemies that had not publicly spoken except in angry denunciation for nearly two decades: the United States versus Iran.

A nation was in thrall as the soccer field became a symbolic battleground for a much larger conflict, in which geostrategic realities were briefly subsumed in the joy of sports. The Americans started strong and Iranians were on the edge of their seats, holding their collective breath, as U.S. strikers aimed four scoring chances in the first thirty-three minutes of play—three of them bouncing off the goalposts.[4] Then, in the fortieth minute, Iranian Hamid Estili placed a header into the upper-left corner of the goal. The effect was like an earthquake ripping along a fault line from the stadium in Lyon, France, all the way to Iran. I was watching with an Iranian family, who leaped out of their seats at the Iranian goal, mouths agape, unable to contain themselves.

Iran had never won a World Cup game. And now it was ahead, against such an opponent! At the eighty-fourth minute, Mehdi Mahdavikia decisively blasted a shot to the right corner of the net, past the diving American goalie. The U.S. side rallied enough to score a header with just three minutes left in the game, but victory for Iran seemed certain.

It was a miracle. The realization of countless Iranian prayers. Iran won 2–1, and jubilation erupted. Even before the final whistle ended the game, Iranians were pouring onto the streets to celebrate, blowing horns, blocking traffic—and boisterously hugging and kissing me, a rare American onlooker.[5] I was lost in the crush of people thronging downtown Vali Asr Square. Shouting. Ecstatic. And overjoyed with a reason for communal happiness, radiant with national pride.

Suddenly I saw a handful of militants who were ready to make their own point from Iran's victory. The men waded into the frolicking crowd with an American flag, tossing out leaflets that read "Down with the USA." They happened to be moving in my direction, and stopped an arm's length away. They hoisted Old Glory onto a pole for burning. As the flag poked up, I watched one young hard-liner brandish a cigarette lighter and set the first threads aflame.

It was a ritual act of denigration and disrespect that had played itself out in Iran countless times since 1979, without censure. But this night was different, and what followed remains one of the most extraordinary scenes I have ever witnessed in Iran.

As the flames began to flicker, the crowd reacted: Revelers reached up and took hold of the American flag, whisking it off the pole and away from the hard-liners, bunching it up and stuffing it under someone's shirt to protect it from destruction. Other Iranians tore up the anti-American leaflets. There was a scuffle that reflected the battle in Iran between right-wing conservatives, who still deemed the United States the "Great Satan," and more open-minded reformists who wanted *their* Islamic Republic to reengage with America and the West.

"This celebration is not because we *beat* the Americans," one young man shouted at me, sweat pouring down his forehead as he fought his way through the melee to pass on this message. "It is because we like to be *with* the Americans."

Was this the same Iran that made burning American and Israeli flags a hallmark of the Revolution? Where Ayatollah Ruhollah Khomeini promised the collapse of American power? Of the voluminous speeches, learning, and venom the ayatollah produced, these few words remain painted on the wall of the former U.S. Embassy: "We will make America face a severe defeat." Also painted there for years, and of more concern to any potential architects of U.S.-Iran détente, was Khomeini's vow: "On that day when the United States of America will praise us we should mourn."

IRAN'S FIRST-WORLD PRETENSIONS HARK back to an ancient era, when the Persian Empire was the indispensable nation of its day. It is the sense of national purpose, of national mission—this heady exceptionalism—that today imbues aspirations in Iran, just as it has throughout the much shorter history of the United States.

Iran has sought to rejuvenate its past strategic glory and influence, beginning with the Revolution's bold declaration that Iran was tearing itself away from the bipolar world dominated by the two superpowers, America and the Soviet Union, in a policy of "neither East nor West." Backed by huge oil deposits and the second-largest gas reserves in the world, Iran spreads "soft power" across the region, from pipeline links connecting the Caspian Sea with the Persian Gulf, to mosque building in Central Asia and greater influence in Afghanistan and Iraq.[6] It leads what I call an Axis of Resistance with Shiite and other militant allies in Lebanon, the Israel-Palestinian conflict, and in neighboring Iraq.

Such ambitions add up to what one Western diplomat told me was "Persian arrogance that sees Iran as the center of the universe."[7] So in modern times, Iranians have easily assumed for themselves America's rhetoric of its own uniqueness. Iranians are certain they will dominate their region as a threat or a power, or both—a point that Iranian Revolutionary Guard commanders are adept at injecting into virtually every news cycle.

It took many visits to Iran before I began to understand—and to accept—some of the parallels to America that Iranians often spelled out for me. The words of President Franklin D. Roosevelt in 1936 ring as true in Iranian ears as they have for Americans, for example, since he declared: "To some generations much is given. Of other generations much is expected. This generation of Americans has a rendez-vous with destiny." [8]

"Roosevelt said the U.S. has a 'rendezvous with destiny,' " a Tehran physicist educated at Yale, Shahriar Rouhani, told me in 2002.[9] "Iran, too, has a 'rendezvous with destiny.' "

Iranians regularly recall how the United States accepted such aspirations for the pro-West Mohammad Reza Shah Pahlavi—when Washington saw Iran as the "policeman" of the Persian Gulf—and speak of their disappointment that today the United States still refuses to acknowledge that the largest, most populous, and most powerful nation in the region should play any role at all in its own neighborhood. One reason is the fear held by smaller or less powerful U.S. allies in the region—Saudi Arabia, Qatar, Bahrain, and the United Arab Emirates, for example—which quake at Iran's weight and rhetoric and Shiite revolutionary influence. Not to mention that most anxious country of all, Israel.

"If the Americans have the right to become the emperor of the world, Iranians think they have the right to be the emperor at least of their region," Javad Vaeidi, the diplomatic editor, explained to me.[10] "If we can find the best way to bring these two hegemons together, it will be good. America recognized this role for the Shah's regime, but as an agent [of the United States], not an ally. If the U.S. can consider Iran an ally, not an agent, it can work. The message to the American government is: You have to accept our existence."

Many of the root beliefs are similar in Iran and America, Vaeidi told me. We were speaking over a takeaway dinner of buttered rice and skewered lamb kebab, with grilled tomatoes and green chili peppers, spooned from aluminum food trays onto plates in a conference room at *Hamshahri*. Amid the satisfying mixed scent of newsprint and meat, Vaeidi was in an expansive mood. Almost too expansive. Months later, under President Mahmoud Ahmadinejad, he would be appointed to a senior national security post. His forthright words to me that night in early 2005 about U.S.-Iran relations complicated his confirmation.[11]

"Consider this expression: 'Your destiny is in your hands,' " he told me. "This is a common thought: Americans see a frontier, they believe it is 'your destiny,' that the world is yours. The same mind and mentality is in Iran; the roots are in the mind of the Iranian people. It is drawn from the Quran. The Lord God will not change the destiny of the people unless they want it. This belongs to our history. We have a vision of the Persian Empire in this story."

Vaeidi was well versed in the views of American analysts and pundits, and had been reading Ken Pollack—one of his articles three times—Zbigniew Brzezinski, and James Woolsey, as well as neoconservatives such as Norman Podhoretz who had long argued for U.S. military strikes against Iran. "The important thing is we have to look for common things," Vaeidi told me. Besides both peoples' belief in their own version of manifest destiny, Iran and the United States had "been able to assert their sovereignty and prove it in their regions." For Iran, the symbol of this independence was the Revolution.

"Before the Islamic Republic for two hundred years, we were humiliated," said Vaeidi. He ticked off the examples. The Qajar period was "made in the British and Russian embassies." Policy during the Shah's rule was "made in the U.S. Embassy." It made the independence of 1979 all the sweeter, he said: "The people are not willing to lose this."

Vaeidi wiped his thin lips and beard with a tissue, then gathered the empty trays and pushed them aside. He called an aide to bring tea, to help wash back the plotting of the "Rumsfeld group at the Pentagon," and to closely examine the words of the Republican senator from Kansas, Sam Brownback, who he said had estimated that only 15 percent of Iranians would firmly support the government in a scrape; perhaps ten million people.

Vaeidi said that was an overestimate of support—perhaps only two million would fight to the death for the Islamic system. But it was a serious underestimate of the number of Iranians who would go to war to defend their country if it were attacked. "Besides the fanatical supporters are other people concerned with the nation, so there *would* be ten million fighting," Vaeidi told me. And far from undermining support for the regime, he calculated that any American military action would boost that 10 percent ironclad support into 30 or even 50 percent.

The conflict was not between two governments, "but two ways of life: the U.S. way of life, and the Islamic way of life," Vaeidi insisted. "The U.S. thinks they must destroy another. . . . In the neoconservative mind, they are dreaming about the collapse of the Iranian regime," he said. But the problem centers on Iran's ambitions for itself and how those clash with America's own global aims. He was still hopeful that two imperial worldviews could live side by side: "The man and woman who have enough ability for war, have enough ability for peace on both sides. In Iran and the U.S., this is the actual deal. We have to have a win-win way."

Iran's hard-liners are convinced that their Islamic system is the closest thing achievable to God's rule—a point of contention for the huge numbers of Iranians who voted against it the late 1990s, for critics of the bloody early years of the Revolution and of its dire human rights record, and for the flood of Iranians who took to the streets in mid-2009 to protest a stolen election.

There have been optimists: "It is only a question of time" before America and Iran are close again, one U.S.-educated Iranian academic told me. "In political science we were taught that no friend is forever, and no enemy is forever. Only the mutual interest is forever." [12]

"Iran has an absolutist, cruel, dictatorial history, in which the ruler always destroyed the aristocracy, so you can easily find people who came from nowhere to high levels of power," explained the historian Reza Alavi, who had been at Harvard and Oxford. [13] "As in the American mind, [there is] the same cultural value of success [and] an extreme individualism. That's why you find so many Iranians adjust so well to America. When they go there, they are like a fish in water."

But of course there are a number of lopsided differences, too, that frame national ambitions, Alavi told me. "America is a country that has been a straight military success until Vietnam. But Iran has not been a military success for—God knows—one thousand years. So our dreams of grandeur are much more pathological."

Governments of God

Yet for those looking for similarities there is much to draw upon. Iran's reformist President Mohammad Khatami set the precedent while making an overture to the United States in early 1998. In a surprise result, the philosopher-cleric had swept to the presidency just months before on a platform of reforming Iran's Islamic system. With a record twenty million votes behind him, Khatami vowed to instill the rule of law, temper radical influences, and ease the Islamic Republic's isolation. He also thought he could begin making amends with America.

In an extraordinary departure from the Great Satan syllabus, the new Iranian president said American civilization was "worthy of respect," in an interview with Christiane Amanpour of CNN.[14] He hailed the Puritans who first set foot in America as a religious people "in search of a virgin land to establish a superior civilization," based on democracy and freedom. The same values, Khatami said, drove Iranians to create the Islamic Republic. Along with "independence," Iran's Revolution from its first moments aspired to couple "religiosity with liberty."

"With our Revolution, we are experiencing a new phase of reconstruction of civilization," Khatami said. "We feel that what we seek is what the founders of the American civilization were also pursuing four centuries ago. This is why we sense an intellectual affinity with the essence of the American civilization."

Such praise came with complaints that U.S. foreign policy had deviated from the pure path. Khatami lamented a "tragedy which has occurred" in the form of a "flawed policy of domination," which caused nations to "los[e] their trust in the Americans." But Khatami had identified a critical similarity. Iranian and American leaders regularly invoke the power of God, to the point of portraying their own conflict as one between dueling theocracies.

Faith is never far in the *Islamic* Republic. It is in the air, staring down from the walls, and is relentlessly on the minds and in the hearts of many Iranians. From mosque to classroom to street corner, you can feel it. There is no tradition of separation of church and state, which pupils in America are taught to respect in *their* republic. In Iran religion *is* the state. By definition, every word, every act must therefore be divinely inspired, a manifestation of God's will.

That was how Ayatollah Khomeini ordained the Islamic Republic when he announced "the first day of God's government" on April 1, 1979.[15] The purity of purpose of the Islamic Republic was to be a beacon of God's rule. "The light of divine justice shall shine uniformly on all," Khomeini vowed, "and the divine mercy of the Quran . . . shall embrace all, like life-giving rain."

Likewise faith is never far away in America, where the Declaration of Independence proclaims, "all men are created equal, that they are endowed by their Creator with certain unalienable Rights." Where every piece of currency and coin is marked with the words "In God We Trust." With hand over heart, Americans pledge allegiance "to one nation under God." Unique in the Western world, presidential speeches end with the simple divine request: "God bless the United States of America."

And despite the line drawn between church and state, Americans have prided themselves on a degree of spirituality—and of setting an example—that has shaped U.S. history from the start. In the words of British historian Paul Johnson:

> They came to America not primarily for gain or even livelihood, though they accepted both from God with gratitude, but to create His kingdom on earth. They were the zealots, the idealists, the utopians, the saints, and the best of them, or perhaps one should say the most extreme of them, were fanatical, uncompromising, and overweening in their self-righteousness. They were also immensely energetic, persistent and courageous.[16]

Among the earliest Pilgrims, John Winthrop arrived near the New England coast, from whence "came a smell off the shore like the smell of a garden."[17] Aboard ship he preached that the New World was

nothing less than a new Promised Land, ordained by God to be a beacon for all the globe: "We must consider that wee shall be as a Citty
upon a Hill, the eyes of all people are upon us."

Few other nations can boast such spiritual underpinnings, or such
broadly self-described spiritual peoples—and of the dangers that "radicals" can pose—as the United States and Iran, where "God's will"
shapes daily decision making. In the American mind, that beatific
thread has never broken. Harry Truman marked the surrender of
Japan in World War II in 1945 with "gratitude to Almighty God," and
said victory was "of more than arms alone. This is a victory of liberty
over tyranny."[18] He had no doubt: "It was the spirit of liberty which
gave us our armed strength and which made our men invincible in
battle."

Decades later in Iran, Ayatollah Khomeini cast his war with Iraq in
remarkably similar terms: "Victory is not achieved by swords; it can
be achieved only by blood," the dour ayatollah said. "Victory is not
achieved by large populations; it is achieved by strength of faith."[19]

DIFFERENCES ARE PRONOUNCED, TOO, I have found. Amer-
icans revere straight talk; Iranians almost never engage in it. Iranians
can be as conspiratorial and paranoid as Americans can be open and
trusting. America is largely a law-abiding society, while Iran is not a
country of laws, but a country that still only aspires to the rule of law.
This is a root cause of the political and social turmoil that has afflicted
Iran for more than a century.

Still, both nations say they act in the name of a higher calling; that
their faith demands goodwill toward others, and good works that
strive for justice. They insist that they pray and work for peace and
the preservation of loved ones and for their fellow man. They insist
that it is the enemy that is "evil" and against God. "[They] are very
similar—they try to use religious language for political targets,"
Hamid Reza Jalaeipour, a reformist editor and political sociologist at
Tehran University, told me.[20]

And that clash is as insistent as it is loud; when they refer to each other they are charging that their enemies act against God's will. When George Bush announced America's War on Terror just days after 9/11, he said: "Every nation in every region now has a decision to make. Either you are with us, or you are with the terrorists." And God had already made His choice, Bush asserted: "Freedom and fear, justice and cruelty, have always been at war, and we know that God is not neutral between them."[21]

After becoming Iran's president in 2005, Mahmoud Ahmadinejad made the counterargument many times. "If Christ were on earth today, undoubtedly he would stand with the people in opposition to bullying, ill-tempered and expansionist powers," Ahmadinejad said.[22] "[U]ndoubtedly he would hoist the banner of justice and love for humanity to oppose warmongers, occupiers, terrorists and bullies the world over."

The competing voices all added up, for both countries, to demagoguery with a dose of the divine. "In the U.S., having a system that thinks religiously is not bad. . . . I prefer people in the U.S. who go to church," conservative editor Amir Mohebian told me in Tehran.[23] "But war between these two people—who think they are acting on behalf of God—is not good. War between believers is too dangerous."

THE DIFFICULTIES OF MAKING peace—or even establishing a truce—became clear that night of the U.S.-Iran soccer game, as I watched the celebration erupt on the streets of Tehran. The Clinton administration had sought to defrost the U.S.-Iran hostility, hoping to build on Khatami's outreach by taking a number of modest positive steps. They weren't the first to try. As journalist Barbara Slavin notes in *Bitter Friends, Bosom Enemies,* "No other country is so fixated on the United States. No other foreign government so aspires to and fears a U.S. embrace. Iran has been dubbed 'the Bermuda Triangle' of American diplomacy for swallowing up good-faith efforts to end the hostility."[24]

The reactions to the June 1998 World Cup soccer game partly illustrate why, ultimately, the mutual overtures failed. Immediately before the kickoff, President Bill Clinton said he and Khatami had "both worked to encourage more people-to-people exchanges . . . to develop a better understanding of each other's rich civilizations."[25] The soccer field was another point of contact, Clinton said: "As we cheer today's game between American and Iranian athletes, I hope it can be another step toward ending the estrangement between our nations."

On the playing field itself, more spontaneous diplomacy was breaking out. Hard-liners in Iran had encouraged their team—it was rumored they had ordered them—not to shake hands or exchange shirts with the Americans. Yet the players very happily shook hands, exchanged flowers and gifts before the game, and went out of their way to treat each other with respect. At the end, after the usual rough-and-tumble of the Beautiful Game, both teams were jointly given the 1998 Fair Play Award from the world soccer governing body.[26]

Moments after the game, as Iranians poured out of their homes, President Khatami took to the radio.[27] His live address was conciliatory and gushed with pride: "Naturally, like the tens of millions of Iranians interested in the fate of the country and the glory of the homeland, I feel happy."

But how did Iran's supreme religious leader, Ayatollah Seyyed Ali Khamenei, react to Iran's soccer victory? With much less generosity. The man who makes all final decisions in Iran, who carries the official title of God's Deputy on Earth, and who is infallible by definition, took a more combative tone. "This has been a beautiful picture of the crusade of the Iranian nation in all the scenes of its revolutionary life," he boasted in his radio message.[28]

Khamenei spoke of intelligence, strength, the sincere and coordinated effort and reliance on God—all of which he had seen on the soccer field. "These were the same exceptional endeavors which during the Revolution and during the Sacred Defense [Iran-Iraq War] and in all the engagements of the Iranian nation with the Great Satan . . . gave victory and honor to our nation," Khamenei said. "Tonight, once again the strong and arrogant contender experienced the bitter taste of defeat at your hands."

• • •

ON THE STREETS AND across the airwaves, the flag-burning metric reflected that clash of views over America. Though ritual burnings had become a fading art form over the years, and chants of "Death to America" less strident, the hard-liners in the late 1990s started to reclaim their territory, leaving behind them a fresh trail of ash from torched American and Israeli flags. "It shows the conservatives are losing public support, and so they put fuel on the fire of America," Ebrahim Yazdi, the Revolution's first foreign minister turned opposition figure, told me. "The issue is not America. They do it only to legitimize their own power." [29]

The bludgeoning anti-American policy *had* always had a broader purpose. It was critical glue that helped hold together Iran's Islamic regime, which made the state of flag burning an even more important barometer—and reaching out for détente even more risky. Yet flag burning was a controversial tool. Khatami had criticized such acts of disrespect, and on the eve of a rally to mark the November 1999 anniversary of the U.S. Embassy takeover, local radio announced that there would be no flags burned. Such calls were useless as the crowd mentality took over.

I watched as militants climbed on high scaffolding to pour gas on eight huge American flags, the largest I had ever seen in Tehran.[30] They set them afire with cigarette lighters to a chorus of chanting. Embers floated down onto the crowd, where clusters of overzealous youth burned other flags—in one case after first ripping into the cloth with their teeth, like rabid dogs getting their piece of a kill. The lexicon of defiance was inescapable, and meant to be, with banners hailing the capture of the U.S. Embassy as proof to Iran's "enemies that [Iranians] would rule themselves, would rule their own fate."

But even at such a pro-regime event, I was surprised at the mix of voices.

"It's my religious duty to be here, to show to the world that America's days are over to oppress the rest of the world," one municipal worker told me, airing the official line.

"Hello, America, hello!" counter-chimed a sixteen-year-old girl with a "Death to Israel" placard. The class of young women draped in black chadors had obviously been given the signs in English—"Islamic Iran has no need for the U.S.," and "Madeleine Albright Shame on You"—but had forgotten the instruction to scowl at real live enemies like me in their midst.

There was much talk, and perhaps even conviction, about "sacrificing my life for the Supreme Leader." But many were clearly tired of the flag-burning desecrations, a point missed by television footage that gave the impression of legions of angry Iranians setting all the country aflame with anti-American rage.

"Oh, America, my love!" shouted a young man called Ardeshir, arms ready to embrace me, as police and militants watched aghast. "It's a joke," affirmed Yara, a photography student. "How can you shout, 'Death to America' when you are wearing blue jeans?"

"I don't believe in flag burning," nineteen-year-old student Samim told me. "Each nation loves their flag because it's a symbol."

"Flag burning disrespects a nation," echoed student Arad.

"We shouldn't do this flag burning, because we *love* the American people," added fourteen-year-old Hossein.

"My sister is in America and she says that's a nice place," explained student Hassan. "I don't know why I should chant, 'Death to America.' Many Iranians live there."

The contradictions applied at the podium, also, to those speaking for the regime. The veteran former Revolutionary Guard commander Mohsen Rezaei said it was "clear" that America did not want relations but instead wanted "Iran to remain a poor Third World nation." His words burst through the speaker system like the rattle of old bullets: "America is a symbol of political discrimination in the world." He failed to mention the dirty detail that everyone knew: The commander's own son had the year before defected to the United States, where he criticized Iranian policy and accused his father of acts of terrorism.

"You hush!" I overheard one man in the crowd berate beneath his breath. "If you really speak the truth, first bring your son from America, then talk to us."

TWO DECADES AFTER THE Revolution, Americans were still very rare in Iran, and it was some time before I felt comfortable answering this question straight: "Where are you from?" Iranians would helpfully suggest that I was German, or Dutch, or from anywhere else, but rarely hazarded to guess "American." I pronounced "Am-riKA" a sinister octave below my normal voice, just to test the reaction.

Wasn't it impossible for such enemies to visit? In fact I had little to fear. People in Tehran—and elsewhere in Iran—can be as rude and unfriendly as in any country. But an American will very often receive greetings of affection and goodwill. I have taken a ride with a dreaming taxi driver who worshipped Humphrey Bogart—portraits of the actor adorning the sun visor of his worn-out car—and discussed pirated American movies with enthusiastic peddlers. When talking privately to many Iranian bureaucrats, I have heard declarations of warmth toward the American people that are effusive, even obsessive.

"People receive so much negative propaganda about Iran," local tour operator Cyrus Etemadi pointed out in 1998, as he told me of the first groups of Americans he had brought to the country.[31] "But when they come here they see that the opposite is true. People invite them into their houses for tea, or to their table to eat." The American women tourists who filled out one of his questionnaires were bowled over: "This has been the trip of a lifetime," enthused one. "The most surprising is the pleasant smile from all the people. Iranians are hospitable. . . . Thanks for being so fun and cheerful and taking such good care of us."

Another traveler, Trygve Inda, was asked by friends before he left home in Reno, Nevada, to bring back Khomeini pictures and "Down with the U.S.A." postcards. He had to FedEx his passport to Canada to get the visa.

"The common perception in America is that Iran is a place of darkness where Americans don't want to be," the computer specialist told me in Tehran.[32] Crossing into Iran was "awe-inspiring," he said. Seeing a couple of images of Khomeini actually smiling—not the typical stern look—put him more at ease. Instead of giving him trouble, border guards giggled with amusement when they saw his American passport, and waved him through. "I've seen a few 'Down with U.S.A.' signs, but you really have to look," he told me. "They aren't on every street corner."

But they did come out in force to mark every anniversary of the U.S. Embassy takeover. For the 2002 event, we in the foreign media were told from the podium to "reflect the truth of what they see here."[33] The gathering *was* instructive, if conducted with less fervor and perhaps less education than previous incarnations. One sign declared DWIN WITE U.S.A., a worse spelling error than the 1999 banner—my favorite—that mangled the word *Satan* to declare: "Down with the Great Stain!"

"This is the day of the braveness and sacrifice of the martyrs. This day was one of the Imam's wishes," an insistent young woman in the crowd told me. Another tried to convince me that "the pupils of all Iran are here," because "this is a lesson to fight against the Global Arrogance." America was accused of using the 9/11 terrorist attacks to "create a new atmosphere to dominate the world. They are fooling the world by using the War on Terror as a pretext to dominate cultures and destroy those that don't agree."

But through all of this, there were an array of viewpoints. One speaker asked wanly that nothing be burned for "environmental reasons," though that did not keep puffs of smoke from rising above the crowd when flags were quietly torched. I heard clapping at the mention of Khatami's name. One girl wore a bandage on her nose—a sign of plastic surgery favored as a fashion accessory by wealthier classes, which rarely had time for the regime ideology and so rarely took part in these official protests.

None of the usual stereotypes seemed to apply. One young man handing out refreshments, upon learning I was American, opened his arms wide in a theatrical move, and said: "American? Ah, welcome!" before giving me two cookies and a small box of juice.

The speaker, a cleric from Qazvin called Ali Khani, droned on. The purpose of the demonstration was "so Americans know we are still alive, and protecting the path of the Imam." Signs waved. People perfunctorily threw trash at a wooden effigy of George Bush riding Israel like a cowboy on a horse. An Iranian photographer who witnessed the upheaval of 1979 leaned toward me to confide his tired contempt: "After twenty-three years, the same slogans!"

"It is a stick with which to beat up your opponents, to say: 'I am the Revolution. I am the one waging war against Satan,' " political scientist Sadegh Zibakalam explained. "It gives you a revolutionary pretext to behave outside the frame of the law. It gives you certain credentials [to] attack [anyone] under the anti-U.S. card. . . . They keep burning flags to show nothing has changed, to say: 'We are still crusading.' "

"We must realize we are losing a lot by carrying the anti-U.S. banner," Zibakalam told me. "Conservatives have not been able to argue why the anti-U.S. stance is good; I can give half a dozen reasons why it is detrimental. The final decision is for the Iranian people. If the majority decides that we will eat bread and water to carry out an ideological war against the U.S. that's OK. But for heaven's sake, let us be aware of what this flag burning is costing us."

The price was right for hard-liners bent on blocking Khatami from reaping the benefit from any deal with the United States. Their strategy was to keep anti-American fervor alive, and it worked. At the United Nations summit in 2000, Khatami did not appear at the photo op for world leaders. He was afraid that he would be photographed shaking Bill Clinton's hand.[34]

From Savior to Satan

To absorb the importance of the anti-American pillar of revolutionary Iran means understanding key episodes in the love-hate history—and how they are viewed and propagated in Iran. That battle is framed by a series of historical events in which Iran has always been wronged, threatened, victimized, and bloodied by unscrupulous, inhumane Western powers—the United States chief among them.

FOR IRANIANS, IT ALL starts with the 1953 coup, when the CIA orchestrated the overthrow of Iran's only popularly elected prime minister and restored a malleable, pro-American dictatorship under the Shah. Early in the Cold War, Washington was fearful that the Soviet Union might try to take over Iran. Prime Minister Mohammad Mossadegh had been *Time* magazine's "Man of the Year" in 1951. The *New York Times* quoted one American official "familiar with the country" who compared Mossadegh's position in Iran "as not unlike that of Thomas Jefferson or Thomas Paine in the early United States." [35]

But Great Britain was the Great Satan back then and was outraged by Iran's nationalization of "their" oil in Iran—which alone had fueled the British economy for three decades.[36] The British press pilloried Mossadegh as a "tragic Frankenstein" who was "obsessed with one xenophobic idea." [37] The nationalization was a popular move by Mossadegh, who was seen at home as a hero. Still, the newly born CIA took over and engineered its first-ever coup d'état, effectively assuming from the British the mantle of number-one evil villain. The result was a tragedy for nascent democracy in the Middle East that would have endless negative repercussions.

"This is the critical event. Up to 1953, Iran loved the West culturally, though it resented Western hegemony," the Western-educated historian Reza Alavi told me in Tehran.[38] The coup told Iranians "the West does not want to share its democracy with us."

"Maybe in your mind it was in the 1950s, and that was ages ago, close to the age of the dinosaurs," one veteran revolutionary explained. "But not really [too distant] in the Iranian context." [39]

The Shah was reinstalled to the Peacock Throne and propped up by the United States with unqualified support and endless weaponry. He aimed to build the fifth most powerful military in the world, and, interestingly with U.S. blessing, to turn Iran into a nuclear power—in energy use, if not also with weapons.[40]

Classified U.S. Embassy documents from the time showed the "Made in the U.S.A." label was a problem. The "government is recognized throughout the country as being one brought in and supported by the U.S.," stated one late 1953 confidential dispatch to Washington.[41] "We have placed squarely upon our shoulders the responsibility for it; therefore, it is of the greatest importance that no stone be left unturned to make this regime successful."

THE SHAH NEVER MATCHED Mossadegh's popular touch, and over time the disparities and injustice were becoming impossible to hide and engendering revulsion and revolt. By the early 1970s most Iranians suffered obscene poverty—there was even starvation in some provinces. By one reckoning, "over 75 percent of rural families earned less than $66 a month and malnutrition was widespread among them."[42] But the Shah created a spectacle in 1971 by spending some $100–300 million on lavish celebrations at the ancient ruins of Persepolis, to mark the 2,500th anniversary of the Persian Empire. He envisioned leading Iran toward an era of "Great Civilization" within twelve years.[43]

No expense was spared in the Shah's ostentatious display, which illustrated how out of touch this ruler was with his subjects. They were kept miles away by "troops with machine guns encircling tent city," according to one Greek guest.[44] This partygoer especially enjoyed a chat with Ethiopian emperor Haile Selassie, whom he found holding a Chihuahua with "such a heavy bejeweled collar he could hardly raise his head."

Guests were deprived of nothing, from the custom-designed Baccarat crystal goblets and chefs flown in from Paris, to the air-conditioned luxury tents with marble and gold bathroom fixtures. A British Foreign Office analyst at the time—in a cable not declassified until thirty years later—called it "the greatest non-event of our time, a creation of royal despotism taking advantage of the bedazzled mass media."[45]

Yet among the claimed television audience of 2.4 billion was a certain exiled ayatollah in Iraq. An ascetic who himself lived on bread and yogurt, onions and garlic, Ayatollah Ruhollah Khomeini wrote a searing protest—among the first bolts of lightning that would electrify Iranians into the building hurricane of the Revolution, which would eventually sweep the Shah away.

"Islam came in order to destroy these palaces of tyranny," thundered Khomeini.[46] The title King of Kings, used by Iranian monarchs, was the "most hated of all titles in the sight of God." The famine meant that to take part "is to participate in the murder of the oppressed people of Iran." The ayatollah raged at the injustice: "The crimes of the kings of Iran have blackened the pages of history. It is the kings of Iran that have constantly ordered massacres of their own people and had pyramids built with their skulls."

ENABLING THE SHAH TO wield such power in the modern age was the United States, which provided the monarch with an endless bounty. "As early as 1943 the young Shah described himself as 'burning' to discuss Iran's 'needs for planes and tanks,'" writes Gary Sick, the principal White House aide on Iran in the late 1970s and during the hostage crisis.[47] The Shah's desire for military hardware was chronic: "That burning interest never subsided; in fact it ripened almost to the point of obsession by the mid-1970s."

From 1950 to 1963, the United States gave $829 million in military assistance, and sold Iran $1.3 billion in new armaments.[48] But a dramatic increase was heralded by the May 1972 visit to Tehran of President Richard Nixon and his aide Henry Kissinger. On the surface, everything went swimmingly: the Shah's prime minister took Kissinger to a government party, where a belly dancer sat on his lap for several minutes. Nadina Parsa was "a delightful girl" who is "very interested in foreign policy," the bachelor Kissinger quipped. "I spent some time explaining how you convert SS-7 missiles to Y-Class submarines."[49]

Yet the next morning a number of explosions highlighted an ominous surge of anti-Americanism. Two sticks of dynamite targeted the

U.S. Information Service offices; an Iranian woman and child walking in the street were killed in a blast that seriously injured the senior U.S. Air Force adviser to the Iranian air force; and a bomb rocked the tomb of Reza Shah forty-five minutes before Nixon was to lay a wreath there. The president's convoy was attacked on the way to the airport, despite taking a circuitous route.[50] Washington's embrace of the unpopular Shah was clearly tarnishing America, too.

But that embrace only grew tighter when those 1972 meetings "radically restructured" the U.S.-Iran relationship to give the Shah access to almost all nonnuclear U.S. military technology, in exchange for Iran playing a "principal role" in protecting Western interests in the region. Pressed on a number of Cold War fronts, Washington was subcontracting regional security to a regional ally. It was a policy that had no precedent, a blank check. Iran would decide its own needs without U.S. interference, Kissinger wrote in a memorandum, and "we will accede to any of the Shah's requests for arms purchases from us."[51]

The rush was on. That year the Pentagon concluded a $2 billion arms deal with the Shah that was, until then, its biggest ever. By 1974, almost half the Pentagon's total arms sales of $3.9 billion were with Iran.[52] "The combination of vast quantities of money, a seemingly unquenchable Iranian appetite for hardware, and formal encouragement by the president of the United States created what can only be described as a stampede," writes Sick.[53] In the first four years alone, "the Shah ordered more than $9 billion worth of the most sophisticated weaponry in the U.S. inventory, and the arms sale program quickly became a scandal."

MANY IRANIANS, FAR FROM believing that the Shah was leading their nation to new glories, felt he was selling its soul to foreigners. And those foreigners were not always model guests. The surge of weapons sales also brought a surge of Americans, whose numbers in Iran from 1970 to 1978 shot up from below eight thousand to some fifty thousand—plenty of them leftovers from U.S. involvement in Vietnam. "The very best and the very worst of America were on display in the cities of Iran," writes James Bill in his history *The Eagle and the Lion:*

> As time passed and the numbers grew, an increasingly high propor-
> tion of fortune hunters, financial scavengers, and the jobless and
> disillusioned recently returned from Southeast Asia found their
> way to Iran. Companies with billion-dollar contracts needed man-
> power and, under time pressure, recruited blindly and carelessly. In
> Isfahan, hatred, racism, and ignorance combined as American em-
> ployees responded negatively and aggressively to Iranian society.
> Iranians were commonly referred to as "sand-niggers," "ragheads,"
> "rags," "stinkies," and Bedouins, and their culture was referred to as
> a "camel culture."[54]

It was a tragic hemorrhaging of goodwill, which had been carefully cultivated by Americans in decades past who had left a powerful
personal imprint. Howard Baskerville, for example, was right out of
Princeton Theological Seminary in 1907 when he journeyed to the
northwest city of Tabriz as a missionary-teacher, joined Iranians fighting in the Constitution Revolution, and led a unit of one hundred fifty,
which was reduced to nine.[55] "The only difference between me and
these people is my place of birth, and that is not a big difference," the
twenty-four-year-old is said to have told doubtful friends.

Baskerville was killed and is remembered as a hero—an American
martyr for Iran, the story goes, shot in the heart. In 2005, President
Mohammad Khatami unveiled a bust of Baskerville in Tabriz.

Also fondly remembered is W. Morgan Shuster. In 1911, he was invited and entrusted by the first parliament, or majlis, to assume the
post of treasurer-general for Persia. Shuster set himself firmly against
the imperial powers the United Kingdom and Russia, and on the side
of the "democrats" in the nascent majlis. Shuster's book *The Strangling of Persia* is dedicated to "the Persian people" for their "unwavering belief . . . in my desire to serve them for the regeneration of their
nation."[56]

Memories of such heartfelt concern did not fade easily. "These Americans and hundreds like them established over the years a reputation for America that was positive and warm," notes historian Bill.[57]

Until the CIA coup in 1953. After that, the relationship began to unravel, with the boost in American numbers in the 1970s creating a new panoply of problems—and reasons for local disgust. In Isfahan in 1975, for example, three American women "dressed in bikini shorts and halter [tops] strolled into the ancient Friday Mosque where, laughing, gesturing and talking in loud voices, they toured the holy place in their own good time," writes Bill.[58] American teenagers roared on their motorcycles through another mosque; "fashionably dressed American women turned over a table in an elegant restaurant because service had been slow; and, as the Revolution was breaking in the late 1970s, an American shot an Iranian taxi driver in the head in a dispute over the fare."[59]

The Lesson of Torture

Anti-American hatred built further over the increasing severity of the Shah's repression, which was covered with Western fingerprints—a point that I saw graphically portrayed in Tehran, in a jail turned museum. The Shah's friends from the CIA and Israel's Mossad had from the 1950s trained Iran's secret police, which tortured and executed dissenters. It was called SAVAK—the Farsi acronym for the National Organization for Intelligence and Security.

The word *torture* here encompasses the acts of violence of a feared internal security apparatus that numbered from three thousand to five thousand, with paid informants pushing it to perhaps sixty thousand strong.[60] Amnesty International noted in its 1974–75 report: "The Shah of Iran retains his benevolent image despite the highest rate of death penalties in the world, no valid system of civilian courts, and a history of torture that is beyond belief."[61]

On their fellow Iranians, says historian Ervand Abrahamian,

SAVAK's torturers were skilled in using techniques from rape and electric drills to

> nail extractions; snakes (favored for use with women); electrical shocks with cattle prods, often into the rectum; cigarette burns; sitting on hot grills; acid dripped into nostrils; near-drownings; mock executions; and an electric chair with a large metal mask to muffle screams while amplifying them for the victim. This latter contraption was dubbed the Apollo—an allusion to the American space capsules.[62]

After the fall of the Shah, the Islamic Republic made sure that such abuses—and the nationalities of those foreigners who helped carry them out—were not forgotten. I saw the iron helmet of the Apollo, still on display as part of the ghoulish exhibits at the downtown Komiteh jail, which had been turned into a museum called Ebrat, which means "lesson" or "example."

When I visited in early 2009, I was surprised at the number of students on the tour, cramming each torture room for an explanation, following the trail of blood-red footprints painted on the floor and stepping into the solitary confinement cells to feel for themselves the suffocating, dark isolation behind thick and heavy metal doors.[63]

The Shah and his queen were remembered, their official portraits in one room overlooking life-size figures applying the tools of torture. And no opportunity was missed to demonstrate a link between this inflicted pain and America: Many of the torturers are unmistakably made up to look like CIA agents, taller and lighter skinned, and dressed like bank executives in New York with white button-up shirts, ties, and even suspenders. They work over wax-figure victims that drip blood from their wounds, sometimes hanging upside down and with backs and torsos burned and lacerated, dirty faces contorted. On one desk is a fake bottle of whisky, a clear sign of "corruption on earth," coming from the West.

Our tour guide was an everyman former inmate with gray stubble. He stopped beside a portrait of an early SAVAK chief: "Now he is in the U.S. and we haven't heard of his death yet, unfortunately. He would like hearing the torture and screams of freedom-seeking people."

The Apollo contraption had a room to itself, where the bucketlike helmet was lowered over the head of the victim, whose wrists were strapped to a chair with bare feet extended. Another American exec look-alike—with stylish tie, his sleeves rolled up for the task—was depicted holding thick cables to whip the feet to a bloody mess.

One inmate, a prominent poet and essayist who spent 102 days in this prison in 1973, wrote that his torture began on the second day:

> My beard is pulled out with a pair of surgical scissors. . . . I am given seventy-five blows on the soles of my feet with a plaited wire whip; one of my fingers is broken; I am threatened with the rape of my wife and daughter [if I don't confess]; then a pistol is held to my head. . . .
>
> I get up but fall down. There is blood all over my feet, and they are already as thick as two heavy mud bricks. The man wields his long wire whips in a circle around my head.
>
> "Get up, you son of a bitch, and stamp your feet on the floor!" [64]

Supreme Leader Khamenei did time here when he was a mere cleric—one of six times he was imprisoned before the Revolution.[65] Here is the mug shot of Khamenei, his prisoner number painted over with the year of his incarceration, 1353 in the Persian calendar, or 1974. It shows a thick, all-black beard and eyes looking through large, slightly askew glasses, straight at the camera with emotionless concentration.

That framed portrait is one of hundreds that hang in four stacked rows down both sides of a long hallway in the jail. As I walked along it, I recognized several regime luminaries. There is former president Rafsanjani (No. 3324) and even Khomeini's oldest son, Mustafa (No. 359), who was killed—Khomeini claimed by SAVAK—in 1977. The many women in the lineup all have headscarves discreetly airbrushed into place, post-Revolution.

Khamenei's old solitary confinement cell is three turns off a dark corridor. I step to the narrow door and see, scratched through the blackened paint, words of a verse about "the prison ashamed of the face of the liberated."

The gift shop sells postcards printed with bleeding and broken bodies, the wax figures from the torture chambers. Among the mementos is a DVD that dramatizes SAVAK crimes as a large CIA symbol moves across the screen.[66] The message is clear, to those on my tour, and to the busloads of students and others who were lining up outside for the next time slot: America collaborated in the suffering of Iranians.

In a side room I was surprised to come across two less conservatively dressed ladies who were *basiji* students. They were just as surprised to find an American here. "Of all places, he *had* to be from America," Fatemeh told her friend Tayebeh about me, unimpressed, her eyes drifting elsewhere, unaware that my interpreter would translate every word. "But I really love the people from the U.S.—they are very straightforward," replied Tayebeh, who wore very un-*basiji* highlights in her hair and too-short sleeves.

I asked them how these displays, showing acts that took place years before they were born, were relevant to them today. We were alone and out of sight, but then a third, older woman called Somayeh, draped in a full black chador, stepped into the small room. The younger *basiji* women were not deterred.

"Those people who were [imprisoned] here really loved something, or they wouldn't have fought for it so hard," Fatemeh told me, drawing the intended lesson from the "Lesson" museum.

But then the older Somayeh unexpectedly raised doubt about the Islamic regime. "It's sad our country is getting back to where it was back then," she said.

Tayebeh agreed: "There could be places like this now; we just don't know about them."

There *were* many places just like that in the Islamic Republic, a number of them secret. Already for a generation, in fact, the regime had distinguished itself with its own flavor of brutality and a death rate—most notably during the "reign of terror" period of 1981–82, and another bout of executions in 1988—that far exceeded that of the Shah era.

"Whereas less than 100 political prisoners had been executed between 1971 and 1979 [the last years of the Shah], more than 7,900 were executed between 1981 and 1985," records historian Abrahamian. "In the prison literature of the Pahlavi era, the recurring words had been 'boredom' and 'monotony.' In that of the Islamic Republic, they were 'fear,' 'death,' 'terror,' 'horror,' and, most frequent of all, 'nightmare.' "[67]

True as that may be, the official narrative of the Ebrat Museum—the one that is widely shared by Iranians—is that the book of torture in Iran was written by the Shah and by SAVAK, with the determined help of America and Israel. *Basiji* students like Tayebeh and Somayeh, as they look at Iran and its cruelties today, were not likely to miss the irony of these words at the museum entrance: "The governments of oppression never learn from history."

THAT IRONY WAS ALSO not lost on one of the actual female guards at Evin Prison in mid-2007. Her visit to the Ebrat Museum "clearly shook her," recalled Iranian-American academic Haleh Esfandiari, who was a prisoner at Evin at the time.[68] Esfandiari spoke often with the guard, and relates: "The museum featured pictures of SAVAK's jailers, interrogators, and torturers. When [the guard] saw the pictures, she told me, she remarked to a friend who was with her, 'Someday, they will put our pictures in this museum.' "

THE SHAH'S REPUTATION FOR brutality was adding to the storm that would consume America's closest ally in the Middle East.

Apparently unaware of this dangerous mix, President Jimmy Carter and the first lady chose to celebrate the New Year in Tehran. At a luxurious and televised state banquet, champagne toasts were raised to usher in 1978. The Shah praised Iran's "unshakeable links" with America, and toasted the "ever-increasing friendship" between Iran and the "great and noble American people." [69]

In his turn, Carter described the very close bond he felt with the monarch, and how impressed he was at the result of twenty-five centuries of history. "Iran, because of the great leadership of the Shah, is an island of stability in one of the more troubled areas of the world," Carter said. Israel had yet to become the best friend and ally of the United States. "We have no other nation on Earth who is closer to us in planning for our mutual military security," Carter told the Shah. "And there is no leader with whom I have a deeper sense of personal gratitude and personal friendship."

Less than a year later the Shah would flee in disgrace. The Revolution and the hostage saga would paralyze much of the Carter presidency and contribute to victory for Ronald Reagan in 1980.

"We know [the hostage crisis] was a blow to American pride. But in the end it didn't change the American way of life . . . the foundation of society was not hurt," explained Ebrahim Yazdi, a pharmacologist from Texas who became the first foreign minister after the Revolution.[70] "But it was different in 1953. [The CIA coup] killed the embryo of democracy in Iran."

That point was made clearly to Bruce Laingen, the highest-ranking U.S. diplomat taken hostage. After a year, he screamed at one of his captors: "You have no right to do this! This is cruel and inhumane! These people have done nothing! This is a violation of every law of God and man!" [71] When Laingen was out of breath, the hostage taker told him in good English: "You have no right to complain, because you took our whole country hostage in 1953."

"Some Kind of Monsters"

For many Americans, it was the seizure of the U.S. Embassy on November 4, 1979, that still creates suspicion of every Iranian action. Invoked in the collective memory are images of revolutionaries storming the iron gates; of blindfolded Americans on TV, the helpless puppets of an evil, terrorist puppeteer. They are images of weakness, of vulnerability. Of the sapping of a superpower's strength.

"Why was it all so important to us?" asked Abe Rosenthal of the *New York Times*: "[B]ecause there was a feeling in this country until the 444th day that it was not just the fifty-two [hostages] but all Americans and, worse still, our very government that had been taken captive and held hostage in that embassy. No amount of reticence, logic, patience, or understanding could assuage that sensation, ever." [72]

The embassy takeover was sparked by the American decision less than two weeks earlier to admit the Shah to the United States on "humanitarian" grounds for medical treatment. Militant students in Tehran saw it as the first step in Washington's plan to destroy the Islamic Republic, to mount another coup like 1953.

"The Americans had been *seriously* engaged in affairs that were *much* more than gathering information, even much more than espionage," Massoumeh Ebtekar told me years later. [73] She had been the spokeswoman for the militant students, a college freshman who had spent her youth in America and became known to a rapt U.S. television audience as "Mary." The documents found at the embassy were taken as proof that the United States aimed to carry out another coup.

"In those days, it was very easy. . . . Regime change was a very simple matter," Ebtekar recalled. "The students had every reason to think this was a very legitimate action that they had to take [or] the Islamic Revolution would face the fate that many other revolutions had—doomed to be totally undermined and destroyed."

For this unlikely Iranian schoolgirl from Pennsylvania, the road from Independence Hall to the embassy seizure in Tehran made perfect sense. Speaking to me in American-accented English, Mary/Ebtekar said that Americans should be the first to recognize the Iranian impulse toward justice and freedom, since those ideals were brought into her life in the United States, and later at an American-style school in Tehran.

She eventually became Iran's first woman vice president. But it was odd to hear this committed revolutionary tell the hostage story with such a familiar accent; if I had closed my eyes, I could have easily imagined the voice of a soccer mom.

The problem was the "contrast between what I saw in Iran, and what I expected to see, and what American policy was in Iran, and what it professed to be, [with] freedom and democracy," Ebtekar told me, sometimes smiling in a black chador that framed her round face in a perfect oval. "I could feel some contradiction here [with] certain values I was being brought up with in that American school. Such as human dignity . . . individual merits, individual rights."

The Revolution was her release, she recalled: "The scenes were unbelievable. The power that it created among the people. The fact that you could see people looking out of their windows—and then closing their windows and pouring out onto the streets and coming. Like a message that transforms everyone, and nobody can resist."

THE STUDENTS WERE IDEALISTIC and naïve, Mary/Ebtekar readily admits, and unaware or uncaring about the personal trauma they were about to inflict—or the mutual U.S.-Iran misperceptions they were about to amplify. Before the seizure, leader Mohsen Mirdamadi revved the students up with a powerful tale of wounded Persian pride. Americans in Iran

had come to expect extra respect, even deference from all Iranians, from shoe-shine boy to Shah. But [Islam] views this as a sin. . . . In our country, American lifestyles had come to be imposed as an ideal, the ultimate goal. Americanism was the model. American popular culture—books, magazines, film—had swept over our country like a flood. This cultural aggression challenged the self-identity of people like us. This was the idol which had taken shape within Iranian society. We found ourselves wondering, "Is there any room for our own culture?"[74]

Some two hundred students swarmed the gates that Sunday morning in Tehran, breaching the locks and chains with long-handled bolt cutters hidden under black chadors. Convinced of the justice of their cause, relates Mary/Ebtekar in her memoir, they "burst into the inner sanctum of a superpower and humbled it."[75]

The takeover did not take long, despite the sprawling size of the twenty-seven-acre compound. A clutch of Americans held out for hours in a secret vault room, furiously shredding documents, destroying codebooks, and smashing communications gear, until students grabbed diplomat John Limbert, put a gun to his head, and threatened to kill him unless those in the vault gave themselves up.[76] When that door opened, the students were angry that so many documents had been destroyed. They set upon Charles Jones, the communications officer. "They kicked me in the ribs, stepped on my hands and held a gun to my head. They wanted to know why I was helping Americans. They thought that as a black man I should be on their side," Jones recalled.[77]

"Many of them had probably never seen an American before. I think a lot of them were surprised to find out that we didn't have horns," recalled Limbert, a political officer who had been a Peace Corps volunteer in Iran in the 1960s, was married to an Iranian, and spoke Farsi.[78] "They didn't know what an American was like, and some probably didn't even know where America is. They expected us to be some kind of monsters."

And reeducating those "monsters" was part of the plan. Hostage Bill Belk was reassured as he was led downstairs and shown—a blindfolded trophy—before a roaring crowd and journalists' cameras. "Don't be afraid. Don't be scared," he was told.[79] "We won't hurt you. We just want to teach you. We will bring you Khomeini's thoughts. We will teach you about God. We will teach the CIA not to do these terrible things to our country."

TWO DECADES LATER, I found an unexpected and surreal link to this period. During a visit to some decrepit student offices in an old house taken over after the fall of the Shah, I came across several rows of beat-up gray filing cabinets from the U.S. Embassy, with their security lock handles for classified material still in place, their locks long gone.[80] One had a red label, OPEN—just as some embassies today still mark unlocked files. Another was stuck with a six-inch-tall portrait of Khomeini, who had promised "severe defeat" to the original owners of this equipment.

Several of the filing cabinets and high-quality bookshelves even eerily had blue and white tabs still attached, which read: "Tehran American School." An embassy logbook for an official Fiat car remained in one drawer.

"Don't write that we took these!" implored one wary student, who was born after the hostage saga. "We inherited them."

BUT IT WAS A powerful legacy with enduring ramifications. In a stroke, with the embassy takeover and Khomeini's blessing, the Revolution's most militant factions solidified their grip, ending a "power struggle to win the support of the masses against liberals like me," former foreign minister Ebrahim Yazdi told me.[81] "They succeeded in pushing aside moderate elements and concentrated power in their hands. And after the [embassy seizure], the policy of suppression and policy of elimination [of opponents] began."

The students were bolstered by continuing large rallies outside the walls. The phones in the embassy—answered by the students with the words "Den of Spies"—constantly rang with Iranians giving encouragement and support.[82] The students set to work cataloging thousands of secret documents they found in those filing cabinets, and painstakingly piecing together the thin strips that had emerged from the shredders in the vault. It all added up to irrefutable proof, they claimed, of a diabolical degree of spy work. The documents were originally published in eighty-five volumes, by one count, and used to confirm fears that America was determined to unravel the Revolution.[83]

Most of the material was run-of-the-mill. For example, the sixty-third volume of the *Documents from the U.S. Espionage Den*—which has the enticing title "U.S. Interventions in Iran," part twelve—included such mundane events as a visit by the American chargé to the agriculture minister and a discussion of French business affairs in Iran.[84]

This volume has few secrets, except for the U.S. Defense Intelligence Agency (DIA) "Intelligence Appraisal" from August 1978, which showed how out of touch Washington's spies really were.[85] The confidential report did tabulate several attacks on official U.S. facilities that "seem to indicate an increasing anti-U.S. tone." Five months before the Shah fled, however, the DIA concluded: "There is no threat to the stability of the Shah's rule, but continuing tests between the government and the opposition are in sight."

And the CIA had been busy. The documents proved that even the first post-Revolution president, Abolhassan Banisadr, was meeting a top CIA agent disguised as a businessman and had agreed to accept a thousand-dollar monthly allowance.[86] They also showed that hostage William Daugherty was one of several CIA agents, a fact he admitted to stunned interrogators. "You're an enemy of our country," the Iranians charged, according to Mark Bowden's detailed reconstruction of the crisis, *Guests of the Ayatollah*.[87]

Enraged, Daugherty shot back: "You guys don't know *jack shit* about the world. This is going to be terrible for your country in the long run." He had never been more angry in his life, and let go his cursing fusillade. "You think you're civilized because you had civilization here three thousand years ago! Well, there's no fucking trace of it anymore. You guys are nothing but animals!"

THE ENTIRE EVENT WAS a "miscalculation" only meant to last a few days, not one and a half years, Abbas Abdi, one of the students who orchestrated the embassy takeover and carried the megaphone that morning to give the command to start, told me years later.[88] I sought him out because over time he had rejected—like many of the militant students—the hard-line worldview and had turned into an important reformist. "We were not thinking of the aftermath. I can't regret a mistake. At that time, we thought we were doing something good," Abdi recalled. Since then, "Everything has changed. Change in the world, our regime has changed; my level of education and understanding has changed. . . . I am older and wiser."

Eventually, in 2002, this key hostage taker was arrested and jailed—ironically—over a poll secretly commissioned by Iran's parliament that quantified the shocking scale of *pro*-American views in Iran. In Iran there may be disgust over hypocritical U.S. government policies in the Middle East, of Washington's talk of democracy while kissing monarchs and dictator allies, of preaching about human rights while being responsible for abuses at Abu Ghraib and Guantanamo, of imperial attitudes that are the inevitable marks of a sole superpower.

But in Iran there was still widespread admiration for America.

The secret poll found that 74.4 percent of Iranians supported dialogue with the United States.[89] And it found that 45.8 percent believed that Washington's policy toward Iran was "to some extent correct"—just months after President George W. Bush designated Iran part of his Axis of Evil.

But truth is a dangerous commodity in the Islamic Republic. Though the "facts" were established by three separate polling institutes—and the survey was requested by the government itself—the result was treason.

Wearing a prison uniform in a Tehran courtroom in late 2002, Abdi was accused of falsifying the results, of selling data to the U.S. polling company Gallup—which the court claimed was linked to the CIA—and of meeting a British "intelligence agent."[90] Among the charges was "acting against the Islamic Republic," thanks to a meeting in Paris with former hostage and U.S. diplomat Barry Rosen in 1997. The hardline newspaper *Kayhan* crowed that authorities had "unearthed the ultimate base of American espionage, and the operations center for a fifth column."[91]

Abdi spent years in prison for canvassing the opinions of ordinary Iranians. From jail he wrote an open letter cataloging the injustices and "lies" of his interrogation and trial.[92] He begged: "At least try to return one shred of my rights to me. . . ." But Abdi had given up.

Iran's cherished Islamic system, known as the *nezam,* was no longer worth his breath to criticize, he said, because it could never improve: "There's no attachment left in me to the *nezam* . . . for which I have strived for nearly three decades."

The Chemical Weapons Connivance

All the U.S. hostages were released alive and unhurt, Iranians like to point out. But to many Iranians, the list of American aggressions against Iran would grow longer. Iranians do not let go of the Iran-Iraq War, and America's decisive support of Saddam's war machine after it invaded Iran in 1980.

It was Iraq's increasingly effective use of chemical weapons that raised Iran's death toll, using American satellite imagery that pinpointed Iranian troop locations. That deadly arsenal was made with ingredients supplied by American and European companies, its use given a green light from Washington that *all* methods were acceptable in the fight against Khomeini. In Iraq's foolhardy war, it was the United States that did much to expand Iran's legions of martyrs. Iranian survivors often told me they had felt the difference on the battlefield, in blood spilled and lungs poisoned.

Many details of the U.S. role were not revealed until years later. "At times, thanks to the White House's secret backing for the intelligence-sharing, U.S. intelligence officers were actually sent to Baghdad to help interpret the satellite information," notes author Alan Friedman in one of the most detailed accounts.[93] As Washington increased its role, the United States "built an extensive high-tech annex in Baghdad to provide a direct down-link receiver" for the satellite imagery.

The CIA used Jordan's King Hussein—who had already been on the Agency's payroll for twenty years by 1977, when that fact was made public[94]—to hand-carry the first set of U.S. satellite images to Saddam in 1982. When Iraq began taking serious losses in the mid-1980s, Washington dramatically expanded its help.

Concerned in 1986 that Iraqi forces were not effectively using the satellite imagery, for example, the U.S. government conveyed a message to the Iraqi leader, via Egypt's President Hosni Mubarak, to step up air strikes. Such Iraqi attacks suddenly intensified, but with an unintended result, writes Friedman: "Saddam gained in the short run, but his escalation triggered an Iranian response that led both sides to target civilian centers over the next two years, contributing mightily to the resulting bloodbath."[95]

And that was not all. By 1987 the CIA was every week flying a planeload of weapons into Baghdad.[96] It also flew spy planes and helicopters over Iranian bases, and eventually "engaged in secret bombing runs," in one case destroying a warehouse full of mines. Delta Force helicopters stationed on barges afloat in the Persian Gulf engaged a number of Iranian vessels, in one case killing three Iranian soldiers.

U.S. personnel engaging in these "black missions . . . weren't confused about what they were doing," said Lieutenant Colonel Roger Charles, a Defense Department staffer who later investigated Persian Gulf secret operations, according to Friedman.[97] "They said they were at war, that their daily actions included combat activities against Iran."

IRANIANS ARE STILL DEALING with the physical consequences decades later. Iraq's heavy use of gas climaxed in April 1988 with a massive chemical bombardment of the Fao Peninsula, Iraq's only port and its access to the Persian Gulf.[98] Iraq threatened to target Iranian cities with gas if Iran did not end the war. According to one CIA report, they were the decisive moves: "Iran's defenses soon collapsed everywhere. Chemical weapons ended the war. . . ."[99]

Khomeini finally gave in. The human toll had been unprecedented in modern conflict, with one million dead and wounded in a war that hadn't even changed the border, just soaked it in blood. Iran had lost up to 60 percent of its military hardware[100] and was running short of zealous new recruits.[101] Khomeini lamented that he himself "would have preferred death and martyrdom" to capitulation, but that the interests of Islam took precedence. He had "no choice" but to "give in to what God wants us to do," Khomeini declared. It was a bitter decision, "but I drink this chalice of poison for the Almighty and for His satisfaction."[102]

While Khomeini's "poison" may have been figurative talk about failing to defeat the infidel Saddam Hussein, for tens of thousands of Iranian foot soldiers, drinking Iraqi poison had been a reality. The continuing agonies of veterans like Colonel Mohammad Akbari are trumpeted in Iran's media, so that Iranians know which enemy—America and the West—they should blame for creating, among their countrymen, the world's largest group of chemical weapons victims.

Colonel Akbari was on one of the most gruesome front lines of the war during the Val Fajr 8 offensive, in which Iran captured the Fao Peninsula in early 1986. Gas was so prevalent that the hirsute soldier had shaved his thick black beard to get his mask to fit better. The Iraqi shelling never seemed to stop. Date palms were smashed. Muddy trenches were death traps. And the Revolutionary Guard officer had to wear a special protective suit around the clock, despite temperatures of 120 degrees with stifling humidity.

"The whole area was contaminated; there was always the smell of rotten fish. This time it was much stronger," the officer told me in late 2002.[103] He was weak, a gray remnant of the strapping and stern-faced specimen shown in his wartime military portrait. Akbari was exposed one night as he walked toward an artillery battery in the dark, and the Iraqi mustard shells found their mark.

"With chemical weapons, you hear nothing," Akbari explained, his words cutting through with a raspy cough. He turned the knob of an oxygen tank next to his couch at home and slipped on a respirator. "I hurried to take my mask, but I realized it was too late." Akbari began vomiting blood. Despite wearing gloves his hands broke out in blisters. Seventeen years later, to cope with what his medical report simply called "severe chronic bronchitis," Akbari had to keep inhalers in his pocket and a humidifier in the room—its steaming presence not far from the clock with the Khamenei picture. He was officially 74 percent wounded, enough to earn the title "living martyr."

Akbari's son, born years after the war, was diagnosed with a nervous disorder attributed to the gas. And Akbari's younger brother, exposed on another front line, had died in 2001. "Nothing is left of me," Akbari pointed out, pulling at his slack pant legs. "I can't laugh or cry. If I get angry, I cough blood."

The Iraqi counterattack was the most sustained of the war up to that point, with chemicals dropped to saturation by thirty-two Iraqi aircraft. "At first we had 2,500 cases but because the mustard gas hung in the palm trees, it went up to 8,500 in a couple of days," a military doctor witness told analyst Joost Hiltermann in the definitive account of Iraqi gas use, *A Poisonous Affair*. "We couldn't decontaminate the area. . . . We kept praying for a rain. . . ."[104]

UN weapons inspectors in the 1990s were amazed to discover the "enormous scope both in terms of scale and breadth" of Iraq's chemical warfare program.[105] Baghdad's "final" declaration in 1997 stated that during the Iran-Iraq War the military had consumed 2,870 tons of chemical agents, most of it in the form of 101,080 munitions. In 1984, an Iraqi general had warned Iranians that "for every harmful insect there is an insecticide capable of annihilating it whatever their number and that Iraq possesses this annihilation insecticide."[106]

On the Iranian side of the front line, the grim human results were mind-boggling. More than one million Iranians were exposed to chemical weapons, and 7,000 died immediately, Iranian officials say.[107] At least 100,000 were "severely injured" by nerve agents like sarin and soman, and blistering agents like mustard gas. Of those, 55,000 are registered and still receive treatment for chemical-related illness, more than two decades after the war.

What makes Iran unique is that detailed medical records often date from the first battlefield exposure and treatment, creating an unmatched resource on chemical effects. Experts from the Organisation for the Prohibition of Chemical Weapons, based at The Hague, responsible for ensuring adherence to the UN-brokered 1997 Chemical Weapons Convention, have held numerous clinical courses in Iran and told me the country "provides a body of experience that really doesn't exist anywhere else."[108]

CIA reports note that Iraq's chemical attacks prompted Iran to con-sider its own chemical, biological, and nuclear weapons options.[109] But while several such American reports also allege that Iran used chemi-cal weapons, in a very limited way—sometimes in a clear effort to lend moral equivalency to the chemical crimes of pseudo-ally Iraq—no convincing information has been found that Iran did so.[110]

Iran's chemical survivors blame the U.S. government as much as Saddam Hussein for their suffering. In Akbari's living room, a por-trait of Iran's two supreme leaders—Khomeini and Khamenei—sits atop a large silver Samsung TV, a gift from a veterans foundation. "All the chemical-wounded accuse the U.S., because without them, Iraq couldn't have made chemical weapons. It was very clear to us, that they were giving this intelligence to the Iraqis. We really blame the U.S. for everything," Akbari told me.

But he had other words, too, which through his coughing he in-sisted I use. They provided hope for reconciliation. "I have no problem with the American people, only autocratic leaders," Akbari said. "I ask you to write this last sentence, because I want Americans to know we are friends with them, not enemies, even though we are chemically wounded."

COULD SUCH RESIDUAL GOODWILL be a foundation to rebuild the U.S.-Iran relationship? Perhaps, if chemical warfare were the only issue. But there are many other layers of antagonism. Concurrent with the Iran-Iraq War in the mid-1980s, for example, another drama was playing itself out that would further widen the U.S.-Iran divide. For despite the close American support for Iraq, Washington was *also* secretly shipping some weapons to Iran, in arms-for-hostages deals that aimed to secure the release—through Tehran's good offices, if they existed—of Americans kidnapped by Shiite militants in Lebanon.

The revelations of the Iran-Contra affair were explosive for all sides, when they finally became public, exemplified on the U.S. side by the rule-bending Colonel Oliver North, who testified that he was simply doing his patriotic duty. Among the most embarrassed was President

Ronald Reagan, who as president-elect in 1980—during the final stages of negotiations for the release of American diplomats held hostage in Tehran—had declared: "I don't think you pay ransom for people that have been kidnapped by barbarians." [111]

President Reagan pledged repeatedly that America would never bargain with "terrorists," and claimed at first that the United States had never traded "weapons or anything else for hostages." [112] The investigation by the Tower Commission had found, however, that under Reagan's watch, the Iran initiative "ran directly counter to the Administration's own policies on terrorism, the Iran/Iraq War and military support to Iran," such that "U.S. policy . . . worked against itself." [113]

It also rebounded on Iran, where top officials found it hard to submit to the Iranian populace—otherwise completely steeped in absolutist ideology about sacred war and "epic" exploits of pure martyrs at the front—that the regime was engaged in secret deals with two of its biggest enemies, the Great Satan and "Zionist occupiers."

Never mind the Islamic Revolution's visceral hatred of America. Never mind how Khomeini's venom spat at the Israeli "cancer." Despite the public war of words, the Jewish state had been wheeling and dealing with its mortal enemy the Islamic Republic for years, privately viewing Iran as a strategic counterweight to its Arab enemies. U.S. intelligence reports from mid-1982 noted one $50 million deal between Israel and Iran for materiel. [114]

This pragmatism—some would call it hypocrisy—was catching. The Israelis and their middlemen were instrumental in convincing key players of the Iran-Contra affair to secretly pursue arms-for-hostages swaps. [115] So deals were pursued, but with limited results and unlimited political fallout. Negotiations always seemed rich with promise, but were only partially fulfilled, if at all. The United States even gave Tehran satellite imagery of the Iraqi war front, at the same time higher-quality American intelligence was already being secretly provided to *Iraq*, about *Iran's* side of the border. [116]

What did arms-for-hostages achieve? In total, in the space of a year to November 1986, Iran had acquired 1,500 TOW missiles and thirteen pallets of HAWK missile spare parts from the Americans via Israel. In return, Washington received the release of two American captives in Lebanon. In the initial deal, with the United States in only a supporting role, Israel had sold 508 TOW missiles to Iran and reaped a single hostage from Lebanon.

"The lesson to Iran was unmistakable," the final congressional investigating report found.[117] "All U.S. positions and principles were negotiable, and breaches by Iran went unpunished. Whatever Iran did, the U.S. could be brought back to the arms bargaining table by the promise of another hostage."

Further shock for the White House came from Ali Akbar Hashemi Rafsanjani, who revealed a Bible signed by Reagan in October 1986, with the handwritten inscription from Galatians: "All nations shall be blessed in you." And to top it all, the whole covert project backfired. In the months after the deals became public, more Americans and Westerners were kidnapped in Lebanon—all of them seen as effective future bargaining chips after the arms-for-hostages saga proved their worth.

FURTHER ANTAGONISMS FOLLOWED. ONE more act looms from history as an unforgivable crime in the minds of Iranians, but left no trace on Americans. IranAir Flight 655 was making its way across the hazy Persian Gulf on a scheduled flight to Dubai on July 3, 1988, when it was shot down by the U.S. Navy's most sophisticated warship, a billion-dollar Aegis cruiser called the USS *Vincennes*. Iranian TV showed heart-wrenching images of bodies and debris floating in the water, and sobbing families of the victims. The Islamic Republic accused the United States of a "barbaric massacre," adding these 290 "martyrs" to the long list of grievances that stoked U.S.-Iran hostility.

An official Pentagon investigation, known as the Fogarty Report, found that the ship mistook the airliner for an attacking Iranian jet. But an in-depth examination by *Newsweek* found that report to be a "pastiche of omission, half-truths, and outright deceptions" that amounted to a "cover-up approved at the top." [118] The incident was a "fiasco," *Newsweek* said, causing the "U.S. Navy [to do] what all navies do after terrible blunders at sea: it told lies and handed out medals."

The central question was how the navy's most sophisticated and expensive surface warship, "designed to track and shoot down as many as two hundred incoming [aircraft and] missiles at once, had blown apart an innocent civilian airliner in its first time in combat." *Newsweek* also found that the *Vincennes* was in Iranian territorial waters at the time, in clear violation of international law—and contrary to the version of events spun to Congress by the U.S. Navy with altered maps.

Inexperience took over the *Vincennes,* such that when the order to fire was given, "the young lieutenant was so undone, that he pressed the wrong keys on his console twenty-three times," *Newsweek* reported. Four years after the event, "a number of the seamen and officers aboard the *Vincennes* that morning . . . are still in therapy today, wrestling with guilt."

The aftermath remains incomprehensible to Iranians. The United States eventually paid compensation but never apologized for the incident. The ship's air-warfare chief won the navy's Commendation Medal for "heroic achievement," for maintaining his "poise and confidence under fire." All crew received combat action ribbons.

The Airbus shootdown "still resonates [in Iran] because it reaffirms the narrative that is already there: the Americans are hypocrites who talk about justice, but when it comes to wars and other people's interests, they always work to undermine it," Iran analyst Farideh Farhi told me. [119]

The United States has "historically proven its intent to weaken" Iran, said Farhi. So despite the fact that Iranians themselves are pro-American, "even among the Iranian population, you can sense a tremendous distrust of U.S. intentions." The lesson for Iran has been clear: "You can't deal with the U.S. from a position of weakness. The only way the U.S. will come around to treat you with respect is from a position of power."

In Need of Enemies

To gain that position, while the United States has projected military power throughout Iran's neighborhood for three decades, the Islamic Republic adopted a strategy of asymmetric warfare. Iran still has a large manpower advantage over all its neighbors. But except for two minor exceptions, Iran's military expenditures have since 1989 been less—often far less—as a percentage of gross national product than every other Persian Gulf state, a figure that in 2007 stood at just 2.6 percent.[120]

That fact never tempered Iran's defiant rhetoric. In 1997, when there were just 20,000 American troops in the region—a fraction of the 150,000 that would be in Iraq a decade later—Revolutionary Guard commander Major General Mohsen Rezaei declared: "Let me send a clear message to the Americans: the Persian Gulf is our region; they have to leave our region. Iran will never start any war, but if Americans one day decide to attack us, then they would have committed suicide. We will turn the region into a slaughterhouse for them. There is no greater place than the Persian Gulf to destroy America's might."[121]

Yet the numbers didn't add up to real danger. In the decade that followed the general's statement, military spending by other Gulf countries was 7.5 times that of Iran. Iran struggled to maintain the remnants of the Shah's arsenal, and sanctions meant new purchases came only from Russia, China, and the former Eastern Bloc. Gulf nations from 1992 to 2006 spent 15.6 times more on new arms deals than Iran. In 2007, when Iran's military spending hit a twenty-eight-year high of $7.3 billion, its chief adversary, the United States—which alone accounted for a whopping 48 percent of all global military spending—was burning through the equivalent of Iran's peak annual defense budget every two and a half weeks, just in Iraq.[122]

The inevitable disparity was "all too clear in the current military balance," noted veteran analysts Anthony Cordesman and Adam Seitz in late 2008.[123] And while Iran had made some progress, its efforts "still do not offset the decay of its aging inventory of conventional weapons, or the wear of wartime operations and constant exercises. Iran is not an emerging hegemon. It is falling behind."

Evident for many years, that reality led to Iran's marginal treatment in a secret Pentagon document called "Defense Strategy for the 1990s," which was leaked to the *New York Times*.[124] The February 1992 draft document was a blueprint for the neoconservative worldview at the end of the Cold War. Created by the office of then secretary of defense Dick Cheney, it said the Pentagon's "first objective is to prevent the re-emergence of a new rival" anywhere in the world. In the Middle East, the aim was to "remain the predominant outside power" and preserve access to oil.

And yet, in all the American reprioritizing of post–Cold War threats, one name hardly features: Iran. The declassified version of Cheney's controversial report barely mentions the Islamic Republic.[125] It simply notes, without alarm, how "we must recognize that regional dynamics can change and a rejuvenated Iraq or a rearmed Iran could move in this decade to dominate the Gulf." But even *that* prospect gets no mention in a string of seven "detailed scenarios" of potential conflicts (leaked once again to the *Times*) that were produced by the Pentagon in early 1992, to plan for the decade ahead.[126]

Among those seven, Iraq played a leading role by hypothetically seizing control of oil fields in Saudi Arabia and Kuwait in a lightning strike. There was a 300,000-strong ground attack from North Korea on South Korea, Russia attacking Lithuania and Poland, a coup in the Philippines, and even "a 'narco-terrorist' plot" in Panama that "threatens access to the Panama Canal, requiring both a Marine amphibious invasion and an airborne assault."

Iran, as a chaotic revolutionary regime still exhausted by the blood drain of its war with Iraq, just didn't rank in the constellation of American threats.

THAT OMISSION WOULD NOT last long.

In the early 1990s Iran was a forgotten villain until a small, ever-embattled American ally in the Middle East decided it needed to wake up Washington to the *real* threat. Anxious that its own strategic utility as a "bulwark" against Soviet-allied Arab states was losing its shine after the Cold War, Israel launched a campaign in 1992 to convince the United States that a new and more dangerous threat had emerged from Iran and the Islamic extremism that the Revolution inspired.

"The fear [in Israel] was that Washington's continued focus on Iraq would disturb the regional balance and enable Iran to emerge as a political—and military—threat to Israel," writes Trita Parsi in *Treacherous Alliance.*[127]

The new policy was an about-face for the Jewish state, which had had close ties with the Shah and had long considered Persian Iran as a strategic wedge against more hostile Arab nations. For years after the Islamic Revolution, Iran and Israel secretly maintained contact. And though sworn enemies today, pragmatism and good taste can still prevail: Israelis knowingly gobble up Iranian pistachios—the largest and best-flavored in the world, raised to perfection in orchards that line the hard, sunbaked desert of south-central Iran—that are channeled through Turkey and are marked as produce from there.[128]

But even as the Pentagon was putting the finishing touches to the rewrite of its "one superpower" strategy—with barely passing reference to Iran—Israel made sure president-elect Bill Clinton got the message of looming danger just days after his 1992 election victory.

"Iran has to be identified as Enemy No. 1," Joseph Alpher, a former official in Israel's Mossad intelligence agency, told the *New York Times.*[129] The newspaper noted that Israel's "catalogue of perceived danger [was] growing fairly long," and that it was Iran's nuclear program—which was still back then in a most nebulous stage—that "really gives Israel the jitters." Israel's own nuclear arsenal, believed since the mid-1980s to number roughly two hundred warheads, was explained by the *Times* "as their equalizer in a hostile zone," a balance that would be "lost" if other nations went nuclear.

The news report also reflected the skepticism both in Washington and for many in Tel Aviv, noting that "why the Israelis waited until fairly recently to sound a strong alarm about Iran is a perplexity."

But no doubt afflicted Israel's Prime Minister Yitzhak Rabin or Foreign Minister Shimon Peres, who, while both moderate by Israeli political standards, spearheaded the campaign to turn Iran into a diabolical threat to world peace—and persuade Washington to act accordingly.

"Our struggle against murderous Islamic terror is meant to awaken the world, which is lying in slumber," Rabin told the Knesset in late 1992.[130] "We call on all nations and all people to devote their attention to the great danger inherent in Islamic fundamentalism. That is the real and serious danger which threatens the peace of the world in forthcoming years. The danger of death is at our doorstep." Fueled by high-octane Israeli rhetoric, the campaign soared into the American strategic consciousness. Rabin said Iran was on a "megalomaniacal" quest to build a "Middle East empire."[131]

Iran certainly did question the right of what it called the "Zionist entity" to exist, and Israel argued "that rhetoric reflected intentions," writes analyst Parsi.[132] Israel Shahak, a prominent Israeli academic, noted in 1993 that the strategy was to "push the U.S. and other Western powers into a confrontation with Iran." David Makovsky, a U.S.-based Israel analyst, noted that Rabin repeated his "Khomeinism without Khomeini" mantra in "every single speech he gave when he traveled. I think he said it a thousand times. He was really focused on Khomeinism."[133]

It wasn't long before the message caught on, though the *Washington Post* noted that the "new rationale" for Israel to warrant greater U.S. military cooperation—by serving as a bulwark against Islamic extremism or Iran's regional ambitions—"is a controversial idea that has not been fully accepted here."[134]

Despite the Israeli efforts, the "skepticism that met their accusation was rooted in a rather simple fact—no one believed that Iran overnight had turned into a major threat to the region," notes analyst Parsi, especially after Iran's heavy losses in the Iran-Iraq War.[135] "Even lobbyists supporting Israel recognized that 'not much' had changed with Iran during the five short years when Rabin went from calling Tehran a geo-strategic friend to his warnings of the Persian menace."

IRANIANS RECOGNIZED THE DYNAMIC of a nation searching for, indeed needing, an enemy. Using the name of the ideological hard-line thugs in Iran that enforce regime diktat, analyst Saeed Laylaz told me how useful such an "enemy" can be.[136] "There are three *hezbollahi* regimes: Tehran, Tel Aviv, and Washington," the government critic said. "They are apparently against each other, but they love each other. They *need* each other. We need a foreign enemy to control the country."

The same was true in the Jewish state, an Israeli expert told Parsi: "You have to recognize that we Israelis need an existential threat. It is part of the way we view the world. If we can find more than one, that would be preferable, but we will settle for one."[137]

That compulsion was magnified on all three sides during the Bush era, when both Iran and the United States were ruled by uncompromising leaders. "Mr. Bush needs Khamenei, and Khamenei needs Bush," the reformist cleric Mohsen Kadivar told me in 2005.[138] "Both need energy, and Iran is a very good energy for the U.S. In foreign policy, both need an enemy."

Yet the Islamic Republic could also be a tactically useful partner, if not yet a strategic friend. After the World Trade Center and Pentagon attacks on September 11, 2001, for example, the United States requested help and Iran's diplomats and Revolutionary Guard quietly provided extensive intelligence and political assistance to the U.S. military and CIA, to improve targeting the Taliban and Al Qaeda in Afghanistan.[139]

Once the Taliban was ousted in late 2001, Iran again proved crucial to getting the victorious Northern Alliance to accept a limited number of cabinet posts and Hamid Karzai as the new president—a critical step toward immediately stabilizing post-Taliban Afghanistan.[140] Iranian diplomats made clear their interest in expanding contacts with the United States. One analyst told me of a "minor love-fest going on" between the Iranians and Americans, as diplomats were meeting secretly and not so secretly to discuss Afghanistan and other issues.[141]

It was a unique moment after 9/11, explained Hadi Semati, a political scientist at Tehran University: "For the first time the U.S. was humanized; the world saw those as human losses. People saw the U.S. not through the eyes of Hollywood, and the U.S. missed that opportunity and went with a jingoistic, arrogant policy. There was nothing but post–Sept. 11 vengeance and paranoia [from Washington], so no one in the region could see what the U.S. is about. . . . It really plays into conservative hands, and not just in Iran."[142]

Any remaining chance of reconciliation evaporated in early 2002, when George W. Bush declared Iran part of his Axis of Evil. Iranian officials considered it a slap in the face, and it had grave consequences for President Khatami and his beleaguered reform movement. The U.S. denunciation became ammunition for hard-liners, who used it as final proof of American mendacity—and of reformist naïveté.

FEAR IN TEHRAN REACHED a peak shortly after the U.S. invasion of Iraq in 2003, yielding perhaps the best opportunity for détente since 1979. The political noise in Washington was about regime change—fueled by vociferous declarations from American neoconservatives and from Israel—which gave Iran every reason to fear. On the ground, taxi drivers in Tehran wondered aloud about quickly learning English because "the Americans are coming!"

So when Iran sent a secret two-page fax to Washington in May 2003, offering dialogue "in mutual respect" on *all* contested issues, it fell on deaf ears.[143] Iran's entire Islamic system, the *nezam,* was clearly alarmed by the real-world demonstration of American troops dismembering in the space of three weeks an Iraqi army that—at least in its prime, and with Western support—Iran had only fought to standstill after eight years.

The Iranian offer outlined a grand bargain: Iran would agree not to pursue nuclear weapons and would open its nuclear program to "full transparency." It would cut support for Palestinian "opposition" groups Hamas and Islamic Jihad, and would "pressure [them] to stop violence" against Israeli civilians. Iran would act to disarm Hezbollah and turn it into a "mere political organization." It would not oppose a two-state solution to the Israel-Palestinian conflict.

The United States in turn would end sanctions and "hostile behavior" and recognize Iran's "legitimate security interests." It would permit peaceful nuclear technology, under strict safeguards. And it would provide "decisive action" against anti-Iran militants of the Mojahedin-e Khalq based in Iraq. Short of the self-destruction of the Islamic Republic, this offer was everything the United States had demanded for years.

Most importantly, it appeared to have the tacit approval of Supreme Leader Khamenei, a point made in a cover letter by Swiss ambassador Tim Guldimann. It explained the provenance of the proposal and how Sadegh Kharazi—Iran's ambassador to Paris at the time, whose sister is married to one of the Leader's sons—had discussed the language and all key points with Khamenei, President Khatami, and the foreign minister.

"There is no country that has more common interests with America than Iran," former ambassador Kharazi told me later.[144] "We still have our [anti-U.S.] revolutionary slogans, but we are not looking for confrontation," he said. "We don't want to be in love with America. [What] is important for us is coexistence with each other, an armistice for the future." In Iranian politics "nothing is impossible," Kharazi added, but the U.S. path must lead directly to Khamenei: "Foreign policy is under [his] direct supervision . . . the Leader is the one who can decide. America should do it carefully."

But the White House of 2003 was emboldened by the swift collapse of Saddam Hussein and on a regime-change roll. In "Mission Accomplished" mode, it ignored the offer.

We will never know how the outcome could have been different, or how far Iran was willing to go to reengage with America—in a moment of existential fear—because the offer was rejected before it could ever be explored. Iran's proposal had been presented to President Bush. While key figures spoke in favor, according to one rendition of the event, "Cheney and [Secretary of Defense Donald] Rumsfeld quickly put the matter to an end. Their argument was simple but devastating. 'We don't speak to evil,' they said." [145]

For years, that had been Iran's exact position, too.

DESPITE ALL ITS REVOLUTIONARY fire, the foreign policy of the Islamic Republic—especially since the mid-1990s—had aimed pragmatically at regime survival above all else. It came down to expediency, the cardinal tenet of *maslahat* in Iran's Shiite and Khomeinist worldview that allowed compromise on ideological "truths" if the alternative would threaten the Islamic system.

An expedient act was Khomeini's decision in 1988 to make peace with Iraq and drink from the "poison chalice," after failing to defeat Saddam Hussein. So was Iran's decision to secretly engage public enemies Israel and the United States to acquire American missiles in the early 1980s, when the Islamic regime had few other sources of weapons to counter Iraq.

Is official hatred of America any different? Is it any more sacred? Is a complete reversal possible of Iran's anti-American mind-set, given the right incentives?

"Khomeini laid the foundation that two plus two equals five," explained a veteran Iranian observer in Tehran, whom I've known for years and shall from here on call the Sage. [146] It was a phrase borrowed from George Orwell's *Nineteen Eighty-four*. Changing reality this way was what Orwell called *doublethink,* and the Islamic Republic modernized and applied it. [147] The Sage explained: "Khamenei spoke in the 1980s and said, 'We don't mean *absolute.*' Khomeini said: 'Shut up. When we say *absolute,* we mean it.' But expediency means to save the Islamic system, if we have to drop prayer, or the Haj [pilgrimage to Mecca], we can do it." [148]

The Sage told me a joke that illustrated how anything in the Shiite world could be justified: "Every night when a mullah got back home from work, after dinner his wife would bring him his medicine. One night the wife was sick. The son asked: 'Daddy, do you want your *arak* [distilled alcoholic spirit]?' The mullah replied: 'Don't name it, just bring it!' That's everywhere."

AS AMERICAN MILITARY FORCES became bogged down in Iraq and then Afghanistan in the years that followed, the leadership in Iran began to recalibrate, correctly calculating that a U.S. regime-change attack was less likely. I watched their harsh and sniping words toward Washington grow increasingly triumphant, as if Iran's exquisite geostrategic chess had somehow brought on terminal American decline.

The hard-line President Ahmadinejad said in a June 2008 speech:

Our beloved Imam [Khomeini], you commanded that the arrogant [powers] of the world must be destroyed. . . . I'd like to say that thanks to your illuminating presence, thanks to your guidance, thanks to your ardent and divine words . . . and thanks to the steadfastness of the Iranian people, today, the cruel and arrogant [powers] have reached a total dead end, and thanks to God, the countdown for the decline of America's demonic power has begun.[149]

The crowd chanted "Death to America" eight times, before the Iranian president added Israel into the mix: "Thanks to God, your wish will soon be realized, and this germ of corruption will be wiped off the face of the world."

The Americans were not impressed—at least not the top brass that knew that Iran, as usual, was more acid than action. "Tehran's feeling pretty cocky right now because they've been able to inflict pain on us in Iraq and Afghanistan," the chief of U.S. Central Command, Admiral William Fallon, said in 2008.[150] And if it were to come to war with Iran? "Get serious," the commander replied. "These guys are ants. When the time comes, you crush them."

• • •

COULD THERE REALLY BE room for U.S.-Iran coexistence when diatribes against America are at their most vociferous at the top of the Iranian leadership?

Henry Precht, the U.S. State Department's country director for Iran in the late 1970s, received a salutary warning about Khamenei—then one of many clerics in the panoply of the new theocracy—from a "liberal" Iranian journalist during a visit to Tehran in October 1979, immediately before the U.S. Embassy seizure. He was told: "There is one you really have to watch out for. Khamenei. He hates you and will never do you any favors." [151]

The Leader's contempt for the United States "has been remarkably consistent and enduring," notes Karim Sadjadpour in an analysis of Khamenei's speeches.[152] "He has very rarely spoken favorably, in public at least, about the United States [and instead], whether the topic of discussion is foreign policy, agriculture, or education, he seamlessly relates the subject matter to the cruelty, greed, and sinister plots of the 'Global Arrogance.' "

Khamenei's reading of U.S.-Iran relations, said Sadjadpour, "appears at times strikingly similar to hardliners in Washington, who believe the two countries represent diametrically opposed ideologies destined for an inevitable confrontation."

I had often heard Iranian hard-liners put their problem with America into a religious context. "We rely on and trust an Islam that does not allow dictatorship, or misusing and abusing others' rights, but the American state is alive with these," Hossein Shariatmadari, the holier-than-thou editor of the hard-right *Kayhan* newspaper, told me in 2004.[153] He was an official representative of the Leader, his office conference table always stocked with the best coconut macaroons in Tehran.

"So our true friendship is starting when one of these changes. Either we change Islam; never. Or America changes, and gets off the donkey of Satan, and we don't see such a thing on the horizon," said Shariatmadari. In Washington it didn't matter which party was in power: "There is no difference between hawks and doves. Contrary to all other countries, in the U.S. these birds share the same nest."

Khamenei's harsh words in late 2008 to mark the anniversary of the U.S. Embassy takeover seemed to bear that out, and left little room for détente, much less friendship. The hatred of Washington was ingrained, Khamenei told gathered students: "Since the victory of the Revolution nearly thirty years ago, there hasn't been a day in which America has had good intentions toward Iran. . . . Our problem with America isn't over one or two global, international or regional issues, which we can resolve by sitting down and negotiating. The problem is like a matter of life and death." [154]

AYATOLLAH KHOMEINI WAS REACHING out from the grave, still stamping the Islamic Republic with his radical imprimatur. But what doctrine could claim airtight belief, when submerged in Iran's fluid society? It wasn't working, for example, for *all* the schoolgirls I came across at the modest prayer hall where Khomeini used to preach, in the decrepit old Jamaran neighborhood of north Tehran. The pupils were clad mostly in black, and sat in a circle on the carpet around their history teacher. [155]

"If it were not important, I would not bring them here," teacher Surore told me of her lesson on Khomeini. "When the kids see it, they will learn it themselves."

And they *were* learning. A banner on the wall spelled out their obligation: "Imam Khomeini is a reality that is always alive." Rays of sunlight filtered through the small windows at the crown of the high roof, its beams catching filaments of dust in the air—small suspended specks that flew floating at anyone's passing. Breaking the reverent silence, I asked the girls why they were there. "To see our Leader," said sixteen-year-old Sarah, stepping forward as her schoolmates twittered shyly behind. "We want to know how our Leader lives—we love him so much."

"It's so beautiful," gushed Maryam, also in Farsi. "Our Leader, his life is very simple."

Their pilgrimage complete, the girls began moving toward the door. As they filed out, Sarah kept toward the back. Then unscripted and in English—so her teacher could not understand—Sarah leaned in my direction, a brim of black hair visible at the edge of her black chador. "It's not *all* our idea about Khomeini, to like him," she said in a hushed tone, as if imparting a state secret. And in fact, she *was* divulging a state secret by questioning a pinion of the Revolution. "This is a very important problem for us." Then flashing a smile and raising her voice in English for all to hear, she said: "Thank you!" Her teacher smiled, too, and they all left happy, unaware that minor sacrilege had been committed.

The doubt of giggling girls from a conservative school hardly constituted a crack in the regime. But it did raise questions about the future—and the willingness of Iranians to accept the legacy of Khomeini's isolation forever.

Appearances could be deceptive, and were not limited to black-clad schoolgirls. On the very night in 1989 that Khomeini passed away, and Iran was awash with a frenzy of mourning, Patrick Tyler was the only Western correspondent in Tehran. He was stopped at a roadblock by a Revolutionary Guard, a "fierce young man" who used the barrel of his AK-47 to tap on the car window.[156] "I slowly rolled down the window to face the muzzle and to gaze into his serious and bearded face," Tyler recalls in his book *A World of Trouble*. "He stooped to draw close and asked in halting English, 'Excuse me, sir, but if you were going to select the best American university to study electrical engineering, which one would you choose?' "

WHAT I FOUND AFTER three decades of revolutionary cant were hardened public views, both for and against America. Witness these two very different reactions from Iranians:

Image One is election day in Tehran, December 2006. Iranians were tired of American officials disparaging the validity of their votes. They remembered the Bush administration spitting about unelected leaders who "spread terror across the world," and staging a "mock election."[157] After 60 percent turnouts the Supreme Leader said the United States had been taught a lesson. "Despite its babbling, your enemy is now humiliated deep inside because of your greatness and the transparency of your democracy," Khamenei said.[158] *Kayhan* referred to "the bloodied face of Uncle Sam."

Iranians were incensed—fully aware that Washington's closest Mideast allies were the least democratic.

"Tell Bush: Forget about Iran, don't set foot here," one older woman—who would only identify herself as an "Iranian housewife and mother"—told me.[159] She was frothing to the point of violence, a six-year-old girl beside her: "If you [Bush] set foot here, we will tear you to pieces, from this little girl to me. When I hear his name, I get shivers of fear. I'm afraid of Bush and I'm even afraid of this guy!" she said, pointing to me, the nearest American. "Your brain is full of shit!"

WITNESS IMAGE TWO, ON the twenty-fifth anniversary of the Revolution, in February 2004. U.S. flags and effigies of George Bush went up in smoke. America was vilified, Zionism decried. But beneath the thin pall of smoke there was a quiet welcome, too, for an American visitor. Two boys who trailed me after the demonstration were especially eager.

"Follow, follow, follow him—you will end up in America!" chanted one.[160]

Shouted the other, racing along behind: "Ask him if he has room in his bag for me!"

2

Scent of Heaven

It is not the martyr himself and his desires that are
important per se, but the role he plays in creating a desire,
a need, a fear—a culture of survivors, bound by blood to the
nation.

—Roxanne Varzi, *Warring Souls*

To UNDERSTAND THE FORCES that drive revolutionary Iran requires entering the world of the True Believer. It is a world that begins with the legend of Imam Hossein, the seventh-century Lord of the Martyrs who rode willingly into a battle he couldn't win, knowing he faced certain death. On the plains of Karbala, Hossein demonstrated the nobility of fighting against all odds, for his belief. To Shiite Muslims he is the epitome of bravery and self-sacrifice, whose tearful mourning on the day of Ashura continues in modern times to be the frenetic climax of the religious year.

The world of the True Believer is further defined by the earth-shaking vision of Ayatollah Ruhollah Khomeini, his 1979 Revolution, and the infallibility of clerical rule.

It is a world that ends—and begins anew—with martyrdom, an act revered as the highest form of Islamic devotion. Soldiers in the Iran-Iraq War of the 1980s did not need to be convinced to sacrifice, but were *eager* to charge forward to their deaths, in holy war, with pictures of Khomeini on their breast. Plenty would do so again in any conflict with the United States—to defend Iran for religious and nationalist aspirations.

For Americans, this may appear a dark and blood-drenched world of pointless loss and unquestioned belief. Indeed, many Iranians have recoiled from the regime's relentless sanctifying of the war—in public sermons and with revolutionary rhetoric that bathed every act in divine light. More than a few Iranians fought simply to protect their country and repel the invasion of Saddam Hussein. Yet those Iranians did not *believe,* and therefore could not fathom the grim calculations, unbending priorities, and rock-hard conviction that characterized the motives of so many of their comrades at the war front.

For the True Believer, this life of constant mourning, resistance, and prayer is a path bright with hope. It beckons toward a brilliant and divinely inspired future, achieved through purity of heart, commitment, and action. This explains how a new generation of warriors in Iran has been formed, how deep their ideological conviction can be, and how they still impose their right-wing politics on modern Iran. They will never disappear.

So this is about the state of the Revolution, with a capital R. About why those Believers still cling to the promise of a pure Islamic state, even claim that they have created one, while many of their fellow Iranians see a Revolution that has gone wrong, that has strayed from its initial ambition of freedom.

During the war at the front, that freedom took flight and soared. Those who die for God do not "feel the pain of the iron" nor "see the Angel of Death—they only see God," preached ranking politician Ali Akbar Rafsanjani, to encourage more recruits in 1981.[1] "[T]hey don't feel any pain when struck by a bullet, an arrow, a spike, [or] a dagger." Again in 1983, Rafsanjani promised divine fruit: "[o]nce the bullet strikes the body of [our warriors] they are carried on the angels' wings [to paradise, where] they reside by the Prophet of God."

Iran's very defense was an act of faith, thanks to the neglect, deep purges, and disarray of the Shah's once-powerful armed forces. Iran's label of an "imposed war" hid the fact that the turbulent—and eagerly fomenting—Islamic Republic was hardly a good neighbor. Iraq's invasion was prompted by "Iran's provocation of Iraq by threatening to take the Islamic Revolution to its territory (by indulging in and lending moral sanction to acts of terrorism against Baghdad)," note historians Shahram Chubin and Charles Tripp.[2]

In the months before Iraq's September 1980 invasion, Iran had attempted to assassinate Iraq's deputy premier, Tariq Aziz, as well as the minister of information. Clashes along the border intensified throughout the spring and summer, and in early September Iran shelled two Iraqi border towns.

Yet in a bizarre contradiction, while repeatedly threatening to topple Saddam Hussein, Iran was also rushing to dismantle its own armed forces, wary of a counterrevolution from remaining Shah loyalists. "Iran was preoccupied not only by internal matters in the post-revolutionary chaos, but by a degree of hubris that rendered it incapable of rational thought," write Chubin and Tripp.[3] "The Iranian leaders' perception of threats, based on their experience in the Revolution and certain ideological baggage . . . bore little resemblance to their actual environment."

Even as Iraq openly mobilized for military confrontation, Iran was

canceling military orders, cutting the already reduced military budget by one third, halving conscription to one year, and seeking to return to the United States the eighty F-14 aircraft together with their *Phoenix* missiles. By August 1979 Iran's helicopter force was largely grounded. . . .

[Purges of up to 50 percent of the officer corps had a] "devastating effect on the army's ability to conduct combat operations." . . .

When the Iraqi attack came with ten divisions, Iran could muster only elements of two divisions and some one hundred twenty tanks near the frontier.[4]

Iran's extreme lack of preparedness turned the war into an immediate emergency—and for a regime still trying to consolidate control, a spiritual opportunity.

"The front was the place to experience life, because death is life's biggest experience," one veteran told anthropologist Roxanne Varzi.[5] "Khomeini told us that the spirit of Islam is in this war. The war front was the best place to practice faith. . . . The front is an expressway to Heaven."

And for more than 200,000 Iranians (and an estimated 150,000 Iraqis) who would lose their lives in the grim trenches, gritty deserts, and across the swampy marshland of the front line during eight years of battle, death *was* their last act on earth.[6] "In Iran, when you are alive you are nothing," conservative editor Javad Vaeidi explained to me in Tehran.[7] "But when you are dead, you are *so* important."

From Father to Son

Remnants of this ideological embrace are not hard to find in Iran, and in my quest I was able to witness how that torch of the Believers was being passed from one generation to the next. Three decades after Khomeini established religious rule, two decades after the end of the war, those who worked so hard to transform Iranian society from top to bottom, to imbue it with daily religiosity and life lived to a higher purpose, could claim some success. All the propaganda, and adherence to the strictest worldview—to the firm belief in resistance and its God-given, purifying quality—was paying off with a crop of new Believers.

They were hardly the majority. The hard-line conservatives committed to these ideals typically could rely on just 20 percent of votes in Iran, though much more in times of national crisis. But I found plenty of evidence of their vitality in the city of Ahvaz in 2007. Forty-five miles from the Iraqi border, the words I heard there were not the rehearsed platitudes I was used to hearing at flag-burning anti-American rallies in Tehran.

I was told that miracles happened in the bleak Ahvaz cemetery where the wind never stopped blowing and the dead slept under ever-whipping Iranian flags. It was a phantasm of endless portraits of young men in the full promise of youth. The grave keeper during the war, Haj Khezeir Bavi, was full of stories of belief and commitment, which provided role models for his three sons. The most powerful was that of Martyr Haidari, interred at the forty-third row, eighth column. During the war, Haidari's head was brought to the cemetery forty days after the rest of his body had been buried.

"It was a miracle when they asked me to take off the stone," Bavi told me, pointing toward a nondescript group of graves.[8] "I saw [Haidari's] body had not decomposed, and a very nice scent came out. The Scent of Heaven came out of it, and was all around this place."

THOSE MEMORIES WERE NOT forgotten. As I explored that cemetery in blinding sunlight, little did I know that it would yield some of the most important interviews I have ever conducted in Iran. I came across these voices by chance while searching, and they were authentic in their belief, drawn from the Iranian soil and its war and its Imam, untainted by the political veneer so common in the capital. To me they explained much about the true heart and soul of Iran—and were concrete proof that revolutionary belief was being transmitted from father to son.

The sign at the cemetery entrance read: "The Land of Heaven."[9] Some marble graves appeared never to have been washed of the ubiquitous desert dust. Others seemed to receive constant care, like the dark slab for Seyyed Ali Akbar Fatemehzadeh, who the inscription said "attained the holy rank of martyrdom" at age seventeen.

Beside it I found a lone young man, lost in homage as he prayed and poured water over the grave. The stone was etched with a well-known chant from the war:

When the sound of Imam Ali is heard by our ear,
The order comes from the soul of God [Khomeini],

"Go to the place of lovers [of God]."

For the love of Him, we go to Karbala.

"He was a great man, the nation owes him . . . because if martyrs were not there, we would not have Iran," Ali Akbar Khoshnazar told me. This young man had been named after that very martyr, a friend of his father who died in a rocket barrage. The teen came often to pray over the grave. "When I come here, my soul relaxes," the eighteen-year-old electronics graduate said. "My father says he was a spiritual person. When he starts talking about him, he bursts out crying."

In fact, the martyr had played a key role in the life of the father, the veteran Gholamreza Khoshnazar. I convinced the son to introduce me that night to his father, a slight man who lived an ascetic life. I was discovering seamless continuity in generational change.

Gholamreza owned a print shop that smelled powerfully of ink and paper. The scale of machinery was large and suggested serious profits. But the "office" in an upstairs loft could not have been more frugal: One telephone on the stone floor, its winding black umbilical cord stuck unceremoniously into the wall. A small table in a corner. No chairs. Few cushions for sitting. Piles of papers. An overworked cluster of thin glass teacups on a tray, with a plastic dish of sugar lumps.

"It's hard to describe—unless you were there," the father told me of the war. "No matter how many times I tell you this is cold," he said, pressing a finger to the floor, beyond the edge of the carpet, "you won't understand until you touch it."

Early in the war, the father was sixteen and sleeping on the roof to keep cool when he saw a twelve-year-old with a machine gun standing guard in his street. "I felt something within, and I thought to myself: 'Why should I be resting here, and the younger one guarding me?' " The next day Gholamreza signed up for the volunteer Basij force at the mosque. His military and spiritual training began immediately.

"When we were at the war front, we would wake in the middle of the night, do our ablutions, and pray," Gholamreza told me of the purity he found there. "It was a very holy spirit in those days."

The father had a close boyhood friend, called Ali Akbar, who had turned Gholamreza on to political books. During the war they fought and studied in turns, and then were together in one offensive battle. Ali Akbar's unit left thirty minutes before Gholamreza's. "He was hit with a rocket and half his face was gone—that was a severe shock to me, because we really liked each other," remembered Gholamreza, his fist-length beard exhibiting a plug of gray. "Then I promised God: if I was given a son, I would name him Ali Akbar."

And that son was the one who led me to this father, sitting here on the floor, hair thinning, pulling a faded red photo album from a red plastic bag, its cover blotchy with mold. It was worn and damaged by water from when he threw it into the river during a fit of trauma a couple of years earlier. The book—and Gholamreza's own sanity, he admitted—were saved by son Ali Akbar. He turned the pages slowly as he spoke, deliberately finding the memories that fit the images. "Some of my friends here have become martyrs," said Gholamreza, pointing out the deceased. There he is, riding a tank in Susangard. There he is in a T-shirt, speaking on a military radio, the man next to him soon to be dead. Or the boys leaning against a dirt berm, preparing to fire a shoulder-held RPG . . .

Gholamreza paused reverently over a picture of Ayatollah Khomeini wearing a black skullcap, a picture given to his family during the war. His admiration was undiminished for the man whose eternally stern countenance has loomed over the visual space of all Iranian Believers. And from that very man the gift of a coin, stuck to the page with yellowing tape, which depicted the Dome of the Rock in Jerusalem. It was presented to Gholamreza by a commander, who said it had come directly "from the Imam."

The coin was a cherished link to the divine. The veteran finally turned the page on this metal memory, as deferentially as any Christian would handle a real piece of the cross.

"Our generation, we wouldn't allow ourselves to be hospitalized or confined to the house; we would go back to the war as soon as we could walk," the soft-spoken Gholamreza told me. It was a high price, willingly paid. To make the point, he pulled up his shirt in an unexpected act of shared intimacy, revealing the mosaic of scar tissue that itched underneath. Multiple wounds from his askew eye to his belly to his hands and knees left him at one point "five percent from death."

As a follower of Khomeini, it was his "duty to be a martyr"—and Gholamreza sought to join their hallowed ranks. He failed and instead became a "living martyr"—a title coined for those viciously injured, who gave their bodies but survived.[10]

"I was not so knowledgeable about martyrdom, and didn't know what a delicious fruit it is," the man lamented. "It slipped from my grasp."

HOW DID THE NEW religious rulers of Iran set about preparing the population to die so willingly for a badly run war? Such glorification of combat and sacrifice was carefully cultivated by the regime from its earliest days. It was an important theme during Friday prayers in Tehran, which set Iran's political and religious agenda, and where preachers such as future Supreme Leader Ali Khamenei would grasp the barrel of a Kalashnikov rifle as they spoke. Khamenei told congregants the prayer leader did so because "Islamic society . . . leans on a weapon against the enemies of God . . . to neutralize the plots of enemies."[11] Friday prayers, he said, were also "a weapon . . . and an expression of power."

Praised from the pulpit were those who had "gratuitously given their blood . . . for removing the curtains of darkness and oppression."[12] As historian Haggay Ram notes about Khamenei's words, it was the combatants themselves who most desired a divine death: "They virtually beg to become *shahids* [martyrs]: they 'cry, they shed tears, and they implore [their commanders], "Take me along to the nightly operation so that I may become a *shahid*." ' "[13]

The regime was investing Iran's modern warriors with the same heroic attributes of the past. "Fighting in God's cause was pure, and contrasted sharply with the avaricious wars of the imperialists," explains historian Saskia Gieling.[14] Khamenei likened this defense of Islam to the "pious deed for which prophets and saints had also fought. . . . Immediately after the war had started, Iranian leaders declared it to be a *jihad,* and they kept on repeating this during the whole war."

As Khamenei asserted weeks after the war began, "Today the sons of Hossein . . . have brought [Hossein's] presence to the arena. This presence is [that] of a nation standing against the political and military machineries of the world." [15] There could be no more powerful evocation than the revered example set by Imam Hossein, of becoming part of Hossein's band of seventy-two Believers, who in 680 A.D. chose death over compromise.

"Even before there was Islam or Hossein, Shia theologians say, the spiritual essence of Hossein's great deed existed as a timeless expression of divine grace," notes political scientist Vali Nasr. [16] In the intervening centuries, the fate of the grandson of the Prophet of Islam has been imbued all the more with spirituality and lessons for the holy warrior: "As a popular Shia saying puts it, 'A single tear shed for Hossein washes away a hundred sins.' "

"Let the Swords Encircle Me"

Songs of war sung with chest-pounding conviction just hours before an attack, with their steady beat and devotional lyrics, helped Iranian soldiers completely commit to the upcoming sacrifice. They saw themselves stepping into the iconic landscape of the Lord of the Martyrs.

On the desert plains of Karbala, legend holds that Hossein saw the insistence of the enemy, tens of thousands strong, to kill him. He spoke these defiant words, baring his chest before their blades: "If the religion of Mohammad will only endure with my death, then *Oh, let the swords encircle me!*" [17]

Iran's holy warriors took themselves to the same dusty plain by singing this chant, which can still be heard today:

Oh soldiers who have your life in your hand, the day of courage
    has come,

Oh Army of God's Spirit [Khomeini], the time of courage is
   nigh,
This force of Islamic believers has come [and stretches] to infinity,
To dispel the enemies—be ready! Be ready!

> *Oh Army of the Master of Time* [Mahdi]—*be ready! Be ready!*
> *For a relentless battle—be ready! Be ready!*

The longing to see Hossein has made all the hearts anxious,
The lovers of Karbala have covered this plain,
In the hearts of these soldiers a new anticipation is born,
Like a solid mountain, full of strength—be ready! Be ready!

> *Oh Army of the Master of Time—be ready! Be ready!* [18]

THE QUALITY OF THIS devotion was shaped by a regime that
portrayed this "sacred defense" with perfectly pitched propaganda
that filled recruiting centers and "spoke" to Iran's devout majority. A
primary tool was film—war footage and powerful personal narratives
from the front line, shot at great risk in combat, then edited, crafted,
and spliced with a level of cinematic genius that has ever since shaped
the work of Iran's world-renowned filmmakers. Dozens of these episodes, called *Revayat-e Fath,* or *Chronicles of Victory,* were broadcast on
state television during the war. Even today their grainy message of
the irresistible call of immortality can be compelling and raise goose
bumps.

The films tap into the deepest currents in Iranian society—just as
the Revolution itself and Khomeini's leadership showed a profound
understanding of that society, with its idealized yearning for justice
and independence. And that reality is one of single-handedly stepping
forward to fight. "I can do nothing for you, besides the prayer I am saying for you," Ayatollah Khomeini told soldiers during the war, while
the men wept for their divine calling. [19] That meant each Iranian had to
make the right decision: "Many statements on God's role in this war

were to the effect that the war was preordained by God but that God left the people with a choice to obey or disobey Him," notes Gieling.[20]

Believers would adhere to the words of the banner I saw in a cemetery: "Martyrdom is the art of the men of God." Another, flapping in the wind, commits to the pinnacle example: "Hossein is my guiding light, and the ark of my salvation." They often use the word "love" when describing their faith. Hossein is the Leader of Love, and among the *Chronicles of Victory* episodes is a film called *Delbakhte,* or "One who has lost/given his heart to love." [21]

When I first learned about this series of war films I wanted to write a story about them. They are still possible to find—try the cramped *basiji* market just south of Revolution Square in Tehran, which is caught in a revolutionary time warp and full of every imaginable ideological poster, memory, and stack of devotional CDs. But the regime is reluctant to share that history with outsiders. I put in a formal request to speak to officials at the Cultural Institute of *Revayat-e Fath,* but it was refused. Surprised and near giving up, I casually asked a few veteran cameramen friends. They made some calls, and unofficially I was plugged right into the world that created *Chronicles of Victory.* It was never far away.

The hour-long *Delbakhte* episode lucidly demonstrates a power of persuasion far more effective than I could have imagined. I cherished such a rare moment; Westerners almost never have access to these films, which tell so much about the mind-set of Iran's Believers today. These episodes are one of the purest examples of regime propaganda, and they worked; I was practically ready to take up a gun myself, to fight in God's war . . .

The introduction shows a bulldozer driver serenely creating a dirt ridge at the front line—one of the most dangerous jobs in the war, with a seventy-two-hour life expectancy—while bursts from machine guns and blasting rockets and artillery shells punctuate the soundtrack. A soldier shoots down an Iraqi jet fighter, which plummets like a fireball from the sky. Comrades cheer as he explains that "it was God who took my missile and hit the plane."

Blue permanent marker across one helmet reads: "Khomeini, I'm saying 'Yes' to your divine call." And then the religious chanting; the quest for Karbala and martyrdom, planted in the mind again like a flag of conquest:

Anyone who craves Karbala, step forward.
Anyone who has the passion in his head, step forward.
Anyone who obeys Khomeini's command,
   I swear to God that he is exploring Hossein's path. . . .
[Cravers of] love and faithfulness, affection and purity, step
   forward.
Karbala is the house of lovers of God. . . .

Words appear on the screen: "Another story from those traveling with the Caravan of Love." And the narrator finds cosmic relevance in the mundane daily life of the front line: "While eating breakfast, we are thinking how we could—from the ordinary face of these moments—travel to the mysterious soul of the moment . . . to know these chosen few, one by one."

In this ideological "documentary," it is mid-1986, the offensive known as Karbala One on the central front; the objective is to recapture the Iranian town of Mehran. Progress has been made. As the Iranians advance, dead Iraqis litter the battlefield. In the film, a student soldier grins at the intensity of it all. He signed up after troops fresh from the front had attended his mosque, setting aside their weapons to pray. "I was ashamed to stay in the city for even one more hour," he tells the camera. "The more we follow this path, the more we grow. This war is a blessing for us. I thank God that now I am standing among these brothers."

Signature techniques of these propaganda episodes enable Iran's soldiers to tell their own stories, to speak of their own beliefs and reasons to fight, to follow fighters—or even an entire unit—from home and small factory to the front lines and then home again, and then back to the war. The picture is deliberately heroic: These are ordinary men, answering the call to wage an extraordinary holy war.

The narrator of *Delbakhte* explains: "The beauty of this is that all these guys view the battlefield as a place to advance your soul, which God put in front of them." Lives are transformed and elevated. The narrator is astonished at the weight of this mission on humble men: "When you see these guys in their normal lives, on fields and farms, you can't believe these are the same guys who history has been waiting for their steps for centuries." There is no higher calling, and this front is the point of departure. "If you are seeking the Savior, brother, try to find him among His soldiers, on the top of these heights, and in the heart of these trenches. . . ."

From the broad theological brushstrokes and frontline scenes in *Delbakhte,* the camera narrows its focus onto a single volunteer, an older farmer called Mr. Molazadeh, who sits in a trench with his unit, his helmet smeared with mud. His face is dark leather, creased by a lifetime of field work, etched permanently by the fierce grit of the front. The man speaks simply and says two of his sons are fighting elsewhere, their aim "to rejuvenate the religion of God." There is no theater, no apparent rehearsal or preparation, just a "random" interview rich with heart, which resonates across Iran's inner landscapes of belief.

"This war is a test," says Molazadeh, as men file past him in the trench. "Those who do not believe in this war do not have faith. They do not think. This war has been imposed, who is the righteous? Is Saddam Hussein right? Or is it this side? They should think. They should sit down and think." The volunteer recounts the Karbala story as if it happened to him, about how Hossein centuries ago warned those with him that they would die. "They did not sleep that night, because of happiness and joy," this farmer tells the camera. "They sharpened the blades of their swords and everybody wanted to overtake each other in the morning [in their eagerness to fight]."

Molazadeh's monologue connects Hossein's historic battle with his own war, in this trench, fighting for the same noble cause. "Now look at how history remembers [Hossein's greatness]. We should be like this, too. These *hezbollahi* children are really like this. They are so sacrificing that they are not scared of any gun or shells; they march ahead like lions."

The camera follows along up the trench as young soldiers slog toward new positions for the imminent offensive. One fighter wipes away tears with his checkered scarf.

THE FILM THEN PICKS up the story several months later, elsewhere in Iran, in Molazadeh's fields. Gone are the helmet and the gun, but not the determination to do God's will in war. Talk is of the rice crop, the rainfall, and yield. Molazadeh wears clothes stained from hard work, a black and white woven skullcap on his head. The discussion turns to the last offensive, the one launched from that trench months ago, toward Mehran. Since then, Molazadeh has been preoccupied, restless.

"When I arrived in my own village, that operation affected my mind so much that I felt something was missing," Molazadeh explains. "I couldn't stay in my village anymore. . . . In that military operation, I have become in such a way that I lost my heart to it, I have fallen in love. I am in love."

The farmer presents his sons. One is still at the battlefront, another just returned. The third is a student, but during the last offensive he sent letters to his father, insisting, "Daddy, I want to come to the war." The father promises that if he does well in his exams, he will be able to fight. "I will never prevent them. Why should I prevent them from going? Our dear Islam is in danger. What value do we have? Even if we live for eighty years, the end of the line is death. Death will come after us, whether we want it or not. . . . So we should at least go after something that will have a future for us."

This is not just a victory of arms, the narrator claims, but of spirit: "What gives meaning to this and other victories of the Army of Islam, is that Mr. Molazadeh and other *basijis* are the torchbearers of a great movement, that after the victory of the Islamic Revolution of Iran is heading toward achieving the holy ideals of the prophets."

The final scenes are a montage, designed to pique the fervor of the audience: Soldiers beat their chests in unison, chanting: "Shout against oppression!" Bullets fire. Grenades burst. Then at night, rockets blast off in dazzling flashes while the war song continues.

It is motivational stuff, with a final poetic word: "The route of the Caravan of Love passes through history," the narrator intones, as a machine gun rapid-fires in the dark, tracers burning an arc toward the enemy. "And whoever says they are devoted to this cause, he is one of those on the Caravan of Karbala."

THE MEN WHO PRODUCED such powerful films were on a mission themselves, just like the soldiers. What could be more crucial to the war effort—to reinforcing the divine legitimacy of the Revolution, as the Imam demanded—than to see images of righteous devotion and sacrifice at the front line, to *see* proof of God siding with the Islamic Republic?

"The cultural architects of this period created a perfect balance by politically exploiting some images while containing others . . . that could potentially undermine the Islamic program," notes Roxanne Varzi in her book *Warring Souls*.[22] "Within the first few months of war, a production of persuasion began, and everything from print to celluloid was used to illustrate the beauty of sacrifice. . . . Martyrdom is nothing without remembrance and without the cultural industry that keeps the martyr alive after death, because what is promised is eternal glory."

The ideological gold dust was not with the regular army. It was in the Revolutionary Guard archives, which include 30,000 hours of audiocassettes, 300,000 pages of documents, 1,300 notebooks, and 20,000 journals.[23] From that collection came a series of photography books published by the War Information Headquarters of the Supreme Defense Council, under the title *The Imposed War: Defense vs. Aggression*. They showed the gallantry and gore of the front line, the devotion and desolation, and the progress of Iran's "heroic fight."[24] "The government kept complete property rights to all war images," writes Varzi. "They knew that the images were the true spoils of this war."[25]

They were best exploited with the narrative power and infinite reach of radio and television. That had been a focus of Khomeini for years before the Revolution, when cassette tapes of his sermons were smuggled into the Shah's Iran and secretly distributed by loyalists. After the Revolution, the media assumed an even greater role. "Of all the organs of propaganda, radio and television are most important," Khomeini said.[26] "If they are reformed, the whole country can be reformed, and if, God forbid, they are corrupted, it can lead a country to corruption. These are more important than schools."

If so, then the greatest television teacher was the documentary film series *Chronicles of Victory*, or *Revayat-e Fath*. It "literally brought the details of the war into peoples' living rooms every night," notes analyst Farideh Farhi. Along with "ceremonies held for the funeral of war martyrs [it] reflected the encroachment of the values of the war front into the daily life of all Iranians."[27]

The undisputed master of packaging this popular and pious image was Morteza Avini, the director of *Revayat-e Fath*, who received all raw footage from the battlefield and created the stories, the image streams, and the multiple layers of sound. Portraits show a bearded intellectual of great intensity whose eyes are piercing behind his glasses. Avini was killed in 1993 by stepping on a land mine while filming along the former front line. At the Tehran Martyrs' Museum a glass case is dedicated to his memory and holds his bloody *chafiyeh* scarf, a pair of shoes with the right heel torn off, and a mangled videocassette, its magnetic tape partly pulled out.[28]

In his writings, Avini explained how his *Revayat-e Fath* crews aimed to overcome the sloppy fakery that accompanied most TV news reports, to get to the untold heart of the story. Avini wrote: "The soldiers would dance for the [news] camera and the commentator would say: 'look at how they sacrifice themselves,' and shahadat, martyrdom, would be taken less seriously. . . . [O]ther directors showed so many people sacrificing themselves that the value of sacrifice decreased. . . . [S]o we show individuals. At the front we were after reality. . . ." [29]

"Avini cared about the human and spiritual aspects of the war and wanted to show these to people," recalled Mehdi Homayoun-Fars, the executive director of *Revayat-e Fath*.[30] He spoke to me in 2007, when he was in charge of documentaries—still shaping attitudes toward the Islamic Republic on-screen—at Iran's twenty-four-hour English-language channel PressTV. It had been a dangerous business. Camera crews considered themselves soldiers and were accepted as such on the battlefield. Each episode begins with a list of *Revayat-e Fath* martyrs who died filming combat.

"Every day you feel death," Homayoun-Fars told me. "Each day you wake up, you are not sure you will put your head down at night." The experience changed those who took part, just as a deep spiritual resonance was imparted by the films to Iranian Believers and non-Believers alike. Critical to success of the *Chronicles of Victory* was a ready-made template.

"This Shiite mentality was one of our main tools to make these films more powerful; it was a cultural benchmark," Homayoun-Fars explained, referring to the annual passion play called *Taziyeh*. "It was something that was embedded in our culture for many years." This ritual reenactment of the Hossein tragedy has been a spectacle in Persia for centuries. In decades past,

> [l]iving tableaux of butchered martyrs stained with blood, their bodies showing simulated amputations, were moved along on wheeled platforms. Mock battles were mimed by hundreds of uniformed mourners armed with bows, swords, and other weapons. The entire pageant was accompanied by funeral music and spectators, lined up along its path, beat their breasts and shouted "Hossein, O Hossein, the King of the Martyrs" as it passed by.[31]

The meaning of such devotion is often misinterpreted in the West as a call to offensive action. Yet despite the historical focus on sacrifice,

modern-day suicide attacks by Shiites—in places like Iraq and Pakistan, where far more than one thousand Sunni Muslims have killed
themselves—have been virtually nonexistent. Veteran film producer
Homayoun-Fars explained:

> There are two things Westerners have not completely understood.
> One is *shahid,* the relationship between Imam Hossein and martyr-
> dom. The other is the concept of the afterlife. . . . We think we are
> now preparing for the next life, the better, real life. From the [ex-
> ample] of Imam Hossein, we believe we should never be bullied.
> I want the people of America to understand the sweetness of this
> message, to understand the afterlife. It's not a message of war.

Psychological Warfare

Ali Ehsan Rajabi is one of those ordinary men transformed by the
ideology of Iran's war into a fearless devotee. He recorded the conflict first with still photographs and then became a video cameraman
for *Revayat-e Fath.*[32] Short but still strong more than two decades after
the Iran-Iraq War, Rajabi easily rekindled the fire in his voice as he
described to me the higher purpose of his fight—of *God's* fight. "They
did not care if they would die or not," he said of the *basiji* volunteers;
he was still awestruck and proud to count himself among them. His
stubbly chin set hard when he spoke. "Even though the enemy was
equipped with state-of-the-art weapons and chemical warheads, we
stood against them. We stood there and resisted. It was a holy act."

Rajabi fought from the age of fourteen or fifteen. His first major
engagement was the 1983 Val Fajr (By the Dawn) offensive along the
southern front. In the face of crippling Iraqi warplane and helicopter
bombardment some hundred thousand Iranian troops were pushed
back, recapturing only a modest patch of their own territory and failing in their primary objective. Then-president Ali Akbar Rafsanjani
had portrayed the offensive as "the final move towards ending the

war." But losses were so heavy that he explained the setback with two-plus-two-equals-five logic: "It is in Iranian interests to spare enemy soldiers who are to serve the future Islamic Republic of Iraq."[33]

None of that diminished Rajabi's sense of common cause, nor his growing addiction to Khomeini's brand of jihad. He remembers it almost as a paradise of purity and conviction. "Because it was my first time in uniform, I had this special feeling of war, so with my friends we started taking pictures of ourselves. There is a humbleness in the faces. We were youngsters, but we knew that our enemy was a very big monster. And the greatness of the enemy created a great spirit among the *basijis*."

Serving as a *Chronicles of Victory* cameraman was a dream and a challenge for Rajabi, who was often in charge of a four-man team embedded with Iranian troops at the front, eating, sleeping, praying, and bleeding alongside them. The team had to be bold or miss the shot. In Rajabi's telling: "This camera was a device through which we wanted to reach the truth, that those involved in the war wanted to reach. So we should get close to these [soldiers] to find out what they were after. This feeling and this need to see gave us the courage to take risks."

Still pressed into Rajabi's memory was the egalitarianism of the Iranian side, of volunteers who had come to the war from every profession—engineers and doctors and grocers and farmers—from each rung of the social ladder. Ayatollah Khomeini had said it was only on such True Believers, and the poor, that he could depend:

This noble people, the true defenders of Islamic values, have well realized that jihad does not agree with luxury. Those who think that fighting for independence and liberation of the oppressed and the deprived throughout the world is compatible with capitalism and hedonism are ignorant of jihad's alphabet. . . .

Only those who have tasted poverty, deprivation and oppression will stay with us to the end. It is the poor and the pious who are the real founders and leaders of revolutions. . . .[34]

These were the volunteers who wrote on their personal effects the slogan: "Here I am waiting for your commands, Oh, Khomeini!" according to the vibrant visual history *Staging a Revolution*.[35] These were the volunteers who reveled in the messages they saw on the billboards at the front line and in its broken cities, "those places where the hearts of our heroes were beating."[36] The quotations from Khomeini that glorified martyrdom, the authors write, "exposed the soldiers to psychological warfare, directed not by the enemy but by the Iranian leadership."

These were the Believers who, upwards of 30 percent of them, would reject help from the government for their injuries "because the pursuit of 'material rewards' undermines the whole notion of serving at the front for the sake of God's pleasure."[37] These were the fighters who signed preprinted postcards home, which read: "My dear ones . . . Don't worry about me. I will never break the firm covenant which I have made with God, since we are men of war; and since Truth is victorious, we, too, are victorious."[38]

I had often heard how the ideological imprint affected families. Rafsanjani once in wartime told a story during Friday prayers in Tehran, in which a father rejoiced at seeing the decapitated corpse of his son, and kissed the severed head. As Rafsanjani told it: "There was not even the slightest sign of emotion on his face. [The father] said: 'My God! I thank my child, my son, for becoming a *shahid* in the way of God.' "[39]

And he wasn't the only father who had "given" his son. The Revolutionary Guard minister in 1984 reported that, in one offensive, 57 percent of the combat forces were schoolchildren.[40] State-controlled newspapers showed photographs of "nearly empty classrooms . . . to glorify the youth who had given their lives for Islam." *Ettelaat* published one gruesome story in 1982, which praised teenagers as young as fourteen for crossing a minefield

like a garden in the morning ready to blossom, to scatter their petals on the wind and take wing. They would pass over the mines, eyes no longer seeing, ears no longer hearing.

An instant, and when the dust settled, there was nothing. Pieces of flesh and bone scattered across the desert, clinging to the rocks. The bodies of youngsters and children in pieces, in bits and pieces . . . strewn over the desert. Sometimes the children wrapped themselves in blankets, rolling themselves across the minefields so that fragments of their bodies would not scatter so, and they could be collected and moved behind the lines, to be raised over their heads in coffins.[41]

Such commitment seems impossible today. Yet witnesses could not forget the signs of fervor. *New York Times* reporter Elaine Sciolino "saw Iranian soldiers ready for battle wearing small gold keys on their uniforms where other soldiers might wear medals [to] take their souls to heaven . . ."[42] One time on the Iraqi side of the front lines, she saw the bodies of a dozen Iranians and the "crude weapons they carried. An Iraqi soldier dumped an Iranian suitcase on the ground. Out poured pocket-sized copies of the Quran, stained with blood," Sciolino wrote in *Persian Mirrors*.

The human wave attacks had a powerful psychological effect on the Iraqis, too, according to one Iraqi officer:

They'd come toward us and reach the minefield. The first one would try to move a mine with his foot and be blown up, but in doing so create a small gap, and then the next one would come, killing himself, and this is how they created corridors. We'd be firing at them with machine guns and other assault weapons and mortars and artillery. There'd be heaps of bodies and our weapons would heat up so much, they jammed. And still they kept coming. . . .[43]

The cameraman told me he understood. "There is a difference between this war and other wars," Rajabi said. "In some wars a lot of people protest so that their children *won't* be sent to war. But here we witness differently: a mother that has a child; a wife that is saying farewell to her husband; a family in which the son *and* father are going to war."

Rajabi could not have been more enamored of his task: "This was so beautiful, their aim was so beautiful that we had no other choice but to film it." He was determined to show these devotees in their "cycle of life and death."

RAJABI ASKED ME IF I had "taken part" in the war in Iraq, and when he learned that I had reported in many war zones from Angola to Afghanistan, as well as Iraq, he said he was "honored" to sit with me. We were both veterans of covering conflict in Bosnia and Lebanon; he as a cameraman, me as a writer and photographer. But the deepest impact on Rajabi's career came from his own war in Iran. When I was still in high school, his mind was seared with war.

Rajabi brought photographs to one of our meetings. Among them was a dramatic black-and-white shot he had taken of a bear of a bearded man, racing heroically with a blanket in a vain attempt to dampen the flames of a Toyota jeep that had taken a direct hit from an Iraqi tank. The man in the picture was Zabihollah Bakhshi—widely known in Iran as Haji Bakhshi—who was driving and had been thrown out by the force of the blast. "This famous car with speakers on top," Rajabi recalled wistfully. Up and down the front lines, it played religious and nationalistic songs "of honor and power" to boost morale. Amid billowing black smoke, Bakhshi's three passengers were being incinerated as the photograph was taken; already dead was a one-legged veteran on a return visit, whom Rajabi had photographed by chance just an hour before, a few miles away.

The man in the front seat was barely alive, his arm resting casually on the edge of the open window, head turning into carbon. He was the target of Bakhshi's rescue attempt. "Fire surrounded him. The door would not open; it was locked," Rajabi told me. "Another photographer and I wanted to help but our hands were burned and we could not open the door."

The place was a well-known intersection called "Three Ways of Death," which *basijis* had renamed "Three Ways of Martyrdom." It was high ground at Shalamche, on the southern front, and with its commanding view was also easily seen and a frequent target of Iraqi shelling. Even as Bakhshi tried to save his passenger, the Iraqi shelling resumed; the jeep was hit three times and turned to ash. Photographer Rajabi was hit in the hand; his Canon camera was pierced, too. His colleague was scarred from shrapnel that struck his right hand, his ear, his kidney.

But despite the flaming wreck, Rajabi's strongest impression remains the aspect of the trapped, near-dead veteran, who whispered prayers to himself as flames took his life.

"When I got near him, he looked out of the window. He was in a spiritual place," Rajabi told me. "I myself felt the heat of the fire. I could not get closer to him because the fire was too much. But he kept looking and he was not asking for help from anybody. Nothing." Rajabi tried to fathom that place, that faith: "Let us see what he is seeing. . . . What he is feeling is definitely something beautiful. Not a negative or dark or black thing. And [because of] his belief, whatever happens is not important for him."

Rajabi was in awe of the new martyrs, and of Bakhshi, who repeatedly flung himself at the inferno to save those trapped inside. The photo has become a well-known image of the war. "They were men of action, not just men of words [who] sit far back from the front lines," recalls the cameraman. "Near the border, the Iraqis knew this car."

Indeed, when I finally tracked down the grizzled revolutionary Bakhshi, years after the event, on his farm thirty miles west of Tehran, he kept portraits of his martyred passengers, and two sons and brother lost in the war, all in one place in his home. "This is the Room of Love," Bakhshi told me:

This is Mohammad Reza. They brought him in a box for me.

He was twenty-one years old.

This is Abbas who was martyred in Fao.

He was eighteen years and two months.

This is my brother. In the Ramadan Operation he was
    martyred. . . .[44]

Bakhshi said that two days after his jeep was destroyed by the Iraqis,
he was back on the front line to make a point: "The guys [Iranian sol-
diers] had lost their spirit. They thought that Haji has been martyred.
Radio Baghdad had announced that they had killed Haji Bakhshi," he
recalls. Waving his arm threateningly, just as he did on that day toward
Saddam Hussein, Bakhshi said he broadcast his own message back to
the Iraqi leader: "I went to the other world, and now I have come back
to take you with me again!"

THE WHITE-BEARDED IRANIAN ZEALOT knew the power
of theater. For more than half a century, Bakhshi had been front and
center in nearly every revolutionary action or pro-regime rally. He
was practically an institution in Iran, a political cheerleader and professional militant. The multiple wounds he received throughout the
Iran-Iraq War added to his renown. There were chemical attacks. A
big scar from where shrapnel tore open his stomach. Another on his
back. Shrapnel once hit his head and bounced off. "It's like cement,"
Bakhshi boasted, touching his sunburned bald head. "I've been blown
up by mines and landed on my hands and feet." He'd been through *five*
cars as a one-man morale booster and feared morality cop.

The septuagenarian greeted me in 2008 wearing a cast on his left
hand, held in place with a sling made of the distinctive *chafiyeh*. Bakhshi had broken his hand days earlier when he fell off his truck during
a crowded Tehran rally to mark the twenty-ninth anniversary of the
Revolution. His other hand was a huge paw, and he used it to pull me
in for a cheek kiss, providing closer inspection of his full beard, large
nose, and single right lower tooth. He was wrinkled, and his eyes focused on many different things. He fancied he resembled Khomeini
from the side, and said, "My grandfather also had a resemblance."

"In war, propaganda and spirit are the most important things," Bakhshi told me. "If they tell me right now that we must go for a protest, I will take off these slippers and run barefoot! Because it's our Revolution. Because it's our country. A person who does not love his country, who does not love his nation, is not human."

One of those oscillating red police car lights was in the living room, ready to speed Bakhshi to any emergency in need of ideological enforcement. The farm was a gift from the regime, as was the huge flat-screen Samsung TV. He watched Iran-Iraq War videos—the "home" video playing when I was there showed Bakhshi sharing lunch with soldiers in a frontline trench.

Bakhshi also enjoyed bootleg Western films, such as Elizabeth Taylor's saucy 1967 rendition of Shakespeare's *The Taming of the Shrew.* "I've watched it three times!" gushed the militant, like a child entering a candy shop. And it wasn't his first exposure to America's silver screen. As a kid growing up in southwest Iran, he saw *Tarzan* and was impressed by the signature cry, "Ahhhhhh!" "We went to the Ahvaz bridge and we imitated Tarzan," laughed Bakhshi. "I shouted like Tarzan and dove into the river. It was really fun for us!"

The broken hand was but the latest battle scar in a life of defiance that began during World War II, and in many ways reflects Iran's own revolutionary path of defiance, violence, and militant belief. When he was just nine, Bakhshi said he saw a British officer kill one of his friends. Incensed, the young Iranian vowed revenge and told his local cleric, "I am going to kill him." The boy put his plan into action after seeing American troops using dynamite to kill fish in the Karoon River. He dove in and threw the fish out to them, eventually making friends with the soldiers, who gave him chocolate bars with nuts. After a month, he had won their trust enough to steal two sticks of dynamite—which he then stuck beneath the vehicle of the British officer.

The explosion killed two men and was officially blamed on a German spy, Bakhshi told me of his violent debut. He then joined the underground Fadaiyan-e Islam (Devotees of Islam), which one historian describes as a "small terrorist organization" pledged to fight "all forms of irreligion." [45] Another historian notes the Fadaiyan was "the first political grouping in twentieth-century Iran to conceive of the goal of an Islamic state and to work actively toward attaining it." [46]

Its first act was to assassinate a famous Iranian secular writer. The second and third attacks killed the Minister of the Court, then the Iranian prime minister.

Bakhshi spent a day in prison for riots surrounding the CIA-engineered coup in 1953. Years later, when he tried to deliver explosives to fellow Khomeini loyalists, Bakhshi found his car being chased in Tehran by SAVAK agents. Bakhshi got away after throwing a brick of cash out the window, creating a swarm of people that slowed his SAVAK pursuers. "Who put this in my mind? God," recalled Bakhshi, relishing the story and its implication of divine protection.

He was protected again in 1987, he claimed, when he helped spark a pro-Khomeini riot during the Haj pilgrimage in Saudi Arabia. Pretending to be a blind beggar, Bakhshi illegally hid a flag under his clothes and stuffed images of Khomeini in a canister meant to spray scented water. When telling the story, he acted it out, showing how he flitted his "blind" eyes so convincingly that a Saudi guard took pity on him, gave him some coins, and led the militant and his contraband directly into the sanctuary. He joked he could "teach the CIA a thing or two" about deception.

More than four hundred died in those protests, including a Saudi soldier Bakhshi bludgeoned to death with chunks of concrete because the soldiers "were killing people." The Saudis had filmed the murder from behind and were after him. He had to change out of his blood-soaked white pilgrimage clothes. "They wanted to shoot me here in the head, but God made the bullet come here," he said, pulling up his robe to show the deep scar on his thigh. To illustrate how he tricked the Saudi guards coming for him, Bakhshi gamely got down on all fours—never mind his broken hand and advanced age—to show me how he crawled forward each time worshippers leaned forward to pray. He stood up again, laughing clownishly at his own cleverness. It was all a game, and Bakhshi had never lost. *"All* of this was God . . ."

Bakhshi was often deployed against regime critics (read "reformists") during the Khatami era. News accounts from the 1990s describe him as a leader of the hard-line vigilante group Ansar-e Hezbollah (Followers of the Party of God). Human Rights Watch in 1996 described him as a "strong-arm leader" who took part in the "violent groups of religious zealots," which "targeted government critics and free-thinkers of all kinds, burning property, beating individuals, and disrupting gatherings." [47] The rights group stated: "Nothing has had a more corrosive influence on the climate of respect for basic freedoms."

Bakhshi led a gang against the state-run Islamic Republic News Agency (IRNA) in 1996, warning through loudspeakers that they would throw staff and parliamentary deputies out the windows for "their disregard for the Revolution's values and supporting the liberals." [48] In 2006, he was photographed with bloodied hands making prints on the wall outside the Denmark Embassy in Tehran to protest cartoons published in a Danish newspaper.

He grew serious when I asked to take his portrait: Bakhshi dressed himself in his "uniform" as ideological cheerleader. It was a camouflage shirt, draped with a bandolier of bullets and green flag, and an aged Soviet sniper rifle, its scope dangling uselessly on a loose bolt. This face and this getup was famously familiar to a generation of Iranians.

"Nothing is more important than spirit in the field of war. Because if there is not spirit in the front line, everyone will retreat," Bakhshi told me. When I departed, Bakhshi was like a rattling caricature and sent me off with a bullet-hanging hug. His last word to me was a war-era accolade: *baradaram.* My brother.

"Mighty Level of Martyrdom"

The high purpose sold well early in the war, when the aggressor was clearly Saddam Hussein. It was more difficult to maintain after mid-

1982, when Iran had repelled Iraqi forces and launched its own offen-sives into Iraqi territory.

"So long as the war was perceived to be a defensive war . . . all the ideological and cultural groundwork . . . remained extremely compel-ling," writes analyst Farhi.[49] "The more the rationality of continuing the war became an issue, the more [it had to rely] on sacred symbols, religious lamentations and mourning ceremonies, and rigid under-standing of religious duties."

An important focus was creating a cult of martyr-celebrities. Their purpose was clear on a white cloth banner I saw strung along the pe-rimeter fence of a military camp that read: "Memories of the war are unending treasures for future generations."

A particular act of courage blasted its way into martyr mythology during one of the biggest early engagements of the war, in Khorram-shahr, which came to be called the "City of Blood."

It was the legend of the boy Mohammad Hossein Fahmideh, who left home in November 1980 without his parents' knowledge, deter-mined to fight for his country. Iranian forces were being pushed back and an Iraqi tank column—aware that Iranian fighters were mostly volunteers and short of antitank weaponry—chose to advance along a narrow channel. The official version holds that, as the Iranian toll mounted, this "true patriot" took on Iraqi armor alone. The young Fahmideh strapped to his chest grenades taken from "one of the nearby bodies and pulled the pin out as he ran and jumped under-neath an enemy tank, killing himself and disabling the tank. This stopped the Iraqi division's advance."[50]

Fahmideh was declared a national hero by Khomeini, who lauded the boy-warrior: "Our leader is that 13-year-old child, that wrapped a grenade around him and went under the tank." The effect of the story was electrifying: "I still remember how his death shocked ordinary people regardless of their political views," recalled Elham Gheytan-chi, now a sociologist at Santa Monica College. "We (students) talked about it in schools, [and] wrote essays about him and the war."[51]

Ever since his death, Fahmideh's boyish face—often depicted under the approving gaze of Khomeini—has adorned the sides of buildings, a 1986 postage stamp, and even school bags for children as an example to emulate. In the dusty Martyrs' Museum in Tehran, a tour guide showed me the glass case dedicated to Fahmideh. It held a small plastic model of an Iraqi tank and a pineapple grenade, alongside what he claimed was a "remaining artifact of the martyr"—a coiled jump rope.

While some in the West construe Fahmideh's action to be the first Muslim suicide attack in modern Middle East history[52]—as a prelude to Iranian *basiji* volunteers stepping through minefields to clear them—in Iran this legend is one of innocence spent for a noble cause. So the site of Fahmideh's grave in the Behesht-e Zahra necropolis south of Tehran (section 24, row 44, no. 11) is hallowed ground for many Iranians.[53] It is elevated slightly on a marble platform and protected by a high canopy, upon which rests a large metal replica of a tank. Inside I looked up, where stenciled on one side are the words of Khomeini about the child patriot: "The blood of our youth overpowers guns." On the opposite side, Khomeini's words again, keeping to the educational theme: "The blood of the martyrs will forever teach the lesson of resistance to the people of the world."

Nearly three decades after the young man's death, I watched in quiet amazement as entire families came to pay their respects, leaning over the cold glass, children extending their fingers to feel the wet sprinkled rose water, to touch the flower petals. The boy Hossein Aghaei spent longer than most reaching out to this martyr, to this model of sacrifice.

"It is of great value to us, because he's a child and gave a great thing for our country," little Hossein told me, setting aside shyness to speak to a foreigner. His schoolmates couldn't believe that the famous Fahmideh rested just two rows up and ten graves away from where his uncle—also a 1981 martyr—lay buried. Fahmideh's story was a lesson in Hossein's third-grade Farsi language book. The moral, this nine-year-old told me, is about "martyrdom, greatness, and overcoming your fears."

It was a powerful lesson, observed Hossein's father, Morteza. "It was something to show to history that someone of that age can stand up in front of the enemy," the veteran told me. "My kid likes him a lot."

Three small girls in Western-style clothes stepped up with their parents and peered down through the glass, where they could read in the carved stone that Fahmideh "reached a mighty level of martyrdom."

The next man hunkered close, and tapped the glass cover with his large silver ring set with an agate, a favorite ornament of religious Shiites.

AFTER NEARLY THIRTY YEARS, the perpetual propaganda power of this shrine had barely faded, though uncertainty still surrounds the story. A blast sufficient to disable a tank would have obliterated Fahmideh; often all that has remained of bombers in suicide attacks from Beirut to Baghdad are solid pieces of skull. Perhaps more important than knowing the contents interred under that stone, however, was how the Legend of Fahmideh came to be.

A Revolutionary Guard commander who fought in Khorramshahr is reported in the 1990s to have explained privately that the story was a blend of two real narratives, spliced together by the regime to boost its propaganda punch. There *had* in fact been a volunteer in the fight, a university student who made good use of the very few RPG-7 rocket-propelled grenades on hand to stop the Iraqi tank column. According to this account,

> [t]he student then grabs a grenade belt and the rest is history, though no one knew who he had been. Naturally it would not do to have an anonymous hero of such propaganda importance. Meanwhile [a boy called] Fahmideh had run away from home to fight but upon arriving in Khorramshahr he was refused any kind of gun since he was considered too young to be able to use it. He then managed to somehow disarm and capture two Iraqi soldiers cut off somewhere in Khorramshahr, turn them over with one of the AK-47s, and kept

the other one for himself. He then later was killed. So they decided
to use his name for the tank episode as well.[54]

Such a fact would be a closely guarded secret, known only to a few
in the Islamic Republic. The continuing potency of that propaganda
was too good to dismantle. A senior Revolutionary Guard officer,
asked quietly about the Fahmideh story on my behalf by a trusted colleague, said there was a precedent for cobbling together such "fabrica-
tions," though he would not confirm this one.

As the Revolution entered its fourth decade, the martyrs were still
being used—and praised frequently by the Supreme Leader—as the
"stars that can guide [youth] to the right path." One of the 476 presidential hopefuls who registered for Iran's ill-fated June 2009 election
was a twelve-year-old boy, a clean-cut kid who submitted his application wearing a suit and button-up white shirt with unruly lapels. He
said he was inspired to be a "leader" by Fahmideh.[55]

That message has filtered throughout Iran's Islamic system, right
down to the village where a former Guard commander in spring 2009
trumpeted the martyrs—one of which had been sacrificed by each
family in the village. Until the war, Iran had to make do with ficti-
tious martyrs drawn from historical myths. But the "emergence of
such heroes [in modern Iran] put our minds at ease," the commander
said, according to an Iranian witness.[56] Chief among them was the
boy-martyr, who had a "great impact."

"Fahmideh didn't just win the battle," the veteran commander told
his village. "He won the entire war."

BUT NOT ALL WERE convinced by the propaganda, nor by the call
to sacrifice in the name of Imam Hossein, who, after all, had died—
heroic though he clearly was—thirteen centuries earlier. "For us, the
war may as well have happened in another country, to another people," a well-educated Iranian from north Tehran told me in 1997.[57]
Even as the war brought a coalescing unity for some, and helped

consolidate the Revolution, its radical strands alienated many other Iranians. Said this north Tehrani: "People who were rich didn't fight and ran away. These [martyrs] were the ones who threw themselves on the mines, and believed they died for something. But those who came back got little respect—it's why they hate us."

That tension, between those who believed to the point of death and those who did not, has defined Iran's debilitating political divisions and its culture wars.

"They all died, for an illusion," said the secular Tehrani. She and student friends enjoyed periods during major offensives when all students would be taken out of class for one or two hours to pray for the soldiers. "We used to love these hours, because we were not studying."

Such sentiment is sacrilege to Believers. Yet the fervor began to fade long before the conflict would end. "Doubtlessly, by 1985–1986 the war had already become a major source of resentment and a burden, rather than a 'divine blessing upon the Muslim nation of Iran,' " notes historian Ram.[58] "A sense of weariness from the lingering war was noticeable in the sermons, as direct references to martyrdom . . . gradually diminished. It seems that the prayer leaders themselves had become tired of being routinely required to elaborate on the combatants' desire for death."

By the time the second set of repeat volunteers was at the front— steeped in the epic propaganda of the regime—they "understood faith in a much more doctrinaire fashion," observes Farhi.[59] "From them emerged a more austere and joyless version of Islam that rejected any kind of compromise with life appearances."

The severe consequences persist today, as Iran writhes under the grip of hard-line rule. Many war veterans became stuck in an "idealized time warp from which they can never escape or evolve," writes Farhi. A second result was overkill: "[I]t could easily be argued that the constant harping on the values generated at the battlefront . . . actually creates resentment and backlash."

Indeed, that resentment could be found even during the war, especially in urban centers where incomprehension about the war "mentality" was so great that soldier-Believers would sometimes go back early from home leave. "[M]any in the cities could not understand and even ridiculed the commitment the volunteers had to the war," adds Farhi.[60] "The kind of constant attention that was being given to the religious and spiritual experience of these young volunteers may have given the impression to others outside the front [that they] had something missing in their heads."

In the last stages of the war, many factors were eroding Iran's effort. Pro-regime newspapers felt obliged to publish photographs of crowded Friday prayer sermons, with many congregants wearing white shrouds to signify their readiness to die.[61] There was a growing sense that the war no longer served the Revolution, but in fact had become a danger to it, notes Gieling: "[C]riticism of the continuation of a war without victory had increased considerably and . . . zeal and enthusiasm [gave way to] loss of morale at home and at the front."[62]

Still, one man had no doubts at all. With "messianic conviction," Ayatollah Ruhollah Khomeini believed that Iran's Revolution would defeat Iraq, the United States, and the West, and score a victory that even the ancient prophets had not achieved.[63] If Iran lost the war, he intoned, "Islam will receive such a blow that it will not be able to raise its head for a long time."

Khomeini's commitment was clear in a story told to Vali Nasr by a grand ayatollah who had known Khomeini for decades. One night when he was "deeply troubled by the war's horrors," the senior cleric found Khomeini alone on a rug, in his garden, beside a small pool. " 'It's not right for Muslims to kill Muslims,' [the senior cleric] began. 'Hundreds of thousands are dying in a war that has no end and no good purpose.' Khomieni made no sound until [the cleric] stopped talking. Then, without turning his head and in even but reproachful tones, he asked, 'Do you also criticize God when he sends an earthquake?' "[64]

I NEVER SAW FOR myself how the fountains in Behesht-e Zahra cemetery once bubbled bright red with water dyed to look like martyrs' blood. They had all been turned off, and after the 1997 political triumph of President Khatami and the reform movement, there were deep-seated complaints about the collapse in such values from the director of the martyrs' section. It was Khomeini himself who declared that the Islamic Republic had been "irrigated" with the blood of the martyrs, that Islam could not survive otherwise.[65]

"There are many things that have lost their color after twenty years. One of them is the color of the fountain. Some traitorous officials claim that the red color is a reminder of the blood shed during the war and since there is no war the fountain should not run red anymore," Hamid Rahimian told author Elaine Sciolino.[66] He was disappointed that the sacrifice brought so little. "Now the ideals we fought for have been buried. The new generation doesn't want us anymore. This country is becoming so materialistic. It is losing the martyrdom mentality."

Part of the problem was what that "mentality" meant to different Iranians. Long after the war, that sense of entitlement earned by service at the front still afflicts hard-liners, resulting in an "us versus them" attitude. In Iran, it is characterized as being an insider (*khodi*) or outsider (*gheir-e khodi*).

"They won't give us access. It's difficult to get through to them," complained a secular woman in Tehran who had made several attempts to understand.[67] "They put up a wall, and in a sense they are right—many people here do not believe in them. But the separation has worked against them," she told me. "I feel a tremendous breakage from the war era and the war dead. They shoved it down people's throats so much, people don't want to know."

These days, schoolkids in north Tehran tell jokes against the martyrs—she had caught her own son doing so.

She told me how, during the Khatami era of the late 1990s, newspapers published letters from martyrs' families asking the regime to stop instrumentalizing them as a political tool.[68] Among them was Hamid Reza Jalaeipour, a reformist editor who lost two brothers in the war and another to a Mojahedin assassin. He wrote in 1998 that his ill mother was tired of hearing constantly of the war that ended years before: "She wants to live. She is fed up with bragging about martyrdom." [69]

"Most people hate the war paintings and don't want to be reminded of it," the Tehran woman told me. "Fundamentalists never allowed their point of view to be put across [to secular Iranians], because of the myths they made about themselves."

Even showing respect is a challenge, said the woman, who had visited Behesht-e Zahra cemetery in a personal bid to make amends. She was respectful, she told me. But her clothes marked her as a *gharbzadeh,* a Western-influenced Iranian. Born in Iran and British-educated, this dual citizen wanted to place flowers on unnamed graves, to honor the fallen. She was confronted by a hostile Believer.

"What are you doing here, with *that* kind of hijab?" the man asked in a tone that said: get out.

"I've come to put flowers on the grave of the young men who died for our country," she answered, taken aback.

He replied: "They didn't die for people like *you.*"

3

Cultural Khatami: "Westoxication"

*As hard as Reza Shah tried, he could not have done what
the ayatollahs have recently achieved. . . . [I]t has gone
so far that today's burgeoning youth, supposedly ruled by
the "representative of God on earth," now even deny the
existence of God himself.*

—Iranian Internet posting, quoted by Nasrin Alavi
in *We Are Iran: The Persian Blogs*

SOCIAL FREEDOMS ARE OFTEN a critical barometer of politics in Iran, and by the mid-1990s simple liberties from budding
heavy metal bands to boy-girl hand holding were signals of broad demand for change.

Ayatollah Ruhollah Khomeini had railed against infatuation with
the West and its poisonous influences, as had ideologues since the
early 1960s. But decades later, demographics were the new driving
force: two-thirds of Iranians were younger than thirty years old and
had no recollection of that cataclysm—the Revolution, followed by
the deprivations and heroics of the war—that had erased music and
ruled out fun. There were still many True Believers, but I spent time,
too, with countless Iranians who wanted the most severe aspects of
the Revolution lifted from their lives.

For those Iranians hungering for reform of the Islamic system, who would so definitely demonstrate themselves to be the majority, the "before" and "after" of hope for change would pivot on Iran's May 1997 presidential election, which heralded the surprise landslide victory of the smiling, erudite, and genuinely warm and well-meaning philosopher-cleric, Seyyed Mohammad Khatami.

Scholar. Optimist. Gentleman—too much so, it would prove, in the vicious battleground of Iranian politics. And with a degree in Western philosophy and the black turban of a *seyyed,* worn by those clerics who could trace their lineage back to the Prophet Mohammad, Khatami could converse in Kant and the ideas of Alexis de Tocqueville. Immaculately turned out, from his wire-rimmed glasses and trimmed, graying beard to the quality cut of his beautiful shoes, Khatami shone from seminary lectern to presidential podium, where he captured the Iranian imagination with promises of restoring the rule of law and civil society and of reestablishing the "freedom" that was always meant to be at the heart of the Revolution.

Khatami had applied those ideas before, during two stints as minister of culture and Islamic guidance. He had finally been forced out in 1992, charged by hard-liners with being too liberal in his freedom-seeking ways.

But by 1997 the time was more conducive to steer the Islamic Revolution and its fading legitimacy into a modern age that would embrace all Iranians and their views, while preserving the glue of the *velayat-e faqih*—the supreme religious rule upon which the Islamic Republic was founded. Voter turnout had dwindled in previous years. Khatami wanted to reinvigorate the Revolution with a dose of tolerance and reemphasize its "republic" nature. Symbolic of Khatami's dreams of hope, change, and of easing Iran's isolation would be his policy of "dialogue among civilizations," which the United Nations, at Khatami's suggestion, declared as the UN's global theme of the year in 2001.

But such soaring aspirations were of necessity kept in check during the 1997 presidential campaign. When approved by the Supreme Leader to run for president, the erudite and friendly cleric from Yazd was considered a no-hoper—but useful in providing a patina of democracy across a broader political spectrum. Change appeared all but impossible. When, well before the vote, I interviewed the regime's handpicked candidate, Ali Akbar Nategh-Nouri—who called the United States a "blood-sucking wolf"—he spoke as if he were already president. The Leader was decrying the "perverse resistance" of intellectuals in Iran to the Islamic Republic. A prime-time TV show denounced academics as Western spies, showing their faces merging with the image of an American hundred-dollar bill.

To fight the cultural "invasion" from the West, parliament had just passed a bill called "Prohibition of Usage of Foreign Names, Words, and Expressions." A UN human rights report concluded that Iran's social climate "is becoming less tolerant."[1] It cited forced newspaper closures, the breakup of a private political meeting, the new TV program aimed at "categorizing targeted intellectuals as social misfits or foreign spies," and a purge of universities, all "done in the name of combating 'social corruption' and 'decadent Westernization.'"

NONE OF THAT WAS news to the disheartened computer specialist I met in Tehran in 1996, when I brought my machine in for repair. Iran had become the "same as the fifteenth or sixteenth century, the Dark Ages," lamented Samira from behind her desk.[2] Was this the "freedom" that Iranians had bled for in 1979, as they toppled the Shah? Was this the "independence" they fought for in crowded streets and shouted, "God is great!" from the rooftops to achieve?

"Samira" is a pseudonym for the woman whose long black robe with Chanel buttons hung on the coatrack, a matching black headscarf tucked over the most tempestuous tangles of her hair. For her and many other Iranians, the Islamic Republic was simply another cage, a novel way to stifle life, this time in the name of Islam.

"If you think about something, it's the Spanish Inquisition. It's here right now. They want to restrict your mind. They want you to think simply, about your house, your food, and your family, so that you will not think of anything else in the world," she told me. (The Shah himself, hardly a paragon of benevolent leadership, made a similar comparison from exile: "Five centuries after the Spanish Inquisition, Iran lives under the terror of its own Torquemada—one far more merciless," he complained in his memoir *Answer to History*.[3] The "explosion of hatred, unleashed supposedly in the 'name of God,' is an insult to God and to our religion," he fumed. Without a trace of irony, the Shah was praying for "our youth, deceived and misguided," and "for those who remain blind to falsehood and deceit.")

And there was plenty of "falsehood" to go around in Iran, just as there had been throughout the Shah's reign. As Samira put it: "You must be a good Iranian citizen to have a good life here. . . . I have to be as they want me to be."

That meant adherence to tough and explicit rules. Manteaus and hijabs were required for women; outlawed were "flashy ones with fashionable cuts, decorated with any exotic insignia."[4] Also taboo were "short, thin or mismatched and glowing stockings," and of course "punkish insignia such as the head of a rabbit or eagle, broken or whole crosses and foreign flags or other pagan symbols, like victory or goodbye signs" on clothing. Illegal too were "depraved, showy and glitzy objects on hats," as well as "necklaces, earrings, bracelets, glasses, headbands, rings, neckscarves . . ." Infractions meant up to one year in prison or seventy-four lashes.

It was a stifling reality that was messing with Iranian minds. "They must hide everything, like the hair under this veil," Samira said, rearranging her scarf with a tantalizing turn of her fingers, which dripped with artificial nails. "If I only lift it, you can see the color of the hair and how long it is, and how I put it up. This is what they are afraid of."

And it was not just hair. "They" were also afraid of the Persian service of Voice of America television, judging by the crackdown that had taken place with the launch of the channel. Samira got a tip-off by phone from a friend; police were swooping in on her neighborhood, hunting for illegal satellite dishes. "Quick!" she was told.

Samira rushed upstairs to the roof, dismantled her prized satellite dish, and hid it away in the nick of time. *Doctor Zhivago* was the last thing she had seen. "Our government attacked us," she told me later, tightening her black veil around her face. "Things are not getting any better." And many others were not as quick as Samira. In the month-long spree, police rounded up fifteen hundred satellite dishes and created a junkyard of them beside a main thoroughfare. The gleaming pile was testament to renewed war against "cultural aggression."

Samira offered me freeze-dried American coffee, in a country saturated with tea. "We used American missiles during the war," she explained, waving away my surprise. "So coffee is no problem." Despite the crackdowns, officials had toyed with easing up. Why? I asked. If the clerics "push too hard, then like a tightly wound coil [angry Iranians] will suddenly explode."

Public and private lives, conflicted. The confusing signals were even felt by Samira's six-year-old niece, who had to pray for the Supreme Leader in school, just as American pupils often start their day with the Pledge of Allegiance: "We have to sing for a man, what was his name? The person on TV with the big black hat?" the niece had asked Samira. But at home there was teasing about that man.

"The Revolution happened to us, but our generation is not honest with itself," said Samira. "There are two cultures adjusting to one another all the time. At school [students] are like [the regime] wants them to be. At home, they are like their parents want them to be."

She was deflated, even devastated. She felt her life slipping away, before it had really started. "Living—sometimes it's awful," she confided. "You must have honesty, or how much better are you than a bird?"

THEN CAME MOHAMMAD KHATAMI'S shock victory on May 23, 1997. No one was more surprised than the regal cleric himself that of the 80 percent of Iranian voters who turned out—that high figure itself was an indication of the enthusiasm for Khatami's agenda—70 percent cast their ballots for his promise of change.

The result heralded a Tehran Spring, and Iran's youth and cultural elites took full advantage, pushing the limits and breaking taboos in a burst of cultural expression unseen in Iran for decades. The dark hues of the Revolution were partly painted over with a palette of splashy new colors. Khomeini's dire dicta, which had defined life in Iran, seemed to recede, including this one: "Allah did not create man so that he could have fun. The aim of creation was for mankind to be put to the test through hardship and prayer. An Islamic regime must be serious in every field. There are no jokes in Islam. There is no humor in Islam. There is no fun in Islam."[5]

Yet as the realization swept Iran that those desiring reform were the clear majority, the reform movement's most ardent supporters began speaking of *irreversible* change. The Islamic system, they believed, now recognized the limits of coercion. So as the Revolution aged, it appeared to be mellowing, maturing, and allowing a new balance between the leadership and those it claimed to lead.

Disillusion ran deep, and it was a key reason for Khatami's appeal. "The earth and the ground moves beneath your feet, and then the result does not match the expectation," a former revolutionary told me, about how he realized his "ideals were wrong" when Iran's clerics sought to impose utopia.[6] He was the Sage whom I met often in Tehran, sipping tea and chewing grapes, inhaling the smoke of his cigarettes and my cigars late into the night, exploring every crevice of Iran's political and social cranium. He had come back to Iran in 1979 after several years in America, expressly to take part in the Revolution. His father had welcomed the Islamists, saying that "maybe the fear of hell will control people and corruption."

Ever since then, the Sage told me in 1999, he had been on a "voyage of discovery." He was troubled by what he found, about how the Revolution's promise of freedom had been smothered by the paranoia and fear of its leaders. All the boasting about "victory," God's will, and divine inspiration masked a deep inferiority complex with ugly consequences. The economy was a wreck, too; clearly clerics didn't double as economists. In the two decades since the Revolution, all that oil money hadn't made Iranians much richer; corruption and chronic inefficiency were preventing progress.

"Now people are tired in their bones of burning flags and Revolution, of fists in the air," the Sage explained. "The problem is Iranians want shortcuts. The Revolution did not give us heaven—so maybe gradual reform is better. For years, they tried to push the religious stuff down throats, and it caused a reaction."[7] One poll showed 45 percent of Iranians had negative feelings toward religion. A government report found that 75 percent of the public and 86 percent of schoolchildren "do not say their daily prayers."[8] There could hardly be a greater indictment of the *Islamic* Republic. Said the Sage: "Twenty years ago, is that the reaction the leaders of Iran wanted? They wanted to train soldiers for Islam, and got exactly the opposite."

And he wasn't the only one saying so. "People are fed up with war and don't believe in religion anymore," an Iranian professional told me.[9] "Before the Revolution, clerics had a big following in Iran. People would make any sacrifice for them. But now the pendulum has swung the other way. Clerics are the losers of the Revolution, and many of them know that. They say they are losing their respect because they are involved in politics."

A student who once thrilled to the call to prayer and ran to the mosque as a child wrote in his blog how his heart had changed:

> The call to prayer, the "Allah Akbar" [God is great] used to make me feel like a stronger person . . . that there was a loving, kind, benevolent God out there . . . greater than all my silly problems . . . But now "Allah Akbar" is the chant of the thugs in the Basij and Hezbollah and fat, corrupt mullahs. . . .
>
> The call to prayer, the "Allah Akbar," still makes me feel like a stronger person . . . but I rarely enter a mosque . . . all that awaits you there are the hypocrites, thugs and oppressors. . . .
>
> We replaced one corrupt monarch with thousands of corrupt clergy . . . yet the only thing they did was destroy our beliefs in the religion they said they were safeguarding. . . .[10]

That collapse in faith was not hidden. Clergy found it hard to hail a taxi if they wore their religious robes. "So many of these guys at the beginning of the Revolution walked around with new briefcases, looking so arrogant—like they had Harvard MBAs," said Louise Firouz, the late American horse breeder and tour operator who lived in Iran for fifty years.[11] She had seen a cleric stuck in the snow in north Tehran and sniggered as she told me of the memory: "He was trying to push out the car and everybody who came past gave him the finger. *Nobody* helped him."

THE BELIEVERS FORGED IN the crucible of 1979 and the Iran-Iraq War had not disappeared. They were as shocked as anyone by Khatami's election triumph, and sent reeling by the new era of glasnost. "Some elements within the right are genuinely afraid of the West, its culture and Western ideals, so feel any mixing . . . would be detrimental to Islam," professor Sadegh Zibakalam told me.[12] And they were preparing to fight back. "Some [right-wingers] still want to destroy the others," said the Sage. "*Compromise* is still a dirty word in Iran. It's bad to be a compromiser."

Conservative leaders were channeling some of the Revolution's most formative thinkers, who for decades had warned of the malady they called "Westoxication"—a destructive obsession with the West and America that had infected Iranians. Declaring in the early 1960s that the "contagion spreads day by day" through "our society," Jalal Al-e Ahmad laid down his treatise against corrosive Western influence.[13] His principles provided important cultural ammunition and have already shaped the defiance of the Revolution for a generation, right up to the present-day inflexibility over Iran's nuclear program.

The cultural disease "closely resembles an infestation of weevils," Al-e Ahmad wrote in his book *Westoxication.* "Have you seen how they attack wheat? From the inside. The bran remains intact, but it is just a shell, like a cocoon left behind on a tree."

The same was happening to Iran and other "hungry nations" of the Third World, Al-e Ahmad argued. Developed, industrialized nations sent manufactured goods along with their "myths, dogmas, music." Centuries of challenging the Western "apostles for 'civilization' " had now "been replaced by rueful, worshipful longing" for the West. Al-e Ahmad accused Iranians of abrogating their own values with West-inspired "lust, stupidity, boasting, and vanity."

He portrayed two civilizations in conflict, with Iran the spineless victim of Western predations: "We pretend to be free just like them. . . . Night and day are night and day when they confirm it," he wrote. "We now resemble an alien people, with unfamiliar customs, a culture with no roots in our land and no chance of blossoming here. Thus all we have is stillborn, in our politics, our culture, and our daily life."

Al-e Ahmad's views were incorporated by another titan of pre-Revolution thought in Iran, Ali Shariati. Even today, Iran's aging revolutionaries credit the Paris-educated Shariati with mobilizing their generation with his blend of Marxist beliefs and modernizing the Shiite passion play. One of Tehran's most important north-south avenues is named after him. "Shariati saw Shiism as a creed of revolution," explains Vali Nasr in *The Shia Revival*:

> Its history told the tale of a grand quest for justice. Its saints were revolutionary heroes. He saw Imam Hossein as a seventh-century Che Guevara and Karbala as a revolutionary drama. Shia history was none other than the famous dialectic of class war, culminating in a revolution. It had all begun in Karbala and would end with an Iranian revolution. In Shariati's thinking, Karbala was . . . a revolutionary act by a revolutionary hero, which could be duplicated in the late twentieth century.[14]

That meant a new obligation of resistance, Shariati taught. "[A]ll Shi'is, irrespective of time and place, had the duty to oppose, resist, and even rebel against overwhelming odds in order to eradicate their contemporary ills," notes historian Ervand Abrahamian.[15]

Shariati created a "genuinely new kind of vision of God's glory" in politics, which "focused on the highest and most compelling God-term of Shariati's generation: 'The People,' " observes historian

Hamid Dabashi.[16] Shariati "became the most popular visionary of his age, the most vigorous proselytizer of revolutionary zeal [who] more than anyone else . . . paved the way for Khomeini's arrival."

Those messages were indeed taken up by Khomeini, who in prescribing Islamic government as a solution said in 1970, "The imperialists began laying their plans three or four centuries ago; they started out with nothing, but see where they are now! We too will begin with nothing, and we will pay no attention to the uproar created by a few [Westoxicated] 'xenomaniacs' and devoted servants of imperialism."[17]

THIS WAS THE HISTORY at stake on a rain-swept day in Tehran in late 1997, when Iran's leaders addressed Muslim heads of state at the Organization of the Islamic Conference. The towering venue had only been completed hours before—builders had to push day and night to finally get it done. Inside smelled of fresh paint, and even as we took our seats in the press gallery, we could see that water from the downpour was leaking through the roof.

The words from the flower-bedecked podium were a study of diametrically opposed views in Iran. First up was the implacable Supreme Leader Khamenei, to issue a warning: "The Western materialistic civilization is directing everyone toward materiality, while money, gluttony, and carnal desires are made the greatest aspirations," he inveighed.[18] "As in the past, today Islam is the only remedial, curative and savior angel."

The result was an epic clash that would destroy the West, Khamenei predicted:

The West, in its all-rounded invasion, has also targeted our Islamic faith and character. In the light of its store of science, needed by all, the West intensely and persistently exported to our countries the culture of laxness and disregard for religion and ethics, a culture with which it is gripped. Indubitably, this ethical quagmire will, on a not-too-distant day, engulf the present Western civilization and wipe it out.[19]

But that was an Old World view. Later the same day, the rain still falling, the leak still leaking, President Khatami addressed the assembled leaders. His tone and ideas were as different from Khamenei as were his effervescent smile and elegant bearing.

"Our era is an era of preponderance of Western culture and civilization, whose understanding is imperative," Khatami said.[20] Muslim nations could not progress unless they "utilize the positive scientific technological and social accomplishments of Western civilization, a stage we must inevitably go through to reach the future."

Khatami explored those ideas further in an extraordinary essay published in *Time* magazine:

Societies unfamiliar with this spirit [of Western civilization] shall never succeed in introducing a positive change in their lives. Many Islamic societies, such as ours, are still regretfully deprived of such knowledge. . . .

For centuries our historical destiny was in the hands of autocratic and capricious governments. . . . Human dignity was not respected, and thought, the greatest manifestation of human character, was contained, and the freedom of opinion was also denied.

We can take Iran as an example. In the past five decades, we have never been successful in our experience with freedom. . . . Some blamed freedom itself for the cause of the instability and even used religion as a mask to justify their shortsightedness. Autocracy has become our second nature. We Iranians are all dictators, in a sense. . . .

Without freedom, the thought sparkling in the minds of thinkers shall be channeled into hidden communities and may emerge one day in the form of bitter and violent reaction.[21]

While those words might have made liberal hearts beat faster in joy, they were prescient—at least in terms of a "bitter and violent reaction"—and challenged Iran's most unreconstructed hard-liners. They knew what sacrilege to expect from Khatami: they had driven him from his post as minister of culture in 1992 for permitting an "invasion" of dangerous ideas.[22] Khatami's five-year tenure at that time is remembered by many Iranians as a "golden era," marked by wide circulation of books and films. It finally foundered on his support of director Mohsen Makhmalbaf, who made films on still-taboo subjects like adultery and suicide, and had, in the words of *Time*, "hinted that tyranny did not end with the Shah's departure."

In his 1992 resignation letter, Khatami was scathing about "violations" that were impeding his "fight against rigidity, ignorance, and backwardness which I consider the biggest calamity for a religious government and the *nezam* [Islamic system]."[23] Khatami blamed "impatient superficial observers [who] won't tolerate, even at the cost of shutting down thought and dismissing legal and legitimate freedom." The future president continued: "The challenge of our Revolution, which claims to save humanity by creating a new superior culture, is heaviest in the cultural domain. . . ."

That historical baggage meant that as president, Khatami had to take special care to reassure hard-liners. His first public appearance after his 1997 victory was to Khomeini's tomb, and then to the Behesht-e Zahra cemetery. His political magic rubbed off even on black-clad traditional Iranians there, who, statistics showed, and as I had found in my own reporting, had voted for his message of change as eagerly as the rest of the country. "He's shining with spirituality," glowed one woman in a chador. "I hope he can do what he says. I liked him from the beginning."[24]

The archradical Ayatollah Ahmad Jannati, leading nationally televised Friday prayers, warned Khatami to heed "first God, second the Leader [Khamenei] and then [third] the demands of the voters. The voters have different demands which should be realized within Islamic and revolutionary limitations."[25] Hoping against hope, the hard-line newspaper *Kayhan* gave Khatami the benefit of the doubt after his obeisance at Khomeini's shrine: "The new president's motto is adherence to the Revolution and the Islamic Republic," the paper said. "The ill-wishers now see that their dreams were nothing but an illusion."[26]

Iran's post-Revolution renaissance was under way. Many Iranians were praying for a new enlightened era. Others were more pessimistic, remembering the lightning bolts cast down by Ayatollah Khomeini in the final months of his life, against "sell-out liberals," "American Islam," and anyone who doubted decisions of the Revolution.[27] He warned: "We should not be influenced by superficial sympathy for the enemies of God . . . and thereby question God's decrees and divine punishments."

Yet the spirit of change, of spreading freedom and fearlessness, would not be denied.

The Kissing Slopes

When young Alireza Mahfouzian stopped mid-schuss and bent his head to steal a kiss from his girlfriend, he quickly looked up—like a child caught stealing sweets—to see if anyone was watching.

Holding hands in public was rare enough in early 2000, because it risked reprimand from watchful morality police. But being openly flirtatious in the Islamic Republic? Well, that was nothing short of revolutionary. Judging by the separate ski lift lines for men and women back then, one might have thought Iran's ski slopes adhered to strict Islamic rules. But when stylish upper-crust young couples started heading toward the pristine summit, inhibitions disappeared as quickly as snowflakes on a warm spring day.

"There is more freedom here than anywhere else," Mahfouzian told me when I finally caught up with the amorous couple.[28] He was nineteen with gelled hair and mirror sunglasses, as if skiing in Colorado or the Swiss Alps. He introduced me to his girlfriend, Golnar Akasheh, whose spandex leggings and jacket redefined Iran's social code.

"Don't worry, this is my wife," Mahfouzian joked.

The pair and their circle of friends were apt symbols of the powerful social forces that were transforming Iran. The growing demands for freedom and tolerance were germinating in places like Dizin, in the Alborz range north of Tehran.

From the summit, Mahfouzian sliced down the mountain, the sun and bright blue sky glinting off the spray of snow crystals as he slalomed back and forth. Akasheh followed right behind, her long hair—anywhere but here completely covered by a headscarf—flowing with little restraint from under her dark beret. He stopped on a hillside knoll. She bumped into him playfully, and then swung an arm around his neck in a brief embrace. With other skiers whooshing past them, they stole their kiss, then smiled broadly.

They hadn't lived through the Revolution. Their lives were not blighted—or inspired—by the war. So instead of looking inward, such Iranian youth had been looking out at the world through illegal satellite dishes and the Internet. And since the Revolution wasn't theirs, they hardly felt bound by its most stringent social rules.

"They are the children of the Revolution [and] they are unhappy," political scientist Zibakalam told me of his students.[29] "They have very high expectations. They are not happy with what their parents achieved through the Revolution. . . . I tell them they have to be realistic. The amount of freedom [they] want and desire is tantamount to a Western state. . . . They are not content with gradual improvements."

Nor were they content with just political progress. Back in Tehran, my friend the Sage spent a lot of time with young Iranians, partly because they were good company, but also to understand what inspired and depressed them. "Now because of what the Islamic Revolution has done, people realize their eyes have been closed to things to be enjoyed. Girls are more aggressive."[30]

"That's why we *love* the Islamic Revolution!" chimed in one young Persian sitting near the Sage, as he rolled a joint, mixing a large pinch of hash with cigarette tobacco. The ashtrays were already full.

The regime had learned the lesson of the first years of the Revolution, when babies were encouraged to bolster the ranks of "soldiers of Islam." Now those "soldiers" were in college, making up an unruly majority of the population, and family-planning courses were required. Condoms were subsidized, and the Islamic Republic was making forty-five million a year in thirty different shapes, colors, and tastes. The factory manager said, "the fancier ones go to the private sector. The favorite color is pink, and for flavor, mint."[31] The UN considered Iran a model for family planning for all the Muslim world.[32] So what was new? "Girls kiss the boy first," the young man told me. Secretly, in parks. In the mountains. In the movie theater. It was something different, he said; women exercising control.

"We're very good at being extremist in many ways, and this is just another way of being ultraradical," the Sage explained.[33] "In the 1960s, women wore miniskirts, but inside they were very traditional; they would kiss, but not on the lips. Now they wear a hijab [to cover their hair] in public, but inside they are all shaken up, and much looser. Relationships are much more advanced."

The friend who rolled a joint would later have "temporary" marriage for a year, a particular Shiite custom that was often utilized, even in increments of an hour or a single day, by the clerical class, to satisfy "needs." Even the Sage, postmarriage, fell in love again and required a temporary marriage license so that he and his girlfriend could travel the country unmolested.

THE SAME WEEK IN 2000 that Mahfouzian and Akasheh were intimate on the ski slopes, reformists scored another political victory. After a high turnout, 80 percent of eligible voters elected a reformist majority to the 290-seat parliament, or majlis. Khatami's efforts had often been blocked by conservative deputies, and reformists now expected more progress. I had watched at dawn on election day while Khamenei's aides prepared his cardboard voting box for the event in the main hall on the Supreme Leader's compound, where he often spoke on the raised platform—with its immaculate cobalt blue background decorated only with a single framed image of Khomeini.[34]

The box was a symbol of democracy, of the power of the people, and these aides took care to get it right. They used masking tape and then delicately stitched together the cloth covering, before realizing they had forgotten to make a slit in the box so that God's Representative on Earth could actually insert his ballot. The aides called for a pair of scissors, unstitched the cloth, then after carving the hole, re-sewed the cover and sealed it with the wax of a white candle. All rectified, the Leader, when he came, went through the motions with a smile of real pleasure on his face, a proud twinkle in his eye, and, on his lips, a call to Iranians to vote.

Some 570 candidates had been rejected prior to that 2000 vote. In future elections, thousands—most of them reformists—would be barred from running as conservatives reasserted supremacy. And yet, until the brazenly stolen June 2009 presidential vote, the Islamic Republic was one of the most democratic nations in the region, where political space was seriously contested.

"We've heard a lot of lies," offered the driver of a taxi that I jumped into after Khamenei voted. It was a typical Iranian-made Paykan: seat covers worn with the residue from thousands of passengers; rear window handles removed; a chain bolted from one side of the chassis to the other to prevent the front seat from shifting too far back—the whole package a hurtling chunk of metal perfect for imposing yourself on Tehran traffic with a nothing-to-lose recklessness. The driver wasn't going to vote.

"For twenty years this regime instilled deliberate insecurity to induce a day-to-day survival," he averred. "Khatami promises to change that. I agree with Khatami's words; he needs to free people from their trap. People worry about feeding their families every day, so don't think about politics. These religious officials in Iran are not really religious. If they were really Muslim, they would not drive such nice cars."

When the election results came out days later, a French diplomat couldn't contain his excitement at the reform sweep into parliament. This was a "major political and historical event" in Iran, he told me. The "very clear, strong and dynamic" election meant "the balance of power has changed."[35]

The changes had been taking place across Iran, long before Khamenei's aides wrestled with the Leader's ballot box. From remote conservative hamlets where rules were easing—to a degree—for boys and girls and their hand holding, to the slopes above Tehran where there seemed to be a surge of fun, signs of change were everywhere.

"Tehran is really controlled, and you can't wear these clothes there," Shadi Peyda, a student skier wearing a loose white scarf and round sunglasses, told me. "Here it is different—everyone is happy, everything is good, the colors are so bright." She noticed too much interest in her artful image among the men, so before setting off she teased: "All women in Iran are beautiful, didn't you know that? That makes them all snow bunnies!"

Skiing had powerful sanction. A billboard in the parking lot showed the Supreme Leader, smiling, next to his own words: "I consider sport a necessity for the health of everyone's mind and body and I agree with it." But while freewheeling teenagers and lovebirds frolicked on the slopes, risks still existed. Just ten days before my visit, there had been a major crackdown when a group of thirty to forty uniformed morality cops—"*basijis* on skis," the Iranians joked at the rhyme—took to the slopes. They enforced compliance with the rules and harassed unmarried couples.

"If they catch you, they take you away and say your coat is too short, your hair is out, and you wear too much makeup," harped Mahnaz, a teenage student. "They tell our parents, who laugh at them." About ten men and ten women were arrested. Mahfouzian was there with Akasheh. "People were scared," he recalled. The couple were given a hard time but finally let go because, by chance, Mahfouzian's sister was there. With such a chaperone, all was legal.

The *basijis* weren't the best skiers, so on most days they kept a low profile, leaving Iran's youth to themselves in the high mountain air. But on crowded weekends, "all the decadent, corrupt, co-ed swooshing about irked the regime" to the extent that finally a cleric was deployed at the bottom of the lifts to lead a noon prayer, according to Azadeh Moaveni in *Lipstick Jihad*. As Moaveni describes, "He stood there with his turban and robes against the gleaming snow, a Grinch-like figure with no purpose but to inject a little Islam into the atmosphere, in case anyone was starting to feel too glamorous." [36]

Such an attempt would never wreck the fun of Milad, a baby-faced friend of Mahfouzian with carbonated hormones. "Look: girls, girls, girls!" I heard him shout as he banged on the inside of the plastic gondola with his ski pole toward a pair of ladies. He had been "very successful" meeting such women and often exchanged phone numbers. One in five saw him again in Tehran. He thanked Khatami for hearing the message of the youth and women and for making such openness possible.

And so did the lift operator, who volunteered about this enlightened president, "He's made this country blossom."

THE DAY MY SKI story was published, I was in the holy city of Qom, to hear about a fracas in New York from the conservative cleric Sadegh Larijani. He had recently canceled his visit to America after an unpleasant experience with immigration officers.[37] He was with a group of half a dozen clerics invited to a seminar at Georgetown University on "Islam and secularism." But all were stopped at the airport, put through an involved fingerprinting process, and photographed from every angle. They were mocked by a U.S. officer when they prayed, Larijani said. "We felt like criminals on the FBI's 'Most Wanted' list."

We were sitting on the floor, drinking glasses of salty, slippery tea—that is how the water comes in Qom. The cleric's mobile phone lay on the floor beside the clear-glass cup and saucer. At the end of my interview, he pulled out a copy of my kids-at-play story printed from the Internet. Suddenly in 2000, a newspaper printed in America was linked to this distant religious city in Iran, via an unpoliced ski run. There was the photo of Mahfouzian with his arm draped over Golnar's shoulders, giving a very un-Islamic thumbs-up with his ski glove.

My decidedly secular translator, Dokhi Fassihian, started to sweat.

"Do you mind if I ask you a question?" Larijani asked, eyeing me carefully. "Do you think this is an accurate picture of Iranian youth today?"

"Well, I think it is one *aspect* of Iranian youth," I answered, as tact-

fully as I could. The cleric knew of many, many more young Iranians who were Believers—and I knew a few myself—who would not
have tasted the fruit of freedom on those slopes; people who would
not have considered it true "freedom" up there, any more than they
would have felt comfortable having sex in public. *His* Iranian youth
would have recoiled from any hint of carnal frivolity, perhaps even
leaped out of their skin to avoid hand holding.

"Dizin is not in all of Iran," Larijani lectured me, his white turban
tilting forward in a degree of seriousness. The tea of Qom was tasting saltier now. "The problem is the problem of youth seeking more
freedom. Your story may have made an untrue picture, because it was
not a full one."

In some ways, the cleric was right. The Dizin ski story *was* not all
of Iran, just a snapshot, focused on the rather crazier side of youth
culture—and the wealthier side at that. But I wondered what Larijani
would have thought if he had weighed that story up with the many
others I had written, with their wide variety of voices from all corners of his society. And I wondered further if, because this was not a
slice of Iran that Larijani had seen much of—much less experienced—
whether he thought it did not exist at all.

I was surprised many times over the years, while relating stories
to Iranians about extraordinary statements or tales I have heard from
their fellow citizens, about how disbelieving they could be—can it be
real?—unless it adhered closely to their own worldview or experience.

Years later when I called Larijani to request an interview, he remembered me. And he refused to talk. He was a member of the conservative Guardian Council, the twelve-seat body that vetted all candidates
for elected office, the key tool for keeping reformists out of government. Larijani would later be named Iran's judiciary chief in the aftermath of June 2009 street protests against a fraudulent election, when
thousands of "rioters" were arrested, many of them brutalized. He
had clearly known how easy it could be to arrest troublemakers when
we had spoken in 2000.

"They let you quote them, using their *real* names?" the cleric asked, incredulous as he looked at the photograph once more.

"They did," I replied to his implied threat. "Is there any reason you think that might be a problem?"

Starstruck Romeo

The way Shakespeare wrote it, the moonstruck lovers Romeo and Juliet are to seal their amorous intentions with a kiss. But when that magic moment came in Iran's first post-Revolution production, no one expected close adherence to the script. Such public physical contact was forbidden.

The miracle instead was that in 2000 the love story was playing in Iran at all. When I saw one of the first showings at the capital's most prestigious venue, the Vahdat Hall, it creatively pushed the limits of the Tehran Spring—with the full and quiet expectation that it would serve as a vanguard for much more change to come.

"Did they touch?" I heard one Iranian theatergoer gasp, after watching Romeo and Juliet pirouette together on stage, apparently arm-in-arm, face-to-face.[38] Later the audience tittered approvingly when Juliet leaned very close over Romeo's dead body and spoke of her love— then brushed his cheek gently with the back of her fingers.

"I don't think we could have gone further," director Ali Rafiee told me afterward, his arms full of flowers given him during a standing ovation. Even the applause was a sign of the times: clapping was also once forbidden, along with chess, women singing in public, and music of all kinds. He was ecstatic. "The former officials did not believe in plays," Rafiee said. "But officials now believe that plays and culture are a necessity. It is a renaissance."

These were the trenches of Iran's "culture wars," where what was put on stage or screen was so important—and seditious—that right-wing vigilantes had attacked theaters for shows deemed too liberal. Compromises were still being made, but Iran's cultural creatives were finding ingenious ways to get their message across. The opulent and carefully choreographed rendering of Shakespeare's love tragedy, for instance, had an Iranian touch. Juliet's hair was tightly covered with a dark brown headscarf—as required by law. But the scarf exactly matched the actress's real hair color, and a waist-length braid of dark hair hung beneath it—was it a wig? Or was it real?

Romeo wore black gloves—a perfect foil against accusations of touching, if any were to be laid. One scene showed Romeo quickly dressing, clearly implying that he had spent the night to consummate the secret marriage with his new wife, Juliet.

"Even if I had permission [to show] more, I would not change anything," the director told me. "In our poetry, all is metaphor and symbolism, and there are plenty of love scenes. . . . I believe in this society. I know the standards."

Khatami's victory and almost-anything-goes sense of freedom was prompting a rebirth in such artistic expression. Outside Iran, that was evident in the number of accolades and awards won by Iranian directors at international film festivals, often for their fresh treatment of humanist issues. More than a decade after the *Revayat-e Fath* (*Chronicles of Victory*) promoted revolutionary ideology during the Iran-Iraq War—using a host of powerful narrative techniques to bring the war and its "sacred" nature into every Iranian living room—independent directors were now, with beautiful storytelling, taking on much broader challenges.

The subjects often appeared plain, but the messages struck deep political notes about freedom and religious rule. The once-banned film *Taste of Cherry*, about a man searching for an accomplice to his own suicide, by director Abbas Kiarostami, shared the Palme d'Or at the Cannes Film Festival in 1997. In choosing the film as its best of the year, *Time* magazine effused: "Kiarostami will find a quiet place and listen to a man's heart right up until it stops beating. And then he will listen some more." [39]

But even the prize giving was controversial in Iran, when Kiarostami exchanged a peck-on-the-cheek kiss with the award presenter,

Catherine Deneuve. "This two-second transgression of Islamic propriety instantly set off a polemical firestorm in Iran," writes Hamid Reza Sadr in his book *Iranian Cinema*.[40] "On Kiarostami's return from France, a welcoming reception at the airport was derailed by angry fundamentalists: Kiarostami was spirited through customs and out through a side door."

Another Iranian phenomenon was Samira Makhmalbaf, the daughter of director Mohsen and at eighteen the toast of Cannes with her film *The Apple*, about freedom seen through the eyes of twelve-year-old twin girls who had been locked up since birth. The film won seven international awards. Its young female director belied every Western stereotype about black-shrouded women in Iran "with her teenage acne, jeans and T-shirt (albeit with the addition of a headscarf)," noted Sadr.[41] She told *Newsweek:* "People ask me, is Iran the kind of place where two 12-year-old girls can't come out and see the world? Or is it a place where a girl who is 18 can make a film about them?"[42]

Her film *Blackboards*, about teachers crossing mountains of northwest Iran carrying blackboards and searching for students, and which she made when she was twenty, won the Grand Jury Prize at Cannes in 2000. It was edited by her highly decorated father, whose own lineup of award-winning titles included *Kandahar*, which won a prize at Cannes the next year—the Federico Fellini Gold Medal from UNESCO—and was listed by *Time* magazine as one of best one hundred movies of all time.[43]

THE BURST OF CULTURAL light wasn't limited to the silver screen. Iranian painters, actors, and authors explained to me that instead of withering from two decades of isolation, Iranian culture had indeed nurtured itself, as if trapped in an incubator. It was a seed waiting to blossom, irrigated this time not by the blood of the martyrs, as Khomeini declared that the Revolution and war had been, but by a refreshing new spirit of expression.

"After Khatami came to power, everything changed," said Manijeh Mir-'Emadi, a painter and editor of a glossy new quarterly on Iranian art called *Tavoos,* or *Peacock.*[44] "It's the beginning of something big happening." The numbers proved it. In the first years of the Revolution, there were virtually no art exhibitions. But by 2000 there were an estimated two thousand contemporary artists, one hundred galleries and culture centers in Tehran alone, and some seventy museums. Newspapers carried full-page listings of cultural events. The budding *Tavoos,* in both Farsi and English, aimed to be the "reference work for Iranian culture, from architecture to photography." And the first editions were marvelous, heavy, and as fat as American *Vogue.*

"We are working to preserve and help Iranian art, to get critical exposure to the outside," Mir-'Emadi told me, as she flipped through copies at her north Tehran house. *Tavoos*'s high quality impressed critics from China to New York's Museum of Modern Art. "We have a lot to talk about and work on, after twenty years of Revolution and eight years of war," she said. "When you have twenty-five hundred years of history, Iranians are used to living with art."

Second-generation Iranians living in the United States were especially interested, as a way of "looking for their roots"—and of breaking down prejudice. "Everybody has a dark picture of Iran from the media, so [*Tavoos*] was a surprise for them, that this came from a country that had a so-called 'dark vision,'" Mir-'Emadi said with a smile. "They can't believe we have all this happening in Iran. People say: 'We didn't know you have sculpture.'"

Yet the buzzing cultural firmament had no match in Iran's regional neighborhood. To most Americans, Iran may have been linked to Iraq, first as joint targets of Washington's "dual containment" policy in the 1990s, and then as fellow members of the Axis of Evil. But Iraq, despite an ancient history that claims Babylon and the Code of Hammurabi—even the fabled biblical Garden of Eden—could not in recent decades boast a fraction of the cultural energy that Iranians take for granted.

And never mind the cultural vacuum of next-door Afghanistan. Homegrown Taliban zealots with Al Qaeda's help, after all, chose to destroy one of Afghanistan's most important historical treasures, the towering Buddha statues at Bamiyan. All that history in those aged lands has just not turned into a vibrant cultural scene, as it did in modern-day Persia. Even had Iraq and Afghanistan not been plagued by war and despotism for decades, it seems very unlikely that either could produce such a multifaceted cultural reawakening as Iran has kept alive, despite sometimes harrowing circumstances.

Some argue that resurgence in Iran was inevitable. "Perhaps you should not give all the credit to Khatami and his coming to power," one Iranian editor told me.[45] "We have been so removed from the outside that Khatami just helped accelerate it with his openness. Compare it to the [Soviet Union's] Gorbachev era. The change would have happened even if he were not in power."

That change included greater immersion in some forms of Western pop culture, too. Long before Khatami, for example, Iranians were secretly getting all manner of American films through illegal video dealers who did their rounds by word of mouth and door-to-door. I caught up with one who had been at it for five years, and had watched his clients' tastes change with the advent of their new president. Unshaven and wearing a polo shirt, he asked that I use a pseudonym— Ali Sufi—and then he turned philosophical.[46]

"Khatami came and started to give freedom, and free space to talk and to think," Sufi told me, as he rifled like an eager smuggler through a black leather briefcase lined with videocassettes. Many were newer releases shot unsteadily in theaters with a camcorder. "Since Khatami, people started to want much more sensitive films—they are tired of arguing. Iranians have powerful feelings. They want to be loved, and want to love something, so they prefer this to action or sex movies." *Titanic* was a blockbuster in Iran, as it was worldwide. So was *Anna and the King.*

Love. Again. In Iran. Not love this time for Imam Hossein. For martyrdom. To be part of a Caravan of Love. Or love of Americans but not their government. Or even love of Khatami and hatred for the "other."

But real romantic, liquid love. Hearts bursting with expectation.

Romeo and Juliet. Joy. Ecstasy as souls blended together. All the things that—except through the prism of religion, or locked away at home—were not permitted in the Islamic Republic. "We are a people full of feeling, love," Sufi told me. Ancient Persian poets had proven it.

Also popular was *Saving Private Ryan*—in part, said war veteran Sufi, "because we had war for eight years, and we can understand it. When I watched that film, it brought back memories of people dying for no reason."

In rejecting Western films, Iran's enforcers had never gone as far as the Taliban in Afghanistan—which used to decorate their checkpoints with shimmering bunches of unspooled video and cassette tape confiscated from passing cars.

But Iran had a long history of film censorship dating to the 1920s, "with theater owners succumbing to the pressure of religious groups worried about Iranians' exposure to Western morals and to the overt sexuality displayed in imported films," notes film specialist Azadeh Farahmand.[47] Later there were efforts to "professionalize and legitimize film censorship," with an official committee in 1950 adopting a fifteen-part set of rules that forbid themes "subversive to Islam and Shiism, [that] instigated opposition to monarchy and the royal family, [that] depicted victorious revolts in prisons, or portrayed illicit affairs. . . ."

While some movies, such as the classic resistance film *The Battle of Algiers* (1966), came off the censored list in 1979, a change of regime did not mean a change of the impulse to control. Both "pre- and post-revolutionary governments displayed a similar concern to suppress themes of political criticism and social dissent," writes Farahmand. "Each regime . . . attempted to regulate the medium in accordance with their own ideological framework."

So in a country where even satellite dishes are illegal—though more or less tolerated—purveyors of illicit Western video culture were taking risks.

"It's very difficult and dangerous to bring these in," Sufi told me, as if he were distributing cocaine straight from Colombia. There was a "mafia" outside Iran, and bribes to customs officials. Smugglers used to carry spools of videotape without their plastic cases, before the era of the easily hidden DVD and ultimately Internet downloads made airport searches pointless. Foreign travelers, flight attendants on British Airways and Lufthansa, even a pilot, were paid good money to be couriers. Iranian video clubs ordered the films from places like Cyprus, Singapore, and Malaysia. Being caught in Iran then usually meant a fine—like the two hundred dollars Sufi paid when police once opened his trunk and found his stash of tapes.

But the risks were worth it, and customer satisfaction was high. Sufi worked for one of the seven biggest illegal movie outlets in Tehran, which rented 3,000 films a week. He could handle 850 a week himself. The club kept just 1,200 of the most popular titles in its archive, and every two or three weeks copied over old films with new ones. Stickers were replaced. And each video cost half a dollar per week to rent, delivered to your door by a traveling war-veteran-philosopher salesman like Sufi, who wandered Tehran with a low profile, as drug dealers do.

Sufi saw himself as a soldier for Khatami's reforms. "I believe that everybody is on the front line of this war, because almost everybody wants reform," he told me, plopping down copies of *Gladiator, The Flintstones II,* and *Music of the Heart,* before stepping out. "Khatami is the one they chose."

THROUGHOUT THE TEHRAN SPRING, conservatives still controlled primary levers of power such as the judiciary and security forces. They also had the majority in parliament, except from 2000 to 2004. But the Ministry of Culture and Islamic Guidance, or Ershad— which issues approvals for all books, films, plays, galleries, and newspapers, just as it accredits all journalists—was firmly in the hands of reformists. The transformation had begun before, in the mid-1990s, as key filmmakers sought to reconnect with their audiences.

Many Iranian films had been "based on a quality of calculated allusion, making their critique of contemporary Iranian society through a variety of metaphoric techniques," explains Sadr in *Iranian Cinema.*[48]

Under Khatami there was a "virtual dismantling of censorship" such that "a new [critical] climate emerged . . . which would have been un- imaginable a few years before."

The new reformist cinema chief vowed to ease the rules, in keeping with Khatami's stated opposition to "any form of cultural repression." A director himself—who had made an anti-Israel film that was the first modern Iranian movie in which actresses did not wear hair covering— Seifollah Dad promised to lift many previous bans, "if the filmmakers have not intentionally broken the law." [49] He vowed also to end "sense- less" restrictions on the export of Iranian films, because they "boost Iran's cultural reputation and bring in hard currency."

Conservative newspapers were up in arms. "We should not send a movie to a foreign festival just because it has a chance of win- ning, but because it represents our Revolution and Islamic culture," *Resalat* scolded, after Makhmalbaf's film *Gabbeh* was nominated for an Oscar.[50] "*Gabbeh* may be a poetic work, but it says nothing about our revolutionary ideals and Islamic values. The movie suits the taste of Europeans and Americans, who have always been after a dark and ugly image of Islamic Iran."

And yet many Iranians had had enough of the Revolution's cant. "After the Iran-Iraq War, men came home to pick up the pieces of their lives," notes Sadr in *Iranian Cinema:*

> Audiences were exhausted by the tragedies of clichéd melodrama and a gradual reappraisal of values produced a new protagonist for the screen. At last, here were films that did not celebrate the his- torically pompous or heroically solemn but concentrated with new- found sophistication on ordinary, prosaic existence. In place of the flamboyant, monumentalizing war films with their abstract ideals, the camera began to look at daily life as if through the eyes of the veteran. . . .
>
> For the first time, heroes had to tackle difficulties—including the questioning of their own faith—that came within their own lives.[51]

Years of backlogged films once deemed too "sensitive" to be officially released in Iran—though always circulated illegally—were now being approved. Among them was a brilliant reel of celluloid called *Snowman*.

I WAS AS EXCITED as any other theatergoer when the cinema lights dimmed. The mostly young audience settled into their overstuffed velvet seats for a treat, buttery popcorn at the ready. For three years *Snowman*—a cross-dressing comedy about trying to leave Iran for the West that finishes with a good heart—had been banned, gathering dust at the offices of Islamic Guidance censors. Finally in late 1997 it was set free, uncut. Theaters were packed. I could barely find a ticket. "I'm surprised they released it," said a student who gave her name as Mojgan.[52] "Maybe they are lifting the pressure because there are other pressures that people are under."

Pressure was working the other way, too, because the release of *Snowman* was not without violence. Militant vigilantes of Ansar-e Hezbollah (Followers of the Party of God), self-appointed defenders of the Revolution, targeted cinemas in protest. On the day the film was to open in Isfahan, witnesses said "bearded radicals attacked the theater [and] shredded posters and attacked moviegoers, including women and children," according to one report.[53] The newspaper *Salam* quoted the manager: "Although the film is being shown in twenty-two cities throughout Iran, the attackers threatened to set the cinema on fire so we were forced to stop showing it."[54]

Though vigilantism has a long history in Persia, the local Friday prayer leader challenged the militants. "If the police and intelligence forces and the governor general's office are unable to deal with them," warned Ayatollah Seyyed Jalaleddin Taheri, "let them tell me, and I will put them in their place."[55] The *New York Times* later quoted an Isfahani carpet merchant about the ayatollah: "He's either mad or brave, one or the other. The important thing is that the film is showing, and that's a big step." In following days the militants returned to "perform triumphant prayers" and addressed a written warning to Taheri: "We are going to fight to the end." [56]

What silver screen sin was so severe that thugs had to beat sense back into moviegoers? Iranian filmmakers have long been adept at making tough points with satire and symbolism. But director Davoud Mirbagheri's *Snowman* crossed a number of red lines at once. The first scene is of an Iranian man in Turkey, who dreams of living in America. Disguised as a bearded academic, he applies for an American visa and is rejected for a third time.

Brokenhearted, he cries out in dismay, "But you don't even know who I am! Do you think I am a bad person, a terrorist?"

Desperate to get to America, the hero tries an even more deviant ploy: he dresses up (convincingly) as a woman. For six thousand dollars his plan is to marry an American man who will take his new "wife" home to the United States for a green card. The iconoclasm cuts deep. To remember their beloved homeland, Iranians in the film break into illegal pre-Revolution songs, prompting the audience to clap irreverently to the well-known beat.

The audience cheered when a character says she wants to live where she will "not get detained because she is wearing nail polish and lipstick." Along the way, however, the hero falls in love with a decent, headscarf-wearing Iranian woman working as a hotel cleaner. They marry and return happily to Iran. The ending is a politically correct paean to Iranians' longing nostalgia for home. At a decisive moment, the hero looks at pictures of family still in Iran. An Iranian friend asks: "You were crying again—were you thinking of Iran, or America?" Another character, who has tasted the semi-Western freedoms of Turkey, says: "I prefer to die in Iran."

The film is called *Snowman* because, as one theatergoer told me, "all the dreams and illusions melt like a snowman." It certainly qualified under the Supreme Leader's caution against "Western materialistic civilization." But many Iranians were lapping up the openness of a new golden age. "There are no more surprises with this new [reformist] government," gushed teenage student Jaber Hosseini. He had seen

Snowman three times on bootleg video before he saw it on the big screen. "We voted [for Khatami] to get these [films] released. Now all Iran has seen it."

IN 2000, THE LATEST film by Mohsen Makhmalbaf was among his most political. It was called *Test of Democracy*.[57] I was shown it by a pair of generous officials at the Ministry of Culture and Islamic Guidance, even while it was being examined by the censors there. To this day, the thirty-eight-minute film remains banned in Iran.

It was not because Makhmalbaf lacked revolutionary credentials. Inspired at the age of fifteen by ideologue Ali Shariati, Makhmalbaf formed an urban guerrilla cell. Two years later he killed a policeman with a knife—breaking the blade inside him. He was trying to steal the officer's pistol in order to rob banks to finance further resistance to the Shah. "As I twisted the knife he cried out, and his cries still remain in my ears. They were the sort of cries I've only heard people under torture make. These are cries you'll never hear in a film . . . the cries of true pain," Makhmalbaf told an interviewer in 1996.[58]

The future director was shot in the stomach. Another bullet ricocheted off the wall as he tried to get away. Then the policeman stepped forward, aimed the gun at Makhmalbaf's head, and pulled the trigger—but the chamber was empty. Before collapsing, the officer smashed Makhmalbaf's skull with his arm. The wounded teenager was caught by passersby as he tried to escape, and was beaten and stabbed. He was sentenced to five years in prison and brutally tortured by SAVAK, which refused to believe that his guerrilla cell had only three members.

Makhmalbaf's feet were shredded by whippings with different-size cables until they would not stop bleeding, and he was subjected to the scream-magnifying Apollo apparatus. His mug shot hangs in the gallery of the Ebrat Museum. Makhmalbaf recalled:

> When they first beat me, I felt as if a tree was being swung at my feet, not a wire. It hurt so much that you felt as if your eyes were

about to explode out of your skull. They'd even tape your eyes tight shut. It was like—you know, when your hand touches something hot, the reflex the body has to that. . . . Well, imagine that sensation in some part of your body every five seconds, imagine that going on from morning to evening. . . .

Makhmalbaf has written about that agony and made films about his prison experience. Early themes idealized aspects of the Revolution—though he later explored tough social issues as his ideals darkened over time and the Revolution failed expectations. One film was an unlikely cross-culture love story about a hard-line vigilante and an upscale north Tehran woman.

But it was *Test of Democracy,* with its poignant simplicity, that could not be released even during the Khatami era. The first words: "This film is dedicated to all who oppose it." There is a discussion of the difficulty of making movies in Iran, of getting a script approved, and of how even if a film is produced, "it will go through so much censorship that nothing will be left."

At once incisive and hilarious, *Test of Democracy* is about imposing one's will on another person. One scene shows the film crew being asked to carry a door across a desert; another records the complaints of a man asked to sell the seat on which he is sitting. The movie drew on recent parliamentary elections but took a broader view of political and religious elitism and the vote of the common man. Looking out on a flock of flamingos on a beach, it is decided, "I'd love to make a film about who will represent these people in parliament."

Addressing the clusters of pink birds with a microphone and speakers, as if he were their candidate trying to win votes, Makhmalbaf makes his most important points in the rhythmic cadences of Persian poetry.

"I don't want to scare you from your beautiful seat," he tells the long-legged flamingos as they nose unconcerned through the shoreline mud:

I'm here to give you the bare facts.
The truth is, [despite] being birds, you don't fly too well . . .
I lead you not to the merry dance of blue smoke.
I lead you not to a plush rainbow, to petty dreams.
Anyone who ever came here lied to you,
    hoping to get one extra act to play.
They've told you how well you fly,
    but I'm here to play this one act, and go.
So, won't you mind if I tell you the truth?
You fly no better than a chicken! Think otherwise?
    Please fly and let us see!

"Don't be offended—some of you are leaving this meeting," Makhmalbaf says, as the birds hop about in the background.

"Please don't let that keep you from flying. Try to fly higher. Make a new record in the history of flight . . ."

"We're testing the feeling of freedom at this time."

Invasion Barbie

To many hard-liners, the most insidious cultural threat came in hot-pink boxes that sat on toy-shop shelves.

Barbie, with her curvaceous body, miniskirts, and platinum blond hair, could not be further from the image of women officially fostered in Iran, where hair must be covered and bodies kept shapeless; where lipstick is a sign of defiance. So naturally, the American icon—one of the most sought-after toys worldwide since her buxom debut in 1959—has been a big hit with a certain slice of Iranian girls.

Just months into Khatami's presidency, the Supreme Leader had marked Women's Week by calling for greater participation of Iranian women in "social and political affairs." [59] But he also warned against copying their lapsed sisters. "A blind imitation of Western women is noxious," Ayatollah Khamenei pronounced. "The feminist movement in the West has only brought sexual promiscuity."

Those carnal escapades could be learned too easily by playing with Barbie dolls, decided the guardians of revolutionary purity. When I first went in search of Barbie and her nefarious influence in 1999, Iranian officials were racing to turn out an acceptable, Islamic answer to Barbie in time for the twentieth anniversary of the Revolution. But the production date for Sara and her brother Dara was postponed for lack of "suitable hair."

"About Barbie, we not only think it is not good for our children here, we think it is not suitable for American children," Majid Ghaderi told me.[60] He was director of the Institute for the Intellectual Development of Children and Young Adults in Tehran, which designed the new dolls. In the past he had decried Barbie as a "Trojan horse" that was full of "Western cultural influences, such as makeup and indecent clothes. Once it enters our society, it dumps these influences on our children." Barbies "only teach consumerism," Ghaderi told me. "Bad influences" included profligate dress, makeup, and an example of "unlimited freedom in relationships . . . between boys and girls."

Barbie was especially pernicious because, on top of all that, she was "a symbol of American culture," Ghaderi said. "The first thing we can do is to teach our children about who they are [as Iranians], about their own culture [so they] reject the bad part [of Western culture] and absorb the good part."

That was not happening. As the Tehran Spring came into bloom, hard-liners were unable to counter every attempt to bend the rules. Smugglers were hiding as many as thirty CDs of music under their clothes when arriving at the airport. From pizza to imitation Nike shoes, it was an onslaught of decadence. "It's not Marx or Hegel— it's Michael Jackson," one government official told the Sage in 1999. "How are we supposed to counter that?"[61] The Islamic Guidance Ministry nevertheless approved publication of the lyrics of Metallica, producing 5,500 copies of "Nothing Else Matters" and other hit songs, when a normal print run would have been 3,500 copies.[62]

• • •

DRAMATIC SOCIAL CHANGE BY fiat started with the father of the Shah, a self-educated army private with an iron will who rose in the ranks and landed a coup in 1921. Reza Shah's reign "can be fairly described as a period of intense hostility to Islamic culture and institutions; what Western authors have approvingly called 'reform' and 'modernization' was experienced by many—if not most—Iranians as a brutal assault on their culture, traditions, and identity," writes historian Hamid Algar.[63]

Among many steps was a new Uniform Dress Law for men that included, besides Westernlike trousers and jackets, a brimmed "Pahlavi" hat. The design was chosen partly "to interfere with the Muslim rule of prayer, which requires the faithful to touch the ground with their foreheads," says historian Ervand Abrahamian.[64] The orders prompted protests that peaked in 1935, when Reza Shah's soldiers burst into the Imam Reza shrine in Mashhad—one of the holiest sites in Shiite Islam—locked all exit gates, took up positions overlooking the central courtyard, then machine-gunned the crowd, killing one hundred people.

But Reza Shah was not finished upending dress codes. In 1936 women were required to remove their covering, or chador, a decree "enforced with considerable vigor," writes Algar.[65] It had quite an impact, notes Christopher de Bellaigue in *In the Rose Garden of the Martyrs:*

> Henceforth, women were to go out bareheaded or not at all. It is hard to overstate the grossness of this edict. . . . In traditional Iranian society, the *chador* had been a shell; its protective anonymity had allowed women to venture freely out of doors, to shop and visit. Now, the police were instructed to rip all head coverings off women in the street. . . . "The effect," says one Iranian historian, "was as if in 1936, European women had suddenly been ordered to go out topless into the street." From then, until Reza was unseated in 1941, millions of Iranian women didn't set foot outside their houses.[66]

Decades later, under the Shah, the imposition of Western culture could still lead to violence, at least beyond Tehran. One American who was teaching at a university in Shiraz in 1968, for instance, remembered a "confused and smoldering resentment" among his students, who came from "very conservative" small towns.[67] It was John Limbert—a Peace Corps volunteer who in 1979 as a diplomat would be taken hostage at the U.S. Embassy, and who in 2009 would be appointed the first U.S. undersecretary of state for Iran, to help President Barack Obama navigate the Islamic Republic.

Limbert recalled how the values taught at the university grated against the students' own:

> They reacted in a number of different ways, sometimes violently. For example, there was an arts festival in Shiraz, and a modern dance performance was put on for the queen. The next evening the same dances were performed for the university students, and this precipitated a full-scale riot. To the students, modern dance was a manifestation of something alien. They didn't know much about it, but whatever it was, they didn't like it. They were going to stop it.

More decades later, there was no stopping the local display of American consumerism. Barbie dolls, at twenty-five to thirty dollars each, shared shelf space with other implants, from Batman and Power Rangers to Snow White and Pocahontas. Iranian educational officials decried Barbie as "like the wooden horse of Troy with many cultural invading soldiers inside it."[68]

To test that theory in 1999, I stepped off a main Tehran avenue into a random toy shop. It was a narrow space, its walls stocked top to bottom with a kids' cornucopia. The owner, Babak, was unimpressed with the shrill denunciations of Barbie. "So much of the discussion of a 'cultural invasion' is useless, with the expansion of global communications, satellite TV, the Internet, and so much information," Babak told me. "If we really care about this 'cultural invasion,' we should be strong enough to influence our own culture, instead of being afraid of [Western] influence on us."

The Iranian-made Sara and Dara dolls were meant to do just that. They were to have an "Eastern look" with brown hair and brown eyes, and Sara wore a removable head covering that showed only the face. Though in Iran these are only allowed in dark colors, Sara would have several bright choices. There would be a handful of costumes of different ethnic groups in Iran, and—in a compromise that mirrored her American counterpart—she would come with a comb.

"Children really don't care much whether they play with an Islamic doll," Ghaderi, the official from the children's institute, told me. "They don't make as big an issue out of it as we adults are making." But at an international trade fair months earlier, children lined up to learn about the new dolls. Interest was high, officials and toy-shop owners said, because any new toy on the market is met with excitement.

Ghaderi was at ease, knowing that the Islamic Republic was creating an alternative: "We were scared about [cultural invasion], but we don't need to be that fearful because we have the capability of confronting it."

POPULAR DESIRE FOR BARBIE, however, tapped into deeper Iranian obsessions about feminine beauty, which has always captivated Persians and their poets. The fourteenth-century mystical poet Hafez wrote a torrent of sensual ruminations on wine, love, and the spirit. Among his lines:

> I cease not from desire till my desire
> Is satisfied; or let my mouth attain
> My love's red mouth, or let my soul expire,
> Sighed from those lips that sought her lips in vain.
> Others may find another love as fair;
> Upon her threshold I have laid my head,
> The dust shall cover me, still lying there,
> When from my body life and love have fled.[69]

Not even Ayatollah Khomeini was immune. He wrote often of his appreciation of beauty—though as a metaphor for divine love and the "wine" of spiritual devotion. A thin volume of his mystical poetry, *The Wine of Love,* was published, but only after his death. In one poem, "The Drunkenness of the Lover," the Imam writes:

> The heart not unsettled by your face is no heart at all. . . .
> The love of your face has cast me into this desert.
>   What can be done? There is no end to this desert.[70]

And in another poem, Khomeini writes of the day he would "be dust":

> I will have abandoned the soul,
>   unsettled by her face.
> I will take the goblet from her hand
>   that increases the spirit.
> I will pay heed to neither of the worlds,
>   bound with her hair.
> I will rest my head on her feet,
>   kissing them 'till the instant of death.
> I will be drunk with the wine of her jug
>   'till the morning of the resurrection.
> I will be a moth, burning,
>   burning all my life in her candle.
> I will be drunk with wine,
>   marveling at her beautiful face.[71]

DURING THE TEHRAN SPRING inspired by Khatami, focus on the face was taking a more materialistic turn. The nose job was the new fashion accessory. Plastic surgery to lift droops, smooth bumps, and taper the problematic Persian proboscis was all the rage, judging by the increasing number of young women—and men—whose noses were graced by gauze bandages and tape. With an Islamic dress code that allowed only exposure of a woman's face and hands, those aspects had to be perfect.

A teenager wearing bright red lipstick beneath her bandaged nose in 2000 told me the procedure had "become an obsession for young Iranians" that few could do without. "It's such a trend that even if people don't get a nose job, they will wear tape for all the attention it brings," Elahe Shirali said.[72]

Her mother, Shahnaz Ganji, understood: "It's very difficult in Iran, because people are so sensitive to noses. People will come up to you on the street and make fun of your nose as you walk by." The standard was high for Iranian women, who regularly asserted themselves to be the most beautiful on earth, their beauty lyricized for centuries. Men often addressed women as *khoshgeleh,* or "pretty one." Some youth invoked Islam's tenet that "God is beautiful, and loves beautiful people."

There were no statistics at the time, but a leading surgeon told me that one hundred nose specialists working then performed thirty-five thousand operations a year. Qualified rhinoplastic surgeons were charging a thousand dollars a head. Doctors felt they were performing a service not limited to a wealthy elite. "The concept of beauty differs in every nation and culture," surgeon Siavash Safavi explained. His office was hung with prints of Picasso, with misshapen noses of every sort, and a Salvador Dali that depicted breasts on horses.

Dr. Safavi was famous for performing Iran's first post-Revolution (and approved) sex change operation in 1985. "Most of my patients desire to change their nose from the age of twelve, and wait four years until they are sixteen," Safavi told me. Some had threatened suicide if they could not get their noses done. Many were pushed by their Iranian mothers, "even if they come for a couple degrees of uplift" to achieve beauty. "The result can be unbelievable and improves every emotion and mood. For people in poor areas, the idea is the same—sometimes I charge half price for them, if a girl needs it emotionally."

Iranians living abroad came from Paris and the United States—where the procedures are much more costly—to take advantage of local expertise honed by daily work. "It's very particular to Iranian girls, that by adolescence a main goal is to be beautiful," asserted Safavi. "It's a value of our culture. There is education and everything else, but beauty is right up there, in every class."

Tehran University student Leyla Jahangari told me she convinced her parents that "she wanted it so much" that it "was affecting my mind." We were at the Golestan shopping mall, a prime pickup place where the fashion-conscious crowd is thick with noses in taped casts and bandages. Vanity comes in large doses here. "The beauty of the Iranian woman's face is considered the most beautiful face in the world," she said, without a glimmer of doubt.

"I was beautiful, but really wanted to change the way I looked. I just did it for myself," Jahangari told me. I couldn't tell if the procedure had made any soaring difference. As she spoke, the mall loudspeakers crackled to life, reminding women to attend to their hijab, to keep every strand of hair covered. Outside the main gate, I saw that the morality squad had picked up a young, unmarried couple. The woman sat forlornly at the back of a police van, the man separately at the front.

"Among my friends, those who can have a nose job do it, and those who can't all *want* to do it," said Jahangari, extending immaculately manicured hands toward a pay phone. She would call to surprise her boyfriend with news that her nose cast was no more. But is it required?

"Yes, you *must* have it in Iran today."

IN THE YEARS SINCE I first visited Babak's toy shop, Iran's vigilant viceroys of virtue over vixens continued to fight Barbie's evil ways. Toy sellers were periodically targeted by morals police who, for instance, decided in 2002 to crack down on "spiritual pollutants." Peddlers with Barbie-embossed trinkets were penalized, import traders arrested.

"They came here and just took away every one of my Barbies," another downtown toy-shop owner told the London *Guardian*.[73] He lost eleven thousand dollars' worth of merchandise and was detained for three days; only a single vinyl Barbie ottoman was left. "I thought the environment was much more relaxed, which is why I opened this shop. Iranians love everything Barbie. I just can't understand it."

There seemed to be a double standard. The *Guardian* reported that a " 'charming [Princess] Diana' [doll] whose natural delights are to be spied beneath a translucent blouse and miniskirt" was still for sale. Ghaderi of the Creative Toys Division was still warning of a Barbie syndrome. "A society may be under the threat of many maladies, each of which could deliver a blow to the social body. But there is always a more dangerous threat, and in this case, Barbie is that *more* dangerous threat." [74]

Those fears hadn't receded by 2008, when I found that the most worrisome items in Iranian toy shops weren't the lifelike pistols and submachine guns racked up in molded plastic arsenals, but again the hot pink Barbie lifestyle.

It was "destructive culturally and a social danger," Iranian prosecutor Ghorban Ali Dori Najafabadi warned in a 2008 letter. But to Barbie was now added a fraternity: Harry Potter, Batman, and Spider-Man. Their appearance are "all alarm bells that . . . need to be stopped." He added: "Undoubtedly, the personality and identity of the new generation and our children, as a result of unrestricted importation of toys, have been put at risk and caused irreparable damage."

Still, Barbie was not going down without a fight. Even my own journalism appeared to have a more licentious flavor, for anyone reading the *Monitor* on the Web. Attached to every one of my Iran stories was a Google advertisement that automatically popped up for IranianPersonals.com, which held the promise: "Meet Single Persians Online!" It included a tantalizing picture of a real-life Iranian beauty, who smiled deliciously while spilling out of her slinky leopard-print bikini top. For a time on the Web, this eye candy sweetened even my most earnest explorations of Iran's revolutionary ideology.

Barbie and her supposedly sinful ways—all that unbridled Western fun, that promiscuous, pulchritudinous promise and the moral free fall encapsulated in a single, eleven-inch-tall plastic doll—were winning.

And it wasn't just on the Web. The mullahs' decades-long anti-

Barbie campaign was only marginally successful. "Barbie manages to reign supreme in the Islamic Republic," writes Porochista Khakpour, an author whose family fled Iran at the onset of war in 1980—leaving behind a room of expensive toys, among them her "beloved Barbie posse."[75] "Iran may be the only place where Barbie has got that somethin'-somethin' to capture young hearts—and enflame adult minds," Khakpour observes. "Now, one hundred careers, fifty nationalities, forty pets, a billion pairs of shoes, fifty thousand makeovers later, Barbie came, conquered and the only place she can go is somewhere else—at least judging from her United States sales, which have been falling for years."

When I stepped back into Babak's busy toy shop in 2008, he had escaped past crackdowns, and had yet to hear officially of new rules limiting the sale of Barbie dolls. There they were: Fashion Fever Barbie and Barbie Glamour Pup, squeezed between Westernized knockoffs such as the Juicy Bling doll and Action Man. "Those kids who watch foreign television and satellite want Barbie dolls," Babak told me.[76]

But of the three to four dolls he was selling per day, only one or two a week were Barbies. Even fifteen years before, an entire shipping container that he imported full of Barbie paraphernalia sold slower than he had hoped. Babak told me it had more to do with the small market and competition from other Western dolls than any government crackdown. More significantly, the rollout of Iran's "suitable" alternative, the Sara and Dara dolls first slated to captivate Iranian children with a wholesome lifestyle in 1999, finally took place in 2002—and bombed.

There were none to be found on Babak's tightly packed wall of toys. He used to carry the dolls, but no longer. "They are very heavy and stiff—[there's] a baby character and a big doll and they are twice the price," he told me. Instead of blocking the influence of Barbie among Iranians, they were chosen as a novelty by Iranians who had seen ads abroad and wanted something "traditional." "But kids who live here, they never ask for it," Babak said. Sara and Dara "are a good idea, if they can make something similar to these [Barbies] with a chador or headscarf. Kids might say, 'This looks cool,' and buy it. As a toy seller, I would prefer these *all* to be locally produced [but] you can't compare. They are different dolls."

What *was* selling in large numbers instead were the real-looking pistols and submachine guns, kept under display glass. There were restrictions on these, too, precisely because they looked so real. In Babak's shop, I saw a turbaned cleric search for a gift, presumably for a child. He wasn't after a doll—not Sara or Dara. But he selected from the toy firepower. He chose a life-size sawed-off shotgun with a pistol grip and red laser beam targeting device.

As I watched the elegantly robed holy man depart the store, his pick of the arsenal in a large, long box under his arm, the shop assistant spoke with a mischievous smirk: "They like guns, the clerics."

The Mischief of Music

As if performing before an arena packed with tens of thousands of rock fans, guitarist Norik Misakian let his lightning-fast fingers electrify the strings of his aquamarine Fender guitar, building the sound of one of Iran's underground heavy metal bands into a full-throated roar.[77]

Driven by the pounding rhythm of Babak Riahipour's bass guitar, Misakian played some chords overhand, and even with his teeth—turning this twelve-foot by twelve-foot rooftop studio in 2003 into a sweating paragon of earsplitting rock music that would make Jimi Hendrix proud. This band was creating a parallel reality that could not be further removed from the hyperreligiosity of Friday prayers and constant preaching of the Revolution. Were we even in Iran?

Behind walls stuck with decibel-dampening Styrofoam—some of it glued to the window—this rock 'n' roll was as rebellious as its Western counterpart. But venues were limited, and suggestive gyrations à la Elvis were out of the question in public. The audience was required to sit, forced to headbang in their seats. It was still an improvement: just years before, band members *also* had to sit, which rather complicated getting full rock expression out of an electric guitar.

And even that was a miracle of openness from the first days of the Revolution, when fun of all kinds was ruled out. It was Khomeini himself who first told the directors of Radio Iran to battle music "with all your might."[78] Khomeini ruled: "Music corrupts the minds of our youth. There is no difference between music and opium. Both create lethargy in different ways. If you want your country to be independent, then ban music. Music is treason to our nation and to our youth."

But could there be life without their music? "No way," Misakian told me, shaking his shoulder-length locks. "We'd be dead," concurred Riahipour, matter-of-factly.

Dead of their own disillusion, perhaps, which had been growing then among Iran's younger generation over lack of jobs, the poor economy, and the eclipsed promise of Khatami's cultural renaissance and stalled political reforms. Khatami had already been in power six years, his reform agenda long before thwarted by conservatives. So this stratum of society was increasingly turning to drugs or other means of escape. During a visit to the more relaxed Caspian Sea coast, the Sage had found an "impressive list" of alcohol and drugs available and did a double take when the "salesman" gave him a Tuborg beer with this apology: "Sorry, I don't have it cold."[79]

It was a big change in a country where actual beer and wine—due to their relative volume and greater smuggling risk—mostly entered Iran through diplomatic pouch. That made the default drink homemade spirit, by necessity. Authorities even went after pharmacies that were overselling medicinal alcohol, after some deaths from Russia-style alcohol poisoning.

"It's no secret it's out there, but how is it tolerated?" the Sage asked. "They can't control it, though they tried so hard, or there is deliberate negligence and they look the other way."

Addiction rates soared in Iran to the highest in the world. The

United Nations reported in 2009 that addiction to opiates stood at 2.8 percent, double that of the next-highest nation, Afghanistan.[80] "If I met a young person, give or take five years, if they had not tried drugs, I would write it down" because it was so rare, joked the bass player, Riahipour.

Tehran officials had revealed for the first time in 2000 that five tons of narcotics such as opium and heroin were consumed in the capital every day, and that the number of addicts had jumped to two million—double the figure for all of Iran in 1998. That was when I talked to a junkie called Ramin who had just bought a hit of heroin in the shadow of the monument in Azadi (Freedom) Square, which the Shah built to honor 2,500 years since the Persian Empire. "Everybody does it, from fifteen years old to fifty," said Ramin, who had just finished a rehab course that cost a hundred dollars and was worried about getting hooked again if he tried his new purchase.[81]

Drugs were so available, Ramin told me, that there was only one conclusion: "I think the government wants this to happen. They don't want people to think." Indeed, drug dealers were reportedly allowed into student dormitories that had been locked down by security forces after riots in 1999, to distribute free narcotics.[82] Neighboring Afghanistan was the top global producer of opiates, and Iran the first stage of the primary trafficking route to Europe. The Islamic Republic in 2007 was responsible for 84 percent of all opium seized in the world, more than eight times that of the next country, Afghanistan.[83] Iran was also the world leader in seizing heroin (28 percent), nearly twice as much as the next in line, Pakistan.

Iranian drug control authorities announced in 2009 that Iran officially had 1.2 million addicts, though the Interior Ministry in 2005 had put the figure at 10 million, or about one in seven Iranians.[84] Another official estimated that year that 20 percent of Iran's adult population was "somehow involved in drug abuse," which included half a million dealers and cost Iran $3 billion to $5 billion each year.[85] Hundreds of clinics and drop-in rehabilitation centers marked Iran's open and progressive effort to tackle the problem.

But desperation was palpable. It extended even to the Behesht-e Zahra cemetery south of Tehran, where the *Washington Post* found that impoverished addicts every Thursday—the day families most frequently visited their dead martyrs—would "sweep in afterward to scavenge the cookies and dates left on the graves."[86]

SUCH FORAGING WAS GRIM evidence of social decay. So mainstream Iranian pop bands—and fringe rock groups like this one I was listening to—were creating important new "space" in which young people could play. The new band—which was to be called Shanti, the Sanskrit word for "peace"—was preparing for their live debut . . . at the conference hall of a local hospital. That also was progress: another popular band that Riahipour helped launch four years earlier never got the stamp of approval.

"We couldn't play publicly," Riahipour told me during a rehearsal break. "Well, we did have one concert—inside the Russian Orthodox Church. They needed the money. You know the Russians." The bass player often played "private concerts" at parties, and had been in dozens of bands. Among them was Assar, a popular Iranian group led by singer and keyboard player Seyyed Alireza Assar, which included a choir and a string section for deeply Persian and religious themes and rhythms. Each of Assar's three albums had sold one million copies. Later that year the band played twenty concerts for a total of forty thousand people. It was quite a change for Assar, a Beethoven devotee and pianist who once dreamed of studying classical music at UCLA, before he joined Iran's budding pop scene.

"Everybody told me I was always crossing the limit in my poems, but I love my people, and love everything about my country, Iran," Assar told me, wearing his trademark thick black beard and ponytail during a rehearsal of his thirty-two-member band.[87] "As an Iranian, a Persian, I try to tell the truth."

On his latest album then, three of ten songs drew their lyrics from Quranic tales about Imam Ali, the revered founder of the Shiite branch of Islam. Such devotion helped Assar steer clear of trouble from the authorities, especially from the *hezbollahi* vigilantes. They could and did stop concerts mid-chord—even if officially approved—if they felt them too demonstrative or un-Islamic.

"*Hezbollahi*s have come to my concerts, but they listened, because of the poems I chose to sing about," Assar told me, between practice sets in a band member's large living room. "Music is not a kind of war, where we are fighting [the Islamic Guidance Ministry] and *hezbollahi*s." He reminded me that Iran has "Islamic rules," and that performers "must understand their people. Maybe [Iranians] like heavy metal—I love it—but it is not our culture. To play that, you must know who is listening to you . . . and this kind of music has side effects."

What I was seeing and hearing from these musicians was pure sacrilege in some quarters. On the tenth anniversary of the Revolution in 1989, a hard-line newspaper ran a special edition that harshly criticized the "very modest social concessions extracted by moderates from Khomeini such as the permission to play some kinds of music on state radio and television, to play chess or to use *eau de cologne*."[88] Just because the war with Iraq was over, the newspaper said, the "wounded snakes of world arrogance led by America" were plotting to undermine the moral and cultural basis of the Revolution:

These plots are far more dangerous and destructive than their war fleets, missiles, air and land offensives and chemical bombs. If we do not pay attention . . . they will destroy us by our very own hand.

[Believers] are angry, disappointed and fed-up with this situation; the singers, dancers, musicians and their friends and cronies, on the other hand, will never be happy with this [Islamic] system. . . . Stop it before it's too late. If you are politicians, you must know that your support is in the Friday prayer congregations, not in music halls. . . .

But that message mattered less and less. "People are looking for a new reality," the Sage told me. He was an amateur musician himself, who first picked up the guitar during high school in the 1960s. "I couldn't find anyone interested in playing with me then, but now it is like a fever."

AND THAT FEVER WAS spreading. A website called Tehran Avenue launched a competition between underground groups in 2002 that turned into a big deal for local bands. On the site was one link, "Setting up a performance: A survival guide," which laid out potential pitfalls ranging from detailed security forms and fluctuating municipal taxes—for "official" dates—to getting caught by the police for unofficial gigs.

The risks were well-known to my heavy metal band, as it crammed into its "other" world roof-studio in an Armenian district of Tehran. It was a small space, full of Misakian and Riahipour and their guitar-hero antics, another bass player sitting on an amplifier, a keyboardist, and a drummer banging away on a black Ludwig set. A backup drum set sat in a corner. The floor was a thick tangle of cables and foot pedals. Speakers and amplifiers and girlfriends filled the gaps. Mobile phones went unanswered and unheard during the thunderous session. We were all sweating, tightly packed and transported to another plane of existence by the power of the music—not unlike Iranian soldiers in the 1980s, who once cried their sweaty tears in cramped dark spaces before battle, overwhelmed by their own chanting and "love" of their imminent epic of martyrdom.

The crescendo of sound peaked with furious abandon and brilliance, as the final notes of the jam session were struck. When relative silence was restored, the window and door were flung open wide, to let in cooler, fresh air. Cigarettes were lit, instruments set down. On the wall was a Fender clock with Roman numerals; a CD on a nail. A portrait of Johann Sebastian Bach—an inspiration to guitarist Misakian, who drew on Bach's classic melodies in his own compositions—hung nearby. There was a printout of the word *GOD* in capital letters.

Keeping this transcendent world closed to all save a few friends was a misery for these musicians. Iran's music scene was still far from the vision outlined in 1997 by Khatami's culture minister, Ataollah Mohajerani, who told parliament: "We have to create an atmosphere where all citizens can express their ideas. Islam is not a narrow, dark alley. Everyone can walk freely in the path of Islam." [89]

Bands nurtured on Western rock still had to contend with vigilantes, however, who equated their form of expression with sacrilege.

"If the *hezbollahis* come, you have to stop," said one member of Shanti. "It's like Texas. Everyone has a gun, and sometimes they just don't like you." *Basiji* and *hezbollahi* thugs were easy to spot, he told me, well before they might shut down a performance by cutting off electricity or beating the audience. "You recognize them immediately, like you can the Ku Klux Klan from their big hats." Just two weeks before, a singer was arrested in the city of Shiraz—onstage—because his music "was too happy, it was dance music."

Bass player Riahipour said that challenging perceptions and prejudices was part of the job, and not just in Iran. He had been on a six-month tour of the United States a couple years before with Googoosh, one of Iran's most famous singers since the 1960s. The Persian equivalent of Elvis, she specialized in pre-Revolution love songs and melancholy ballads, and was branded an infidel by Khomeini. She now lives in exile, but many in America were amazed by the Iranian musicians performing with her, when they played sizable venues such as the twenty-thousand-seat Staples Center in Los Angeles.

"Some of them couldn't believe we came from Iran," laughed Riahipour. "They thought all Iranians were bearded [militants] with Kalashnikovs."

The Pickup King

Stuck in Tehran traffic, the young driver with goatee, shades, and a roving eye spotted his targets—two lanes over. Oozing self-confidence, he rolled down his window and motioned to the surprised passenger in the next car—me—to roll down both my windows, so he could deliver his pickup line directly. The young women, coiffed in headscarves but clearly of a liberal, Westernized persuasion, peered across at their suitor. Unimpressed, they drove on.

"Oh well, I guess they weren't interested," Siavash told me, ending with a shrug of the shoulders another attempt at a secret liaison in Iran, where the official limits on male-female contact had by 2005 turned even traffic lanes into passion-laced zones.[90] He failed with the ladies in that attempt, but before Siavash moved on, I took down his phone number and we met up later for multiple cappuccinos. "Siavash" is a pseudonym for a handsome mechanical engineering graduate who back then spent his days fulfilling his military duty. It was a twenty-month waste of time, so pointless that in the barracks he heard "some grown men crying at night."

But Siavash was assigned to blessed Tehran, not some hopeless desert border post. So after hours he took pleasure in the unexpected softening of social strictures in the Islamic state. When we met, he described in hushed tones the quiet streets where young men "park" cars with girlfriends, preferably on rainy nights when windows would steam up and you could "have fun safely." Tehran, Siavash told me, was like a number of cities rolled into one, with "different islands [of permissiveness] around town." There were nightly parties stewed in alcohol and drugs. A hit of heroin cost less than a box of cigarettes, though Siavash was fastidious. He never touched alcohol or drugs, or even smoked—earning not just the trust of his parents, who would sometimes step out while he had a female "guest" at home, but also the trust of potential pickups.

His tactics did not always work. A few days before we met, on the road during a rainstorm, he had pulled over to offer a woman a ride, and tried this line: "Hey, will you marry me? You look beautiful when wet!" A "major problem" was how many young women remained virgins, he said, noting that "deflowering is a dangerous thing to do—they can take you to court, for a fine, or if accused of rape, they are going to kill you." Still, he found many triumphs, including some with women ten years his senior who were "looking for fun."

Much depended on the quality of your car, which spoke of the promise of a cash-rich good time. "Ninety-nine percent of them are sluts"—just as he was—Siavash asserted. "It depends on you, how brave you are, and be ready to hear their 'no' in a very bad way. But we are having fun here. I like my town; I like my country. I'm trying to be positive. Lots of people have left Iran." Siavash told me he was a "shy guy" during high school. These days he was trying to turn every day into a "good hair day."

And this lady hunter was not alone. Some of these tastes were evident in a bestselling lexicon of coded slang used by highway date hunters like Siavash. During on-the-road pickups, "hubcaps" were a woman's bottom; a "zero kilometer" was a virgin. Women in skin-tight, thigh-length "Islamic" manteau jackets had their own language and signals, and downloaded erotic images to spice up their mobile phones. At one party, an art student with a revealing net top was eager to show me her Nokia with its screen-saver shots of Angelina Jolie in a series of poses, her breasts covered whenever a phone number was dialed.

Hard-liners and undercover morality cops—people who would have pasted Siavash as an apostate, if they caught him—had tried to legislate a stricter dress code. They crashed mixed-sex parties, arrested girls flashing too much ankle and makeup, and scolded those resting sunglasses on their heads. The government deployed mobile flogging units in more laid-back Caspian Sea coast towns, to dispense immediate justice.

Iranians were reacting, sometimes boldly, soon after Khatami won in 1997. Witnesses reported young people fighting back with rocks and bottles against security men who tried to arrest one of them at a beach resort on the Caspian Sea.[91] Over time cultural clashes would lead to very serious violence. Khatami's initial victory and what it said about the desires of Iranian society was a step into uncharted territory. "After the election, we can feel that the Iranian nation has no more fear," said Ali Dehbashi, the editor of the arts and culture review

Kelk.[92] "They dropped their fear and are thinking that they can affect their own fate. If you see something beneath the surface, it is because of this self-confidence. This is something new."

Khatami's momentous victories were taken as a license for secular and Western-leaning Iranians to reach beyond the rules. And where they led, others followed. One student who spent five years at a provincial university in the ancient and remote city of Maybod—which she called a "nasty hellhole"—wrote in a 2003 blog of the change she had witnessed:

> I remember when I started my course at that so-called university . . . we must have been the first group of single girls entering that God-forsaken place and setting up on our own . . . so many times coming home and washing the spit of passers-by off my clothes . . . they could just not tolerate our shameful headscarves . . . without exception then, all the [local] women used to wear chadors. . . . They say that things are changing and extremists are getting more tolerant . . . a friend of mine even thinks we started a revolution here. . . .
>
> It's been just five years, but the same shopkeepers who would refuse to serve us if we were not wearing a chador now have teenage daughters who dress more provocatively than we ever dared to. . . .[93]

One close observer of this underground awakening was the Iranian-American journalist Azadeh Moaveni, who moved from California to Tehran in 2000. "I decided I wanted to live like them, as they did, their 'as if' lifestyle," she writes in *Lipstick Jihad*.[94] "They chose to act 'as if' it was permitted to hold hands on the street, blast music at parties, speak your mind, challenge authority, take your drug of choice, grow your hair long, wear too much lipstick."

She describes a mixed party for a teenage cousin, full of "the pre-meditated exposure of so much flesh," thanks to strict official rules:

It hadn't been a birthday party so much as a pushing and shoving match with the Islamic Republic; a cultural rebellion waged indoors against the regime's rigid codes of behavior. Those codes banned young men and women from interacting casually together, attending soccer matches, studying at the library.

When they were finally permitted a few hours in each other's company, they scarcely knew what to do, or how to behave.

BY 2005, AS KHATAMI'S two terms drew to a close, an uneasy balance prevailed. The unpopular right wing had shifted tactics, hoping that discontent over the failure of Khatami to fully deliver on promises of freedom, openness, and the rule of law would help their cause. Conservatives seemed to have determined that social flexibility was a price they had to pay for their political survival. That meant a new laissez-faire attitude from the right wing, a calculation easily recognized by the incurable Casanova, Siavash.

"The conservatives are getting clever—people are free in the street, holding hands and wearing less hijab," he told me. "[They] want to show that voting for reformists is not going to solve your problems; that if you vote [for reformists] you are going to be punished." That calculation appeared real. "This regime allows people to do what they want, so the army of the people has returned to its bases," analyst Saeed Laylaz told me.[95] "Maybe [people] do not like the regime, but they don't hate it. They don't accept totalitarianism anymore, and the regime accepts this."

Yet there were limits. The political realm was becoming, again in 2005, tightly controlled. Internet bloggers were getting prison time. Scenes of mixed-sex frolicking during the important Ashura holiday, which mourned the death of Imam Hossein, brought religious ire against "a handful of hoodlums and promiscuous elements that ridicule our sanctities," in the pages of the hard-line newspaper *Jomhuri-e Eslami*.[96] "In this disgraceful event, which was like a large street party, [girls and boys] mocked Muslims' beliefs and sanctities in the most shameless manner," the newspaper lectured. "Some long-haired guys would openly cuddle girls creating awful immoral scenes. Fast, pro-vocative music . . . nearby gave the street party more steam." Vigilan-tes were there to break up the lovefest in affluent north Tehran.

AND THERE WERE MANY other times when the hard-liners scored. I was once sitting down, for example, to a milkshake thick with dates with a young woman, when out came her story of being prevented from flying from Tehran to London in late 2004 because she wore no socks.[97] An athlete who had medaled at the Asian Games and was "waiting for Prince Charming," she usually wore mascara, plucked her eyebrows, and even blithely kissed me on the cheek when we met on the street—an extraordinary risk that I was shocked she even attempted.

For the airport departure, she thought she had taken the pre-caution of looking as conservative as she could. She hadn't put on makeup, though her designer eyebrows and striking beauty would have prompted an initial prejudice. Female airport officials slapped handcuffs on her and took her to a nearby court to sign documents. When she complained, one woman shouted, "Don't you be smart, bitch!"

"Where does it say in the Quran you must wear socks?" my friend asked in amazement.

"You're going to say you are sorry, in court!" came the uncompro-mising reply. The plane was already gone. The young culprit with the bare ankles was given a choice of punishments: a $150 fine, one hun-dred lashes, or two months in prison. Her mother arrived to bail her out—uncharacteristically dressed in a full black chador, sans makeup. She pleaded that the family (though indeed well-to-do) "did not have enough money for socks," and were a *"basiji* family" that staunchly supported the Revolution. The mother paid in cash to release her daughter, rescuing her from the deep conservatism that persisted be-neath the veneer of social permissiveness.

Lamentation: "This is the Iran we live in—they are so rude."

• • •

BUT "THEY" ARE NOT always so successful at curbing illicit appe-
tites, as evident in the future adventures of the Pickup King, Siavash.
The young conscript who had sought young women from the driver's seat of his car had formalized his woman-hunting ways. By late
2007, I found him to be living proof that "anything is possible in Iran,"
though his sex-saturated private life might surprise even the most
open-minded Iranians.[98] His day job was sales manager at a large office
supply company, wearing a suit as he watched the failing economy
damage his bottom line. Deals were down 30 percent in the previous
six months, and had plummeted 200 percent over four years—most of
that since Iran had been hit with UN and American sanctions over its
nuclear program.

But for Siavash, the real playing field extended beyond the office.
He was still exploring the ways and wiles of the opposite sex. He had
been bodybuilding for a couple years and told me that women were
"an adventure, not just sex." He likened himself to the mirror-scoping
narcissist played by Tom Cruise in *Vanilla Sky* (2001), reminding me
that Cruise's character's nickname was "Citizen Dildo." Siavash picked
me up in his modest black car, its interior awash with the man's perfume as Mark Knopfler's luxurious *Shangri-La* played on the stereo.

"I'm still the kid I used to be. I'm still chasing women," laughed the
twenty-eight-year-old libertine, remembering the "quiet roads" where
couples steamed up car windows on rainy nights, unmolested. And
Siavash was enthralled as ever. In his job, he said, formal dress made it
"easier to get close to women—it's an ace." He gave women his card
once or twice a day. In the parking lot. On the sidewalk. "It's closing
the deal. I ask them: 'What are you looking for in a man? Money? To
take you to my place, where I can give you good sex? Whatever you
want . . .' " he explained. "We have a rule in business: for one good
sale, you must have ten prospects."

And he was closing deals. Siavash was known as a *dokhtar-baz* in Persian, one who is into women. To start, the pair might drive to a private
place, to kiss in the car. Siavash was expected to spend "good money."
In many of his recent conquests—for that is how he saw them—

foreplay wasn't a factor. "It's really easier with married women," he told me, because they have their other lives to attend to. "You don't need to spend much time with them, but go straight to sex."

The fact that Siavash still lived with his parents complicated his libidinous lifestyle, though they seemed exceptionally open-minded about his transgressions. Siavash said his younger brother—who was then doing his time as a soldier—is "beautiful" and "women love him," though also "more emotional, he's more about love."

His father chided him: "It's not like your room is your castle. So remove the condom box from the kitchen table."

His mother chided him: "Why do you meet so many older women? It's not your future."

"They have trust, and I'm just enjoying myself," Siavash explained. "I would love to join women of the same age, but they are not so open."

The astonishing confidence of Siavash enabled him to navigate Iran's fluid social rules while keeping his distance from politics. An anonymous blog entry spoke to the dynamic:

> Have you noticed that everything that Iranians do is considered illegal and is banned by the regime? In reality, everything is outlawed . . . Listening to music or watching a film. The clothes you wear, what you drink, the games you play . . . What you read and write.
>
> [So] the way people live their lives is illegal. Perhaps there is no other country in the world where there is such a cultural gulf. . . .[99]

As journalist Christopher de Bellaigue observed of his several years living in Iran, "By setting very demanding standards of Islamic virtue from its citizens, the Islamic Republic has made criminals of millions of them." [100]

WHEN I BROUGHT IT up, Siavash bristled at the label *gharbzadeh*—the morally mesmerized, Westoxicated youth decried by the religious establishment. "Maybe [I am], but it's not like I have a George

Clooney poster on my wall. I don't worship him!" he protested. "I like Hollywood, but sometimes I feel like it is propaganda."

Propaganda like *Sex in the City* and *Lost,* to which he was addicted— watching ninety to one hundred episodes once in a single month. Siavash ordered American films online from a Tehran company, for motorcycle delivery to his front door. And every time a hot prospect called, Siavash's mobile phone rang out with the pop song: "I'm too sexy for my love, too sexy for my love . . ."

The Mall: The New Front Line

Milad Mall—home turf for Iran's prosperous and disillusioned social elite—is a place where two worlds collide. On one side in this upscale Tehran hangout are young, free-spirited Iranians, radicalized beyond politics against Iran's Revolution and its hard-line rulers.

On the other: feared enforcers of the regime's Department of Vice and Virtue, who routinely targetted improper garb and pop music, and shut down trendy shops for selling tight-fit women's apparel and men's ties.

As far as Hossein was concerned, his clothing shop for women was the front line of Iran's simmering social war. Seven years into the rule of President Khatami, women shopping there in 2004 were reprimanded and even detained by overzealous morality police for showing too much hair. Hossein was ordered to stop displaying "too much red and pink" in the Valentine season—colors known to be "screaming" in Iran because they are so bright and happy.[101]

"I feel so sorry and hateful, to see these very stupid people who are destroying their own country with their own hands," moaned Hossein, who wore a thick silver necklace and long, slicked-back hair. Recently detained for his tattoo, he likened the social clash to "friends choking each other, and throwing themselves into a dark pit."

His parents and grandparents believed they were "tricked and deceived" into fighting for the Revolution, said the twenty-two-year-old shop owner, and that it was the "biggest mistake they had ever made."

A week earlier his girlfriend was pulled over on the road, and while she was being held the *basijis* wanted to get her phone number. He said she was also stopped by the police, who demanded sex or they would take the car. "This happens to everyone," he asserted. "It was true of all *basijis*, police and morality guys"—so he claimed—that they would "offer sex to girls" held in detention in exchange for going home sooner.

The result, regardless of the truth, was a social chasm. Hossein told me: "[Hard-liners] made a very small world for themselves, and have been bombarded with ideas from people above them. The ideology has penetrated their minds. They are just followers and obedient. They do not know what the real world is."

True Believers in the Revolution and its divine clerical rule argue the opposite is true, of course, and accuse such Westernized and secular Iranians of being the ones detached from reality. That week I was canvassing the mall, in 2004, conservatives were on the verge of re-capturing parliament. The hard-line Guardian Council rejected more than two thousand reform-minded candidates as "unfit" to stand. Key reformers were boycotting the vote, including Iran's Nobel laureate and best-known human rights lawyer, Shirin Ebadi. Text messages were zipping from one cell phone to the next, warning that "the ballot boxes on Friday are the coffins of freedom. Do not take part in the funeral of freedom."

More than one hundred reform legislators had directly challenged Supreme Leader Khamenei in a letter. "The popular Revolution brought freedom and independence for the country in the name of Islam. But now you lead a system in which legitimate freedoms and the rights of the people are being trampled in the name of Islam," they wrote.[102] "Institutions under your supervision—after four years of humiliating the elected parliament and thwarting (reform) bills—have now, on the verge of the parliamentary elections, deprived the people of the most basic right: the right to choose and be chosen."

The social and political fault line had become so pronounced, and the value systems so mutually incomprehensible, that both sides had taken to protesting the other in the most niggling ways. One student registering for college wrote in her blog:

> The first thing they noticed was my make-up!!! [Scrawled] across my Conduct Form: HEAVY MAKE-UP!!! And started telling me that I would be answerable for this in the after-life!!! Is wearing make-up cannibalism or something?!!!
>
>   What about all our corrupt government officials? Will they ever be answerable to anyone?!!! [103]

At the mall, shoppers reveled in the uniform of the Westoxicated: shrinkwrap-tight "robes" above the knee and kerchief-sized head-scarves. Mixed into this secular, affluent world was respect—even yearning—for Iran's top enemy, America. It could not be further from the poorer, religious areas of south Tehran, where the Revolution first took root and still commanded a faithful following. Silver-bedecked shop owner Hossein said most of the mall's morality cops were cut from poverty-stricken cloth: "Only ten percent come with ideology; the rest because of economic shortages or jealousy and haven't seen this kind of thing in their lives. It's a different world."

"[Hard-liners] think the same about us, as we do about them: that we are animals, imitators stricken by the West, and on the wrong path," explains Hossein. "That is what I think about them—they are such animals."

Another shopkeeper would not give his name and pulled me aside to whisper like a coconspirator. "There is too much pressure under this tyranny—we can't talk. Even a word, and tomorrow you are not here," he told me. "They have a gun at our heads. They have the power, and we can do nothing." Vice and Virtue officers had recently insisted that neckties be removed from storefront mannequins, and they broke a CD playing music, even though it had been officially approved. Else-where I had seen the breasts of female mannequins crudely hacked off with saws, the gaping holes then covered with brown packing tape, Taliban-style.

As a partial concession to the demands of Vice and Virtue, one saleswoman now wore more conservative covering over silver-tinted hair. But it was draped over a tight manteau and blue jeans. Her eyes were ringed with thick mascara. Rose-colored nails matched glossy lipstick, completing the garish display.

Painted beauty? No.

Gaudy protest? Yes.

"They come here in plainclothes as shoppers, ask for the price of a tie, then go out and bring uniformed officers," the woman told me, her voice a hissing whisper. As we spoke, everyone stopped in shock when two men with beards entered the shop. There was a sigh of relief when they were recognized as friends. "I have my own beliefs, and they have their beliefs, and that is all," the saleswoman said. She doubted one of "their" most cherished tenets: "They are not true about that, 'the last drop of blood,' " she scoffed. "We're all Muslims here, but there are hard-liners, and there are normal people."

The saleswoman knew that any relaxation of the dress code was "one hundred percent reversible" and so kept her hopes in check. "When people in charge are that powerful, they can tell me: 'Wear this today, and don't wear that tomorrow.' " A boyish salesman added: "They have no logical reason why we can't sell a tie. It's a piece of cloth. So it's a protest. . . . It's chic to buy a tie, and chic to be against them."

I found architecture student Somayeh shopping with her sisters, wearing the full Westoxicated *gharbzadeh* getup. "We fear [hard-liners] because they can make trouble for us with lashings, or put us in prison," Somayeh told me. She was on the lookout for police as she spoke, her darting eyes framed by a ski goggle sunburn. "Islam is not just about covering your hair and not drinking alcohol—it's also about not telling lies. Some [hard-liners] are worse than those who don't cover themselves. Islam says: 'Don't deceive each other.' "

Her sister Parisa took up the theme, full of disdain. "Their Islam and their state are different from the ones we know," she told me.

Parisa and her young friends once said their prayers regularly. But no longer. Coincidentally, just days before, the reformist writer Ebrahim Nabavi had pointed out that precise irony in a blog: "Is it not strange that after decades of institutionalized religious education, Iran's youth are totally apathetic about such matters and have the keenest social and cultural leanings to 'American ways' in the Islamic world?" [104]

The conservative recapture of parliament was casting a pall on the future, the shopkeeper told me. "Our society is like a cage now. They have taken our freedom," the man complained, exasperated. Shoppers were passing by, couples flirting subtly among them. "Girls and boys coming out like this are only pretending to be free. What do you call liberty? Uncovering your hair? This is not freedom."

He praised the Revolution and "true" Islam, but said both had been corrupted by the Islamic Republic. "What we see right now is not Islam. In all the world, people deal with computers and technology. In Iran it is only social pressure and using force," he told me. "True liberty is expressing your idea. . . . This is the atomic age, and each person knows better if they are on the right path. I know what is right or wrong. I don't need anybody else to tell me.

"We are the majority, we think, but in front of them we can do nothing. They are much more powerful. We are a burned and finished generation."

IN THE BLACK-AND-WHITE WORLD of Iran's hard-liners, the word "compromise" was not part of the lexicon. The term "enemy" dominated instead, and was applied as often to profligate fellow Iranians—such as those whining at Milad Mall—as to purported American spies. Mohammad Hossein Azemi, a dedicated revolutionary and a city clerk from western Iran, told me he knew how to deal with enemies. [105]

"I want to put a very strong fist in the mouths of those who talk rubbish," Azemi told me, scorning those privileged Iranians who detested clerical rule. "They are not our brothers. Those who drink alcohol and use drugs—do you think they are human beings? I hope they recognize their sins, and recommit to the Revolution. They have the power to choose the right path."

Both sides were convinced they spoke for the majority, but they hardly recognized or respected how the other half lives.

"They are not reformists—they are all pagans," said Yaghoub Ramazani, a Revolutionary Guard and veteran of the Iran-Iraq War.[106] His brother died a martyr on the battlefield—a fate he considered the "ultimate death in this world," and wished could have been his. "They make no difference to us at all, and their numbers are not as high as you think," Ramazani told me at Friday prayers in Tehran. People were "free to do what they want in their own house," but he believed that "immoral" acts of some fellow Iranians "put national security at risk." He lauded the recent beating by vigilantes of senior reformist officials, who he said were "related to America; the U.S. Embassy knows them."

"It is possible the propaganda of the enemies affects the hearts of the ignorant," Ramazani admitted. For him, the example of Imam Hossein's sacrifice on the plains of Karbala centuries earlier was evidence enough to be against democracy. "In [Shiite] Islam, we have the culture of Ashura, of seventy-two disciples in front of thirty thousand," he said. "If foreign countries talk of democracy as the majority winning over the minority, Islamic culture proves the opposite."

Reformists had been "tricked by foreigners" to believe otherwise. "It is our duty to convince [Westernized Iranians] to do good things," said the strong-nosed Ramazani, who declined to give his rank or current job but wore the black beard of a Believer. "Maybe we are sad about what they do in their hearts, and tell them—and if they still don't listen, we have to hit them with the impact of a hammer. Our law specifies, according to Islam, what to do with them. It may be fines, it may be prison, it may be lashings. Whatever I say is the view of people all around."

A group of like-minded ideologues had, in fact, gathered around us outside the university gates before prayer time, and began to chant

"God is great" in unison. "[Ramazani] reflected the true words in our hearts," affirmed Safar Esfandiareh, a carpenter with worn hands and a scar on his wrist. "When we have such people in our country, we do not fear the U.S., the West, or even the reformists."

YET VIOLENCE WAS NOT accepted by all Believers. Reformists "are on the wrong path, but hitting and arresting people achieves nothing," said Alireza Yazdanbash, a young, unshaven *basiji,* a student in south Tehran whose favorite sport was judo.[107] He had no uniform, and had dark eyes and bad teeth. "When I see them, I just feel sad and thank God for who I am. God burns them enough, according to their sins," he told me. We were talking in Freedom Square before a rally. A Revolutionary Guard officer strode past, barking a warning to the *basiji:* "Your enemy is here. Be careful!" he said, referring to me, an American journalist with a notebook.

"Whatever I do, I do because of God. I want to be closer to God," Yazdanbash told me. "Whatever the Supreme Leader says, that is right."

With uncommon candor, Yazdanbash acknowledged that hardliners like him were fighting a losing battle: "Tehran is a big city, we can't control it all. You can't talk about 'winning' or 'losing' [against reformists] because everyone is responsible for their own sins."

The Renaissance in Retreat

What happened to Iran's cultural renaissance? What happened to those who defined the Tehran Spring? To the promising blossom of the Revolution's quarter-century peak of cultural openness? Its petals began to wilt under the harsh heat of conservative rule, as it returned in 2004 and 2005.

Just as the privileged Alireza Mahfouzian—the skier I first found copping an illicit kiss with his girlfriend in 2000—was one symbol of social change in Khatami's Iran, his story proved even more instructive as it played out over the years. Mahfouzian had always been an active combatant in Iran's culture wars. When he graduated from high school, the police shaved off his too-radical long hair. He was in court twenty times for social infractions and boasted that he knew the courthouse "room by room."

He was sentenced to seventy-five lashes, with shirt on, in the mid-1990s, after a woman—in a bid to extort money, he says—accused him of having sex with her. He was also sentenced to thirty or forty lashes on his bare back for an alcohol infraction at a family party. Friends told him to take photos of his lacerations and apply for political asylum.

"I was very angry for a year. I thought: 'Why do they have to do this? There are other ways of punishment. Why do they use this violent, old-fashioned way?' " recalled Mahfouzian, while offering chilled beer in his parents' plush apartment in 2005.[108] "Why do we have such laws? And why do we have such people to carry them out? I went through this dark period—I tried to leave everything behind, to turn my back on the country and try to go to America." The lashings, family bankruptcy, and love problems prompted a period of "crazy" moves that included becoming the youngest Iranian to get a parachuting certification.

"Then I came to my senses," Mahfouzian says. "I like this place, and want to live here. So I had to adapt myself and accept certain things." Ski partner Akasheh was long gone: she had been in a hurry to get married in 2000, and he wasn't. Then he was run over by a car, an accident that broke both his legs and left him with an artificial kneecap and metal pins. While he recovered in a hospital, Akasheh left him. Many girlfriends and five years later, Mahfouzian had an interior design business that put him in contact with more middle-class Iranians and some officials. The experience changed him. He remained a party animal but had become a more circumspect one.

"We must realize we live in an Islamic country—we should accept that the [leaders] up there have their own tools to push," said Mahfouzian, heavyset and more thoughtful than before. "It's not that I hate or dislike the rulers, but I understand this is their way of imposing power."

The impact of the Khatami awakening depended upon whom you

asked. "If you ask teenagers, many have a dark image of what is happening," said Mahfouzian. He now had a longer perspective. Indeed,
just as some conservatives had lowered their sights about force-fitting
a restive population into some seventh-century template of Islamic
perfection, many youths had also adjusted their expectations in grudg-
ing recognition, even accommodation, of hard-line forces in Iran.

It was time for another round of beer, and he poured it.

Those youths who refused to acknowledge that hard-liners play
such a decisive role in Iranian society—for better or worse—had been
"reckless in their life, and they crash," said Mahfouzian. "I was the
same. You must decide: Will you grow up and adjust? Or stay reckless
and destructive?"

Mahfouzian and other former foot soldiers of reform knew that the
change they voted for a decade earlier, with hopeful hearts and overwhelming majorities, was no more than a cruel memory. The promise
of democracy *and* Iran's Islamic state existing together was proving
impossible to attain.

"They are walking away from the state. They are pushing away
politics," the sociologist and reformist editor Hamid Reza Jalaeipour
told me.[109] "I call this the 'Era of Rethinking.' These days Iranians are
thinking how they can find a better way."

Mahfouzian was distracted from those earlier dreams, anyway,
because he was too busy trying to save his new fast-food restaurant.
"Business is not so good. There is no optimism," said the older and
wiser entrepreneur when I found him again, in 2007.[110] He poured a
couple of double scotch whiskies, straight. Not only was the stagger-
ing economy taking a toll, but the health ministry had been putting
out "a lot of bad propaganda" about how fast food was unhygienic
and unhealthy.

Mahfouzian was now wearing a closely cropped *basiji*-style beard;
his hair was receding fast. He got stuck in an argument with his new
girlfriend about the state of social repression. He had his lashes for
alcohol, but said "it was the law." She had just been caught, sent to
court, and given a two-year suspended sentence for speaking in the

street with a male classmate. As a university student in a remote town, she was outraged: "If I even have a single conversation, they will come the next day." Mahfouzian was mellow: "As I age, I feel I have more freedom."

But he also had the freedom to lose money from a small establishment that was popular but facing long odds. On the takeout menu I found the mixed brain and tongue sandwich—wrapped in silver foil, with a packet of ketchup on top—an especially tasty concoction. They were parts of a famous Persian specialty that is boiled and usually eaten by men very early in the morning. Sheep eyeballs. Cheek skin. Throat cartilage, to crunch with that tasty boiled tongue. *Kaleh pache* in Persian. Inflation had eaten away his profits. Erratic supply meant items like tongue weren't available every day. ("The cows are cold," was one supplier's winter excuse.)

A few months later, the girlfriend was out of his life. And the fate of the pizza and sandwich shop hung in the balance.

"We have this five thousand years of civilization, but it is no credit to us," lamented Mahfouzian, who expected to be forced to close "unless there is a miracle." He had to raise the price of a pizza 60 percent. His ambition of launching a chain of shops inside and outside Iran had evaporated. At twenty-eight and unmarried, the trained industrial designer also failed to get a European visa to attend a building exhibition—and said he wanted to hit the German Embassy with a Molotov cocktail.

But this onetime cultural guerrilla had come to terms with staying in Iran—despite the right-wing regime and its ruthless restrictions—while enjoying plentiful girlfriends and a new SUV. "Since I was a kid, I was after that, and I got it," said Mahfouzian, making a crude gesture with one hand forming a circle, the other inserting a finger.

"If the financial situation were good, Iran would be one of the best places to live," Mahfouzian affirmed. A steaming Jacuzzi bubbled in the basement. The luxurious apartment gleamed with gilt objets d'art. On the coffee table was a black stone ashtray with a sensuous sculpture of two nudes, a young woman sitting in a man's lap. Mahfouzian poured a third scotch. On the sound system "Adagio for Strings," by the Dutch artist DJ Tiësto, perfected the moment.

"Our country is moving ahead with these [conservative] beliefs," said Mahfouzian. "We can either move with them, or move out. We have no other choice."

Achieving that level of resignation was a victory for the regime, which from its first days had sought to create a believing—or at least accepting—battalion of youth. It would prove a fleeting victory. And it was hardly complete. Here they were, in all their scotch-sodden submission: Iran's modern-day "soldiers for Islam."

FOR MANY, ANGER TRUMPED resignation. Parvaneh E'temadi was one of Iran's best-known artists, and her latest work in 2004 was a striking collection of montages, made up of portions of photographs of the ancient metal death mask of Agamemnon, laid upon colorful backgrounds. The work was hanging beautifully in the Golestan gallery—where I met her—but the bespectacled E'temadi felt she was being suffocated. "This [political] war doesn't exist for us—it's fundamentalist versus fundamentalist. . . . I hope they eat each other up, and we finish with them," E'temadi told me.[111] "Everything is politics. You can't avoid it; it follows you everywhere."

The artist was worried that her latest book, already at the publishers, would not be approved "before the system changes. Maybe they will stop it. That's the fun of it, it's never boring," E'temadi said, with cutting wit. "The more difficult, the better it is for us. When you lose everything, you are better. . . . There is something about this nation: suppress these people, and they will grow."

BY 2004 FRUSTRATION WAS also infecting the layout rooms of *Tavoos,* or *Peacock*—the sophisticated and glossy quarterly magazine that saw itself as the "guardian of Iranian art and culture." I profiled it in 2000 as a harbinger of cultural renaissance. But the last issue was printed in early 2001. Seven more had been completed, though cash was too short to have them printed—and low-interest loans that required official approval had not come.

"When you have conceptual art in Iran, you should have mass media together, to discuss these paintings and issues and artists, and ask, 'What is the meaning of it?' " editor Manijeh Mir-'Emadi told me.[112] "We keep working, and nobody can stop us," she said, with a flash of defiance. But it hardly qualified as optimism. Conservatives in Qom were angry with the magazine. And Mir-'Emadi was angry with them. "They know nothing of modern art," she told me. "It's like sharing a beautiful sculpture in a poor area. Poor people look up and say: 'What is the meaning of that?' "

"To tell you the truth, I am a little bit tired," confided Mir-'Emadi. She flipped through one fine copy of *Peacock*, every page redolent with art and color and promise and ambition, heavy with the weight of expensive foreign ink. "How can I trust them? They don't understand what is going on in there." Careful as she is with images, she could never be careful enough. "Even this modern painting can raise questions. At the Islamic Guidance Ministry, or in Qom, someone says, 'This picture means revolution. It means such and such.' I don't trust them. They will cut my head; I will lose everything."

Mir-'Emadi was beside herself and had sent out a letter of apology to subscribers. It promised "strength to continue . . . despite the obstacles we face."

THOSE OBSTACLES ALSO ATTENDED the 2004 premiere of the film *Marmoulak (The Lizard)*, which humorously explored one of the most sensitive subjects in Iran: the ruling clergy. The movie follows a thief who steals clerical robes to escape prison, and then gets unexpectedly wrapped up in life as a holy man. While poking fun at the foibles and privileges of the turbaned class, the cutting-edge comedy also delivered a deeper religious message that anyone can reach God.

I went to a private screening attended by several hundred people, among them a number of religious families and clerics. Afterward, I watched a mullah corner director Kamal Tabrizi. "You make people laugh, but you give them a green light to ridicule the clergy," Hojja-toleslam Mustafa Elahi scolded the director.[113]

"You're wrong," replied Tabrizi. "This is a very religious film."

"The film *was* great—I was laughing so hard that I could hardly hold my turban on my head!" the cleric cut in, cracking a smile. "I saw myself in it. But you focused more on making fun of the clergy, and not enough on scenes of repentance and returning to God."

The face-off showed how far Iran's cultural landscape had opened in the quarter century since the Revolution. Elahi was not a charitable man, at least when it came to Westerners. When I spoke with him afterward, he was gruff. He admitted he had been a *nofouzi*—literally an "infiltrator," in this case someone employed by the regime to spy on other clerics. When I asked for his name, he first gave me a false one. Then he gave another and declared: "Don't try to find me. Never contact me again."

Signs were multiplying that openness was in peril—or at least subject to far stricter interpretation. For the conservative side, liberties had just gone far too far. "Some films in festivals are rewarded just because they are against our state. We reprimand them, but that's all we do," Hossein Shariatmadari, the macaroon-eating editor of the hardline newspaper *Kayhan,* told me.[114] His pages had been critical of *The Lizard.* The Ministry of Culture and Islamic Guidance, controlled by reformists, "has broken the rules before," he told me. "For sure" the new conservative parliament would enforce those rules more strictly.

Criticism from the right didn't prevent the movie from winning best film at Tehran's prestigious Fajr Film Festival. "I wanted to take a critical look at the clerics, to show it is possible to be critical of this class of people, but in a balanced, proper way," director Tabrizi told me. "I was not sure at all [of official approval]. I was waiting for trouble."

The Lizard drew its name from the underworld thief-cum-cleric, who can climb any wall and has a lizard tattooed on his shoulder. When he escapes prison, he immediately finds himself up against popular disdain for clerics, when he tries to hail a cab on a Tehran street.

Mirroring reality, no one stops—and one driver swerves to hit him, eliciting the curse "I spit on your soul!"

Boys joke that Reza Lizard's turban is on backward and are shocked when he responds with gutter cursing, before catching himself to say, ahem, "I hope God will help you."

While on a train trying to get a counterfeit passport to flee to Turkey, Reza Lizard is mistaken for a cleric newly assigned to a remote village mosque, and is forced to play the role. He doesn't know how to lead prayers or practice Islam, but his humorous prison/preacher earthiness wins him a wide following.

At one description of God as "compassionate and very kind," some in the audience hiss disapproval. In the final speech, Reza Lizard makes a tearful appeal to local inmates—before his cover is blown and he is arrested. He says "the doors of the prison may be closed to you," though "God does not belong to good people only."

With acerbic blade and laughter, the film cut so deeply, cleverly, and cleanly into Iranian society that is was a box office smash. Cinemagoers lined up at theaters across the country for weeks to watch *The Lizard*. Until it just proved too popular for those clerics who really do rule Iran.

Overnight, all public screenings were banned.

THAT WAS A STATUS familiar to U.S.-trained independent filmmaker Farzad Motamen, who began his career making documentaries during the Revolution. He was in the change-is-irreversible camp but was under pressure when I met him in 2004.

"I don't think things will change a lot—they can't take back the little democracy that people have got, they just can't set the society back," Motamen told me as conservative control expanded.[115] He thought a "little democracy is not a problem for them." But freedom was relative. Clerical rule had made him "used to living with these limitations."

When not directing his own films, Motamen was teaching. "My students make amazing films, but you can't show them anywhere," the director told me. "They don't accept any limitation. They are inspired by drugs, rock 'n' roll, and free sex and you can't show it. We watch them, and I say, 'It's a good film. Take it to your home.' "

And censorship was encroaching, again. An experimental film of the Iran-Iraq War made by a friend was banned, even though he had cut eight minutes out of it. Motamen set aside one of his own projects after submitting the script to the Islamic Guidance Ministry ten months earlier. Official script readers insisted upon strategic changes that "made it shit" and demanded a director of the ministry's choosing.

"They won't let me make it, because it is critical," Motamen said. "I'm not interested in any control [by them]."

But he had to take interest in his predicament. He had made forty documentaries, then two experimental films. Then he had to "go commercial" on a third film that he didn't want to make, in order to "pay the rent."

And still there were issues. Endless issues. Motamen had to cut out the 1966 Nancy Sinatra ballad "Bang Bang (My Baby Shot Me Down)" from the soundtrack—due to its lurid female singing voice— and replace it with the much less suitable Elvis Presley song "Viva Las Vegas." He had to slice out a shot taken at a distance of a woman removing her shoes, because there was also a man in the room. Motamen complained: "They imagine what is *not* in the film!"

And he was asked why his lead actress smoked cigarettes.

"She's a femme fatale!" Motamen howled in exasperation. "She is supposed to kill people, use drugs, have wild sex, and I just have her smoking cigarettes. Just leave me *alone*!"

4

Political Khatami:
The Enemy Within

Those who are trying to bring corruption and destruction to our country in the name of democracy will be oppressed . . . they must be hanged. We will oppress them by God's order and by God's permission.

—Ayatollah Ruhollah Khomeini, 1979

AFTER THE 1997 ELECTION of Mohammad Khatami, hand-to-hand combat ensued between two political armies in Iran, their camps loosely called "conservative" and "reformist." Both lay claim to the territory of the Revolution: either as adherents to its sacred ideals, devoted to infallible clerical rule—my Leader, right or wrong—or as progeny of the natural evolution of the "freedom" promised by the Revolution.

Both camps have been certain of their path, certain they spoke for the majority even when election results proved the opposite. Hard-liners threatened and used violence because, they warned, "people are getting further from God. Too much liberty given to people is corrupting them."[1] At the same time liberal reformists—including top grand ayatollahs—began to fundamentally question the wisdom and utility of religious rule in a modern, democratic age.

The two-term presidency of Khatami (1997–2005) was more popular than any single political trend in Iran since the Revolution. To
know how it disintegrated—to see how it was stopped by conservative political maneuverings, the application of physical force, and the
reformists' own overstretch and arrogance—is to understand why
hard-line rule would return.

Working against the reformists was their own determination to restore the rule of law, and therefore to play by the rules. Their right-
wing opponents felt no such compunction, unleashing vigilantes—a
time-honored Persian practice—and using every coercive tool of the
regime to reimpose their will.

The root problem was two legitimacies: the religious one claimed
by the God-gifted Guide, the "Supreme Leader" who in title if not authority since 1989 was Ayatollah Seyyed Ali Khamenei; and the democratic one of President Khatami, whose landslide election victories
affirmed deep popular yearnings for change. During the first decade
of the Revolution, under the charismatic rule of the "Imam" Ayatollah Ruhollah Khomeini, there was little distinction between these two
sources of power. They led to the same place. But after Khomeini's
death, they became two separate tines of belief—and legitimacy—
that would ever after be in conflict.

Khomeini had himself ensured this legacy of uncertainty. His
speeches and edicts "zigzagged between a messianic notion of politics and a more utilitarian view . . . for defending the interests of the
people," writes historian Daniel Brumberg.[2] "Khomeini's vision of Islamic government had no single foundation, no one core logic. The
notion of a divinely inspired activist-prophet who implemented God's
laws was important to him."

But so was the need for a "political ruler" to act for the people.

Khomeini complained in 1979, for instance, that the first draft of the
constitution did not specify aspects of clerical rule. Its framers "want
freedom but without Islam," he charged.[3] "We hate freedom without
the Quran. . . . We hate their saying: Islam without the clergy." The
final version, therefore—with an extra clause affirming Khomeini in

the post—enshrined the overarching role of the *velayat-e faqih,* the all-powerful Guardian Theologian who was to reign as God's Deputy on Earth. But it also required the Supreme Leader to be supported "by a decisive majority of the people."[4]

Those provisions were scrapped when the constitution was rewritten in 1989, specifically to enable the far less qualified and less charismatic Khamenei to ascend to the post. But still part of the vocabulary was the vote of the people and the legitimacy it bestowed, the gold standard set by Khomeini himself. On the eve of the Revolution, Khomeini declared that "only through the departure of the Shah and the transfer of power to the people" would peace return.[5] The new Islamic government, he promised, would be "confirmed and supported by the people [with] their full and active participation."

So the Islamic Republic has always pushed hard for high voter turnout, portraying it as a religious obligation that confronts the "threat of the enemy." I heard it repeatedly over the years: "Khomeini's famous standard is the vote of the people," as one Iranian newspaper editor told me. "Those who do not believe in the people's vote are not correct at all."[6]

Yet Khomeini did more than anyone to promulgate and popularize the primary role of the *velayat-e faqih.* In doing so he buried the "quietist" tradition of Shiite clerics, who had always kept their distance from politics, and replaced it with a radical hands-on interpretation that incensed many senior clergy. Any ambiguity was erased toward the end of Khomeini's life, when those powers were made "absolute." In 1988, Khomeini even proclaimed that the *velayat-e faqih* was "the most important of the divine commandments . . . and had priority over all derivative commandments, even over prayer, fasting, and the pilgrimage to Mecca."[7]

This declaration "squared the circle in religious terms," noted one astute analysis.[8] "By raising obedience to the *velayat* to a theological imperative, Khomeini sought to overcome the traditional Shiite distinction between the world of religion . . . and the world of politics. The sacred and profane had become one; all government orders henceforth bore the full weight of holy writ."

The response of Khamenei (who was then president) drew the battle lines for Iran's future political warfare, by placing the self-declared deity of the Guide above democracy. "The commandments of the *vali-e faqih* are . . . like the commandments of God," Khamenei had said.[9] "The Mandate of the Jurist is like the soul in the body of the regime. . . . What right do the majority of people have to ratify a Constitution and make it binding on all the people? The person who has [that] right . . . is the ruling jurist. . . . Opposing this order then becomes forbidden as one of the cardinal sins, and combating the opponents of this order should become an incumbent religious duty."

But Khamenei, since becoming Supreme Leader himself in 1989, has lacked both the charisma and religious gravitas to carry his exalted title. It has complicated his political position, not least with senior theologians in Qom who far outrank him in learning. As one observer pithily put it, "You can't force people to believe that, simply because the representative of God has died, the man now sitting in his chair is the new representative of God." [10]

AS I WAS MAKING my first visits to Iran in the mid-1990s, cracks were evident even before Khatami's reformist victory. That was clear in the uninspiring basement offices of the tolerated but illegal opposition Freedom Movement. Its newspaper was banned. Meetings were attacked by vigilantes. Supporters were in prison.

Its leader, Ebrahim Yazdi, the Texas pharmacist and first foreign minister after the Revolution, dutifully tape recorded our conversations. His finely apportioned hands fiddled with the device, so that proof was available for Iranian intelligence that, as he met with an American, he was not plotting to overthrow the regime.

The Revolution's main point was "liberty and freedom," he told me.[11] "[The people] wanted an Islamic Revolution, but they are faced with a government of the clergy. Now they are confronted with harsh measures by those who consider themselves the sole representatives of God on Earth, the sole interpreters of religion, and the sole combatants. . . . So any opposition voice is being silenced; any unorthodox view of religion is being crushed and suppressed," Yazdi said. "We are trying to find a new embodiment for the old values. One can't resolve the difference by repressing them."

The gray-haired dissident said the hard-line agenda was simple. In religion they were "backward, reactionary, and narrow-minded." [12] Politically, "they don't believe in any kind of democracy. It is against Islam to them, so it is blasphemy. They want complete, totalitarian control." The cassette player continued recording, its spool of magnetic tape slowly turning as it filled with our words. Yazdi was certain of one thing: "Democracy will eventually win in Iran. They must recognize this fact."

Of course conservatives feared that possibility, so resistance was fierce from the start. Tolerance had always been a rare element in Iran's political periodic table. Far more commonly found in Persian ore was defiance and resistance. Dictatorship and dominance. Obedience and submission. Students were asking their professors what the revolutionary slogan "Independence, Freedom, Islamic Republic" actually meant in practice—and whether those were still valid aspirations, or had been achieved already and they just missed it.

"Unfortunately the official history is so much rhetoric and superficial that the young generation does not believe in it," Tehran University political scientist Sadegh Zibakalam told me. [13] A weathered revolutionary himself, with a narrow face and sharp eyes, he could easily explain the evils of the Shah. He had been imprisoned for two years by SAVAK in the downtown jail where the Supreme Leader was also locked up. His mug shot still hangs today in that extensive gallery, at the jail turned museum called Ebrat (Lesson), with its wax figure torturers. The Shah personally pardoned Zibakalam, thanks to an Amnesty International appeal—a result unlikely to be repeated in revolutionary Iran, where Khomeini ridiculed the rights organization as "Travesty International." [14]

Zibakalam said the regime "made it a fantasy, a fairy tale—that the Shah was so bad, and the ayatollahs so good. They made it black-and-white. Now we are gradually reconstructing." But that process was laying bare real divisions between the hard-line right wing and the reformists, which "both have support of substantial parts of the population," Zibakalam told me. "We have reached a point where neither side can do without the other. It's a recipe for violence."

Challenging the Guide of God

The scale of the division was clear in the spontaneous celebration that greeted Iran's unexpected qualification in the World Cup soccer competition in November 1997, months before Iran would actually beat the United States on the soccer field—and I would witness the dramatic rescue of the American flag from burning. Because no one expected Iran to qualify, no one foresaw that people would pour onto the streets, where I saw them flaunting Islamic restrictions. Men and women openly danced, homemade vodka was poured into paper cups, wads of money were thrown from rooftops, flower sellers and chocolatiers gave away their inventories, and some women removed their headscarves.[15]

"If I was a conservative cleric, I'd be quaking in my shoes, because the security forces lost control of Tehran for five hours," a Canadian diplomat told me.[16] "It was a revolution," one Iranian told me, mindful of the special meaning of that word.

BUT THE FLOWING HAIR and sheer disrespect of hearts younger than the Islamic Republic were only the most obvious problems. The protest that cut the deepest against the *velayat-e faqih* and most angered Ayatollah Khamenei came not from dancing soccer fans, but from one of the most powerful ayatollahs in Iran, whose religious rank and status far outweighed that of the "Supreme" Leader.

There are only a handful of grand ayatollahs in the entire Shiite

Muslim world. And for many years in the 1980s, the diminutive Hossein-Ali Montazeri was the one designated to be Khomeini's successor. He was a "source of emulation"—a *marja-e taqlid* who commanded a significant following and had the respect of his peers—while Khamenei as president was still only a mid-ranking *hojjatoleslam*. During the Shah's time, Montazeri had been imprisoned several times for speaking out, and banished to a remote town. From 1979 onward, Montazeri was in charge of exporting the Revolution. Khomeini hailed him as "the fruit of my life."

But Montazeri's history of rebuking injustice continued. In 1988 he wrote letters to Khomeini, criticizing the execution of several thousand political prisoners. In 1989, he marked the tenth anniversary of the Revolution with unprecedented critiques.

"I agree with the new generation of the Revolution that there is a great distance between what we promised and what we have achieved," Montazeri told *Kayhan*.[17] "[T]he denial of people's rights, injustice and disregard for the Revolution's true values have delivered the most severe blows against the Revolution to date."

In his speech to mark the day itself, Montazeri further questioned the conduct of the "sacred" defense of the Iran-Iraq War: "Did we do a good job during the war?" he asked.[18] "Our enemies, who imposed the war on us, emerged victorious. Let us count the forces we lost, the young people we lost, how many towns were destroyed . . . and then let us repent recognizing that we made these mistakes. On many occasions we showed obstinancy [*sic*], shouted slogans, and frightened the people of the world who thought our only task here in Iran was to kill."

Khomeini was furious. Montazeri was removed as the designated successor, stripped of his rank as grand ayatollah, and smeared in a venomous campaign.[19] Portraits of Montazeri were taken down and collected from offices and mosques, the high security walls dismantled around his office in Qom, his guards removed. "The same preachers who, just a day earlier, had asked their congregations to pray for

Montazeri as the 'sublime jurist' and the 'hope of the Imam and the People,' now had to explain why he had to go," writes Baqer Moin in *Khomeini: Life of the Ayatollah*.

God's will had clearly made a U-turn.

"It breaks my heart and my breast is full of agonizing pain when I see that you, the fruit of my life's labor, are so ungrateful," Khomeini wrote in a letter to Montazeri, its contents kept secret for a decade.[20] Montazeri was going to hand Iran over "to the liberals" and had provided "valuable services" to the enemy, Khomeini wrote. "You have inflicted heavy blows on Islam and the Revolution. This is a great act of treason."

Just as painful for Khomeini was the letter he was obliged to write to senior clergy—with whom he had always had a testy relationship. The Revolution was "successful in most aspects," and so was the war, Khomeini argued.[21] It was another example of Orwellian math: two plus two equals five. Never mind that Khomeini had likened his signing of the cease-fire in 1988 to drinking "poison." Nor, as his son Ahmad reported, that after agreeing to the cease-fire, Khomeini "kept hitting himself with his fists saying 'ah,' " could no longer walk, and never again spoke in public.[22]

No, Khomeini now told the clergy, it had all been a triumph:

With God's assistance we have not been defeated and conquered in any way. . . . Each day the war brought a blessing which we used to the full. Through the war we demonstrated our oppression and the aggressor's tyranny. Through the war we unveiled the deceitful face of the world-devourers . . . [W]e broke the backs of both Eastern and Western superpowers [and] consolidated the roots of our Islamic revolution.

. . . we do not repent, nor are we sorry for even a single moment for our performance during the war. Have we forgotten that we fought to fulfill our religious duty and that the result is a marginal issue?[23]

All of Khomeini's rhetorical attention may have tamped out the flames lit by Montazeri, but it was a temporary fix. Montazeri was neither silenced nor intimidated, and his discontent was reignited by Khatami's 1997 victory.

This time his target was the all-powerful *velayat-e faqih*, and the credentials of the man who held that post. Khamenei should "supervise, not rule," Montazeri said: "*Vali-e faqih* should not interfere in all affairs like the Secretary General of the Communist Party. I established *velayat-e faqih* myself and now they call me anti-*vali-e faqih*. . . . Coercion by authorities and officials has made people disgusted with clerics. . . . The red line is [only] God, the Prophet [Mohammad] and Immaculate Imam. There are no red lines except these." [24]

Such insubordination was blasphemy to devotees who knew the Supreme Leader's post was wholly divine and therefore deserved unquestioned obedience. No matter Montazeri's own towering theological credentials. Nor his ironclad revolutionary history. Right-wing vigilantes in Qom stormed Montazeri's house and religious school, and that of another senior cleric who had spoken in his defense. For five years the dissident ayatollah would be under house arrest, the doors of his prayer hall chained shut, its windows broken, security cameras eyeballing every passerby. Anyone could see the graffiti on the wall outside, as I did: "Death to the anti-*vali-e faqih*."

The regime prepared treason charges, and the Supreme Leader struck hard. Khamenei belittled Montazeri as a "politically bankrupt, pathetic and naïve cleric who has taken an erroneous and clumsy stance against the spine of the revolution." [25] He declared of dissidents: "If what they have done is illegal, which it is; if it is treason against the people, which it is—then executive and judicial officials should carry out their duty about these individuals." [26]

But Montazeri's words had merely crowned months of mounting criticism by moderates aimed at the theocracy, and calls for at least some of Khamenei's powers to be transferred to the elected president. Khamenei chose to trumpet his infallibility. Those who questioned his authority "were enemy agents, even though they might not be conscious of it."[27] Iranians should keep their perspective, he said: "You should get to know who the enemy is. World arrogance is the enemy, America is the enemy, the Zionists are the enemy."

EVEN SO, THE DAMAGE had been done. Khamenei's rule and the *velayat-e faqih*, under his supposedly "divine" stewardship, had been knocked from its pedestal. But criticism still wasn't safe. Student leader Heshmatollah Tabarzadi, who had the temerity to call at a rally for a reduction of Khamenei's powers, was set upon and severely beaten, his group's office vandalized.[28] Khatami marked his first one hundred days in office like a playground monitor, by appealing for "a safe environment so that everyone, including dissidents who respect the law, can enjoy their liberty."[29]

And Iranians found much to discuss about the Supreme Leader who had in the past denigrated his own qualifications. As Elaine Sciolino relates in *Persian Mirrors:*

> When I interviewed Khamenei in 1982, he said that no one man could ever replace Khomeini as Supreme Leader, predicting that instead a council of three or five religious leaders would have to rule. He certainly didn't portray himself as a candidate for the job. Indeed, in a rare unguarded conversation just months before Khomeini's death, Khamenei confided to a foreigner, "I'm not qualified to be Supreme Leader. It's not the proper place for me."[30]

History shows in fact how reluctant Khamenei was to take on the role of *rahbar,* or Leader, in the first place. I had heard that never-before-seen footage of the emergency debate, held within hours of Khomeini's death in 1989, had been aired publicly for the first time. Nineteen years after the event, those internal deliberations made up the final episode of a sixteen-part documentary on state-run IRIB TV in 2008.[31] I bought my copy at a small CD shop for less than a dollar, though it was worth far more as a window on the uncertain business of transferring God's authority from one mortal to the next.

In the film, the narrators build suspense by describing how the Assembly of Experts—saddened by the death of Khomeini—was at a loss about who was qualified enough be the next Supreme Leader. But Ali Akbar Rafsanjani was about to share a secret with the chamber, and "say things that show that even in this vital moment, the Imam did not leave his people alone," as he had "pointed to the correct path."

The cameras showed a young-looking Rafsanjani taking charge and telling several stories. In the first, a small group had pressed Khomeini about his choice of successor, when the issue of Montazeri "had become very hot." They were worried that no one else combined the necessary extent of clerical learning and revolutionary background.

Sitting at the front of the chamber, Rafsanjani recounted: "Imam said: Why do you think you don't have anyone suitable? Mr. Khamenei."[32]

"On that day, we thought Imam was just trying to convince us that there are other people, and we are not in a deadlock," Rafsanjani told the assembly. "We decided not to tell anybody; Khamenei himself insisted we don't talk about this anywhere else. He told me, 'I don't want to see you telling this story to anybody.' And I didn't."

Rafsanjani gave another example, in which he privately "really prodded" Khomeini on the issue. "He told me in that meeting that when you have someone like Khamenei, why do you think you have a problem?"

The documentary shifts to an interview with an ayatollah who had been witness to Rafsanjani's words. The cleric said, "Hearts were suddenly changed in the [assembly] by the intervention of God."

Yet the one man still unconvinced was Khamenei himself. He had prayed early that morning, and "implored God, with much begging" that if choosing him as Leader would be harmful, God should "do something so that it doesn't happen." Remarkably, Khamenei sought to block his own appointment. At the moment of decision in the chamber, he looks despondent, holding his face in his left hand, fingers in his beard. He asks to speak but is almost denied by ayatollahs shouting that the "issue was settled" and "there is no need for speaking."

But Khamenei insists, and ascends the podium to argue against his own candidacy. "Listen, gentlemen, I . . . regarding this issue . . . Gentlemen in this issue . . . ," he stutters, trying to come to terms with the moment. Clerics shout him down. "I'm against this, anyway," Khamenei says, then turns and steps down.

All rise in favor of Khamenei as Leader, to chants of "God is great!" The chairman reassures them that Khamenei had "never made concessions to the Global Arrogance," that "with this decision the hope of our enemies . . . will be turned to hopelessness."

THE GROUND HAD ALREADY been prepared during the final months of Khomeini's life to enable a man of such mediocre religious standing as Khamenei—yet with undoubted revolutionary credentials—to become *vali-e faqih*. In the name of expediency (the ever-useful trait, *maslahat*, of compromising principles to save some other "sanctity"), Khomeini simply erased the requirement that the Leader be a *marja'* in the Shiite faith. Until then, the constitution stipulated that only a "just and pious *faqih*," who was "qualified to act as *marja'*," could hold the position.[33]

Also removed was the one explicit bridge between divine rule and the principle of democracy: the Supreme Leader no longer had to be "recognized and accepted . . . by a decisive majority of the people."[34] Instead he would be appointed by "experts elected by the people" and, hopefully, be "possessing [of] general popularity."

To further paper over Khamenei's clerical shortcomings, upon assuming the role of Leader his rank was upgraded overnight to ayatollah. But to this day his qualification to be an official *marja'*, a "source of emulation" in the Shiite faith who has his own authority and disciples and can issue religious edicts—bestowed by some senior clerics in December 1994—is heavily disputed among grand ayatollahs. Desperate to boost his standing, Khamenei had presented himself in Qom but was refused the high spiritual title of *mojtahed*. A joke in Tehran then held that Khamenei "paints" his gray beard white, to fit in with the older ayatollahs.[35]

So Khamenei's tenure as Leader has been consumed by the rather worldly role of balancer of factions in Iran, instead of continuing the far loftier work of Khomeini, who came to be seen, in the words of one historian, "to millions of Iranians . . . like the Old Testament prophets, as the *bot-shekan,* the idol-smasher, and as *the* Imam, the religious and political leader of the community."[36]

The Pedigree of Violence

Shortly after Montazeri's stunning criticism of Khamenei and his house arrest in late 1997, I visited Qom to hear from one of his fellow grand ayatollahs, Nasser Makarem Shirazi. Speaking to me in offices not far from Montazeri's embattled compound—where police had to use tear gas to end the vigilante assault, and plainclothes agents loitered to keep a close watch on anyone even passing by the low metal door—Shirazi said the dispute should be resolved by law, not on the street. He admitted an impact: "The best way to undermine the position of *velayat-e faqih* is to have someone revolutionary . . . do it," the full-bearded grand ayatollah told me.[37] But he dismissed any real threat to clerical rule: "We think we've been through a lot more than this."

Yet this was not just a theological debate, confined to the elaborately tiled and yellow-bricked shrines and seminaries of Qom. Young people were complaining that their vote had limited value. "Many of those who were [revolutionaries] with Khomeini now have children who ask them: 'What bullshit are you telling me?' They see *velayat-e faqih* as a tool to keep others from power," a Swiss diplomat told me, noting President Khatami's embattled position.[38] "The Persian mind turns against those who hold power. Khatami won, but if he doesn't keep up the momentum it will be dangerous, because the people will turn against him. Here [in Iran], the father who does not impose himself is disdained."

And hard-line elements *were* imposing themselves in Khatami's place. First among them were militants of Ansar-e Hezbollah (Followers of the Party of God). Their clandestine patrons were the hardest ayatollahs. Over the years I have glimpsed these sinister vigilantes in action, streaming to their targets on motorbikes, young bearded men frequently wearing religious headbands and with clubs and sticks and thick lengths of chain. They had published a manifesto in 1995, taking out full-page newspaper ads to announce: "Until our throats be cut, we will fight the supporters of the West and of anti-fundamentalist tendencies."[39]

Their impact was far greater than their very small number of core fighters would suggest. The street-level bloodletting and brutishness applied by Ansar and other shadowy *hezbollahi* groups during the Khatami era deeply affected the efforts of reform activists. Michael Rubin notes in one of the few detailed studies:

> Vigilante groups pose serious challenges to Iranian reformers and to any future rapprochement between Iran and the West. Every political and social crisis in Iran sets back the clock and gives hardliners an excuse to roll back reform, ostensibly for the sake of preserving internal stability and national security. . . .
>
> Few hardliners find it in their interest to renounce power voluntarily, realizing they will not likely win at the ballot box without compromising on their more radical positions. Vigilante groups . . . create an alternative—a way for hardliners to forestall reform without having to take direct responsibility for the violent acts precipitated toward that end.[40]

SUCH "PRESSURE" GROUPS HAD featured in Iran long before the Revolution marshaled them against its blaspheming opponents. "The root of [this] violence is very simple: The mullahs of Iran for centuries relied on small groups of acolytes, vigilante groups, to enforce their fatwas [religious edicts]," professor Reza Alavi told me in Tehran.[41]

"In villages, that is how mullahs ruled and enforced. When they took power in Iran, they put this on a gigantic scale," he said. "These techniques were used by fascists of Europe. Islam has been an extremely violent religion. The first four [Shiite] imams were assassinated, and violence has been a tool of political Islam almost since the first day."

Scholars record how even at Shiite holy shrines in Iraq, Iranians carrying books about a minority school of thought in the eighteenth century were "obliged to cover them up for fear of attack."[42] Also in the late 1700s, ranking clerics increasingly asserted "the function of the religious scholar as arbiter and enforcer of the law," notes historian Hamid Algar. That lesson was learned "most effectively" by the son of one of the most prominent Shiite Iranian luminaries of the day, who "was constantly accompanied by a number of armed men who would immediately execute any judgments that he passed. The example . . . was to be followed by numerous Iranian *ulama* [clerical communities]."[43]

Ranking clerics ordered the deaths of numerous followers of various Sufi orders from the late eighteenth century.[44] One cleric who in 1844 claimed to be the "gate" to the missing Twelfth Imam was banished, then finally executed in 1850, as his followers "engaged in rebellion in various parts of the country."[45]

Conflict burned between rival schools of Shiite belief from the early nineteenth century, over the case of a popular cleric who claimed to have direct contact with long-dead imams, and was labeled an infidel. The controversy "continued to inspire sporadic but violent clashes" until the early 1900s.[46] And in 1905 a "minor war" erupted between rival believers in Kerman over control of the city's religious endowment.

During World War I, Iranian clerics issued fatwas calling for resistance against invading Russian and British forces, and even mounted militias and "jihad movements."[47] One of them, launched in 1917 to take on both the central government and foreign forces, mustered six thousand men and is considered the "first guerrilla movement in modern Iranian history."

That tradition was never broken. It wasn't too big a leap from those impulses to the creation in 1945 of the militant Fadaiyan-e Islam (Devotees of Islam), which was the first to aim for an Islamic state and to rely on violence to get there. Among members was the grizzled "Haji" Bakhshi, that surviving cheerleader of the Iran-Iraq War front I had met with his bandoliers of bullets and broken hand, who as a boy had blown up the British officer with American dynamite.

Half a century ago, the Fadaiyan-e Islam was an important precursor to modern-day vigilantes, and its constituency was the "religiously oriented segments of the disaffected urban poor; hence the radical methods they used," records historian Algar.[48] "The most conspicuous method used by the Fadaiyan was the assassination of persons considered dangerous to the interests of Islam and Iran." Though the Fadaiyan were dispersed after the CIA's 1953 coup—its leaders "manfully undergoing severe and prolonged torture" before execution, according to Algar—"their example of militancy did . . . foreshadow the rise of Islamically oriented guerrilla movements of the late 1960s and the 1970s."

The vigilante tactic was also used by the secular Shah, whose dictatorship was so complete that Washington insiders snidely called Iran a "one-bullet state."[49] In 1978, in an effort to stop the cycle of forty-day mourning periods that invariably drew more protesters onto the streets—and made more martyrs—SAVAK created its own Underground Committee of Revenge. It "sent threatening letters to the lawyers and writers prominent in the human rights movement," accused them of being American stooges, and kidnapped and beat some activists, while bombing a number of offices, writes historian Abrahamian.[50]

The Shah's single-party showpiece Resurgence Party also "set up a vigilante force called the Resistance Corps, staffed it with policemen in civilian clothes, and attacked meetings organized by student groups, the Writer's Association, and the [Mossadegh-founded] National Front. In one such attack, the Resistance Corps, pretending to be irate workers, seriously injured thirty people who were celebrating 'Ayd-i Qurban (Day of Sacrifice) in the private gardens of a National Front leader."

Violence had become a necessary and acceptable tool. "For Believers, this goes to the heart of belief," a Western-educated political scientist told me.[51] "There are theological and ideological justifications, because the defense of the *nezam* [Islamic system] is a sacred duty. So violence can be used. A lot of people have done it for twenty years, so it is a normal part of statecraft, like a bureaucrat signing a paper: 'If there is a danger, it has to be taken care of.' It could start from intimidation, all the way to killing."

One reason was that key figures on the right aspired to a "pure" Mohammadan society, a throwback to the idealized seventh-century rule of the Prophet. "These people are the Shiite Taliban," one professor told me.[52] "They very much believe in the divine right of rule. They believe in people, so long as the people follow the Leader—it's religious fascism."

Some heavyweight theologians felt otherwise. "This Islam does not allow anyone to kill a cat, much less kill a human being," Grand Ayatollah Yusef Saanei told me in Qom, his eyelids flitting as they often did when he spoke.[53] The problem was not with Islam, but with implementing it. "I believe that someday, all the people in the world will say Islam is democracy, and democracy is Islam."

But that someday appeared a long way off. Iranians may have been fighting for democracy for more than a century, but it was so alien to Iran's traditional culture of despotism that the Persian-language equivalent of the word *democracy* was only coined in 2001, halfway through the Khatami presidency: *mardom salari,* or "people-ocracy," with the suffix *-dini* sometimes added to make it "religious" democracy.

Hard-liners proved repeatedly that legal restrictions meant nothing to their foot soldiers. Khomeini had made clear that securing the system—*hefz-e nezam*—was the "highest" obligation for a Muslim, a higher priority than even prayer and fasting. They believed it, so anything was allowed. As former foreign minister Yazdi put it, "The Shah was state terror [but] after the Revolution there was naked violence, naked terrorism."[54]

Khomeini told Yazdi that for the Revolution to endure, "sometimes it is needed to . . . kill someone."[55] Khamenei was a Believer, too, and stated during one Friday prayer sermon, "When the Islamic state has to deal with bullying, aggression, riots, and instances of lawbreaking, it must be tough and decisive. It must deal with the matter violently. It must not be frightened of the word violence. . . . When the Prophet of Islam issued orders to have some individuals killed, he did not whisper those orders into someone's ear. He spoke out openly and in public. . . ."[56]

That mind-set girded the use of violence throughout the Khatami era. In September 1998, for example, Khamenei spoke of the need to purge "deviationist interpretations" and "negative and destructive teachings of Western freedom."[57] The next day Khatami's interior minister, Abdollah Nouri, and culture minister, Ataollah Mohajerani, were both physically attacked by eighty militants after Friday prayers. A passerby quoted Mohajerani's wife shouting: "Stop it! Leave him alone! You are killing him!"[58] Ansar denied it conducted the beatings, calling them "regrettable" and "suspicious," while suggesting they were the work of reformists themselves who wanted to benefit from "chaotic conditions."

The hard-line strategy was to maintain constant crisis.

My friend the Sage—a former radical revolutionary himself—spoke to one *hezbollahi* the day militants had broken up a prodemocracy demonstration in 1998. He asked, "If the people are against you, will you step aside?"[59] The militant said no: "This is a fact, that always the righteous in history are the minority." Just the night before, the *hezbollahi* and his senior officer had debated how many Iranians might turn out if an open-air concert were held in Tehran by Googoosh—Iran's pre-Revolution pop star. The militant estimated three to four million; his commander, thirty million, or nearly half the population of the country. "That's why we are willing to die for our cause," the militant concluded. "Even if we have to strap grenades onto ourselves and go into a crowd of bad people."

Those "bad people" were the ones who found a hero in Grand Ayatollah Montazeri, whose years of house arrest in Qom had only enhanced his reputation as a dissident. He had become a "symbol of the ills plaguing the Islamic Republic and a model of the ideal, plainspoken cleric [who] was a crusader for people's rights and liberties," note Geneive Abdo and Jonathan Lyons in their book *Answering Only to God*.[60]

Montazeri's house arrest had lasted five years, but these two journalists managed to elicit an eight-thousand-word fatwa from him, by fax, in early 1999. In Iran, they noted, it was the equivalent of receiving a detailed critique of the Soviet system from the dissident physicist Andrei Sakharov during his exile in Gorky. While still under lock and key, Montazeri said it was his "religious duty" and in the interest of the Revolution to tell the truth and "defend the legitimate rights and freedoms of the people."[61]

"No one can claim to have access to the absolute truth," Montazeri wrote. Islam "does not recognize the concentration of power in the hand of a fallible human being." Many of the regime's current rulers had been his pupils, Montazeri wrote: "I am very sad and sorry to see [today] there is no tolerance in the Islamic society [and] the children of the Revolution . . . are being sent to jail on a daily basis under various pretexts."

The cleric noted that he had "spent a lifetime" fighting for people's rights and the honor of Iran: "In a condition where I am being treated like this, what can others expect?"[62]

Poisoned Pen-Holders

Of the many figurative front lines that carved their way across Iran's political and cultural battleground, few were as literal as the white building on Africa Street. Wire-mesh screens were bolted across windows to deflect grenade attacks (there had already been one by late 1999). And the structure was ringed by a tall wrought-iron fence with sharpened tines. These were the fortresslike offices of the reformist newspaper *Khordad*, where journalists saw themselves on a mission to liberalize Iranian thinking.

"This is the most important battlefield," said Emadeddin Baghi, a bearded columnist who once trained as a cleric and in coming years would do stint after stint in prison.[63] He had big, welcoming hands and wore his shoes loose to easily remove for prayers. A master of shifting metaphors—and of striking fear in some hard-line hearts with his pen—Baghi told me of the importance of journalism: "The press today is like a bottle of life for reformists: If it is not broken, reformists will stay; if it is broken, they will not."

Hard-liners were trying to break that bottle. They had shut down six newspapers in the previous year, and *Khordad* looked like it might be next. Its embattled director, Abdollah Nouri, was a popular senior cleric and former interior minister and vice president—the one physically attacked with the culture minister after Friday prayers in 1998. He was now in court facing charges of apostasy. It was all part of the Fourth Estate growing up in Iran, Baghi told me. "To me it is natural, like a baby learning to walk. You fall and stand up."

But these risks were far greater. Five reformist intellectuals—three of them writers—had already been assassinated. Student protests had been brutally put down. Journalists and reform activists were being imprisoned. The most recent closure had been *Neshat*, the third newspaper in a series of shuttered titles put out by the same reformist team. The editor, once severely beaten by vigilantes himself, was arrested and thrown into Evin Prison.

WHAT DROVE THESE EMBATTLED writers to push the limits, to embrace their defiant vision of press freedom? A firm belief that the glasnost they were forging—and risking so much for—could not be reversed. Writer Baghi was philosophical yet energized, sitting in his office where four out of six fluorescent strip lights didn't work, a faded map of Iran on the wall, brimming ashtrays fighting for desk space with bowls of sugar lumps, used tea glasses, and a very old phone. His work had done much to expose the regime's hand in the killings.

"When you see your country unwell, it is your natural obligation to treat it. And when you enter the press, this is a case of life and death. Once you make that decision, you know no fear," Baghi told me. And in the case of defeat? "We don't call it martyrdom, in which you lose your life for God. We call it *isar,* which means you sacrifice your power, influence, title, and prosperity in a religious way."

The results of this journalistic audacity were unique in Iran. People often stood in line before dawn to get a six-cent copy of their choice of reformist newspapers. Khatami's emphasis on press freedom meant three times as many titles to choose from. "In the past, nobody was buying papers because there was no *reason* to buy them," an Asian diplomat explained.[64] "Those journalists have been very courageous and undergone much suffering to print these things."

And those things were drawing fire from the far right, the reason for grenade grates over the windows. Entire newsrooms had been upended by rampaging thugs. But the papers had their allies, too. The closure of *Salam* newspaper sparked, in July 1999, six days of violent student unrest. Afterward the Assembly of Experts accused the media of "revealing their disbelief in the Leader, the Prophet, and the clergy." It blamed a "number of pen-holders" for supporting the "enemy" during the student unrest.

Yet few reformist journalists questioned the legitimacy of the Revolution itself, or whether Iran should have a pious state. Like Khatami, they argued for a flexible interpretation of Islam that combined religion with liberalism, pluralism, and the rule of law in a civil society.

"We are against revolution from above, and we're against revolution from below," Hamid Reza Jalaeipour, publisher of *Jameah (Society)* newspaper told me.[65] I was speaking to him in mid-1998, just as *Jameah* had become Iran's latest—and most targeted—title on the newsstand. He called it the "first civil society newspaper in Iran," and it didn't last long. Born in February, its daily print run of 50,000 expanded to

300,000—which could sell out in an hour—before its license was revoked in June. The paper had been aiming for a million. But Jalaeipour was charged with printing "insults . . . and publication of lies to agitate public opinion."

The crime in fact was quoting the unreconstructed Revolutionary Guard chief Brigadier General Yahya Rahim Safavi as he lashed out against President Khatami's policies in April 1998. Initial reports said the comments were made in public in Qom, and other newspapers ran portions of the speech. Iran's armed forces were taking a political stand—something that Khomeini had always forbidden.

"Newspapers are published these days which are threatening our national security. They contain the same material as American newspapers," Safavi had said.[66] And he was just warming up.

"Liberals have entered the foray with cultural artillery. They have taken over our universities and our youth are now shouting slogans against despotism," Safavi said. "We are seeking to root out these antirevolutionaries wherever they are. We have to behead some and cut off the tongues of others. Our language is our sword. We will expose these cowards."

The general criticized Khatami for weakness, exemplified by his policy of "dialogue among civilizations." He said he had told Culture Minister Mohajerani that "his way was threatening national security." Mohajerani replied that "no one had the right to suppress a thought just because he is opposed to it. Human beings are born to think."

Khatami fought back, too, when he spoke before the Revolutionary Guard officers himself. "The society cannot move forward with narrow-mindedness and through creation of an atmosphere of terror," Khatami said.[67] "True Islam means that all fair beings willing to coexist in an Islamic society are dear. . . . We should show this in practice and establish justice throughout the nation."

While Khatami's words evaporated without a trace, those of Safavi were given new life in print—and then in the courts. Safavi's lawyer reportedly told the court the speech was "internal" to the Guard, and therefore confidential. Jalaeipour was banned from publishing for a year and fined five thousand dollars, but when I found him he was still publishing until the final verdict on the first of seven newspaper titles he would work through during the reform era. Eventually he would be driven out of newspaper publishing entirely.

Jalaeipour was an unshaven prime example of a revolutionary turned reformist. He called himself and the other founders of *Jameah* "religious intellectuals." They had believed in the 1979 Revolution and in changing the world with Islam. But they were taken aback by the totalitarian turn of the regime, and now believed in a more democratic interpretation. Jalaeipour had the credentials: He was imprisoned by the Shah and spent eight years as a Revolutionary Guard soldier himself. He survived the bloodied front lines of the Iran-Iraq War, but two of his brothers did not; a third was killed by the Mojahedin. He sold his father's shop in the bazaar to come up with the cash for his original 17 percent investment in *Jameah*.

"We believe in dialogue, and are against the closed mind and the closed society," Jalaeipour told me. The paper boldly pushed the limits of press freedom. *Jameah* had been critical of the snail's pace of Khatami's reforms. It gave front-page treatment to President Bill Clinton's comments about possible "reconciliation" between the United States and Iran, which other papers buried inside or ignored. It planned to put in a request to interview Clinton.[68] *Jameah* was also packed with sports and Hollywood gossip. Conservatives feared the paper, he said, "because it could shape public opinion."

Mohsen Sazegara, a founder of the Revolutionary Guard who helped launch the newspaper, told *Time* magazine, "People read *Jameah* because we don't lie." The surge of readers gave these newsrooms a real sense of power—and an unreal sense of their own ability to prevail.

Editor Jalaeipour predicted: "Today we are in a democratic atmosphere, and revolutionary ideology is not forever." But that would have been news to Ayatollah Khamenei, who in 1998 condemned the reformist press as the "crawling cultural advance of the enemy."[69] That was as good as a direct order to the Revolutionary Guard. "American dollars are turning into articles in liberal newspapers," warned Guard commander Safavi.[70] "If such cultural sedition reaches an intolerable level, the [Guard] will act under duty and confront anti-revolutionary groups in whatever disguise."

Among the most dangerous to the regime was Akbar Ganji, a former Revolutionary Guard intelligence officer—and later a well-known dissident and imprisoned hunger striker—who wrote a series of groundbreaking stories about intelligence agents involved in the murders of intellectuals.

"Some people in this country play with this issue of death," Ganji told me.[71] "Some people like football, some people like murderous games. To reach for something, you have to pay for it." With his thin, short hair and stubble, Ganji seemed an unlikely iconoclast, sprightly but serious, as if the regime had already got the better of him. The investigative journalist had done prison time and seemed to be pushing for more. A sweeping new press law before parliament would give the police, Intelligence Ministry, and judiciary the right to veto publication licenses and empower judges to overrule jury verdicts on the press. For the first time individual journalists would be held accountable, not just their directors.

One friend of mine was already caught in the maw. He had been ordered to turn in his press card and was accused of espionage.[72] Intelligence agents appeared with a warrant—portraying themselves first as couriers, with a parcel he had to come downstairs to sign for—then searched his apartment. They took his passport, a stack of his news reports, and a toy pirate's flintlock pistol that he had rescued years before from a garbage pile. The agents labeled that item "antique gun"—to this day he still has the useless relic, with a Revolutionary Court tag and case number attached to the grip. They took away his illegal satellite dish, as well as a pornography magazine left behind by a friend, and they opened and poured three cans of beer down the kitchen sink—scolding him that it was "illegal."

During questioning at the Intelligence Ministry, the agents focused on small, silly things, prompting my colleague to believe the case was not serious, but only the agents proving their worth to their superiors. He was asked why he—in the presence of foreign journalists—had once "revealed" what everyone knew already, that Iranian journalists had contact with the Intelligence Ministry. He was told he had "challenged" the ministry when he had refused in the past—due to the presence of his mother and sister—to allow his place to be used as an intelligence stakeout to eavesdrop on suspect neighbors across the street.

The interrogators appeared severe, making a show during the interrogation of ordering the journalist's file: *"Bring the file!"* an agent bellowed. He flipped its pages throughout, but when my friend was able to catch a glimpse, he saw that the pages were blank. He was lucky. In this case espionage charges were eventually dropped, the press card reinstated.

"WE ARE REACHING A stage of democracy that has a cost," crusading journalist Akbar Ganji told me. He pointed out that thousands had died or disappeared to disrupt dictatorship in Argentina, Chile, and other Latin American countries. By comparison, Iran's casualties had been few. Ganji said he hoped Iran's model would be like the 1989 bloodless "Velvet Revolution" of Czechoslovakia—a phrase that would obsess Iranian intelligence chiefs and military commanders for years to come.

"We opened the door [of press freedom], and all these genies jumped out," Ganji said. "The power-hungry leaders are trying to catch them and put them back, but they can't. These genies are instead duplicating themselves, causing people to have new goals, expectations, and demands."

And while those hopes grew, Ganji had one aim: "We will write, write, and write until we find the truth."

"Khatami, Where Are You?"

Feeling the promise of those expectations was the new crop of students, unborn during the street clashes of the Revolution. Students had proven their ability to change history in Iran—their takeover of the U.S. Embassy in 1979 being just one example. Now Khatami's victory, his message of openness and law and civil society, and the newspapers that spread those ideas were an intoxicating elixir on college campuses. Every year "Student Day" marked the 1953 killings when U.S. vice president Nixon visited Tehran, and the Shah's police shot dead three student protesters.

Remembering that day in late 1997, one of the most influential and controversial philosophers of Iran's reformation, Abdolkarim Soroush, ascended the podium. He was a former revolutionary ideologue who had served for four years on Khomeini's Advisory Council on the Cultural Revolution—a group of seven tasked with changing curricula and "cleansing the universities," which was responsible for expelling numerous professors and students.[73] In 1980, Ayatollah Khomeini had railed against "imperialist universities" that had only trained students to be "infatuated by the West."[74] Professors were "brainwashing and miseducating our youth." Khomeini closed universities for three years; Soroush had been a key player in the purge.

But since then, Soroush turned against the "divine right" to rule. From the 1990s he had become renowned as the Islamic Martin Luther, and as a result his appearances increasingly drew hostile vigilantes from Ansar-e Hezbollah. Once he barely escaped the clutch of militants who had a noose ready for lynching.

Student Day signified both the quest for knowledge and fight against injustice, and a student "should correctly know what is the manifestation of injustice in this time," Soroush said.[75] "In our time, loyalty to human rights" should prevail: "The faithful students should also know the injustice done to the religion and repel it. To commit violence, to spread hatred and crushing criticism, and to want students to be bowing . . . sycophancy, spread of superstition, and putting power above righteousness in the name of religion are exact cases of injustice. . . ."

When asked about the success and dynamism of student movements, Soroush quoted Ali Shariati, that key pre-Revolution ideologue whose work inspired so many to resist the Shah in the name of Shiism. Shariati said that students enjoy the "blessing of deprivation," such that they had not yet sacrificed their ideals to "fame, bread, welfare, power, and wealth."

"This freedom from burdens is the secret of the success of students," Soroush said, before challenging the sanctity of divine clerical rule: "Regrettably some in our society have interpreted [*velayat-e faqih*] as if it is an area of absolute powers and rights without any duty and responsibility. . . . To be superior does not just mean having more rights. It also means to be more responsible."

The students were listening. And so were the militants, whose idea of "responsibility" meant going after promulgators of such sacrilege. Soroush events were often attacked—one lecture hall where he had just spoken had been burned down—and when I found him in late 1997, Soroush said he had to "smuggle" himself to keep safe.[76]

"The only thing: I am able to breathe—this is the only thing," Soroush told me. "They dislike me because I'm a religious person; if I were secular they would not be afraid. But religious ideas from religious people are very influential." President Khatami may have heralded a cultural renaissance and wellspring of political hope. Yet the violence showed how little had changed: "Thugs came with flags and physically attacked—that demonstrates very clearly to me no change. [Hard-liners] have not taken and are not willing to take the message of the elections," Soroush said of Khatami's ballot box success. "The election showed that the situation can't remain, despite the wishes of those elements."

The dissident was talking blasphemy against the *velayat-e faqih*. "Religion is infallible, but those who interpret it are not," Soroush told me. "To borrow from a Marxist phrase, 'Time is not on their side.' "

• • •

MONTHS LATER, KHATAMI BASKED in a fifteen-minute ovation during the rousing rally that marked the one-year anniversary
of his election. Young supporters repeatedly interrupted their hero's
speech with calls of "Khatami, we love you!"[77]

But the contours of conflict were already clear, so the president
called followers to use "patience and forbearance" to establish freedom within the law—and avoid going too far.[78]

"Desired and legitimate freedom may come under attack from
those who disagree with the essence of freedom and who are by nature attached to prejudices. . . . They think that the only way they can
survive is through the elimination of their rival," Khatami said. Freedom "does not mean anarchy," but hard-liners should take care.

"Let me declare myself clearly. The destiny of the religion's social prestige today and tomorrow will depend on our interpretation
of the religion in a manner which would not contradict freedom,"
Khatami warned. "Whenever in history a religion has faced freedom,
it has been the religion which has sustained damage. Even if justice has
contradicted freedom, justice has suffered. When progress and construction have curtailed freedom, they have been undermined."

Khatami was aiming to find a new balance, because "it is not freedom if only the people who agree with those in power . . . are free.
Freedom means the freedom of the opposition," he said. "The art of
government is not to eliminate the opposition [but] to compel even its
own opposition to behave within the framework of the law."

SEVERAL BATTLES STAND OUT from the state-sanctioned thug-
gery of the Khatami era; ironically, the first serious clash came just
two days after those presidential platitudes. Khatami had warned
reformists against going too far. "We have to understand what kind
of freedom we are after, and understand the reality of the country
we live in," he said. That wasn't enough for the hard-line newspaper
Jomhuri-e Eslami, which complained of "radical and diversionary slogans" at the rally.[79] "Such slogans did not help to bring hearts closer.

There is a fear that they will only intensify mutual recrimination and open the way for those who want to disrupt peace."

That fear was quickly realized—but with violence from the right. Some two thousand students holding a prodemocracy rally in Laleh Park downtown were attacked by sixty to one hundred vigilantes from Ansar-e Hezbollah. Police did nothing for twenty minutes, then tried to restore calm with bullhorns, saying that the rally had been permitted by the Interior Ministry: "Please allow them to continue." [80]

The hard-liners—whose ranks eventually swelled to about four hundred—"heckled the police." Students fought back, shouting: "Long Live Freedom" and "Taliban, Taliban, this is not Afghanistan."

Canisters of tear gas rained down; twenty students were injured. One *hezbollahi* shouted: "We don't want freedom. Freedom will lead to a day when veils will be dropped and the Americans will return to Iran. Freedom will lead to a dead end. We will continue to fight against such a trend and will not allow it." [81]

After the confrontation, reported witness Afshin Valinejad, "students regrouped and fixed speakers broken during the melee. But they then abandoned the effort to resume the rally after the Ansar-e Hezbollah poured gas on the truck carrying their equipment and injured the driver." [82]

Before Khatami was elected, the right wing warned that the changes he wanted would unglue Iran's revolutionary society, that "peace and tranquility" would disintegrate from constant tension. Like a self-fulfilling prophecy, actions of Ansar were making that happen. "The risk of a backlash is great, but instead of coming to terms with the reality that twenty million Iranians are behind Khatami, [conservatives] are choosing to ignore that," the Sage told me.[83] The attacks "display the biggest worry of the conservatives that things are getting out of hand and that nothing is sacred anymore. They are trying to get back to the 'good old days' when they were in control, and there were a limited number of voices."

· · ·

BUT THAT CONTROL WAS not restored without more, much more, violence. It was touched off in early July 1999 with the passage of a draconian draft press law by the conservative parliament, which gave hard-line authorities new powers to muzzle the increasingly irreverent media and punish journalists. The key to keeping Khatami's agenda high in the public eye had been reformist newspapers. Among a list of vague new restrictions was any violation of "Islamic values" or tarnishing the reputation of senior clerics. Almost immediately, the popular pro-Khatami newspaper *Salam* was shut down, under the pretext of publishing a secret Ministry of Intelligence memo that had called for those very press restrictions.

Late that evening, two hundred students staged a peaceful demonstration against the *Salam* closure, then retired for the night. What happened next created a storm of outrage.

At 3 A.M., some four hundred Ansar-e Hezbollah and Basij militants and police burst into the dorms, beating students mercilessly while they slept and throwing a few from windows. A number of students were reported dead, dozens were hospitalized, and scores arrested. Afterward, according to journalists on the scene, "dorm rooms resembled bombed out shells in the war zones of Lebanon or the Gaza Strip. Blood-spattered walls had caved in and windows were shattered, covering the floors in glass." [84]

The students' peaceful protest had "handed the conservatives the chance to create enough horror so that no student would dare to protest again," write journalists Abdo and Lyons. "The students, too, had waited for such a moment to validate their grievances with the system: There was neither law nor order in the Islamic Republic. Freewheeling hooligans sanctioned by the state would stop at nothing to quell political dissent."

There was almost universal condemnation—a phenomenon that surprised many. In their first reaction, Ayatollah Khamenei's representatives chastised "members of law-enforcement forces and irresponsible elements."

"Even the rightists are condemning this as unacceptable," Shirzad

Bozorgmehr, then deputy editor of the *Iran News,* told me.[85] "So some believe that this could be the beginning of the end of these little extremist groups that did whatever they wanted and got away with it." The press law was affront enough, he said, but true to form the hardliners "immediately went too far" and closed down *Salam.*

In fact, six days of rebellion would witness a definitive defeat of the students, prove the efficacy of those vigilantes, and demonstrate that conservatives would use every lever—and length of chain—to win. During the protest, students chanted, "Either Islam and the law, or another Revolution." They boldly shouted against the Leader, blaming Ayatollah Khamenei for the acts of the vigilantes: "Ansar commits crimes, and the Leader supports them. O great Leader, shame on you," the students cried.[86] "Death to despotism! Death to dictators!"

None of it changed the outcome. The Revolution had rarely seen such internal combustion. Student leaders were trying to protest the undemocratic excesses of the Islamic system, not overthrow it. But that message was lost in violence that harked back to clashes earlier in the Revolution, when Khomeini ordered his three-year university closure. Back then, he told students to "not resist or try to sabotage" the process of Islamization.[87] If any did, he would "instruct the nation as to how to respond."

Khomeini would declare: "It is not Western power we must fear, it is Western ideas." [88]

NEARLY TWO DECADES LATER, the hard-line descendents of that viral need to purge "miseducated" students held tight to their truncheons. Among those arrested in 1999 was Mohammad Reza Kasrani, who told the BBC of four days of police beatings to the soles of his feet with a cable—that favorite practice of the Shah's SAVAK—and a month of "psychological torture." He said it was all part of a successful regime effort to "create an atmosphere of terror" in Iran:

> At one stage, I heard the voices of my parents from another room. They were told that I was going to be executed. Then I heard my

mother faint and then my father cried and begged them not to kill me.

I heard them say to my parents: "For this bastard, you should not even read Quran after his death."

I said to God: "I am going to be killed for my country's freedom and for my religion, now my parents cannot even mourn for me."

Later, when I was freed, I found out that they played the recorded voice of my parents from another room. They put me in a situation where I was totally convinced my parents were being tortured.

Before I was arrested, I always believed that we could criticize the Islamic establishment by peaceful dialogue and that the officials would reform the system.

But after my arrest, my belief has completely changed.[89]

Behind the crackdown was an assumption of longevity of the regime. One student from Shiraz later wrote about how he tried to get to Tehran for the protests.[90] Before even leaving Shiraz, he was pulled off the bus by police, blindfolded, and questioned:

He asked his questions very calmly. Until, that is, he said: "Do you know that if we arrest you in the demonstrations you will be put away for ten years?"

And I said: "Do you think these people will be around another ten years?"

Suddenly he got really angry and said: "You son of a bitch! Do you want me to empty this gun in your head, so then you'll realize who'll be around for another ten years?"

I said, "No, I'm sorry," and started groveling.

The cold metal gun against my head gave me a feeling of helplessness. I knew I could do nothing. . . .

Amid the ongoing street battles of 1999, the image that emerged as icon was that of Ahmad Batebi, a Persian prince with long black hair and a protest headband, who held up the bloodied shirt of a fellow student who had been shot as a warning to other students. The photo was on the cover of the *Economist* yet would prove to be an image of defiance, not victory.

That photograph evoked the 1979 Revolution itself, in its visceral anti-Shah urgency—an ironic fact that would have enraged hard-liners all the more. But neither Batebi nor the students he epitomized would triumph. The first Batebi knew of the image was when the judge put the British magazine before him in court and declared: "You have signed your own death sentence."[91]

Batebi was sentenced to death and from prison wrote a letter to the judiciary chief detailing abuse. Whenever he protested his treatment, he wrote, he was told that "this is the land of the *velayat* and that I should be blinded and not allowed to live here."[92] His testicles were beaten with a metal cable, his teeth kicked in with a boot, his head plunged into a drain full of excrement, until he inhaled into his nose and mouth. Batebi concluded his letter with a quote from the Prophet Mohammad: "A ruler can remain without believing in God but never through oppression."

Batebi's death sentence was commuted to fifteen years in prison, then ten. By early 2008, he had spent a total of eight years behind bars. Speaking later to the *New York Times,* Batebi described being strapped to a chair and cut, his jailers rubbing salt into the wounds.[93] Twice he had been taken to the gallows, blindfolded. Once he passed out from fear when the noose had been around his neck for forty-five minutes; the next time prisoners on either side of him were hanged. Out of prison for treatment after several seizures, the thirty-one-year-old made a dramatic escape from Iran through the mountains to Iraq, using a Kurdish underground network of people traffickers.

His Iranian interrogator tracked Batebi down in northern Iraq, calling him on a cell phone issued by the UN: "We know where you are. You must turn yourself in," Batebi was told. Allowed into the United States, his reply to Tehran on his blog was emphatic: "Your hands will never reach me," Batebi taunted, with a link to a photo of him in Washington, standing in front of the domed U.S. Capitol.

. . .

DURING THAT SCALDING SUMMER of 1999, the dreams of
Khatami and his twenty million voters were caught in a revolutionary
brawl. It was an "unpredictable" situation, but an "unavoidable labor
pain" attending Iran's new birth, the dissident Ebrahim Yazdi told me
on the first day of protests.[94] He was optimistic. But then the student
protests escalated, along with the overwhelming desire by hard-liners
to crush them.

Portraits of the Supreme Leader were torched; security forces were
struck with stones. The students produced a communiqué with fourteen demands to make Iran's theocracy more accountable. "Those
who have based their rule on the principle of conquest [through] terror are now facing the consequence of their atrocities," the students
wrote.[95] "There is such a volcano of national rage erupting in the university, as the eternal vanguard of freedom, that if demands of this nation are not heeded by the tyrannical forces, the flame of this inferno
shall burn all the present authorities in this regime."

Elaine Sciolino of the *New York Times,* who had also covered the
Revolution, was in Tehran and watched the peak fifth night, which
continued "with a frenzy" of beatings.[96] "The vigilantes attacked with
stones, sticks, chains, metal cables, knives, and meat cleavers as well
as their traditional green batons. The cleavers reminded me of the
butcher knives carried by black-clad women in the days after Khomeini's victory, when they called for revenge against the Shah's generals."

From her front-row seat at two such formative events of the Islamic
Republic, Sciolino noted that the student protests "did not seem like
another revolution. In fact, the demonstrations showed not how close
Iran was to the flowering of a second revolution, but how far."

For days, Khatami did not speak, despite the express pleas of students. They expected his support at such a crucial juncture. The protests and counterattacks had spread across Iran. "Khatami, where are
you?" students in Tehran begged.[97] "Khatami, your students have been
killed!"

And when Khatami finally did comment, it sounded like a betrayal.

He calmed his loyalists, and condemned the "deviation" that had led rioters to "aim . . . to inflict damage to the foundation of the system and engender violence, tension, and disturbance in society."[98] Students had said they were not to blame. Rioters "must be stopped and we will withstand them," Khatami vowed.

In his first reaction, Supreme Leader Khamenei said the "bitter incident hurt my heart."[99] Then he said the violence would be stopped—with more violence. Officials had been "emphatically instructed to put down the corrupt and warring elements with insight and power," he said. "My *basiji* children in particular should maintain their full alertness . . . and everywhere they are needed, terrify and crush the wicked enemies."

There was another day of brutality during which Ansar vigilantes shaved their beards to "change their look" to better infiltrate the crowds, students later told me.[100] That was followed by a large but listless pro-regime counterrally, with the usual offering of "every drop" of blood to the Leader.

And then it was over. The tally was five or six dead. Hundreds wounded. Some fourteen hundred arrested. Countless curses against the police, the vigilantes, the Supreme Leader—and for the first time, Khatami. Banks and shops were burned, windows smashed. Police cars and motorcycles and buses were overturned, and some burned, along with the Friday prayer platform at Tehran University.[101]

But that was not all: Khatami's commitment to reform was under fire. Student leaders were hunted down, arrested, and sometimes sentenced to death. "The clear lesson for vigilante groups like Ansar-e Hezbollah was that no matter how strong the popular feeling to the contrary, a manufactured crisis could provide an excuse for the further erosion of civil liberty and reform," notes Rubin, who was in Tehran at the time.[102]

Reformists were disgusted. Many said the hard-liners had "hijacked" the student riots. After the first four days of protest, it was a "very strange soup" that flooded the streets, one moderate government official told me.[103] "For True Believers, it's God's assignment for them [to stop reformists]; they believe it is a holy duty. They misused religion."

AND IT WORKED. AS I spoke to students in the coming months, there was clear disappointment that all the bandaged, broken heads and bloodshed had brought so little benefit. I met clandestinely with several students in a Spartan dormitory in east Tehran. They said they now had to work "underground," even though their actions were not illegal, at least under Iranian law. The blue-jeaned Pejman—not his real name—was a top member of the largest moderate student group, Daftar-e Tahkim-e Vahdat (Office of Fostering Unity). He had secretly videotaped many hours of the demonstrations, and made an instructive film for fellow activists.

"If you want to say the students were taught a lesson, then it's not the first lesson of this class, and it won't be the last," the mechanical engineer told me.[104] "I can't judge if it was a setback or not, because the story goes on. But until now I don't think anything positive has come from it. None of our demands, like removing the police chief, have been met."

This dormitory was similar to those that had been raided by vigilantes: simple bunk beds, chairs, a desk, a table, vines growing from a pot climbing up toward the ceiling. Inexplicably taped on the wall was a yellowed newspaper photograph of film star John Wayne—the all-American frontiersman who survived a gunfight or two.

Pejman was still loyal to Khatami, calling him "our teacher." But the students were divided and disillusioned. "Iran is not suitable for revolutionary change; in this country it leads to negative results," he told me. "So the solution is reforming slowly, maybe even taking two steps forward and one step back, with at last a positive result. It's better than revolutionary change—and a negative outcome."

"We learned a lot of lessons from this incident, that populism did not have a result," added another engineer. All these students had been under pressure from their parents to stop, for their own safety:

"We should not have war in the streets—we should have war in newspapers and ballot boxes."

Pejman was despondent: "I hope that my grandson will live in a free society." Others nodded their agreement, but it was a far-off, plaintive dream. "I want to change and reform the culture, then everything is possible."

REFORMISTS WON CONTROL OF parliament decisively that February 2000, but the violence of the previous summer dampened spirits. "The reform strategy is silence," editor Hamid Reza Jalaeipour told me, after the latest of his newspapers had been shut down.[105] "The hard-liners want a chaotic situation, because they have special, extraordinary powers. But with silence they have nothing. They are waiting for any pretext to bring out the tanks."

The Sage was reserved. "People got the message that going onto the street is not the way, because it just plays into the hands of the hard-liners," he told me.[106] "The reformists are lowering the flame. They want to allow the storm to pass, and they hope they will survive until they can get to the parliament." The bodies of those who died in the 1999 unrest were quietly returned to their families, reportedly only after relatives promised to keep quiet—and in the case of at least one student shot in the head, many months later.[107]

The one-year anniversary of the bloody assault on the dormitory showed how much fire was gone from the protest—and how distant this generation of students had become from the embassy-seizing militancy of 1979. This newer group planned to mark the day of their evisceration with a "flower power" strategy, in which they handed out long-stemmed gladioli. They sent bundles of the flowers, in pink and red, to senior hard-line clerics—including one linked to Ansar-e Hezbollah—and to the security forces and state-run broadcast media.

"We will confront fists with flowers," student leader Ebrahim Sheikh told me.[108] "We are soldiers against violence. We have our pens and our voices only, and with violence would lose to those people with knives who are more powerful."

But on the first anniversary in 2000, radicals on both sides took each other on. Dozens were wounded by thugs wielding broken bottles, amid clouds of tear gas and the smashing of bus stop and shop windows. Ansar-e Hezbollah dominated the fight. By midnight, I saw how hundreds of vigilantes armed with clubs and lengths of electrical cable had taken over Revolution Square, and on their motorcycles chased down any potential reformists.[109]

Before the standoff, Khatami had limply told conservatives not to impose their views. "We must not expect people to behave as we like, and [threaten] to suppress them if they don't," he scolded, like an exasperated schoolteacher. "People must be allowed to speak freely and criticize their government. If people are left unsatisfied, this will one day lead to an explosion."

Indeed, the first detonations were already taking place. And Khatami was not able to demonstrate, to the majority of Iranians who had voted for him, that there was any democratic give in the calcified edifice of the Government of God.

The Court of the Clerics

The jury of eight turbaned clerics sat along one wall, as low-key as if judging a high school debate. The site of this historic confrontation in November 1999 was a converted living room in a luxurious north Tehran house, a Shah-era mansion seized by revolutionaries, its two empty swimming pools a reminder of past frolicking. The audience shifted in plastic chairs, stood packed at the back, or stacked up along the curving wooden staircase.[110]

On trial in this modest "courtroom" was nothing less than the reform movement itself, and its promise of more social freedoms and the rule of law.

Those aspirations were manifest in the man in the dock: the supremely short, sharp, and immaculately turned out Abdollah Nouri—for years a trusted representative of Ayatollah Khomeini, more recently a high government official, subject of a vigilante beating, and reformist director of *Khordad* newspaper who had received the most votes in recent local elections. The gray-bearded Nouri had been targeted by conservatives before, in mid-1998, as Khatami's interior minister, for his handling of pro- and anti-reformist rallies, and for allowing U.S. academics to visit Iran. President Khatami had defended Nouri as "one of the most competent ministers," whose absence would "harm both the government and the nation."[111]

But right-wing parliamentarians pressed on. In 1998 it was impeachment. During those proceedings, one accused Nouri of leading Iran toward divisions as severe as those that tore apart the former Yugoslavia. Nouri was opening Iran to "suspicious groups" with such a destabilizing impact that "no stone will stay on top of the others."

The fight still raged one and a half years later, as the white-turbaned cleric sat in court, facing Iran's inquisition with arms crossed, a reservoir of arguments ready, to counter new charges of apostasy, undermining clerical rule, and advocating the renewal of Iran-U.S. ties. This case was the highest-profile example yet of hard-liners turning Khatami's "rule of law" mantra into a tool of their own. In this simple room, rival clerics were dueling to determine Iran's future. Each argued that victory of their opponents would cause the Islamic regime to crumble.

Nouri was expected to do well in upcoming 2000 parliamentary elections and serve as the next speaker of the majlis. Either that, or in Iran's Darwinian eat-your-opponent political swamp, he would be removed from the election and swallowed by prison, charged with acting against God. The transcript of Nouri's spirited defense became a bestselling book. He rejected the legitimacy of the Special Court for the Clergy but said he attended proceedings out of "respect" for the system. Even conservative newspapers commented on how Nouri had put the process itself in the dock.

"Listen," scolded the judge, who was but a teenager during the Revolution—when Nouri had been carrying out sensitive orders of Imam Khomeini. "The reason why we convened this court is not to give the accused a platform from which [he] can continuously cross-question the court."

The prosecutor read off the forty-four-page indictment like a sermon that grew more strident with every crime. There was talk of "enemies of God" and "deviations," of "insulting and confronting the Imam's view." Nouri's newspaper *Khordad* had pushed far beyond the limits of press freedom.

"In truth, who here is trying to challenge our Islamic system [*nezam*]?" Nouri asked the court, its members sitting at wooden tables, a box of tissues before them. "Is it me, or is it those who ignore our constitutional laws, who try to set Muslim against Muslim, to create false barriers, to foster conflict and confusion?"

The prosecutor was livid, my translator relating his response this way: "You can fuck off with your constitution. I can tell you about Article Five Hundred of the sharia [Islamic law], and that says, despite all your fancy arguments, I'm telling you by our definition [your view] refutes the Imam's view and Islam." Throughout the trial, Nouri had dissected the system, challenging the court on all manner of issues—asking, for instance, how it was possible for Iranians to be "more Palestinian than the Palestinians" in opposing an Israeli-Palestinian peace deal.

Then, heretically, he declared there had been more freedom under the Shah, suggesting that the current regime was probably not configured the way that God—and the people—wanted. The judge was getting testy, too, and finally sentenced Nouri to five years in prison on fifteen counts. Khatami could do nothing and abided by the "legal" ruling.

Ansar-e Hezbollah vigilantes celebrated by warning that reformists would be the first victims of any further "provocations," a statement praised in the pages of the hard-line *Kayhan*.[112] After the trial, a Saudi-owned newspaper reported an assassination plot against Nouri. It quoted a former Ansar militant saying he had gone to the northeastern city of Mashhad to kill him. By one account: "The activist revealed that a security officer approached him shortly before Nouri delivered his sermon to say, 'The plan has changed. Do not do anything.' "[113]

Years later and out of prison, Nouri ended his silence with the foreign press, still brave and defiant. He told me how the court case was a victory, how the reform movement was in fact the true and natural progression of the Revolution's slogan of independence, freedom, and the Islamic Republic.

"I want to say the Revolution itself was a reform, so this reform does not conflict with anything in the Revolution." Nouri's trim beard was all the more gray as he spoke in the book-lined study of his home.[114] "The most important thing for the Revolution is to defend the human being, so people could have their human identity."

The court's judgment was irrelevant, Nouri said, compared to the platform it gave him: "It actually enlightened the thoughts of the public—it created enlightenment," he told me, sitting confidently in a tight gray robe. Prison forced activists to "measure" their mottos, Nouri said. But there were many reasons for disappointment in the collapse of the reform movement, among them that "there is only one Nelson Mandela in the world."

All that Iran had back in 1999 was Khatami. Despite his electoral mandate, the president seemed powerless to stop the anti-reform onslaught. I heard how Iranians nicknamed him the Smiling Nun or the Emperor's Consort "because he is relegated to opening flower shows."

"What do you do if you are pro-Khatami?" a French diplomat asked me. "You preach for the law, but if the law is used against the people's will, then there will be a real risk of violence."

Reformists still wanted to believe that their clear superiority at the ballot box would eventually turn the tide, regardless of what Khatami actually delivered—or what the right wing threw at them. "Even if tomorrow they impeach Khatami, it doesn't mean the end of the change. . . . They can't turn the clock back," one reformist official told me. "And getting Nouri out of the picture does not mean they won. It's gone beyond Khatami. Either way, the conservatives lose."

Yet if the right wing saw their defeat as inevitable, their bold attacks didn't betray it. The conservatives "are very nervous, and they won't relinquish their position without a fight," a European envoy told me. "They have a limited perspective. They don't travel much or meet people from outside. So inside them is still the root of the Revolution—and it's a formidable force."

ANOTHER LEGAL DRAMA EVOLVED from the July 1999 dormitory raids by police and vigilantes, and the subsequent student protests. The Supreme National Security Council had immediately launched an investigation and found that fourteen previous illegal student demonstrations had taken place, which justified the violent response.[115] Some of the legitimate, uniformed security forces testified that vigilantes ran the show, "using foul language [and] reproaching them for not attacking and for not being harsh with the students." The report did not name Ansar-e Hezbollah but discussed how the militants had received word of the pending attack in order to mobilize for it.

When it came to the court hearing, the involvement of Ansar was set aside, while top police officers were pinned with blame—one for acting in a "maladroit manner." Of the twenty security men in the dock, no vigilante was among them. Despite that injustice, looking back it is clear that the extraordinary nature of this trial—of all these court cases, their sensitive subject matter and their large measure of openness—was due to Khatami's positive imprint on politics. Accountability in public was something very new, even when the "law" was abused for political ends.

Every word of the proceedings made it into print, as the police officers defended themselves. Witnesses included a number of wounded students, on crutches, bandaged, or wearing casts. One student said he was beaten with metal rods and cables and pistol-whipped by an attacker in civilian clothes. "He then threatened and forced a passing driver to open the [trunk] of his car, and tried to force me while handcuffed and with my whole body bleeding into the back," the student said. The hail of stones from fellow students to prevent him being taken away meant he was put into one of the attackers' own cars and "repeatedly they would point an empty pistol against the side of my head, pulling the trigger and saying: Where is Mr. Khatami to help you now?"[116]

Reformists were not happy with the verdicts. The police chief who had directed the raid was acquitted. During the hearings, hard-line supporters had showered flower petals on thirty-six-year-old Brigadier General Farhad Nazari, and greeted him with religious chanting like a senior cleric. Officially some two hundred students had been injured and one died, and the state was ordered to make compensation payments to thirty-four students. The key lawyer for the students was arrested. One witness was beaten in a nearby alley shortly after he testified. And many of the students were themselves facing charges.

No vigilante from Ansar was brought before the court, and only two police officers were sentenced. One got two years in prison for beating students; another got three months and a $120 fine for stealing a student's electric razor.[117]

AMONG THE FIRST KEY reformists to fall to conservative prosecutors was the respected mayor of Tehran, Gholam Hossein Karbaschi, who in eight years had overseen a thirtyfold increase in city revenue, set aside fifteen times more green space for parks, and built new highways to ease congestion in the second-most-polluted city in the world. Look anywhere in the crowded capital in 1997 and the mayor's Midas touch was evident. Tehranis spoke of him as a miracle worker who transformed the city of twelve million. Traffic lights worked, road signs were accurate, and within minutes of a storm municipal workers were on the streets sweeping up leaves and debris. Around every corner, it seemed, Iranians pointed to something and said with pride: "Our mayor did this."

Karbaschi was a strong Khatami supporter and had run his election campaign, so corruption charges were quickly leveled. But when I met the mayor in his aerie-like office atop the municipal building, he could not have been more confident, certain that Khatami's overwhelming vote count would prevail.

"The people have had a good experience in Tehran, and their logic will overcome this propaganda," Karbaschi told me.[118] Aerial photographs of Tehran covered the walls, and two Mont Blanc fountain pens sat atop his broad desk. With his oval glasses and gray-black beard trimmed very short, the mayor exuded a refined efficiency and political effortlessness.

"Those who lost their place and position in public opinion are very much worried," said the mayor, dismissing the pending charges as political, in a country where the corrupt ways of some clerics spawned the saying "The longer the beard, the deeper the pockets." Karbaschi said, "The most valuable thing Khatami did was talk about law and order. Those opposed to him always take illegal actions, so it is very good for him if everything is done according to the law."

The mayor's eleven-day detention in April 1998 touched off violent street protests. When Karbaschi's trial began in June, the charge sheet listed fraud and embezzlement and "despotic and dictatorial behavior."[119] Rival demonstrators faced off outside, with critics shouting: "Death to the mayor! Death to inflation!" Karbaschi denounced the corruption charges as "lies" and "political scheming."

Yet the mayor made the mistake repeated often by the titans of reform. He shrugged off the threat from the far right, saying that neither he nor Khatami's government had anything to fear from hard-line opponents. "They are not strong at all, because their strength is [not] related to the people," Karbaschi told me. Hard-liners "appear strong and well-organized, but they are not. On the contrary, supporters of the president are day by day becoming stronger and more hopeful." He did recognize that 30 percent of Iranians did not vote for Khatami, "so there will be some conflicts."

And indeed there were. Six months later, the mayor of Tehran was in jail.

The Assassins

The would-be killers wore motorcycle helmets when they approached Saeed Hajjarian, the political maestro and Khatami adviser who in 2000 had just orchestrated the reformist sweep in parliamentary elections. As he was stepping into the municipal building, they handed him an ordinary letter—some request for a job. When Hajjarian paused to read it, the men shot him once with a pistol before escaping on a high-powered motorcycle the size that could legally only be used by the Iranian police—outlawed to anyone else because in the past they had been used for quick getaways in political killings.[120]

The bullet entered Hajjarian's left cheek and lodged in his neck. The man lived, but the daylight assassination attempt—on the steps of a landmark government building where spit-and-polish guards kept constant security but failed to chase the assailants—reminded Iranians of dark forces still lurking, and of how little Khatami and his legions of voters had yet achieved. No one claimed responsibility for the shooting, but there was no doubt who was to blame.

President Khatami called the perpetrators "terrorists" and declared: "The enemies of freedom wrongly believe that they can attain their goals by assassinating a pious intellectual who was serving the nation." The Ministry of Culture and Islamic Guidance, run by reformists, said, "Bullets cannot halt the trend of the establishment of democracy in Iran." Even the Supreme National Security Council called an emergency session within hours and set up a special operations center, saying, "Those who chose Hajjarian to be their assassination target knew they would create a crisis in the country by doing so."

The campaign to undermine the reform movement with violence and political killings was well under way. Ironically, Hajjarian was a former ideologue himself, a student hostage taker credited with founding Iran's notorious Ministry of Intelligence, and then a deputy minister from 1984 to 1989.

But he had a change of heart—like so many other once-radical revolutionaries—when he saw the ideals of his Revolution turn toward despotism. Besides advising Khatami, in the reform era he was managing editor of the cutting-edge newspaper *Sobh-e Emrouz*, and critical in exposing the death squad in the Intelligence Ministry responsible for a series of killings that would become known as the serial or "chain" murders. He knew their secrets, because he had once been their boss.

The killings peaked in late 1998, with the leader of an opposition party, Dariush Forouhar, and his wife, Parvaneh, murdered in a way that was clearly meant to horrify. "The assassins stabbed him eleven times, turned his body toward Mecca, and left the blood to collect in a pool around him. Parvaneh was upstairs getting ready for bed. She was stabbed twenty-four times. Afterward both their bodies were hacked to pieces," recalled Shirin Ebadi, the future Nobel laureate who was part of the legal team that had brief access to the intelligence files on the case.[121] Not long thereafter, three more secular intellectuals were murdered, two of them pro-reform writers. Target lists circulated with the rumors about who might be next.

Ebadi was shocked by the contents of the voluminous chain murder files. "The material was dark with descriptions . . . passages where a killer, with seeming relish, told of crying out '*Ya Zahra*,' in dark homage to the Prophet Mohammad's daughter, with each stab," she writes in her memoir.[122] Her blood ran cold when she came across this line: "The next person to be killed is Shirin Ebadi." The document was a conversation with an assassin requesting permission from the minister for the murder. He was told: not during the fasting month of Ramadan, but anytime after.

"But they don't fast anyway, the mercenary had argued; these people have divorced God," relates Ebadi. "It was through this belief—that the intellectuals, that I, had abandoned God—that they justified the killings as religious duty. In the grisly terminology of those who interpret Islam violently, our blood was considered halal, its spilling permitted by God."

Such killings had not been common inside Iran since the earliest years of the Revolution. Their return in 1998 rocked the nation and became a key test for Khatami. A shadowy new cabal took for itself the name of the old Fadaiyan-e Islam, and expanded it. The "Mostafa Navvab's Devotees of the Pure Islam of Mohammad" promised more bloodshed: "The revolutionary executions are a warning to all those whose pens are in the service of foreigners and want Iran to return to foreign domination." [123]

IRANIAN AGENTS HAD IN fact mastered the art of political murder, in the course of killing scores of dissidents and regime enemies abroad over twenty years, from Washington to Pakistan, the majority in Iraq but many across Europe.

"Iran's global assassination campaign was predicated on the simple principle that for opponents of the Islamic Republic there can be no safe haven anywhere in the world," concluded the most detailed examination of the cases, by the U.S.-based Iran Human Rights Documentation Center.[124] It tabulated more than 162 killings abroad until 1996, when they came to an end on the eve of the Khatami era (there was one more in Iraq in 1999).

"These attacks have been carried out on the authority of the Supreme Leader of the Islamic Republic and have been planned and coordinated at the highest levels of the clerical establishment," the report found. It quoted Ayatollah Khamenei congratulating Rafsanjani's intelligence minister, Ali Fallahian—the subject of three outstanding international arrest warrants, and who has since run for president—for his "great achievements in combating and uprooting the enemies of Islam, inside and outside the country."

From the first days of the 1979 Revolution, former officials of the Shah's regime were hunted down and executed for "corruption on earth." Internal battles and a "reign of terror" grew to a peak within two years. As he so often did, Khomeini set the tone: "Criminals should not be tried. The trial of a criminal is against human rights. Human rights demand that we should have killed them in the first place when it became known that they were criminals." [125]

The political assassinations abroad would include some spectacularly bold strikes. One was carried out by a black American convert to Islam called David Belfield, or Dawud Salahuddin, who was recruited to kill the former Iranian Embassy press attaché and vocal regime critic Ali Akbar Tabatabai in Bethesda, Maryland, in 1980.[126] He dressed up as a mailman to get close to his target and has lived unhappily as a fugitive in Tehran ever since.

Other regime opponents were gunned down on the streets of Paris and knifed or shot in their apartments in Bucharest and Istanbul; they were picked off across Iraq, by bullet and by grenade.

Among the most headline-grabbing attacks was the 1991 killing of former prime minister Shapour Bakhtiar, who lived in Paris under twenty-four-hour police guard. Two Iranian agents entered with one of Bakhtiar's aides to "meet the famous exile," as described in *Time*, which examined a string of cases:

> As soon as [the secretary] went to the kitchen to make tea, one of the visitors leaped at Bakhtiar and, according to the autopsy report, struck a "mortal blow" to the throat. The secretary was similarly dispatched. With two knives grabbed from the kitchen, the assailants hacked at their victims' throats, chests, and arms so savagely that a knife blade was broken. An hour after arriving, [Bakhtiar's aide] calmly collected the trio's passports, and the men drove off in an orange BMW. The guards failed to notice that [the two visitors'] shirts were drenched in blood.[127]

European investigators pursued trails of clues from that case and others through France, Switzerland, Austria, Germany, often Turkey, and then to the highest levels of government in Tehran.

Time acquired a copy of a 1993 execution order for the Shah-era minister and anti-regime activist Manouchehr Ganji, who, among alleged crimes, had "bamboozled the masses to rebel against the Islamic Revolution."[128] The order states that a fatwa had been requested from the Supreme Leader, who replied with these words: "Because he is at war with God and God's Seal of the Prophets [Mohammad], and has ignored the divine decrees and orders . . . the aforementioned is corrupted and an apostate and spilling his blood is permissible. For the purpose of protecting Islam and the Muslims, this corrupted root must be cut off as soon as possible so that it can serve as an example for others."

That one execution order written by Iran's prosecutor general linked together Khamenei, then-president Rafsanjani, the head of the judiciary, the Foreign Ministry, and the Intelligence Ministry, whose operatives were given the job. "The agents that successfully discharge this duty and kill the corrupted . . . will receive a significant monetary sum as a bonus, in addition to rewards in the afterlife," the execution order read. The final instruction: "After finishing the operation destroy all related correspondence."

THEN THE MINISTRY OF Intelligence easily turned its attention to voices of protest inside the Islamic Republic with the chain murders of late 1998. At last the extrajudicial brutality was impossible to ignore. President Khatami managed to cleanse the Intelligence Ministry, forcing an admission of guilt that is considered a high-water mark of the reform era. Khatami vowed to investigate and was for once enabled by the Supreme Leader, who did not block the search for the perpetrators.

The result was a partial reversal of unaccountability that had prevailed for two decades. The Ministry of Intelligence issued a statement: "A few of our colleagues—irresponsible, devious, and obstinate persons—were among those arrested." [129] The acts of these "traitors" were "quite contrary to the holy mission of the Intelligence Ministry and we condemn it."

Saeed Emami, a deputy minister of intelligence, was charged with running the "rogue" death squad and was among ten agents arrested. Mystery still surrounds his death in prison in June 1999, which was officially called a "suicide," caused by "drinking hair removal cream" while taking a bath.

The lawyer Ebadi was suspicious and asked her staff to buy one of each brand of hair removal cream available in Tehran. "Every single one of the bottles they brought back was labeled 'no arsenic.' It seemed impossible to commit suicide with any over-the-counter depilatory on the Iranian market," she recalled.[130] Emami doubtless knew many dirty secrets, but his death—at his own hand, or some-one else's—was not likely faked. Ebadi went to the funeral to find out and met the bereaved wife: "I took one look at her red-rimmed eyes, felt her unsteady hand in mine, and knew that her husband was dead."

Iranians were doubly stunned. First by the murders, and second by the mea culpa. For many, it was the most hopeful sign that reform was possible in the Islamic Republic. "It would be wrong and naïve to say the Revolution failed, because the very fact the Intelligence Ministry must confess is a fruit of the Revolution," professor Sadegh Zibakalam explained.[131] "So it appears that the Khatami government was not as weak and powerless as many observers believed it to be," he told me.[132] "They decided they had no alternative but to let the people know what's happening—the truth."

Little did reformists know that they were witnessing the high point of Khatami's power—a standard, with the Leader's collusion, that would not be repeated.

"The Islamic Republic learned that it was a house divided: the rift in the regime helped produce the scandal; the scandal in turn widened the rift between the regime and the people," concluded Ebadi.[133] The outcome "made killing less cheap, and less easy. It forced the Islamic Republic to check its excess, to discard extrajudicial killings, as it had discarded mass executions a decade prior. If the words did not stick so in my throat, I would call it an evolution."

SUCH SHOCKING OFFICIAL REVELATIONS would not have been possible without the groundbreaking and risky work of investi-gative journalists like Akbar Ganji, who had vowed to "write, write, and write until we find the truth." Ganji was publishing one exposé after another about intelligence ministry involvement in the kill-ings, and dark tales of right-wing abuse of power that led straight to

Minister of Intelligence Ali Fallahian. The assassination squads had secretly been given religious sanction by hard-line clergy.

A measure of the impact of these revelations could be found in the disorderly offices of the publishers Tarh-e No, which in 2000 were stacked high with freshly printed books smelling of ink on paper, the promise of literature and enlightenment, and—in Iran's volatile political atmosphere—of subversion.[134]

In a market that normally sells three to five thousand copies of any book, Ganji's *The Red Eminence and the Gray Eminences* was, in just four months, already in its twenty-ninth printing and had sold 160,000 copies. It was a collection of hard-hitting factual newspaper columns about the political murders, death squads, and the misdeeds of former president Ali Akbar Hashemi Rafsanjani and his powerful family. It followed the book *Dungeon of Ghosts*, another collection of articles that referred to Fallahian, without naming him, as the "Master Key" to the chain murders. The work was a bold challenge to once-untouchable forces in Iran and paved the way for further investigative work by others such as Emadeddin Baghi.

But when I visited the publishing house in 2000, Ganji was already in prison. So too was Baghi.

As a former Revolutionary Guard intelligence officer, and a close associate of Hajjarian, Ganji had access to damaging inside information. Analysts compared the impact in Iran to America's Watergate scandal, with Ganji playing the role of Woodward and Bernstein, the two *Washington Post* reporters who exposed the political break-in and cover-up that eventually led to the resignation of President Richard Nixon.

"Ganji was the first, in a highly intimidating atmosphere, to put his life on the line to investigate these forces," said Reza Alavi, the Harvard- and Oxford-trained historian in Tehran.[135] "It's the everyday life of the people [at stake]: the essentials of life, liberty and the pursuit of happiness." The work broke a tradition of self-censorship, and a number of other taboos.

Even the purchase of the book was a political act favoring reform.

The "Gray Eminences" of the title were the death squad intelligence operatives. The "Red Eminence" was a barely veiled reference to Rafsanjani, who had been at the center of power in Iran since the Revolution. Ganji challenged his record and, with former hostage taker Abbas Abdi, exposed the corruption of the first family. The result was that in the next election, Rafsanjani, who conservatives calculated would easily assume the speakership, barely made it into parliament at all. Deeply humiliated, he later gave up his seat.

But demystifying the process of political murder in Iran carried its own risks, because of the Revolution's history of violence. For Rafsanjani, that also included coming to terms with an outstanding German arrest warrant, due to his alleged involvement in ordering the 1992 killings of three Iranian Kurdish dissidents and their translator in the Mykonos restaurant in Berlin.[136]

"It is dangerous if the full truth is upon us," noted a Swiss diplomat in Iran.[137] "How do you deal with the past? An amnesty? Do we want a full light on what Iran did in the 1980s? We saw what happened when Rafsanjani was nailed for Mykonos—all the system backed him. . . . There are many other corpses in the cellar," he told me.

But it went further than that. Not even the accusers had clean hands. Many reformers had themselves played important revolutionary roles that involved violence and compromises. "How do you [reconcile] people to the right of Genghis Khan, and to the left—most were implicated in the Revolution, and did things not so charming. Rafsanjani says: 'Who are these reformists, Ganji and Hajjarian? I prevented them from killing *more* people,'" the diplomat said, referring to the fact both ranking reformists had grim intelligence histories.

In the face of unrelenting attack, Rafsanjani had indeed counterattacked. "Some of these gentlemen disguised as reformers and liberals made problems for us due to their extremism," he told the newspaper *Iran*.[138] "You wouldn't imagine how much I suffered in trying to curb their excesses—hangings, trials, and confiscation of (private) property in the early years of the Revolution."

That was Iran's conundrum. "If you as an individual have done wrong things, and you know about it, and then for [eight] years you go through a war—it weighs on your conscience," the diplomat said. "For a whole society, how do you carry all that baggage? What do you do? [You] try not to disturb the quiet waters."

IN CLASSIC REGIME STYLE, conservatives played down the significance of the blockbuster. "Ganji's book did quite a bit of damage, but Ganji is not the first revolutionary who became antirevolutionary," said Hassan Ghafouri Fard, a Kansas-educated right-wing member of the Supreme Council for Cultural Revolution.[139] The 160,000 copies were "not important" relative to Iran's population then of sixty million, he told me. "We [conservatives] never denied that two or three or five percent of the people are antirevolutionary and don't believe in religious government."

Near the top of that antirevolutionary list was Ganji, whose pious commitment during the early years of the Revolution turned to anger—and then feisty energy thrown into his investigative efforts—at the corruption and violence of the 1990s. "It's going to be very bad for him, because he knows all the secrets," Hossein Paya, the publisher of Ganji's bestseller and other reformist titles, told me in those ink-scented offices.[140] He gave me posters of the covers of Khatami's and Hajjarian's latest books. Paya had already sold one hundred thousand copies of the transcript of Abdollah Nouri's "trial of the century," which was called The Hemlock of Reform, "hemlock" meaning "poison."

When Ganji's book was first released, it had literally sold out before it could be placed on store shelves—a fact that Ganji was pleased to hear when he could still telephone Paya from prison. "Even homemakers have read this book," he told me. "The average in society, people who vote."

Ganji spent six years in prison and became Iran's most renowned dissident after spending more than seventy days on hunger strike. He wrote Manifesto for Republicanism, in which he called for a separation of religion from politics, a secular democracy—and for the Supreme Leader to step down. He starved himself to the verge of death and had to be hospitalized. The example galvanized a worldwide effort by human rights groups to free him.

Writing during solitary confinement in Evin Prison in mid-2005, on the nineteenth day of his second hunger strike, when his weight had already dropped from 77 to 58 kilograms, Ganji stated that he had been deprived of every connection to the outside world, including "the open air." He attacked the "Orwellian" language of the regime:

> Let it be known that Akbar Ganji will not cease his hunger strike until he achieves his goal of letting the world know that there is a committed democracy movement in Iran. Forcing repentance letters on prisoners is the method of Stalin's interrogators, inherited by Iranian Stalinists.
>
> Today my broken face is the true face of the system in the Islamic Republic of Iran. My ravaged body exposes the regime's oppressiveness.[141]

Ganji inspired one aging academic friend of mine in Tehran. We began to speak about the firebrand in late 2005, after Mahmoud Ahmadinejad's election as president. I had been critical, noting that Ganji's writings had become increasingly extreme, that his call for Iranians to boycott the 2005 presidential election helped ensure a conservative victory. One analyst had told me that Ganji had "helped fuel a lot of radicalism." But this academic suggested that Ganji himself would have gotten 80 percent of the vote if he had been a candidate.[142]

The academic's eyes began to well up with emotion. He said Ganji's self-destructive steadfastness should be seen as resistance—à la Imam Hossein and the epic Battle of Karbala. And so Ganji deserved respect for challenging authority.

"He is a danger. He inspires me. Courage is something all Iranians admire," my friend told me. He had recently made a speech, he said, and felt Ganji's spirit: "I lashed into the regime. I lashed into Khatami," he said. "What gave me the courage to do it was the image of this man."

• • •

ALSO INSPIRING—AND ALARMING—to many Iranians was the 2000 near assassination of the architect of reform, Saeed Hajjarian. After the conservative defeat in parliamentary elections, Hajjarian had made several provocative statements, and received numerous written death threats—some from extremists reportedly linked to the previous killings of intellectuals. Hajjarian told me years later that he had been warned by the interior minister that both he and former minister Abdollah Nouri were next on the target list—but Nouri was by then already "safe" in prison.[143]

And they weren't the only targets. Outspoken art gallery owner Lili Golestan told me she was sixth on a list in which the first four had already been killed. Former foreign minister Yazdi told me in early 1999: "I am at risk. Last year I was arrested for twelve days. I was told the next time they would kill me in the street. To kill us in dubious ways is easy. What can we do?"[144]

By coincidence on the morning of the Hajjarian assassination attempt, *Iran News* published an editorial—which hit the streets just hours before the 8:35 A.M. shooting. It asked the intelligence and security services to take precautions "before the actions of some extremist and prejudiced individuals threaten the security of the country once again and endanger the lives of our cultural architects."[145]

The editorial reminded readers that the arrest of the death squad the previous year had yielded a list of names of two hundred cultural, artistic, and media figures to be murdered "over a period of time."

WHILE RECOVERING IN HIS bed at home in July 2000, Hajjarian received a few student leaders. It was some months after the assassination attempt, on the first anniversary of the student unrest, when the new tactic was "flower power."[146] In a gesture of solidarity, the students spent the day visiting high-profile "victims of violence" and their families. I was alongside as they crowded around the man whose mind had helped create the hopeful firmament of reform. He was sitting up in his pajamas, his body broken and partially paralyzed from the bullet that had been shot into the left side of his face. Therapy exercise equipment hung over the bed from the ceiling, to develop arm strength.

Except for the scar tissue, Hajjarian wore the requisite stubble of beard—what self-respecting revolutionary bothered to shave? There were some flowers in the small Tehran apartment; the students held a poster: "Say 'No' to Violence." Hajjarian flexed his right hand. But speaking was not easy.

"I am very optimistic, even though I should be pessimistic after the assassination attempt," Hajjarian told the students, his voice a hiss over the exhale of breath required to get the words out. "I do not want to underestimate this catastrophe—I think we should call it looting. They attacked students and beat them to death, and threw them out of windows," Hajjarian said. "It's like a tumor in one's brain, and one is always suffering, in pain. . . . But this pain can't be silenced. We can't kill it in a rush. We need to find a slow and enduring solution. This is not easy."

Hajjarian recited a poem about time being the only cure for all aching hearts. It was important that the students not "let this pain become too enduring."

"You should have gone to the cemetery. The victims of violence are lying there. Then you should have come here, to me, who is half alive," rasped Hajjarian.

After the meeting, I asked this injured oracle about the prospects for reform. More presciently than most, he told me that victory for prodemocracy elements "depends on the reformers, and how they will make use of the opportunities now here. If they don't do it right, there is a good chance the conservatives will regain their position."

HAJJARIAN WAS RIGHT. CONSERVATIVES were on the march, and in coming years would retake control of parliament and seize back the presidency. And reformists would contribute mightily to their own downfall. As they became marginalized, reform personalities—Hajjarian among them—often insisted that they had learned innumerable "lessons" from their failures. They had to connect their intellectual platform to the average Iranian. They had to focus on improving daily life. A common refrain: "You can't eat human rights."

But when I saw Hajjarian in late 2007, there was little sign in Iranian politics that the fragmented remnants of reform had descended from their intellectual heights, to broaden their appeal.[147] President Ahmadinejad was instead winning over Iranians with his talk of economic "justice" and street-level populism.

Hajjarian shuffled into our meeting, helped by two men, one on either side holding a hand. His legs were not working. He had lost more weight. He wore a gray argyle sweater and white hospital shoes. But inside that broken, incapable body, Hajjarian's mind was as incisive as ever. He reached back to the early Revolution and gave lament about how "charisma becomes routine" in leadership.

"You realize those high slogans of the Revolution are not easily attainable," Hajjarian told me, his barely audible voice more air than words. "It needs reform." Rafsanjani and then Khatami "realized that you can't move the Revolution ahead with just slogans. We believe freedom needs competition."

Hajjarian was getting tired as he spoke. His open hands grasped a cup of tea with little certainty, fingers straight. Hajjarian complained about "mobocracy," the idea inserted into the mainstream by Iranian conservatives that the United States and West were behind the reformist wave—and therefore had to be stopped in the name of the Revolution. At all costs.

A tear rolled down Hajjarian's cheek when he recalled the attempt to kill him; how he had been warned, and how it was such a close call. The actual bullet is still in the court file, he said. It had been "just an ordinary day" when he was handed that request for a job by the men wearing motorcycle helmets.

In the years since, Hajjarian had persisted with his trademark strategy of applying "pressure from below, negotiation at the top." In Iran, that required a certain faith, he told me: "You have to believe despotism can be reversed."

. . .

STILL BELIEVING IN THE dream of reform was the young audience that gathered in the basement of a party office in 2008 to mark the eighth anniversary of the assassination attempt on Hajjarian.[148] The event was crowded, but very highbrow intellectual, as professors discussed the impact of Hajjarian's thought. The survivor himself had not yet arrived, but there were other survivors who found their seats, the wounded veterans of Iran's Battle for Reform. One man came in—I don't know who he was—his blinded eyes covered with scar tissue, his left hand missing, a plastic sack hanging from his stump. He tapped his way forward with a cane and had a young man at his side as a guide.

Key reformers were there in the cramped, low-ceilinged room, all packed around tables at the front. Their martyrs were invoked. But most of the analysis, while perhaps correct, was impenetrable. Hajjarian, it was said, had deconstructed the "Sultanistic regime" and found no separation between the government and the *nezam* (Islamic system), so that criticism of the government meant criticism of the *nezam*. Human rights were analyzed, and the point made that any religion "against the people's inner will" could not be a "holy religion."

Those were among the least technical points. My interpreter Pedram Khodadadi finally gave up in disgust on the real-time translation. "Haven't they learned anything in all these years?" he asked me. "This has *nothing* to do with people's lives!"

But worse was to come. Hajjarian—the man whose shooting was being commemorated by this very event—had arrived at the back and he began to shuffle his way forward slowly, one assistant holding his arm to ensure forward movement and not a sudden downward collapse. There was a brief pause in proceedings, but it appeared more a function of ignorance than of appreciation. No round of applause. No special reaction or even recognition as Hajjarian moved in silence. That young audience had no idea that right there before them was the icon of their veneration.

There was no doubt now. Conservatives had won.

Hijacking the Revolution

Few Iranian politicians better exemplify how soaring hope for change would turn to despair than Fatemeh Haghighatjou, the youngest female candidate in the 2000 parliamentary elections. As a freshly minted lawmaker on the pro-Khatami ticket, she was part of the reformist landslide backed by one million Tehran votes.

I first joined the thirty-one-year-old candidate when she was stumping on the campaign trail.[149] In a taxi on her way to a grassroots political meeting, Haghighatjou was draped in a black chador, its layered black-brown-gray making her as anonymous as any Iranian woman following the stringent Islamic dress code. But she had a radiant smile—not so common among overserious Iranian politicians—and a Nokia mobile phone cord clipped beneath her chin, for constant calling.

Speaking in a large south Tehran restaurant, Haghighatjou confidently represented the growing vanguard of both women and young voters. At the town hall meeting, she turned into a populist firebrand, brandishing her brown leather handbag and its decorative chain clasp with the same take-no-prisoners vigor that Margaret Thatcher once did.

Her message was simple, but aptly illustrated the profound changes sweeping across Iran: The Islamic Revolution had been hijacked by self-serving clerics. Only voting for reform could reestablish its promise of freedom and democracy.

"I am happy to be among you, people of Tehran," Haghighatjou began, implying that her conservative opponents were out of touch. She was short and had beautiful, expressive hands that punctuated her points and augmented her arguments. Addressing first the women and then, separately, the men—to standing-room-only audiences both times, beneath a portrait of Khomeini and the restaurant clock—she explained the mechanics of voting and why it was so important. She promised the women, all but their faces shrouded in black, that she would work toward equal rights—as promised by the Quran, she said—and for youth programs.

"They believe the people's role is unimportant, but I believe it is the people who can decide," Haghighatjou told the two hundred women. "They don't understand that people want to participate."

One black-clad woman in the audience asked her, "What does your family think of you taking on the ayatollahs?"

The candidate's reply: "They're positive. They're used to it." She had been active as a student leader, with all its dangers.

Q: What do students want?

A: Freedom—freedom of expression and thought.

Q: Wasn't that promised by the Revolution?

A: It was the slogan of the Revolution, but because of the war we couldn't fulfill these goals. [Now] freedoms are the top priorities.

The women filed out, and then Haghighatjou stood before some 250 rapt men. A young man asked about the obstacles before Khatami.

"I believe it is the people who can make a decision for themselves," the candidate said. "This is not my idea, but that of Ayatollah Khomeini." She paused with the microphone to adjust her chador reverently, as she invoked the Imam's name. "We are going toward the goals of the Islamic Republic: independence and freedom; but today the framework has changed."

Haghighatjou was a doctoral candidate at Tehran University with a background in vocational counseling, which gave her an unusual window on different strata of Iranian society. Because shaking hands between men and women is forbidden, politicians working the crowds at election time had to "press the flesh" in other ways. "You must communicate with people, by talking and listening to them," Haghighatjou told me. "Your body language is more important than shaking hands."

Clapping hands was more acceptable, and Haghighatjou was applauded frequently. "People are very excited," my translator Saeed Kousha whispered as we watched, "because now they understand their power, and are doing something about the conservatives. They see [conservatives] begging for their vote."

Haghighatjou was speaking to these voters in a conservative bastion of south Tehran. Already extralegal actions had marred the first term of the Khatami era: the mass shutting of reformist newspapers, the court cases, the vigilante violence and student protests, the chain murders of dissident thinkers. Yet like any good politician, she had the answers. "Conservatives divide society into two parts. Look how it is said by our Prophet that 'the people are like the ends of a comb—they are all equal,' " she said. That meant "if the *hezbollahis* have a right [to impose their views], all people have the same right."

After Haghighatjou spoke, a brief argument broke out as she prepared to leave. The local campaign organizer didn't want her to take a taxi without a security guard. Another candidate—the sister of a cleric who challenged conservatives—had received a death threat.

But Haghighatjou was fearless, and waved toward me and my translator, saying breezily, "Don't worry, I'm with them."

THE YOUNG CANDIDATE EASILY won her seat in the first—and only—reformist parliament. But when I caught up with Haghighatjou again just a month before the new, boisterous majority took its seats in the majlis, the gravity of the popular election "coup" was settling in and provoking anxiety.[150]

A strong old-guard backlash—evident in previous days with the closure of more than a dozen pro-reform newspapers, the jailing of editors, and annulment of some election results—pointed to severe challenges ahead. I had seen graffiti on walls in Tehran which read, "The newspapers against Islam should be shut down," sprayed in poor penmanship and misspelling the word "against" in Persian.[151]

The Sage said his country needed "a bridge between reform and hard-line bastards, someone who can stop the bloodshed."[152] He didn't share the optimism of reform activists. It was after midnight in his small apartment—he never turned off the ring of flame on his gas stove, which kept the tea piping hot. We were working together through a large bowl of fat, purplish grapes with bitter seeds. Candidates had deemphasized their clerical credentials and presented themselves as doctors and engineers.

"Now there is a growing awareness that we are the owners of the Revolution, and that the *hezbollahis* went the wrong way—they thought they owned it for years," the Sage explained. "But reformists are too self-confident."

As Haghighatjou prepared to take up her duties in parliament, she hoped to avoid that very trap. "I know there will be hard work and a heavy responsibility on my shoulders," Iran's youngest new deputy told me, in her quiet voice. "I am a bit concerned about whether we can fulfill the high expectations of the people." While she spoke, she held her chador closely around her face in conservative fashion, Yves Saint Laurent buttons flashing on her sleeves. Reformists finally controlled two pillars of power in Iran—the presidency and parliament—but hard-liners still gripped the ones that mattered: the military, security forces, and the judiciary.

Haghighatjou thought the most important challenge would be reconciling "different interpretations of Islam"—quite an assignment, in Iran's viciously contested political space. "Obviously people prefer our interpretation of individual and social rights and pluralism," she told me. She spoke confidently about the reformist worldview, noting how Iranians had clearly rejected methods that "used religion to take power and finish with their enemies."

Conservatives were wrong, she maintained. "We witness a lot of Quranic verses about individual rights and freedom of the people. We look at how our religious leaders and imams behaved. The first Imam Ali was really defending the rights of opponents [and] was a very democratic political leader. . . . Democracy and Islam can completely go together."

Which meant, Haghighatjou said, that there could be only one result: "It's a fight we have to win."

That very afternoon, students were holding a sit-in. "Khatami, Khatami, we love you! We support you!" I heard them chant.[153] "Death to dictatorship!"

THE RAW MATERIAL OF President Khatami's power—and of Haghighatjou's hope—were poll numbers never before witnessed in the Islamic Republic. Not only did Khatami win with 70 percent of the vote in 1997 (with a near 80 percent turnout), he started his second term in 2001 with a boost to 79 percent of the vote (though only 66 percent turned out)—despite all the violence and political tension. Further, Fatemeh Haghighatjou's crop of reformists swept into parliament in 2000 on the wave of an 83 percent voter turnout.

Iranians wanted change, and that desire cut through all society. Even at Behesht-e Zahra cemetery, resting place of Iran's revered martyrs, I was astonished in late 2002 to find nothing but reformist voters.

Among them, dressed all in black and to all appearances cut from Iran's most conservative cloth, was Zeinab Bolooki. She sponged off the white marble tombstone of her son and sprinkled it with a mother's love and red flower petals. Like so many I had met at this cemetery, this mother said it was an "honor" that her son Iraj "was chosen by God to be a martyr."[154] But the second sentence was not about devotion to the Supreme Leader Khamenei. It was about President Khatami and his transformative promise.

"We voted for Khatami—every Iranian voted for him—and we hope one hundred percent that he does his [reform] agenda," said Bolooki's husband, Morteza Ahroon. He lowered a copy of the Quran from his eyes for a moment to speak, while standing next to his son's grave. And what if hard-liners carried out their vows to continue blocking that agenda? "It's like when we go to the battlefront," the father told me. "We are committed to the end."

This family's support of reform showed how deeply Khatami's influence had penetrated, even among bedrock supporters of the regime like these. The reaction should not have been a surprise. Many of the usual conservative blocs such as martyrs' families, the Revolutionary Guard, and clerics were known to have voted in the same large percentages for Khatami as did the rest of society. One government poll showed that 84 percent of the Revolutionary Guard voted for reform.[155]

"It's like a volcano coming up, which you can't see until it blows," one Iranian professional told me. "Then we can really get rid of them forever. The taboos are broken now. . . . The conservatives are losing the basis of support."[156]

BUT THOSE PORTENTS DID not all lead to an eruption, despite three key events in 2002. The first was Iran being labeled a charter member of George W. Bush's Axis of Evil. A British diplomat called it "a case of sledgehammer diplomacy" that had "badly damaged Khatami personally" and raised substantial pressure on the regime.[157]

The other two events seemed, on the face of it, to make a stronger case for reform, but ultimately exposed the impotence of President Khatami. In July 2002, the long-venerated Friday prayer leader of Isfahan resigned, penning as he went a ferocious attack against the ruling clerics whose "deviations," he said, were undermining Islamic rule. The departure of Ayatollah Jalaleddin Taheri from a post bestowed upon him by Khomeini himself was a stunning blow. He was the same senior cleric who in late 1997 took on vigilantes after they attacked the Isfahan theater showing the film *Snowman*. Reformist newspapers published the letter in full, before all media were ordered not to mention it—prompting the reformist newspaper *Norouz* to leave blank space on its pages where it had planned to report on reactions, including a statement of support for the cleric from 125 members of parliament.[158]

Ayatollah Taheri wrote that he could not close his eyes to "tangible realities, and witness the stifling pain and unbearable suffering of people who were seeing the flowers of virtue being trampled, values collapsing, and spirituality being destroyed."[159] He denounced the continued house arrest of Grand Ayatollah Montazeri and lambasted the Ansar-e Hezbollah vigilantes, who had broken up some of Taheri's own sermons, as "louts and fascists, who are a mixture of ignorance and madness, but whose umbilical cord is connected to the center of power, and who are completely uncontrolled and beyond the law."

Taheri accused clerics of being corrupt hypocrites and a "gang of shroud-wearers," and in his despair he made the regime shudder: "When I remember the promises and pledges of the beginning of the Revolution, I tremble like a willow thinking of my faith."

Hard-liners were appalled and suggested that reformists had manipulated the aging cleric's mind, forced him to sign the letter, or made it up themselves. Taheri's office had to confirm that the theologian had written the angry epistle by his own hand.

The third telling event of 2002 was a death sentence for "apostasy" imposed upon the liberal academic Hashem Aghajari—a war veteran who had lost a leg and a brother to the Iran-Iraq War—for suggesting reform of the clerical establishment. Even right-wing commentators condemned the death sentence as too harsh for simply calling for reform and criticizing the blind following of clerics—statements that had boiled down in the charge sheet to "insulting Islam."

"The Revolution should not eat its own children," the reformist *Etemaad* newspaper suggested in an editorial. Even Montazeri weighed in despite his house arrest. He said the "harsh and unjustified death sentence was the best way to deal a blow to Islam."[160] Montazeri accused "a minority in the country of toying with the lives and reputations of others, in order to preserve their own power and positions."

The standoff spilled into the streets, where students demanded that Aghajari's death sentence be lifted. *Basiji* militiamen provoked several minor-level clashes with the students, who chanted, "Death to the Taliban, in Kabul and Tehran!" and openly questioned the rule of Khamenei's office of *velayat-e faqih*.[161] Top reform leaders nervously warned students to avoid violence to prevent a "state of emergency." A letter signed by 750 people demanded that Khamenei be put on trial; an Iranian analyst told me that Iran was "at a crossroads" and that the "far right only understands force." [162] Thousands of hard-line militiamen reacted, demonstrating in front of the old U.S. Embassy, chanting: "Hypocrites, hypocrites, take shame and leave the university!" [163]

Thrown into this volatile mix was the arrest of former hostage taker and reform strategist Abbas Abdi—ironically on the exact anniversary of the U.S. Embassy takeover—whose polling company had found overwhelming popular support for U.S.-Iran dialogue. The incarceration of someone of Abdi's stature, combined with apostasy charges against a veteran who had endured as much wartime sacrifice as Aghajari, said much about the anxious state of the Government of God.

"Come on, man, these people are part of your family," the Sage fumed. "If you call Abbas Abdi an enemy—a man who is a True Believer—there will be a shortage of words for the majority of Iranians!" [164] Indeed, Iranians had once widely respected clerics. In the 1970s some would take gum out of their mouths when a holy man passed, or chastise someone if they kissed a mullah's hand after drinking alcohol. "But now this is more and more clear, that religious hard-liners see people as a piece of shit," the Sage told me. "From the corner they are in, they say, 'We don't like you!' "

Far from strengthening Khatami's hand, the constant confrontation was eroding faith in the reformist mandate. Pilloried as ineffective, the president had prepared two legislative bills to challenge conservative power, and stated: "Only dictators fear democracy." [165] Yet a French diplomat pointed out what was becoming obvious: "The basic problem since Khatami was first elected, is that if you take the reform process to its logical end, you get regime change. The big question is: Are we closer to an open fight, where eighty percent of the people will tell the rest that they are a minority?" [166]

THE DEATH RULING AGAINST Aghajari was making waves across the Islamic system. Parliament speaker Mehdi Karroubi—lining up two-thirds of Iran's elected deputies behind him—expressed "disgust at this shameful verdict." Khatami said it "never should have been issued."

The surprise was only that the students were not taking bolder steps. "With that kind of backing," the Sage told me, "the students should have burned Tehran down three times over." But there was a warning, too: Supreme Leader Khamenei vowed to deploy "popular forces to intervene" if the power struggle did not ease.

Student rally, Day 4, Tehran University,
November 2002

Demonstrators called for separation of mosque and state, and more accountable clerical rule. But afterward I was sought out by a student dressed in conservative all-black: "I just wanted to speak in favor of the judiciary," she told me. "This decision [to execute Aghajari] has been taken by all the people of Iran. [The reformers] are questioning my country, my religion, and my beliefs, and I object to them. We respect freedom, until it violates the freedom of others. Freedom of speech has its limits." [167]

Student rally, Day 5, Amirkabir University,
November 2002

From the podium: "I ask you not to let those [militants] who want to interfere, to take advantage of this demonstration: This event has been created by them, by the arrest of Abdi, and the ruling against Aghajari," the first speaker said to one thousand students—far fewer than the thousands that had marched earlier in the week. [168]

Police bolstered their ranks on city blocks around the campus, a known political hotbed. Thugs moved in the area, low profile and ready to beat back this manifestation of "Satan's infantry," as Rafsanjani called them. The students were apprehensive. There were posters of Aghajari with an inscrutable look; students had hung a noose from the podium to illustrate the stakes.

Mehdi Habibi, head of the local Islamic student union, was speaking: The rulings were "against thinking" and made by those "making their living from religion. Defending Aghajari is not defending a [reformist] faction, but defending the freedom of expression." The students fidgeted, expecting a blow. Out of the corner of my eye I saw several plainclothes thugs milling on the margins, letting their presence add to the tension.

Student leader Habibi spoke: "For years, the clerics put themselves in a position of holiness, and wouldn't tolerate any criticism," he said. "The clerics [must] not let the demands of the people be sacrificed to fascist interpretations of religion."

REGIME RAMROD RAFSANJANI WARNED factions to stop wrangling, because it was making the United States "greedy for Iran"—the specter of a foreign threat another weapon against dissent. From the pulpit of Friday prayers:

> I would like to tell the White House . . . explicitly that they must be certain the Islamic Revolution in today's Iran is many times stronger and mightier than in those early days when you started your plots to render our Revolution impotent.
>
> You [the American people] should know that there is only a very small number of people in our country who pay any attention to your words. These individuals are weak, and they will desert the scene at the moment they sense the smallest danger. . . .[169]

VIOLENCE ERUPTED AGAIN IN June 2003, a leaderless expression of anger confined to less than one square mile in Tehran. Witnesses like the Sage spoke of an unaccustomed resolve, of how a paltry student demonstration had exploded into running battles and urban warfare that for a week—with first-ever chants to hang the Supreme Leader—became loaded with significance for the future of the Islamic Republic.

It started when several students decided to boycott their dinner in protest, according to one student, Sassan, who took part.[170] "More students came, and brought logs to burn," he told me. Closed-circuit traffic cameras caught their action, and the next day, pro-regime militants tried to secretly penetrate the group. Students took them hostage and found they were carrying pepper spray. One middle-aged man had spurred the students on, Sassan recalled: "This is the revolution—tomorrow there won't be a regime!"

Within a few days students made up only a fraction of thousands of protesters who faced off against thousands of security and vigilante forces. Recent polls had shown that 90 percent of Iranians wanted change, and 70 percent wanted dramatic change. Disenchantment was further fanned by anti-regime satellite TV channels based in the United States, which beamed Farsi-language reports—and real-time details of where clashes were taking place, and encouragement to join them—back into Iran. The message: "There are millions of people out there. Why are you staying at home, watching me?"

During Friday prayers, Rafsanjani warned young Iranians "not to be trapped by the evil television networks that Americans have established." Yet the regime could not quiet the din of supportive honking horns that blared across those Tehran nights.

"It's a sign, [like] those small and relatively minor noises that can be heard when a dam is cracking," Yale graduate Shahriar Rouhani told me from Tehran.[171] "The engineer knows that this is not a joke [and] could result in a major catastrophe."

Washington then stepped in, which only lent credence to Tehran's knee-jerk charges of U.S. meddling. The White House decried "the use of violence against Iranian students" and made clear the United States "supports their aspirations to live in freedom."

Among witnesses, the Sage had only to step outside his door to taste the event. He described the war zone, and its import: "In daytime, it's quite normal; at night there are killings and the highest level of hatred. What's going on is different from a demonstration—nobody is calling for it, or organizing it; it's a general call for dissent." The students had been no more than a "triggering device."[172]

"Unbelievable scenes of violence near my home—two hundred meters away!" he reported. "Young people using sticks attacked a group of Islamic militants, set fire to their motorbikes, and beat the shit out of them—for a while everyone was dancing around the fire. Young people used knives, cables, sticks, stones, and bottles to throw. Both sides showed a high level of violence. . . ."

"Do you hear the horns?" he asked me suddenly, as the blare from outside his apartment made its way through the windows.

Why were they out there? "This buildup of frustration, and resenting the fact that Khatami is not capable of doing anything," he told me. In the previous month "salt was added to the wound" when four MPs went to deliver speeches in cities outside Tehran. "But in all those places Ansar-e Hezbollah turned up and stopped these people from speaking. It was another show that reformers were losing rapidly what was left over from the power they used to have—they can't even deliver a speech. It contributed: 'Wow, see where we ended up.' "

Journalists had been sent a very unusual fax from the Islamic Guidance Ministry, or Ershad. The Sage read me a copy: "In order to avoid possible danger, please do not be present at the scene of sporadic clashes in Tehran. If you don't follow our advice, this office cannot help you at all."

The previous two nights, many Iranian journalists had been arrested, beaten, or detained. All had complained to Ershad, which "did its best for them" to get them released, the Sage said. Yet some had misinterpreted the new missive as an order not to cover the news. In fact it had a far more sinister meaning: the situation had spiraled beyond government control. The street—and all the shadowy arms of revolutionary grip, from militias to vigilantes to a host of intelligence agencies and their battalions of prickly agents and thugs—was taking over. "It means we *really* cannot help you" if you get picked up, the Sage said of the Ershad letter. "We can't do *anything*. It seems the hard-liners are serious about crushing this movement."

The *basijis* would attack without ceasing, and now the other side was showing the same resolve. "Last night there was a young fellow in the street, after midnight," the Sage said. "I asked him, 'What is going on in your neighborhood?' two streets to the south. He replied, 'The mothers of the *basijis* are being fucked tonight!' "

For the first two nights police controlled the *basijis*. But then they did not. On the fourth night, some *basijis* were seen actually wearing police vests, to rein in some vigilantes.

"The hard-liners see two types of people in Iran now: either defending the Islamic Republic, or pro-American," the Sage told me. "So [to them] all these people protesting are paid or unpaid agents of the Americans. It's very black-and-white."

The Sage lamented how after six years of reformist rule, public protests could so quickly spiral into violence. Even if reformists were to set a prearranged plan to follow a certain route, slowly and peacefully, he said, after one hundred meters "the people become crazy, a mob mentality takes over, they forget about the plan . . . there are fires all over the place and things are broken."

Even the Sage was at a loss to explain.

"Young people say, 'This is just the beginning, we have started it, and we are going all the way to the end.' But if you carry on the conversation, they have no idea about what the end should look like. . . . It is very dangerous," he said. "I was scared to shit talking to these young people. There is such a determination in their eyes and their behavior. They are fearless; they are ready for combat. It's like [urban] warfare."

As for the hard-liners, "there is no sign yet that they recognize the danger, that they need popular support to survive, and that they must come to terms with at least part of the demands of the population," the Sage told me. He had just days earlier spoken to one vigilante: "Deep in his mind, he was convinced that the majority of people are with them," the Sage said. "He refused to recognize that all over Iran there is this wish for a more open society—it was his big failure— [along with] his love of his ideology. He would go to great lengths to defend his ideology. The way he approached his religion, it must be one hundred percent true, so there is not room for any different, modern interpretation. No, no, no."

The Sage was still amazed, and repeated for me the narcissistic chants of the vigilantes, as simple as those of high school cheerleaders: "Who is the best? *Hezbollah!* Who fights the most? *Hezbollah!*" Groups of fifty men on twenty-five bikes moved very effectively along the urban front line. But when protesters isolated one or two bikes down a side alley, those militants were suddenly very vulnerable.

There was an important psychological deflation, too, the Sage surmised. "There is a big difference between the *basijis* these days and twenty years ago," he noted. "During the Iran-Iraq War, there was a feeling that we were not only fighting Iraq, but the biggest powers in the world behind it. You define yourself by your enemies, and those were the superpowers back then," the Sage said.

"But these years, they are fighting young people who put gel in their hair, or girls showing hair, or nose jobs. That's the enemy. So it's demeaning, and not at all elevating for their self-image. The only way they can face it now is saying they're fighting these agents of America in our country."

"The Sound of Military Boots"

I found how disgust over the low-grade political and cultural combat had permeated the highest theological levels at the religious center of Qom in late 2003.

"Islam is the religion of peace, of rights, of justice, not tyranny, violence, and prisons—let alone terrorism and killing people and torture in prisons, even if this torture is putting them in solitary confinement," Grand Ayatollah Yusef Saanei told me, his tired eyes testimony to numerous theocratic battles.[173] "All these things are against Islam. . . . I don't think Iran can be presented as an Islamic example."

One poll by the Tehran Medical University had found that 72 percent of respondents thought the reform process was over, 38 percent wanted Khatami to quit, and nearly a third wanted all of parliament to resign.[174] Apathy was spreading like mustard gas in a World War I trench, but Khatami declared democracy the "only alternative." Hardline Friday prayer leader Ayatollah Ahmad Jannati simply dismissed the president's words, telling Iranians: "They are lying. Do not be fooled by them. Leave democracy alone."[175]

Presidential aide Mohsen Mirdamadi, the head of parliament's National Security and Foreign Policy Committee and a former leader of U.S. Embassy hostage takers, had been set upon in the central city of Yazd by fifteen thugs who repeatedly kicked and pummeled him. It was one of a number of vigilante actions.

"They are criminals . . . and wild wolves," said Grand Ayatollah Saanei, who had once been Khomeini's head of judiciary but was now a reformist.[176] Above him on the wall were the framed words of Khomeini, who said he had "raised Mr. Saanei like a son of mine." Holding forth with his stringy beard, he told me that Islam and democracy were an "exact" fit, though "it needs a lot of time, because all those people in theological schools do not think the same way."

Saanei shook his head, disappointed at "the violence of those who have the power, and [their] tyranny." He was rueful: "No one will listen to me." He would "pray to God" against the vigilantes: "They are hateful."

COMPLAINTS SEEMED TO BE the spirit of Qom. Grand Ayatollah Hossein-Ali Montazeri had finally been released in early 2003, after five years of house arrest for questioning the Supreme Leader's legitimacy. Revolutionary Guard and intelligence agents had finally decamped from rooms inside Montazeri's compound, and mostly kept outside. This legend met visitors without a turban, wearing only a simple skullcap. He was surprisingly short—both in height and in time spent with any foreign correspondent. I made my pilgrimage, threading my way through the layers of agents and cameras that still watched this troublemaking cleric.

Iran's leaders "are not fulfilling the promises of the first days of the

Revolution," Montazeri told me.[177] The Guardian Council, designed to ensure that laws complied with Islam, had taken a "radical" step in rejecting thousands of candidates "and is doing the opposite of what it was supposed to do." In another interview he had said, "If people are not satisfied, the establishment is not legitimate. . . . The authorities should increase their tolerance . . . and allow the new generation to choose its future." [178]

When speaking to me, Montazeri issued a call to action. He read a Quranic verse: "God will not change the position of any man, until they decide to change themselves." Then the cleric laughed, finishing our meeting with a saying of the Prophet Mohammad, that the ruling power will be what you make it.

Conservatives had their counterattacks ready: reformists were infidels determined to destroy the Islamic system; reformists had in fact mounted violent attacks upon themselves and blamed it on right-wing vigilantes to gain public sympathy. All their points demonstrated how, after a quarter century of *perfect* Islamic rule, two plus two could still equal five, and often did.

"It is very clear," the hard-line editor of *Kayhan* explained.[179] Hossein Shariatmadari—an official representative of the Supreme Leader, the man with the best coconut macaroons in Tehran—claimed there were few signs of any violence coming from the right. He blamed "extremists among the reformers" and said the beating of Khatami's aide fell into this category, as a clever diversion because reformists couldn't explain "wasting the budget for seven years" and "not paying attention to people's demands."

The same dynamic had been at work during the 1999 student protest, the editor claimed, after students rampaged out of control chanting slogans, occupying streets, and "stopping women with veils and insulting them."

"Faced with such incidents, it's natural that someone loyal to the *nezam* [system] feels it his duty to stop these people," Shariatmadari told me, his voice free of doubt. And it was easy to tell the difference between the godless thugs of reform and the righteous enforcers of Belief. "*Basiji* forces will never attack those who are innocent—a woman or passersby. This is a characteristic of those *basijis* and *hezbollahis*," asserted Shariatmadari. "When we see that a student is attacked with a knife, it is clear this can't be the work of a good Muslim"—and therefore by definition could not be the handiwork of pure-hearted regime loyalists.

Orwell could not have said it better.

IN THIS IDEOLOGICAL STORM, it was perhaps no surprise that news of an Iranian winning the Nobel Peace Prize was buried on official newscasts, if mentioned at all, in December 2003. Human rights lawyer and activist Shirin Ebadi—resolute, pugnacious, a perennial thorn in the side of the whimsical judiciary, *and* a woman—won the most coveted international prize for peace. But Iranians would have been lucky to catch it on their local news, for that event ranked twelfth on state-run TV at 7 P.M. that night. Bigger news included the Iran trade fair, American soldiers killed in Iraq and then Afghanistan (two stories, to illustrate U.S. weakness and the comeuppance of occupation), and an earthquake in Taiwan.

When the Nobel Prizes finally came up, Ebadi's name rated but a brief mention at the end, after extended talk about the chemistry and physics prizes, and then a denigration of the Peace Prize by explaining that other recipients included global reprobates such as Israeli premiers Yitzhak Rabin and Shimon Peres, and former U.S. president Jimmy Carter.

The 9 P.M. broadcast was even worse: Ebadi's triumph was again twelfth on the lineup, but the Nobel story flew by in thirty seconds, with no mention of Ebadi at all.

"I wish I had received a golden key, rather than the Nobel Peace Prize, to open the doors of prisons," Ebadi would later say, making clear that her moving honor had not moved the regime.[180] "I am one drop in the ocean of the freedom-seeking people of Iran, and I feel I have to take this prize and submit it to the Iranian nation," she said. A cartoon in the reformist *Shargh* newspaper showed the Nobel medal emerging from a thicket of thorns.

"Conservatives are very frightened by this new phenomenon of Ebadi winning the prize," said Hamid Reza Jalaeipour, the reformist editor and sociologist.[181] "When someone like Ebadi focuses on human rights, according to conservatives it means they are against God; it's an antireligious activity."

The death threats would indeed pile up against the diminutive campaigner as years went by. Her offices would be attacked, her assistants jailed. Ebadi was routinely vilified in the right-wing press. The uncompromising *Jomhuri-e Eslami* felt obliged to fuss over Ebadi's clear disrespect for Iran's all-important social rules so many miles away in Norway, when she collected her prize. "It must be noted," the paper wrote gravely: "Ebadi shook hands with the BBC man who interviewed her." [182]

AFTER THE YEARS OF street violence and hard-line counterattacks, what happened to the fighting spirit of the youngest reformist elected to parliament in 2000, Fatemeh Haghighatjou? Did she still hold fast to her sense of mission, imbued with ideals of justice and democracy? What fate her belief that the Islamic system could be reformed without violence? How fared her conviction that Khatami's huge electoral mandate—and hers, too, reinforced by so many Tehran votes—could transform the Revolution?

In just over a year, the freshman lawmaker watched her youthful hope turn to hopelessness, the battering she suffered emblematic of how hard-liners triumphed over the first—and only—reformist parliament in a generation. By August 2001, a notoriously hard-line prosecutor had slapped Haghighatjou with a twenty-one-month prison sentence for, among a long list of charges, "misinterpreting" Khomeini's words. Thirty MPs had been summoned to the courts in the previous year; she was the third sentenced to jail, despite immunity for parliamentarians. In 2004 the outspoken deputy was officially barred—along with 2,500 other candidates and eighty sitting deputies like her—from running for reelection.

When I saw Haghighatjou then, on the eve of that 2004 parliamentary vote, she had been acquitted of one charge, which meant ten months off the sentence. She had also been detained, and taken part in a three-week sit-in at parliament to protest the rejection of so many candidates. A mass resignation of 120 deputies deepened the crisis. MP Mohsen Mirdamadi, so recently targeted by a vigilante beating, announced the joint decision to resign. Of Iran's apparently indestructible and inflexible hard-liners, he said, "They want to cover the ugly body of dictatorship with the beautiful dress of democracy. We had no choice but to resign." [183]

An editorial in the reformist *Shargh* newspaper said that accepting the "imposed" conditions of the Guardian Council "is ultimately realization of the slogan: 'Death to reformists.' " [184] The demure Haghighatjou was now well aware that the challenge went beyond politics. She and her fellow reformists were at war.

"There are two options: either [conservatives] are destroyed, and finally destroy the Islamic system, or they change their behavior toward people," the soft-spoken deputy told me, her unflinching eyes locking on mine. [185] "I believe in the proverb 'Power corrupts, and absolute power corrupts absolutely.' That is our main problem now."

The original vision espoused by Khomeini—that the people's votes were a top source of legitimacy—was "not the view of the Supreme Leader today," said Haghighatjou. "I don't believe in the extralegal power of the Supreme Leader, or anyone."

As Haghighatjou's dreams disintegrated, she had come to believe that "reforms within the state are impossible." But she was quite sure those reforms were also inevitable, eventually. She was married by then—sporting a pearl wedding ring—and was a new mother. She heard many complaints from the university students she taught about the failure of reform. She wore her many-layered chador with elegant ease, though her frustration oozed from every pore.

"I couldn't have predicted for a single moment that such difficult things were awaiting reformists . . . that the conservatives would use all the legal and illegal means, while we limited ourselves to the legal," Haghighatjou told me, in calm, measured tones. "They don't believe in the wishes and will of the people at all. They look at people as instruments to use whenever they want. I admit we were naïve about this fact. Everything goes back to the base of our calculation, which was the law."

The former optimist joked that she would find "new friends in prison" whenever summoned for her sentence. The order hadn't come yet. As I took photographs of her after our talk, I commented on her broad grin. "I'm happy to be out of the *nezam* [system]," she said. "That is why I smile like that!"

PRESIDENT MOHAMMAD KHATAMI HAD decried Iran's "culture of despotism" and "dictatorship," but failed to leverage his popular mandate to curb the power of unelected conservative bodies. Haghighatjou and the majority of Iranians who had voted for change were dispirited. The president finally admitted so in an apologetic speech in mid-2003. "If you had pinned your hopes on [the reform movement] and we were defeated . . . at least know that we did not lie to the people and we did not betray them," Khatami told students.[186]

He offered another mea culpa months later. "I am not sure I have been able to fulfill all my promises," Khatami said in his speech to mark the Revolution's twenty-fifth anniversary.[187] "I had a lot of psychological pressure from enemies both internal and external." I barely saw a single portrait of the president poking up from the huge crowd during that speech. Khatami had spoken of his difficulties, looking out upon countless images of Khomeini and Khamenei.

But none of those admissions was enough. Fine words of apology—heartfelt as they certainly were—could not temper the rage of young reformists, the dashed hopes for change that turned willingness to take risks for democracy into despondent resignation. Khatami was accosted on Youth Day 2004 by student representatives. Among them was Somayeh Tohidloo:

Dear Mr. Khatami,

Do you remember the student dormitory [attacks]? That day, in addition to the brutal injustice we endured . . . instead of our attackers, our fellow students were imprisoned. You were silent and told us to be silent too. . . .

When they condemned our professors to death you were silent . . . from then on, one by one, our classmates en masse were sent off to jail and you were silent . . .

Mr. Khatami . . . [y]our ultimate achievement was to destroy a tidal wave of hope—my generation voted for a reformist agenda in two consecutive elections . . . I say today, with conviction, that you are the guilty party.[188]

Reformists were wrecked. The president's brother knew it. "Our main enemy now is our disappointment," Mohammad Reza Khatami told me.[189] "We can't change the reality of the country with dreams." But, he maintained, "the movement has infiltrated all our homes, and turned our children into a generation completely different from us. Maybe this is our biggest achievement."

There was no denying that change had occurred, from the cultural renaissance to political civil war. But it did not temper the excesses of the regime, according to one Western-educated analyst who traveled the country widely. One of his close friends had been killed.

"They believe in death, in murder—in righteous murder," the analyst told me, his anger catching in his throat.[190] "But they won't tell you that. They will say, 'Our fatwa says this, our fatwa says that.' You are dealing with fanatics; it's the same the world over. . . . Iranians are very cultured and hospitable and polite, and *you* often are not dealing with a group of brutish, impolite people—but those people really are." The result, he said, was that "an organized minority [hard-liners] have more power than a disorganized majority."

The Sage mused that over the previous century, Iranians had missed several chances to embrace more democratic rule. "Somehow that bird flew away, we couldn't keep it," he told me.[191] "Perhaps we in our hearts did not have sufficient appreciation or love for democracy, and that's why we lost it." He drew parallels between the optimism that fed the Revolution in 1979 and the hopes that had soared for reform—the triumphs of both events incomplete and unenduring.

"We were radical revolutionaries, and thought *that* was the only way to change things," the Sage told me.[192] "We were children. The idea then was, 'It couldn't get worse. Let's get rid of the Shah, no matter what happens.' But then, it *could* get worse."

ANALYSTS WERE CHARTING THE reasons for defeat. Many pointed to the suffocating press laws implemented in the last days of the outgoing conservative parliament, in the spring of 2000. Reversing those restrictions was the top priority of the incoming reformist deputies, who had convened urgent meetings to prepare for the vote. Overturning the press law was central to the reformist agenda. Until, that is, Ayatollah Khamenei intervened with written instructions—even as the legislature prepared for debate on the floor of parliament. The Supreme Leader ruled that the new bill was "not legitimate" nor in the "interests" of the Revolution.[193]

"If the enemies infiltrate our press, this will be a big danger to the country's security and the people's religious beliefs," Khamenei wrote, in a letter only made public and read in open session under extreme pressure from pro-reform parliamentarians.

The deputies were dumbfounded, and the shouts, shoving, and partial walkout that ensued prompted the speaker to turn off the microphones and make repeated calls for order.

"The critical event that ended the reform of Khatamism was when the Great Führer [Khamenei] ordered the parliament not to discuss the press law," one Iranian professor told me.[194] "That was the end of reform, when these people buckled under. On that day MPs should have gone on strike. They never succeeded in justifying why they accepted this. Khatami's brother said he heard news that *hezbollahi* black shirts were standing ready to move in on the parliament. And conservatives just noted wisely how easily they got away with it. Like a lot of schoolboys, if you are punched in the nose and you don't even try to punch back. . . . They showed themselves to be absolutely spineless."

Amir Mohebian, an editor at the conservative newspaper *Resalat*, had predicted the reformist collapse years earlier. "Instead of controlling people's expectations, [reformists] raised them," Mohebian told me.[195] The biggest mistake had been the out-of-control June 2003 demonstrations, which were shocking in their resolve, but were disorganized and fizzled. "They used their last card when they took to the streets. They couldn't do anything, and lost the biggest tool of politics: the bluff," said Mohebian. After that, "we understood they lost all chances. A loaded weapon scares one person; an empty weapon scares two people."

But the right wing had limits, too, and "their time was over," asserted Mohebian.[196] "Hard-liners are like dynamite: you can destroy things with them, but you can't build things with them."

That matched the view of Khatami's closest advisers: "The distance grows on both sides," Vice President Ali Abtahi told me.[197] "One side believes the conspiracy grows every day, and the enemy gets stronger every day. These people believe that Khatami is a traitor. Then there are people who say we need to be faster, that we need a new Revolution now. [Yet] anything that leads to violence will reverse the result." Already the speed had been too fast, Abtahi said, because it "led conservatives to believe that we wanted to eliminate them."

The reformist "defeat" didn't necessarily translate into a conservative "victory," however. "Reformists feel increasingly it's a lost cause. But if you talk to the other side, they feel it is a lost cause, too," the Sage told me. Khatami had "portrayed a new brand: a powerful man who is not despotic." And while it was a new image, it failed to solve the riddle of whether the Islamic Republic was more "Islamic," or more "Republic," or could balance both. It was the same riddle—the same clashing debate—that would soar to prominence again in 2009, with heavy bloodshed and protests in the streets, over an election stolen by regime hard-liners.

"After twenty-five years we are at the end of attempts to legally reform the system, and there are real fears and worries," said the Sage.[198]
He pronounced "a dead end: if you don't want another Revolution,
and [if] legal reform doesn't work, nothing is left but a miracle."

And Iran had already *had* its miracle—back in 1979.

"Khomeini came and said, 'All people are free; they are born free
and will live free,' " recalled the Tehran computer specialist I had met
years before, the one with the Chanel buttons on her chador, artificial
nails, and a pseudonym.[199] "Everyone thought, 'Ah! Here is democracy.' But after two or three or five years, slowly . . . ," Samira had
said, her voice trailing off. Back then before the Revolution, SAVAK
had been killing citizens. And these days, its acronym changed by one
letter, to VAVAK, an intelligence cell of "revolutionaries" from inside
had been killing people. Students had no money, no jobs, no future.
Yet anyone with a beard got a job.

To Samira, the *velayat-e faqih* says, "I know all." She mocked: "Maybe
you *know*, and you *are* a genius." But it didn't make sense to this
educated professional. She asked: "For sixty million people, only one
person can think, only one person can decide?"

FOR YOUNG IRANIANS WHO dared hope for something different, for something less severe, for a system more inclusive: for them,
that legacy of using "force" was proving impossible to escape. Stretch-
ing back decades, national episodes of brutality far outnumbered
those flashing moments of collective bliss. And beyond the obvious
paroxysms, Iranians had routinely been afflicted by a gnawing chronic
culture of violence—whether imposed from outside by war or occupation, or erupting internally through the Revolution or reaction to
reform.

A blogger called "arareza" described it this way in early 2004:

The girls of my generation will never forget their head teachers tug-
ging hard at tiny strands of hair that somehow fell out of their veils
to teach them a lesson. The boys of my generation will never forget

being slapped five times in the face for wearing shirts with Western labels on them . . . all of us have hundreds of similar memories . . .

My generation is the damaged generation. We were constantly chastised that we were duty-bound to safeguard and uphold the sacred blood that was shed for us during a revolution and a war. Any kind of happiness was forbidden for us . . .

My generation would be beaten up outside cinema queues or pizza restaurants . . . punished in the public parks; kicked and punched in the centers of town by the regime's militia . . . I will never forget the militia's Toyota vans and the loudspeaker announcements in Vali Asr Square: "We will fight against all boys and girls!"—shouting those exact words!

Who can forget?[200]

ON THE EVE OF Iran's June 2005 presidential election, the candidate choice illustrated the confusion among those Iranians who wanted change. Khatami's legal limit of two terms was coming to an end. Reformists had settled on a bland, unelectable choice, Mustafa Moin. Cleric Mehdi Karroubi was promising cash handouts. Regime phoenix Rafsanjani was trying to rise from the ashes again, to prevent the spread of "Islamic fascism" in Iran.

Reformists were so discredited that an attack just days before the vote—by thirty vigilantes against a meeting of five hundred people in Qom, which left reform strategist Behzad Nabavi injured—was portrayed as a sign of rising fortunes because it showed they were still relevant, that reformists were still *worth* attacking.[201] The *hezbollahi*s threw tear gas, eggs, and other projectiles. When they surrounded Nabavi, the reformist crowd screamed back at them: "Death to the Taliban in Tehran! Death to the Taliban in Qom!" It was the worst beating that Nabavi had suffered since his seven years in a SAVAK jail.

"These actions reveal the nature of our opponents [but] maybe we should thank the militants," Nabavi joked at a press conference days later, sporting cuts, a black eye, and torn shirt. "People tell me: 'If they had killed you, Moin would win 100 percent.'"

As voting day neared, candidates across the spectrum vied for support by rekindling reformist fantasies of change. The calculation was that Khatami's 79 percent voting bloc was out there, if candidates could convince them to turn out. Front-runner and two-time former president Ali Akbar Hashemi Rafsanjani—who portrayed himself as a centrist "experienced captain" who could pilot Iran away from the treacherous waters of radicalism—showed how far some felt they had to go.[202]

At a campaign meeting in a north Tehran prayer hall, I watched the audience clap as Rafsanjani spoke, swooning about the middle ground. Never mind the lingering questions over corruption or links to political murders; this regime perennial was polling twice the support of his nearest rival. He had also quietly sent an unambiguous message to Washington via the Swiss Embassy that he could deliver better U.S.-Iran ties.[203]

"Nobody is willing to [believe] anything but moderation and reality," Rafsanjani told supporters. His Shah-era mug shot was on the wall of the prison downtown, too. "Don't be worried about radicalism; this is [just] a [passing] wave."[204]

Hard-line newspapers complained that not one of the many candidates spoke of Islam—it clearly wasn't good politics. "Not only do they forget about the important things in the country," railed *Jomhuri-e Eslami*, but candidates showed "the authorities as incapable, as traitors to each other, and [that they] consider conspiracies and foreign enemies to be myths. We confess that we never predicted a day when enemies would succeed in making the faithful fight against the children of the Revolution."[205]

If nothing else, Khatami's legacy had brought a "divine" political system right down to earth. Reformist politics and the language of freedom dominated the debate. At the end of his tenure, Khatami claimed that some part of the ruling system could be criticized "without fear. Although criticisms may still have costs, the mentality is such that all are in awe of the prevailing freedoms."[206]

It certainly looked that way, momentarily, on the ground. On the

eve of the vote, Rafsanjani campaigners oozed an impression of openness, trying to convince doubters that there were good things to come
if their man won. Hundreds in rich districts of Tehran were treated to
live outdoor concerts, with both men and women onstage at once—in
a country where any music in public had been restricted for decades.
I watched a crowd of young Iranians mob the metal gate entrance,
where teenage campaign volunteers behaved like bouncers at a night
club—doing face checks to guarantee a high quality of "clientele."

But cynicism had set in. "Everybody knows this is temporary, and
only for the election," said Samira Ghorbani, a graduate with a token
headscarf and red lipstick, shouting over the amplified music.[207] The
election "makes no difference, so there is no reason to vote."

As the crowd clapped to the beat, I was asked not to photograph
people enjoying themselves too much in public. "We're trying to
make it so in the future, there will not be problems with the police,"
explained Hamid Hosseini, a Rafsanjani volunteer with a goatee.
Groups of young people outside the venue roared along the street in
cars covered with Rafsanjani stickers, each paid six dollars a day to perform the service. "This is just to fool people," an engineering student
with a lip stud told me. "People will not be fooled."

Indeed, not enough voters bought into the illusion. Rafsanjani's
aides had warned shrilly that a conservative victory would mean "Islamic fascism." But Rafsanjani was crushed by a wild-card hard-liner: a
blacksmith's son by the name of Mahmoud Ahmadinejad.

Rafsanjani was never convincing and never even left Tehran to campaign. Mustafa Moin, the lackluster reformist meant to carry Khatami's torch into the future, did not even make it to the second round
of the vote. Yet at a reformist election rally in a soccer stadium before
voting day, there were moments of excitement and some prescient
warnings.

The disillusion had not taken hold in Nahid Molavi, a twenty-one-
year-old history student I saw draped in an Iranian flag and with her
fists clenched defiantly at the rally. "I support the one who values
freedom," Molavi said of reformist Moin.[208] "I came because I love

freedom, because we are Iranians, and we will decide," she told me. Thousands of people had turned up to hear the voices of reformist personalities; scores of young people raced around the infield trailing Iranian flags and plastered with images of Khatami. Molavi said, "This flag is sacred to all of us, and while we are here, democracy will not die."

But such conviction belonged by then only to a distinct minority. Among the speakers at the rally was Fatemeh Haghighatjou—the onetime youthful lady lawmaker whose democratic views had proven so unacceptable to the Islamic *nezam*.

"Until a few days ago, I intended to boycott the election. I considered it unjust and illegal," Haghighatjou told the rally, her beautiful hands holding the rim of the rostrum.[209] "But as we approach the day of the election, the more my ears are hurt by the sound of military boots. So today, [as] I hear the military march, I also anticipate the sound of bullets" of a new crackdown.

"So today, remaining silent is wrong," declared Haghighatjou, sounding the alarm. If reformists stayed at home, a hard-liner would win. Everyone had to vote. Cheers erupted: "The election is our chance to express the thunder of freedom!"

5

Ahmadinejad: The Messiah Hotline

We see the hand of this holy management every day.
God knows that we see it. I don't exaggerate. . . . Iran's
nuclear achievement is the biggest miracle in contemporary
history. . . .

  The big powers are still astonished. . . . They all have
become united, and applied the severest methods, but Iran
has become nuclear before their eyes, despite their will. It is
not an accident. We behold the hands of Imam [Mahdi], we
behold it in many occasions.

—Mahmoud Ahmadinejad, May 2008

IDEOLOGICAL. HARD-LINE. AND A pious, political fire-bomb committed to the principles of the Islamic Revolution. The simple-living President Mahmoud Ahmadinejad is a man who struck fear into the hearts of Iran's reformists and rekindled hope in those that brought him to power: the legions of Iran's often-overlooked religious poor, and puritanical militarists.

The phenomenon of Ahmadinejad's pole vault to the presidency in June 2005 shocked and mortified Iran's political elite. They did not appreciate the magnitude of resentment against reformists for failing to fulfill promises of change. And few predicted the willingness of Iranians to back a fire-breathing maverick who had promised to take Iran back twenty-five years in time, to the splendid "roots" of the Revolution.

Ahmadinejad's ascent also marked a critical step in a carefully plotted neoconservative revival, which gave hard-liners control once again of every formal lever of power. This president ushered in a new era of leadership for the most right-wing ideologues of the Revolutionary Guard, the Basij and the clergy, which they aimed to make permanent. Their project to reestablish *total* control would take years more—and would require, in 2009, one more violently contested presidential election. Along the way, Ahmadinejad took a post endowed with limited power, gathered much more power in his hands, and boldly created for himself a near-imperial presidency.

THE 2005 ELECTION REVEALED two distinct leadership styles— and very different political worlds—as the two presidential candidates cast their ballots within an hour of each other in Tehran, in the final round of voting.

Ali Akbar Hashemi Rafsanjani had been at the center of power for a quarter century, and his campaign video was set in his expansive north Tehran compound.[1] Yet it sought to portray a modest family man, and was deliberately shot like a handheld home movie to give the impression of peering into his private moments.

The video showed Rafsanjani reading in the garden, his face lighting up with grateful appreciation when his wife brought a plate of chilled watermelon. It showed Rafsanjani the soccer fan watching a game on TV. Here was a modern man surfing the Internet with a grandson at his knee. It showed a global power broker whose every word made headlines—setting newspaper printing presses whirring as they churned out the news he made. The election video showed a man whose granddaughter walked into his den wearing innocent white shoes, hoping for some attention. The little girl—in fact, an unrelated actress—cracks open the door and peeps in. Rafsanjani smiles and takes her for a walk down a tree-lined avenue—an Iranian idyll.

That is, unless one was appealing for votes among the multitudes of poor Iranians, who clogged lower-class warrens in Tehran and across the country. Ahmadinejad's low-key campaign contrasted sharply with the $5 million spent by Rafsanjani on flashy posters and concerts. Even his campaign video was a deliberately humble affair, which brilliantly evoked pious priorities. It showed the aspiring president demonstrating his ascetic lifestyle and giving a tour of his modest, working-class home, where he sits down cross-legged in front of the tablecloth, or *sofreh*, laid out on the floor. Ahmadinejad's son is asked, in an obvious dig at the luxurious lifestyle of the main opponent, "Do you have a sauna and Jacuzzi?" The son replies: "What are those?" [2]

After the first round of voting, Ahmadinejad had thanked Iranians for getting him through to the second round, saying they "created a relationship between hearts, and this is my way." [3] And with one more round of voting to go, Ahmadinejad felt the need to strike moderate tones. "I know Iranian culture, and I know how to relate to the Iranian people—this is a great gift from God," he said. He called the first-round vote "a day of friendship and brotherhood."

Ahmadinejad said freedoms would continue, and that nothing would be imposed: "Freedom is the spirit of the Islamic Revolution. And in our religious democracy, this is much greater than you can imagine," the candidate said. "Every day that passes in the Islamic Revolution, the place of freedom shall be more clear and enlightened."

ON THE FINAL DAY of voting, the two distinct political styles played out in practice. [4] First came Rafsanjani. Like a strutting monarch, he swept alone into Jamaran prayer hall, breathing the rarefied air of affluent north Tehran, on sacrosanct ground where Khomeini used to preach. We reporters and photographers had been assembled in an orderly row behind a piece of string to observe this perfectly scripted act of democracy.

Wearing immaculately pressed robes, Rafsanjani was a picture of decorum, the emperor deigning to exchange a few words with his subjects, exuding benevolence. He voted perfunctorily, nodded respectfully to election officials, inked his finger, and cast his ballot. Then he paused at the podium and addressed the cameras. Speaking with a savior's certainty, he said he was "destined to serve the Revolution until the last day of my life. I intend to play a historical political role, to stop the domination of extremism."

We dutifully recorded his words. But it was already too late. In another part of Tehran, Iran's political clock was being turned back.

I raced to the middle/working-class district of Narmak in east Tehran, where religion, poverty, and regime loyalty were serving up a surprising mix of voters. I made it just in time to catch Ahmadinejad. An unlikely contender who had cast himself as a man of the people, the candidate had refused to move into the Tehran mayor's mansion in 2003 and listed his only assets as a thirty-year-old car, a much older house, and an empty bank account.

So quickly after Rafsanjani's elite performance, I found myself packed tight into the small, crowded, stuffy-hot hall that was attached to Ahmadinejad's neighborhood mosque. With fellow photographers, I perched on the edge of a stage. But chaos erupted the moment God's candidate arrived, as if a grenade had been tossed into the tangle of people. Mobbed by photographers fighting each other to get a clean shot, the stubby populist cheek-kissed and bear-hugged supporters as he forced his way toward the ballot box.

His divine duty done, he finally put up his arms—the pad of his right index finger stained with the purple ink of democracy—and sternly ordered journalists to back off. Iranians could not remember when, if ever, they had such a high-ranking politician who could also conjure such a personal, populist touch with Iran's "common man." No other Iranian politician had played such a hands-on role, as a magical man of the people.

"First comes God, and second comes Ahmadinejad!" shouted one exuberant housewife, Sadat Nassiri, moments after her hero voted. Her own finger was stained with ink, and as proof she poked it out of her black chador. She avoided the candidate crush by standing outside the mosque, on an American flag that had been painted on the street years before, to be easily trampled underfoot. She told me of her hope: "He says he wants to be friends of the world. He speaks from the heart. He helps people for the sake of God."

Ahmadinejad emerged from the sweating mass inside the mosque, squeezing out a side door only to be dwarfed by an array of microphones, the elaborate blue tiles a perfectly Persian backdrop.

Declaring his pride in being Iran's "little servant and street sweeper," Ahmadinejad vowed: "Today is the beginning of a new political era for the Iranian nation." But only he could have known then how different it would be.

BEHIND THE SUNKEN EYES, patchy gray-black beard, and populist Mr. Rogers zip-up Windbreaker was a man quite convinced that he was God's choice, destined to lead the Islamic Republic at the moment of the triumphant return of the Shiite Messiah, the Mahdi. In the process Ahmadinejad would throw Iran back to those early days when the Revolution was in a fight to save itself, when it first entrenched a brutal "securitization" to eliminate enemies. Ahmadinejad's initial burst onto the national stage came only with critical help from the Basij militia and the Revolutionary Guard, and a word-of-mouth campaign from key hard-line clerics.

In their conservative project, it was not enough to simply defeat reformists at the polls—or at least *appear* to defeat them. They had to destroy the reform movement altogether, using the ballot box and head-cracking baton to remove its taint from Iran's revolutionary blood.

Still, there seemed to be as many reasons to vote for Ahmadinejad as there were votes cast for him. The majority dismissed critics' predictions that he would impose "Islamic fascism" upon Iran, that he was a radical Islamist whose "Iranian Taliban" would reverse the years of loosening social restrictions under Khatami. Ignored too were the endless jokes—and fears—that Ahmadinejad had plans to divide sidewalks with curtains into separate lanes for men and women. Or about how the careful parting of his hair was meant to segregate male and female lice. One friend told me that already more jokes had been made about Ahmadinejad than about every king, premier, shah, and president during Iran's previous 2,500 years, combined.

Ironically, despite Ahmadinejad's fierce loyalty to the Islamic system (*nezam*), he was seen as the anti-establishment choice, taking on the ultimate insider Rafsanjani, who had been tarnished by past charges of corruption and links to political killings. "He never wears a tie—the unmistakable sign of modernity. And since Islam forbids the frivolous sensation of a razor blade on a man's face, Ahmadinejad's beard is also part of his persona," writes political scientist Abbas Milani.[5] "All aspects of his appearance are intended to signal the sharp tension between moderns and traditionalists."

For some, Ahmadinejad appealed simply because he was not a cleric. He may have been more stridently religious than most holy men, but that did not prevent Yaghoub Balali from voting for him. "No more clergy!" the taxi driver told me on election day, joyfully explaining his vote with a twist of his hand above his head, as if he were unwinding a turban. "Everyone I know is voting for Ahmadinejad; all Tehran is voting for him."[6]

For many Iranians, it was his populist message of economic "justice," of bringing Iran's oil wealth to the table of every Iranian, as well as Ahmadinejad's evident incorruptibility, that seemed to cut across Iran's social divide. One woman told me how, when she was destitute and out of work, she had appealed directly to Ahmadinejad, when he was mayor. He took an interest, wrote a letter, and she got a job serving tea for the municipality. "He helps many poor people," she said, still in awe. Another family of teachers told me they voted for Ahmadinejad because he had improved school supplies and the education system.

"He's concerned about people and knows the pain of this society much better than the others," said Mahdis Pournikoo, an eighteen-year-old student laden with makeup and a tiny headscarf—signs that would normally mark her as a reformist voter. I asked if, under the new regime, she feared a tightening of social rules, which in the past involved beatings for such dress.

"Maybe there is a need for a little bit of restriction," Pournikoo told me, self-consciously pulling her headscarf up to cover more hair. "Anyway, we know how to restrict ourselves." Groups of motorcyclists— normally used by shadowy hard-line vigilantes to intimidate—handed out flowers to Westernized young people in north Tehran, in an apparent bid to reassure them that a crackdown was not on the cards.[7]

Despite the swelling support for Ahmadinejad, I spoke to many people who had voted for Rafsanjani out of desperate hope to avoid an archconservative president. One of those was Mona, a young woman overly dolled up and standing in line to vote *against* Ahmadinejad. The bright red of her lipstick had been hurriedly applied and extended beyond the line of her lips. "We must vote, because the situation will get so much worse . . . We must try harder for democracy," she told me. "People who did not vote last time are voting this time."

Or they did not vote at all. "Why should I vote for my unfortunate future?" asked one angry man. "You talk to the *basijis* to get the real truth . . ." Another asked me: "Why do you interview the guys with beards?" Yet another die-hard boycotter would be quoted by Max Rodenbeck in the *Economist:* " 'I have voted once in thirty years, and that was for the creation of an Islamic Republic,' says an old gentleman who deals in real estate. 'I'm not going to get fucked again.' "[8]

While Ahmadinejad's rise stumped the political elite, it made perfect sense to those who lived near the mayor and reveled in his homespun image. "He is a wonderful person; he is my neighbor," said Mehdi Gomar, an English-speaking twenty-two-year-old with a goatee and wraparound shades, who lived a block from the president-to-be and had a job as an industrial engineer with the Iranian Atomic Energy Organization.[9] Few would appear less likely to join the mayor's bandwagon, but Gomar told me the threats of imminent social crackdown were all "lies." "I know he has lots of experience to be president,"

Gomar said. "I'm sure he is absolutely better than Rafsanjani. All my family is voting for him."

Masoud Hadizadeh felt the same way. "His house is there, next to mine. He is my neighbor. He is just like us. He is very available to us," Hadizadeh told me. "Honesty, honesty is the most important thing to us. I don't think he will make big social changes. Once you give freedom to people, you can't take that from them."

REPRESENTING THE PATCHWORK OF Iranians that swept Ahmadinejad to victory were bearded ideologues and black-shrouded women and uniformed Revolutionary Guard soldiers, mixing night and day with Westernized youth and the nonreligious, outside the president-elect's humble home. They voted for a populist who had vowed to fix an ailing economy. Or they voted against clerics. Or against the establishment. Or to return to those cherished, defiant, and self-reliant "roots" of the Revolution.

But of the multitude of Iran's political factions, none was behind him. Institutional support for the mayor's unlikely bid to be president came only—and ominously—from the Revolutionary Guard, their *basiji* brethren, and the chain-wielding militants of Ansar-e Hezbollah. And they would all be well rewarded. Ahmadinejad was the first Iranian president beholden to no political group, only to his fellow ideologues, both in uniform and out. His close ties to the Guard and Basij stretched back to the Iran-Iraq War, when for two years Ahmadinejad served in the Revolutionary Guard, based in the Hamzeh Headquarters near the Iraq border. There he befriended fellow hard-liner Esmaeil Ahmadi Moghaddam, who would later become the Basij commander and Iran's police chief, and would in 2005 spearhead *basiji* and Guard support for Ahmadinejad's election.[10]

Trained in guerrilla tactics, the new president had been associated with a daring raid far behind enemy lines to Kirkuk, Iraq, in 1987. Journalist Kasra Naji, in his biography *Ahmadinejad: The Secret History of Iran's Radical Leader,* says details are "hazy," but that Ahmadinejad was part of the support team. Kirkuk "was by far the most dangerous operation he had taken part in," and marked a big change after his usual duties of "engineering roles such as building bridges and erecting fortifications."[11]

No pictures have ever been made public to clarify Ahmadinejad's war experience. But throughout the campaign he carried the mantle of the *basiji* and his status as a war veteran, steeped in the memories of the martyrs. And during the war he had made connections with a number of key Revolutionary Guard officers who would grow into influential leadership roles—and prove invaluable to fulfilling Ahmadinejad's political aspirations.

Widespread disappointment among the warriors after the war helped Ahmadinejad mobilize True Believers, according to U.S.-based political scientist Abbas Milani.

> When the war ended, and the Revolutionary Guards and the Basij returned to their cities and villages, they were shocked by the corruption that had transformed many of the revolutionaries in the clerical leadership into very rich men. Some had enriched themselves by virtually taking over industries that had been confiscated from the old regime. Others had become rich as the result of the war itself—from selling ration cards or receiving kick-backs in black-market arms purchases. While some Revolutionary Guard commanders and Basij leaders soon acquired wealth of fantastic proportions themselves, the more devout members were deeply disturbed by it and began to plan for a return to the pieties of the early days of the revolution.
>
> Ahmadinejad was among them.[12]

In that context, notes Milani, the eight years of the Khatami era "further convinced these devout Islamists that the very soul of the revolution had been compromised."[13] So Ahmadinejad spent that time working to burnish his anti-reformist credentials, becoming a "trusted figure of the fringe of Islamic zealots" of Ansar-e Hezbollah, writes biographer Naji.[14]

Ansar and Ahmadinejad shared discipleship of some of the most extreme ultraright clerics, such as Guardian Council chief Ayatollah Ahmad Jannati, and Ayatollah Mohammad Taghi Mesbah-Yazdi, who approved of violence against opponents. Ansar militants provided plenty of that in their attacks against reformists. "As [Ansar] stepped up their activities, Ahmadinejad seemed to get closer to them," writes Naji. "He became a regular speaker at their secret internal gatherings."

More publicly, Ahmadinejad and "younger members of the religious right were determined to reverse their humiliating defeats at the ballot box," adds Naji. In one speech the future president said: "This is the time for a cultural war. We have to direct the minds of our youth towards the basic principles, methods and the values of the Revolution. We have to lay down Islamic guidelines for governance. . . ."[15]

It was Ayatollah Mesbah-Yazdi who helped spearhead the revitalization of the hard-liners, a project that the wealthy and influential cleric took on with "energy and strategic foresight," notes historian Ali Ansari.[16] Ridding Iran of the "heresy of reform," as Mesbah-Yazdi saw it, would take time:

> The reformists had always believed that while the conservatives might dominate in the use of coercion—unleashing vigilantes when necessary—they themselves would always win the argument. Mesbah[-Yazdi] wanted both to retain control over the street and win the argument.
>
> Thus was cultivated a new generation of articulate conservatives who would present the case for authoritarianism. The failure of reform, the case ran, was not caused by the violent obstruction of conservatives, as reformists charged, but by the failure and inadequacy of the very idea of democracy. . . .
>
> The notion that all could participate in politics was nonsense.[17]

The new argument was a reversal after decades of received revolutionary thought. "This was a highly elitist philosophy that went against one of the central myths of the Islamic revolution: that of its inherent popularity and mass base," writes Ansari. This new think-ing flowed from the proven electoral pull of the reformists—and the angry disillusion that attended their failure.

"[H]ardline conservatives like Ahmadinejad are haunted by Kha-tami and what he achieved. Ahmadinejad's much-remarked populism is a direct response to the genuine popularity Khatami generated," adds Ansari.[18] "[T]he broader aim of the conservative faction is to show that one of their own can do better; to shatter the bond between the reform movement and the populace and forge a new bond between the people and their own ideology. Ahmadinejad was to be the hard-line conservative populist who would capture the public imagination."

WITH SO MUCH AT stake, reformists cried foul over the skewed results of that 2005 election victory. How could Ahmadinejad have made it to the second round of voting, when support was lean even in the northwestern province of Ardabil, where Ahmadinejad had once served for three years as governor-general? His former constituents were unimpressed: only 44 percent of eligible voters turned out, and gave him fifth place out of six in the first round of voting.[19]

Mehdi Karroubi—the former parliament speaker and cleric, with a perfectly sculpted white beard—went to sleep the night of the first round in 2005, with enough of a lead in the initial count to expect that he easily made it into the second ballot. But he woke to find that official figures put him behind Ahmadinejad by less than one-fifth of 1 percent (.18 percent) of the vote. Karroubi decried a "bizarre inter-ference" in which "money has changed hands," told people to vote again anyway in the second round, and prophesied: "The fanatics are coming, and people are not going to enjoy peace and security any longer."[20]

The main reform candidate, Mustafa Moin, did far worse in the re-sults, and also issued dire predictions. "Take seriously the danger of fascism," he warned. "Such creeping and complex attempts [at vote manipulation] will eventually lead to militarism, authoritarianism, as well as the social and political strangulation of the country." In a letter to the Supreme Leader, Moin's advisers called on Khamenei to stop "the coup d'etat that was going . . . through its last stages." [21]

Even Rafsanjani, the winner in the first round, complained about the results and told the Leader privately he was going to pull out of the election. Khamenei persuaded him to stay in, but Rafsanjani spoke publicly of an "organized interference" that caused a "soiled" result.[22] He knew right-wing forces had marshaled themselves for victory, and he derided "those who are wearing the cloak of Islam inside out and are deceitfully engaged in defrauding the people by trying to portray their sick thoughts as original Islamic culture, and impose it on others."

Rafsanjani was defeated. But few questioned the relative magnitude of the final tally, in which Iranians lavished the hard-liner Ahmadinejad with 61.6 percent of the vote, compared to Rafsanjani's lackluster 35.9 percent.

"I feel betrayed," middle-class voter Mohammad told me. "No one even knew Ahmadinejad before this. How could he come from nowhere without cheating? All those who voted for him have ties to the regime."

"It's a mini coup d'etat," the Sage told me, still in shock after the election, as he rolled a cigarette.[23] His double-nested teapots were hot on the gas burner well past midnight. There was much to talk about. "Something bigger has happened . . . it's a movement, not to say anti-regime, but it's anti-establishment. Ahmadinejad happened to offer a window of opportunity for all the poor, and people who feel deprived."

SO HOW DID IT happen?

"Ahmadinejad's victory represents a fooling of the public, by creating a war between different classes of rich and poor," explained Mohammad Atrianfar, then chief editor of the reformist newspaper *Shargh* and senior political adviser to Rafsanjani.[24] Speaking in plush glass and wood-paneled offices—marking a man who clearly was a player—Atrianfar told me that five months before the election, the

Basij and Revolutionary Guard created what he called a "Basirat (Insight) Plan" to undermine front-runner Rafsanjani's credibility. They showered Iranians with leaflets that portrayed Rafsanjani and his family as filthy rich and out of touch with ordinary Iranians—which was not a big leap. Then two months before the vote, *basiji* militants were each instructed to list ten people that they knew and convince them to vote for Ahmadinejad.

"So the *basiji* acted just like a political party, which is illegal," Atrianfar told me. "A person with few prospects can't come from the city as a technocrat, and get sixty percent of the national vote, without going through an organization. And there *is* no organization besides the Basij that could do it." Such stories were widespread in the aftermath of the election about how Ahmadinejad squeezed into the runoff.

Rafsanjani had made clear that if he won, he intended to curtail the powers of the office of the Supreme Leader. So Khamenei "suggested" to Guard and Basij commanders that they vote for Ahmadinejad, and take family members with them.[25] Indeed, a friend of mine who worked in Tehran told me that, weeks before the vote, the cleric linked to his government technical office told all staff they had to "think about" voting for Ahmadinejad.

While other candidates appealed to the Leader to stop a "coup," the decision had already been made to engineer victory for Ahmadinejad, rather than fellow conservative and former high-ranking Revolutionary Guardsman and national police chief Mohammad Baqer Qalibaf, who had portrayed himself too much as a Westernized *Top Gun* pilot, wearing sunglasses and voicing values that smacked more of reform than revolution.

"In fact only days before the country went to the polls, the fate of the election was decided at a high-level meeting" at Khamenei's residence, reports Naji, drawing on two well-placed sources.[26]

"In order to secure the blanket conservative control of all branches of the Iranian government, the leaders had to look at where the grassroots support already lay. And here was Ahmadinejad's key strength: the Basij. Many members of the voluntary militia were already campaigning for the mayor of Tehran," writes Naji. "Ahmadinejad was the candidate who most closely captured their blend of fervent Islamism, conservatism, and militancy."

When the father of Iran's Revolution, Ayatollah Khomeini, created the Basij, he called for a "twenty-million-man militia" to tackle both external and internal threats. Today they number in the millions (anywhere from three to twelve million active members, with six hundred thousand in armed paramilitary units), with a powerful ideological presence across society, from indoctrination camps run by the Islamic Revolutionary Guard Corps (IRGC) to university students, tribal, and factory units.[27]

But Khomeini had also explicitly forbidden political activity by each one of Iran's armed forces. In 1982, the New Army Statute codified that rule, and Khomeini declared that "the duty of every soldier in every garrison is that he should not be ruled by politics."[28] Any interference in politics would "certainly destroy the prestige and honor of the armed forces." Khomeini later reinforced that order, saying that all armed elements "should not enter into any [political] party or groups, and steer clear from political games."[29]

But those diktats had been losing their potency since the Imam's death. The Guards themselves did not hide the fact of their intervention. The deputy chief of the IRGC, General Mohammad Baqer Zolqadr—one of the senior officers Ahmadinejad worked with during the war, and who would become his deputy interior minister—told a group of Basij commanders that "in the current complex political situation, in which both foreign pressures and internal forces were trying to prevent us from forming a fundamentalist government, we had to operate with complexity."[30] Ahmadinejad's victory was no "accident," he said. "Fundamentalist forces, thank God, won the election thanks to their smart and multi-fold plan and through the massive participation of the Basij." The plan was apparently called "moving with lights off" so it would not be spotted by rivals.[31]

But it certainly was spotted. Adding to the complaints of disenfranchised non-hard-liners, outgoing President Khatami gave a detailed secret report to the Leader that described "the misuse of the logistical, financial, and human resources of the Guard and the *Basij*" in the 2005 election.[32]

The picture of what happened became clearer over time. Someone claiming to be a *basiji* from Qom, for example, boasted on the Internet that he had used eight birth certificates of dead people to vote eleven times for Ahmadinejad.[33] An officer had come from Tehran especially to instruct local *basijis* on the secret operation, he wrote, and told them that reform candidate Mustafa Moin had been selected by the United States to serve as Washington's puppet.

"The commander told them that they were duty bound to use all means available to ensure that the right presidential candidate was successful," writes journalist Naji of the episode. "Trickery and cheating were justifiable weapons. For the commander and for the Basij, the election was a war, no different from the violent battles of the Iran-Iraq conflict or the Revolution itself. And in a war in defense of Islam, any action necessary was righteous."

Those instructions seemed to be a partial dry run for the far more blatant stealing of the June 2009 presidential vote, which would reinstall Ahmadinejad but spark the largest antigovernment unrest since the Revolution, and deal a severe blow to regime legitimacy.

In Qom in 2005, this *basiji* was told that he had to help manipulate the vote in order to avoid the following scenario: "In the aftermath of the election . . . millions of people were supposed to come out on the streets to celebrate. During the chaos, the revelers would call for the downfall of the Supreme Leader. At this point the U.S. would enter dramatically and militarily, claiming to bring democracy but actually subjugating Iran and furthering its global hegemony."[34]

The City of God

What could Iranians expect from their new "incorruptible" hard-line president? Several months before the vote, I had examined the effectiveness of Ahmadinejad's Tehran city council, as a case study of modern fundamentalist rule in Iran. Hard-liners hoped that their example of efficiency in the capital would translate into support for conservative factions nationwide, though when I wrote the story the mayor barely had 1 percent backing for a presidential bid, compared to other potential candidates.

Hear the voice of a city engineer, turning from joy to lamentation, as he leaned over a map of Tehran, pointing out to me a segment of freeway to the northeast—the strip of concrete where he had experienced an unlikely political epiphany. Back in 2003, hard-liners had just taken control of the city council and promised to turn Tehran into a "model Islamic city." Ahmadinejad was their leader. With revolutionary zeal the council quickly overcame bureaucratic hurdles and finished the Sayyad Shirazi freeway project, which had been stalled for years. But the impressive start did not last.

"My colleagues and I were so happy because our job was having a direct impact on improving people's lives," the engineer told me, his finger at the spot on the map.[35] His glasses and gray hair added to the image of a well-meaning servant of his city since 1991. "I became hopeful and thought: 'Here comes a group that I do not like, but has the connections, the will, and the ability to get something done.' "

And get things done it did. Even while Khatami was still president— his cultural renaissance still playing itself out—the council began to turn cultural centers and art galleries into mosques, and canceled "un-Islamic" programs. Prostitutes were chased off the streets. The municipality gave interest-free loans to newlyweds.

The editor of *Kayhan,* Hossein Shariatmadari, was ebullient in late 2003. The city council was "an example people are very happy about these days," the archconservative told me over tea and macaroons.[36] Council members "live simply, are highly educated, have low salaries, and work sixteen to seventeen hours a day. In a word, they are only working for God's satisfaction."

Mayor Ahmadinejad—who had a doctoral degree in traffic management—pushed plans for a monorail to ease traffic congestion. Gone were the days of council infighting that marked previous reformist administrations. Ahmadinejad was entered in the World Mayor 2005 Internet contest with three hundred other mayors. Supporting comments claimed that he was the "best mayor" in Tehran's history and part of the "modern forward-looking management" bringing "twenty-first century reform" to the city.

But then it all started to go wrong. Ideological nepotism began taking a toll, and this new team was falling into a familiar trap: ignoring previous efforts by city technocrats and experts, disgracing political rivals, and starting from scratch.

"Immediately after [hard-liners] came, there was progress," the engineer told me. "But this new group overemphasized ideological credentials in projects. When there is a push to finish a project for a big revolutionary anniversary, it gets done," he added, folding up the Tehran map. "Otherwise, there are problems."

Another key motivator was spite. "They had a very suspicious view of the reformers who came before, so began to reexamine everything and began chasing shadows, even at the cost of bringing a project to a stop," the engineer said. "The higher priority is to put into disrepute Khatami's people."

"The loyal servants of the Revolution needed constant nourishment," writes journalist Kasra Naji of the city contracts that went to the "mafia-like politico-military machinery" of Tehran.[37] "This naturally accentuated a culture of 'us' and 'them' and spread corruption among those Ahmadinejad and the religious establishment regarded as reliable insiders, while deepening the alienation of those not overtly or particularly religious. . . ."

There were other controversial changes, too. Within months of becoming mayor, Ahmadinejad declared that seventy-two city parks, squares, and universities in Tehran would be used to bury and remember the newly found remains of martyrs from the Iran-Iraq War, a policy that he kept up as president. Though contentious, the moves brought a number of political benefits to Ahmadinejad.

"This extraordinary idea, sensational and media-grabbing, stunned the more refined citizens and many members of the political elite, who publicly balked at the idea that Tehran should be turned into an ad hoc cemetery," writes historian Ali Ansari.[38] Yet even those veterans who did not like the idea "nonetheless concluded that Ahmadinejad had cleverly raised public awareness of their experiences." And the pursuit of this policy "in the face of stiff protest bolstered his credibility as an action-oriented man of the people who cared little for his popularity, and was genuinely concerned for the ignored and the dispossessed."

Hard-liners were pleased, including Brigadier General Mir-Faisal Baqerzadeh, head of the Foundation for the Preservation and Propagation of the Values of the Sacred Defense—the same man who would later block my visit to the former battlefields.

"The memorials are symbolic places where a spiritual relation between the people and the martyrs will happen," Baqerzadeh said to mark the unveiling of a new site at a university dorm—the latest in what he said were 460 sites for graves across Iran.[39] "Martyrs, especially unidentified ones, have such a rank and holy place, which one can't describe with words. Today repairing, renovating, building, and erecting memorials for martyrs is in a way fighting the enemy."

But there was a big public outcry—including noise from some clerics. Video footage showed violent clashes that resulted from these high-profile acts, as *basijis* carried their most sacred, flag-draped remains for reinterment into the political hotbeds of university campuses. Polling showed 82 percent of students opposed the moves. In one case, six hundred to seven hundred students who "attempted to create a human chain" around the graves to stop the reburials clashed with two hundred who were in favor.[40] Many saw a more sinister, repressive motive.

"By burying the bodies of the martyrs on university campuses, they can destroy every freedom-seeking movement under the claim that the blood of the martyrs is being disregarded and trampled upon," warned student leader Reza Delbari. "Under the [pretext] of a renewal of support for the martyrs, universities will be turned into [military zones] by military and militia groups."

Such moves may have won points in the conservative corridors of power. But in Tehran, the result of greater conservative control was more traffic and more pollution in a chaotic city choked with people. Amir Mohebian, political editor of the conservative newspaper *Resalat,* was not impressed. "The city council is a model of working without tension, but people expect more than no tension—the council needs brilliant works, a brilliant plan." [41]

There was little chance of finding that with a city council elected in February 2003 with just a 12 percent turnout. The majority of Iranians who wanted reform did not turn out in that local vote. I had even heard a number of conservatives complain that the city council was not a suitable model for the rest of the country.

"There is a faction in Iran—call them the Taliban—whose cultural view is closed, who do not believe in freedom of expression or participation," Mostafa Tajzadeh, a deputy interior minister under Khatami, told me two years later, as the presidential elections loomed. [42] "If they thought this [city council] was doing well, their first presidential candidate would be Ahmadinejad, but he is fourth" on the list of conservatives. There had been extravagant promises: "They very famously said: 'In forty-five days, we will repair all the streets,' but never in Tehran's history has it been this bad," said Tajzadeh. "Our society and our people do not believe they can solve the big issues of the country."

As time went on, notes Kasra Naji, "The relationship between the Guard and the municipality was so close that it was difficult to say whether the Guard was supporting Ahmadinejad or *vice versa.* Many of the development projects of the city were awarded to the Revolutionary Guard, which by now had developed into a gigantic military/industrial conglomerate. In return, the Guard provided the municipality with money and other help. This included removing all barriers to projects that had remained dormant. . . ." [43]

In a city where Iran's security forces control one-sixth of the turf, good relations are key. The real reason—it turned out—that the Sayyad Shirazi freeway had ground to a halt before Ahmadinejad took over in Tehran was that the Revolutionary Guard owned the land but did not approve of the previous, reformist mayor. Now that "their" man Ahmadinejad was on the job, they were letting it happen.

"They just sold the city to the armed forces—this is the biggest damage done to the city because of their inefficiency," *Shargh* editor and former head of the city council Mohammad Atrianfar told me.[44] Reformers, too—"those who became fat"—had made mistakes and were partly to blame. But they were the epitome of efficiency compared to this right-wing crew. And Ahmadinejad (and Atrianfar got this right) was a "conflict seeker."

YET RADICALS OF THE right wing not only survived, they triumphed. Ahmadinejad's 2005 victory marked their ascent. Like him, these ideologues were nonclerical veterans of the 1980s Iran-Iraq War and were often far more politically and theologically uncompromising than many clerics. Ahmadinejad called it a Third Revolution, after the 1979 Revolution and then the seizure of the U.S. Embassy, which Khomeini had declared the "second" Revolution.

Pundits pronounced the reform movement dead, though the wise among them knew that the widespread desire for change remained to go forward in time, not *backward*. "How do you fill that gap between reform and the people, and transfer this into a popular movement?" asked analyst Karim Sadjadpour in Tehran.[45] "Now you have tens of millions of Iranians who share the ideals of reform, but feel they have no political representation. The Iranian street is like a sleeping elephant: this enormous reservoir of energy and will for political, cultural, and social reform that is not being tapped into right now."

Those words were prescient; four years later that energy would unleash itself in the prodemocracy Green Movement. But long before Iran's latent reformists had reason to reunite into a real political force—as they would in mid-2009—the new president's aides went out of their way in 2005 to reassure anxious, West-leaning liberals that Ahmadinejad was not about to impose a Talibanesque dark age. In one memorable interview, Ahmadinejad's flamboyant culture adviser, Mehdi Kalhor, stepped well beyond the dreams of even the most radical reformists. When asked about the rumor that curtains would be installed on sidewalks to separate men and women, Kalhor scoffed and said Ahmadinejad "wants everyone to be joyful," and that his efforts aimed to "prevent the government from interfering in private lives."[46]

Kalhor promised that press clampdowns were over. He endorsed total freedom of live music and the return to Iran of singers and actors who played "illegal" music from exile. Satellite dishes—also still illegal—were "inseparable from people's lives," he acknowledged. Women were "free to choose their dress."

His short-sleeve shirts and unruly shoulder-length gray hair—kept in check with greasy pomade—made him an unlikely Ahmadinejad acolyte. And there was a backlash, immediately. One hard-line MP called instead for a "cultural revolution" to counter greater openness, and said the president should crack down on "badly veiled" women wearing "un-Islamic and immoral cloth." Kalhor was obliged to retreat, stating that his earlier words were "not the words of the president." This about-face hinted at the divisive and aggressive internal politics and foreign policy that were to come.

Ahmadinejad would scrap like a street fighter with parliament over his ministerial appointments, many of them underqualified loyalists and ideologues. He battled fellow conservatives, creating powerful enemies. He attacked "certain decision-makers within the Islamic establishment, whose hearts and minds are set on countries far beyond our borders but pretend to support the Islamic Revolution"—a not-so-subtle rebuff of Rafsanjani and his past promise to end the U.S.-Iran estrangement.

Ahmadinejad praised his ministerial choices as competent devotees close to God, then fired and replaced them—because of incompetence, not impiety—at an unprecedented rate. Ahmadinejad churned through four candidates for oil minister before one was even deemed acceptable, a fact he blamed on "certain gangs" inside the ministry.

At yet another confirmation debate in Iran's cavernous modern parliament building in 2007, I heard exasperated deputies ask the obvious question of the president. Moaned one: "Do you have unlimited people to replace them? When they learn and gain experience, you change them!"[47] The previous oil minister who finally made the grade was pious and spoken of highly for three months—until he was sacked. "What happened? We ask you, why did you remove the last one? Why [also] did you remove the finance minister?"

Candidates passed the piety test, and proved they had at least that qualification when speaking to parliament before their confirmation votes. Oil candidate Gholam Hossein Nozari invoked the *basijis*, the martyrs, and prisoners of war who had "done very great things." Nozari told the well-known story of a girl whose martyred father came back in a dream to sign off on her school grade report. He asked: "Is it not right that martyrs are supervising our jobs?" Nozari then reached even higher: "O God, I am your small servant, and satisfaction of righteousness." He called on the families of martyrs to "please forgive our mistakes" and hailed the martyrs themselves, and "all who worked with an empty table with no expectation of any position."

After prayer time, images of Ahmadinejad filled the screens above the austere parliament chamber, larger than life as he pitched at the podium for his new choices and his right as "coach of the team" to make endless adjustments. The president said he was fond of the young candidate for industry minister: "I am proud of him, a *basiji* kid from the lower level of society" who was a "pride of the university" where Ahmadinejad lectured on traffic congestion.

So both men were confirmed in their new posts, to serve as more like-minded ideologues—as surely righteous as they were often unskilled and inexperienced. But piety was not the only criterion; so was politics. The purge exacted by Ahmadinejad squeezed out an "intellectual elite" deemed "liberal-leaning and ideologically Westernized," according to the book *Iran and the Rise of Its Neoconservatives*.[48] Hardliners claimed that, for Iran's *mostazafin* (downtrodden), "such matters as civil society, democracy, economic reform, women's rights, and human rights were irrelevant."

But the result was amateurish and predictable: "The failure to reappoint well-qualified senior officials or diplomats has been considered as part of Ahmadinejad's agenda to clean the state of the so-called 'liberals' who had not paid enough attention to the values of religion and the revolution. Removing key figures from office, around six hundred in total, has had a direct bearing on the performance of the government. . . ."

Such decisions may not have made ministries any more effective or well run, as experienced bureaucrats lost their jobs. But it *did* make them more ideological. Ahmadinejad slotted fellow veterans of the Revolutionary Guard into key security posts and as provincial governors, one after another. (Khatami had presided over a similar transformation of nearly all governors and many district managers. In the words of one Khatami official: "We drew personnel mostly from the education ministry; Ahmadinejad is bringing people with security and military backgrounds.")[49] At one point in 2009, thirty-four former IRGC officers held senior-level positions in Ahmadinejad's government.[50]

And they had a very specific agenda. "Within Iran, the key target of the Third Revolution was the ruling elite and their ideology of democratic Islam, [which was] seen as un-Islamic, and therefore unacceptable," writes biographer Kasra Naji.[51] Ahmadinejad's new choices for Supreme National Security Council (SNSC)—which handles nuclear negotiations and other sensitive issues—moved in swiftly before Khatami's team could even clear out their desks, notes Naji. "Several top officials were removed from the SNSC and were treated as little more than traitors by the incoming president's men. Safes were broken into, computer hard drives confiscated, and telephones tapped."[52]

SIGNS WERE GROWING OF the increased IRGC role in politics. By one count, 91 of the 152 new deputies elected to parliament in 2004 had IRGC backgrounds.[53] The Guard had long been the keeper of Iran's most important secrets, including its nuclear facilities and ballistic missile arsenal. The expanding IRGC role with hundreds of industrial projects was portrayed as a logical extension of its mandate for postwar reconstruction, bestowed by Rafsanjani in the 1990s. But the once-pristine motives of the IRGC and the Basij beneath them were turning commercial. Often front companies and opaque commercial structures hid the true extent of Guard involvement.

"Back in the '80s, it was a very pure force, ideologically. Very Islamic. But now the whole thing is about making money," said Mahan Abedin of the Center for the Study of Terrorism in London.[54] Yet there were limits to slipping standards, he added: "The IRGC can never be allowed to get too corrupt, because that would endanger the system as a whole. It still is seen as a prime ideological force, the strong arm of the Islamic Revolution. So its ideological health is very, very important to key people in the regime, and they watch it very, very carefully."

"This 'Praetorian Guard' has been a cornerstone of the conservatives' survival and comeback strategy since 1997, and has been substantially rewarded by Khamenei," note the authors of *Iran and the Rise of Its Neoconservatives*.[55]

Those rewards came also from Ahmadinejad. Within months of his presidential victory, the government had dished out $10 billion in contracts, bypassing the requirement that all such contracts be put to public tender because it was in a rush to get the work under way.[56]

The biggest contracts were given to the IRGC's main engineering company, Khatam al-Anbia, which along with its subsidiaries was estimated to employ twenty-five thousand people.[57] They included a $1.3 billion deal to build a 560-mile natural gas pipeline, a no-bid $2.5 billion contract to finish two phases of the vast South Pars oil field, and a further $2 billion to build new lines of the Tehran metro. From laser eye surgery and dental work in one of many IRGC clinics or its main hospital, to running Tehran's new Imam Khomeini airport—and shutting it down on opening day in 2004 to force out a Turkish-Austrian consortium—the Guard had a lock on Iran's economy and, increasingly, its politics.

In total by 2007, the IRGC had won some $12–15 billion worth of business—sometimes in areas like hydrocarbons where it had little experience.[58] While that often squeezed the private sector out of civil projects, from bridges and tunnels and dams to pipelines, the IRGC had plenty to offer. "The Guard has mobilized its equipment stock-piles, wartime medical know-how, weapons-building capability, and cheap military labor to become the contractor of choice on many government projects," noted Kim Murphy in the *Los Angeles Times*.[59]

Combined with Ahmadinejad's combative commitment to Iran's nuclear programs and fierce denunciations of the West and Israel, the "roots" of the Revolution were being seeded anew, just as the president had promised. Yet senior clergy in Qom were far from convinced.

"The sensitivity is not about transferring power from the clergy to others, [it] is because of the shift from the clergy to the military," Seyyed Reza Boraei, a cleric close to Khomeini for a quarter century, told me in Qom.[60] "The political atmosphere is moving toward militarism," affirmed Mojtaba Lotfi, a cleric who—when not imprisoned—helped run the office of Grand Ayatollah Montazeri.

That concern echoed in Tehran, as the Guard extended its grip. "Half of the government are [Revolutionary Guard]," an economist in Tehran told me ruefully.[61] "They are too close to holding power, and if they take full hold, maybe they won't need anyone—even Khamenei." With words more prophetic than he could have known, he added: "They are impatient to take political power. This is one of the biggest dangers of the next two decades."

The Most Divine Devotee

None of those concerns bothered President Mahmoud Ahmadinejad, whose bulletproof self-confidence stemmed partly from certainty that his leadership had divine backing—and that the return of the Mahdi, the Shiite Messiah, would happen on his watch. Every speech he made was crowned by prayer for the Mahdi and calls for his speedy return.

Months before his 2005 election victory, at a time when polls showed virtually no support, Ahmadinejad predicted his own victory. "You will see, on the day of the election, I will be the winner—I have no doubt about it," the candidate said, according to witnesses who shared that fact with conservative columnist Amir Mohebian.[62] "People change, and we can calculate [politically] why he won," Mohebian told me. "But this [gives a] kind of self-confidence. Mr. Ahmadinejad thinks he has a mission."

As much as a year before the vote, it was rumored that Ahmadinejad had told those close to him that there was a higher purpose to *this* presidential election, that the Mahdi would use it to choose who would lead for him. Another rumor was that, as mayor, Ahmadinejad had secretly tasked the city council with reconfiguring the capital to prepare a suitable route for the Mahdi's return—a rumor publicly denied, like the others.

Yet Ahmadinejad kept letting slip that he had a special relationship. The president, for example, talked about the aura that wreathed him when speaking at the United Nations in New York when he addressed the General Assembly for the first time, in September 2005. "From the beginning of time, humanity has longed for the day when justice, peace, equality, and compassion envelop the world," Ahmadinejad told the audience of world leaders. "All of us can contribute to the establishment of such a world. When that day comes, the ultimate promise of all divine religions will be fulfilled. . . ."[63]

Later in Tehran, Ahmadinejad shared his views of that U.N. moment, stating that he had "become surrounded by a light" throughout the speech, as if possessed by a celestial spirit.

"I felt that all of a sudden the atmosphere changed there, and for twenty-seven to twenty-eight minutes all the leaders did not blink," he told Ayatollah Javadi Amoli, in a private meeting caught on grainy video.[64] "I am not exaggerating when I say they did not blink; it's not an exaggeration, because I was looking," he said. "They were astonished, as if a hand held them there and made them sit. It had opened their eyes and ears for the message of the Islamic Republic."

It was pure conviction. Converted into political power.

The president's certainty would not have surprised Supreme Leader Khamenei, who reportedly spoke about it with Ahmadinejad. By one account, "During his swearing in ceremony the newly elected president casually expressed to [Khamenei] his expectation that his tenure as president was only temporary and that he would be handing power over to the Mahdi. 'What if he doesn't appear by then?' asked the Supreme Leader, amused. 'I assure you, I really believe this. He will come soon,' " came the answer.[65]

IT WAS NOT THE first time the legend of the Mahdi had been used for political purposes. During the Iran-Iraq War, to "mobilize as many people as possible, Iranian leaders made use of Messian[ic] expectations of the Iranian population by stressing that participation in the war effort would hasten the appearance of the hidden imam," notes historian Saskia Gieling.[66] "The war was presented as part of a program of active preparation for the appearance of the hidden imam; the war would pave the way for his return."

Back then, officials repeatedly referred to Iran as the "land of the Remnant of God," one of many Mahdi names. Soldiers sometimes told stories of seeing a "manifestation" of the Mahdi or speaking to him. Friday prayer leader Khamenei claimed in 1980: "I am convinced that the holy presence of the [Mahdi], who was present and gave his help during all our great struggles through long years, will also be here in this war which was imposed on us by the mercenaries of arrogance and imperialism. . . . The Lord of the Age sees all this beloved and pure blood. . . ."[67]

Yet many argue that the recent resurgence of Mahdaviat thinking signifies deep problems. "Apocalyptic politics in Iran originates from the failure of the Islamic Republic's original vision [of] a utopian promise to create heaven on earth through Islamic law and theocratic government," writes analyst Mehdi Khalaji.[68] As that promise "ceased to attract the masses" in the past decade, Tehran "has turned to an apocalyptic vision that brings hope to the oppressed and portrays itself as an antidote to immoral and irreligious behavior."

The failure of reform was a critical catalyst in "politicizing the Mahdi cult," says historian Abbas Amanat.[69] "As [Khatami's] government was riddled with inefficiency and indecision and his rhetoric of civil society, the rule of law, and the 'dialogue of civilizations' weakened, the new spirit of messianic expectations and popular religiosity came to capture the public imagination and reflect its overall disillusionment with the unfulfilled promises of the Islamic Revolution."

CLUES TO PENETRATING THIS mystical worldview are found in the legends of the mosque at Jamkaran, sixty miles south of Tehran. Beneath the beautiful turquoise-tiled minarets, hordes of the faithful prepare for the return of their Messiah, turning Jamkaran into the second-most-visited religious locale in Iran.

"Few Shi'i scholars before the twentieth century accepted its authenticity," notes Amanat.[70] "The transformation of Jamkaran into a major pilgrimage site is indeed a telling story of the conservative appropriation of diffuse messianic beliefs . . . by manipulating the public imagination and its disillusionment with the country's state of affairs."

Pilgrims can pick up prayer beads on their way to the ornate entrance. But finding space inside the crowded mosque was not possible for many—and forbidden for non-Shiites like me. I watched pilgrims take up their positions for prayer, throughout the entranceway at night, down the stone steps, and across the grounds outside. The expectations here are of direct communication with the divine, and are the same ones that were shaping Ahmadinejad's every decision . . .

CLOSE UP INSIDE THE adjoining prayer hall in Jamkaran, for those who believe, the devotion is real. Tears streamed down the cheeks of two thousand Iranian men ripe for the return of the Mahdi, the Twelfth Imam they expected would soon emerge to bring justice and peace to a corrupt world. On their knees in tightly packed rows, men readied for revival. Eyes upward and arms open to receive God's promised salvation, right now. From a position at the front and taking photographs, I felt I had stepped into a Christian revivalist meeting that promised healing and redemption; many wept as they awaited their Messiah. These Shiites are led by a religious storyteller, whose lyrical song speaks of tragedy on the path to salvation, prompting cries of anguish and joy.

For two hours, the bearded Mahdi Salahshur relentlessly rallied his listeners around the belief in the all-powerful Twelfth Imam. He sat in the only chair, ten rows back amid that sea of red-eyed sweating supplicants, kneeling and brought by his words to ecstasy and agony in turns.

"Don't let the wish stay in our hearts! Come on, come on! I have a fear of not seeing you!" Salahshur told the crowd in a poetic, longing voice.[71] "Everybody wants to see the Lord and Master of the Age! Mourn, raise your hands."

People chanted. Men cried, wedged shoulder to shoulder. Sweat began to pour.

"Those who sinned, cry more!" came the order. "Don't let me down in front of the martyrs . . ."

Salahshur's voice steadied as he told a story of a faithful friend killed during the Iran-Iraq War. The friend dreamed that Imam Hossein, the Lord of the Martyrs, the Leader of Love, who showed the way in the seventh century, had appeared to him and said he would take him away.

"The night before he becomes a martyr, he was crying," Salahshur recalled, expertly raising the emotional heat. His friend worried that he was not "pure enough" to stand before the martyrs.

"If they ask, 'How do you justify yourself?' I have no answer," Salahshur quoted his friend saying. That night, he died.

"Ya, Imam of the Age! I ask you to swear, whom [do] you love more?" said Salahshur, sitting calmly with hands folded, his choking voice alone pulling the heartstrings of the crowd.

Then, imploring: "For heaven's sake, take us away in a way that we can look at your eyes [without shame]!"

The storyteller, or *maddah*, cooled the crowd with a lengthy standard prayer, the Tavasol, and then began more stories to magnify emotion. One was about Zeinab, sister of Imam Hossein, captured and abused when she was brought to Damascus.

"Aye, cry! Love your own crying!" Salahshur howled. "Akhh, [it is so bad] I want to die! I want to die!"

The crowd approached meltdown. "Ya, Imam of the Age, our apologies! All of a sudden, people were throwing stones at Zeinab from the top of the buildings. . . . I hope God will prevent my family ever suffering the same. . . . Why are your clothes torn off? Why are you chained?"

The audience burst, wailing at the injustice. A pilgrim in a wheelchair reached for the sky, begging heartily to feel Mahdi's presence, insisting that he not be left behind, on earth. He didn't want to let the storyteller go, nor the rapture ever to end—none of them did. I had rarely seen such force of belief. As I was taking photographs, one man took off his green headband—its red-lettered words spelling "Hail to the Mahdi"—and jammed it into my hand as a gift, taking care to wrap my fingers around it.

Even before the last lilting note of the night could fade, well after midnight, burly guards surrounded the *maddah,* linking arms to protect him—not from assassination, but from adulation. As he rose above the tear-stained crowd, devotees surged forward trying to hug, kiss, or touch him.

After leading the emotional journey, he was ecstatic himself, when he got safely to a back room. "Sometimes I feel they don't need me," Salahshur told me. "They are wired to God in their hearts."

Then, like a celebrity leaving a backstage exit, the *maddah* put on a gray *basiji* militia jacket, pulled the hood over his head in semi-disguise, and stepped out the side door and back into the real world.

EVEN THOUGH MAHDAVIAT THINKING was popular in some quarters, it was deemed empty superstition and a folk religious practice by many. "Apocalypticism . . . has been always a marginal trend within the clerical establishment. The return of the Hidden Imam means the end of the clerical establishment [so] they do not propagate the idea that the Hidden Imam will come soon," writes analyst Khalaji, who trained at the Qom seminary.[72] "Not one" of Khamenei's speeches, for example, "refers to any apocalyptic sign or reveals any special eagerness for the return of the Hidden Imam," notes Khalaji. "But in the military forces . . . apocalypticism has a very strong following."

While some might like the idea of a president who believes his leadership is under divine "management," as Ahmadinejad has said, Shiite religious texts ban all claims of revelations about the Mahdi's return, or of seeing him, and warn against "false prophets." The punishment for "fooling" people is so great, notes one text quoting the Prophet Mohammad, that "hell's fire and its occupants are crying." [73]

The Mahdi himself, apparently in a final letter to his last ambassador, had this warning: "I will be absent so much that some people will start lying about seeing me . . . anyone who will say from now on that they are in contact with me is a big liar." [74]

That final instruction has meant that Mahdaviat claims throughout history have been met with caution—just as many senior clergy disparage those by Ahmadinejad's government. "They take advantage of Islamic religion and [the Mahdi]—they exploit them," the ranking dissident cleric, Grand Ayatollah Hossein-Ali Montazeri, told me in Qom. [75] The result "makes people fed up with religion and is wrong."

The Mahdi's eventual return is an article of faith for Shiite Muslims. But turning that distant "one day he will come" into a current expectation is something else—and very political. Posters began to appear in Tehran shortly after Ahmadinejad became mayor, which read: "He's Coming." But only a fraction of Iranians actively prepare for that moment.

Tradition holds that the Jamkaran mosque was ordered built by the Mahdi himself, during a dream revealed to a "righteous" shepherd one thousand years ago. Legend has it that written prayers dropped into a well (which, local guides admit, at least to a foreigner, has no religious basis) will be divinely answered. The president's office denied rumors that all members of Ahmadinejad's first cabinet had signed a letter of devotion to the Mahdi that was then dropped into the well.

That legend is a superstition that even Ayatollah Khomeini refused to associate with. Still, in a well-known speech called "Awaiting: The Religion of Protest," the pre-Revolution ideologue Ali Shariati turned the tradition of passive waiting on its head. "Expecting [the Mahdi's return] means protesting" against the status quo, Shariati explained, and not just through prayer, but by "flag, sword, chain mail, and jihad." [76]

So since the Revolution, the Mahdi was often touted as intervening in Iranian politics. Ayatollah Khomeini, despite little time for the legend of Jamkaran, was not beyond invoking the Hidden Imam. "Why should we worry? The owner of this country is the Imam [of the Age] Zaman," he told parliamentarians in 1981. [77] Early in the Iran-Iraq War he told the Revolutionary Guard: "You are now under the protection of God and the Imam Zaman. They protect you personally; a letter listing all your activities is being sent to Imam Zaman on a regular basis." [78]

But sightings surged during the Ahmadinejad era. That was evident when the octogenarian Ayatollah Ali Meshkini spoke after more than two thousand reformist candidates (among them several dozen sitting MPs) were barred from running in 2004 elections. As chair of the Assembly of Experts, he "informed an incredulous public that an angel had been sent by the Hidden Imam to the Leader with the names of the winning candidates." [79] The ayatollah claimed that seven months before the vote, the angel had brought a list of candidates for Khamenei to sign.

Ahmadinejad's cabinet by 2006 had earmarked $17 million for improvements at Jamkaran. There was talk of a direct train link from Tehran across the arid hills and desert flats to the elegant turquoise-domed mosque, which lay just east of the religious center of Qom. "It has been transformed from a very small and modest mosque to a colossal holy shrine" that the custodian says attracts sixteen million pilgrims each year, notes Khalaji. [80]

Visiting foreigners are welcome, but also treated with deep suspicion. On my first visit, I was immediately detained for questioning when I started taking pictures outside. Security agents sat me down at a white plastic table in an upstairs room at the complex and subjected me to their well-honed impulse to proselytize—which is not common among typical Shiite believers. The questions often turned toward my own beliefs, and I was asked to fill out a form: Did I believe in the "final battle" between the forces of good and evil? Did I believe in the second coming of Christ, or of the Mahdi?

It was suddenly clear. They really wanted to know if that same mental model of "return" was in me, as it was in them. They wanted me, a foreigner from the West, to confirm that I shared their belief structure.

With a string of anodyne answers, I at least convinced them that I was not *against* their brand of Messianic fervor. I was given a packet of Jamkaran salt, an agent as a guide, and told I could not photograph the actual well itself, though pilgrims busily shot as many images as they liked with cell phones and cameras. Here I saw many from Iran's poor and less-educated, who voted heartily for Ahmadinejad, lined up by the hundreds to receive food, and settled in family groups on blankets outside. With hands over their hearts in a mix of awe and obeisance, they approached the radiant mosque for evening prayers.

"Good intent and moral purification" is what can bring Believers into contact with the Mahdi, though lack of "moral rectitude" meant he remained hidden to most people, writes Amanat of the ritual.[81] According to the Jamkaran website, "If reports of the deeds of the Shi'is that every week are presented at his sacred threshold were not laden with such grave sins that are displeasing to His Excellency [the Mahdi] . . . his distance and separation would not have been [so] prolonged."[82]

THE OPENING OF THE famed "well" is covered with a two-footsquare, green-painted grill of metal bars, to prevent burning candle wax from falling through to the dry hole below. Pressing lips and foreheads to the bars—which are scratched with devotional graffiti— believers slipped requests to the Mahdi on preprinted prayer notes. The Mahdi did "not read the notes, he reads the hearts," said my guide as we neared the hallowed hole. He explained that the well itself was not real, has no water inside, and is more of a pit that doubles as a large mailbox for the Mahdi.

Mosque staff dug the well decades ago to accommodate the tradition, my guide admitted, taking care to repeat that there was no religious basis for the myth. Every week staff entered the subterranean chamber, collected the prayer papers in sacks, and transported them elsewhere to empty into natural streams, in keeping with guidelines that they touch actual "running water."

That devotion worked for some. At night, pilgrims on the half-lit asphalt apron in front of the mosque shared with me stories of extraordinary healing.

"When you come here, you get your [prayer] request fulfilled, if you are clean and pure," Fatemeh told me, speaking through a small gap in her head covering as she tended to a red pot of boiling rice.[83] The portable stove put out a strong smell of gas. Her family was holding vigil on a blanket, the minarets lit up and glowing behind them. She attributed a significant healing of heart palpitations ten years earlier to a Jamkaran visit, but said the "Mahdi does not allow me to talk about it with anybody else."

Such healings were carefully documented at Jamkaran, and a doctor is on hand especially for the purpose. "We don't take anything based on sayings," my guide told me. Yet pilgrims are not limited to the poor or infirm. A young man with a thin beard told me he had come to Jamkaran thirty times since he was a kid. "Whatever I wished up to now, it was fulfilled," said Mohammad Hamid Fathongharib, from the not-too-distant city of Kashan. "I get so lighthearted. I can tell the [Mahdi] whatever I want. I feel like a bird . . . every time I feel cleansed." He said that "everyone" he knew came to Jamkaran.

One young couple—he was a banker in Qom, and wore a stylish suit—told me they had their prayer answered after coming forty Tuesday nights in a row. Now they had another request and would be here forty times again. "We Iranians have very strong beliefs, and this is a holy place," said Mahdi Abdollahi, holding a late-model motorcycle helmet as he stood near the mosque entrance. "I don't think it's a matter of [presidential] propaganda to crank you up. It depends upon your own belief."

Critics—many of them from the clerical class—accused Ahmadinejad of playing politics by manipulating public sentiment. "They pay more attention to the façade of religion, rather than the jewel of religion," Mohammad Ali Ayazi, a professor at the most influential seminary in Qom, told me.[84] "Having sincerity or honesty does not make any difference to the results. It's very dangerous, a person exploiting religion for political achievement, because everyone has their own relationship with God—it makes me sad that someone would endanger that."

Ayazi sat in the large library room of his office, laden with row upon row of books. He estimated that only 20 percent of Iranians focused so much on the Mahdi's imminent return. "Because this gentleman [Ahmadinejad] does not have political legitimacy, they have to use religion to motivate the public," Ayazi told me.

Such manufactured authority was "not a good departure point," added Ayazi, because it left no room for failure. He compared Ahmadinejad's dilemma to George Bush's invocation of God when explaining his reasons for invading Iraq: "Now if [Americans] are defeated in Iraq, what is [Bush] going to do? And what will happen to this slogan?"

The Iranian president faced a similar dilemma. "Nothing connects with the audience like the vocabulary of imminence," said Kurt Anders Richardson, an expert on Shiite theology at McMaster University in Ontario.[85] "It's great to live with imminence if you believe. It changes everything: it supercharges politics, it supercharges ethics and collective feeling. Also it's a great antidote to worldly distractions. Instead of fear instigated by morality police, you have euphoria, a profound enticement," Richardson told me in Tehran. "Clearly these people are motivated by the belief they will be privileged to see the return of the Mahdi in their lifetime."

But believing that "extraordinary faithfulness can hasten the Imam's return" is a catch-22. "Obviously generations of belief have not hastened" the Mahdi's return so far, Richardson explained. And most importantly, the politics of imminency, especially when attached to a government, or a politician who claims to act on behalf of the Mahdi, "must yield superior results."

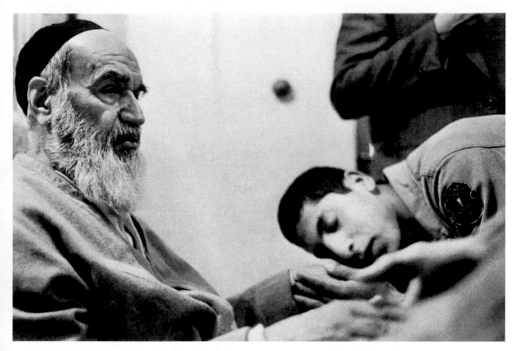

Devotion: "Only those who have tasted poverty, deprivation, and oppression will stay with us to the end."
—Ayatollah Ruhollah Khomeini MAHMOUDREZA KALARI/SYGMA/CORBIS

Sacred War: "If we died, we still won—martyrdom is the highest aim." —Dr. Alireza Zakani

U.S. Support Against Iran: "For every harmful insect there is an insecticide capable of annihilating it." —Iraqi General ALI KAVEH, *THE IMPOSED WAR* (VOL. 4)

Veteran: "I want Americans to know we are friends with them, not enemies, even though we are chemically wounded." —Col. Mohammad Akbari

Haji Bakhshi Fights the Flames, 1986: "They were men of action, not just men of words." —Photographer Ali Rajabi COURTESY OF ALI RAJABI

left: Genius Director: "At the front we were after reality." —Morteza Avini www.shahed.isaar.ir

right: Chronicles of Victory: "This war is a test. Those who do not believe in this war do not have faith." —Soldier Molazadeh ᴅᴇʟʙᴀᴋʜᴛᴇ, ʀᴇᴠᴀʏᴀᴛ-ᴇ ꜰᴀᴛʜ

Regime Cheerleader: "In war, propaganda and spirit are the most important things." —Haji Bakhshi

Martyr Namesake in Ahvaz Cemetery:
"When I come here, my soul relaxes."
—Ali Akbar Khoshnazar

Fahmideh Grave: "It is of great value to us,
because he's a child and gave a great thing for
our country." —Admiring Boy, Hossein

Voting Reform: "We have never been successful in our experience with freedom."
—President Mohammad Khatami

Enemies: "Our problem with
America isn't over one or
two [issues]. The problem is
like a matter of life and death."
—Ayatollah Khamenei

Stealing a Kiss: "There is more freedom here
than anywhere else." —Alireza Mahfouzian

Underground Heavy Metal: "Music corrupts the minds of our youth. There is no difference between music and opium." —Ayatollah Khomeini

Another Band: "Music is not a kind of war, where we are fighting . . . *hezbollahis*."
—Musician Seyyed Alireza Assar

Defining Freedom: "Girls and boys coming out like this are only pretending to be free. What do you call liberty? Uncovering your hair? This is not freedom." —Shop owner

Resolute: In the West, "money, gluttony, and carnal desires are made the greatest aspirations. . . . Islam is the only remedial, curative, and savior angel."
—Ayatollah Khamenei

Basij Militiamen: "We are seeking to root out these antirevolutionaries wherever they are. We have to behead some and cut off the tongues of others." —IRGC chief Rahim Safavi

The Challenge: "There is a great distance between what we promised and what we have achieved."
—Grand Ayatollah Hossein-Ali Montazeri

Reformist Expectation: "They believe the people's role is unimportant, but I believe it is the people who can decide." —Candidate Fatemeh Haghighatjou

Student Protester Ahmad Batebi: "You have signed your own death sentence." —Iranian judge REUTERS/JAMSHID

Supreme Leader: Opponents should "open their eyes and see the enemy." —Ayatollah Seyyed Ali Khamenei

Seeking Justice: "Do not think giving me the Nobel Prize gives me the key to open all prison doors." —Shirin Ebadi

above: Old Guard Decorum: "Destined to serve the Revolution until the last day of my life . . . to stop the domination of extremism."
—Ali Akbar Rafsanjani

left: Populist Mahmoud Ahmadinejad: "He's an angel! This guy's an angel! I'll give my heart to him, if he wants it. I'll even give my eyes for him."
—Loyalist

Mohammad Khatami Roughed Up: "Liar! Liar! Death to the person against the *velayat-e faqih*!"
—Militant Opponents

Awaiting the Messiah at Jamkaran: "Sometimes I feel they don't need me. They are wired to God in their hearts." —Religious storyteller Mahdi Salahshur

From Vigilante to Peacemaker: "The message is that this country is for everyone, with different political tendencies." —Masoud Dehnamaki

Renaissance: "When [Ahmadinejad] became president, the Revolution was reborn. . . . The Leader thinks the same." —Cleric Morteza Agha-Tehrani

Influencing Votes: "Another Spring Is Waiting." —Pro-Ahmadinejad poster of election "morals committee"

Westoxication: "I have friends [who] wake up in the morning, shouting and angry. I hate [the regime] the most, but I just tolerate." —"Tooska" COURTESY OF "TOOSKA"

Roxana Saberi Arrested: At moments of potential U.S.-Iran engagement, "you have a hard-line faction in Tehran—the spoilers—who have a long history . . . of provoking [crisis]." —Karim Sadjadpour

Blood Reverence for Mir Hossein Mousavi: "He can be our savior. We hope, with the people's vote, their good choice will bring a bright future." —War Veteran

Voting for Change: "If Mousavi does not win, it will cause big damage to society. You will see angry people, it will be dangerous." —"Siavash"

Mousavi Rally: "If there were really freedom [under Ahmadinejad] there would not be so many people here." —Grandfather Mohammad

Defacing Ahmadinejad: Iranians want the "truth [or] the volcanoes that are fueled by people's anger will form in society." —Ali Akbar Rafsanjani

Greatest Crime: "These days and nights a turning point is being forged in the history of our nation." —Mir Hossein Mousavi

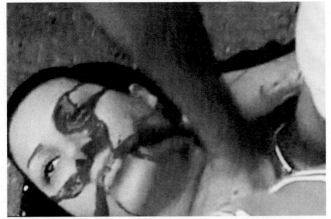

Angel of Iran, Neda: "The taste in my mouth changed. . . . I felt angry. I felt that this was it. Blood cannot be ignored." —Witness to Killings ANONYMOUS

Fight and Fight Back: The "riots took us to the edge of a downfall [and] pushed us into a new phase of the Revolution." —IRGC chief Mohammad Ali Jafari NIACINSIGHT .COM

Show Trial: "This technique of fomenting coups is so planned out that . . . it can stealthily and quietly complete the stages of a Velvet Revolution." —Court Indictment

FARS NEWS/AFP/GETTY IMAGES

Great Expectations: "This ingenious idea of green. . . . Suddenly with a little piece of cloth, you could say so much. . . . Underneath the apathy there was something, waiting to be led, to be awakened." —The Sage

Shrine of the Imam: "We will provide you water and electricity and bus rides free of charge. . . . We will exalt your souls." —Ayatollah Khomeini

"The Mahdi will rise, and it's a reality that needs [study] by religious science," Seyyed Hadi Hashemi, a black-turbaned senior cleric in Qom, told me.[86] "But if you say, as Ahmadinejad says, 'We should construct an avenue in Tehran for the Mahdi to arrive,' this is only fooling the public."

SPREADING THE WORD OF that arrival is the point of the twenty-four-hour Messiah "hotline," where adherents can call to have their questions answered. Need to know when the Mahdi is coming to save mankind? Need to know what signs to look out for that will herald the return of perfect justice?

Just call the hotline. Or log on to the Bright Future News Agency at www.bfnews.ir to get the latest religious readout—all part of the effort by Believers freshly rejuvenated by presidential passion to spread their message of the Mahdi's imminent arrival. Launched in 2004, the Bright Future Institute in Qom was the eighth of its kind in Iran designed to study and even speed the Mahdi's return. It quickly became the largest and most influential.

"People are anxious to know: When and how will he rise? And what must they do in order to receive this worldwide salvation?" explained Ali Lari, a keen-eyed cleric at the Bright Future Institute.[87] "The timing is not clear, but the conditions are more specific. There is a saying: 'Whenever the students are ready, the teacher will come.' "

While he waited for that glorious moment, Morteza Rabaninejad sat at a new computer, wearing a new headset plugged into the institute's hotline, answering five calls and ten letters a day, from devotees thirsty for Mahdaviat knowledge.

"Would you please explain all the signs of rising? What are the things we must do to make the Mahdi rise earlier?" were questions scrawled on one postcard with prepaid postage. "Good works" was the answer; a pure heart and personal devotion could make it happen. Good spiritual citizens would receive divine reward.

There was bubbling optimism thanks to the expanding political attention from the president's office. "Mahdaviat is a code for the Revolution, and is the spirit of the Revolution," institute director Masoud Pourseyyed-Aghaei told me.[88] "It's the code of our identity, [and] I think this belief has been increasing."

Countering the doubters was the job of the Bright Future News Agency, which began churning out reports in late 2005. "There is a gap between us and the popular media," the young editor in chief, Seyyed Ali Pourtabatabaei, told me, sitting in his tiny newsroom.[89] "We started the idea of a Messiah news agency of the Mahdi [because] we thought we needed a news agency to publish *his* news."

Surprisingly, in this conservative bastion, Pourtabatabaei had campaigned for Khatami in 2001 and did graduate work in human rights. But he respected this hard-line president, too, very much. "We think the world is a place for peace, not war. We visited our president [Ahmadinejad], and I asked him about nuclear weapons. He laughed and said: 'Does our religion allow it? Imam Mahdi does not like nuclear weapons.' "

THAT ASSERTION DID NOT wash with American evangelicals who were busily turning Iran into an issue of fear and daily prayer. Some use forty-five categories—from liberalism and natural disasters to "beast government"—to predict the "end time" when holy people will experience "rapture" and go straight to heaven.[90] The category for "Persia (Iran)" had been at the maximum number of five since "President Bush warned that Iran is seeking to produce nuclear weapons." In total, the ever-adjusting "Rapture Index" was at 164; anything higher than 160 meant "Fasten your seat belts," because of the high level of prophetic activity.

One reason the Christian "Rapture Index" had been so high, of course, was Ahmadinejad's own fervent beliefs and angry pronouncements, which by the time they reached American pulpits had swept away any Mahdaviat message of "good works" and "pure heart." The Iranian president's every noisy word fed the fears and dire expectations of Christian millenarians like nothing else.

"Their 'ultimate objective' has clearly been established by the president of Iran, the new Hitler of the Middle East," writes Texas pastor and fervent Christian-Zionist John Hagee.[91] His fire-and-brimstone preaching attracts a congregation of nineteen thousand and a global radio and television audience of tens of millions. DVDs for sale on his ministry website include one called *Harry Potter: Witchcraft Repackaged,* which helps young readers cope with "occult resources."[92]

In his own book *Jerusalem Countdown,* updated in 2007 to account for Ahmadinejad's fiery presidential rhetoric, Hagee argues that World War III has already begun. Iran's "persistent attempts to acquire nuclear weapons" have combined with "evil leaders [who] have publicly declared that they will use violence—any kind and any degree of violence possible—to reach Islam's highest goal: a successful holy war against the United States, the *big Satan,* and Israel, the *small Satan.*"[93]

Hagee stated that Tehran had the threat all figured out and—using language eerily similar to that of Iran's own hard-liners—that it had to be stopped: "If Iran gets nuclear weapons, America will see nuclear suitcase bombs that will have the ability to kill 1–1.5 million people per atomic blast. Just because you can't imagine it happening, don't be foolish enough to believe it can't happen, because the enemies of America and Israel are working night and day to make it a reality. It is the 'sudden storm' President Ahmadinejad of Iran dreams about."[94]

On Israel—which Hagee says "belongs to God himself" because it "is the only nation created by a sovereign act of God"—history was in danger of repeating itself. Hagee writes:

[C]onsider that in 1935, Hitler said, "Kill the Jews!" No one listened, and his rhetoric became a hellish reality. Today, the president of Iran, Mahmoud Ahmadinejad, is saying, "Kill the Jews." Ahmadinejad is trying to put nuclear weapons together to bring a nuclear holocaust in Israel. . . .

Iran with nuclear weapons will transform the [U.S.] Roadmap for Peace program into a racetrack to Armageddon.[95]

Hagee kept up the blast against Iran's Holocaust-denying leaders in a subsequent book, *In Defense of Israel*. "The viewpoints of these radical terrorists are past the point of being dangerous and now are easily considered delusional and insane," he writes.[96] "To call them madmen is justified. To attempt to negotiate with them is beyond naïve. It is time to consider a military pre-emptive strike against Iran's nuclear facilities."

Hagee was among a lineup of American authors sounding the alarm. Mark Hitchcock's *The Apocalypse of Ahmadinejad: The Revelation of Iran's Nuclear Prophet* promises a "well-researched expose" and has an eye-catching back cover.[97] "Meet the world's most dangerous man," it reads. "He stands only five-foot-four and smiles incessantly. But behind that charismatic persona beats the heart of a genocidal terrorist."

Hitchcock's book resurrects old falsehoods such as Ahmadinejad playing a "major role" as a "ringleader" in the 1979 seizure of the U.S. Embassy. It quotes one former hostage claiming that Ahmadinejad threatened him in one interrogation session: "We know where you live. We know that you have a handicapped child. We know what time he gets picked up for school. We know where. If you don't answer our questions as we like, we are going to chop off his fingers and his toes and send them one by one to your wife in a box."[98]

Even the U.S. government has concluded that Ahmadinejad played no appreciable role in the hostage crisis. Yet Hitchcock says that the Iranian president's past "makes Saddam Hussein look like Santa Claus."[99] Hitchcock touches up his portrait with tailor-made quotes such as this one from Israel's Prime Minister Benjamin Netanyahu, who said, "The real danger is that Iran could become one gigantic suicide bomber."[100]

But the conclusions are based on Ahmadinejad's own damning statements. Hitchcock determines, reassuringly, that "for certain" Ahmadinejad is not the biblical Antichrist. "However, having said that, vicious, cruel, arrogant dictators like Saddam and Ahmadinejad do strikingly foreshadow what the Antichrist will be like," he writes.[101] "Menacing madmen like Ahmadinejad do give us a small window into the Antichrist's character. History is littered with the lives of despotic dictators who prefigure what the final great man of sin will be like."

There are many parallels between the worldviews—and choice of bombastic language—of the religious right wings in both America and Iran. On the U.S. side, "fundamentalists are deeply pessimistic about the prospects for world order and see an unbridgeable divide between believers and nonbelievers," writes historian Walter Russell Mead.[102] They "are downright hostile to the idea of a world order based on secular morality and on global institutions such as the United Nations." Fundamentalists in the United States, furthermore, believe "that Christ's return will precede the establishment of the prophesied thousand-year reign of peace. Ultimately, all human efforts to build a peaceful world will fail."

SHIITE RELIGIOUS WRITINGS TELL of the events surrounding the Mahdi's return in sweeping and often gruesome end-of-time terms, similar to those used in the Bible's book of Revelation. The Bible describes a final cosmic war during which Jesus Christ returns as the Messiah, and wins, to rule for a millennium. The Four Horsemen who herald the Apocalypse bring Pestilence, War, Famine, and Death while riding on steeds white, red, black, and pale. The Bible explains: "And power was given unto them over the fourth part of the earth, to kill with sword, and with hunger, and with death, and with the beasts of the earth." [103] When the Messiah returns, "out of his mouth goeth a sharp sword, that with it he should smite the nations. . . ."

The harvest of Revelation is manifest in the "great winepress of the wrath of God," which yields a sea of blood rising "unto the horse bridles, by the space of a thousand and six hundred furlongs." [104] (According to one American Christian Believer: "That would be a 200-mile-long river of blood, four and a half feet deep. We've done the math. That's the blood of as many as two and a half billion people.") [105]

Events of Armageddon are equally as grim in the Shiite Muslim version. "Shiite apocalyptic tradition has bloody visions about what will happen when the Hidden Imam returns," writes analyst and former seminarian Khalaji.[106] Citing traditional texts, he explains: "[W]hen the Mahdi appears, there will be two kinds of death, red and white, each claiming a third of the world's population. The red death will be from the Mahdi's sword and the white will be from the plague, leaving only a third to survive. In some [texts], the Mahdi will kill two-thirds of the world's population, and he 'will clean the earth from nonbelievers and deniers [of Islam] . . . he will continue to kill the enemies of God until God is satisfied.' "

In one Shiite scenario, the forces of evil would come from Syria and Iraq, and clash with forces of good, which would come from present-day Iran. The battle is meant to commence at Kufa—the Iraqi town near the holy city of Najaf, which in the aftermath of the 2003 U.S. invasion became the base of the Iraqi anti-American cleric Moqtada al-Sadr.

Legend holds that the evil commander named Sofiani, and the anti-Mahdi known as Dajjal (the "false messiah," comparable to the Christian Antichrist), would both be killed. The forces of good would be led by a "man from Khorasan"—a province in northeast Iran (from which Ahmadinejad does not come, but the Supreme Leader does). The Mahdi would return at Mecca and fight on behalf of Muslims. His victory would bring a government of God for a period of "seven," according to one reading. But seven months, years, or even millennia, is not clear.

One hadith text details a conversation in which the Prophet Mohammad explains that even while absent, the Mahdi would benefit his followers "just as people still benefit from the sun on a cloudy day."[107]

At the Bright Future Institute, the currency of expectation was being traded. "The Imam of the Age will have victory, and all the world will support him, except some regimes and governments that are racist regimes, like Zionists," director Pourseyyed-Aghaei told me. The result will be global dominance of Shiites, the "oppressed of the world. Believing in the Mahdi and the savior . . . is superior to nuclear energy in the hands of the Shia. The power of the Shia is bound to this—not a nuclear weapon."

The Populist Potentate

While Ahmadinejad told Iranians that his "divine" government had the omnipotent Mahdi on their side, the president left nothing to chance when it came to his own penchant for populism. Unlike any Iranian politician before him, Ahmadinejad sought the presence of ordinary Iranians, listened to them, and—in what would become one hallmark of his presidency—received millions of letters from them. So many millions of letters were collected, asking for money, or a job, or praising this tireless champion of social justice, that the president had to create a special office to handle them.

The strategy caught many Iranian critics off guard. Historian Ali Ansari writes that

> few within Iran actually understood Ahmadinejad, and that in trying to make sense of this self-proclaimed charismatic national savior, several of his opponents fell victim to his greatest personal asset: an extraordinary and protean charismatic personality cult that defies attempts to understand it and successfully mystifies its subject to outsiders. It acts as it own validation; as long as the initiated, the believers, understand, it hardly matters, indeed is positively a good thing, if everyone else does not.[108]

Watching Ahmadinejad work a (friendly) crowd or an audience was a lesson in communing with the common man. In Iran, his populism was one of his most potent political tools. Ahmadinejad is a two-faced demagogue: he sears the West with his anti-American and anti-Israel rhetoric (never mind blasting domestic political rivals) yet at home is capable of soothing scenes with constituents.

One example I witnessed was the unscripted aftermath of local elections in December 2006, when Ahmadinejad stepped outside after casting his ballot.[109] The president's polished black Mercedes was waiting for him, along with scores of citizens. He was immediately thronged by black-draped women and some men, who had waited while clutching pens and scraps of paper to write notes requesting assistance.

This was the same middle/working-class east Tehran neighborhood, Narmak, that was proud to have turned a blacksmith's son into a president. Some cried. Some gave him their notes, which Ahmadinejad dutifully gathered into an increasing stack. One woman shouted "Hi!" to get his attention.

"Wait your turn!" the president replied, in a deliberately comic tone that sparked laughter through the tight crowd. Despite the crush, Ahmadinejad took out his own pen and notebook to write down personal details of some of the needy. To get a better view, I climbed up a concrete utility pole, holding on with just my legs while taking photographs. State TV caught it on film, and for days afterward, Iranians—starting with the room cleaners at my hotel—expressed delight at the footage. But in the circle of those surrounding Ahmadinejad, their notes held up to him with outstretched arms, the encounter was a brush with greatness.

"He came out of the heart of the people," said Soosan Jalili, whose note asked the president to find a job for her daughter, a blind university graduate. "If you put all the [Iranian] presidents on one side, he is something else. We've never had one like this."

Another woman said the president had remembered by name her son, Mahdi, who had worked on his campaign the previous year. "He still knows everyone here," Fatemeh Jamshidi told me. "We always pray for him."

"These people are the pillars of the government and the Revolution," Fatemeh Erfanian told me. She put her phone number on her note so the president could solve her husband's "problem." She expected a reply, and almost certainly would receive one: "He promised me. And we believe his promises."

One woman complained to Ahmadinejad that he had not replied to her letter. He asked what it was about. She had asked him to find places in medical school in Iran for her two sons, who were studying medicine in Azerbaijan. The president said he had replied, but that Iran had too few places at medical schools, so there was nothing he could do. Ahmadinejad turned to speak to others clamoring for attention, but that answer was not good enough for the woman. She interrupted again to say so.

The president turned back to her, and replied sharply, "I already answered you. And what are your sons doing in *Azerbaijan,* anyway?" The crowd laughed at Ahmadinejad's well-calibrated jingoistic jibe and his put-down of the too-persistent mother.

At times, the president could get carried away with his populism. He once gave out both his office phone number and e-mail address, so "ordinary" people could contact him, without apparently thinking first that the phone line would immediately be jammed, as it was for months.[110]

Still, even in this neighborhood, there were detractors. "These people are a minority in Iran," a goldsmith called Reza told me as he stepped among the women and conservative men. He was speaking in English and leading his daughter by the hand. The "majority" were angry because of rising inflation, unemployment, and drug addiction, he said, and they didn't expect any solutions. "Whatever the Iranian government does [domestically], it is like flogging a dead horse. It does not have any effect."

That would be news to one man, who raised his voice above all others, to get to the president. "He's an angel! This guy's an angel!" he shouted as he made his way through the throng and security guards. "Nobody accepted me but this one . . . He went through a lot of trouble to get me a job. I'll give my heart to him, if he wants it. I'll even give my eyes for him. He has given me much!"

The presidential motorcade finally pulled away, the smiling president delivering one last respectful tip of his head toward these loyalists, placing his right hand over his heart, before stepping into the car, its door sealed by security guards.

"Ahmadinejad is like the truth. He's from here," Hassan Hosseini told me as the convoy disappeared around the corner. "You saw the example: he stood for an hour and answered every question. He could have just driven off."

BUT THEREIN LAY THE greater problem, because personal promises could only reach so far. Expectations could not have been higher, when Ahmadinejad was elected, that he would use the oil windfall "to initiate an extensive program of infrastructure projects; putting people to work, increasing salaries and rejuvenating the industrial base," writes historian Ansari.[111] "As the man thus responsible for the resurrection of the Iranian state, Ahmadinejad's legacy would be untouchable."

Iranians who expected some share of their nation's oil money to end up on their dinner tables—or more specifically, as the president promised, on the mats called *sofreh* laid out on the floor and upon which families sometimes eat—were disappointed that the value of any extra cash they were given was diminished by an economy in free fall.

Ahmadinejad's first four-year term did witness a bull run of the highest oil prices in history, at nearly $150 per barrel for the black gold that accounted for some 80 percent of government revenues. That surge brought at least $250 billion—a figure greater than the $173 billion earned during the eight-year presidency of Mohammad Khatami, and double the value of all of Iran's pre-Revolution oil earnings combined.[112]

But it was squandered—to the point where parliament deputies twice sought to shorten Ahmadinejad's term. "While Qatar, Saudi Arabia, the United Arab Emirates and Kuwait now boast Sovereign Wealth Funds worth hundreds of billions of dollars, [in mid-September 2008] an unreleased Central Bank report leaked by an Iranian parliamentarian estimated the Islamic Republic's own future fund to be only $7 billion," notes analyst Michael Rubin.[113]

Indeed, Iran was the one global oil exporter whose economy during this period turned to crisis mode. Sets of international sanctions over

Iran's nuclear program added to the burden. Soaring prices meant that nearly seven hundred thousand more urban Iranians fell below the poverty line in 2006 alone, and despite all the president's populist talk, the gap of "social injustice" grew wider for the first time in more than a decade.[114] The president had spoken of bringing "a fundamental reform" in the economy so that "business would become unsafe for profiteers."[115] He reveled not only in his populist antipoverty measures, but also in his ignorance: "I pray to God that I will never know about economics."[116]

And that skewed wish was coming true every day for beleaguered Iranians. "Upon taking office, [Ahmadinejad] promiscuously handed out grants and subsidies; when they were not approved by the state budget office, he simply ordered the banks to issue more currency," notes Laura Secor in the *New Yorker*.[117] "He injected billions in oil revenues directly into the economy, dipping into the country's savings to do so. Liquidity increased by nearly 40 percent in the space of a year. . . . Within a year of Ahmadinejad's election, the inflation rate was the fourth highest in the world, after Zimbabwe, Uzbekistan, and Burma."

Among economists like Hossein Askari, Iran's "record of economic failure since the revolution is astonishing," with real per capita income lower and income inequalities wider.[118] Since 1979, oil production dropped 30 percent while dependence on oil revenue has only grown. "Preoccupied with day-to-day survival and short-term popularity, the regime in Tehran has foregone policies to achieve sustained economic growth and development," writes Askari.

Ahmadinejad was simply the latest to impose his economic incomprehension on Iran. Consulting no one, he ordered that interest rates be brought down. His sudden decision to raise the minimum wage by 60 percent, for example—while certainly well intended—meant that hundreds of thousands of Iranians were forced out of work by employers who could no longer afford them.[119]

The value of oil exports had nearly doubled, to $50 billion and then $60 billion in the first two years of Ahmadinejad's presidency.[120] But central bank figures showed that he had withdrawn $35.3 billion and then $43 billion those two years from the oil reserve fund, when his own development plan called for just more than $15 billion spent each year. Countless cash handouts were eaten up by inflation. In 2007 alone, Iran spent $56 billion on imported goods—a 50 percent increase over three years before. Dozens of economics professors signed one letter, and then another and another, warning of coming catastrophe.

"To Ahmadinejad, the economists' pleas were not advice: they were a challenge and had to be met head on and defeated," writes Kasra Naji.[121] Portraying economists as a "number-crunching elite bereft of human compassion," Ahmadinejad "saw himself as actively doing things in the real world to alleviate genuine suffering and hardship. For him, this was more important than kowtowing to the false gods of economics and the market."

Anger erupted in June 2007 when the government tried to ease sub-sidies on gas prices and impose strict rationing. Iran may have 10 per-cent of the world's proven oil reserves and 15 percent of its natural gas—the second-largest global reserve—but its refining capacity is small. Iran imports 40 percent of its gasoline, at an annual price tag of $4 billion. In an extraordinary act of mishandling, authorities gave three hours notice that the new rationing would start at midnight. Riots broke out and nineteen gas stations were torched.

"Unfortunately, Mr. Ahmadinejad did not fulfill his promises to poor people," the economist and critic Saeed Laylaz told me.[122] "This social unrest is an immediate and direct consequence of those policies. . . . And at the moment, the social structure of this country is abso-lutely fragile and sensitive about economic issues."

Iranians had good reason to be concerned, since Iran's National Audit Office revealed in early 2009 that $1 billion in oil revenue had not been paid back into the treasury by Ahmadinejad's government from the 2006–2007 budget.[123] One vice president dismissed the find-ing as an "accounting error," prompting the Audit Office to angrily denounce the administration's "insufficient answers."[124] The auditors also cited two thousand spending violations in the 2008–2009 budget.

The president criticized the reports for tarnishing the reputation of his government—which they surely did.

But for Believers like him, economics often boiled down to ideology and politics. Merchants in the traditional Grand Bazaar, for example, might avoid taxes or export their goods for free if they worked closely with the government. Or they might run into trouble if they did not, according to a carpet dealer who took the precaution of speaking to writer Laura Secor beside a Tehran river, to avoid being overheard: "After elections, he claimed, police came around to check *bazaaris'* identity documents for the stamp confirming that they'd voted. 'If you did not vote, they decide you are in the group that disagrees, and they write down your address and everything. They can close your shop.' "[125]

The economy of the Islamic Republic was blessed anyway, according to Ahmadinejad, who in late 2008 said the global economic downturn was a "creation" of the United States—and he knew why. Iran's president said the crisis "is the result of [American] behavior, the result of [America's] distancing from divine rulings, the result of trampling morality, the result of aggression and lying. The only solution is a return to morality."[126]

AHMADINEJAD'S ELECTION-DAY VOW OF a "moderate" social policy also fell victim to a string of right-wing ministerial choices. He seeded all levels of government with hard-liners and former veterans of the Revolutionary Guard. No Iranian president in recent memory had faced so many scathing and frequent attacks from so many Iranian factions, especially in Tehran, nor created so many powerful enemies, over issues that ranged from imperious management and "inept" economic policies to snooty gibes from elite critics about lack of "intellectualism."

Despite all this, Ahmadinejad's bold political moves succeeded in increasing the power of Iran's presidency.

"Ahmadinejad just broke all the rules," one Iranian journalist told me.[127] "Whatever he does, he's always giving orders, giving commands—it projects an image of power." He also provided an antidote to what many Iranians saw as the wishy-washy ineffectiveness of President Khatami in coping with the conservative assault and vigilantes willing to use violence. "Ahmadinejad did not come out of nowhere," the journalist said. "He was a reaction to how government was run in the Khatami era. Khatami could not do his job. People wanted a stronger president, after a weak president. [Ahmadinejad] knows that."

Never mind the endless criticism in Tehran; Ahmadinejad and his ever-changing cabinet had another strategy for winning the next election that reached far beyond the capital. In the span of four years, the president made two high-profile visits to each of Iran's thirty provinces, handing out gifts, cash, projects, promises, and political attention to areas long neglected by previous presidents. It amounted to a perpetual reelection campaign and allowed Ahmadinejad to do what he does best—speak to ordinary Iranians. An added bonus was creation of an archive of photographs of the leader/candidate, swarmed by supporters everywhere he went—so he could be seen as a magician attempting to solve the problems of ordinary citizens, and not as the cause of those problems.

"One of the many purposes of Ahmadinejad's populism was to show [that he and the right wing] were simply too popular and successful to be dismissed," writes historian Ansari.[128] "The [fundamentalists] were confident about the capacity of the population at large to be repeatedly won over by populist policies, and about the extent to which the effective and occasionally ruthless exercise of power would act as a reminder of authority."

Of all those provincial visits, Western journalists were allowed to witness only a handful. On one of the earlier trips, the BBC was told *not* to film the crowds, and while they were there they heard more than a few complaints sent the president's way. Many of the ten million letters accumulated by Ahmadinejad throughout his first term, after all, were complaints.[129]

And the very need for them was drawing fire. The moderate newspaper *Mardomsalari* called the provincial trips a "backward step" drawn from the first days of ancient Greek democracy.[130] It noted that if even half the letters had been acted upon—and Iranians often told me how requests were answered with an envelope stuffed with cash— then inaction on the other half would cause a "feeling of despair and mistrust in those who have been neglected." The newspaper said it was far better for the government to improve the economy for all, by lowering inflation and boosting jobs and growth, to abrogate "any need for writing letters."

THERE WAS A LARGE amount of cash handed out, and on the November 2007 trip that I joined I also counted bicycles, toys, and plenty of shrewd politics.

I was granted permission to visit the conservative town of Birjand, eight hundred miles southeast of Tehran, concurrently with a presidential trip. Birjand, the capital of South Khorasan province, in 2005 had boasted the highest percentage of Ahmadinejad voters anywhere in the country. In fact, as pointed out by defeated candidate Mehdi Karroubi, the province managed to produce 298,000 votes in ballot boxes, from just 270,000 eligible voters.[131]

Etched into the desert at the base of dun-colored crags, Birjand was rewarded for its loyalty with the first presidential visit to any province. Now the second round of provincial visits was under way, and Birjand was on top of the list.

For me the journey was a logistical nightmare, since my permission did not come through until Ahmadinejad was already there and providing pablum to the masses. I was scrambling for air tickets in Tehran while Iran's demagogue was declaring to an appreciative crowd that the just-released U.S. National Intelligence Estimate, which concluded that Iran had halted a nuclear weapons program in 2003, was "a victory for the Iranian nation." The Iranian people, he vowed, "will not step back one inch."[132]

I flew at midnight to Mashhad, then after arriving at 1 A.M., jumped into a taxi and subjected my translator Dariush Sadeghi to a six-hour overnight drive to Birjand.[133] We arrived just after dawn and received a frosty welcome from the president's men and the traveling Iranian press corps. The president was doing nothing else public, we were told, at least nothing that I could see and report on. He was meeting the governor, and then privately with citizens, and later attending an evening prayer session—which I *might* be able to attend.

The only good news was that in Birjand there was only one hotel to get coffee and breakfast. Several of Ahmadinejad's advisers were there, run ragged themselves from days of driving around the province, as they did on the eve of every presidential journey, to check up on projects, cut through red tape, and inaugurate projects completed in Ahmadinejad's name. On each trip outside the capital, the president held a cabinet meeting locally. I was presented with a copy of a report listing more than two hundred projects initiated by the president in the province. He was spending millions more during this visit alone, on everything from new petrochemical factories to shantytown improvement. He had already promised that 40 percent of Iran's budget for the next fiscal year would go to rural areas.

Local officials were sold. "The amount of projects and development in the past two years is equal to the entire history of the province," said Abolfazl Noferesti, the press chief for the governor. His boss was appointed by the president, and he said the projects launched in 2005 were 20 to 90 percent complete. His job was to be sure residents knew who to thank. "People get very happy and thankful to the president and to God, when they see these projects being implemented," Noferesti told me. "One of the reasons that Mr. Ahmadinejad is in the heart of the people is because whatever [he] promises, he follows it up until it is implemented. . . . People will observe the results of these projects during his presidency, they will taste it"—and vote for him again.

Noferesti was too young to be a veteran of the Iran-Iraq War, yet he wore a white *basiji* scarf with its trademark black crosshatched design, a *chafiyeh*. He was wearing it in the picture that appeared that morning on the front page of the local Birjand newspaper, as he stood just behind the president. I noted the significance of the scarf and asked him if he was a *basiji,* and possibly a veteran. No, he wasn't a veteran, he admitted. But he wore the scarf with pride, he said, because being a *basiji* was a "state of mind."

THE IMPLICATIONS OF AHMADINEJAD'S carefully calibrated long-term election campaign were not lost in Tehran. "There are only two ways Ahmadinejad can be defeated," a political scientist told me in the capital.[134] "Another [reformist] mass vote, or Supreme Leader Khamenei fully withdraws his support for Ahmadinejad—and I don't see either one happening." The president, he said, "is getting smarter on how he spends money, targets his campaigns, and at negative campaigning."

Ahmadinejad had recently taken to calling critics of his nuclear policy "traitors."[135] "People are beginning to realize he is really messing up the economy," the analyst told me. "But the only people [who see it] are the urban middle and educated class. Those people do not have the votes, or the will to challenge him."

"Power is the same as liquid: if you can't gather it, it will go the other way," the conservative Amir Mohebian, of *Resalat,* told me.[136] "I thought Ahmadinejad is not an experienced politician. But he has shown he knows well the functions of power," said Mohebian. "Every act he takes now is for the next election."

And on the hustings in Birjand, the president and his advisers knew what they were after. National TV showed Ahmadinejad being driven in a modest car very early one morning to a poor section of town. Standing on the street, people reached out to shake his hand and share their problems. He responded by placing his arms on their shoulders in solidarity, like the son of a blacksmith who also happened to have a Ph.D.—a down-to-earth performance that few clerics in Iran would have been able to match.

Another scene showed Ahmadinejad addressing local clergy, praising the Revolution's immortal icon, Ayatollah Khomeini. Next he was in a poor family's house, sitting with a mother as she grieved for two sons martyred in the Iran-Iraq War. The president's body language was pitch-perfect. He sat with head down and knees together, hands clasped respectfully in his lap as the woman told the former Revolutionary Guard officer, "I'm sure you remember the Imposed War . . ."

Evidence of that personal touch was combined onscreen with footage of ministers at ribbon-cutting ceremonies to inaugurate completed agricultural projects and a water treatment plant, or breaking new ground. Similar visual imagery attended every provincial visit, and it had been effective.

Ahmadinejad was "very creative" with tailoring his message to local sensitivities, the Sage told me.[137] In Zanjan, for example, a provincial capital in northwest Iran famous for its knives as well as its seedless grapes, Ahmadinejad told a rally, "I received a gift of Zanjan blades. Let's cut the hands of aggressors with Zanjani knives!"

So the legions of poor and pious were, at least in late 2007 when I visited Birjand, still willing to give their hard-line president the benefit of the doubt. That was clear to me during the evening prayers. They were not expecting an American, much less one with a camera. When I arrived outside the Hossein mosque, the most conservative institution in a most conservative town, I was told it was not possible to enter. Men were streaming in, past the security guards; old men with rubber shoes and canes and stooped backs, who clearly preserved their souls with prayer at this mosque every day; and young men, including a boy who had a letter for the president tucked between the buttons of his shirt, who ogled the novelty of such a foreigner.

(Just an hour before, I had been forced to move out of a threadbare hostel—the only other place in town to stay, except for the hotel taken over by the presidential entourage. The frightened family owners said they did not have the right forms to accept foreign guests.)

While security guards radioed their superiors to confirm that I was to be shut out of the prayer service, a man with a blue suit and an enemy air loudly told me off: "You should go back to America. Everyone here supports Ahmadinejad!"

There was heated debate about my presence. Finally one of the president's own security guards arrived, and he recognized me from

Tehran—perhaps from climbing the telephone pole? Much more debate, and finally a decision. I would not be allowed to take my camera, so I left it with the intelligence agents at the door. Another agent was tasked with taking me in and led me by the hand. Inside the first door, at the edge of the carpet, we took off our shoes and put them in clear plastic bags to keep with us. The air was permeated by the rich and unpleasant spice of thousands of malodorous feet. We squeezed through the next narrow doorway, past a Plexiglas partition, into the inner sanctum, where people were clustered so tightly that their sweat dripped despite the cold night.

There was electricity in the air, in anticipation of a divine moment. Many men wore *chafiyeh* scarves of the Basij. I was led toward the back of the large hall, and found just enough space to drop down onto my knees, with all the other Believers. More were trying to get in, pushing at the Plexiglas, making it bend. A man tapped his large ring against the glass repeatedly, to get someone's attention. Tempers rose. A woman had fought her way into the men's section to be in the presence of her knight, but she was clawed back by other women to behind a thick green curtain.

Then Ahmadinejad arrived, like a rock star. There was a collective intake of breath as the crowd jumped to its feet and leaned forward to catch a glimpse of their favorite firebrand. "Sit down! Sit down!" implored the imam of the mosque, before finally giving up to announce: "The friend of the Imam has come!"

It was a perfect blend of piety and politics. Like most Iranians there that evening, I did not even physically *see* the president; the diminutive populist was lost behind his security guards, a gaggle of aggressive cameramen—the traveling press, with no foreigner among them—and those toward the front who had surged forward. Still, along with all the Iranians there, I *felt* his brief presence. To show me what it looked like, one Iranian photographer who had seen me deprived of my camera kindly picked his way to the front, shot some frames, and brought his camera back so I could see the image of Ahmadinejad sitting in the front row, reading a leaflet.

It was probably the handout given to all who entered that night, a four-page black-and-white campaign propaganda sheet that was a first template of Ahmadinejad's bid for reelection in 2009. It used cherry-picked statistics to demonstrate how "active" his administration was and how superior in every way to the previous reformist government. The "Notice of the Day" section credited Ahmadinejad with "removing the depredation from the face of this desert province," and listed a university, gas pipeline, steel plant, and construction of twelve thousand residential units among dozens of projects that "brought the admiration of all people of this area" for the president.

Under the heading "Secrets of the Successful Ninth Cabinet," the leaflet listed diplomatic "greatness" and pride restored to Iran with its nuclear defiance, and its achievement of enriching uranium. The populist approach was "correcting" previous misdirections of Khatami.

There was a long list too under the heading "Ninth Cabinet, the Cabinet of Firsts." Here Ahmadinejad's radical changes were given full flower, with a string of claims of variable veracity, some of which had little to do with his miraculous government. His was the first cabinet to travel to all provinces, and had doubled key budgets. Non-oil exports "soared" 41 percent. Foreign investment (in just two years) had jumped to $27 billion, compared to just $12 billion in the previous twelve years. The suspension of uranium enrichment had come to an end—though left unsaid was the fact that this was decided during the Khatami era.

"For the first time" the government answered millions of complaint letters, the leaflet read. Twice the number of schools had been constructed—and the education budget tripled—compared to the last year of the Khatami cabinet. Nine times as many fuel-efficient vehicles were on the streets . . .

And there was more. All these changes—and the maverick president who supposedly made them happen—were backed by God's Representative on Earth. Beneath a photo of Ayatollah Khamenei, a message praised the president as a "pious man, brave, clean-handed, principled [and] extremely active," whose "firm decisions serve people

[and] highlight the aims of the Revolution." The Supreme Leader said this government was "destined . . . to solve the people's problems" and to "obey Islam," while proving that "the Revolution is still at the peak of its slogans."

The Leader enthused: "I thank God that the President, [his] working cabinet and the government of service" is what "the nation wants, the men whose sleeves are up and belted for service to the people."

THAT MESSAGE OF DIVINE labor had clearly been getting out. Hear the voice, as I did, of one man who made a comparison to the missing Shiite Messiah, the Mahdi.

"Ahmadinejad is the best president that we have ever had. . . . He is an angel, the envoy of the Imam of the Age [Mahdi]," one sandwich shop owner told me in the town of Sarayan, an hour's drive north of Birjand.[138] "But still our town has lots of problems," he complained. This man was a war veteran and surrounded by crates of empty bottles and too-sugary orange drink, as he slapped together my sandwich of processed meat and mayonnaise. He had been refused a second loan to expand his thirty-year-old eatery into a guesthouse. The man pointed ruefully at the upper floor of his place, where an unfinished upgrade had been halted years before, rust overcoming the reinforcement bars protruding from concrete on the roof.

Nevertheless, this citizen saw the president as the man trying to solve his problems. It was local officials who were the villains, whom Ahmadinejad would sort out if he knew about them.

"You have to have a friend to have your request approved. Problems, problems . . . ," the shop owner said of the governor's office. He was not convinced by all the official projects the presidential entourage had been talking up: "It's all decoration. They had some projects they just started, but nothing gets done."

THAT'S WHAT I HAD thought, that this list of projects was little more than an Iranian version of a Potemkin village, with its shiny false shop fronts, when I spoke to Mehdi Kalhor in Birjand. He was

Ahmadinejad's senior press and culture adviser—the same one with long, greased gray hair who, around election time in 2005, had so memorably promised that his hard-line president elect's aim was to "prevent the government from interfering in private lives," and that women were "free to choose their dress."

Wearing a short-sleeved checked shirt, his wide face with its broad, pushed-down nose crowned with a single thick line across his forehead, Kalhor said he still believed everything he had said in that interview. "Nothing" in the presidential campaign—including those words—happened by "accident."[139] "We are not conservative. Do I look conservative?" he asked me over his omelet. "They *look* conservative, but in their thinking"—he nodded to his fellow advisers, then pointed to his own head—"they're not." He said he had tried to delete twenty-seven years of false impressions about the Islamic Republic and had received "lots of good feedback from that interview. It is still rebroadcast—our fax machines ran out of paper!"

Kalhor's conglomerate thinking was useful insight into the minds that were running Ahmadinejad's presidency. From nuclear politics and outreach toward America, to the meaning of "freedom," Kalhor was a study of remarkable assumptions, belief, ignorance—even flexibility. "We think the best medicine to remove the fears in the world is to create kindness and love and friendship," he told me. "These superpowers have few material needs, but inside they are depressed. It's been thirty years that the West did not laugh—it became mechanical. Westerners buy laughter, like you buy sandwiches. Cats live better than that. Dr. Ahmadinejad's idea is 'Look at yourself from the other side.' Inside of us, we are laughing heartily."

The West was in decline anyway, he told me in English, and partly because the Holocaust—the death of six million Jews during World War II at the hands of Nazi Germany—was a "scenario" that had been allowed to "take hostage the heart of humanity, and that's a dirty thing. That's a dirty, satanic thing. What Israel did in Palestine is worse than the Nazis."

America and the West have "a complex of fear and hatred,"

Kalhor insisted. "You can see that through their cinema, their diplomatic talks. So when Mr. Bush talks of bombs and weapons, his words are like weapons. . . . We don't need the West at all. Maybe we needed it for technological needs, but not anymore."

At first he was disparaging of U.S.-Iran dialogue. "There is a fact in psychology: you see yourself in the people you are confronting," Kalhor said. "If someone gives the Americans a bunch of flowers, they immediately take it to an X-ray machine to inspect it. Because they did the same thing, giving gifts which were bombs. The normal people are pure people, and they received the message of Ahmadinejad."

But then he was more hopeful: "We are very optimistic and positive about the American people. This is not propaganda, it is heartfelt belief."

Also heartfelt was Kalhor's belief that he and his fellow aides and ministers—and of course, Ahmadinejad—were on these provincial trips following in the footsteps of the Prophet, who "was living this way, working with the farmers and laborers." Kalhor said, "What comes from deep inside people is what God is."

And he was finding it there in South Khorasan province, where he had been pressed into agriculture duty. Kalhor said he visited several farms, including an experimental irrigation project that makes narrow clay tubes to seep moisture to crops—cutting to zero the 75 percent of water normally lost to evaporation, and minimizing soil depletion. Ahmadinejad "went through this process of evaluating problems from the village level," Kalhor told me. "He can't go everywhere so he sends us to check [on needs], and we report back to him."

The president himself had visited the site two years before, but no money had come. "It wasn't going anywhere. It was stopped at the gates of bureaucracy," Kalhor said of the project at Bideskan, one hundred miles to the northwest. "I came back to Birjand and spoke to the president. In two and a half hours it was resolved; before it would take twenty years." Such intervention made good politics, Kalhor admitted: "What's happening in our country is not hidden to ourselves—we know who gets the vote and who doesn't."

But how real were these claims of the president's men? I asked to be allowed to go to the experimental irrigation project the next day and was surprised when permission was given. During an unscripted visit to the farm, the director was effusive. The day before, he had received a large infusion of cash that would enable operations to expand twenty-fold, creating more than eleven hundred new jobs—with credit going to Ahmadinejad.

"It was so fast—yesterday I was called by the governor's office to collect the money," said Mohsen Hedjazi.[140] Outside his solar-powered office, rows of experimental crops demonstrated increased yields from less water. The pilot project was already churning out fifteen thousand hollow clay tubes each day, and after the cash infusion planned to increase staff from seventy to 1,200 in four months.

"Dr. Ahmadinejad is very interested in energy conservation projects, so he directed his attention to this," Hedjazi told me.

I asked: Did the president make his dreams come true?

Hedjazi did not hesitate: "Yes."

AND SOUTH KHORASAN WAS not the only place where the president was making hearts race. As part of a five-day presidential visit to Fars province several months before, Najmeh Bozorgmehr of the *Financial Times* found a similar mix of enthusiasm, awe, overspending, and complaint as Ahmadinejad hopped between twenty-four cities and towns, tirelessly making promises and pressing the flesh.[141] It was one of the very few provincial visits ever attended by other foreign media, and prompted Bozorgmehr to conclude that the punditocracy in Tehran, which had already concluded that Ahmadinejad was politically sunk, was engaged in "wishful thinking. His rivals have a tough challenge ahead."

"Thousands are held back at the gates of the Artesh (army) stadium by soldiers, who warn people they could die under the pressure of the crowd inside," Bozorgmehr reported about the first day. "Behind the podium, many people have been laid out on the ground after passing out.

" 'Let me die, but see the president,' said Morteza, a tearful 12-year-old boy who had been stopped at the entrance."

During that single tour the president made $3 billion worth of promises, including $2 billion in soft loans—which were especially popular in the provinces—and $1 billion of spending that Ahmadinejad planned to take from Iran's oil stabilization fund. Throughout, Bozorgmehr writes, Ahmadinejad's "language was uncomplicated, devoid of political and economic jargon, and sometimes peppered with jokes. 'He's as miserable as we are,' a tearful woman named Robabeh said in the town of Fasa. She desperately tried to fight her way to the president to 'kiss his hands and feet.' "

"Noble Americans"

Yet such successful efforts were hardly resurrecting the Revolution. President Ahmadinejad spoke brashly as if the Islamic Republic were still following an ever-higher trajectory, with every Iranian lined up behind him, battalions of Believers unified in their determination to win an Islamic, anti-Western victory. But even Ahmadinejad's mastery of *doublethink*—George Orwell's term "for holding two contradictory beliefs . . . and accepting both of them," in a "vast system of mental cheating"—could not hide Iran's litany of economic problems.[142]

When he addressed the crowds in Tehran on the twenty-ninth anniversary of the Revolution, in February 2008, Ahmadinejad had to admit to still wrestling with high unemployment and soaring prices. "Despite all developments and progress achieved throughout the Revolution, we are at the start of our journey. We are facing structural problems," he said, that require "major reform and surgery."[143] And the list of issues was formidable: taxation, banking, distribution, import and export, and Iran's hugely expensive subsidies.

Later he would justify the delays this way: "Do you think that [economic] justice is implemented immediately, as soon as we speak of justice? Do you think we can put everything right by just issuing a circular? This is not the case." [144] Achieving justice is "the most difficult phase," he said, in "establishing the divine state."

There were no such difficulties on the world stage, however, where the Islamic Republic was taking on the Global Arrogance over its nuclear program and preparing to launch rockets and a satellite into space.

"I ask the people's view. Would you agree if your officials give in, surrender or compromise over the nuclear issue? Would you agree to give up one iota of your nuclear rights?" the president bellowed. "No!" the crowd shouted back. "Nuclear energy is our absolute right!" [145]

Ahmadinejad had thanks to share, as well. "I want to express my special gratitude to our Master, Imam Mahdi, in front of Iran's grand nation," he said. "Turning Iran into a nuclear nation hasn't been a normal event; it is equal to the victory of the Revolution. . . . Who gave spiritual guidance to Iran [during the Revolution] and guided Iran step by step until its grand victory? The same thing [Mahdi's guidance] is happening in the nuclear issue."

But Iran's nuclear prowess was more than just a divine happening; it was also a political club to beat reformists who had negotiated with the West. Ahmadinejad railed against Iranians who "decided to sit down with the enemies," which had only encouraged those enemies to pursue "harsher policies against Tehran." The president said those Iranians were traitors, not "part of the Iranian nation," and that Iranians would "throw them away."

IT WAS AHMADINEJAD'S UNASSAILABLE hard-line credentials—and reliance on such divine support—that gave him confidence to talk freely with "enemies" himself. A remarkable episode of U.S.-Iran outreach came from the Iranian president's own pen, when in his first year in office he wrote to President George W. Bush. The first of its kind from Tehran to a U.S. leader since the Islamic Revolution, the eighteen-page missive focused on American hypocrisy in world affairs, and how liberal democracy had "failed" in the West. [146]

It was an extraordinary look into Iran's hard-line mind-set. Riddled with religious references and rich in self-righteousness, the letter spelled out Ahmadinejad's view that Bush's America was acting contrary to divine teachings. He warned—quite prophetically for Iran, it would turn out—that "history tells us that repressive and cruel governments do not survive."

To many American ears, the letter was an outrageous harangue from a religious fanatic, whose lack of diplomatic tact showed with every phrase. The list of complaints was long, from U.S. troops in Iraq, "their hands stained with the blood of others," to blanket support for Israel. Ahmadinejad wrote of "an ever-increasing global hatred of the American government."

"The people will scrutinize our presidencies," the Iranian upbraided his American counterpart. "Did we defend the rights of all people around the world or impose wars on them, interfere illegally in their affairs, establish hellish prisons and incarcerate some of them?" asked Ahmadinejad, without a hint of irony about the Islamic Republic's own grim human rights record; its history of lethal meddling beyond its borders; or its complete disregard for the "truth" when it saw fit.

"Did we bring the world peace and security or raise the specter of intimidation and threats? Did we tell the truth to our nation and others around the world or present an inverted version of it? Were we on the side of people or the occupiers and oppressors?"

U.S. officials dismissed Ahmadinejad's ruminations as the screed of a sanctimonious hypocrite. No one in the Bush administration saw fit to respond directly, which surprised many Iranians, because aside from Ahmadinejad's accusations the letter also affirmed that both sides shared many values. Indeed, few would argue that the events at Abu Ghraib and at Guantanamo Bay, or in the CIA's "rendering" of terrorism suspects to third-party nations for harsher treatment and torture, was the best face of America.

Despite that severe scolding, Ahmadinejad's letter was a concrete step—deliberate ink upon paper that could in no way be interpreted as a slip of the tongue—by Iran's top elected leader to "speak" to an

American president. And this came from the pen of not just any Iranian president, but the most hard-line yet produced in the history of the Islamic Republic.

Few could charge this firebrand populist with trying to destroy the Islamic system by caving in to the West; by capitulating to the Great Satan. Yet Ahmadinejad's predecessor Mohammad Khatami, despite his vast popular mandate, was crushed under suspicion of his motives for making even the most tentative efforts to reach out to America.

When Khatami had spoken warmly of "breaking down the wall of mistrust" with America, it was ridiculed as high treason, a corrosive threat to Islamic rule. But years later, when Ahmadinejad took far more substantial rhetorical and even physical steps toward Iran's archenemy—praising American values, while trashing the hypocrisy of U.S. government policies—there was little murmur from Iran's far right. As a bona fide hard-liner, Ahmadinejad could toy with the volatile U.S.-Iran relationship and reach out to Americans publicly as none had before. And he wasn't done. Six months after writing his letter to Bush, the Iranian president in late 2006 penned another—this time to the citizens of the United States.

ADDRESSING THE "NOBLE AMERICANS," Ahmadinejad's letter was an extraordinary catalog of the similarities he saw between Iranian and American values:

> While divine Providence has placed Iran and the United States geographically far apart, we should be cognizant that human values and our common human spirit, which proclaim the dignity and exalted worth of all human beings, have brought our two great nations of Iran and the United States closer together.
>
> Both our nations are God-fearing, truth-loving and justice-seeking, and both seek dignity, respect and perfection.
>
> Both greatly value and readily embrace the promotion of human ideals such as compassion, empathy, respect for the rights of human

beings, securing justice and equity, and defending the innocent and the weak against oppressors and bullies.

We are all inclined towards the good, and towards extending a helping hand to one another, particularly to those in need. . . .

The pure human essence of the two great nations of Iran and the United States testify to the veracity of these statements.[147]

Ahmadinejad's words were a great leap away from the time-tested term *Great Satan,* and they prompted a surge of speculation about the apparent willingness, finally, of Iran's archconservatives to explore an opening with America. Yet without the slightest nod to Iran's own constant complaints about American meddling in Iranian affairs, Ahmadinejad stepped deeply into U.S. domestic issues, lecturing about how "civil liberties in the United States are being increasingly curtailed. Even the privacy of individuals is fast losing its meaning. Judicial due process and fundamental rights are trampled upon. Private phones are tapped, suspects are arbitrarily arrested, sometimes beaten in the streets, or even shot to death."

The Iranian president made no mention of how those points applied very much to Iran, nor how its own human rights record had deteriorated during Ahmadinejad's tenure—from jailing students and women's activists to being second only to China in worldwide executions, with at least 346 in 2008.[148] Still, with all the reassurance of a hectoring superpower leader himself, Ahmadinejad lectured that a change of ways could ease "hatred of America": "I am confident that you, the American people, will play an instrumental role in the establishment of justice and spirituality throughout the world. The promises of the Almighty . . . will certainly be realized. Justice and Truth will prevail and all nations will live a true life in a climate replete with love, compassion and fraternity."

Ahmadinejad ended with a verse from the Quran, a line that evoked the proselytizing letter Khomeini had sent to Mikhail Gorbachev in 1989. The ayatollah, just months before his death, tried to convert the

Soviet leader to Islam, and told him that "from now on communism will only . . . be found in the museums of world political history." Islam, Khomeini said, "can easily fill the vacuum of religious faith in your society." [149]

Likewise, Ahmadinejad reassured Americans that "those who repent, have faith and do good may receive salvation."

ON THE SURFACE, THE political theater of the twenty-ninth revolutionary birthday party in February 2008 was at its usual fever pitch. Freedom Square was packed with a kaleidoscope of color and patriotism on a day most Iranians do not only consider a "regime" holiday, but also a national one, akin to the Fourth of July in America. All of Iran's social and political divisions were therefore on display, and I found a growing despondency that, despite years of hardship, the Revolution had failed to live up to its promise.

The hard core were still plentiful—I marched for three hours along packed streets and past deafening loudspeakers that spouted anti-American slogans as I tried to get to the square.[150] Crowds of poor fought over free packets of juice handed out from the back of trucks. Volunteers in roadside stalls also gave out free bowls of bean stew, the steaming contents sometimes spilled onto the street in splashes of sticky brown goo. Emergency workers showed their fitness by rappelling down the side of the Bank Tejarat building. And the anti-Americanism was notably virulent; after three decades, a critical animating force remained simply rhetorical hatred of the Great Satan.

On the streets, I saw a pair of young boys with one of the few "positive" messages on their hats: "Our lives for the Leader." But on their balloons was written "Death to America." And as I walked with my translator, the loudspeaker truck moving beside us was painted with anti–Uncle Sam images. It was all an exercise in pure negativity, supposedly driven by religiosity.

"We swear on the blood of the martyrs, we will *kill* you, Bush!" the loudspeakers screeched with certainty. Again, and again, and again. I had heard that endlessly over the years, but perhaps not with such resolute determination—or mindlessness. The regime of course declared an "epic" turnout, and it had some reason to be pleased.

The Bayuni family, for example, spent days preparing for the annual anti-American effigy contest. First prize: a gold coin stamped with the hallowed image of Khomeini. One of their entries showed Iran choking America and Israel; another showed the United States capturing all of the globe except Iran, which was protected by barbed wire. They decided not to burn those effigies, said wife Sara, "to see what the United States will do with the world." Countless other effigies and U.S. and Israeli flags—sometimes I wondered if they did not outnumber the Iranian flags—were incinerated.

BUT MANY OF THE ordinary Iranians I spoke to were tired. The widespread show of nationalist support was real, though mixed with disappointment, voiced from unexpected quarters, that the Revolution had strayed far from its original promises of freedom, justice, and prosperity.

Take for example government employee Reza, a religious man I found wearing a headband in a propaganda tent, where televisions looped videotape of street scenes from 1979. He had a few days of stubble for a beard, and though too young to have taken part—he was a toddler at the time of the "Glorious Victory"—he looked the part of a Believer. At first he gave me platitudes.

"What is certain is people are happy because they can choose the people they want, based on voting, not on dictatorship," Reza told me.[151] He thought vetting of candidates was necessary to "make sure they support the *nezam* [Islamic system]." I detected some doubt, but turned away, expressing an interest in the video and some leaflets. Outside on the street, Iranians streamed past on their way to Freedom Square. I turned back to Reza and pressed him on how the Revolution had measured up. He didn't flinch this time.

"Personally, I feel sad about the way things are going because I have better expectations for my country," Reza confided. He was religious, but his face was worn beyond its years. "I'm a government employee.

I work very hard all year just to earn enough for the next rent rise, and still I do not have a weekend free to be with my wife," Reza told me. Many Iranians like him had to get second jobs to make ends meet. I was constantly riding with taxi drivers moonlighting from their day jobs as professors and engineers. "I don't have peace of mind. With all our natural resources, I have nothing. I feel disappointed."

I was surprised at such words, from a government employee. But Reza was quite sure that the Revolution's potential was being ruined by its loudest proponents. Ahmadinejad had raised the perennial problem of mismanagement to new levels. Reza was shocked that thirty sitting members of parliament had been disqualified from running in the upcoming vote. "If they are not qualified, what the hell are they doing there?" he asked. "If someone has been a vice minister and made big deals worth billions—after being qualified and serving the system for thirty years—what makes him suddenly not qualified? This is a very questionable fact. He does not change overnight," Reza told me. "They choose you for a job based on your loyalty to the Revolution. Not because of your expertise."

There were plenty of other Iranians who thronged those streets in a bid to revitalize the Revolution, or to show devotion to the Supreme Leader. Or because they felt duty-bound. "Many people have sacrificed a lot for this Revolution, so we came to give it a rebirth," one high school student told me. He was with several Western-looking boys from his class, all of them laughing and enjoying the day. Among shorter hair and crew cuts favored by religious *basiji* militiamen, there were also many long- and spike-haired young men like them.

"We have come to defend our Revolution, to show that we are backing it," said Alireza Dadpour, a fellow student with an Iranian flag draped over his back. "A lot of blood was spilled. We want to honor that." His father had taken part in every Revolution-era protest—for a Revolution that, he said, "ended oppression and beatings."

One woman had never missed an anniversary march in twenty-nine years, and was there to support "my country, my religion, and my Leader." Her son had been sacrificed in the Iran-Iraq War. Akram Azari

Khameneh carried a portrait of the Supreme Leader and said she did not care that two thousand reformist candidates had been shut out of the upcoming parliament elections in order to ensure continued conservative control of politics. "What matters to us is our Leader. Whomever Khamenei accepts, we will accept," she told me. "You can see this with your own eyes; ninety percent of people believe this way. This march proves it." Those who believe otherwise, she acknowledged with disdain, "are also living in this country. I hope God will help them."

One skinny young boy sang hard-line chants pledging fealty to "the Imam" and hailing "blows against imperialism." Reza Akbari was not even born when the Revolution celebrated its tenth birthday. But he was certain that there was no room for reformists in *his* Islamic Republic. "They are not Iranians. They are very stupid. They don't listen to the clear commands of the Leader," the boy told me. "The Iranian people are so smart they would never give the power to those people."

Less convinced of the Revolution's rectitude was another woman called Akram, who I found having a picnic with her family on the grass near the monument to 2,500 years of Persian history, after the rally peaked with Ahmadinejad's bellicose speech and had begun to disband. She had brought her son and daughter to every anniversary celebration since they were babies. But over the years that bright treasure had lost much of its shine.

"We are the followers of Khomeini's path [and] we like this day. We wait for this day. We long for it all year," Akram told me. "[But] we've had a lot of hardships since the Revolution," the mother said. Her now-grown children and their aunt circled around her, sitting on pages of newspaper to keep dry on the damp grass. The grounds were littered with a detritus of political posters and bottles.

Daughter Maryam said the rally would "show our might to the enemy," though she had concerns. "We support the Islamic system [*nezam*] when there is justice, but what is going on now we don't like. It's injustice." And she had her own problems, besides. "As a girl I have no future. I am a student but do not know about a job." Politicians across the political spectrum had let this family down—or was it the *nezam* itself, still trying to be genuinely "revolutionary," that failed to meet the aspirations created so many years before?

"When Ahmadinejad was a candidate we had hopes, but neither he nor the Revolution fulfilled expectations," said Akram. Street cleaners were already picking up the trampled trash, scooping up the ash of burnt flags of "enemies" abroad—the official focus of the rally that, this family said, should have instead addressed real grievances at home.

"Hope is with God," Akram told me, voicing resignation. "We have no hope in these guys anymore."

Iran's Rise and Rise

Ironically, while skepticism grew for many Iranians about the state of their Revolution, conservatives found reason to celebrate. They had locked in their hold on parliament in the March 2008 election. And the likelihood of an American attack on Iran seemed to evaporate overnight, with the release in late 2007 of the U.S. National Intelligence Estimate, which concluded Iran had stopped a nuclear weapons program years before. The result was renewed regime triumphalism, and for hard-liners a taboo-breaking boldness.

"The conservatives feel a very strong sense of power in themselves, especially after the NIE report. . . . They feel the chance of war against them is gone," Iraj Jamshidi, then political editor of the reformist newspaper *Etemaad*, told me.[152] "The reality is that the Islamic Republic feels itself at the peak of its power since the Revolution, and the foreign threat does not exist anymore."

Iran's power had indeed been on the rise, helped in large measure by Washington's own policies. The toppling of the Taliban in Afghanistan in 2001 and the overthrow of Saddam Hussein in Iraq in 2003 removed Iran's two most implacable regional enemies. The Islamic Republic also found success extending its influence by forming, leading, and supporting what I call the Axis of Resistance—an anti-American, anti-Israel coalition that included Iran-backed Hezbollah in

Lebanon, Hamas in the Palestinian territories, Shiite militants in Iraq, and ally Syria.

The influence of that ideological alliance was further bolstered by the thirty-four-day Israel-Hezbollah war in the summer of 2006, which saw several thousand Shiite militiamen fight Israel's much-vaunted military machine to a standstill while raining down Iranian-made rockets into northern Israel. U.S. secretary of state Condoleezza Rice attributed the violence to the "birth pangs" of a "new Middle East." Washington rushed more lethal weaponry to Israel while putting off calls for a cease-fire, and couched the fight as a regional standoff between the United States and Iran. Hezbollah chief Sheikh Seyyed Hassan Nasrallah called the result a "Divine Victory." [153]

In Tehran, the Supreme Leader was ebullient in his praise of Hezbollah: "What you gave as a gift from your unique resistance and jihad to the Islamic nation is beyond my capability to describe," Khamenei said.[154] "You showed that through the help of God military superiority is not based on arms, weapons, fighter planes, tanks, or warships, but on the power of beliefs, jihad, and sacrifice accompanied by wisdom and resourcefulness."

The Axis of Resistance was handed another "victory" by Israel's offensive against Hamas in the Gaza Strip in December 2008–January 2009. A hugely disproportionate reaction to Hamas rocket attacks, it left some fourteen hundred Palestinians—roughly a quarter of them children—dead in the space of twenty-two days.[155] Thirteen Israelis died, four of them in friendly-fire incidents. Besides Hamas and military and civilian targets, the Israeli assault also struck UN facilities, left hundreds of thousands of Palestinians homeless, and saw indiscriminate use of white phosphorus munitions in civilian areas. Israel was roundly condemned for its brutal tactics by human rights groups and the UN, as well as by some of Israel's own soldiers, for a conflict with a death ratio of one hundred to one.

It was a propaganda coup for the Axis of Resistance, which was seen by some as partial fulfillment of Ayatollah Khomeini's order to "export" the 1979 Revolution. That promise is encapsulated on the brass plaque to be found today at Khomeini's old prayer hall of Jamaran, in north Tehran. It reads: "It was this very modest and humble house that became a *qiblah* [center] for the hearts of millions of Muslims in Iran and throughout the world and disturbed the sweet dreams of the tyrants in the world."[156]

In Tehran, that is how it looked to conservative activist Hamidreza Taraghi: "When Imam Khomeini said, 'Export the Revolution,' he didn't mean sending people to the country and by war converting people by force to their beliefs. He meant this idea [of resistance] should be expressed in the world."[157]

In Beirut, portions of which—along with much of southern Lebanon—had been flattened during the 2006 Israeli air strikes, Iran's full spectrum of influence had resonance. "For Hezbollah, and even for Iran, [the] play for power in the region serves an ideological aim," analyst Amal Saad-Ghorayeb told me in the Lebanese capital.[158] "Their influence over the Palestinians does not mean they want to spread Shiite Islam in Palestine. It's to confront Israel and the U.S. It's to spread resistance; *that* is the religion they want to spread."

While the Axis of Resistance against American hegemony included non-Shiite actors like Syria and Hamas, its leadership fell naturally within the purview of Shiite theology, honed by its history of an embattled minority "resisting," and cradle-to-grave indoctrination. "Hezbollah is fully immersed in this religious ideology," said Saad-Ghorayeb. "There are people who have been raised by mothers who want them, encourage them, to sacrifice themselves. The medium of Shiite Islam—it's a very valuable mobilizing tool."

Supreme Leader Khamenei knew the stakes and was confident. In May 2007 he declared that a "great war of wills" was taking place.[159] Iran standing up to the United States and the West had "exploded a powerful bomb in world politics that is a hundred times more powerful than the [atomic] bomb the Americans exploded in Hiroshima," Khamenei declared. "Even the Europeans are speechless before this oppressive America, but the Iranian nation by its actions and stances has placed a question mark over all the rules and principles of this oppressive power."

The fact that Ahmadinejad was seen across the region as a bold hero and figurehead of resistance—who often polled just behind Nasrallah as the most admired leader—was a balm to the regime. "Everybody has understood that Iran is the No. 1 power in the world," Ahmadinejad boasted in early 2008.[160] "Today the name of Iran means a firm punch in the teeth of the powerful. . . . Today the message of your Revolution is being heard [around the world] and even in the United States itself."

WHILE ECHOING IN WASHINGTON, that bracing confidence was also spilling over into domestic politics in Iran. After what conservatives saw as the frightening treachery of the Khatami era, they vowed they "will never [again] allow themselves to lose a major election," predicted editor Jamshidi, who was among reformist candidates barred from running in March 2008.[161] He was rejected for being against the Islamic system and having a "bad reputation," a claim usually reserved for armed robbers. "I've never been to a police station, either as a witness or a suspect," Jamshidi told me. "Yet now I'm known for a 'bad reputation.'"

Lobbying of the Supreme Leader led to a reinstatement of 850 of the 2,200 rejected candidates, but the fix was in. Many conservatives were also embarrassed by the scale of disqualifications. Khatami called them a "catastrophe." "They were not rejected because they were reformists, but because [they were] proven not to believe in the constitution or are disloyal to the *nezam*," asserted Taraghi, the conservative politician.[162] "They can be in society, but they should not hold power."

"The potent combination of nationalism, ideological zeal, and fear of foreign interference has closed down the political space," a political scientist in Tehran told me.[163] "This is a deliberate and pre-engineered clearing the way for Khamenei to ensure conservative dominance in Iranian politics for years to come. They want to finish what they have not: getting rid of any reformist inclinations [and giving] a message to reformists not to contemplate a presidential comeback" in 2009.

AMONG THOSE DEEMED TOO dangerous for politics was Elyas Hazrati, a veteran lawmaker elected four times who had sixteen years of parliamentary experience. The stocky newspaper editor should have been a shoo-in candidate, but was one of the many liberals rejected, in his case for supposedly being "against Islam."[164] His newspaper, *Etemaad*, was critical of Ahmadinejad, and in Hazrati's words, "assaults [his government] on a daily basis."

Hazrati had the bearing of a street fighter, and the regime clearly considered him to be one, though not of the useful variety. He had taken part in pro-reform protests and spoken out for Iranians challenging the regime. In his office hung a large photograph of Hazrati in the dock of Iran's criminal court, which imposed an eighteen-month suspended sentence on him in 2006 for "campaigning against the Islamic Republic." The office receptionist, on her computer, had a screen-saver picture of Mohammad Khatami, smiling.

"Conservatives are very scared of the popularity of the reformists and have many differences among themselves," Hazrati told me. "Reform is the only way to maintain the Revolution, because we believe in its goals and ideals. The current [antidemocratic] situation is a major deviation from the Revolution."

In fact, all sides proclaimed reverence for the Revolution and the ideals of Khomeini. But who truly carried the torch was the focus of vicious debate, with rivals accusing each other of being "enemies" of the regime bent on destroying it. The discourse showed the profound confidence of Iran's most radical right-wing factions.

"In twenty-nine years, they didn't have the courage to talk this way," the reform-leaning Grand Ayatollah Saanei told me in Qom. His eyes were dark with too much blood and fatigue, and glazed.[165] "But now [hard-liners] have full control and they have no competitors inside or outside Iran."

One rule laid down by Khomeini forbade the military playing any role in politics. And one unwritten rule prohibited criticizing Khomeini's family. But that did not stop the Revolutionary Guard commander Mohammad Ali Jafari from creating a furor. "To follow the path of the Islamic Revolution, support for the principlists (conservatives) is necessary, inevitable, and a divine duty of all revolutionary groups," he told officials of the Basij before the parliament vote.[166] Jafari noted that conservatives already controlled the executive and legislative branches, and "if the Basij members want to preserve this current and develop it, they must eliminate weak points."

Those words brought stinging rebuke from across the political spectrum, even from fellow hard-liners like the macaroon-favoring editor of *Kayhan,* who called it a "faulty declaration" that is "against the clear guidelines of the late Leader ordering Armed Forces not to intervene in political rivalries."[167] But the message was already delivered, to those in the Guard and their Basij brethren who needed to hear it.

Among those who spoke out was the respected grandson of the late Leader, in a rare public comment. "If a soldier wants to enter into politics, he needs to forget the military as the presence of a gun in politics means the end of all dialogue," said Seyyed Hassan Khomeini, a mid-ranking cleric in charge of his grandfather's mausoleum.[168] "Those who claim to be loyal to [Khomeini] should be very sensitive to this order, which was directly given by him." Noting that the Leader of the Revolution had put great store in voting, he criticized the mass disqualification of candidates—among them another Khomeini grandson. "No one can prevent the people from deciding their future."

The hard-line counterattack was swift and unprecedented. A website very close to Ahmadinejad's office went after Khomeini himself—a target long off-limits. Under the headline "The Secret of the Red Cheeks of Seyyed Hassan Khomeini," the Nosazi website wrote that Khomeini had received a seventy-five-thousand-dollar BMW and lived in luxury in northern Tehran, where he would "never leave" his steam sauna but "have the luck to see the problems of the poor and needy with [his] red cheeks."[169]

The backlash was fierce. Fellow conservatives warned that allies of Ahmadinejad had gone too far. *Kayhan's* influential editor, Hossein Shariatmadari, told the president in print: "Beware of infiltrators and enemies [reformists], but mostly ignorant friends that are more dangerous in an Internet site pretending to support you and your government." [170]

From Qom, the dissident Grand Ayatollah Montazeri continued his scathing criticism of antidemocratic moves. Hard-liners "want the government and parliament to be all the same, the people to be one with them, and they put others aside," he told me.[171] "They weaken the Revolution and they weaken Islam."

The aging holy man seemed indefatigable. His offices in Isfahan and Mashhad had been closed, and cameras placed by intelligence agents looked down every street. But at least the Revolutionary Guard was no longer camped inside the compound, as they had been for five and a half years. The short man—once the "fruit" of Khomeini's life— wore a knit skullcap and had shaved his head, but still missed the tufts of his ears.

Often described in print as being "disgraced" after his fallout with Khomeini, Montazeri still had large influence as a Shiite theologian. In a back office, a shoulder-high safe with two keyholes in its gray door was testimony to the value of Montazeri's charity as one of the highest ranking Shiite *mojtaheds,* or sources of emulation. In another room, I saw clerical administrators thumbing through the large, numbered green volumes that listed the thirty- to thirty-five-thousand followers whom Montazeri helped support and put through seminary studies.

Montazeri was angry at the abuses he saw beyond the confines of this religious world, where the Revolution he had done so much to create was being corrupted by second-class tyrants. "They have the power and they want to scare people," he told me, breaking his schedule briefly to talk in his study. "At the beginning of the Revolution, they had the power of belief." But now Iranians blamed clerics for failing to fulfill the promises of the Revolution.

"The owners of the country are not four or five people. The Shah made the same mistake; now they are making this mistake again," Montazeri said. "Because people saw the opposite of promises [of the Revolution], all this eventually turned to dust. People have brains."

Montazeri delivered those razor-sharp words while sitting calmly behind his small desk, stacked with books as usual, one of them opened toward him on a tilted reading stand. But there was far more physical agitation elsewhere in the clerical community, where anger over the insults to Khomeini's grandson was blamed for the sudden death of Ayatollah Mohammad Reza Tavassoli, the former head of Khomeini's office, who fell dead while making an impassioned speech about it in front of the Expediency Council.

The newspaper *Kargozaran* praised him with the headline "Defending the Imam Until the Very Last Moment."[172] It quoted the brother of Rafsanjani as saying that the ayatollah had died attacking those with "fossilized minds."

The Mahdaviat Tour

Among those might have been President Mahmoud Ahmadinejad, whose obsession with the imminent return of the Shiite Messiah had sparked a revival of Mahdaviat thought in official circles. This much was clear during the fourth annual conference on Mahdaviat doctrine in August 2008, which had expanded from very humble origins to the preeminent conference venue in Tehran. It was organized by the Bright Future Institute, whose clerical director Pourseyyed-Aghaei had told me years earlier that Mahdaviat thinking was "code for the Revolution."

Now from the podium, the cleric praised the presidential patronage. Without Ahmadinejad's favor "we would not have such a conference of this size; it is beyond me and my friends," Pourseyyed-Aghaei told the gathering of a couple of hundred.[173] "The president's office removed all our problems."

I knew that to be true, because I had received a late-night call in Istanbul less than thirty-six hours before the meeting began, from Qom, from the young director of the Bright Future News Agency, whom I had met and had quoted in my earlier stories. Editor Seyyed Ali Pourtabatabaei invited me to the conference and said they wanted to give me a "journalism prize"—and that the president himself would be doing so. I nearly fell out of my chair. Weren't these the same sensitive stories that helped keep me shut out of Iran for nearly a year? But then I relaxed—there was no way they would issue an American a visa in time, a process that normally took weeks.

"Your visa is already at the airport," he continued. And for good measure, they instructed the Foreign Ministry to issue another one at the Iranian consulate in Istanbul. I was still in shock when I arrived in Tehran the following morning before dawn and was whisked into the VIP lounge with an American academic expert on Shiism from McMaster University in Canada, who had submitted a paper for the conference. Professor Kurt Anders Richardson and I were driven by official car to Tehran, with Pourtabatabaei sitting in the front seat, craning his neck back to talk.

"We thought there was no way you would get the visa in time," he told me, with a knowing smile that lit up his young features. It was clearly meant to be, he confided: "We think the power of the Mahdi was helping to get you here on time."

Who was I to contradict him? For it was by far the easiest visa of the thirty or so I had ever been granted for Iran. The reason for the invitation was not because of my main story about the Mahdi's Jamkaran mosque—the one that quoted clerics saying the president was cynically using religious superstitions for political ends—but because my story on the twenty-four-hour "Mahdi hotline" had caught their attention, and the president liked it. "That story brought *everyone* to Qom to see us," Pourtabatabaei claimed. "Christiane Amanpour of CNN, all the journalists came with your story, asking, 'What is this?' "

The surprises kept coming. Within two hours of arriving at the hotel, I was on a bus heading to the conference center with other delegates, one of them from Indonesia, who, disconcertingly, had a picture of the Supreme Leader on his mobile phone. At the center of the vast, high-ceilinged conference center—the same leaking one rushed to completion in 1997 for the Islamic summit—was a flower arrangement taller than a man. It was dominated, appropriately, by birds-of-paradise and other colorful varieties that matched the array of clerics, academics, and officials in attendance to honor the Mahdi and the "science of waiting" for his return.

"Although eleven hundred years have passed [since the Mahdi's departure], each hour can be a century for those who feel," Pourseyyed-Aghaei told the conference. "Mahdism is the secret identity of the Shiite," he said, which explained "secretly why" the Revolution started. Government had "one purpose, to pave the way for the appearance of the Mahdi," and the Islamic Republic was blessed with that mission, the cleric said. "We will deliver this government to the Imam [Mahdi]."

Ahmadinejad arrived while Pourseyyed-Aghaei was speaking, and all eyes turned as he made his way to the front, right hand raised like a holy man bestowing a blessing. "The True Believer and popular president of Iran—a president we are proud of!" announced the cleric. "He does believe in the Mahdi and its vital teaching. He believes Mahdism is the message of peace and love, contrary to what some propagate as violence."

It was the week of celebrating the Mahdi's birth, an auspicious time that Ayatollah Mohammad Emami-Kashani, who'd taken over at the podium, marked by asking, "What does God favor the most?" He quoted the Prophet Mohammad saying, "The only thing is to wait." Ahmadinejad stifled a yawn in his front-row seat, where he looked small as a child in the arms of the high-backed and wide green leatherette chair.

Kashani wrapped it up: "We hope this Islamic system will be concluded by the appearance of Imam Mahdi. We hope this time next year, we will have the appearance of the Mahdi."

The president stepped onto the stage, and beside him—even shorter, slightly stooped, and far more fragile—stood the hard-liner's hard-liner and head of the Guardian Council, Ayatollah Ahmad Jannati. A wisp of a man in his eighties, he once said non-Muslims "cannot be called human beings but are animals who roam the earth and engage in corruption." And after Ahmadinejad's controversial 2007 visit to Columbia University, he took the president's performance as a cosmic sign that "the situation is going to be ready for the return of the Hidden Imam." [174]

The two men began handing out forty-one trophies and certificates to those who had submitted papers on Mahdaviat thought—and to a lone journalist. My name was called, I stepped across, took the president's hand, and he gave me a cheek kiss, his beard brushing against mine as he pulled me closer, his left hand on my shoulder. Ahmadinejad seemed especially pleased to see an American among this group. As we shook hands, I asked him in freshly coached Farsi for an interview—a souvenir with which to remember the Mahdi's birthday. He agreed, though the interview would never materialize.

I was still pinching myself, pleased at my good luck—and not just because the trophy had two supernatural golden wings giving it flight to another world. Nor because I now had an official citation that identified me as a specialist in "waiting" for the Mahdi and praised the accuracy of my reporting on Iran—a document that could prove useful the next time I was arrested.

Far more important was the window this conference would provide into the mind-set of the Mahdaviat elite, including Ahmadinejad, the parliament speaker and former nuclear negotiator Ali Larijani, and Iran's obese armed forces chief of staff, Major General Hassan Firouzabadi, who were also in attendance.

Due to the controversy and even open ridicule they can generate, Mahdaviat ideas are not often detailed in public. But this conference was an exception, and the president and Larijani gave uncommonly candid pictures of their religious thought models. I now have no doubt that Mahdaviat beliefs, for them, are all-pervasive and dictate every action. The aim is to pave the way with good works—while facing off fearlessly against the global injustice that these men *know* the Mahdi requires to be confronted.

After hearing the words of so many high-ranking devotees, it became clear to me that many of the rumors—though often officially denied—were very likely to be true. Did Ahmadinejad leave an empty place setting for the Mahdi at his dinner table? Were important meetings held on Fridays, so decisions could be made in the Imam's "presence"? As mayor, had Ahmadinejad secretly ordered plans for a reconfiguration of Tehran streets to provide a suitable place for the Mahdi's arrival? One ranking cleric suggested establishing a "Ministry of Waiting" to prepare for the return.

Ahmadinejad had himself stated: "If someone loves the Imam, he/she is reborn. This is real life and life without [love for Imam] is meaningless. . . . That person's life is empty, even if he conquers the world. Just like Mr. Bush. He is valueless. If you believe in Imam [Mahdi] you will notice that the superpowers have no magnitude."[175] Ahmadinejad explained how he kept his composure while under verbal insult from the president of Columbia University, Lee Bollinger, who introduced him as a "petty and cruel dictator" in New York in 2007. "When I was there I was certain that my master [the Mahdi] would come and direct the scene due to the poisonous environment that they had made."[176]

The president later spoke of his thoughts and divine support in those moments: "Dear God, what plan do you have for punishing [those who] are being so rude and so offensive? After all, it is not customary in any part of the world to invite the president of a country and then swear at him. This is very stupid."

Ahmadinejad said that had made him laugh, and he had then called upon the Mahdi: "O dear Imam, I am sure you will manage the events and turn this scene into something which will eventually be beneficial to Islam. I know you would . . . after all we were at the heart of enemy territory," Ahmadinejad recalled. He had been told that five hundred million people—"practically everyone," he said, one-twelfth of the world's population—had watched the speech on TV. "I want to ask you this: Could this scene be managed by anyone but the Lord of the Era?"

Ahmadinejad was still convinced, later in 2007, when he said, "[L]et me tell you something that I can see. There are some people who sneer when we say these things because their hearts are empty of faith. They are the modern idol worshippers. They are the modern Satan worshippers. They put on an intellectual demeanor; they don't understand as much as a goat about the world."

AHMADINEJAD WAS ONLY THE latest Iranian leader who took his cue from on high. Among the Shah's grandiose official titles was "Pivot of the Universe" and "Shadow of God." [177] Though Iran's last monarch made considerable efforts to curtail the powers of the clergy, he stated that throughout his life he had received "messages" and "visions" from the prophets, imams, and even God.[178] He claimed: "I am accompanied by a force that others can't see—my mythical force. I get messages. Religious messages . . . if God didn't exist, it would be necessary to invent him."

Ayatollah Khomeini, of course, redefined what it meant to be a divinely inspired leader. And now Ahmadinejad was the latest incarnation. From the podium at the Mahdaviat conference, he declared that the Mahdi would destroy unjust rulers who "are not connected to the heavens [and] separated their ways from the almighty prophets"— meaning the United States, Israel, and the West.

Those "oppressive rulers" had in Iraq left more than one million dead; in Israel "imposed several wars on the region and thousands of assassinations"; and in Afghanistan, "under the pretext of freedom," had bombed wedding ceremonies, turning people to "blood and dust." Only the Mahdi could restore justice, said Ahmadinejad, though Believers would have to work hard: "We should do our best and if we change our hearts, if we change our ideas . . . then that great auspicious event will happen."

THE PRESIDENT'S MILLENNARIAN CONVICTION pushed Iran's Mahdaviat industry out of the shadows. Even Ahmadinejad's website, www.president.ir, had a supernatural feel, with heavenly billowing clouds on the home page and the smiling president waving toward the words "God hasten the return in health and in victory."

But the enemy was never far away, as illustrated by the booths at the 2008 Mahdaviat conference in Tehran. One was run by the website www.armageddon.ir, which had already been hacked twenty-eight times by Israeli computer experts. The purpose was to draw attention to the cultural poison seeping from the West, especially from violent video games. On display was Call of Duty 4: Modern Warfare, a first-person shooting game that was a global bestseller in 2007 and depicted military operations in an anonymous Middle East country after a U.S. invasion. The young man in the booth—who happened to be a college student in America—pointed out one scene, where "most of the bad people are going to the mosque, so they have to attack the mosque." Never mind the secret atomic bomb in Baghdad that goes off before it can be found.

"We introduce the game, and tell them this is how it affects people's minds; how we have to wake up to this," said the student, who asked me not to use his name or U.S. college affiliation. "We're trying to give them the knowledge, how the governments of the West are trying to fight this way."

The influence was insidious, even if not obvious. The situation was similar, he claimed, to the 2007 film 300, the graphic novel–style treatment of the Battle of Thermopylae in 480 B.C. It portrayed heroism of three hundred Spartan warriors fighting to the last man against a massive Persian army of 120,000 murderous barbarians and monsters. The tiny band of Spartans is finally defeated after three days because of treachery, not because they couldn't outwit, outfight, and outkill the invading enemy.

Iranians and their officials alike were outraged. "Such a fabrication of culture and insult to people is not acceptable by any nation," a government spokesman had said. "[Iran] considers it a hostile behavior which is the result of cultural and psychological warfare."[179]

"It's like 300," the student told me. "Over there [in America] they look at it as a movie, but here they say it will stick in the back of [American] minds. So in the future, if you have to fight with Iran, people will say: 'You remember *them*?' "

THE MAHDAVIAT TOUR OF 2008 left Tehran to visit the Jamkaran mosque and the "Light of the Return" arts and cultural festival in Qom.[180] The road was thick with pilgrims marching to the mosque with green flags and devotion in their hearts for the Mahdi's birthday. The president was not the only patron of the superstitions at Jamkaran, according to a book released during the conference, *Mahdaviat and Complete Peace: Quotations from Dr. Ahmadinejad Regarding the Mahdi*.

Tucked in its pages was a recollection by Hezbollah leader Sheikh Seyyed Hassan Nasrallah of a meeting he had had years earlier with the Supreme Leader. Khamenei tried to encourage Nasrallah during a rough patch for the Shiite militia, and then added:

> In running the affairs of the country, I sometimes have difficulty solving issues and there is no other way left. To my friends, my staff and my entourage I say: "Get ready, we are going to Jamkaran." We set off for Qom, and we go to Jamkaran mosque. After speaking and praying to the Master [Mahdi], I would feel that a hand from the hidden world leads me, and I reach a decision there, and in this way the problem is solved and I implement the decision.[181]

When we arrived at Jamkaran, it was plain that with Ahmadinejad's presidential support and cash, building expansion had taken off. The wardens, struggling in their royal blue shirts to bring order with multicolored fly whisks, were overwhelmed by the number of pilgrims. The Iranian leader of our group—which could not have had higher official approval—was hauled in for questioning by intelligence agents while we loitered, boldly taking pictures inside the mosque. He had to explain why he had permitted a group of camera-laden foreigners into the mosque sanctuary. We were led back outside, where tents encircled the vast compound and pilgrims sought relief from the hot sun.

Just down the road in Qom, it was cooler in the large basement space of an office block, at the "cultural" festival. Endless stalls were manned by devotees selling books, CDs, and DVDs to propagate the faith, to push for expectations of imminence. One stop was a prize draw, in which participants answered questions about the Mahdi. There would be five winners, one each night, of a gold coin. A group of schoolgirls ticked off the multiple-choice answers to such questions as "Why is the Imam of Time considered proof of God?" and "What does 'awaiting' mean?"

I was drawn to one booth with a large movie poster of *Lord of the Rings* (showing Frodo Baggins staring at the glowing Ring of Power from the J. R. R. Tolkien trilogy). There were other posters of Nostradamus and Western video war games. The booth was called "The West and Mahdaviat," with a subtitle: "Enemies of the Culture of Mahdaviat."

I asked the cleric what Tolkien had to do with the Shiite Messiah, and the point of the exhibit. "It's to introduce the youth to what the West does to devalue the Mahdi and create hatred of the Mahdi," replied Musa-Reza Javanshir, his shoes off and out of the way, his turban white. They were, he said, all signs of the immorality and chaos that would one day be put right by the divine return. "We believe in Christianity as a divine religion [but] they want a dead Islam, an Islam that is a quiet voice, not a loud one against their oppressive actions."

To ensure that children received an accurate view of Mahdaviat thinking, the Islamic Guidance Ministry had printed the fourteenth edition of *Sunshine*, a cartoon book full of stories, poems, and games about the Mahdi. It asked readers to "travel through time" with two boys—their eyes welling with tears of joy on the cover—as they "witness the events that will happen in the hours of the reappearing of the Imam of Time."

"Hello, kids! I'm your friend Ahmad, and we will travel . . . to the future. You should come with us, too," welcomes one of the first story panels. The Mahdi's face is portrayed as a bright light emanating from beneath a turban. The purpose of the comic book is for "the friends and the seekers of Islam and the correct path" to increase their understanding of the "Beholder of Time . . . so that one day we will be a soldier of that Holy One."

Call it Mahdaviat Lite for children. Though one scene shows Shiite prisoners centuries ago being tied up and whipped—"torture" is the word used by the schoolgirl telling the story—it concludes that "obeying the requests of the holy ones" and praying for the Mahdi's early return "will make the Imam's heart happy and will make his return earlier."

IN IRAN, SUCH EXPECTATIONS were becoming daily fare—and the regular butt of jokes—as the president and his aides stated with increasing frequency that the Mahdi was at the helm. Among a number of claims, the president was quoted in 2005 telling officials concerned with overspending: "Don't worry, Imam [Mahdi] is going to come in two years and all the problems will be solved." [182]

Critics found voice in a July 2008 newspaper article that listed many of these "deviant" claims about the presidential proximity to the divine. "Do you believe that these remarks can excuse the government from its mismanagement, inflation, increasing prices, dissatisfaction, and the protest of people?" wrote Rasoul Montajabnia, a cleric and deputy head of a rival political party. [183] "Now that three years have passed [since Ahmadinejad claimed the Mahdi would come in two years] and these promises have not been fulfilled, who is responsible for damaging the beliefs of the people and the youth?"

The article quoted one member of parliament who said the Supreme Leader "seriously" confronted Ahmadinejad about this two-year prediction, and that upon exiting Khamenei's office Ahmadinejad was livid: "He thinks that I'm *his* president, [but] I'm the president of Imam [Mahdi]."

Another influential cleric was scornful about claims that the Mahdi was "managing the affairs of the world" and that the hard-line government was his tool: "Imam [Mahdi] certainly does not approve of 20 percent inflation, high prices and many mistakes, and if Mr. Ahmadinejad's remarks are correctly interpreted as [Mahdi's] management of the country, we must blame Imam [Mahdi] for many of the mistakes, which inflict irreparable damage on the faith of the youth."[184]

The Super Superpower

The Government of God could hardly boast superior results. But Ahmadinejad nevertheless transformed the source of his inspiration into political self-confidence. Certain that divine victory is inevitable, he has rejoiced at what hard-liners believe to be God's hand behind the demise of American power, from Iraq and Afghanistan to Gaza.

Ahmadinejad may have reached out to the Americans in several unprecedented ways—through letters, and saying the United States could be a "good friend" of Iran if it changed its ways—but long gone were the respectful sentiments of President Khatami and his call for a "dialogue among civilizations." "Ahmadinejad was convinced that negotiating with the West was a fruitless exercise and that the only approach of any merit was that of robust confrontation," writes historian Ali Ansari in his book *Confronting Iran*.[185] The West only respected strength:

> He was not interested in whether the West conceded anything. On the contrary, a state of continued tension and confrontation was desirable, and the criticism of the West was to be actively sought. This was a return to the early glory days of the Revolution, when Iran had stood alone and "America could not do a damned thing." If Iran drew criticism from the West, it merely confirmed the righteousness of Iran's position.

Ahmadinejad was pushing Iran's triumphs as part of an unstoppable historical advance. It was this president who defiantly likened Iran's

nuclear program to a speeding train without brakes; whose combative rhetoric had brought Iran perilously close to war with the United
States and Israel; and who at a carefully stage managed presentation in
April 2006—in which dancers in traditional costume carried glass and
metal vials said to hold Iran's first quantities of enriched uranium—
announced, "Iran has joined the nuclear countries of the world." [186]

One year later, to mark National Nuclear Technology Day, which he
had proclaimed, the president boasted with "great honor" about how
"our dear country has joined the nuclear club." It was this president
who locked such defiance into the fabric of daily life, when Iran produced a new fifty-thousand rial note, the largest denomination at the
time, with an atomic symbol overlaying a map of Iran. It is adorned
by the words of the Prophet: "If knowledge is to be found in the heavens, the Persians will go and get it."

And in fact science, military innovation, and stepping up domestic weapons production were all focal points for the Ahmadinejad
presidency. Iran trumpeted one success after another, claiming new
technological prowess in everything from homemade radar-evading
torpedoes and embryonic stem cell research to nanotechnology. Rhetoric and defiance soared to new levels in 2009 on the Revolution's thirtieth anniversary, which official media dubbed the "Day of God." That
week Iran had launched its first homebuilt satellite into space, joining
an elite scientific club of just nine nations—and significantly boosting
its ballistic missile knowledge.

"Congratulations to the nation of Iran and all the freedom-seeking
nations of the world," Ahmadinejad said for a launch that sent a message of "peace and hope." [187] Television footage showed the president,
flanked by generals and officials, signaling the launch by speaking on
a white telephone. The men repeated "God is great" four times, with
little conviction. Ahmadinejad then reached for the second coming,
shouting as the rocket began soaring into space: "O Lord, hasten the
return of the Mahdi!"

• • •

I WAS SURPRISED DAYS later to see a towering replica of the Safir-2 rocket put on display in Freedom Square for the raucous thirtieth anniversary rally, along with several air balloons cube-shaped like the Omid (Hope) satellite. The real Omid was a silver-box-like affair that appeared, from images on state-run TV of it being assembled in the lab, to have the basic guts of a 1950s-era transistor radio, with D-size batteries and wires held in place with black electrical tape. Iranians gawked appreciatively at the life-size rocket, its blue fins numbered with white Roman numerals. The Iranian flag painted near the top turned it into a nationalist treasure.

"It shows our power," student Mohammad Hazarian told me, standing with his camera at the base of the Islamic Republic's metallic phallus.[188] "Our country doesn't want to fight with anyone, so this technology defines who we are."

That was how Ahmadinejad saw it, as he took to the podium after a brief walkabout in the crushing crowd of cheering, flag-waving Iranians. "Today, with God's grace, the Iranian scientists have broken the chains of humiliation and the scientific monopoly of the world arrogance [the West]," the president said of the space program.[189] Indeed, that metal box with its pencil-size silver antennae was orbiting at 155 to 250 miles above the earth, fifteen times every twenty-four hours. State-run TV repeatedly played the Iranian national anthem while showing a video graphic of the launch, the first-stage engine falling off, and then the satellite slowly spinning while circling the globe and sending messages back.

And there was more, much more to declare. "I officially announce today that the Iranian nation is a superpower, real and true," said Ahmadinejad. "I must announce with a loud voice, with God's mercy, with God's help, through the resistance of the Iranian nation, the shadow of threat has been removed forever," he boasted. Sanctions had no impact, the "heaviest" imposed in history, he claimed—clearly unaware of Iraq's excruciating experience in the 1990s. Western militaries had failed to unseat the regime.

The Islamic Republic of Iran, Ahmadinejad told his people, had demonstrated that all enemies combined were "weaker" than Iran. Never mind the voices of disillusion I was hearing in the crowd. Unmentioned also were concerns that the West was trying to foment a bloodless Velvet Revolution in Iran. Presumably that danger had passed, too, since the president reassured his countrymen of their hard-earned invincibility.

Mahmoud Ahmadinejad was leading the divine nation of Iran on a Messianic march, and nothing would stop him.

"Today the world is on the verge of entering the era of thought, logic, and negotiation," he proclaimed. "We have to announce with loud voice that the era of control of oppression and vulgar disrespect has come to an end."

From his platform stacked with flowers—and standing on a step to raise his stubby height to the level of the microphones—Ahmadinejad crowed that Iran had achieved a new peak:

> They brought military force and threatened [us] militarily. They thought that they can [break] a nation that has found itself, has discovered its own power, is linked to the Imam and *velayat* [religious leadership], is linked with God. . . .
>
> From now on, which power in the world can be found that has the courage to threaten the Iranian nation? It is impossible for anyone to [even] think in their mind that they can threaten the Iranian nation.

6

In the Name of Democracy

The Big Powers, and among them especially the United States, have since long ago been busy scheming. And preceding them was Britain. For a long time now they have been putting together the sporadic bits of information and intelligence which they have gathered about the various countries of the world and specifically those upon which they have preyed.

—Ayatollah Ruhollah Khomeini, 1981

We are not, like Allende [and Mossadegh], liberals willing to be snuffed out by the CIA.

—Friday prayer leader Ali Khamenei, 1981

DEEP WITHIN THE ISLAMIC system, preserving and protecting Iran's growing power was turning into an obsession— one that hinged on total *internal* control. Paranoia about being undermined by enemies inside and out was fed, after America's 2003 invasion of Iraq, by simmering talk in Washington of conducting "regime change" in Tehran. If that change was not to come at the tip of the Pentagon's military spear, then it would surely come—quietly, but inevitably, it was believed—through means of a Velvet Revolution: a popular uprising, financed and coordinated by the United States and the West, that would use civil society democrats and intellectuals to erode Iran's Islamic theocracy.

Lessons from the Dark Ages

The framework of that fear can be found half hidden in the writings of Iran's most hard-line voices, which provide a historical justification for opposing liberalism of all kinds—and for taking on modern-day reformists at all costs. Tucked into the pages of the vigilante Ansar-e Hezbollah newspaper *Ya Lesarat al-Hossein* and other right-wing publications are self-serving descriptions of Andalusia, the Muslim kingdom of medieval Spain that for nearly eight hundred years flourished with brilliance and an all-inclusive Islamic civilization.

Called by a tenth-century Christian writer the "Ornament of the World," Andalusia and its capitals of Toledo, Cordoba, and finally Granada became powerful symbols of enlightenment on the dark edge of Europe in the Middle Ages.

"In its moments of great achievement, medieval culture positively thrived on holding at least two, and often many more, contrary ideas at the same time," writes historian Maria Rosa Menocal.[1] "This was the chapter of Europe's culture when Jews, Christians and Muslims lived side by side and, despite their intractable differences and enduring hostilities, nourished a complex culture of tolerance."

The result was a "deep-seated vision of complex and contradictory identities that was first elevated to an art form by the Andalusians" and shaped modern Europe far beyond its era and geographical borders, writes Menocal. Andalusia was the place where "the bright lights of the world, and their illumination of the rest of the universe, transcended differences of religion."

But Andalusia as an Islamic center was slowly destroyed. It was torn apart by intra-Muslim civil war, the destructive intolerance of Islamic fundamentalists from North Africa, and an ever-encroaching Christian Crusade—a war of "reconquest" waged by what proved to be superior fighters backed up by a powerful and aggressive Catholic pope. In 1492 the final bastion of Muslim rule at Granada was eliminated.

It was an ignominious end to what is universally seen as a historical peak of Islamic civilization. Even Ayatollah Ali Khamenei, when addressing Islamic leaders in 1998 in Tehran, spoke highly of the "brilliant civilization" of Andalusia:

> Western historians overlook and neglect this grand and unprecedented uprising, transformation, and revolution in science, culture, and civilization and link the history of science from ancient Greece and Rome to the Renaissance, as though science and civilization had died for a thousand years. . . .
>
>   But the truth is that the Middle Ages was a period of darkness, ignorance, and consternation only for the West and Europe, but for the Islamic world, which was several times larger than Europe by ranging from Andalusia to China, this was a period of illumination, awakening, and academic sublimation and boom.[2]

That legacy made the loss of Andalusia painful for the Islamic world. But Western historians have not ignored this period. On the contrary, writes one, a recent increase in the scope and intensity of research means that the "history of al-Andalus is better known and understood than the history of any other part of the pre-modern Muslim world."[3] Still, Iran's hardest-line ideologues have drawn a selective and often unbalanced lesson from Andalusia and its collapse, to justify their own intolerance of the moderation and reform launched by the election of President Mohammad Khatami in 1997.

The historic strength of Andalusia lay in its ability to unite ancient Greek, Roman, and Eastern scholarship—from Aristotle to Indian mathematics—and attract intellectuals from all over the known world, who came together to study side by side. But far from holding up Andalusia as a shining example of Muslim wisdom and tolerance, modern-day Iranian hard-liners choose to portray Andalusia as a massive "defeat" for Islam.

For them, openness and "freedom" diluted the true faith and fatally weakened it, erasing Islam from Europe in the process. For them, the "bitter story of Andalusia" is a warning that must be applied today to the threat from reformers and the "cultural onslaught" from the West. In April 2009, *Resalat* reinforced that view, in an article titled "Cultural Defense, Antibody for Andalusian Policies."[4] Its writer explained that the "enemies of Islam are still thinking of conducting the same method in order to take control of Iran and so reach their evil aim. The fact is that today's policy is to Andalusia-ize Iran. . . ."

Such political interpretations of the fate of the Muslims in Spain centuries ago have popped up sporadically in the Islamic Republic. The 1994 preface to Khamenei's lengthy "Discourse on Patience," for example—published on the Supreme Leader's own website—was written by Seyyed Hossein Alamdar. He spells out the roots of the modern conflict:

> The war between total belief and total blasphemy is going on fiercely on all fronts; namely militarily, economically, and culturally. The most severe among the three is the cultural onslaught being waged by the enemies. . . .
>
> The Islamic "Andalusia" (modern Spain) was snatched away from the Muslims by using this tactic. We must wake up before history repeats itself. The enemy has already intruded within the privacy of the four walls of our dwellings. Even the so-called cartoon video films for children and the paper wrappings inside chewing gum packages are not immune, and intermingled with their Satanic sexual onslaught, without mentioning the other horrible means at their disposal.[5]

Tracts sounded the alarm in hard-line publications and defined the enemy in medieval terms. " 'Freedom,' a phrase so sweet, so beautiful, and so holy, [but] a look at the history of Andalusia shows that the phrase 'freedom' directed this civilization from liberation to re-captivity," stated one *Ya Lesarat* article.[6] The "sun started to set over

Andalusia," it argued, when ruling Muslims permitted Christians to keep practicing their religion, to teach and to do business. The author drew a direct parallel with the unbridled openness of Iran's reformists:

> Freedom to proselytize under the guise of "freedom of speech and thought"; freedom to train Muslims under the cover of operations of foreign NGOs [nongovernmental organizations] and . . . freedom in trade . . . under the guise of promoting foreign investment . . . in recent years have been taking place so professionally that it is unprecedented in the history of Muslim countries since those times.
>
> The agreements and pacts that put the economic, cultural and political pulse of the land of Andalusia in the hands of Christians and followers of non-Islamic sects are once again implemented by the advocates of freedom.

One week later, *Ya Lesarat* published another analysis, "Enemies and the Policy of Andalusiazation of Iran." The writer explained the dangers:

> What is most visible, and can be felt, and has the closest similarities and fundamental bond with the bitter story of Andalusia, is promotion of the sexual and immoral part of the cultural invasion. . . .
>
> In Andalusia the enemy, in addition to weakening and demolishing the strong faith of the people, started promoting drunkenness and increasing sexual need, then it freely put at the disposal of Muslim gatherings its alcoholic drinks and beautiful girls, and it wasn't long before a big Islamic civilization was burned in the Christian's fire of revenge.
>
> Today also, the enemies of the Islamic Revolution, after tasting defeat in other fields, have adopted the policy of Andalusiazation of Islamic Iran and have armed themselves with the same weapons; because the passage of time does not change the path to honor or dishonor a nation.[7]

Similar formulations—often nearly identical, always warning of the dangers of Andalusia-style tolerance—continue to appear in Iran's conservative press. Yet it is a selective reading of history.

While Western historians note periods of "decadence," none of which were unusual or exceptional for the times, they attribute the disintegration of Andalusia to far more overwhelming strategic and military concerns.

After all, in Andalusia things were different from the start in 711 A.D., when Muslims first came. Andalusia, the Iberian peninsula, was already Christian. Part of the Roman Empire, it was then part of the Holy Roman Empire, run inexpertly from Constantinople before being ceded to Christian Visigoths. The foundation of its eight-hundred-year longevity was the initial tolerant takeover, which did not destroy what was already there. When the Muslims arrived, under moderate Syrian leadership, they left the Christian communities intact and gained the affection and respect of those they conquered, ruling by example rather than by fear.

Even the eighteenth-century English historian Edward Gibbon, in his *Decline and Fall of the Roman Empire,* while noting that "many partial calamities were inflicted by the carnal or religious passions of the enthusiasts," concluded that "if we compare the invasion of Spain by the Goths, or its recovery by the kings of Castile and Aragon, we must applaud the moderation and discipline of the Arabian conquerors." [8]

AT THE PEAK, WRITES historian Maria Rosa Menocal, it was in Andalusia "that men of unshakeable faith . . . saw no contradiction in pursuing the truth, whether philosophical or scientific or religious, across confessional lines." [9] And it was not just cultural, but military and administrative, with Christian mercenaries and Jews in government.

As Chris Lowney writes in *A Vanished World,* "Medieval Spain's Muslims, Christians and Jews embraced and rejected each other's faith traditions and customs, fought alongside each other and against each other . . . and somehow forged a golden age for each faith." [10]

But trouble lurked beyond Andalusia's northern border, where Christians, growing in strength and increasingly centered on Vatican power, fretted over the "loss of Iberia to the Moors." And trouble lurked between Muslims as well, where after three centuries of accelerated progress and flowering, a failed succession struggle meant that al-Andalus disintegrated into a number of small, independent, and often competing states.

Menocal explains the impact: "Bitter civil wars among the rival Muslim factions of al-Andalus began in earnest in 1009, and for the subsequent two decades they tore apart the 'ornament of the world.'"[11] She writes: "Appalled contemporary observers rather poignantly called those self-destructive years the *fitna*, 'the time of strife.' A culture that not long before had been at the peak of its powers was brought low not so much by barbarians at the gate as by all manner of barbarians *within*—within its own borders and within the House of Islam."

The result, writes Hugh Kennedy in *Muslim Spain and Portugal*, was "a period of weakness and conflict when the Andalusis proved incapable of finding a structure of government, which would enable them to resist the increasingly aggressive Christians from the north."[12] And another factor was emerging: "Christian military superiority over the Andalusis, which became so painfully apparent as the eleventh century wore on, was already becoming obvious."

Contemporary writers were "painfully aware," writes Kennedy, "that Andalusi political society was fundamentally sick, but they, and those who felt like them, were unable to resolve the tensions which were tearing it apart."

FOR IRANIAN HARD-LINERS, THIS period is the source of the moral decrepitude of Andalusia. One critical case caused a Muslim provincial prince to make an unwise alliance with a Christian king and finally lose control of the city of Toledo in 1085. "The fall of Toledo was to have dramatic effects on Islam, its power and civilization," writes historian Salah Zaimeche.[13] "But first it raised some far reaching questions on the causes of Muslim weakness. In various poems of the period the blame fell both on the rulers, for their indolence and preoccupations with their own pleasures, and on the Muslim community which had lost touch with the practices of its faith."

Zaimeche quotes several examples. One verse chastises Andalusian rulers: "Their minds were occupied with wine and song, and listening to music." [14]

Another writer says of those kings, "By God, I swear that if the tyrants were to learn that they could attain their ends more easily by adopting the religion of the Cross, they would certainly hasten to profess it! Indeed, we see that they ask the Christians for help and allow them to take away Muslim men, women and children as captives to their lands." [15]

Still, despite the current narrative in Tehran that Andalusia succumbed to a Christian "cultural invasion," there were more substantial realpolitik reasons for its erosion. The fall of Toledo prompted the defeated Muslim prince to look abroad for reinforcement, asking for military help from fundamentalist Muslim Berber tribesmen called Almoravids, who were building their own empire in North Africa. "These fanatics considered the Andalusian Muslims intolerably weak, with their diplomatic relations with Christian states, not to mention their promotion of Jews in every corner of their government and society," writes Menocal. [16]

The Berbers arrived and duly defeated the offending Christian king of Toledo. But they stayed on, creating "their own dour and intolerable kingdom," notes Menocal. "For the next 150 years, Andalusian Muslims would be governed by foreigners, first these same Almoravids, and later the Almohads, or 'Unitarians,' an even more fanatic group of North African Berber Muslims likewise strangers to al-Andalus and its ways. . . . [Andalusians] had irretrievably lost their political freedom."

IT IS IRONIC THAT those who occupy the hard-line political space in Iran today claim that reform-style *tolerance* destroyed Andalusia, when in fact it was hard-line *intolerance* back then that further divided society and made Muslim defeat more likely. Embattled reformists in

Iran these days understand the dynamic. In fact, Iran's current ideological battle and its violent results in many ways echo the events of centuries ago.

"The Almoravid attempts to impose a considerably different view of Islamic society on the Andalusians provoked relentless civil unrest," writes Menocal.[17] "In 1109, not even twenty years after these newcomers had been invited in as allies, anti-Almoravid riots broke out in Cordoba following the public book-burning of a work by al-Ghazali, a legendary [Persian] theologian whose humane approach to Islam, despite its orthodoxy, was too liberal for the fanatical Almoravids."

The consequences were made lethal by Pope Urban II, who in 1095 proclaimed a new crusade to recover the Holy Land, which expanded the papacy's vision of desire far beyond the walls of Jerusalem. As historian Charles Julian Bishko points out, for Christian warriors from that time on, "innumerable bulls of indulgence . . . equated in importance and spiritual privileges anti-Moorish combat in Spain with that against the Saracens of Palestine."[18]

Andalusia was not undermined by tolerance, but was caught in the pincer of puritanism that inexorably closed in from north and south. "Both Christians and Muslims developed an ideology of Holy War, or *jihad*," notes Kennedy.[19] "Both sides believed they had God and right on their side."

THE ANDALUSIAN PERIOD OF Spanish history was not a failure. Even though Muslim rule came to an end, it lasted eight hundred years: twice as long as the British Empire, and more than three times as long as the American republic so far.

Of all the reasons given by Western historians for the destruction of Andalusia and its tradition of tolerance, not listed is too much tolerance. Nor too much religious freedom. Nor opening society to such a degree in those Middle Ages that a cultural "onslaught" induced terminal decay.

When the Spanish kingdoms finally expelled the last Muslims from Granada in 1492, it was the same year Spain would "discover"

America, and the influx of wealth from the New World would make Christian Spanish power feared throughout Europe. Spain's gift to the reunited kingdoms of Iberia, however, was the Spanish Inquisition—a brutal tool of Christian religious enforcement that has a parallel or two in modern Iran.

"Satanic Plots"

Those hard lessons drawn from Andalusia—and their uncompromising impact on Iranian politics today—led not to modern enlightenment, but to deeper fear of Velvet Revolution. Of a moral corruption so great, and of corrosive influences from the West so strong, that the Iranian system would crumble from inside.

The bloodless 1989 Velvet Revolution that overthrew communism in Czechoslovakia was the model, and the namesake. But there were more recent, explicit examples of locals using Western "prodemocracy" cash, ideas, and training to topple undemocratic regimes, from Serbia to Central Asia. In Iran, the CIA had launched a $2 million campaign in 1995 to broadcast anti-regime propaganda. But all efforts were stepped up at the end of that year with a new, secret appropriation of $18 million.[20]

Brainchild of then House Speaker Newt Gingrich—who had railed noisily about the need for a strategy "designed to force the replacement of the current regime in Iran"—the covert operation became public almost immediately. The *New York Times*, which broke the story, noted "the CIA finds itself required, against its better judgment, to plan a 'secret' mission, with its cover already blown, in a region where American policy has suffered failures and fiascos." President Bill Clinton approved the operation, the *Times* reported, on condition that it "seek only to change the behavior of Iran's Government, not to topple it."

Within days Iran's parliament earmarked $20 million of its own to counter the "secret" U.S. effort. In Tehran, one deputy charged that the United States was "a renegade government whose logic was no different from Genghis Khan or Hitler."[21] The Iranian counterespionage cash would be used to "uncover and neutralize US government conspiracies and interference in Iranian affairs." From that day on, hard-liners had a perfect pretext to crack down on opponents and reformists of every kind.

Never mind that the first point of the U.S.-Iran Algiers Accords, signed in 1981 to end the hostage crisis, was explicit: "The United States pledges that it is and from now on will be the policy of the United States not to intervene, directly or indirectly, politically or militarily, in Iran's internal affairs." [22]

The infusion of dollars would have a big impact in Tehran. I first saw glimmers of it in 1998, when Dr. Alireza Zakani—the Basij chief of Tehran University and veteran of the Iran-Iraq War, who had first told me of the revolutionary magic to be found at the former front lines—insisted that hard-liners were not afraid of this American meddling. [23] Instead they tried to attract the Westernized "minority" to their own conservative way of thinking, Zakani said, to give "guidance" and to convince all "except those who pull a gun on us."

"I'm sure our enemy, whoever they are, are investing in these minority groups," Zakani said. He cited the $20 million, and a bill in Congress (which failed) that aimed to remove Iran's only armed opposition group, the Mojahedin-e Khalq (MKO/MEK), from the U.S. State Department's terrorist list. "It's not a surprise to us. There are different factions in [Iran, and] we as fundamentalists believe we should make the rest aware. . . ."

But those men believed the Islamic Republic had never been more imperiled than it was during Khatami's reformist experiment, imperiled by the hands of fellow Iranians—the liberal and the weak—who were suckered into believing that the United States and the West had wise solutions and benevolent aims.

So the regime set out to learn. Not long after Khatami's victory in 1997, Supreme Leader Ali Khamenei ordered a wide-ranging examination of the "decline of all dictatorships, especially . . . the decline of communist regimes, because they understand that they are very similar to communist regimes," said Mohsen Sazegara, a founder of the

Revolutionary Guard and an acolyte of Khomeini during his late 1970s exile in Paris. Sazegara had by the late 1990s embraced the reform movement, published some of the most cutting-edge reformist newspapers, done time in Iranian prison, and finally moved to Washington.

"They have explained to Ayatollah Khamenei, for instance, how even Nelson Mandela got power in South Africa. How Vaclav Havel got power as a writer. How Yeltsin got to power," Sazegara told me in the spring of 2008.[24] "And [Khamenei] thinks he can avoid the mistakes of other dictators. This is the way that all dictators think. They don't understand that the mistakes are not from the dictators—the mistakes are from the dictatorship."

Sazegara was sitting incongruously at a Starbucks in Washington, D.C., changing his specialty contact lenses, which he had worn all day, accidentally spraying solution onto the table where I stirred sugar into my Grande-size cup of coffee. I grabbed a number of napkins to help him clean up, while he continued about the Islamic Republic's self-education. From Czechoslovakia's Velvet example to the Philippines People Power revolution of 1986, there were lessons for Iran. Khamenei had also analyzed how American tactics facilitated this process.[25]

"According to those studies, they think that all these changes in regimes are conspiracies, that they are *made,* [by a] universal enemy that rules every country in the world," Sazegara told me. "So they think that all Velvet Revolutions were preplanned by the CIA."

Supreme Leader Khamenei himself spoke in 2000 of those lessons—and how the Islamic Republic would not succumb.

I have now reached the conclusion that the United States has devised a comprehensive plan to subvert the Islamic system. This plan is an imitation of the plan that led to the collapse of the former Soviet Union. The US officials intend to carry out the same plan in Iran, and there are enough clues in their selfish and often hasty remarks made during the past few years indicating that they aim to do so. However, the enemy has made certain mistakes in its calculations. . . .[26]

The results of the Leader's analyses were applied immediately. That self-awareness accounted for a number of the brutal actions that began in the Khatami era, from the arrest of high-profile—even aging—dissidents, to the serial killings of intellectuals and their political wives.

"They think that if Nelson Mandela had a very good reputation for [his] long term in prison, so they think in Iran, 'Who can be Nelson Mandela, with a good reputation?' " explained Sazegara. "If for instance Vaclav Havel is a playwright, and he becomes the alternative, so they try to kill any writer who might be popular. . . . If Corazon Aquino was the wife of a political activist [assassinated opposition senator] Benigno Aquino in the Philippines, they want to kill [Iranian dissident leader Dariush] Forouhar . . . [and] they killed his wife as well, because they were afraid that his wife was a political woman—that she becomes another Corazon Aquino in Iran."

Even Sazegara's own high profile as an outspoken editor of the reformist *Jameah* had drawn attention. He said he was told by Saeed Hajjarian—the former senior intelligence official turned reform strategist, who survived the assassination attempt on the steps of the city hall in 2000—that Khamenei kept a list of "potential Yeltsins." Soviet leader Mikhail Gorbachev was seen as sincere, but Yeltsin "was a CIA agent."

The dots were easily connected by the regime's overly smart intelligence. The *Wall Street Journal* was seen to be "run by Zionists, this is another tool of imperialism. So if [the *Journal*] interviews me, they say, 'Ha! They're going to make a Yeltsin!' " said Sazegara.

"Hajjarian told me: 'Mohsen, I have been informed that on Khamenei's list of Yeltsins, now you are at the top of the list.' He said, 'Very soon you will be arrested,' and he was right."

FEAR THAT VELVET REVOLUTION was being planned by Iran's enemies in the West was only the latest conspiracy theory to grip the authoritarian leaders of Iran, where such paranoia—and the very real historical examples that lay behind it—long predated the Islamic Republic.

In 1892, Lord Curzon finished his voluminous *Persia and the Persian Question* with the observation that the "natives are a suspicious people" who would "see a cloven hoof beneath the skirt of every robe." [27]

The Shah was also prone to countless conspiratorial flights of fancy. Historian Ervand Abrahamian notes how his memoir "reads like a long nightmare full of shadowy figures out to knife him." [28] The Shah charged that key players were the British and Americans—despite providing the Shah with blanket military and political support from Washington, and the CIA's role in restoring his throne in 1953—along with the media and major oil companies. All formed a "strange amalgam" bent on discrediting him in an "organized effort." [29]

"For the next twenty years students and media echoed the same anti-Iran themes intermittently, whenever the West felt my wings needed clipping," the Shah complained in *Answer to History*.[30] He said "the British meddle in everything" and "had their people everywhere, hoping to exercise some control no matter what happens. This is a policy Britain has never abandoned, not even today." [31] No connection was too far-fetched to matter, since the British "had their fingers in strange pies." In recounting a failed 1949 assassination attempt, the Shah noted darkly that the British Embassy gardener was the father of the mistress of the would-be assassin.[32]

In an almost uncanny omen of the paranoia that would later plague the Islamic Republic, the Shah ascribed the 1963 Tehran riots to an"obscure individual who claimed to be a religious leader." That cleric was none other than Ayatollah Khomeini, who the Shah claimed "it was certain . . . had secret dealings with foreign agents." [33] Likewise, the Shah stated that "Western" sources had told him of payments "to Iran's clergy" by the CIA of an astronomical $400–$450 million annually—which were supposedly stopped by President Jimmy Carter in 1977.[34]

Even as the momentum of the Revolution's demonstrations began to overwhelm the Shah in late 1978, the cloistered leader was convinced that only the CIA could have orchestrated such mass popular protests.

"The Shah told [Secretary of State Henry Kissinger] he didn't see how it was possible for a bunch of ignorant mullahs to lead demonstrations so precisely organized and so effective. There must be some other force leading them," recalled Henry Precht, the Iran country director at the State Department from 1978 to 1980.[35] "He concluded that the CIA must be behind them. He asked why the CIA would do this to him. Why would they turn on him? . . . I was dumbfounded. This was the man we were relying on to save our terribly important interests in Iran. He was a nut."

To this day, I am surprised by how many Iranians inform me, with total conviction, that the *real* truth is that Washington engineered both the fall of the Shah *and* the victory of the Islamic Revolution. As Abrahamian explains, in Iran "the paranoid style permeates society, the mainstream as much as the fringe, and cuts through all sectors of the political spectrum."[36] The Imam was a big practitioner.

During the Islamic Revolution, Khomeini found "plots" here, there, and everywhere. "The world," he proclaimed [in 1984], "is against us."

"Satanic plots" lurked behind liberal Muslims favoring a lay, rather than a clerical, constitution; behind conservative Muslims opposed to his interpretation of *velayat-e faqih;* behind apolitical Muslims who preferred the seminaries to the hustle-and-bustle of politics; behind radical Muslims advocating root-and-branch social changes; behind lawyers critical of the harsh retribution laws; behind Kurds, Arabs, Baluchis, and Turkomans seeking regional autonomy; behind leftists organizing strikes and trade unions; and of course behind military officers sympathetic to the Pahlavis, the National Front, and even President Banisadr.[37]

Decades later, that neurotic mind-set fit perfectly with the growing awareness that Tehran was next on Washington's list for regime change. Not only had the Pentagon used overt force to topple Saddam Hussein in Iraq and the Taliban in Afghanistan, but also a template had been established of promoting regime change from *within,* where a dose of Western prodemocracy assistance could tip over old-style dictatorships. I reported on several of those "color" revolutions and heard telling voices, some of gratitude for U.S. intervention, and others of warning.

Understanding how they happened is necessary to accurately perceive the security obsession in Tehran, as it grew from the late 1990s. The history of past Velvet Revolutions is the key to the turmoil of 2009 in Iran—right down to the opposition use of the color green—and why the regime fought back so hard against those hundreds of thousands of Iranians who took to the streets, demanding: "Where is my vote?"

IN EARLY 1997, I watched Serbia's feared riot police deploy silently across Belgrade like dark storm troopers, streetlights glinting off rain-drenched helmets, truncheons ready.[38] For years street protests against Balkan strongman Slobodan Milosevic were met by brute force, tear gas, and, sometimes, a charmed stoicism.

Tens of thousands of protesters had been on the streets for fifty days already, rallying against Milosevic's failure to recognize opposition victories in local elections. A mob of whistling and dancing prodemocracy demonstrators advanced, their nonviolent resistance driven by blaring rock music. The marchers filed within inches of the wall of plastic riot shields, asking the police to join them.

Some of the women went further, brandishing their lipstick to paint the riot shields with hearts and arrows like valentines. One kissed the clear plastic, leaving the delicious red imprint of her lips for the fidgeting troops to ponder.

"We will win, because they are with us," she told me. Peering over the edge of one shield, she asked a charmed policeman, "You are, aren't you?"

But it wasn't enough. Baton charges would send the democrats home. The man renowned as the "Butcher of the Balkans"—engineer of bloody ethnic wars across the former Yugoslavia, from Bosnia and Croatia to Kosovo, and whose actions created the term *ethnic cleansing*—hung on through debilitating sanctions and even a seventy-eight-day NATO bombing blitz in 1999 to force Serbian units out of Kosovo.

So to shift the balance against Milosevic, Washington and European donors infused Serbia with cash and prodemocracy expertise. When introducing the $100 million "Serbian Democratization Act" to the Senate, cosponsor Jesse Helms said it "has but one purpose—to get rid of the murderous regime of Mr. Milosevic."[39] President Bill Clinton pledged another $10 million during a visit to Sarajevo, with these words: "Serbia will only have a future when Mr. Milosevic and his policies are consigned to the past."[40]

At first, the intended beneficiaries were anxious. The regime "portrays the leaders of the opposition as NATO servants, and that's not helping us," politician Zarko Korac told me in Belgrade in 1999, presaging the complaints I would later hear from Iranians.[41] "Their message is: 'What NATO didn't get through bombing, it will get through the opposition.'" Serb democrats despaired. "We are tired of being seen as cash-and-carry spies," opposition politician Nenad Canak told me. "Talking about the history of democracy in Serbia is like talking about a vegetarian crocodile. It sounds nice, but does not exist."

All that changed in September 2000, when Milosevic overplayed his hand and blatantly rigged his last election. Activists had orchestrated a massive voter turnout. They were armed with the U.S. and European cash—$25 million in the previous year from the Americans alone—that helped energize a combative opposition press, unify a fragmented opposition, and galvanize a critical and bold student movement called Otpor—Resistance—which used an uncompromising clenched fist as a symbol. The spray-painted slogan began to appear everywhere: *Gotov Je!* He's finished!

Those young Serb revolutionaries couldn't have known it at the time, but the example of Otpor—of its grassroots mobilization, U.S. and Western support, disciplined nonviolence, and sheer determination—would create a model for peaceful political change that would reverberate in every so-called Velvet Revolution thereafter. Ten years later, the parallels with the Islamic Republic and actions of Iran's opposition Green Movement were easy to find.

In Serbia the effectiveness of this strategy was demonstrated in how change took over the town of Vladicin Han, population nine thousand, a place like any other in southeast Europe where factory workers were told how to vote—or else. "Serbian television used its monopoly to ram home a simple message: Milosevic or mayhem," wrote Roger Cohen in the *New York Times Magazine*.[42] Among those who resisted was twenty-year-old Davorin Popovic, whose support for Otpor drew the attention of the burly local police chief, just weeks before the election. The senior officer put his hands around the young man's neck, bruising it with his tightening fingers, in Cohen's telling:

> "Are you a terrorist?" the policeman screamed, his breath thick with alcohol. "Who is your leader? Where does your money come from?"
>
> Davorin felt terror and rage rising in equal measure, but recalled the message of his Otpor training. Do not respond to violence. Overcome your fear, because when fear disappears the regime loses a central pillar of its power. Remember that violence is the last sanctuary of the weak.

The young Serb was one of a several Otpor members beaten that day, prompting widespread disgust in the town. "Parents, relatives and friends of the students turned away from the regime that they had grudgingly supported but that now indulged, before their eyes, in gratuitous violence against unarmed kids," recounted Cohen. Similar incidents across Serbia "moved people to a new courage, as more than two thousand Otpor activists were detained. 'Nobody could ever convince me that Milosevic would go,' says Davorin's mother, Dragica Popovic. 'But this beating changed my ideas.' "

Otpor had formed a year earlier, from the remnants of those shield-kissing students I had met. It had grown to seventy thousand members, with extensive U.S. support. Of the American millions pumped into Serbia, hundreds of thousands went directly to Otpor for everything from organizing techniques to T-shirts. An official from the International Republican Institute (IRI), which spent $1.8 million in Serbia the year prior to the vote, met Otpor leaders up to ten times in Hungary and Montenegro. The IRI organized a four-day seminar at the Budapest Hilton for twenty more senior Otpor leaders, where they were trained by retired U.S. Army colonel Robert Helvey in nonviolent methods of resistance and undermining state authority.

In Belgrade, new recruits were set up with mobile phones, spray paint, leaflets, posters, and Otpor T-shirts adorned with the defiant fist. "I was happy," said the activist who opened the branch at Vladicin Han. "I felt like a revolutionary going home to spread the word." [43]

And that word was shaped more than anyone else by Gene Sharp, an American political scientist whose work on nonviolent resistance since the early 1970s served as the action template for challenging authoritarian regimes. Sharp developed a list of "198 Methods of Nonviolent Action" for would-be regime changers.

Portions of his book *From Dictatorship to Democracy: A Conceptual Framework for Liberation* were translated into Serbian, just as in years to come they would be translated into Russian, Georgian, Kirghiz . . . and Farsi. It became the handbook for every subsequent attempt at Velvet Revolution.

Copies "became a *samizdat* passed around Otpor's branches in the last months of Milosevic's rule," noted Cohen. Key passages resonated in Serbia, just as they would in Iran: "Dictators require the assistance of the people they rule, without which they cannot secure and maintain the sources of political power," writes Sharp.[44] "If, despite repression, the sources of power can be restricted or severed for enough time, the initial results may be uncertainty and confusion within the dictatorship. That is likely to be followed by a clear weakening of the power of the dictatorship. Over time . . . [t]he dictator's power will die, slowly or rapidly, from political starvation."

In Serbia, the protests built to a peak. Thousand of miners went on strike. A thirteen-mile-long convoy of angry citizens—driving in two lanes and led by a bulldozer to remove police checkpoints—began rolling toward Belgrade from the opposition town of Cacak. Men armed with crowbars and hammers simply pushed police cars off the road.

"Mothers kissed their sons, and husbands told their wives: 'Here are the keys, and there is money,' as if they knew they might not come back," a Cacak local called Alexander told me, as the smell of Belgrade's partially burned parliament building still hung in the air.[45] We were standing beside the incinerated chassis of a car painted with the words, "He's finished!" a pig's head placed on top. "They were determined. It took ten years, but then they came to Belgrade to do their job."

Otpor had been instrumental in beginning that long work, in the words of one activist, "to get rid of Serbia's cult of leaders and messiahs."[46]

It was a triumph—for Washington.

And for the ideas and methods of peaceful resistance that would overturn one dictatorship after another, until they erupted a decade later into the jubilant expectation of imminent change, in Iran's own June 2009 effort at Velvet Revolution. But of course the guardians of the Islamic Republic, just like those who protested against it, were drawing their own lessons from history—and were determined to stop it. Those Eastern European regimes that managed to halt the process of Western-funded reform were to prove especially instructive to Iranian hard-liners, for the brutality of their resolve.

A KEY EXAMPLE WAS Belarus, where voters reelected their authoritarian leader Alexander Lukashenko in September 2001. The scale and nature of American and Western help to anti-regime forces gave weight to Lukashenko's claim that he was a target of regime-change meddling. He learned from the fate of Milosevic. "During the election campaign, the Belarusan official media were mobilized to discredit the Serbian revolution," notes analyst Vitali Silitski.[47]

I was in Minsk before the election in 2001. "It would be dark, scary, and awful without that [U.S.] money," Anatoly Gulayev, deputy editor of the independent newspaper *Den,* told me.[48] "Very few [opposition] newspapers live without that help. We should admit it and be grateful for it. American help gets to the point."

Months before, a hush-hush meeting at the State Department brought together U.S. officials responsible for Serbia and Belarus, to see what lessons from Belgrade could be applied to Minsk. While it was against U.S. law to fund foreign political parties, American and European grant money was flowing to an array of prodemocracy and civil society groups, newspapers, and political awareness campaigns.

"The U.S. is helping facilitate [opponents] who are already there. The money lets them be more active," Thomas Carothers, a State Department analyst, assured me.[49] "If you have an election and there are some gray areas where you can help out, this is a different ballgame from the Cold War," he said. "You can't throw it all in one bin and call it U.S. 'neo-imperialism.' The world has changed."

The fall of Milosevic "proved to Lukashenko that even a semblance of competitive elections can be a threat to an authoritarian regime," writes Silitski.[50] "Lukashenko's determination to prevent an electoral revolution was countered by the opposition's own efforts to imitate the Serbian scenario."

U.S. ambassador Michael Kozak was singled out as "an expert in ensuring Washington's favored candidate wins elections."[51] And it was true. In 2000, Washington spent $24 million in the bastion of the "last dictator in Europe." In 2001, it spent more. "To me, [the aid] is nothing to be embarrassed about if you say you want to develop an open, civil society," Kozak told me.[52] "What we want to see is a change in the system. . . . We made no secret about it."

So the lifeline of support to prodemocracy activists was used as a pretext to crack down—just as it would be later by Russia, and eventually Iran. Critics told me that even if the opposition had won the

2001 vote, it would have had a hard time shaking a "Made in the U.S.A." label. That was a point Lukashenko made: "We will not have Americans telling us what to do . . . we cannot be brought to our knees."[53]

He accused the United States and the West of "sleazy election techniques" and read out a list of opposition leaders paid by the U.S. Embassy to "remove" him. Lukashenko accused the top European diplomat in Belarus of being the opposition's "chief of staff," for successfully uniting disparate factions.

But Velvet Revolution failed in Belarus, because the regime acted quickly—and with resolve—against all would-be democrats. Belarus was the first, noted Silitski, to have "brought the policy of preemption to perfection."[54]

I WAS ALSO ON the streets of Tbilisi in November 2003, in the hours after Georgia's "Rose Revolution," where among the endless banners some U.S. flags were held high, waved in gratitude for Washington's role in facilitating democratic change.

"We are so grateful to the U.S. and European Union, our friends that have supported us," top opposition strategist Giorgi Baramidze told me, after protesters angry with fraudulent elections stormed parliament.[55] "We can now teach our children how to defend democracy, using Georgia's 'Rose Revolution' as the example."

U.S. officials pushed diplomatic buttons before and throughout the crisis, explicitly warning the government of the dangers of a forceful crackdown against demonstrators protesting a blatantly stolen election. Washington had committed $2.4 million to the vote, as part of a ten-year investment of $1.3 billion aimed at building civil society in Georgia—a huge investment in a small Caucasus outpost of the former Soviet empire, the birthplace of Stalin and renowned as much for corruption as for its wines and fruit.[56]

And it wasn't just the U.S. government. The Open Society Georgia Foundation of American billionaire George Soros had a staff of fifty in Georgia and a budget of $2.5 million.[57] Soros himself plays down his role, but the foundation had flown then opposition leader Mikheil Saakashvili and youth leaders to Serbia to learn from the Belgrade veterans about nonviolent change.

The world had seen it happen before, and in Georgia the similarities were striking, right down to the distinctive clenched fist symbol of Otpor in Serbia, borrowed almost identically by the Georgian student movement Kmara (Enough!). It received training from Otpor veterans who spread the word. There was a flood of Western cash, though half the population of just five million lived far below the poverty line. And now a telegenic, young, U.S.-educated opposition leader had become president.

"In the end, this was done by Georgians—it was not done by Americans—and that is vital to everything," Mark Mullen, the director of the Georgia office of the U.S.-government-funded National Democratic Institute, told me.[58] "There's always a temptation to get out in front." But Mullen was reportedly there when the opposition took control, inside the parliament itself with the opposition leaders, dispensing advice in real time.

U.S. ambassador Richard Miles was ebullient, and before briefing journalists he let out a big sigh of relief. He had also been chief of mission to Belgrade in the late 1990s, when the anti-Milosevic ground was being prepared.

"Now that it has reached a seemingly successful result, one of the things you have to say is that all of this election hoopla, largely financed by the Western community, [helped] raise public expectation that this would be an honest and decent election," Miles told us.[59] The effort had "exposed the public [to] what people were doing to cheat them of the full weight of their ballot," he said. "You could see the cheating going on right in front of your eyes," which caused widespread indignation and "dangerous" street action, Miles added. "It appears to be an exercise in almost pure democracy."

Except that, as one Georgian friend told me, "in many minds, the new leadership is equal to the U.S.A."

. . .

ANOTHER AUTHORITARIAN REGIME STEALING an election. Another Velvet Revolution, colored orange. Another T-shirt-ready slogan; this time, "It's time." *Pora*.

Anyone who doubted that a line could be drawn from Georgia's Rose Revolution to the Orange Revolution in Ukraine in 2004 needed look no further than the rose that opposition leader Viktor Yushchenko sometimes held in his hand during huge rallies of hundreds of thousands of Ukrainians, night after night in Kiev. Or the Kmara activists who had come in support, wearing Pora hats and shirts and waving Georgian flags, and with long-stemmed roses clenched in their teeth.[60]

The model was now familiar, of how Western-supported "democracy guerrillas" could defeat the unpopular old order by "banishing widespread fear of a corrupt regime," noted Ian Traynor in the *Guardian*.[61] The tactic had failed in Belarus. "But experience gained in Serbia, Georgia and Belarus has been invaluable in plotting to beat the regime of Leonid Kuchma in Kiev," wrote Traynor. "The operation—engineering democracy through the ballot box and civil disobedience—is now so slick that the methods have matured into a template for winning other people's elections."

The Orange Revolution was part of a bigger global strategy, wrote David T. Johnson, the U.S. chargé d'affaires in Kiev: "It is true enough . . . that Uncle Sam is up to something. And not only in Ukraine, but . . . around the world.[62]

The numbers showed the level of Washington's commitment. In the two years prior to the Orange Revolution, the Bush administration spent more than $65 million for "democracy building."[63] Most of the cash was funneled through large organizations that specialized in election and media training and exit polls. A well-oiled machine was ready to take advantage of any electoral fraud. For example, the opposition newspaper *Ukrayinska Pravda*—operating with the assistance of the National Endowment for Democracy—published telephone intercepts from the headquarters of regime favorite Viktor Yanukovich, which exposed blatant manipulation of the results, and how government operatives even sparked scuffles by deploying an "assault group." [64]

"Neither the level of forgery nor the quantity of violations has any precedents in the past. It's a fact," the newspaper concluded. "The authorities have made a farce of the Ukrainian elections."

That was expected by Pora students, who were ready to respond nonviolently, after literally duplicating the work of their Serb brethren. One activist explained: "The Bible of Pora has been the book of Gene Sharp, also used by Otpor, it's called: *From Dictatorship to Democracy*. Pora activists have translated it by themselves." [65] They had also written to Sharp, and his Albert Einstein Institute funded the printing of twelve thousand copies.

Wary of too much publicity, U.S. officials and the prodemocracy groups downplayed their impact. "There's this myth that the Americans go into a country and, presto, you get a revolution," said Lorne Craner, a former State Department official and head of the International Republican Institute (IRI), which in 2003 had received $25.9 million to push prodemocracy programs in Ukraine and fifty other countries. [66] "It's not the case that Americans can get two million people to turn out on the streets. The people themselves decide to do that."

The Iranians were listening closely.

AND SO THE "DEMOCRATIC" drumbeat went on, with similar tales of critical American and Western support compiling more evidence of the tactics of successful upheaval.

The Tulip Revolution gripped the poverty-stricken Central Asian nation of Kyrgyzstan, after corrupt parliamentary elections in March 2005 prompted street protests—and this time some violence—that ultimately caused President Askar Akayev to flee. American and European donors were there, with the United States giving $12 million in 2004, as well as support for the usual panoply of prodemocracy organizations such as Freedom House. It provided a printing press—often with newsprint paid for with U.S. money—for opposition newspapers.[67]

One edition prior to the vote stoked outrage by running photographs of the president's huge new home, which was under construction. Electricity was shut off just as the newspaper was about to go to press with a 200,000-copy special issue. The next day, the U.S. Embassy sent Freedom House two generators to deploy there.

In a 2005 tabulation of "successes," the U.S. Agency for International Development (USAID) connected the dots. "The Kyrgyz rulers were not, after all, the worst of the regional rulers," it stated.[68] "But the Kyrgyz people had seen the democracy movement succeed in other ex-Soviet republics—the Rose and Orange Revolutions were inspiring democracy advocates around the world."

BUT THESE VELVET REVOLUTIONS also grabbed the attention of other authoritarian regimes, prompting Tajikistan to pass new rules limiting contact between foreign diplomats and civil society groups. Opposition groups and press were subjected to fierce violence from Azerbaijan to Uzbekistan. An opposition delegation from Kazakhstan was in Kiev during the Orange Revolution, among the roaring crowds to study "democratic" Ukrainian methods before their own 2007 election.

"If our authorities make the same mistake, using vote-rigging and [state] resources, the people will take to the streets," the chief Kazakh delegate said.[69] "The ideas of the Rose and [Orange] Revolutions are beginning to penetrate Kazakhstan." But they didn't penetrate far. Kazakhstan outlawed its major opposition party, and in June 2007 the parliament passed a law giving the president lifetime powers, privileges, and immunity.

Moscow also clamped down on civil society assistance with renewed vigor. In mid-2005, the head of Russia's FSB security service—the successor to the KGB—charged that several NGOs, including the U.S. Peace Corps, were "conducting intelligence operations under the guise of charity."[70] Nikolai Patrushev further charged that think tanks were using educational exchanges and civil society projects to work for "regime change." Reinforcing the message in 2006, President Vladimir Putin warned Russian secret services to be vigilant, to prevent "attempts by foreign states to use these organizations to interfere in Russia's internal affairs."[71]

Yet Washington was unrelenting—and unabashed—in its pursuit of George W. Bush's stated "ultimate goal of ending tyranny in our world."[72] It was spending $1.2 billion per year on "prodemocracy" efforts. In a flashy full-color newsletter called *Democracy Rising*, USAID trumpeted a "new wave of mass demands for democracy," from Kiev to Kabul, which had "stunned the world."[73] The propaganda was saccharine sweet: "One picture summed it up: in the cold dark night of Tbilisi, Georgia, as people marched towards the seat of government to protest a fraudulent election, one firm hand held up a model of the Statue of Liberty. Millions are asking for the rights that statue represents: elections to choose their leaders and freedom of speech, press and religion."

But such boasting had a negative impact on those who still lived—like Iranians—under authoritarian rule. "As many surviving autocratic leaders see it, the great mistake of their fallen colleagues was to tolerate social and even political pluralism, believing that it would furnish them with a respectable democratic façade without endangering the stability of their regimes," wrote the Belarusan analyst Vitali Silitski.[74] "The lesson drawn by these autocratic survivors is simple: They must step up repression."

For the most hard-line regimes, argued Silitski, survival was ensured "not just by sporadic reactions . . . but by *preemptive* attacks that eliminate threats before they arise." That lesson was being learned—and increasingly applied—in Tehran. The 2005 victory of the ultra-conservative Mahmoud Ahmadinejad was the ideal corrective, in the minds of hard-liners, after the dangerous and pluralistic ways of reformists had left Iran more vulnerable than ever before to its own Velvet Revolution.

"Happiness for the Youth"

At first there were only subtle signs of the changes to come, of the looming new "securitization" of the regime by its most fervent Believers.

For one heavy metal rock band, the eclipse of freedom began the very day that Ahmadinejad was voted into office in June 2005. The band received a phone call from a nervous official at the Interior Ministry. Their performance had been scheduled to take place at the ministry—a sanctuary of powerful security and intelligence agencies, which sometimes doubled as an unlikely music venue—but it would have to be called off. Speaking from the heart of the security bureaucracy, the official told them: "We can't guarantee your security."[75]

Stunned, the rockers thought they were witnessing the start of a long-expected tightening of the social restrictions that had eased under President Mohammad Khatami, now that conservatives once again held the main levers of power in Iran. When I spoke to the band members one hundred days into Ahmadinejad's tenure, they weren't sure what to expect. "Very little has changed so far," said guitarist Amir Tehrani. "We are expecting it, but it hasn't come. Yet."

In fact, three months after Ahmadinejad's victory, Iranians had seen relatively few signs of a rollback of Khatami's hallmark tolerance. One fascinating example was at the Fourth Islamic Women's Games, just weeks after the presidential election. Organized by Faezeh Rafsanjani—the liberal daughter of Ahmadinejad's main rival, who was a frequent target of hard-liners—the opening ceremony included one routine in which men and women were on the field at the same time.

Militants of the Ansar-e Hezbollah did not intervene to stop it, and the reason was important enough for the vigilantes to discuss it in their weekly newspaper, *Ya Lesarat al-Hossein*.[76] If Khatami had still been in power, the newspaper explained, Ansar would have felt "obligated" to stop the obscene display. But under the new Ahmadinejad crew it was acceptable, because this trusted ultraconservative would never allow such a sacrilege to spiral out of control. There was no difference whatsoever to what had taken place on the field itself. But Ansar's decision *not* to react violently was determined by who was in charge at the top.

Iran's cultural elites were hardly reassured. Beyond the small rehearsal rooms of underground heavy metal bands, mainstream musicians were also feeling the pressure of uncertainty. I wanted to look at the opposite end of the musical spectrum, and so attended a concert in Vahdat Hall—the plush venue where almost a decade earlier I had witnessed the groundbreaking Romeo and Juliet courtship onstage. Before the music began, the conductor of the classical music ensemble wanted to send a message, in fact a plea, to authorities.

"Please clarify the position of music one time—just once!—so we know what to do about it," Alireza Mashayekhi, the veteran conductor and composer of forty-four years, told the audience on International Music Day.[77] He then turned to conduct one of his own powerfully rhythmic, unconventional works for percussion and piano. Just three months into Ahmadinejad's term, there were no turbaned clerics in the audience, but several men wore once-forbidden Western ties. The revolutionary ban on music back in 1979 was so severe that musicians had had to hide their instruments. It took an edict from Ayatollah Khomeini himself to convince some that it was safe to begin playing again—at least traditional music and martial songs to boost the war effort—though harsh restrictions applied.

On that day in 2005, musicians were probing the limits but had low expectations. "Music is the very beginning of the human being, the dances of the galaxy," the director of the Tehran House of Music, Kambiz Roshanravan, told me.[78] "The music we are performing now is a [test] to find out how they will react, how the new government is thinking."

A mix of official answers came soon enough. In December 2005, the Supreme Council for Cultural Revolution, chaired by Ahmadinejad, notified the state broadcaster of "twenty-three strategies for improving the quality of radio and TV activities."[79] They imposed tougher restrictions that required: "Observing Islamic and religious rules, avoiding decadent and Western music, emphasizing legitimate music and refraining from spreading violence and decadence." But national radio still broadcast Celine Dion, Elton John, and others.[80]

Then there was this, one month later, when the minister of culture and Islamic guidance spoke at the closing ceremony of the Fajr Music Festival in Tehran: "We promise to invest in the music which helps man during his desperation," he said.[81] "The dividing point between the decadent and rich music is that the latter, which is created by worthy musicians, drives man to the sky while the decadent music pins him to the earth and takes his flying wings away."

Enforcement on the ground varied, but further directives were issued. In early 2008, another circular banned pop music altogether and obliged radio to "reverse the current policy" of 70 percent music and 30 percent speech.[82] In mid-2008, the Ministry of Culture justified its policy of never showing pictures of instruments on TV by saying, "Promoting music is not part of the Islamic and Iranian values." [83]

AHMADINEJAD HAD IMMEDIATELY BEGUN appointing men with hard-line Revolutionary Guard and Basij backgrounds who were hardly committed to letting Iranians play and hear what they wanted—indeed, most flatly opposed the modest freedoms that had flowered under Khatami. Their definition of "freedom," that tenet of the Revolution's most important slogan, was very different from that of reformists'. For them, freedom meant freedom *from* the corrosive influences of the West. It meant freedom *from* the advance of globalization. It meant the freedom to stay locked in a revolutionary time warp, where piety alone, and isolation—not competence, or global awareness—was the answer to every problem.

"This country is really going to get dangerous; I can see the chain murders returning," predicted one Western-educated academic, shortly after Ahmadinejad's triumph at the polls.[84] He was despondent. The result was a throwback to a bloodier dark age, he told me. "I can see a period of extreme right and left . . . between democracy and

Islamic totalitarianism. With the failure of the Khatami movement, people are confused. People are so tired of the Revolution, [but] can't think outside the [Islamic] system. People are still not at the point of saying: 'Goddammit, we're going to take up arms.' "

That moment of popular insurrection would come years later. But meanwhile, there appeared to be a de facto truce on the streets, during which hard-liners refrained from a broad crackdown—though from the outset they targeted certain activist groups. Students were near the top of that list and felt as hunted as ever. Just months into Ahmadinejad's reign, I met the leader of one mainstream student group, the Office for Strengthening Unity, in a hotel lobby, over tea and dry cakes. The judiciary had a month earlier made a surprise announcement that imprisoned students would be released. But not one had yet been freed, despite that headline-grabbing announcement.

"Even during [the rule of] President Mohammad Khatami, a shadow government was suppressing the student movement," Reza Delbari told me.[85] "After Ahmadinejad, the hidden government revealed itself, and came forward to openly take part in the action. . . . I could say it is worse than before."

One of Delbari's fellow student leaders, Ali Afshari, had already spent three years in jail, 350 days of that in solitary confinement, for "threatening national security" during the 1999 protests. Yet after the announcement that students would be released, Afshari's file was reopened and he was sentenced to a further six years in prison. "The university is still suffering from the [1999 protests] shock," said Delbari, who attended Amirkabir University, the same technical institution that produced so many revolutionaries in 1979. "As soon as students begin to unify, they receive another hit."

With such a large portion of Iran's population below the age of thirty and unemployment high, I reported that how Ahmadinejad and his team of ideological Islamists handled this group—many of whom rejected theocratic rule—would tell much about the inclusiveness of his presidency. In fact it would be only a few months before student activism would prompt a violent government response. Even at that early moment in Ahmadinejad's tenure, signs pointed to a determined effort to reshape the thinking of Iran's restless youth.

LEADING THE CHARGE WAS Mehrdad Bazrpash, an Ahmadinejad adviser on youth whom I met in the well-appointed presidential offices in downtown Tehran. He was a "youth" himself and looked out of place in this seat of power. He bore the distinctive features common to many of Iran's ideologues: pale skin, sunken eyes, and the patchy beard of a young man who had never applied a razor to his face. He gave the impression of spending as much time at prayer in the mosque as in the classroom, and he wore his piety on his sleeve.

Bazrpash used no notebook; there was nothing to indicate in this office that pen or paper—much less a computer—played any part in his daily work. A former head of Basij at Sharif University, Bazrpash was anxious that I quote him correctly, but the e-mail address that he took time to etch into my notebook failed to work.

Ahmadinejad's big plans for youth were evident during his campaign, this apparatchik told me. "During the elections, sixty to seventy percent of the president's slogans were about affairs of the youth," he said.[86] "What is important . . . is to create enough opportunity . . . to let their capability flourish." Iran's young people had proven themselves in nuclear science "without depending on outside powers." They had excelled in stem-cell research and won international science prizes.

But Bazrpash defined "joyful and happy youth" in religious terms drawn from the "sacred" Iran-Iraq War of the 1980s. During the previous eight years under Khatami, he claimed, many youth had strayed from these ideals. His job was to set it right. "We talk all the time about wrong interpretations of what made youths happy in the past," Bazrpash said. "With the right tools, we can define what is happiness for the youth. . . . It's the job of the state to create and transfer this culture of sacrifice to these youngsters."

Those tools included "correct [TV] programs," especially during religious festivals. Also planned were more public sports facilities. Parliament had approved a $1.3 billion "love fund" to give newlyweds a head start. "Our programs should be acceptable to all kinds of youths," Bazrpash told me. "We are pursuing an advanced . . . and happy country, and the existence of these youths is the source of joy and happiness. We will introduce the model of happy, young Iranians to the world."

(Bazrpash would have to wait for that result. It wasn't long before he was appointed, at twenty-eight years old and widely criticized for his inexperience, to be executive director of the large vehicle maker Pars Khodro [SUV models] and then its parent company, Saipa. Two years later in July 2009, Ahmadinejad named Bazrpash a vice president for youth affairs. Though reportedly unhappy at being shifted away from the captain of industry fast track, by spring 2010 Bazrpash, as head of the National Youth Organization, launched a new website with courses designed to lower the rising divorce rate by educating young couples about successful marriage—from sexual problems to happily-ever-after.)

BUT NOT ALL YOUNG Iranians were ready to tune in—even those who had given Ahmadinejad the benefit of the doubt in the 2005 election. Mehdi Gomar was Ahmadinejad's young neighbor with wraparound shades who *looked* like a reformist, who in the flush of the vote had called his archconservative candidate a "wonderful person," who told me the rumors of a social crackdown were all "lies." [87] One hundred days on, Gomar was less certain of Ahmadinejad. A tae kwon do expert and an engineer who had previously worked for Iran's atomic energy agency, he arrived at my hotel in a slick car, wearing a very fine suit with a hands-free telephone earpiece dangling from his pocket.

"A lot of people believe in these [religious] ceremonies, but a lot have different ideas," the engineer with Western tastes and flexible political views told me in English. [88] He waxed nostalgic about Khatami's more laissez-faire attitude, and then made a prescient prediction: "I don't think this [Islamic] system will last more than ten years more, because a lot of people are not satisfied—they only tolerate it."

Ahmadinejad had promised moderation. But one week before I

spoke to Gomar, the cultural body the president headed had banned imported films that they said promoted secularism, feminism, drugs, alcohol use, and violence. Gomar hoped Ahmadinejad would improve. He confided his concern that the *basiji* militia would take Ahmadinejad's electoral mandate as a license to crack down. "Many [*basijis*] are children; they are not mature enough. They think they can do what they want."

INDEED, THE *BASIJIS* WERE increasingly active—and media savvy. I watched in September 2005 as they sought to maximize news impact by waiting for hours until live TV cameras were rolling before staging a pronuclear rally in front of the British Embassy.[89] Ready-for-camera vitriol was spewed; U.S., British, and Israeli flags were burned; some of the hundreds of protesters gathered buckets full of stones.

"Our aim is to use this [nuclear] energy, and our nation will not let us forget it!" thundered a Tehran University Basij leader from the podium. "Confrontation with those bullying Western governments is our legitimate right. They should know that not only the interests of the U.S. and Western countries will be jeopardized, but American territory itself shall not be safe from our *basijis*."

Eggs, tomatoes, and stones were hurled at the building, and police used tear gas to keep protesters back. Calling the British Embassy a new "den of spies," the student *basijis* vowed to repeat the U.S. Embassy seizure of 1979, then angrily stormed toward the gates and implanted bloody handprints onto the polished brass embassy plaque.

Their message of preserving Iran's nuclear rights was one of the few issues that echoed across the political spectrum with any semblance of national unity. On the sidelines of the *basiji* demonstration, I had spoken to several young reformists who were there to apply for visas to the United Kingdom, before the violence prevented them from entering the building. They knew it was Iran's "inalienable right," under the terms of the Nuclear Non-Proliferation Treaty (NPT), to peaceful nuclear technology. They backed Ahmadinejad's bellicose and uncompromising stand.

"I may not believe in most of what the *basiji* and *hezbollahi* do, but on this issue, you can't divide the country," said Ali Farbod, an English major at Tehran University with gel in his hair and a strip of goatee. "We all believe [nuclear technology] is our biggest right. It is the people who want it, not the government. The people are forcing this, and we will not stop until we reach this step."

"How can North Korea, India, Israel, and your country [the United States] all have it, and we can't?" asked Mohammad, a tour guide with long hair and black sunglasses perched atop his head. He was not a typical Iranian ideologue. "This technology is for our progress, our prosperity—it is our right."

In the Name of Defiance

But unity in the pursuit of nuclear power did not translate into blanket support for Iran's divisive president, who spoke often about how the multitude of freedoms granted by the Revolution were unmatched by any other nation. Ahmadinejad railed about the failure of Western democracy, and held up Islamic Iran as a perfect example. In one typical interview, the president claimed: "In Iran, we have this absolute freedom. People can express themselves . . . and there are no limitations imposed on them." [90]

Yet Ahmadinejad's limited commitment to free expression came into sharp focus after a December 2006 speech at the prestigious Amirkabir University. The vicious retribution by security agents in the months afterward would provide a chilling foretaste of violence to come.

The incident was the first serious public outcry against Ahmadinejad and came as he spoke to young *basijis*, many of them bused in for the event. The speech was disrupted by non-*basiji* students who had forced their way into the venue. The president was used to basking in the adulation of adoring crowds during his provincial trips. But these students were angry at the curbing of civil liberties, deepening economic problems, and relentless anti-West rhetoric.

The students, Nazila Fathi reported in the *New York Times,* had "an additional and potent source of outrage: the president's campaign to purge the universities of all vestiges of the reform movement."[91] The newly appointed head of the university had already ordered the destruction of the office of the Islamic Association, a center of student politics since 1963 that had become pro-reform. More than one hundred liberal professors were forced into retirement and "many popular figures were demoted," according to Fathi.

At least seventy students had been suspended for political activities, thirty more were given warnings, and one Ph.D. candidate was barred from completing his work. They were forbidden from printing anything but official news reports in more than two thousand student publications. They could no longer hold meetings—as during the Khatami era—nor invite reformist figures to speak.

"It's not that simple to break up a president's speech," Alireza Siassirad, a former student political organizer, told Fathi. "I think what happened at Amir Kabir is a very important and a dangerous sign. Students are definitely becoming active again."

Student leaders said the protest was not planned in advance. They jeered the president, held his picture upside down, and burned three portraits while chanting, "Death to the dictator!" One banner read: "Fascist president, the polytechnic is not for you."

"The interruption provoked a furious melee in which punches were thrown and a shoe was hurled at the bemused president," reported Robert Tait of the London *Observer.*[92] "Eyewitnesses described [Ahmadinejad] as looking bewildered and close to tears as the upheaval unfolded. Yet amidst it all, he issued a riposte of lasting resonance. 'Everyone knows the real dictator is America and its servants,' he shouted in response to the 'dictator' chants. Those present recall him accusing his hecklers of being paid agents of America and warning that they would be confronted."

Ahmadinejad was forced to cut his speech short and make a hasty departure. The president's security guards fired a stun grenade to block pursuers. But "angry students stormed [Ahmadinejad's] car, kicking it and chanting slogans. His convoy of four cars collided several times as they tried to leave in a rush," the *Times* reported.

Key students involved went into hiding. Ahmadinejad's website played down the protest, suggesting that the president had a "good feeling when he saw a small group amid the dominant majority insulting him without any fear."[93] The president stated that the dissident students should not be punished. But within months fifty-four students were expelled—ostensibly for poor grades—and their expulsion orders were accompanied with documents signed by the university chancellor making them eligible for military service.[94]

Eight leading activists were then arrested and charged with circulating four campus publications that had irreverently cast aspersions upon the reputations of hallowed Shiite imams, claimed the Supreme Leader's post to be less than sacred, and alleged that the highest number of prostitutes per capita in Iran could be found in the religious center of Qom. Family and friends derided the publications as forgeries. Four scanned copies of the publications' logos were, in fact, found inside the briefcase of a Basij student.

"The government wanted to confront the Islamic Students Committee in such a way that other student bodies around the country would be intimidated," one activist said.[95]

Five students were released. Relatives of the three who remained alleged that their sons were tortured to gain confessions. Interrogations conducted by teams of up to eight men could last forty-eight hours at a stretch. "Physical assaults," Tait reported, were "interspersed with insults and psychological abuse."

Interrogators whipped their feet with cables and students told Tait of threats of rape, though none seemed to have been carried out:

They would take off your clothes and one would sit on your legs and talk about how he was going to rape you. Then they would say: "He's not worth raping. It's better to use a bottle or a hot egg." They would then bring a bottle and start hitting it into their hands so you could hear the sound. Or they would say, "Today we will rape you with the hot eggs." They would hand [freshly boiled un-shelled] eggs from one to the other and eventually you would have to eat it.[96]

A letter by parents to Iran's judiciary chief prompted an investigation, but officials publicly denied ever using torture. When the parents met with Tehran's notorious chief prosecutor, Saeed Mortazavi, the official rebuked them with these words: "It is for me to say whether they have been tortured and I say we have not yet tortured to know the meaning of torture."[97]

Closing "Vulnerabilities"

Each of the "color" revolutions had provided more evidence to Iranian hard-liners of their vulnerability, and of the proven prodemocracy tactics of the West. So Ahmadinejad and his Revolutionary Guard and Basij backers began to "securitize" the regime, systematically and with force. During the first two years of Ahmadinejad's reign, the government "carefully controlled its more vocal opponents, [but] endeavored not to antagonize the vast middle of the political spectrum, those Iranians who, while unhappy with the status quo, bear its burdens quietly," wrote analyst Farideh Farhi.[98]

But preparations were under way for a strategic change. Just months after Ahmadinejad was elected, state-run TV reported that Basij forces in eight cities had launched exercises to "confront [urban] unrest"—the first in a number of such training missions.[99] And from spring 2007 a more public calculation prevailed, with a crackdown that touched a broad spectrum of Iranian society, from drug dealers to a former nuclear negotiator. The portrait-burning students of Amirkabir University had been among the first to feel the bite.

"A newly security-conscious state, bordering on paranoid, has indeed emerged," wrote Farhi. "The salient changes under Ahmadinejad have occurred in the three key ministries of Intelligence, Interior, and Culture and Islamic Guidance, from the top of the chain of command on down. The transformation of these ministries is striking precisely because great energy was spent under Khatami to render them less intrusive in Iranian life."

The new minister of intelligence, Gholam Hossein Mohseni-Ejei, for example, had been a "leading figure in prosecuting reformist clerics and politicians, as well as suppressing press freedoms," during posts in the judiciary, according to Human Rights Watch.[100] As prosecutor general of the Special Court for the Clergy, he was in charge of cases against top reformist clerics during the Khatami era. He also sat in the judge's chair during the trial of the popular mayor of Tehran, a key Khatami ally.

Mohseni-Ejei was accused—by dissident journalist Akbar Ganji and former interior minister Abdollah Nouri, among others—of ordering the death of Pirouz Davani, one of the dissidents killed in the 1998 chain murders.[101] And there is the mysterious story from 2004, in which Mohseni-Ejei physically attacked and bit reformist journalist Isa Saharkhiz on the shoulder.[102]

But this minister was on another mission, too, in his new post: to overcome the stigma of the purge the Intelligence Ministry was subjected to during the Khatami period, after the death squads were found within. As Farhi explained, "The aggressive approach taken by Ejei's Intelligence Ministry is a grasp at redemption, an attempt to prove to the various power centers in Iran that the spymasters can solve the country's problems."

One step was the arrest of Hossein Mousavian, a former senior member of Khatami's nuclear negotiating team, on charges of passing sensitive nuclear information to Britain and Japan—an arrest that sent the chilling message that *anyone* could be found a traitor. Mohseni-Ejei justified the arrest to parliament, telling deputies that Mousavian was "guilty as far as the Intelligence Ministry is concerned."[103] Ahmadinejad echoed the same certainty in public, though Mousavian was released after ten days, given a two-year suspended sentence, and eventually even given a semi-official apology.[104]

The new minister of interior, Mustafa Pour-Mohammadi, had an even more controversial past. At the end of the Iran-Iraq War in 1988, he was part of a three-man "Death Committee" at Evin—each prison had one—tasked with purging unrepentant regime opponents, most of them members of the Mojahedin-e Khalq (MKO/MEK). All told, between 2,800 and 3,800 were executed, many of them at Evin, where Pour-Mohammadi was the chief intelligence official in charge of their questioning.[105] The regime has never acknowledged this bloody episode. But in his memoirs, Grand Ayatollah Hossein-Ali Montazeri—who was heir-apparent to Khomeini at the time—recalls meeting Pour-Mohammadi and his committee and urging them to stop the executions during a holy month.

Instead they were eager to kill. One replied: "We have so far executed 750 people in Tehran, and we have identified another 250 people. Allow us to get rid of them and then we'll listen to you . . . !"[106]

During the 1990s, when Iran assassinated scores of opponents abroad, Pour-Mohammadi was the director of foreign intelligence. And in 1998, as a deputy minister, Pour-Mohammadi was implicated in ordering the chain murders of the five dissidents. A parliamentary investigation was unable to complete its work because it "led to certain people whom we did not have the power to deal with."[107]

According to Human Rights Watch, a source with firsthand knowledge confirmed that "investigators implicated Pour-Mohammadi and even an arrest warrant was about to be issued for him."[108] Instead a deal was done for him to step down.

These men were the type of proven security veterans resurrected by President Mahmoud Ahmadinejad, who had come to power with a view of the coercive capacity of the state—and when it should be applied—very different from that of his reformist predecessor. Ahmadinejad portrayed himself a smiling, pious populist, and famously dismissed during his election campaign women's headscarves as a real problem: "Don't we have more important things to deal with?" he asked.

But the new president's spiritual mentor—shared by many in the new government—was Ayatollah Mohammad Taghi Mesbah-Yazdi, the hard-line mastermind of the conservative resurgence. He was a proponent of the use of force and had no time for democracy in a system where God had already chosen the best.

"The government follows its goals by force of arms," against those who question the path of the *nezam,* said Mesbah-Yazdi, a cudgel of a man with a rounded nose and eyeglasses who gives off the air of an errant uncle.[109] "Those who violate the law-based regulations will be forced to accept them with the help of law enforcement organizations."

His reading of the role of *velayat-e faqih*—as a leader who derived his legitimacy straight from God—left little room for the vote of the people. "Government legitimacy has never depended upon others' wishes [because] it has been a divine issue and has taken place by [divine] appointment," said Mesbah-Yazdi. Reformist officials, he once proclaimed, "are mercenaries of foreigners and they've shown their hand."[110]

MESBAH-YAZDI'S LETHAL INFLUENCE STRETCHED very far, and was a case study of how religion in Iran could justify extreme violence. It would prove a critical framework for Ahmadinejad and hard-liners to follow when putting down the June 2009 protests.

An informative example that made few waves abroad was the case of six *basiji* militiamen brought to trial for five of eighteen deaths recorded in Kerman in 2002. Shocking details of the killings had been in the newspapers: A married woman thought to be "loose," stuck in a pit and stoned to death, her body then taken to the desert to be eaten by wild animals. An engaged couple going to inspect the home they were to rent after their marriage, stopped in the street while walking together, drowned in a ditch and dumped in the desert. A man buried alive after bludgeoning with a rock. Still others "drowned in a small house pool: gang members took turns to keep them under water by standing on them until they drowned," according to reports.[111]

Iran's Supreme Court in April 2007 reversed guilty verdicts that had been rendered by three lower courts. The court found that the *basijis* "considered their victims morally corrupt and, according to Islamic teachings and Iran's Islamic penal code, their blood could be shed." [112] Iran's penal code states that murder charges can be dropped "even if the killer identified the victim mistakenly as corrupt."

During the trials, the killers did not hide the fact of the heavy influence of Mesbah-Yazdi. The ringleader had even met with the cleric to ask for guidance sometime in 2001–2002, and was told to return that evening to hear the ayatollah preach. Mesbah-Yazdi was explicit that night, and said, "If one calls somebody to virtue and warned him against committing a sin three times but that person still fails to fulfill his commitments, then his blood may be freely shed." [113]

In court, the killers claimed they had given their victims multiple warnings before taking their lives. Another defendant described listening to a speech of Mesbah-Yazdi on a cassette, about how to deal with sinners. He paraphrased the cleric in court, saying that if two warnings are ignored and the sinner "repeats his wrong action, this person's blood may be shed [easily]. Whoever kills him is a holy warrior on God's path and if it didn't suit society's taste and [the killer] was executed, he would be a martyr on God's path. This sentence is repeated twice in the cassette. I took it to a cultural institution and found out that the written text of this speech exists there." [114]

These killers were certain they were acting for Islam and would be exonerated by God, if not by the judicial system. "It was like a pain in my chest," proclaimed one of the *basijis* in court. [115] "Why should we allow a revolution for which so many martyrs paid with their blood to go to waste at the hands of such individuals?"

These violent episodes demonstrated what steps ideological militants could take, if given a clear religious justification for action—as so many *basijis* and vigilantes received in 2009, when charges of rape and brutality in secret detention centers emerged. Journalist Kasra Naji notes the disturbing moral of the Kerman case: "Although the killers were not so interested in checking up on the facts [of guilt] relating to their victims, they were very keen to ensure that they killed in accordance with the Quran as they interpreted it."[116]

The judicial leniency was a sign of how Iran's Revolution was casting back, after a quarter of a century, to a period of supposed ideological purity. The elements were in place for retrenchment. As Naji observes, "With the Kerman killings, a conservative hardline religious judiciary, murderous moral zealots and inflammatory violent rhetoric all combined to undermine the rule of law and to accept extra-judicial executions backed by the spurious theological rulings of President Ahmadinejad's mentor."[117]

THE SPREAD OF SUCH brutalizing influence coincided with news of increasingly "devious" actions from Washington. The public "prodemocracy" funds set aside by Congress for Iran, which began modestly in 2004, grew to $66 million in 2007 and $60 million in 2008.[118] Never mind that most of the cash was spent on Farsi-language broadcasts, and very little inside Iran. To resurgent conservatives, it was the seed money for Velvet Revolution.

Reports surfaced of increasing American intelligence and military activities, even inside the Islamic Republic, and of planning for a strike against Iran. A second U.S. Navy aircraft carrier battle group was sent to the Persian Gulf, along with a Marine Expeditionary Unit, adding to the U.S. military punch that already accompanied U.S. forces in Iraq and Afghanistan, and the U.S. Navy's Fifth Fleet, based in Bahrain.

Iranians began to joke that the inexplicable policy of replacing all street signs in Tehran—which had been in both Farsi and English for years—with ones *only* in Farsi script was to confuse American troops, should they ever arrive on those streets. Throughout 2007, senior U.S. officials and commanders ramped up accusations that Iran was waging a "proxy war" against America in Iraq by sending explosively formed penetrators (EFPs), rockets, and trained militants across the border.[119] The result in Iran, said U.S.-based Iranian analyst Kaveh Afrasiabi, was a "national security paranoia."[120]

And the chance of a U.S. military strike only seemed to grow as the months passed. By late 2007 Congress had agreed to "fund a major escalation of covert operations" against Iran in a classified $400 million presidential finding signed by President Bush.[121] It was "designed to destabilize [Iran's] religious leadership," Seymour Hersh reported in the *New Yorker*. U.S. Special Operations forces had been conducting cross-border operations since 2007. Wrote Hersh: "Many of the activities may be being carried out by dissidents in Iran, and not by Americans in the field."

THOSE DEEPER RUMBLINGS OF subversion were no secret to the Iranians, and gave added incentive to a forceful response. Supreme Leader Khamenei sparked things off in March 2007 when he repeatedly urged Iranians to resist the West's "psychological warfare."[122] Iran's writers and opinion makers "should be watchful and must not follow the enemy's targets, consciously or unconsciously," the Leader warned. "Because whoever undermines people's trust in the system's authorities and in the future . . . has helped the enemies."

The internal crackdown began to gather pace in April, when 150,000 people were stopped or detained, many of them women for insufficiently covered hair and tight-fitting clothes. Men were rounded up for bad attitudes and "big hair" Western haircuts, honed at barbershops that were shut down for providing "deviant" long, spiky, and gelled styles. Eyebrow plucking for men was banned.

The target list expanded beyond the usual spring cleanup. Intelligence chief Mohseni-Ejei described the "enemy's new policy" as organizing civil society groups like women and students. "(The enemy) has taken a few groups to other countries to train for conducting soft subversion," he said. The plan was to divide Iranians from their government by imposing economic pressure and "heavy propaganda . . . to portray the government as incompetent and to disappoint the public."[123]

Mohseni-Ejei warned: "Anybody who works against the *nezam* and aims at subversion . . . will be confronted."[124] And so they were. Some three hundred teachers were imprisoned for demanding higher pay and sometimes held for months; bus drivers were arrested for union organizing; thirty-three women were arrested for staging protests calling for equal legal rights, five of them sentenced to up to four years of jail time.[125]

Professors were warned by the Ministry of Intelligence against contact with Western colleagues, to prevent them being recruited as spies at "so-called scientific conferences."[126] From then on, several academics I knew in Tehran would not permit their names to appear in print, or even meet me in any but the most secretive ways.

"Ahmadinejad has repeatedly stated his goal of purging Iranian society of secular thought," said Hadi Ghaemi, then an Iran analyst for Human Rights Watch.[127] "This is taking shape as a cultural revolution, particularly on university campuses, where persecution and prosecution of students and faculty are intensifying with each passing day."

If the aim was to hamper Iran's civil society, it was working. "People don't want to come to conferences, they don't even want to talk on the phone," said Abbas Milani, the Director of Iranian Studies at Stanford University. "The regime has created an atmosphere of absolute terror."[128]

IN TEHRAN, AUTHORITIES WENT out of their way to publicize that spring 2007 crackdown on crime. To some extent it was popular with the public. Cameras followed cops on nighttime raids against drug dealers that netted hundreds in a single night. Iranian media plastered their front pages with images of masked, black-clad police arresting, humiliating, and parading criminals, forcing some to drink from distinctively shaped plastic water jugs used in toilets. But state-run TV also showed a woman wearing a black chador telling a Westernized one that her fashionable outfit was not appropriate for an "Iranian woman."

"Our decisive confrontation will continue in Tehran until the very last thug," declared the head of the capital's police force, announcing more than 1,100 arrests in May 2007.[129] "The Iranian police and judi-

ciary should act in such a way that anyone who dares to touch a ma-
chete starts to shiver," added Tehran's prosecutor Mortazavi. Women
with "bad hijab" were fair game, too, he told *Etemaad* newspaper:
"These women who appear in public like decadent models, endanger the security and dignity of young men."[130] Parading the accused
in neighborhoods was done with his approval because "we wanted
people to see them."

One news report stated that officials were targeting " '*arazel va
obash*,' literally 'rascals and villains' who are accused of disturbing
the peace in low-income neighborhoods [like] thugs who brandish
machetes, extortionists, rapists, the owners of 'vice centers' as well
as those who drink alcohol in public."[131] In Farsi, these thugs were
known as *chagoo-kesh,* or "knifepullers."

The morality dimenson of the crackdown wasn't as vicious as
the early 1980s, when female Revolutionary Guards had reportedly
thrown acid in the face of women with improper Islamic covering, or
said, "Let me take off your lipstick," only to use a Kleenex with a con-
cealed razor to cut their lips.[132] But as it wore on, it became clear this
was not just another episode of enforcement. It was part of a broader
strategic plan to protect the regime from "vulnerabilities" that could
be exploited by archenemies like the United States.[133]

"The girls are not the target," an Iranian journalist told me, noting
that many women were still deliberately flouting the rules.[134] "The
core reason is dealing harshly with thugs. Now they are preempting—
they are keeping a potential [threat] from growing. They are looking
at modern history [and] going onto the Internet."

WHAT LINKED COMMON CRIMINALS with the security of the
state in 2007? One unforgettable precedent: the CIA coup of 1953.

Crucial to success back then were the mobs organized by CIA-paid
agents that had taken over the streets. The British government had
secretly worked since World War II with the three Rashidian brothers, who received twenty-eight thousand dollars each month to cre-

ate crowds, plant news stories, buy off parliamentarians, and influence public opinion.[135] These brothers then became U.S. "assets."

As planning for the Operation Ajax coup got under way, all those assets were turned against the popular prime minister. The CIA station in Tehran was given $1 million from Washington to use "in any way that would bring about the fall of [Mohammad] Mossadegh."[136] They worked with a mob organizer called Sha'aban "the Brainless" Jafari and relied on another pair who controlled a network of more than one hundred subagents. All engaged in a pre-coup destabilization campaign to "create, extend, and enhance public hostility and fear" of the government, according to the once-secret CIA history.[137]

On the morning of August 17, 1953, crowds swelled to tens of thousands. "Gangs of thugs pretending pro-Mossadegh sympathies were making their way from the slums of Tehran's south side toward the center of town," notes Stephen Kinzer in *All the Shah's Men*.[138] Writes historian Mark Gasiorowski, "Genuine [communists], who did not realize this was a CIA-financed provocation, also came out into the streets, as did other Iranians. These crowds created chaos in Tehran, tearing down statues of the Shah and his father, Reza Shah, attacking Reza Shah's mausoleum, and throwing stones at mosques."[139]

The violence intensified the next day. Mossadegh finally ordered the police—whose commanders were close to the coup organizers—to step in. The *New York Times* reported: "The troops appeared to be in a frenzy as they smashed into rioters with clubs, rifles and night sticks, and hurled tear gas bombs."[140]

The final showdown—and the final proof of what thugs in Iran could achieve, in the pay of "foreign agents"—came on August 19, 1953. Every event of this coup had so far been a surprise, with Iranians almost always unaware that American hands and cash were at work behind the scenes, causing them to think in a certain way, to perceive the "spontaneous" violence in a certain way—as coming from this side, and then that side—and also to react in a certain way. Even senior ayatollahs had received tens of thousands of dollars of CIA money, unaware that it came from foreigners. Iranians were on the street taking part in paid-for protests, ignorant of the fact that CIA cash had helped guide them there.

Defying political gravity—because in reality Mossadegh still had widespread popular support—the mercenaries were paid to change Iranian history. "That mob that came into north Tehran and was decisive in the overthrow was a mercenary mob," stated Richard Cottam, who was part of the Operation Ajax staff in Washington.[141] "It had no ideology, and that mob was paid with American dollars."

Proof of that came in the smoldering aftermath of the climactic fight at Mossadegh's home. "About three hundred people died . . . half of them in the final battle at Mossadegh's house," writes Kinzer.[142] "Some of the civilian victims were found with 500 rial notes still in their pockets"—the American paymasters of the mob "had distributed the notes that morning to dozens of their subagents."

DECADES LATER, THE STEALTHY effectiveness of those tactics fed fear in the Islamic Republic that it was all happening again. Now, hard-liners charged, it was reformist Iranians who were undermining the security of the regime—often without knowing who they were *really* working for.

Iran's security services raised their anxiety higher by surfing the Internet, where they became familiar with the writings of American regime-change neoconservatives like Michael Ledeen—a fact I heard from several right-wing sources in Iran. Ledeen had argued in 2007, for example, that with U.S. support "we could liberate Iran in less than a year."[143] An Iranian journalist paraphrased for me those ideas, as they were perceived in Tehran: "In the war with Iran, the U.S. will not be the foot soldiers" but will "just provide the trigger" for Iranians to rise and topple the government.

Though dismissed by many Iran specialists as a serial regime changer far removed from the realities of Iran, Ledeen captivated Iranian hard-liners as if he were spelling out the secret truth of U.S. policy. Ledeen's analysis assumed that Iranians were ready to risk another violent, full-blown Revolution to rid themselves of despised clerical rule—to start with, a more than contestable point. I had frequently heard from Iranians that they wanted change, but not at the risk of serious violence. And Iranians wanted to do it themselves.

"The question is, how?" wrote Ledeen.[144] "The answer is, the same way we brought down the Soviet empire, by exporting the American democratic revolution, by adopting the methods that have successfully been used against dictators from Moscow and Belgrade to Beirut and the Philippines. The best strategy is to support the Iranian people against the mullahs they so hate."

Yet there was no recognition that the underlying ideology of Iran's True Believers was made of rather sterner stuff than that of communists. "We defeated the Soviet empire at a time when only a small minority of its people were willing to fight for freedom," Ledeen wrote.[145] The logical conclusion, he asserted, was that the job should be easy in Iran, where "we have upward of 70 percent of the people on our side."

To Iran's own neoconservatives, such interpretations were electrifying proof that conspiracies were afoot and attempts at Velvet Revolution were under way. Khamenei told police academy cadets that "only those who cause problems for people should feel insecure," yet they "must strongly continue with the 'social security plan' [crackdown] so that its goals are institutionalized in society."[146]

"The 'soft' revolution allegation is distinctive for being the only external security threat given credibility in Tehran," observed British journalist Robert Tait, resident in the capital during that 2007 crackdown.[147] "While speculation about a US or Israeli strike on Iranian nuclear installations and other facilities has reached fever pitch in the West over recent weeks, in Iran the possibility is publicly dismissed." U.S. forces were bogged down in Iraq and Afghanistan, "so having given up the idea of toppling the regime through military action, the official narrative goes, the US is trying to destabilize it by stealth."

• • •

IN ONE OF HIS first acts as Iran's new Revolutionary Guard commander, Mohammad Ali Jafari raised eyebrows in September 2007 by stating that his top priority would be containing internal dissent. Lauding the change as "new strategic guidelines" laid down by the Supreme Leader, Jafari said, "The main mission of the IRGC from now on is to deal with the threats from the internal enemies." [148] The Basij force would henceforth come under Revolutionary Guard command, to cope with increasingly complex threats. He said, "We don't have the right to remain silent." [149]

Jafari's declaration was public confirmation of what was already clearly visible to Iranians: that Revolutionary Guard control was spreading across all aspects of Iranian society. It harkened back to the earliest years of the Revolution, when "securing the system [*nezam*]" was deemed the highest obligation, even above prayer and fasting. The difference was that, unlike both 1953 and 1979, the regime had now recruited legions of security forces and loyal vigilante groups whose job was to ensure that the *nezam* endured, and to achieve "victory through creating fear." [150]

This, in the eyes of many reformists, was the real silent takeover of power in Iran. Ebrahim Yazdi, the foreign minister turned dissident, explained it as a "velvet coup d'etat," with the Guard seizing more and more power. "The philosophy is that you terrorize people in order to succeed. Ahmadinejad represents this line," Yazdi said.[151] "To survive you have to continuously create episodes that justify political repression."

Such ends justified the means because Iran was under attack, the influential cleric Seyyed Abolhassan Navvab told me in Tehran. "The U.S. planned two wars against us, a hard war and a soft war," Navvab said:

The hard war, it is only intimidation and slogans. But the soft war, it goes more toward reality [by provoking] social, cultural, ethnic, and religious conflicts. It is not a flood, but this is a very slight rain that is continuous, and when it washes away it has ruinous effect. If you take it seriously, the level of danger drops. If you don't take it seriously, the danger is there and it is firm.[152]

The impact of such beliefs was widely felt. "I have never seen Iran like this in twenty-eight years," one Iranian political analyst who spent time in the United States told me.[153] "Early in the Revolution there was mass jubilation, and repression was very targeted . . . Now it's a systematic intimidation, and they are very good at it. The whole security environment is intended to really suffocate or torpedo any possible change from within."

And the regime *was* good at it. Beyond intimidated academics, Iranians even began refusing invitations to lunch in Tehran where Western diplomats might be present. Attendees at the queen's birthday party event at the British Embassy were harassed as they left the compound. A final report of BBC correspondent Frances Harrison in mid-2007, as she left after three years in Tehran, illustrated the scale of change. While numerous officials had attended the going-away lunch of her predecessor, Jim Muir, not one—not even those from the press office, who are often very helpful on a personal level—came to her BBC farewell lunch. "I did not take it personally," wrote Harrison.[154] "The atmosphere is now one where Iranians are afraid to mix with foreigners for fear of being accused of spying."

The Supreme National Security Council (SNSC) had been sending out by courier a mounting pile of edicts to newspaper editors. As I sat in the office of one editor, he opened the top drawer of his desk to reveal a collection of brown envelopes, stamped with the SNSC seal, and then swore me to secrecy. Iranian news organizations were receiving direct orders: they could no longer report negative news about social unrest, the failing economy, gas rationing in the world's fourth-largest oil-exporting nation, the impact of sanctions on Iran, the nuclear program, the arrest of dual-citizen academics—the list went on.

The regime issued a dark warning. "There are some signs of a creeping coup in the press," proclaimed the Minister of Culture and

Islamic Guidance Mohammad Hossein Saffar-Harandi. "When we say a creeping coup in the press, it means a person is moving within a framework of action to overthrow the *nezam*."[155] Journalists knew what that could mean, for it was Ayatollah Khomeini himself who had taken exception to press coverage in 1980 and called the president and government officials to him. "Why do you not stop these newspapers?" Khomeini asked.[156] "Why do you not shut their mouths? Why do you not stop their pens?"

INTELLIGENCE AGENTS WERE TAKING exactly that kind of proactive approach, keeping a close eye on Iranian dual-citizen journalists working for foreign media. For *Time* correspondent and author Azadeh Moaveni, her secret government minder, Mr. X, became "perhaps the most important person in my Iranian life."[157] She was expected to inform him of all her writing plans and would be summoned to "secluded, anonymous apartments, empty hotel rooms in unmarked establishments [which] created the theater of intimidation," she writes in *Honeymoon in Tehran*.

Mr. X clawed his way into every corner of Moaveni's life, as she juggled her job, a pending marriage, and pregnancy. He or his fellow agents followed her. When she bought a ring for her mother, and a family friend went to pick it up, the friend was called back to the shop the next day and questioned by two security agents about his ties to Moaveni. They demanded to know where she received the money for such expensive gifts. Moaveni fretted about whether to tell Mr. X about the incident: "By not telling him, I risked losing his protection against a sinister arm of another branch of government."[158]

Mr. X was obsessed with secrecy, insisted that their meetings never be disclosed, and frustrated Moaveni: "Once, exasperated and angry, I stopped circling around what I wanted to say and just blurted, 'How can you expect me to trust you with the identities of my sources when your ministry just two years ago was *murdering* people?' "[159]

Moaveni thought she had finally found a way of escape the haunting presence of Mr. X, after she was married, by explaining that her husband did not approve of their meeting alone in such remote places. Mr. X was livid and demonstrated how hypocritical the servants of the Islamic Republic could be.

"What right does your husband have to interfere in our work? Our work is *amneeat*, security," he said, as if lecturing a child.[160] Their back-and-forth did not budge him. She writes: "Mr. X had said in stark terms that security concerns, whatever that meant, took precedence over Islamic correctness. That pretty well summarized the ethos of the regime: security over everything—over development, over the ethical values of Islam, over the rights of its people."

THOSE RIGHTS WERE BEING challenged also for Maziar Bahari, an Iranian-Canadian filmmaker and writer for *Newsweek*. "I'm not supposed to tell you this, but I met Mr. Mohammadi. In fact, I met three Mr. Mohammadis in four days," Bahari wrote in 2007.[161] "Mohammadi is the nickname of choice for the agents of Iran's Ministry of Intelligence—the country's equivalent of the CIA."

Ordered to meetings in nondescript hotel rooms while working on a story about activist women and students, Bahari provided a semilighthearted glimpse. Mr. Mohammadi—each one of which insisted their meetings never be divulged—had evolved from agents in years past, into a polite being who plied his journalist with endless tea, Nescafé, and juice. He even smiled too much, as he questioned Bahari about his main concern, "that the American fifth column, disguised as civil rights activists, scholars and journalists, is destabilizing the Islamic Republic."

Bahari was wary nonetheless. "He has killed many people in the past. And you know he is capable of violence again if he thinks it's necessary. Mr. Mohammadi's counterparts in the numerous parallel security apparatuses (intelligence units of the judiciary, Revolutionary Guard, and the police) still have not caught up with his methods." Bahari notes that arrested students and labor activists had been beaten with electric cables and batons.

But *this* Mohammadi's effort was listless. "His bosses have come up with a conspiracy theory and asked Mr. Mohammadi to validate it. He is a smart man and has been down this road many times since the 1979 Islamic Revolution. It's never worked in the past [and he] knows that he's wasting his time and mine," explains Bahari. "He wraps up our session with a few farewell sentences that all other Mohammadis use: 'I hope you don't think it's personal. There are people who want to take advantage of your good intentions. We just want to protect you.' And then he delivers the punch line: 'We know where you live.' "

The next Mohammadi is a little more engaged about the risks to Iran. He doesn't smile as he asks Bahari to envision America in the same predicament that Iran faces. The intelligence agent tells him:

[I]magine if Iran has 250,000 soldiers in Canada and Mexico (roughly the number of US soldiers in Iraq and Afghanistan) and then allocates a budget to help civil rights movements in the US, let's say to the Black Panthers or to a Native American movement, wouldn't Americans be paranoid? We know our problems better than anyone, and we do our best to tell those who are responsible about the social maladies. . . . But this is Iran. It takes ages for anything to happen. In the meantime we have a vicious enemy to deal with: the US. It's determined to topple our government by any means necessary. As Tom Clancy says, the US is: "A Clear and Present Danger."

"THIS IS A COMPREHENSIVE security plan for the whole [Islamic] system, not just Mr. Ahmadinejad," Saeed Laylaz, an analyst and former deputy minister, told me in Tehran in 2007, as the crackdown continued.[162] It was being pursued on three levels, by first "attacking ordinary people" to boost the police presence on the streets; then going after student activists and intellectuals; and finally by arresting nuclear diplomat Hossein Mousavian on espionage charges as a warning to other high-ranking personalities.

All of that was very far from the campaign promises of Ahmadinejad, who had gone out of his way to reassure Iranians that a victory for him—and the entire militant hard-line cabal behind him—would not bring to power the "Islamic fascism" and "Iranian Taliban," as his enemies charged.

The veteran dissident Ebrahim Yazdi was sure the crackdown signaled something very different. "This is the [present system's] last bus. What its precise destination is, I don't know," he told me.[163] "But my prediction is that it will end similarly to the old Soviet system. That didn't end through a revolution—red, orange, or velvet—or through an outside military attack. More than anything, it ended because the collective Russian leadership came to the historical conclusion that the continuation of that system was impossible. It will not be a revolution. It will be gradual. But ultimately, it will be democratic."

The Living Velvet Revolution

Caught along the way was Haleh Esfandiari, whose freedom came to an end in the dead of night in late 2006. Three intelligence agents in identical olive drab uniforms, wearing hunting knives on their hips—and one with a disconcerting grin on his face—forced her taxi off the long, empty highway that leads from Tehran to the Imam Khomeini Airport, an hour's drive south of the capital.[164]

An Iranian-born scholar and director of Middle East programs at the Woodrow Wilson Center in Washington, D.C., the sixty-seven-year-old grandmother told the "robbers" to take everything—except her plane ticket and Iranian and American passports, so she could still fly out of Iran. But that was, in fact, what they were after—to prevent her from leaving the country. Her nightmare began with the rough words of one of the culprits, when he told her to squeeze between the narrow back seats so she would not observe their departure.

She protested that there was no room. "Get down, you bitch," the agent ordered, "or I will smash your skull; I will kill you. Do as you are told."

And then they were gone. But this was no ordinary robbery, as Esfandiari found out in the following weeks as she tried to replace her passports. She had been visiting her ailing ninety-three-year-old mother in Tehran and seemed an unlikely threat. But Esfandiari found herself stuck in a web of suspicion spun by the Ministry of Intelligence. Her apprenticeship was about to begin, into the obsessions of Iran's security services about Velvet Revolution.

Esfandiari was one of a number of Iranian-American experts who would be arrested in 2007, accused of being "agents" and of using U.S. funds to undermine the regime. Her experience, described in her book *My Prison, My Home,* lays bare the minutiae of neurosis that had been afflicting Iran's Islamic system, taking hold like a degenerative disease for years while the regime kept up its façade of impervious power. In Iran it was the ignorant mixing of reality and unreality, the weight of suspicion that left little room for reason, much less for truth, that shocked Esfandiari.

"I felt the country I had cherished all my life was no longer mine. I had loved Iran with a passion. I loved its brilliant blue sky and its brown earth. I loved the desert and the sea," writes Esfandiari.[165] "Yet these horrible people had made me feel alien in my own homeland." Her work for decades of bringing Iranians and Americans together—work meant to enhance mutual understanding, and encouraged by the previous government of Khatami—was now an act of treason that had trapped her, cheek by jowl, with the darkest phobias of the Islamic Republic.

At the top of the list for her interrogators was the Woodrow Wilson Center, where she worked in Washington, and the fact that its director, Lee Hamilton, had been a longtime congressman and chair of the House Foreign Affairs Committee. For the Ministry of Intelligence, that was evidence of the "revolving door" between government and civil society organizations.

It wasn't long before Esfandiari realized her interrogator Jafari didn't believe a word she said. " 'You're talking about the surface things, the superficialities,' he insisted. 'We want to know about the core, the kernel, the hidden layers. Tell us about the hidden layers.' With alarm, I began to see the shape of Jafari's fantasies and the case he was trying to build against me," she writes.[166] To him, the Wilson

Center was just another tentacle of the U.S. government. "There was virtually nothing that didn't feed Jafari's insatiably suspicious mindset or that he couldn't fit into his conspiracy theory." [167]

Esfandiari was "recruited, not hired," she was told, and the fact that her program had first been called the "Middle East *Project*"—with her job title a "consultant"—was also, to Jafari, no coincidence. During a raid of her apartment, Jafari was selective. He took with him an invitation to mark the coronation of the Shah in 1969—nearly four decades earlier—but "showed no interest in a framed letter from the minister of agriculture of the Islamic Republic honoring my father for his services to the field of Iranian botany. Jafari was adept at cherry-picking his evidence," writes Esfandiari. [168] Jafari even started taking away some clear white wrapping paper, stating, "There's invisible ink writing on it." She laughed out loud and told him it was really just wrapping paper. He left it behind.

Hard-liners in the Ministry of Intelligence were convinced they had caught a "big fish," a mastermind. [169] Interrogator Jafari had a voracious appetite for information—most of it available publicly on the Internet. "Like some manic agent of the Soviet secret police or the East German Stasi, he was intent on amassing detailed information, no matter how insignificant, on every Iranian I had ever known," recounts Esfandiari. [170] "Along with his colleagues, he imagined that if he piled up enough information and stitched it together in charts and timelines, he could finally figure out America's plan for overthrowing the Islamic Republic."

Esfandiari had some female prison guards who became sympathetic allies. But others were more disagreeable. One she called Sour Face was sure she knew the *truth*. "Every one who comes here, including you, thinks they are innocent," she lectured Esfandiari, getting "so worked up that foam formed at the corners of her lips." [171] "None of you are innocent. Islamic justice doesn't make mistakes. All of you are here because you are guilty and you don't want to repent."

Also clear to Esfandiari was that the much-praised purge of the Ministry of Intelligence in 1999 after the chain murders—one concrete achievement of Khatami—was more form than substance. The hard-liners "simply moved elsewhere, setting up a parallel intelligence operation . . . to repress Khatami's nascent reform movement," writes Esfandiari.[172]

The first detailed report on this Parallel Intelligence Apparatus, or PIA, noted in 2009 that it was "not a specific entity or organization, but a network of law enforcement, security and intelligence units that conducted clandestine operations against targeted individuals in an effort to weaken and silence the reform movement in Iran."[173] They grew as a direct result of Khatami's effort to clean up the Ministry of Intelligence, or MOI, according to the U.S.-based Iran Human Rights Documentation Center: "The PIA initiated their campaign to crush the reformist movement following the purges. . . . Many of the security personnel that were purged from the MOI were ultimately absorbed into the PIA."[174]

In their new capacity, these hard-line agents—filling slots within intelligence units in the Supreme Leader's office, judiciary, IRGC, vigilante groups, and elsewhere—were able to act with even greater impunity and set up "a system of secret detention facilities in which they subjected their targets to long interrogation sessions, solitary confinement and torture."[175]

Though their existence was always officially denied, these agent networks and secret facilities would later be used to devastating effect against protesters in June 2009. But their initial purpose during the Khatami presidency was to "relentlessly and systematically engage in measures to silence pro-reform voices." Relying upon a "striking pattern of brutality," the report states, the "PIA's objectives were two-fold: to end the activities of the targeted individuals, and to make examples of them in order to intimidate other political activists, dissidents and members of the reformist camp into submission."[176]

USING TIME-HONORED METHODS, STATE television in mid-2007 broadcast a program of "confessions" of Esfandiari and fellow Iranian-American Kian Tajbakhsh, a U.S.-educated urban planner who had been crisscrossing the country working for Iranian ministries, the World Bank, and the Open Society Institute—the same George Soros organization active in previous Velvet Revolutions. Earlier footage of Canadian-Iranian philosopher Ramin Jahanbegloo—detained for four months in 2006 and accused in the right-wing media of serving the CIA and Mossad as "one of the key elements" of the U.S. plan for regime change—was mixed in to make a cohesive argument.

These academics were accused of "serving the enemy," whether they knew it or not. The "confessions" were a surreal déjà vu from the first years of the Revolution. Back then, people from across the political spectrum were "brought in front of the cameras to make confessions," historian Ervand Abrahamian told me.[177] "It was a routine thing: you made a video. It [was so common] it became a joke."

Called *In the Name of Democracy,* there were two parts of fifty and thirty-six minutes each, which deftly spliced images of those "soft" revolutions in Serbia, Georgia, Ukraine, and Kyrgyzstan with segments of interviews. One edition began with footage of Gene Sharp—that acknowledged godfather of nonviolent regime change—in his office library. The entire plot, as explained in the films, was driven by tens of millions of dollars paid by the U.S. government to undermine Iran. The films showed activists across the former Soviet Union planning for demonstrations, elections, and finally regime overthrow with the help of Americans and their money. And it drew the inevitable link to Iran, where American think tanks were plotting regime change again.

"The impetus comes from die-hard people around Ahmadinejad, the former Revolutionary Guards, people who now dominate the intelligence services," Abrahamian told me. "They practiced this under Khomeini, so they are really going back to the old methods [that] did work. . . . It also tells Iranians to beware of anyone from abroad who is talking about human rights. So even if you are not involved in regime change . . . you would be tarred with the same brush."

In the film, Esfandiari spoke of facilitating scholarly exchanges, networks of Iran experts, and meetings at international conferences—all of which had been encouraged during President Khatami's "dialogue among civilizations" tenure. Plucked from solitary confinement and looking pale and emaciated, Esfandiari wore a black headscarf while sitting on a couch beside a plant.

"What was my role here?" she asked.[178] "In the course of these years, when you put these number of meetings back to back, you would come to the conclusion that, willingly or not, a network of connections would be formed." Esfandiari later explained that the Intelligence Ministry had "spliced two disparate sentences of mine" to indicate that her purpose was to bring "fundamental change" in Iran.[179]

Other segments showed Tajbakhsh speaking with notes about his work for Soros, in a wood-paneled office setting. He spoke of an "overt" Soros program, and then other "dimensions" that included creating nongovernmental organizations and bringing Iranian contacts to Europe.

Jahanbegloo stated that the Wilson Center "receives most of its money . . . from the US Congress," and spoke of conferences where he met Americans and some Israelis "who were mostly intelligence agents."

The new art of Iran's increasingly media-aware intelligence services, the films included President Bush during a speech, promising to ensure that "the untamed fire of freedom will reach the darkest corners of our world." The first movie also showed Russian president Vladimir Putin—who had clamped down on NGOs across Russia over concerns of similar, Western-sponsored unrest—complaining about such prodemocracy efforts.

After showing scenes of street violence abroad, and then in Iran, the narrator asks, "How are Velvet Revolutions led? Which country is next?"

Esfandiari described how her center was a "highway" for Iranian speakers to come to the United States, to find fellowships and provide analysis. The U.S. government would also provide some money for research. The aim, she said, was "to create a little change in decision-making bodies inside Iran, a sort of change from within."

· · ·

COLLEAGUES AND FAMILY MEMBERS decried the interviews with the prisoners, who had not been able to meet with lawyers for weeks. They were "coerced" and nothing more than "propaganda," they said in a statement. Esfandiari's daughter, Washington lawyer Haleh Bakhash, dismissed the "KGB-style television 'confession' . . . a typical secret-police job of deception, vicious in intent yet clumsily contrived," and made clear her mother "sounded wooden—unnatural and coerced." [180] Writing in the *Washington Post,* she said, "When the television program ended, I felt contempt for my mother's jailers and interrogators. But I was filled with admiration for my mother [who] preserved her dignity, held her head high, and did not lie."

It was a convincing show in Iran, one analyst in Tehran told me. "They didn't say anything that would amount to a confession," he said. [181] "However, when put together with the [Velvet Revolution] documentary, very, very professionally, with the comments of [all] the individuals, it did give you a feeling: 'Ah, these guys were working together in a network that is so extensive and [well established] that it would be able to topple the regime."

And there was no doubt that the regime's respect for the power of cinema—first voiced by Khomeini, and used to great effect with the front-line *Revayat-e Fath* episodes during the war—remained. The Supreme Leader himself in 2006 told filmmakers: "Your influence is many times as much as . . . that of a clergyman or a preacher or writer. If I say that your influence is ten times as much, it is surely more. Therefore, you can see that there is a great difference between the influence of a well-produced motion picture and the influence of the pulpit!" [182]

Still, *this* propaganda film didn't impress everyone in the target audience. "They haven't made any serious confession," said Nilufar, a Tehran housewife. [183] "I see the whole thing as being stupid. Anybody that has been deprived of sleep and tortured would say anything they want."

After the broadcast, state radio gloated that the "wide reaction by

Western media and governments" to the case "indicates a calculated conspiracy to topple the [Islamic] system in Iran."

In fact, the imprisonment of these dual citizens demonstrated something else. It was put clearly to me by Iranian-American expert Karim Sadjadpour, whose own computer hard drive was unceremoniously copied by Iranian agents at the airport when he had last left Tehran in mid-2005. Sadjadpour later received warnings against returning to Iran and was active in trying to secure the release of jailed colleagues. He said hard-liners were making a Machiavellian calculation.

"Whereas Khatami and the reformists said our best security is people's happiness, [this hard-line] worldview is that it is much better to be feared than loved," Sadjadpour told me.[184] "Their behavior is much more out of desperation than of strength. It doesn't show that you are very confident about your place as a regime, when sixty-seven-year-old women are being suspected of undermining Iran's national security."

After her release in Tehran, Haleh Esfandiari had become a celebrity. From a government clerk who told her, "We are so proud of you," to four university students who said she was their new "role model," Esfandiari wrote that "numerous encounters with strangers on the street suggested that the footage of the Ukrainian and Georgian 'velvet revolutions' had exactly the opposite effect than the one the government had intended."[185]

At her local greengrocer, "A woman in a black chador gave me a big smile and said: 'We are so happy you are out. May God burn them in hell.'"

" 'Inshallah,' added the greengrocer. God willing."

ESFANDIARI WAS RELIEVED THAT the regime's Velvet Revolution propaganda appeared to have so little impact. But she did not expect the regime itself to forget the gravity of its own charges. Yet one year after she returned to Washington, she received a formal invitation from Iran's UN ambassador to attend a reception for President Mahmoud Ahmadinejad.

"The irony was overwhelming," writes Esfandiari. And it was also telling, of the whimsy that can color Iran's security game:[186]

> The very government that a year earlier had branded me a spy, an agent of Mossad and the CIA, an enabler of "soft revolution," and a threat to national security was inviting me to appear in the same room with the Iranian president and perhaps to engage with him in idle chatter . . .

But I should not have been surprised. Iran's leaders are heedless of the damage they inflict on the lives of individuals and families. They assume everyone else is as indifferent to basic human decency as they. They pretend to forget what they did to me—and the worse torment they inflicted on countless others.

"Apolitical, Amoral, Demoralized . . ."

Battered by the culture wars that marred the Khatami era and smashed the reform movement, many of its former foot soldiers simply withdrew from politics. But the regime did not stop its effort to entice them to the polls in the March 2008 parliamentary elections, to provide another "epic" turnout that would prove to the world—once again—the divine perfection and popularity of Iran's Islamic state.

No one doubted that conservatives would maintain their majority, especially after the Guardian Council rejected more than 2,200 reform-minded candidates. The regime machine pushed all the usual get-out-the-vote buttons. Supreme Leader Khamenei declared the election a "great test of dignity and sovereignty" for the nation.[187] Voting, as it had been throughout the life of the Islamic Republic, was a "religious duty."

Even former president Khatami called for a high turnout, arguing that every reformist seat would chip away at hard-line dominance. "The vote is the ultimate criteria," he said.[188] "Those who do not believe in the vote are not friends of the people."

But when I asked a few Iranians who had voted for Khatami in the past, I found that few were listening to their fallen hero now—most had given up on elections. The vast demographic that had once dominated electoral politics was instead marked by apathy. Iran's young people may have made up two-thirds of the population, but they seemed terminally discouraged by the poor economy, the triumph of hard-line conservatives, and the sad conviction that their vote changed nothing.

The cultural guerrilla Alireza Mahfouzian—that girlfriend-kissing skier and victim of multiple lashings for social infractions, who was trying to make a go of it selling brain and tongue sandwiches—told me he wasn't stepping near a polling station.

The pickup king Siavash—that Persian Casanova who trawled for women in traffic jams and cherished American films and Western culture, the prince with the "I'm too sexy for my love" ringtone—told me he could not care less about this election.

And political choice was something that one Tehran law student and painter, who chose the pseudonym Tooska, told me she had given up long before. She voted in 2005, to try to stop Ahmadinejad and "Islamic fascism," but it did little good. She wasn't going to vote again.

How did Iran's young people—70 percent of the population, so many of whom felt no affinity for the Islamic Republic as it was then constituted—manage to live with their current reality?

"The Islamic system [*nezam*] will exist for all my life, at least," Tooska told me, as we sat in one of her favorite coffee shops, a frequent target of morality police.[189] "It certainly affects my life—I just tolerate it. I oblige myself to tolerate what I can't change. You can't be angry every morning, all the time, with the fucking country. I have friends [who] wake up in the morning, shouting and angry. I hate it the most, but I just tolerate."

But Tooska's rage did rise about the double standard she saw imposed by the demands of whimsical power and official faith. "I don't think they really believe what they say," she said of the regime leadership. "There are some rules in Islam they don't follow. They shouldn't be rich, they shouldn't womanize, they shouldn't lie—moral things.

I am not a religious person, and I don't do those things. But they say, 'Don't do,' and they do it."

So like many liberal Iranians, both exhausted and disgusted by politics, Tooska refused to vote in March 2008 and had instead created her own parallel universe, a semi-underground cultural life.

In *that* world existed all freedoms.

"Everyone hates [the hard-liners]—not just me," Tooska told me. "But my circle of friends is a very little minority. In my minority, it's not freedom, it's my right. I can paint whatever I want."

Tooska chafed at the headscarf, and drank plenty of alcohol—she had polished off an entire bottle of Smirnoff vodka with two friends, playing poker, the night before we first met. She smoked forty cigarettes a day. Tooska worshipped Western film directors, as evidenced by the bank of DVDs in her apartment. Tooska's older sister was married and lived in London, volunteering at a well-known art gallery.

Tooska was the anti-*osulgara,* the anti-principlist, and described herself irreverently as *la-eek,* a religious nonbeliever. She could wear her headscarf tight and right, and when black it projected an unsmiling soldier-of-the-Revolution edge. More often she wore her hijab loosely neglected, framing with stylish flair (if she had not shaved her head) a baby face of soft features, full eyebrows, and thick lips.

In Tooska's wallet, along with an image of her latest boyfriend, she preciously kept a small black-and-white photograph of her grandfather, a cleric who wore a white turban and carried the title "Friend of God." It's no more than a worn passport photo, showing a handsome man with dark skin and alert eyes, his trim beard sprinkled with white, above an open-necked shirt and cloak. He died fifteen years before Tooska was born. She told me she keeps it there "because I think he looks like me." And certainly there was a resemblance between this beauty of the present and her decades-dead ancestor.

When growing up, Tooska's father only permitted listening to classical music. His uncompromising diktat extended to books. Only science and nonfiction were allowed in the house, and no fiction save for J. D. Salinger—because her dad had translated it. Tooska was forced to take violin instruction for ten years, and recalls grim lessons learning "sad" classical music from a legless cripple bound to his wheelchair. "You can imagine a hyper ten-year-old girl," she says, still relieved it is over. "I couldn't bear that."

So Tooska's laptop computer was loaded with a musical smorgasbord. Often when we met during subsequent visits to Iran, usually late at night or in the early hours of the morning, her computer would play an eclectic musical mix, reflecting love and longing. Ricky Martin to Vivaldi. "Nights in White Satin" to James Blunt's "You're Beautiful." She sings along to Santana, and to the hauntingly lyrical voice of Israeli singer Yasmin Levy, with her emotional repertoire that mixes flamenco rhythms sung in Ladino, the language of the Jews forced in 1492 to flee—along with Muslim Andalusians—medieval Spain.

Tooska pleasured also in the ruminative flow of film scores. And once she made a point of playfully queuing up for me a gift from her boyfriend, the seductive back-and-forth, man-and-woman song "Yes Boss," by the Danish band Hess Is More:

> *Hello Sweet Pie.*
> *I am really glad you could make it.*
> *I think we should get straight to business.*
> *Show me what you've got.*
> *It's all yours . . .*
>
> *Yes, Boss, I'm on the mike.*
> *I'll try to give you what you like.*
> *I can be soft, I can be hard.*
> *Let me do the B part, please, please . . .*[190]

A mischievous smile lit up Tooska's face, as if she were sharing a secret. And indeed her musical canon was full of surprises. On another visit I found her grooving to some of the most hard-line religious chants, ideologically pure Shiite Iran, tracks that she kept on her cell phone. Her fiercely religious ringtone always drew stares.

Sitting in her tiny Tehran apartment at three o'clock one morning, smoking long, slim cigarettes after a night waiting tables, Tooska rested her body—a marvel of youth and Persia that could easily be the subject of the nudes that she painted; a capable machine, when cared for, that had won prizes in national martial arts competition. But she hadn't worked out since she lost a karate match months before, and took the job at an arty hole-in-the-wall restaurant that served exquisite ratatouille.

In the fight Tooska had been hitting well, but her opponent managed to get in three strikes to the neck with her foot. "I fouled her the worst I could do," Tooska admitted. "I was so angry. There was blood in my eye." No longer training, she was missing the rigor of the mats: "My body needs it—it's asking for me," she told me. "When I do karate I am so happy, so full of energy. But no more."

Tooska was as impulsive as she was obsessive, and will again one day heed the calls of her coach and return to the gym, knotting her karate brown belt at her waist. In a fit of depression after a messy breakup in 2007, she carved her left arm with a knife. Tooska's key ring had a scorpion set in plastic, to help her confront a phobia of cockroaches: "This is what I fear most," she said of the choice bauble.

This night she was eager to share, to listen again to her favorite ideological chants in modernized electronic versions—like Christian rock, Shiite style. She sang along, translating the meaning of the insistent religious beat, lighting cigarettes. The place it takes her could not be further from James Blunt's high-pitched love songs, but these Iranian lyrics clearly touched Tooska's twenty-two-year-old soul:

> Some days I think my sins have done something to me,
>   so I feel guilty in front of you;
> From my shame, I can't even look at you,
> My eyes are closed.
> My heart burns from my sighing . . .
> I think about the day they took me.
> I remember crying out from the pressure of the grave,

I remember the torture on my body,
I think about two angels asking me, and I see myself silent.

I think about it, weak because they hit my body,
So they ask me, who is your god?

Tooska was taken aback and enthralled at the same time, wondering where this rough voice could come from, from what part of a man's throat. "Listen to his words, this violence!" she said, before singing further along. She meant no disrespect. "You know what I like about this Islamic music? I listen to these things, and no one does that. Because I think it's very special. It's very exciting. It's very monotone—just a guy shouting, and there is no music, maybe some things they use [for rhythm]. It's violent. It's impressive. From his voice you can get what you want. It's very powerful."

Such a lesson in religious hardness seemed unlikely in this studio apartment, from a Westernized Iranian woman who—if appearances were anything to go by—had discarded all devotion. Tooska's knowledge was incomplete, but her spiritual desire was real.

"Listen to this one. It's my favorite. It's beautiful. It's sad. Very sad. I listen to this one on repeat," she told me, switching to another track on her phone. "He's calling someone called Uncle Abbas, who is the son of one of the Imams—I don't know which one. He's famous." Yes he was: Abol Fazl was the standard-bearer of Imam Hossein on the plains of Karbala who fought valiantly in the Ashura battle centuries ago. Tooska said there were techno versions of these songs that had an even wider appeal, among Iran's many godless youth.

"They turn it very loud in their cars," Tooska told me as the beat took hold of her. "Because you know, in Ashura people just go out to see each other. It's a party. We call it a 'Hossein Party'—it's the name for Ashura. The fact that's it's religious is important for me, because it's one of the impressions of that song. Even if it were Christian, or anything, I would like it. But the fact that it's Muslim—this is important. Because it has some factors of Islam: it's violent, you know, it suits. It really does."

BUT SUCH DABBLING IN religious cadences was not enough to convince Tooska to vote again for the so-called *Islamic* Republic. She had become, along with fellow nonvoters Siavash and Mahfouzian, further evidence that the "dream of democracy in Iran is dead," for those critics who believed Iran's century-long struggle for democracy was close to "final defeat." According to political scientist Abbas Milani, "Young Iranians, these skeptics say, have become nothing short of Nietzsche's 'Last Man'—apolitical, amoral, demoralized, selfish, and hedonistic."[191]

The Sage was depressed about such a widespread boycott of the March 2008 vote, decrying it as a gift to conservatives, which completed their work of stamping out reformist influence—with the help of reformists themselves. For the Sage, creating parallel realities was just denying reality.

In his small top-floor apartment in downtown Tehran, we ordered out for pizzas. They came, greasy as usual, with oven-browned cheese and packets of ground chili and ketchup to sprinkle and squirt across the top. The Sage bit into a modest slice as he identified one worrying characteristic in "the mind of the people." There was little middle ground, he said. Iranians practiced "either total obedience or riots and resistance."[192]

Both could be dangerous, the Sage complained. And very often, for Iranians, those extremes stemmed from misperceptions of reality, or irrational decisions, or trying to keep up with the Joneses—or a combination of all three. Of several examples, he told me of a family that spent a thousand dollars on a gravestone of Brazil granite. It was a family whose patriarch made just a scratch more than one dollar each day—one "Khomeini," as the green ten-thousand-rial note with an image of the Imam is sometimes called. They would be considered among the most vulnerable, the most needy in society.

"It's all about appearances—to have the highest model, even though we are miserable as a result," said the Sage, reaching for his glass of tea between slices of pizza. "For some strange reason, people allow themselves to have expectations that have no relation to reality. Something only available in a dream world, they say: 'I want it now.' "

By purchasing the gravestone, the family had "put themselves under pressure for something which is useless: a stone," the Sage told me. "They are playing like they are someone else. What's common is the denial of reality [that pretends] we aren't what we are."

The Sage fell into a contemplative mood as he stepped into the kitchen to pour more tea. "I *believed,* pre-Revolution. But that's *out,*" the Sage lamented. He poured concentrated tea from a smaller kettle into our two glasses, then diluted it with boiling water from a second kettle. No sugar.

"What's *in* is to fly—to act as if you are high up there. This is why people give [parliament] seats to the conservatives. They detach themselves [from reality] and live in a fantasy world."

FOR THE SAGE, THAT "fantasy" included the belief that voting was useless, and that conservatives would somehow recognize that the majority of Iranians wanted change, if that majority stayed at home on voting day. Already the right wing had wisely engineered every advantage for itself, and there was no disguising the official preference for the "principlist" faction supporting Ahmadinejad.

Banners at Friday prayers in Tehran before the vote proclaimed: "If you want a nation of Islamic solidarity, we should follow the *principles* which we share and not waste our time on side issues." [193] Instead of using the usual word for "ideals," *armanha,* the banner used the word *osul*—a deliberate sign of backing for the *osulgaran,* the "principlists." Another banner read: "Following and sticking with *osul* will lead to an increase in power."

Belting it out at the podium, the vitriolic Friday prayer leader Ahmad Khatami preached that voting would "nip seditions in the bud," and then went much further. First he told a laudatory story about how

President Ahmadinejad had traveled much more freely in Iraq during his recent visit than George W. Bush could.

"When Bush is traveling in the region, even the stewardess on the flight does not know where they are going," the black-turbaned cleric crowed, his gloating tone unmistakable.[194] "But we clearly state the agenda of President Ahmadinejad."

And what about the candidates themselves, and their campaigns? "Do not be cheated by these slogans," the ultraconservative cleric warned. "The *right* people should be chosen, based on the sayings of the Leader, which clearly show us the way. Is he religious? Or pretending to be religious? Protect our Leader; make the Imam of the Age [Mahdi] happy for us."

On the eve of the vote, conservatives spoke with knowing confidence. Reformists would never win—this election or any future one—because they had "desecrated" Islamic Republic values during their weeks-long sit-in at parliament to protest the mass expulsion of candidates. "Anyone who is a True Believer does not accept that. . . . This conduct has been indefensible and paved the way for the enemies' abuse," Shahabeddin Sadr, a hard-line Tehran MP, told a press conference.[195]

It was simple, said fellow hard-line parliamentarian Ali Asghar Zarei. The Islamic system was indestructible, and the latest UN sanctions only showed "that Westerners are blind and dumb towards Iran's realities."

Sitting beside those two men was none other than Dr. Alireza Zakani, the veteran front-line doctor I first met in 1997—the Tehran University Basij chief who first told me about the "magic" of the martyrs in the former Iran-Iraq War battlefield, who gave me a checkered *basiji* scarf with a bloodstain. I had tried to track him down many times over the years, with no luck. After reading my story back then, he had complained to my translator Nahid Hosseinpour because I pointed out that not every Iranian believed as deeply as he did. In my defense, she replied that he would not find a Western journalist who would write with greater understanding and get it into the newspaper.

Zakani appeared hardly changed, though he had aged with the physical depletions of his faith and the stress of national politics in Iran. The handshake with his right hand was still weak from paralyzing wounds; his kindly face was framed by short gray stubble and gold wire-rimmed glasses. Zakani's dark forehead scar—from prayer, not war—was still split in two. These days he was more MP, in his suit jacket and top-buttoned white shirt, than *basiji* ideologue and war veteran.

But Zakani was still 100 percent True Believer.

Just as he was that day more than a decade earlier, when he first described to me his front-line epiphanies, the surrender of Iraqi troops from the marsh reeds, and how it all locked within him an ironclad commitment to the Islamic Revolution. When we talked alone days later—he had quite a fine silver watch peeking out from under the sleeve of his gray suit jacket—Zakani told me of his dream. "The society we have in mind has development and construction, an increase in spirituality and religious belief, under the wing of freedom and independence," he said.[196] All that would send "a message of peace and friendship to the world."

Zakani's gray hair had a tight cut, and he spoke as if Ahmadinejad and the hard-liners were just starting out and had not already been in power more than two and a half years.

"We are at the beginning of the way," the parliamentarian said. "Now we have laid the groundwork and it will take time for this planning to take effect" to remove financial disparities. The *osulgaran* (principlist) view "is like a new plant that has flourished, that has just come out of the ground," Zakani asserted. We were meeting in a grimy political office downtown, which clearly had not received any of Iran's oil money. "I hope it can solve the problem it faces. It will take years."

The biggest danger wasn't foreign threats—which the scarred veteran dismissed, because Iranians were "awake and active and aware"— but the fact that Iran had distanced itself from the main goals of the

Revolution. Zakani's war experience was invaluable, he said, in understanding the problem. "The hardships of *those* days taught us to withstand the difficulty of *these* days, and to choose the best path to these goals," Zakani said, his eyes as sharp and his nose set as strongly as ever.

"We don't say all the achievements of the West are bad. The West has many hardworking people who left great things for humanity," Zakani told me. "[But] when we say 'freedom,' we don't think that is an achievement of the West. Islam gives a better meaning of freedom."

As for Westoxicated Iranians, they could not rule. "We oppose them [as] decision makers to decide the path of the country. . . . We don't have problems with them, except those dependent on outsiders. This is very ugly for us," Zakani said. He did not understand how some Iranians had "lost themselves" in their infatuation of the West. Those "dependent" on foreign countries, he was quite sure, deserved no mercy.

THE DECISION OF THE people on voting day was a foregone conclusion. Conservatives were out in force, in keeping with Khomeini's instruction that I saw printed on a banner strung across a main avenue: "Elections are a holy duty." [197]

Many reformists stayed home, after so many of their candidates were barred from running. I spoke to Iranians standing in line to cast their ballots. And also to six men standing in the morning sun drinking tea on the sidewalk fifty yards from one polling station—an ornate and very old blue-tiled prayer hall overcome by the aging and overused neighborhood all around it. They weren't voting, they told me, because "we don't believe in them anymore."

From tomatoes to rent, prices had soared with an inflation rate of 19 percent. Iran's nuclear defiance had brought several sets of UN and American sanctions, and nearly war. But that didn't stop Ashraf Banoo Rahimikia from casting her vote for allies of Ahmadinejad— and racing to a downtown Tehran polling station before it closed just to do so. She was not alone and helped conservatives achieve a 70 percent majority in parliament, with a 60 percent turnout of eligible voters.

"We like Ahmadinejad [despite] all the problems. Prices have gone up, but I will vote for him again. He understands people," Rahimikia told me.[198] Life was hard; she had raised two children alone since her husband died in the Iran-Iraq War. "Though people are against him, he is one of us. We don't have high expectations from him, but he is fighting and that is good enough for us."

Such sentiment would have been balm to the Supreme Leader, who had clearly supported Ahmadinejad's faction. Khamenei pronounced that the "epic turnout defeated the enemies' craft and cunning and turned their psychological warfare . . . into an empty bubble."[199] *Kayhan* crowed that Iranians had once again "entrusted" parliament to the principlists.

But questions were raised about the integrity of the vote. Official observers from reformist groups were made to leave some polling stations as counting began. Journalists were ordered to leave the Ministry of Interior, which ran the election, before the count. And while polling stations were meant to be free from party materials, I was surprised to see, affixed below some ballot boxes, posters from the "morals committee" of the official election commission, which showed a photograph of Ahmadinejad and a field of red flowers, with the promise that "another spring is waiting."[200]

"This was not a real election, it was completely engineered," one reformist voter told me after seeing the initial results. "This is fixed and that's sad. Once people start giving up on elections, that is the end."

I EXPECTED SUCH DOUBT from many young Iranians, and from those in the reformist camp. But I was not prepared for the depth of disillusion that I also came across, unexpectedly, among those who sacrificed the most for the Islamic Republic. Just days after that March 2008 vote, I was at Behesht-e Zahra cemetery, picking my way slowly among the graves, when I looked ahead and stopped in my tracks. Several slabs away, one man was hunkered over and crying, wearing a suit and sitting on a small stool. He clearly spent a lot of time here, tearfully attentive to one stone in Section 27.[201]

I watched from a distance, at first. The man's mobile phone was on the grave, playing music like a radio. He was relatively young, not a veteran himself. But one whose heart was here, who would have understood the slogan I had just seen on a poster pasted up by the "Basij of Sobhan Mosque," which read: "The martyrs are the stones along our way, so we don't get lost."

I edged closer, and when I entered his consciousness, he looked at me quizzically, through reddened eyes. With a nod he allowed me to join him, and then we talked. It was his older brother, the martyr who lay at our feet, who had insisted on volunteering to fight. The man's fondest memory was not of the weaponry his brother brought home from the front—impressive though the assault rifle was to a seven-year-old. It was instead the day in 1982 when Khorramshahr—the City of Blood—was liberated from the Iraqis. The brother had not even signed up yet to fight, but he was so excited at the victory he bought ice creams for the whole neighborhood and distributed them from a cardboard box.

That became an annual family tradition: eating ice creams on Khorramshahr's day of freedom.

"When he wanted to go to the war, my dad wouldn't let him," recalled the mourner, wiping away his tears. His brother had been nineteen and had replied: "If you don't let me go, I will jump in front of a car and kill myself." Two years later a piece of shrapnel tore into the son's head. His brother said he was proud. Others from the neighborhood had returned early from the front, afraid. But his brother had stayed on and came home in a coffin, his duty fulfilled to God and country.

The man ran the tips of his fingers through the rose water he had sprinkled on the white stone, tracing the etched calligraphy. It was a poem:

Let me kiss your hand, O mother,
   who raised me to be free.
Come and look, Daddy,
   see that your child has wed.
I'm going to the first night of my marriage happy . . .
Tell my dear Mother, a martyr never dies.

The loss was worth it, this man said, for the Revolution. But that's where his pride stopped. Did he feel any pride today, for what the Revolution had become?

No, was the answer. And it tore at his heart.

"A lot of things get undermined," said the man, resigned, sitting up straighter as our talk turned to politics and away from the war. When his brother died, the family was offered an apartment in town. The mother chastised the official who made the offer, with the words, "I didn't give my son's blood for money."

The Iranian shook his head. Clean-shaven, he worked as a technician in the paint section of a car factory. The ideological underpinnings that sustained him for years had obviously been giving way for some time.

The reasons behind his family's level of commitment to the Islamic system, to this nebulous *nezam,* were now being questioned every day. "A lot of people say, 'Why did we start a Revolution?' People are asking themselves this question," the man told me. The government—everybody, in fact—was "undermining it. And they are doing a lot of things in the name of the Revolution. Literally, they are cutting people's heads off in the name of the Revolution."

7

The Rising

We are up against a person who says black is white and four times four equals five. He looks into the camera and lies with self-confidence. There is nothing worse than when a government lies to its own people.

—candidate Mir Hossein Mousavi, June 2009

IN THE MONTHS LEADING up to the June 2009 presidential election, President Mahmoud Ahmadinejad aimed for a second term, to make conservative rule of Iranian politics a permanent reality. Iran's security chiefs, most of them hard-line cohorts of the Supreme Leader and Ahmadinejad, had been acting on their declarations that the biggest threat to the Revolution came from inside.

Campaigners of all kinds, from labor leaders and journalists to students and women, were accused of endangering national security and fomenting Velvet Revolution. High on the target list was Nobel Peace Prize winner Shirin Ebadi, whose Center for Human Rights Defenders was shuttered in December 2008. Then on January 1—in a menacing start to Iran's tumultuous 2009—vigilantes swarmed Ebadi's apartment and offices as police looked on. They spray painted black and red graffiti across the walls outside and defaced the office sign. Ebadi deliberately did not remove it, "so everyone will see it," she told me later with characteristic grit.[1] The challenge "makes me stronger."

That choice probably also suited the hostile crowd of militants who painted the message—their handiwork part of a bid to unsettle Iran's best-known human rights lawyer. "Ebadi, death to the witch of America," read the scrawl on the garage door, the word "witch" misspelled in Farsi. Nearby was another message: "Shame on the holder of the pen of the enemy."

"The people who accuse me of working with the U.S. know themselves that it is not right," Ebadi told me. Since winning the Nobel in 2003, she had received numerous death threats. Recently there were false rumors that she had forsaken Islam, worked with the enemy, and was a CIA agent, thereby "providing their supporters the excuse to engage in my physical elimination and assassination." [2]

The lawyer had often been critical of the United States, too, over abuses at Guantanamo Bay and Abu Ghraib. But her work was counterrevolutionary as far as the self-declared arbiters of Iran's ideological purity were concerned. And this was not new. A decade earlier, Ebadi had told the *Monitor*, "Any person who pursues human rights in Iran must live with fear from birth to death, but I have learned to overcome my fear." [3]

The renewed pressure in 2009 told more about the regime's lack of confidence than it did about any real threat from outside, she said. "This will not lead me to leave Iran or to give up my work. What I am doing is based on the law, and they can't stop me," Ebadi told me. [4] "A government that is powerful is more open to criticism. [This one] is scared."

The regime was seeing the ghost of regime-change past and confusing it with democracy. "As for what is called a soft or Velvet Revolution, we have no crime by that name on our legal code," Ebadi once said. [5] "What has happened in countries such as Georgia is simply the victory of one political party over another. When a political party is active, it tries to achieve power and Iran has always claimed that it gives power to political parties to act. So why should they be so sensitive over this question of a Velvet Revolution?"

In fact, Ebadi resented Washington's "prodemocracy" spending in

Iran, saying it "damaged the human rights situation in Iran." What was true too was that it was also damaging her. Seyed Mohammad Marandi, the head of North American studies at Tehran University, said Ebadi and the women who had launched the One Million Signatures Campaign to reform laws that discriminate against women were seen by some Iranians as sellouts.

"The problem is Ebadi and those people going for the signatures are not seen as homegrown activists," Marandi told me.[6] "[People] think Western interests are behind it. . . . So they feel they have no place here. They are seen as people getting funding from abroad."

The UN General Assembly had just passed a resolution expressing "deep concern at serious human rights violations" in Iran.[7] Iranian officials insisted that every one of the 346 offenders executed in 2008—the count of Amnesty International, and the highest in the world after China—were in accord with the law. In the months prior to the June 2009 vote, Amnesty described stepped-up "arbitrary arrests and harassment" of more than 220 people in one three-month period.[8]

Mohsen Sazegara, the revolutionary turned editor and critic who helped found the Revolutionary Guard, was despondent at the encroaching repression. "We unfortunately have gone back to thirty-five years ago, like 1972, 1973—the Shah," Sazegara told me from his exile in Washington.[9] "In those days, [the Shah] was a simple believer, too. He believed that he could run a country by dictatorship. By SAVAK—his secret police—and army. Ayatollah Khamenei has gone back to that policy. A dictator. One person, ruling a country with the Ministry of Intelligence and the Revolutionary Guard. That's it."

Years earlier, before he was forced to leave Iran, Sazegara had written to the Leader pointing out how "Iranian despotism" had returned despite the Revolution—and that one day Khamenei would have to take responsibility.[10] But now it was too late to reverse such a precarious, shortsighted policy. The Shah had made a similar mistake.

"[Khamenei] thinks he has all the power, and he doesn't need any [other] participation. When you marginalize social groups, sooner or later they will come to the scene of politics suddenly, sometimes with an election, sometimes for a demonstration," Sazegara predicted.[11] "Sociologists call it a revolution. If it's violent, it's a violent revolution. But if it is nonviolent, then it is a Velvet Revolution. That doesn't make any difference. It is not correct anymore to call this a mullah regime. You have to call it a police state. We have gone back to our traditional twenty-five hundred years of despotism."

The only difference, he said, was that the "old" despotism had been legalized by the Revolution, enshrined in Article 5 of the constitution as supreme rule by the "just and pious *faqih*."

"This is a regime that creates two absolutes: The absolute power of the regime, and the absolute weakness of the people," Sazegara told me. "And that's the reason they can say to the people of Iran: 'I am absolutely powerful, because I can confront the United States. And all the power in the world to persuade the people [otherwise] is useless. If you fight against me, I can close any newspaper, I can jail everybody.' "

That had turned Sazegara into an activist, someone who really was gunning for a Velvet Revolution in Iran: "It's my duty, and the duty of people like me, to prepare the tools, the organizations for the people, to facilitate their movement, as much as we can."

BUT CAMPAIGNERS IN TEHRAN were still looking to make change within the confines of the Islamic system, the *nezam*. And despite the critics and threats, among the most active was the grassroots effort to improve the legal status of women, to make it equal with men. Volunteers trying to get one million signatures for a petition were often detained by police. High-profile attempts to hold street protests were shut down with scores of arrests.

"They know our population is seventy million, so if we gather one million signatures, it is nothing," the campaign leader, Parvin Ardalan told me, speaking in her tiny apartment.[12] "The important thing is, the action we do is increasing consciousness in society and thinking of equality." The steps taken against the group and multiple court cases had raised its profile. But the website of the One Million Signatures Campaign had been blocked twenty times. A spike of interest came when Ardalan was named winner of the 2007 Olof Palme Prize, then prevented from collecting it when she was ordered off the plane in Tehran moments before takeoff. Ardalan's passport had not yet been returned months later, when I met her.

But hanging proudly on the wall was her prize citation, which hailed the diminutive activist for "making the demand for equal rights for men and women a central part of the struggle for democracy in Iran." She had been sentenced to six months in jail for "spreading propaganda." The campaign also won the 2009 Simone de Beauvoir Prize for women's freedom, but the group decided—given the atmosphere in Iran—that it could not accept the thirty-thousand-euros prize money. Officials asserted that parliament had already taken several steps to redress gender inequalities and slowly expand women's rights. Ardalan told me that was no coincidence.

"We are now powerful. Of course, we didn't do anything, but they are afraid of us," she said, noting with a matter-of-fact smile that by early 2009 some two hundred thousand signatures were already collected. "We are changing discourse on women. They attack us . . . but they must adhere to the law. Of course we couldn't gather one million signatures, but one million people know about us."

The Iconoclast

Can these divisions in Iranian society be bridged? Are there examples that reach—even tentatively, however imperfectly—across the divide?

One of the least likely illustrations of what may be possible is the legendary hard-liner turned film director Masoud Dehnamaki. This slight, black-bearded former militant with sharp eyes and formidable commitment was, from the late 1990s, one of the most feared characters in the panoply of enemies of the reform movement.

A veteran of the Iran-Iraq War who was wounded three times, Dehnamaki has kept those memories close. His office years ago was made up to resemble the front line with a sandbagged bunker, helmets, and gas masks—and a sign requiring pre-prayer ablutions before entering. "I keep it like this because we are the generation of the war, and we don't want to forget its values in the daily routine," Dehnamaki told the *Monitor* in 1999.[13]

During the Khatami era, Dehnamaki was a founder of the Ansar-e Hezbollah vigilantes, edited a string of radical newspapers (one was called *Jebheh,* or *Front*), and finally created the Ansar newspaper *Ya Lesarat al-Hossein.* In the late 1990s he wielded a club—and the pen of his newspapers—to provoke lethal clashes with students and to attack reformists, mobilizing fellow vigilantes on their motorcycles and reigniting the use of violence in the reformist age.

Back then, political moderation was a disease to Dehnamaki, who told the *Monitor,* "When you see some people here dressed in American-style clothes, you are seeing the bullets of the West."

He was a key player in the storming of student dormitories at Tehran University in July 1999; several students died—sparking six days of unrest. Dehnamaki was detained and interrogated. The official investigation held Ansar responsible and found that the sheer presence of such a "famous member" of Ansar "was provocative, because students recognized him." And Ansar kept at it, in 2002 even declaring a "holy war" to rid Iran of prodemocracy reformists.[14]

Footage from the late 1990s shows Dehnamaki making a speech wearing a green military jacket and a black *chafiyeh* scarf, and a much thicker black beard. He is identified as the general commander of Ansar. But during interviews with me over several years, Dehnamaki was reluctant to talk about his head-cracking past. I insisted on an explanation, and finally he talked—if elliptically.

"I always remember something that I heard in my childhood: try not to be the wave, but the wave maker," the former militant told me in 2008.[15] "Creating Ansar, and leaving it, had a reason. . . . My [violent] methods did not meet well with their intentions."

He had told the *New York Times* about the seeds of his transformation, about how his fellow soldiers "gave their lives for ideals that never materialized." "There was a time that I believed that the people were the problem. But that was a mistake. The real problem are our rulers, who have become used to corruption and cannot fulfill the promises of the early days of the Revolution about social justice and equality." [16]

Dehnamaki turned out to be a serial iconoclast, and remained so even as he began trying out new weapons, turning to film to examine Iran's taboo social problems in a way that especially angered conservatives. His 2004 film about two soccer teams was a political allegory about rival political trends, which showed the teams *playing* each other, not *fighting* against each other. "In my film . . . I announced the end of the era [of violence]," Dehnamaki told me.

The former hard-liner wrote an open letter to Ahmadinejad, warning against his "fundamentalist and backward supporters," those people "who reduced promotion of virtue and prevention of vice to fighting against women's dress, and ignored justice in society." [17]

Greater impact was in store, as Dehnamaki's past right-wing credentials enabled this man to challenge prevailing myths about the Iran-Iraq War. Perhaps only he, among the pantheon of Iran's gifted film directors, could get away with the irreverent portrayal of the war in his 2006 blockbuster *Ekhrajiha (The Outcasts)*. In taking that tack, he revealed like no one else could how the sanctity of the "sacred" war was being redefined in Iranian society.

Dehnamaki had in fact leaped across Iran's political divide, from hidebound regime enforcer to the director of a groundbreaking film that raked in a record $1 million in one month, with a total take of $2.5 million. *Ekhrajiha* is based on many of the unlikely young volunteers Dehnamaki came to command during the war, a reflection of reality that does not jibe with the official version that every recruit was a pure-hearted fighter for God.

Cloaked in comedy, *The Outcasts* tells of a gang member named Majid "Suzuki" who gets out of prison, and he and several friends—irreverent misfits, junkies, and thieves who are disdainful of the official revolutionary zeal of the time—decide to prove themselves by signing up to fight.[18] When the men finally make it to the front line, they are dismissed by self-declared Believers who are supposedly ready to become martyrs, and who fight in God's name, out of spiritual devotion. "Their presence destroys the order of the war," one officer confides to another about the misfits.

In the process, Majid the thug is transformed. He risks his life, stepping across a minefield that has already claimed several soldiers. Some characters who appeared much more religious turn out to be cowards or weak. One religious man hides during a firefight and asks for divine explanation: "God, why did you bring me here to show me that they changed and I didn't? God, you've won."

Ekhrajiha elicited stinging criticism when it came out; Dehnamaki's former Ansar comrades denounced it as irreligious and countered it with their own documentaries. A soldier who fought alongside Dehnamaki during a 1987 offensive went to see it with the director. "As I was watching the film, I got angry," Said Abu Taleb, a parliamentary adviser, told Babak Dehghanpisheh of *Newsweek*.[19] "I kept turning to him and cussing him out. I said, 'What is this, you idiot?' I thought the movie was insulting to veterans. It's also an insult to the Holy Defense movies."

Still, he acknowledged a shift from Dehnamaki's past club-wielding ways: "Someone who used insults and shouting to get his message across has now moved on to something more sophisticated. Someone who wanted to push his views by force is now using art. That's very important."

Ekhrajiha had a spellbinding effect on the audience. "The message is that this country is for everyone, with different political tendencies," Dehnamaki told me of the film, when I first met him in 2007.[20] "It's breaking the clichés, and many people did not like that. In *Ekhrajiha* we knew how to play with those red lines [about the official version of the war] but did not cross them."

The Sage was especially impressed at the film's unexpected social-bridging qualities. Dehnamaki had provided a "recipe of salvation," he said, for Iranians deeply divided between hard-liners—many of them veterans who looked down on those who did not make similar sacrifices—and reformists, who sometimes deemed the war a historical footnote with little connection to their Western-leaning lives.[21]

"In the audience you had all-chadored [black-cloaked] women, and bad-*hijabi* girls [with loose headscarves]," the Sage told me, still marveling. "He brought them together, side by side."

THE POWER AND APPEAL of Dehnamaki's work lay in harnessing the extremes of Iran's revolutionary experience, of reforging the one-dimensional portrayal of the war into a universal message.

"I'm stuck between the blades of a pair of scissors," Dehnamaki told me.[22] And he of all people knew how dangerous, in Iran, that sharp place could be. I asked if he worried about his own safety. "The person who used to step on mines has no fear. Does he have any fear?"

The *Ekhrajiha* trilogy focused on how the doubt that had been sweeping Iranian society was due to incorrect practice, not to faulty ideals. "I'm not disillusioned. Disillusioned people usually sideline themselves," Dehnamaki told me. "*I'm alive*. That is exactly the reason I am being attacked so much. They would love me to sideline myself so they can put me in a museum."

Points of Peace

Also attempting to bridge Iran's ideological divide—and redefine the meaning of the Iran-Iraq War—was Dr. Shahriar Khateri, director of the Tehran Peace Museum. Was that possible in an Islamic state where endless acres were dedicated to war dead? Where endless tears of mourning and pride had fallen for loved ones lost in the "sacred defense"? And where endless sermons had turned martyrdom into the highest form of worship?

In that soil, planting a seed of peace by opening a museum that showcased the horrors of war was never going to be easy. Yet the Peace Museum was dedicated in mid-2007 and opened in early 2008.

"The people of Iran always hear about the glories of war, when we were invaded, but they rarely hear of the devastation of war," Khateri told me.[23] He was one of Iran's top experts on the impact of chemical weapons and volunteered to fight at the age of fifteen. "It's not easy.

People charge that you are damaging the morale of those who will stand against the enemy. . . . A few officials still believe that peace is the same as surrender, because we are a country under permanent threat from enemies."

Hard-liners recoiled at the very idea. But the Peace Museum's volunteers were hardly typical peaceniks. They were former soldiers, victims of Iraqi chemical weapons attacks, and as committed as ever to the defense of their homeland. The museum had workshops for children, students, and the public to learn about the suffering caused by the war and chemical weapons. It had a studio to record oral histories of Iran-Iraq War veterans—modeled on those made by survivors at Hiroshima.

"Dozens of my close friends were killed in the war and hundreds were wounded, so I really respect their cause," Khateri told me. During the war, Iranians were told they were soldiers of God, fighting Iraqi infidels. But then Khateri received a lesson in universal suffering. Years later, when his group collected and returned remains of Iraqi soldiers to their families at the border, he saw unexpected similarities that made his heart turn against war and toward peace. The official narrative was wrong, that Iraqis were non-Believers.

"They call them 'family of martyrs,' just as we do," Khateri told me of the Iraqis. "It was really shocking psychologically to see those mothers, just like Iranian mothers, crying with photos in their hands, candles, and Qurans."

BUT CONVINCING THE "OTHER" in Iran is never easy—and may not always be possible. For art gallery owner Lili Golestan, understanding the conservatives who wanted to shut her down permanently—and the effort of trying to work with them—had consumed untold energy over the years. The once-fearless voices for cultural change had been squeezed to a whisper during the ideological retrenchment under President Mahmoud Ahmadinejad. The restrictions, the ignorance, the exclusionary mind-set, and capricious control of a tentacular regime over even the smallest, most inconsequential details were all proof that "worse" was always a possibility.

After engaging in cultural battle for decades, Golestan was depleted. The violent fracas over Ahmadinejad's 2009 reelection was a fight for air, after years in which the cultural space had been increasingly sucked of oxygen. Her cynicism was ingrained. When we first met in 2004, this elegant woman told me that any appearance of openness under Khatami was an illusion: "The deep thing is this Revolution, and the belief has not changed."

In the intervening five years, that belief had been revitalized and imposed anew. "They are always present," Golestan told me the day before the disputed 2009 election.[24] "They are always asking: 'What are you doing? What are you thinking? Why do you do this?' It bothers me very much. Always, I clash with them." Golestan said this milieu of regime enforcers was "coming from another planet."

But was it possible to coexist with them?

As a veteran cultural warrior, Golestan had received death threats during the chain killings of intellectuals in the late 1990s, when she was brave enough to hang even seminude paintings in her small gallery space. On the hit list thrown over the wall into her overgrown north Tehran garden, her name was sixth—the first four had already been killed. In mid-2009 I breathed deeply of the scent of that same garden, as I walked through and was welcomed into a large old house brimming with fine art and objects of exquisite beauty.

But Golestan's refined tastes—and her education and erudition— could not have been in starker contrast to those militants who would soon be on the streets, breaking heads full of thoughts like hers with batons, so that they could continue imposing their divine judgment upon Iranian society. Over the years, from Albert Camus to Gabriel Garcia Marquez, she had translated thirty-eight books. Five of them were permanently banned, some since the Shah's time. She hung a new exhibit in her gallery every week, and so had to be in frequent contact with the cultural filters of the Islamic Guidance Ministry.

"Before Ahmadinejad I would go there and talk with them, and they would listen to my opinion," Golestan told me. "But after Ahmadinejad, I don't go there because they don't understand me. We are two different people. We can't speak peacefully. They don't like me."

Those frustrations were founded on countless whimsical uncertainties, such as her Farsi translation of the 1968 cult French book *Mortelle (Mortal)* by Christopher Frank. "All the young people like it; in Iran it's famous, about a city made of glass, in which everyone can see each other—like here," explained Golestan. "For every movement you must get permission, you must have three pieces of paper and get it signed. They sew a smile on your mouth and everyone smiles in this town. At the end of the book, two lovers rip their smiles off and they die."

Her translation was censored by the Shah. Then after the Revolution it was published. By May 2009 it was in its tenth edition and had received approval three times during Ahmadinejad's time. Then on the morning of a Tehran book fair, Golestan was told: "Your book is out of the question; you can't sell it here." She was stunned. "I don't know why. I just laughed. I'm not going to argue with them anymore."

Thousands of book titles and films were being reassessed. The once acceptable was turning seditious. The Ministry of Culture and Islamic Guidance boosted the number of censors to keep up; hard-line parliamentarians wrote a scathing report of how hundreds of un-Islamic book titles had been permitted during the Khatami era. As author Kasra Naji notes,

Tolstoy's *Anna Karenina* was lambasted for having "spread the culture of drinking, normalized relationships between unmarried couples, undermined spiritual values, removed the stigma attached to sin, propagated vulgarity, promoted unethical traditions and glorified the aristocracy." Time and again, authors—new and old, domestic and foreign—were rejected by the censors with bland and vague expressions, such as "worthless," "lacking content" or "inappropriate." [25]

And when it came to art, the president himself had little time for anything but the products of the Revolution. "We want art that is on the offensive. Art on the offensive exalts and defends the noble principles, and attacks principles that are corrupt, vulgar, ungodly and inhuman," Ahmadinejad told state-run TV shortly after winning the 2005 vote.[26] "Art reaches perfection when it portrays the best life and best death. . . . Is there art that is more beautiful, more divine, and more eternal than the art of martyrdom? A nation with martyrdom knows no captivity."

"Captivity" was a relative term for cultural activists like Golestan, who were in despair. She told me the limitations of official taste testers were a problem:

The atmosphere is very sad; for the writers and painters, they are all very disappointed. You can't make a plan for the future—even one month in advance.

[Hard-line censors] are very poor and small and with nothing in their personality. They are not dangerous for me. I see them like a human being who has nothing: not culture, art, money, good food, good looks—they have nothing. I'm not against them, really. If I can do something for them [personally], I will do it.

We are all depressed because they can't do this, they can't do culture and art, because they don't know it, they are not educated in it. They don't let you come close to help, and we don't like to be close to them.

Years before, Golestan had said she was "against" President Khatami because "he didn't do anything." She had less time for Ahmadinejad, who was "sick in his mind. A megalomaniac, and he lies." More years of hard-line rule seemed impossible to contemplate. "We are tired now. I am tired. I don't have any energy. I don't have any more power to fight," Golestan told me.

They had summoned one of her artists for a talk. "The paintings are all portraits of young girls," the ministry official had told the artist. "Why are they so sad? We are making a very good atmosphere for you. They must laugh. Promise us to paint happy people next time."

The Return of the Reformists

Reformists had been the first victims, from the late 1990s, of the determination by conservative forces in Iran to reconquer, and hold for good, every layer of power in the Islamic Republic. Khatami had served his two terms as president and finished a defeated, discredited man.

Reformists needed a new figurehead. But months away from the 2009 presidential election, no new savior had emerged. Desperate, and sure that severe economic hardship and brutish political infighting among conservatives might jeopardize Ahmadinejad's chances, key reformists began to lobby Khatami to run again. Despite his failings, Khatami was one of the most recognized politicians in Iran. And after four years of Ahmadinejad, Khatami had again become one of its most popular.

Khatami procrastinated, saying publicly that he would only run if Iranians promised—this time—to scale back their expectations. Then he said he wouldn't run if Mir Hossein Mousavi—an architect and painter who had been prime minister during the 1980s but had been away from politics for two decades—would take up the reformist banner. Mousavi refused, at first.

Still, the political operatives who dreamed of a renaissance for reform were impatient and already hard at work laying down the foundations for a campaign that they hoped might challenge Ahmadinejad. In December 2008, two months before either man publicly announced his candidacy, this cadre of reformists secretly chose a color—green—that would eventually build into the opposition Green Movement.

"The color green is the color of good government, of Imam Hossein, of Imam Ali, of Islam," said Ebrahim Mehtari, a software engineer and one of the tight cell of seventeen young intellectuals—part of a broader secret group of eighty-eight—that were close to decision making.[27] They served as behind-the-scenes architects of the opposition campaign, and many would later end up behind bars. Choice of the color green first became public nearly seven months before the June 2009 vote, when hundreds of thousands of copies of posters—150,000 in a single day—were printed that showed Khatami, as president nearly a decade earlier, bestowing a green sash upon Mousavi.

Symbolically, the image showed the men as powerful and equal politicians, so the image would resonate no matter which one finally chose to run for president. And because both men were *seyyeds,* or direct descendents of the Prophet, the image also signified that Iranians were "waiting for the *seyyed* to come," Mehtari explained to me.

"We were looking for a symbol. This picture was mass distributed," Mehtari said. Ever after, when the opposition candidate addressed a rally, someone would approach him at the podium and place a green scarf around his neck—a moment of pageantry that was widely used in campaign films and television advertisements. The Green Movement was born, even before it had a "leader." Choosing a color or other powerful symbol to rally around was near the top of Harvard academic Gene Sharp's checklist for nonviolent regime change.

"One of my wishes is to meet Gene Sharp," Mehtari told me many months later, after he was forced to flee Iran. "The hand of a person like Gene Sharp, who has created such a nonviolent theory to guide people's power, should be kissed."

KHATAMI MET PRIVATELY SEVERAL times with the Supreme Leader and told him he felt an "obligation" to run again for president. Ayatollah Khamenei, who had provided Ahmadinejad much public support, apparently advised Khatami not to enter the race.

"Almost everyone knows of that last meeting with the Leader— they know the Leader said not to run, but [Khatami] said he will run," said Isa Saharkhiz, the reformist editor who had once, memorably, been bitten by the minister of intelligence.[28] "It shows that Khatami is tougher than before."

But was he tough enough? On the eve of the Revolution's thirtieth birthday, Mohammad Khatami announced his candidacy. He declared it "our duty to correct the current situation," though he cautioned that nobody could perform a "miracle" or "play the hero."[29] Activists like Saharkhiz—who had in his living room a photograph of Khatami presiding at the wedding of his son—were gushing in their excitement. The philosopher-president would overcome the reputation that "he's a good guy, but he is weak," Saharkhiz told me. "It is the slogan of the reformists, the 'New Khatami.' "

But the challenges to reformist resurgence were daunting. I obtained a British diplomatic cable dated December 1, 2008, that was marked "Restricted." Even the British were underwhelmed.

"To hardliners the reformist is at best a dupe, and at worst a Zionist-American-British spy," the cable read.[30] When in power, reformists "hardly helped themselves" and "played their hand badly." They neglected the economy and "lacked, and continue to lack, the networks and organizations the hardliners and conservatives rely on: eg the Basij militia, and the mosques. The reformists' powerbase is small, and focused on middle-class intellectual urbanites, who are very much a minority in Iran."

"The reformists are now disorganized, and rely on one totemic figure: Khatami himself," the British cable pointed out. "Optimistic reformists say that Khatami's popularity might be able to overcome any election rigging attempts by the hardliners. But pessimistic reformists doubt that the hardliners will ever again allow a reformist victory. Khamenei has in recent years made public comments doubting the suitability of people with reformist ideas for high office, especially on national security issues."

Still, the British Embassy wrote that "the future of reformism in Iran might be brighter," due to "significant underlying trends in Iranian society that could challenge the hardliners' ability to dominate the regime." Noting the "huge population bulge" of Iranians between eighteen and thirty years of age, the report said the regime was not coming close to providing the 1.2 million new jobs per year necessary to employ them. "Managing youth disaffection might require social reforms with political repercussions," the cable noted, adding that Iranians now had more news sources that "challenge the regime's narrative of what Iran should be like."

Nevertheless, the British cable ended on a pessimistic note, a diplomatic reflex honed by decades of trying to make political predictions in Iran. Reformists "might prove unable to harness these trends, and end up failing to make political change happen," it read. But reversing apathy would not be easy and "in any case, the continuation of these trends may provoke the hardliners to tighten their grip on power."

ALL MIGHT DEPEND UPON the personal mettle of the "New Khatami," which was tested the day after he announced his candidacy, when he joined the throngs marching to Freedom Square to mark the anniversary of the Revolution. I went, too. Entire families walked for miles to the event in Tehran, holding placards that read "30 Springs of Freedom, 30 Years of Pride." They chanted, "Death to America!" until they were hoarse.[31]

State TV was unrelenting on the afternoon news broadcast that I saw on IRIB Channel 1. It devoted twenty-five minutes to scenes of Tehran and huge rallies across the country, but with primary emphasis in every city on the shouts of "Death to America." Footage included an Iraq-inspired shoe-throwing contest, using posters of American and Israeli leaders as targets.

But also displayed on the street that day was the painful polarization that would shape the June 2009 presidential race and its bloody aftermath. I was with a handful of photographers who found Khatami's unmarked car stuck in traffic. He finally stepped out, immaculately dressed in matching black turban and black robe draped over a dark blue clerical tunic. Surrounded by five or six bodyguards, Khatami walked quickly the two blocks to the main body of marchers, collecting surprised Iranians along the way.

Upon arrival, the former president stepped into the thick, moving crowd. It was the same crowd we had already been stuck in for much of the morning, at times making almost no progress. In there you were completely at the mercy of the people around you. In our relative anonymity, we were safe enough. With a controversial celebrity like Khatami, however, this crowd presented new dangers.

As Khatami and his nervous entourage passed through the sea of faces, many Iranians hailed him, commenting repeatedly on how well dressed the cleric was. But there were others who yelled, "Liar! Liar!" and young ideologues who loudly questioned his devotion to Iran's Islamic system. I saw them surging forward to within inches of Khatami's face, grimacing in anger, pointing their fingers and yelling, "Death to the person against the *velayat-e faqih!*" The menace was palpable.

Khatami stoically weathered the onslaught, though the ring of people around him thickened to become almost impenetrable. Most other photographers had dropped away, unable or unwilling to muster the exertion required to keep up while keeping cameras safe. I sweated profusely through my rain jacket—it was a humid morning, and overcast—and often had no choice but to hold my camera aloft to take photographs of the scene immediately before me. Changing my camera lenses was almost impossible, as was even getting to the second camera that hung from my shoulder.

The scrum was turning dangerous, and I watched fear begin to creep across the faces of the bodyguards—and then to Khatami himself—when they realized they had lost control. A few right-wing troublemakers began deliberately ramming Khatami's group from behind, adding to the chaos. Other men drew closer holding sticks, recognizing that within reach was an enemy, trapped. Khatami's bodyguards, their faces contorted by growing concern, tried to maintain a protective ring, but to no avail. The powerful momentum of the crowd—like an unstoppable undertow pulling the swimmer beneath the waves and farther out to sea—brought the candidate face-to-face with his opponents.

This former president was no longer untouchable.

Seeking sanctuary, the entourage moved toward the nearby gates of Sharif University, but was refused entry by security guards in an act of political callousness. With no choice but to continue being swept along with the crowd, several Khatami supporters joined the body-guards to try to keep Khatami safe. Worshipful Iranians reached out to shake his hand and touch him, as if his very garments held healing properties. But hard-liners threw wads of paper and other objects, and reached out, too, with their hands, in one case knocking off the former president's glasses.

As I photographed from less than a yard away—fighting to keep my camera above the melee, knee and shin bleeding after being caught between the crowd and a parked car, my toes crushed repeatedly by countless Iranian shoes—it seemed that Khatami's heart was no longer in it, that perhaps he was questioning his decision to run for office again. If this first day was any indication, the election campaign was going to take much stomach and require overcoming physical fear.

Eventually Khatami made it into a cramped streetside kiosk set up for the anniversary. It was a metal frame draped in a blue tarpaulin. Amid the continuing pressure, he was at least able to sit down on a plastic chair. His bodyguards kept the crowd at bay at the front, even as plastic chairs and tables were trampled and broken by the mob. I was by the side and was able to quietly prevent—by bracing my arms along two sides—people getting in from that direction.

Khatami sat, very much alone, his glasses fogged with steam, the kiosk under siege.

Unseen by all but him in the emotions of the moment, I instinctively reached down to shake Khatami's hand. It was soft—would a philosopher's hand be anything else?—but also clammy and of uncertain strength at that moment. He was not a young man. His eyes had already betrayed bewildered surprise at the energy unleashed by his reception, from both sides of Iran's political divide. But then as suddenly as we had arrived, a rear exit was found in the tall steel-barred fence and Khatami was whisked away to safety just as the crowd engulfed the kiosk.

The pro-Ahmadinejad shouts and fist shaking that rose immediately were swiftly matched by Khatami supporters in a noisy face-off, impromptu and right there on the street.

"The policy [Khatami] has would take the country to a dead end; with Ahmadinejad our standing in the world has only risen," hard-line chanter Esmail Abdi told me. "This is not just the word of one student, but millions of Iranians." Voters, he said, "will question making friends with imperialism."

"Most of the people you see here are the friends of Khatami," countered Mehdi Rajaei, an engineer who had taken up the shout for Khatami. Banker Hamid Jalali also yelled for Khatami and then praised him. "Ahmadinejad thinks he is strong with ten million votes, but Khatami got more than twenty million," he told me, still sweating from the heat of the crowd and the effort of staying close to the only man he thought could save Iran. "People are angry with this economic situation and think Ahmadinejad's policies are wrong. People are one hundred percent going to . . . turn away from Ahmadinejad."

IN CASE THAT HAPPENED, the Revolutionary Guard was getting prepared. A few weeks after Khatami announced his candidacy, IRGC commanders began stepping up their warnings about a "soft revolution," and how the Islamic Republic had to be ready. The elections were still months away.

"Next to military hardware, the enemy is utilizing other resources such as Velvet Revolution and psychological warfare to corrupt the Revolution," warned Ali Saeedi, the Supreme Leader's representative to the IRGC.[32] In announcing a seminar titled "The Role of Spirituality in Asymmetric Warfare," he pointed out that during Iran's 1979 Islamic Revolution, Khomeini used some of the same tactics and "was able to overcome both the dictatorship in Iran and the American hegemony and rule in the region by relying on soft power."

Mohammad Ali Jafari, the overall Guard commander, also announced the launching of a "Pious Basijis Plan" meant to "confront soft threats."[33] Speaking to Basij commanders, Jafari said "today's war is a cultural war" and that the "most important and essential responsibility of the Basij today is to confront soft threats and the enemies' cultural war, which is silently targeting youth."

The enemy had "employed all its capabilities and resources to shake the faith of our youth," Jafari warned. "Which rational mind would decide that we set aside operations appropriate to confront this kind of threat, or that we do not make it our first priority?"

The Clenched Fist

Iran's election was getting under way just as another one had recently concluded, thousands of miles away in the United States. The reign of George W. Bush, proclaimer of the Axis of Evil and a president who never missed an opportunity to fulminate at enemies like the Islamic Republic, was over. And elected as his successor in November 2008 was Barack Obama, a black American and a Democrat who had promised to sit down and talk with Iran—a man whose middle name just happened to be Hussein, a match for the patron saint of all Shiite resistance, Imam Hossein. This was a man whose averred preference was to solve problems with diplomacy instead of military strikes.

That was quite a change in Washington, and it caught Iran's hard-liners off guard. It was much easier under Bush, the "enemy" par excellence, to revive the anti-American rhetoric of the Revolution, to cast the Great Satan—and its ever-ally Israel—once again as the undisputed source of all injustice and suffering across the Middle East. For Iran's ascendant conservatives, the Bush presidency could not have played a more helpful role. Bush was seen as an irrational and bloodthirsty actor bent on depriving Iran of its national and nuclear rights. Steady talk in Washington of regime change was a gift to hard-liners, who had no doubt where they stood as archenemies—nor that they were targets for Velvet Revolution.

But that simple "with us or against us" world disappeared when Obama took the helm. Now President Obama threatened to call Ahmadinejad's bluff and follow through on the Iranian president's oft-stated offer of dialogue, offered if only Washington would first "change its ways." Ahmadinejad had sounded despairing in August 2008, when he told Charlie Rose of PBS that he had "created golden opportunities for the U.S. government" to engage, such as approving ambassadorial talks in Baghdad.[34] "But what have we seen from the other side? Nothing. . . . What should a president do?"

Obama set a new tone toward friendship in January 2009, one week after his inauguration. "If countries like Iran are willing to unclench their fist, they will find an extended hand from us," he told Al Arabiya television.[35] "It is very important for us to make sure that we are using all the tools of U.S. power, including diplomacy, in our relationship with Iran."

The Islamic Republic began sending mixed messages back. Obama had already come under fierce criticism in Iran for making little comment during a December–January Israeli blitz against Gaza that killed fourteen hundred Palestinians, most of them civilians, compared to thirteen Israelis. Portraits of Obama, who was still only president-elect, were trampled upon and burned in Iran.

I noticed something else, though, in Tehran that February. Ayatollah Khomeini's most uncompromising words, which had codified anti-American ideology and been painted on the U.S. Embassy walls for decades, had been quietly painted over. There was blank space now, where once it read: "On that day when the United States of America will praise us, we should mourn."[36]

But a little paint job does not in a splash change a policy of perpetual defiance. As Obama reached out, the regime was wrestling with a deeper existential question: Was it really ready to set aside thirty years of official hatred for the "Great Satan"?

"Some people think this is the time to solve the problem with the U.S. in a balanced way," conservative editor Amir Mohebian told me.[37] "But others think the hostility against the U.S. after thirty years is a main element of our identity, and if we solve it we will dissolve ourselves."

Suspicion remained among the right-wing elite. "Our viewpoint is, the U.S. strategy to Iran has not changed, but the tactics have changed," explained Hamidreza Taraghi, a conservative politician.[38] "When the U.S. says to open your fist, our fist has always been in defense. It's the U.S. that has always had its fist clenched." He claimed that Washington's regime changers were still hard at work, only weeks into Obama's tenure: "The CIA has continued its soft plans to overthrow the Islamic Republic," Taraghi told me, and the "drumbeat of sanctions is continuing."

Obama's lack of leadership over Gaza was unforgivable for Hossein Shariatmadari, the diminutive editor of *Kayhan* with the lion-size hard-line roar. For the first time, there were no coconut macaroons. But on the wall were now two large maps of Israel and Palestine, one covered with arrows showing Israeli military moves.

"The people of the world see what is happening, and see Mr. Obama's silence, [so] how can they expect any change?" Shariatmadari told me.[39] He said the Americans had created a "new problem every day" for Iran for years. "With all this, the U.S. has been an enemy of ours, so there exists no room for friendship."

Yet President Obama persisted, making his first move during the Persian New Year festival in March 2009. In a videotaped message to the Iranian people to mark Nowruz, the American president used the spring "moment of renewal" to remember the "common humanity that binds us together." He called for a "new beginning" with Iran, in which "the old divisions are overcome."[40]

"Nowruz is just one part of your great and celebrated culture. Over many centuries your art, your music, literature and innovation have made the world a better and more beautiful place," Obama said. "We know that you are a great civilization, and your accomplishments have earned the respect of the United States and the world."

Obama noted it would not be easy to get beyond the rancor. "There are those who insist that we be defined by our differences," the new American president said. "But let us remember the words that were written by the poet Saadi, so many years ago: 'The children of Adam are limbs to each other, having been created of one essence.'"[41] The same quotation, in flowing Farsi calligraphy, hangs on the office wall of Iran's Nobel Peace Prize laureate, Shirin Ebadi.

With uncharacteristic speed that signified the importance of

Obama's gesture, Supreme Leader Khamenei replied the next day with a lengthy speech in Mashhad. But as followers chanted, "Death to America," Khamenei seemed among those insisting on defining the U.S.-Iran relationship by its differences. The Leader cataloged long-standing grievances and cases of U.S. "arrogance," and even charged that Obama had "insulted Iran" from his first days in office.[42] Khamenei was seeking to both lay down parameters for the debate in Iran and limit future anger among hard-liners that American's Great Satan status might be shifting.

"Right from the beginning" of the Islamic Republic, the Leader charged, the United States would "provoke" opposition groups and "support terrorism" in Iran:

> In any parts of the country, where there were grounds for disintegration, the United States had a hand, we noticed their money, and at times their agents. This cost our people much. Unfortunately this continues. . . .
>
> This is how they treated the Iranian nation for thirty years, and now the new US government says that they would like to negotiate with Iran, that we should forget the past. They say they extended their arm towards Iran. What kind of hand? If it is an iron hand covered with a velvet glove, then it will not make any good sense. . . .

It was an unremitting list too ugly to overcome. But at the end Khamenei offered a thread of hope, when he said, "You change, and we will also change our behavior, too."

Officials in Washington were unimpressed, and headlines and many analysts read the speech as a rebuff to Obama. Yet some recognized that Khamenei's response was a carefully calibrated bid to tell the Americans that further pressure was pointless, if talks were to begin. Either way, the American bid could not have been more different compared to the Bush White House, from which the president lambasted Iran's unelected leaders as men "who suppress liberty at home and spread terror across the world."[43]

"All these things are extremely serious, and Iran and the U.S. have begun to talk," analyst Farideh Farhi told me.[44] "The reality is you have a new [U.S. leader] who has talked about change, so the question is, what does that change involve? If it's sticks and carrots, or the change involves more and more *robust* sticks and carrots, it's not going to go anywhere."

And thrown into the mix was a new problem. The American-Iranian journalist Roxana Saberi had been quietly arrested in late January, after living six years in Iran freelancing for the BBC, NPR, and Fox News. Her press card had been revoked, and this friend of mine had been working on a book. But now at a delicate time of possible U.S.-Iran rapprochement, the former Miss North Dakota—who had placed ninth in the Miss America pageant—was sitting in Evin Prison, charged with "spying activities under the guise of being a reporter."[45]

Her father, Reza Saberi, traveled to Tehran, where he said his daughter had been "deceived" into making false confessions that she later recanted in a closed-door trial, before being sentenced to eight years in prison. Bitterly angry, Roxana Saberi started a hunger strike.[46] She was losing weight and sometimes suicidal, her father said. Obama was "deeply disappointed" at the verdict. But such attempts to derail détente had been expected.

"Whenever there are moments of potential confidence-building between the U.S. and Iran, you have a hard-line faction in Tehran—the spoilers—who have a long history, dating back to the 1979 hostage crisis, of provoking an international crisis in order to forward their domestic political agenda," noted Washington-based analyst Karim Sadjadpour.[47] Those hard-line factions very openly state that any opening to the United States "would lead to the demise of the entire [Islamic] system."

As journalists do, Saberi had made a copy of an official report that she came across while doing translations for a government think tank—a long, out-of-date analysis of U.S. intentions in Iraq before the 2003 invasion. Prosecutors said it was classified—though it had no such designation stamped on it.

"I was under severe psychological and mental pressure," Saberi said, when released after more than three months in prison.[48] "I was very afraid, and my interrogators threatened me and said, 'If you don't confess to being a U.S. spy, you could be here for many years—ten years or twenty years, or you could face execution.' "

So she made a videotaped confession, in a bid to get out sooner. That confession, according to Saberi's defense lawyer, included a description of a secret meeting with a CIA agent identified only as "Mr. Peterson," who had tried to recruit her.[49] This piqued my interest, as my mind raced back to my dinner with Roxana many months earlier at a Chinese restaurant in Tehran. Of course, I was no agent, and therefore could not have tried to recruit her. And in fact, she reassured me later, the "Mr. Peterson" in question was someone else entirely. "My confession was false and I thought I had to fabricate it to save myself," Saberi told NPR. "So I don't really want to say any more about this person, because it was false."

What was true was that Roxana Saberi had been a victim of a right-wing mind-set that felt threatened by the chances of a U.S.-Iran thaw. "If the hard-liners had their way, I would still be in prison today," she told NPR. But pragmatists had won the day—this time—by reaching "the conclusion that it was more costly to keep me, amid all this international pressure, [than] to release me."

THAT SAME POLITICAL FACE-OFF began to dominate Iran as the presidential election loomed. If Mohammad Khatami had any illusions about the difficulties—or risks—that lay ahead for his candidacy, they were dispelled by *Kayhan*. The unrelenting hard-line mouthpiece showed how far Khatami's anti-reformist opponents might be willing to go to keep him out of the race. In a front-page editorial, *Kayhan* compared Khatami to Benazir Bhutto, suggesting he might share the same fate—assassination—as the U.S.-backed former prime minister and Pakistani candidate who died in a bomb blast in late 2007. *Kayhan* charged that reformists planned to "change the regime and remake its essence"—a charge that amounted to treason and blasphemy.[50]

Was that a threat to Khatami's life from the self-declared protectors of the Revolution? Or simply more hard-line hot air meant to dissuade Khatami—who might well disrupt conservative plans for perpetual dominance—from running for president? Or was it a signal to regime apparatchiks that, if Khatami were to be killed, there was plenty of justification for it?

It would be for Khatami to decide whether his life was worth trying to bring democratic change, a second time, to the Islamic Republic. The fact that he was forced to make such a grim calculation said much about how militarized and fearful Iranian politics had become during the reign of Ahmadinejad and its internal enforcers, the Revolutionary Guard.

But that was the knives-drawn milieu with which the former prime minister Mir Hosssein Mousavi was all too familiar, from his leadership days in the 1980s. He had withdrawn from politics for twenty years to pursue his talent in painting and sculpture, and to eventually head Iran's Academy of Arts, which is today housed in an open-access building that Mousavi himself designed. The gray-haired revolutionary was notably uncharismatic and appeared a bland choice, a wild card who had little hope of firing up the public imagination.

It was difficult to use the word *reformist* to describe Mousavi, because Iran's political landscape had turned upside down during his absence, and little was known about what ideas and resolve may have incubated in the meantime. But at least he was more acceptable to conservative factions than Khatami, whose galvanizing presence threw conservatives into paroxysms of spitting rage.

So hard-liners breathed a sigh of relief when Mousavi chose to run and Khatami gave him his full support while dropping out himself. "All four major candidates are in line with the *nezam*," the prominent conservative Askar Owladi told Iranian television executives and government officials meeting just two weeks before the vote.[51] "So we do not feel concerned about who will be our next president. We should make sure we can maximize the turnout because that high turnout can ensure and secure the future of our system."

The caretakers of the Islamic Republic were again pushing for mass participation as a legitimizing force. Khamenei said election day would be "one of the Iranian nation's big tests before the eyes of the enemies."[52] Those enemies were bent on showing that the vote had "little enthusiasm and poor turnout," he said. "The first priority is not to choose either this individual or that. The first priority is your presence in the elections. Your presence strengthens the state."

THAT WORN-OUT BROMIDE BEGAN to gather new meaning as the prospect of ousting Ahmadinejad started to catch on among those reformists and non-hard-liners who had long ago given up on politics. Steadily, Mousavi's campaign rose on that hope. As it became clear that change was a real possibility—if Iranians turned out en masse—the "presence" of Iranians was no longer in doubt.

Street demonstrations began to materialize at night, led by young people who just weeks before had barely even heard the name Mousavi. Who were toddlers or less when Mousavi finished his premiership in 1989 and the post was abolished. And who had never until then associated the chosen campaign color of green with anything but flags flown during Islamic religious events. The sudden surge spoke to the depth of despair and desperation that Ahmadinejad's presidency had instilled in many Iranians.

The incongruity could not have been greater, of young women swooning over the political promise of an aging man, visibly nervous in crowds, who did not like to be photographed because he was self-conscious about his bulbous nose.

After all, Mousavi sounded as uncompromising as all the others back in the 1980s, vowing that the Islamic Revolution had to be spread throughout the "entire world." His views on freedom of speech in 1983 matched those of *hezbollahi* vigilantes today: "Anyone can think in their hearts, but whoever speaks out or acts against the Revolution would see the system fighting him with all its strength."[53] Likewise in 1987, Mousavi had told parliament, "There will be no reconciliation on our side with the US."[54] *Time* magazine back then stated that "fervently anti-US radicals like Mousavi are sharply at odds with pragmatists."

But over the years Mousavi had matured and mellowed, like so many of Iran's original revolutionaries, and embraced a more pragmatic and inclusive path for the Islamic Republic, both inside and out.

"One of my slogans is 'Freedom from Fear,' " Mousavi said on state television as his campaign began to gather momentum. He knew as well as anyone in Iran what revolutionary "tools" could be deployed by the archconservative enemies of change.[55] " 'Fear' does not have only a physical meaning, rather, peace of mind should be created in the society."

The Lincoln-Douglas Damage

President Mahmoud Ahmadinejad kicked off his campaign combat with vows to continue retrenching the values of the Revolution while ensuring that the disastrous reformist policy of détente stayed dead. "We have to build an Iran that will have a role in directing the future of the world," Ahmadinejad told a screaming crowd of fans at his first rally.[56]

But rhetoric and reality rarely relate in the Islamic Republic. Elections in Iran are dangerous because their pressures can yield unpredictable results. And the Supreme Leader must have known he was taking a risk by approving six head-to-head debates between the four presidential candidates before the vote. If he thought that Iran's modernity and democratic credentials would be showcased, he could not have predicted that the charge and countercharge of the debates—led with rhetorical flourish by the irrepressible pot stirrer Ahmadinejad, as he tore down every Iranian government since the Revolution except his own—would shock Iranians with their candor and sheer vindictiveness.

I watched the Ahmadinejad-Mousavi face-off on TV in the company of several young Iranians, including journalist Tara Mahtafar. She was with a few friends who ordered takeout sandwiches and soft drinks, then flopped down on couches and chairs to watch the show.

The Iranians were soon gripped and aghast.

The divinely inspired Government of God, as Ayatollah Khomeini had once so loftily proclaimed the Islamic Republic, seemed hardly that after the drubbing it received in the debates. Instead, if these senior officials of past and present were to be believed, the regime had made countless errors, was utterly corrupt, and had been mismanaged throughout its thirty-year history by dictatorial leaders. The normal sanctimonious veneer was wearing thin.

At the prime-time debate, the usually calm Ahmadinejad was visibly nervous, more than I had ever seen him. Where was his Columbia University confidence, which he said came directly from the Mahdi's guiding hand? The president complained that Mousavi accused him of being a dictator, "but do you remember," he chided, "your own time in power?"[57] Mousavi countered that Ahmadinejad's "method is leading to dictatorship."

For ninety minutes, both candidates denigrated each other's past records, portraying their opponent as dangerous for the future of Iran. They were both viciously effective, despite the clinical setting in which they sat on opposite sides of a round table, separated by a spray of flowers and a mediator who merely kept time in the verbal sparring. Mousavi accused Ahmadinejad of causing instability in Iran with his "adventurism, heroics, and extremism." The hard-line president had "undermined the dignity of our nation" with his caustic anti-West, anti-Israel, and Holocaust-denying remarks.

Ahmadinejad said all the other candidates had ganged up on him, three to one, and that his record had been subject to unprecedented "lies and defamation." He claimed that his administration had done the work of several, and that Iranians were now "among the most beloved people on the planet" because of his government's ethical standards.

Ahmadinejad boasted that he had rescued Iran from the degradations caused by the corruption and foolhardy policies of his predecessors. He asked about the huge wealth of two-time president Ali Akbar Hashemi Rafsanjani—a clear violation of the debate rules, which forbade hurling allegations against anyone not present. He stated that his own ministers were humble and pious. He portrayed Mousavi as a puppet of Rafsanjani and claimed that the former president had shown his true colors by secretly sending a message to the leader of a Persian Gulf state shortly after Ahmadinejad was elected, which said: "Don't worry, within six months this government will fall."

Ahmadinejad further charged that the two terms of reformist Mohammad Khatami had been marred by capitulation to the West on the nuclear file, when Iran agreed to suspend uranium enrichment and permit intrusive inspections—decisions that were, in fact, made by key figures of *all* factions, including the Supreme Leader. Khatami had helped Washington in Afghanistan during the 2001 war and in making peace afterward, but was rewarded with the Axis of Evil. By contrast, Ahmadinejad claimed, his own uncompromising stance meant that even Bush eventually gave up thoughts of regime change, and Barack Obama was ready to talk.

"So who endangered the regime?" Ahmadinejad asked, using the sarcastic and combative tone that marked many of his words.

Mousavi sat poker-faced throughout each fusillade. Then he derided Ahmadinejad's foreign policy, asking why, for example, the president kept saying the United States was weak and "about to fail," yet made four visits to New York and wrote two letters to George Bush and the American people. Mousavi said the incendiary nature of Ahmadinejad's Holocaust remarks had yielded fierce international reaction, yet "he comes back and this was like a heroic epic. How was this an epic?" Instead, Ahmadinejad's ferocity against Israel—most recently at a UN conference on tolerance that caused Western delegates to walk out during the Iranian's speech—had been called a "blessing" by supporters of Israel by increasing global support for the Jewish state.

Ahmadinejad then hit below the belt with a move that many Iranians thought went too far. He brandished the intelligence file of Mousavi's wife, and said her two master's degrees did not add up to a

Ph.D. and therefore she should never have been allowed to be a university dean. That was rich, coming from a man who derided degrees as mere "scraps of paper," when one of his own candidates for interior minister was caught trumpeting a forged degree (complete with misspellings) from Oxford.

The body blows continued. Mousavi pointed out: "Everyone's upset, productivity is down, inflation is up, and [there is] unlawful expenditure from the public purse." He noted that the president had been dipping into the treasury to pay for his programs and dissolved the organization meant to provide checks and balances. "It's in the interest of everyone in the country, including yourself, for you not to do these things."

Iranians were in shock. "They are destroying the entire Islamic Republic!" exclaimed journalist Mahtafar as she watched the debate, transfixed.[58] "All the dirty laundry of the Islamic Republic is coming out. All the realities people talk about, but never leaders. It makes everyone look bad."

"It's a battle," concurred one of her friends when Mousavi spoke of his disgust at how Ahmadinejad repeatedly acted "above the law."

And indeed, the ugly debate broke all rules of courtesy and restraint, helping to turn Iran's 2009 presidential election into an ideological and personal-attack free-for-all. Rival candidates produced rival statistics, each vowing that their numbers were truthful. Mousavi took Ahmadinejad to task during a subsequent debate with another candidate.

"We are facing a phenomenon: a person who can stare at the camera and say outright lies to people," Mousavi said. "When the president sits here and lies, nobody confronts him. I'm a revolutionary and speaking out against the situation he has created. He has made the country full of lies and hypocrisy. I'm not frightened to speak out. Remember that."[59]

Mousavi was echoed on the street. A student called Morovati told me: "We don't want such an impolite, unpleasant president," she said, part of a crowd of noisy Mousavi supporters taking on rival Ahmadinejad loyalists, who jeered from across the street.[60] "Our president has put us down in the eyes of the world. People want democracy instead of dictatorship."

Tears at the Shrine

But Morovati had only one vote, and in Iran's political system it was rather less important—or perhaps irrelevant entirely—than the one vote cast by the Supreme Leader, Ayatollah Seyyed Ali Khamenei. In the Islamic Republic every event has a political dimension. So it was no surprise that barely a week before the presidential vote, Khamenei would comment on the upcoming election as Iranians marked a dual twentieth anniversary: the death of Ayatollah Khomeini and the transfer of power from the Revolution's first Supreme Leader to its second one.

Devotees had gathered at Khomeini's shrine under the hottest of suns. They were there to remember what to many was a divine loss—and to recall the most frenzied funeral in Iran's living memory. Gorban-Ali Baqerzadeh's grief for the Imam back then in 1989 carried him twenty-five miles, barefoot.[61] He arrived to a scene of millions of black-clad Iranians beating their chests, throwing dirt on themselves, and passing out in the extreme heat—despite fire trucks dousing the churning masses.

Dozens died and more than ten thousand were injured during days of mourning, heat exhaustion, and collapsing. Revolutionary Guards lost control as Khomeini's coffin was being carried, the lid removed and pale white knees of the Representative of God on Earth exposed to a material world, as the funeral shroud was shredded by countless hands reaching for a remnant of the sacred cloth.

"We cried," recalled Baqerzadeh, his beard now white but his devotion undiminished. "We cried a lot for this person who was an exceptional, very religious person, who was so close to God, and worked for the success of Islam." In 2009, along with thousands of others, Baqerzadeh had walked for days to reenact his grief from two decades before. But this time the event was as much a show of force by supporters of Ahmadinejad as an anniversary. Soldiers searched the men entering the shrine and stood on scaffolding near the entrance to shout out that no green scarves, ribbons, or T-shirts—the campaign color of Mousavi—would be permitted inside. Campaign posters of Mousavi around the shrine had been defaced—I saw one brutalized by a blue ballpoint pen—while portraits of Iran's current and past Supreme Leaders on the right-hand side of the same posters were untouched.

Baqerzadeh told me that he was "one hundred percent" for Ahmadinejad, as other anniversary pilgrims who gathered tightly around nodded their agreement. "My heart says so, too, because [Ahmadinejad] has the outlook of the Imam [Khomeini]. He has a spiritual way, and continues the way of the Leader and understands the oppressed."

I came across a small gaggle of Mousavi supporters, who said they didn't like the president's "looks." Amir was a student with gel in his hair and a green headband, who was surrounded by hostile onlookers the moment he stopped to tell me, "All the young people are for Mousavi because we want freedom."

"Freedom," the key slogan of the Revolution. The ideal iconized by Khomeini in word, if not deed. But this conservative crowd at the shrine believed freedom was already in abundant supply in the Islamic Republic.

"For Imam Khomeini, freedom was not control or oppression," said Mehdi Daheshi, an apprentice auto mechanic who was only an infant when Khomeini died. He wore a pale pink shirt that contrasted with the dark hues all around. "The Imam said the word that came from the Quran, and this belief is the heart of the people. I wish I could have been there helping Imam, been by his side and sacrificed for his goals. Khomeini wanted to show freedom to the people of the world, and as time passes, the number of countries that think about this independence [from the West] are growing."

THEN KHOMEINI'S SUCCESSOR, KHAMENEI, arrived by helicopter to speak at the shrine. He was introduced with the chant, "The hand of God is on our head; the Leader is with us." He spoke flawlessly, as usual, with just a small paper for notes held in his non-paralyzed hand. He praised the "freedom-seekers" of Iran and Khomeini's work to "rejuvenate Islam."

Khamenei also told the crowd there had been much pointless speculation about which candidate he supported for president. He portrayed himself as the benevolent godfather, above party politics, and stated that he had "one vote, and only one vote" and would not play favorites. He quieted men shouting that Ahmadinejad "gives energy to the heart of the Leader," saying they should obey the rules against politicking at such a sacred place.

But despite that nod toward neutrality, the Supreme Leader had already made clear many times that he wanted Ahmadinejad to win. As early as 2006 he called Ahmadinejad the "most popular [president] in Iran in the last one hundred years." [62] Speaking a month before the election, in May 2009, he declared: "We should elect those who have popular support and who live in a simple and modest way [and] are pained by the pain of the people." [63]

Days later, Khamenei further boosted Ahmadinejad in a nationally televised speech. "Be careful in your choice. Do not let those come into office with people's votes who would want to surrender to our enemies and make the nation lose its dignity," the Supreme Leader warned. It would be a "catastrophe" for Iran to elect anyone "who thinks about endearing himself to some Western power," he said.[64] "[Vote not for] those who would want to flatter the West and the bullying Western powers in order to gain a position in the international arena. These things are of no value to the Iranian people."

In the parlance of Iran's revolutionary politics—and the fact that all Ahmadinejad's opponents called for a less aggressive foreign policy, and even for talks with the West—Khamenei could only have been throwing his weight behind one man.

And on this hot day at Khomeini's shrine, he once again revealed his hand. Khamenei referred—not by name, but clearly taking sides—to Mousavi's comments against Ahmadinejad's foreign policy during the presidential debate the night before. Khamenei said, "I do not accept the sayings of those who imagine that our nation has become belittled in the world because of its commitment to its principles. . . . [T]his path will continue until final victory."

Press access to the main interior courtyard was limited to a tiny group, so unaccredited journalists like me were refused entry. My translator Pedram Khodadadi and I listened to the lengthy speech anyway, sitting on newspapers and holding campaign leaflets above our heads to deflect the heat and bright sun on a crowded patch of grass outside the shrine amid thousands of Iranians. Soon after the Leader was finished, three identical military helicopters took off from the next parking lot, one carrying its divine cargo back to Tehran, with two outrider decoys on the same flight path.

The math teacher from northern Iran who was sitting nearby had turned to us a couple of times during the speech, eager to talk. When the Leader was gone I asked what he had to say. Gholamali Rostami was another war veteran, with scar tissue all over his left arm. He supported Mousavi but was not sure his man could win.

"The intelligent people who can think, they don't vote for Ahmadinejad," Rostami told me. Then he cast his eyes upon the devout pilgrims he could see in every direction, and added, "With this support Ahmadinejad could win, because the main pillars of the Revolution are with him."

Trouble in Paradise

I wanted to test that theory, and another one: that President Ahmadinejad's sixty provincial trips had secured him universal support in Iran's rural vastnesses. Analysts often presumed that reformists had little chance of victory in the provinces, where Ahmadinejad had spent so much time and money, lavishing underdeveloped areas with cash and thousands of development projects.

So in the week before the vote I returned to Birjand, the modest provincial capital eight hundred miles southeast of Tehran, which I had visited one and a half years earlier when Ahmadinejad was there, receiving rock star treatment everywhere he went. This was the Ahmadinejad stronghold where voters in 2005 favored the firebrand in higher percentages than in any other city.

So no one would have been more surprised than Ahmadinejad himself to see the exuberant welcome that I witnessed being given to his main challenger, Mir Hossein Mousavi, who by chance arrived in Birjand just thirty minutes after I touched down at the airport.[65] Electricity of expectation crackled in the air as hundreds of green-clad supporters—some young men wore green face masks to hide their identities—awaited the arrival of their unlikely new hero. And they were not all starry-eyed students stepping into Iranian politics for the first time.

Those waiting included war veteran Gholamreza Ghanbari, who lost both his legs in the Iran-Iraq War and considered Mousavi a fellow veteran "in the war with me," because he was Iran's premier at the time.

"He can be our savior," Ghanbari told me. "We hope, with the people's vote, their good choice will bring a bright future and restore Iran's national dignity."

The veteran had personally met Ahmadinejad twice during Birjand visits, and by his own conservative appearance and war experience, Ghanbari might have been reasonably expected to be an Ahmadinejad supporter. But "nothing changed" after the president's visits, he said. Many manufacturing companies like his had shut down. "He didn't solve the problems. He speaks very well [but] hopefully there will be a change."

MOUSAVI WAS MOBBED IN Birjand from the moment he stepped out of the airport terminal. Two cows and a number of sheep were slaughtered to honor the former prime minister, and as he passed bloody handprints were slapped onto the hood of his silver SUV to offer a traditional form of protection to the man hailed by supporters as their savior-in-chief. The convoy could barely move because of the number of people lining the roads.

I jumped out of the crammed photographers' truck—all of them Iranian shooters, with no other foreigners—to get a closer look. I was engulfed in the energy at street level, and the visceral imagery of the bloody handprints. One sacrificial cow with blood gushing on the roadside was bound by all four hooves to a cable and lifted by crane to become a swinging totem of political hope as the convoy crept forward.

When Mousavi stood up through the sunroof, Iranians lunged forward to touch his outstretched hands, or held up babies in search of a blessing as the motorcade inched along. Smiling wanly as if embarrassed by the attention, the candidate was taking in what analysts had been calling a fresh surge of support. Indeed, several weeks earlier this candidacy did not exist at all. Any suggestion that Mousavi had a chance at winning—even seven days before—would have been contrary to all received wisdom of Iranian politics.

Yet acolytes of the uncharismatic artist/architect—who had chosen painting over politics for twenty years—were calling it a Green Wave, after the campaign color. While reformists rejoiced at the level of excitement, even comparing it to the one that swept Khatami to his first landslide in 1997, hard-liners began to see the bones of a Velvet Revolution stitching themselves together.

But these new Mousavi adherents were not Westoxicated dreamers. They were angry over the tanking economy and the president's failure to fulfill extravagant promises, and even repelled by the head-to-head debate just days earlier in which Ahmadinejad's knife-twisting criticism did little more than officially expose the regime's previous misdeeds and the corruption of top leaders. They did not appreciate attempts to drag Mousavi's wife, Zahra Rahnavard, into the fray.

The result in Birjand was an evening opposition rally in which thousands of wildly cheering, green-draped supporters welcomed their candidate in a sports arena with deafening cries of support. "Death to the dictator!" rang out against Ahmadinejad.

We photographers barely got in, after a long and fast drive from the airport, once Mousavi's convoy pulled away from the main clusters of roadside supporters. We clung to each other in the back of the small press pickup truck, holding on to belts or sitting on one another's legs, unable to move for the tangle of limbs and cameras, most still standing up. At the first burst of speed, the Iranian sitting precariously next to me on the edge of the truck rolled helplessly backward. I caught his arm and belt just quickly enough to haul him back from certain injury on the road.

My translator Pedram Khodadadi—who most certainly was having second thoughts about this latest adventure—was in agony, his arms reaching out to others gone numb, legs falling asleep in his crouched position under the weight of all the photographers. The journalists who had been traveling regularly with Mousavi told us the uptick in energy at rural political rallies could easily be measured day by day.

In the sports arena, standing at the podium above the pandemonium below, Mousavi addressed those in the five-thousand-capacity arena. The temperature was a sweltering fifteen degrees hotter than the warm night outside.

"The heat in here is the heat rising toward freedom!" Mousavi told the throng, who sweated in their physical effort of standing up, waving flags, and shouting. "Birjand is known as a city of culture. [Conservatives] came here to buy you people with money, but they could not." Since the debates, Mousavi's statements at rallies had shed their earlier politeness for more direct attacks; Ahmadinejad and his crew were "delusional fanatics."

"The people are on the scene today and they will change the atmosphere of lies and treachery, lies in the name of the Islamic Republic, lies in the name of Islam," Mousavi thundered. "The worst corruption is to lie to the people in the name of Islam. Is it correct . . . that you stick your head in people's private documents and private lives?"

The crowd erupted again. And Mousavi delivered more. I had already soaked through my shirt, and even my backpack, standing on a barrier—legs braced against the metal bars and other people—to get a better look.

"This country was built on the blood of martyrs," Mousavi reminded these loyalists. "Is this the message of the martyrs, that you step over everything for the interests of your group or your family?"

Mousavi addressed Ahmadinejad, who had once been so popular in this town, "You ask why you are being called a dictator. What is a dictator? Isn't it a person who stands against the law? You don't follow any rules."

When Mousavi finished, he stepped down behind the podium and the crowd pushed forward, over the barriers. Pressing him against a brick wall as he tried to leave, dozens of supporters touched his white hair, rubbing their hands on his head and suit as security guards tried to prevent the candidate being caught in the physical crush.

Outside and gulping fresh air, I found a grandfather called Mohammad who had brought his daughter, granddaughter, and other family to the raucous rally—and had waited for five hours. I asked why he was there.

"Freedom," the patriarch replied. "If there were really freedom [under Ahmadinejad] there would not be so many people here." He said the last time the president had visited Birjand—the same "rock star" trip in November 2007 that I had observed—local schools and universities were closed and people told to go to his rally. By contrast, Mohammad told me, surrounded by several members of his family, "these are real people in this place. For love, we will give our lives."

In the afterglow of the event, several students told me they felt the same way. "God forbid if [Ahmadinejad] becomes president again; it will be unlivable," said business student Mohammad Ahmadi. "He's caused people's views of him to deteriorate. People are more thoughtful now."

"This is a very important day," added student Hamidreza Jalayeri. "We want another Revolution. We have many expectations of our future leader."

Those were the very expectations once carried by Ahmadinejad, too, when he had won so many Birjand votes in 2005. Among those voters was Mehdi Hassan-Khani, a young taxi driver who had recently withdrawn his six-hundred-dollar investment from a presidential housing scheme that yielded nothing after three years. Ahmadinejad "did nothing," he told me, so he was switching his vote to Mousavi—like many other Birjandis.

But those did not include Hassan-Khani's father, whom I happened to meet later. He was still voting for Ahmadinejad. He told me why: "They gave half the city of Birjand natural gas, which it didn't have before."

Mousavi's campaign manager in the city was Mehdi Ayati, a former member of parliament. He told me that Birjand was such a conservative stronghold that Mousavi had not planned to visit until after the first round of voting. But as the wave of enthusiasm grew toward an outright victory in the first round, his campaign advisers decided to fly him in earlier.

"We have called this very fast movement the Green Wave, and it has developed in all cities," Ayati told me. "Ahmadinejad made very nice speeches, but he did not act well at all, and that is what led to this great wave against him. We hope Mousavi will be a man of action, and make up for four years of Ahmadinejad."

Ominously, it wasn't just Mousavi supporters out that night. Shortly after the rally broke up, I watched as a group of thirty to forty motorcycles—with two or three young men riding on each—roared down the road carrying Ahmadinejad signs, not unlike the right-wing Ansar-e Hezbollah toughs who once had attacked reformist rallies. These ones, in fact, were flying a yellow flag of the Lebanese Hezbollah militia.

A young government worker on the dark sidewalk was not impressed as he watched the motorcycles drive past. Hossein turned to me and vowed not to be intimidated: "Those things are not effective anymore, because people have seen the true face."

AND THE FACE OF change in Birjand could not be hidden by the local vigilante squad driving en masse through town, like a South Khorasan chapter of the Hells Angels. The divisions in the city were as clear as the storefront glass, with new doubts raised about Ahmadinejad even in this once-indomitable outpost of support.[66] By the metric of storefront posters, public support appeared split roughly 50-50. But I found the retail demographics to be telling. Those posters for Mousavi mostly graced shops selling mobile phones, flowers, and glittering toys, many of them from the West. They often played on the fact that "Mousavi" was part of Ayatollah Khomeini's name and signature pattern, too, and referred to the candidate as the "Scent of Imam."

One poster had a particular impact on women: It showed Mousavi clearly holding the hand of his wife, Zahra Rahnavard—an unprecedented though not illegal act for married couples, which said much about the former university dean's reputation as a supporter of women's rights.

Ahmadinejad posters were more often affixed to shops from different strata: those selling car parts; plumbing, electricity, and basic building materials; and hole-in-the-wall businesses. On those the incumbent was praised as the one who understood the "pain of the people." One image showed the president on his knees drinking water from a bowl offered by two older women clad all in black. On the side it read: "We believe in you."

Birjandis were well aware that the victor in the imminent vote would shape Iran's view of itself and the world—and the world's view of the Islamic Republic. He would set the tone on a range of geostrategic issues, from how to engage President Barack Obama—and possibly ease thirty years of anti-American hostility—to whether to scale back nuclear defiance or anti-Israel diatribes.

Birjand had not been alone in raising doubts about Ahmadinejad and his populist plans. Najmeh Bozorgmehr from the *Financial Times* had been on a second presidential trip, many months before, to the Persian Gulf coastal city of Bandar Abbas. It was a repeat visit for Ahmadinejad, and in an article called "President a Hostage to His Promises," she found that "the second time round, he is being held to account." [67]

Bozorgmehr followed Mohaddeseh, an angry mother of four girls, to the presidential rally. Her first letter to Ahmadinejad about her dockworker husband losing his job was answered by the president's office—but only with advice that they could sue the employer and get a $320 loan. The banks told her that two government employees had to sign as guarantors on the loan.

"Other women in the crowd complained of similar answers to their letters and claimed only people with good connections had received loans," reported Bozorgmehr. There had also been trouble at a large local chromite mine, in which workers had not been paid for eleven months, and one of their number was killed during a protest—an event that was hushed up. Residents of Bandar Abbas were "bitter" that they had seen so little benefit from the fact that one-third of the world's oil exports passed by their strategic city, by ship at the neck of the Strait of Hormuz.

During the rally Mohaddeseh "shouted to the president that her family could not afford to eat red meat even once a month." She was sure the president would solve her problem if he personally read her second letter, the one she was delivering at the rally. If not, she said, she was going to vote reformist. That was a decision already made by some Iranians, according to an Iranian poll in September 2007—nearly two years before the actual vote—that found that 56 percent of those who voted to elect Ahmadinejad wouldn't back him again.[68]

But what about fealty to the Revolution? Or the president's self-declared backing of the Twelfth Imam? The reason for the falling popularity was simple, wrote U.S.-based analyst Abbas Milani. It was due to "the failure of nearly every aspect of Ahmadinejad's program—including the failure to fight corruption or improve the economic plight of the poor."[69]

THE DAY AFTER THE Mousavi rally in Birjand, I paid a visit to the local Ahmadinejad campaign headquarters, where I found a deep sense of resignation. In a nondescript apartment, one worker sat on the floor folding campaign newsletters. Another attached Iranian flags to wooden poles to be carried by motorcycle outriders in the convoy that would greet a high-level cleric arriving later in the day to campaign for the president.

"Everything we do is out of love for Ahmadinejad," campaign worker Hassan Shamshiri told me. It took several attempts before he—or anyone there—consented to being quoted by name.[70] He laid out a fluorescent banner five yards long that he said was donated by citizens who "love" the president. The banner read: "He's Ahmadinejad, he is manly in jihad / The heart of all the nation campaigns for him." Stuck to the wall, a black pro-*hezbollahi* poster had the words "You are descended from flowers, humbleness and light / You are the Mahmoud of Time, in the greatness of the land . . ."

And on it went. "Just like Ahmadinejad, we work twenty-four hours a day, seven days a week," Shamshiri told me.

But these campaign workers had been working less happily, as support for Mousavi began to surge. They told me they had sent observer-spies to the steam-hot Mousavi rally I had witnessed the night before, and dismissed it as an impressive-looking small crowd in a small place. But more damaging were Mousavi's well-founded accusations that Ahmadinejad was using incorrect statistics and "lies" to falsely burnish his record. There had been a collective national gasp, for example, when Ahmadinejad in one of the television debates had claimed that inflation was less than 15 percent, as part of a series of graphics that all showed positive trends.

Rivals cried foul, accusing the president of presenting Iran as a place where "all the fields are green and all the flowers in blossom." Newspapers then published the real inflation rate, which stood at 23 percent. Almost immediately, the website of the government statistics office was temporarily disabled, as were all links from the site of Iran's central bank. The fight over facts prompted the appearance of one new poster at pro-Mousavi rallies: 2 x 2 = 10.

The charges of lying by both sides also fed a surge of mobile phone text message jokes. One said that Ahmadinejad was capable of telling twenty lies in forty minutes. Another made light of Iran's disappointing draw against North Korea in a key soccer match; it said that, according to the "Iran Statistics Office," Iran had in fact won, 12–0. Yet another text message pretended to quote Ahmadinejad saying that Iran beat North Korea, 2–0, adding: "I have the documents to prove it!"

Now even Ahmadinejad's own campaign staff in Birjand seemed to have resigned themselves to the defeat of their street-fighting president. "It's a pity," one despondent volunteer confided, "that the best man won't win."

WHEN ASKED, SUCH CAMPAIGN helpers could not describe a single benefit that the president had brought to the city or South Khorasan province. But one leaflet detailed the official tally: seven hundred miles of new natural gas lines laid in the province, with 5,800 new branch lines. Fuel consumption had become more efficient (obviously thanks to the president!). The number of electricity lines had increased by half; the number of villages linked to the national grid was up by 20 percent.

Rival candidates charged that such numbers were either padded, made up, or had nothing to do with government. But in Birjand, where state-run TV was the source of most news, all statistics portrayed a man of untiring effort, and the ideological machinery was working nonstop. So Ahmadinejad could still claim strong support in this former stronghold. I returned to the same Hossein mosque—known locally as the most political and important in Birjand—where I had witnessed the president receive his rock star welcome more than a year and a half earlier, where I heard the audience gasp at his arrival, leaving the local top cleric to simply exclaim that the "friend of the Imam [Mahdi]" had arrived.

Now it was nearly prayer time, days before the presidential vote. Men arrived at the entrance, with arms dripping wet from their ablutions, of washing to above their elbows. They stopped at a wooden box full of small clay disks—all of them just a couple inches across or less, stamped with images of religious shrines—upon which to place their forehead as they prayed. Some men chose their *mohr* carefully, flipping through several before they found one shaped to their liking.

Inside I waited for the imam, Seyyed Mohammad Baqer Asadi, as he sat on the carpeted floor and attended to the needs of another customer, a young man who had a pressing question. Before answering him, the cleric picked up his large Quran from its wooden reading stand, closed the book, and then opened it randomly to see what guidance might happen to appear on that page. It was traditional bibliomancy called *estekhareh,* disdained by some clerics as irrational and akin to spiritual gambling, but a method sometimes used by Supreme Leader Khamenei. Persians sometimes even used volumes of the poetry of Hafez for the practice.

Then the cleric turned to me. The heavy prayer scar on the middle of Asadi's forehead was the most prominent feature of his face, a revelation itself in folds of dark brown and gray skin. It was easy to see why, when I looked down and saw the cleric's huge *mohr,* an eight-sided chunk of clay several inches across and with a dark stain in the middle.

"It gives a very humble and popular feeling when people can talk to their president face-to-face," Asadi told me.[71] "Our policies are not different from our religious beliefs, and our Revolution comes from Islam. Other presidents were clerics, so technically they were more religious. But for Ahmadinejad, he's trying to show he believes."

And it was working, the cleric said, tipping his black turban forward to scratch the back of his head. "In general, people are not dissatisfied, especially the youth. Maybe the youth are even more for Ahmadinejad," he posited. "A lot of youth pay attention to his courage and standing up [to the West]."

Outside and across the street, in a sandwich shop decorated with three Ahmadinejad posters, I found one of those who counted himself satisfied.

"Compared to a couple years ago [when] no one thought of getting a home or getting married, [now] with all the money pouring in, people can make their own shop, get jobs, and get married," Mohammad Reza Bahdani, a thin-bearded city water worker, told me. "If Ahmadinejad gets to be president again, the problems of the poor people will be solved." Bahdani was waiting for his sandwich to be made and cast his mind to the missing Imam. He said the president had the help of the Shiite Messiah, whose name he constantly evoked.

"Previous governments were turning away from Islam and becoming irreligious, but Ahmadinejad—with the help of Imam Mahdi—has got more people around religion again," Bahdani told me. Despite Mousavi's respected premiership in the 1980s, he had since gone "in the wrong direction. God willing, he will not win. If he does, we will really understand the people have not awakened yet."

BAHDANI WAS PART OF the president's base of pious poor, who most lauded Ahmadinejad's efforts to bring social "justice" by spreading Iran's wealth even though, in reality, the redistributive benefits remained mere tables for many. They were the ones who later that afternoon formed the bulk of the convoy to welcome Morteza Agha-Tehrani, a hard-line cleric and the senior moral and "ethics" adviser to Ahmadinejad's cabinet. He was a follower of the most hard-line of Iran's clerics, Ayatollah Mesbah-Yazdi—that intolerant cleric whose guidance had prompted *basijis* to kill "morally corrupt" Iranians in years past, who detested democracy and was credited by some analysts as the man who engineered the post-Khatami resurgence of the right wing.

With some higher education in Canada and the United States but an unreconstructed conservative, Agha-Tehrani had published a book that, according to one description, "gives instructions for meeting the Hidden Imam and methods to petition the Mahdi at Jamkaran mosque." [72] He was filmed during a 2007 sermon saying, "Throw away these filthies [reformists] as you would a tissue that you use to wipe a baby's bottom. And don't get close to them." [73]

As Agha-Tehrani arrived in Birjand, young men outdid each other to plaster their motorbikes with portraits of Ahmadinejad and roared off with Iranian flags flying to usher the cleric into the city. [74] This remained a God-fearing, revolutionary town: the convoy passed a faded billboard that praised heroes of the war. It showed a column of soldiers marching to the front line, while beside them another soldier stood by, in uniform but on crutches, his right leg missing. "I told him not to go," the sign reads. "He just laughed and left."

HUNDREDS OF PEOPLE PACKED the entrance of the mosque to hear Agha-Tehrani laud Ahmadinejad from the pulpit. Conservatives who turned out were showered with propaganda leaflets that portrayed Ahmadinejad as an angel birthed from their earth. One "Special Edition" page of newsprint was headlined: "Rejuvenating the Imam's and Revolution's Words." It described Ahmadinejad as the "most hardworking president of the world," noted the Leader's acclaim that this was the best government in a century and listed statistics about this "much-loved child of the nation." The tally included 3,000 working meetings, 60 provincial and 65 foreign visits, 1,000 speeches, 150 press conferences, and 55 interviews with the foreign press.

A small sidebar was titled "Latest Opinion Polls." Taking a series of liberties with the truth, it stated that despite the "volume of harsh criticism" at home and abroad, a number of "wide-ranging statistics and many opinion polls" indicated that "the rise of votes toward Mr. Ahmadinejad has been exceptional and he will beat other opponents by a wide margin in the first round."

The president was heralded in what were claimed to be "statistics of the government"—a surreal collection that sounded like a Soviet progress report on the latest Five Year Plan. The figures portrayed Iran's steel production increasing by more than one-third, with a 950 percent boost in aluminum output and 400 percent for copper. Investment in natural gas more than tripled; retiree salaries had more than doubled; the floor space of sports facilities was more than five times larger; new "housing for the poor" had increased 1,800 percent, while the Internet "penetration rate" in society had expanded elevenfold, though the raw figures on the page actually showed a 350 percent increase.

Another leaflet on pink paper praised the government's "special attention to waiting" for the Mahdi, and for mentioning their "admiration for the Remnant of God" in all global forums. Yet another poster—produced by the "Supporters of the Government of Love"—trumpeted Ahmadinejad as the "crystalization of the justice-seeking of a nation."

It was all too good to be true for one young man, a Mousavi supporter wearing a green armband just seventy-five yards from the entrance of the mosque. He was standing at the door of a mobile phone shop, and angrily shouted about the conservative crowd: "They are not Iranians!"

But inside the stifling mosque, support for Ahmadinejad was solid as Agha-Tehrani climbed the stairs, sweating, to the preacher's seat. While he perched there trying to control his sweat—we in the audience were trying to cool down, too, after the strenuous fight through the crowd to get inside—Agha-Tehrani was introduced by a local official. "For the long life of Ahmadinejad, say a *salavat!*" the man said, prompting the audience to respond with the words that praise the Prophet's household. Up high, the microphones weren't working properly, so the broad-faced Agha-Tehrani waited while they were fixed, wiping his brow.

It was so tight on the floor that the local intelligence agents, once they spotted me, passed up a sheet of paper, from one person to another, to write down my name and details and pass back for inspection my press card and letter from the Islamic Guidance Ministry.

Agha-Tehrani described this as a "religious event" and not a political one, declaring that if anyone died in the crush to get to the mosque—or indeed during the hurly-burly of the election campaign itself—he would be considered a religious martyr.

Immediately, of course, the "religious event" turned political and Ahmadinejad was praised from the start for his brains and his courage. No accolade was too much for this hero of the Islamic system. He knew how to talk to the enemy. Iraq and Afghanistan were proof that "whenever [the United States] comes into a country, they will never allow it a good time. Here we have security. We really have security." Nobody threw stones at shops. It was the out-of-control opposition—

those *reformists*—who were responsible for any violence the audience might hear about. "The people who make insecurity do not belong to this president," Agha-Tehrani said, giving his forehead another wipe.

A box of tissues had been handed forward, along with a glass of water.

Here was the passion of politics on the right, steaming and devout, and malodorously scented with polyester socks and cheap, overused shoes removed and carried inside by every congregant, to avoid them getting lost or stolen if left at the door.

Agha-Tehrani told some homespun stories of Ahmadinejad, about how he was just like you—the men sitting before him, men whose foreheads are marked from decades of prayer, men whose doubts do not extend to their religious faith, men who very often would have struggled to care for their families.

"What else do we want from our president? We are honored he is with the people," Agha-Tehrani said. "One day after prayers, I met the president . . ."

It was a meal, and someone had ordered chicken. But Ahmadinejad wasn't having any of it. "I bring my own food from home," the president told the cleric. Using a "crappy iron pot," Agha-Tehrani said, the president had brought onions and tomatoes to make his own salad. "Having this kind of simple life, it's good." Agha-Tehrani reminded the audience of the president's lack of wealth: "When Mr. Ahmadinejad became president four years ago, you saw his belongings. Compare that to now. . . . [H]e does not give anything to himself."

The Iranians here knew that and appreciated it. As they listened, a couple of clerics rudely answered their mobile phones and talked, disrupting the political sermon.

"When [Ahmadinejad] became president, the Revolution was reborn. . . . The Leader thinks the same," the white-turbaned Agha-Tehrani told these voters. There were two ways to respond to an attack, he said. "Some go into defense mode, and just try not to get hit. But some like Mr. Ahmadinejad are always in attack mode. When somebody wants to punch him, he is ready and will punch them first."

"If every one of us became an Ahmadinejad," the cleric preached, "our country would be very successful."

The Green Tsunami

Back in Tehran the streets were alive with a level of political excitement unseen for a decade, but the definition of "success" depended very much upon whom you asked. Day by day, momentum was building behind Mir Hossein Mousavi—and the promise of change that he embodied for his supporters, whether realistic or not. They wanted to kick out Ahmadinejad and realized that their past nonstrategy of simply withdrawing from Iranian politics had achieved nothing, except to hand conservatives one victory after another.

The Sage had been waiting years for this realization to dawn on his fellow citizens. When it finally came, he was shocked by the enthusiasm with which reformists embraced Mousavi, taking to the streets in their thousands every night for hours to cheer the chances of change. The preponderance of political partygoers were green-clad Mousavi supporters, roaring up and down Tehran's streets in motorcycles and cars, shrieking until their lungs gave way.[75] But Ahmadinejad loyalists were also out in force, flying the national flag—the president chose the red, white, and green colors of the flag to be their "purity" colors. Everyone seemed to have a mobile phone held up in the air, taking photographs and video to record the exceptional scenes that everybody knew could never last.

Iranians told me repeatedly how surprised and impressed they were as Iranians from both camps found each other at main squares in the capital and talked and debated in the most civil manner. There was no hiding the expanding support for the white-haired old-timer Mousavi, who was hardly known for moderation during his tenure as premier in the 1980s. Still, sometimes there were shouting matches, intimidation, and bullying. Late one night I watched a couple of vigilantes with cheap "Police" vests over their street clothes charge several Mousavi supporters and pummel them with their fists, just like old times.

Time magazine writer Nahid Siamdoust told me she also witnessed prevote violence from Ahmadinejad supporters on bikes, who wielded razor blades late at night, slicing at Mousavi motorcyclists as they passed.[76] She saw one shocked victim—with green Mousavi wristbands—whose forearms were slashed with two parallel slices, deep and both three inches long, which bled profusely as his friends took him away to the hospital.

The Sage was in awe. "It's going in a swing, in a big way, totally to the extreme," he told me in his apartment as the vote neared.[77] "This ingenious idea of green: it is such a small thing, and it caught. Suddenly with a little piece of cloth, you could say so much, against Ahmadinejad, and all the problems. Underneath the apathy there was something, waiting to be led, to be awakened."

And yet, once awakened, the surge for Mousavi carried its own risks, the Sage warned. "It's amazing, fantastic, and we are having it! But the Green Wave should expect to be disappointed. In the minds of people, they expect reforms compared to [Khatami] twelve years ago."

HOW POWERFUL WERE THOSE expectations of change, for greater freedom? Polls in Iran are notoriously inaccurate, and I remember the pollsters I spoke to in 2005 who complained to me that Iranians were very reluctant to share their true political views with a stranger. I had begun my story with the words "Pity the Iranian pollster . . ."[78] But among the very few convincing results for me came out less than a week before the 2009 vote—and therefore it was one of the only polls to incorporate part of the last-minute surge for Mousavi.

Newsweek reporter Maziar Bahari—the consummate professional whose Intelligence Ministry minders so often reminded him that "we know where you live"—had seen "government-funded polls" that indicated that Mousavi would win 16–18 million votes, compared to just 6–8 million for Ahmadinejad.[79] If correct, it meant that Mousavi could win in the first round, and represented "a tidal shift from just four weeks ago, when public polls showed Ahmadinejad ahead by 50 percent," Bahari reported. Many voters were casting ballots for the first time, expressly to kick out a man they saw as reckless. Perhaps more surprising were the poll findings that it was not just angry youth feeling their political power for the first time.

"Even Iran's Revolutionary Guards and members of the country's vast intelligence apparatus seem to have come around to this position: a large majority of them also plan to vote for Mousavi, according to the government poll," Bahari reported. That point was backed up by interviews he had conducted with "military and intelligence officials." Older cadres remembered Mousavi's careful steering of the economy during the Iran-Iraq War, and Bahari heard complaints that the president's "erratic economic and foreign policies have made the country less secure."

Ahmadinejad was "alarmed by the poll," wrote Bahari. In previous weeks the "president's campaign had become secretive and withdrawn. His usually media-friendly advisers have turned off their cell phones and barred staffers from talking to reporters."

And it wasn't the only such poll. One source close to Ayatollah Khamenei told Lindsey Hilsum of Channel 4 News about "private polling for the Supreme Leader," which also indicated Mousavi winning by a two-to-one margin.[80] The source gave a provincial breakdown, saying he expected the result would stand—and implying, at that point, that Khamenei had accepted the outcome.

I TOOK MY OWN microsample to help gauge the scale of this political transformation. And sure enough, all three of the Iranians I had featured in a story more than a year earlier about apolitical, disappointed reformists—each had refused to vote in the March 2008 parliamentary election, considering it useless—were this time going out of their way to vote.

Tooska, the law graduate and painter of nudes who once took pride in her distance from politics, told me that this election was "different."[81] She was the one who had explained before that she had to "oblige" herself to "tolerate what I can't change." Now, on the eve of the election, her world was a different place and looked like it could be altered for the better. Every night for a week, Tooska had headed out with friends after midnight to join the throngs of other boisterous Iranians filling the streets to shout, honk, and chant their support for Mousavi.

The vote had turned into a referendum on the performance of Ahmadinejad and his cabal of archconservatives, and Tooska was certain now that her voice would be heard. Rollicking in the car as it lurched forward in bumper-to-bumper traffic on Vali Asr Avenue, Tooska let her headscarf fall back as she explained why, this time, she was taking part. Motorcycles roared past, trailing green ribbons of Mousavi's Green Wave, the riders hurling insults at the president. Tooska had a green ribbon tied to the windshield wiper.

"Like Mousavi, I feel the danger we are in," the young karate ace said. The scenes on these streets were inconceivable just a few weeks earlier; even those in the crowds were staring in disbelief, repeating that they had never witnessed such a political outpouring in their lives. "During these four years [of Ahmadinejad], everyone is unsatisfied with the *nezam* [Islamic system]," Tooska told me, her eyes riveted to the public party scene that enveloped the car. "This time, change is necessary because [the situation] is worse than ever."

Tooska's views were echoed by Alireza Mahfouzian, the onetime culture warrior, girl-kissing skier, and brain sandwich shop owner who had never voted in a national election before—not even for Khatami. The increasingly stout Mahfouzian was not going into the streets wearing green, nor shouting against Ahmadinejad. But this time he was going to vote for Mousavi—and was taking his mother along with him to make sure she voted, too.

"There are many reasons I don't like Ahmadinejad," the young man said when I tracked him down.[82] Mahfouzian wore expensive jewelry and drove a very expensive car that he happily admitted was a tool for meeting women. It seemed to be working. "There are a couple I have now that are so beautiful even I die when I see them," he told me.

But he was also in deep new trouble after a late-night fight with a gang of construction workers, in which he was knifed. "I beat the first one up and then ten of them jumped on me." He pulled up his white Giordano T-shirt to reveal the healing wound on his left shoulder, where the blade had penetrated two inches. The gang had bribed the police to forget about their knifing, and to instead press Mahfouzian on an alcohol infraction. That would feel especially painful, with a sentence of thirty or forty lashes on his bare back.

"Mousavi is like an anesthetic they put up, like Khatami was," Mahfouzian said. He didn't think Iran would change much for the better after the election, and he said he liked Ahmadinejad's attention to science, from Iran's nuclear and satellite programs to stem-cell research. But the catastrophic state of the economy nearly sunk his sandwich shop, in which he had recently—and with relief—sold his stake.

He drew a parallel with the anti-Bush support for President Barack Obama in the 2008 U.S. election. "With Ahmadinejad it is exactly the same," Mahfouzian said. "The main problem is, we don't have freedom, and because we don't have freedom, we feel the problems more."

Also experiencing a rebirth of political engagement was Siavash, the Pickup King and Persian Casanova whose life was undergoing many changes. Among them was a semipermanent girlfriend, after years of one-night stands and temporary quests with Iranian women, married and not. His telephone with the brash "I'm too sexy for my love" ringtone had been stolen, its jingle not reinstalled on his new iPhone, which set him back nearly a thousand dollars; worth it for "the look," he said.

"I'm settled down and dating only one girl. It's good practice for the future," Siavash divulged when we met for sandwiches during his lunch break from his job selling office equipment.[83] Siavash was still buzzing from taking part in the human chain formed by Mousavi supporters along a green ribbon from the top of Tehran to the bottom, a twelve-mile stretch of Vali Asr Avenue that is the longest street of its kind in the Middle East.

"It was the experience of a lifetime—it was so beautiful. I was so happy to be there," Siavash told me, using True Believer inflections that I was used to hearing from Ahmadinejad supporters or war veter-

ans when discussing the return of the Mahdi, or the blood of the martyrs. Reform was the new religion of this man, when it was possible.
"Nobody planned it. People just came out, not because they believe
[in Mousavi], but because they want something to be stopped."

What he had seen on the streets, he said, could change Iran. "I believe this is bigger than [Khatami's movement]," Siavash told me, adding thick ranch-style dressing to a large chicken salad. He wore a suit
along with a tie—an uncommon feature, except for the most Westernized Iranians—and sported a green ribbon tied around his right wrist.
"Let's say the wave out there is bigger. This green color is a branding.
I don't have to have a poster on my back—just put this on my wrist."

Mousavi was "not a perfect choice," Siavash admitted, and many
on the streets chanting his name were not even born when the former
prime minister was in politics. But they had cause: "The most important thing of all is to stop what is happening in the last four years in a
democratic way."

He blamed the president's economic mismanagement for a 50 percent drop in his office sales over the previous year. And Siavash blamed
Ahmadinejad for giving the morality police a "free hand" to hassle
people for un-Islamic dress, and for his aggressive foreign policy
toward the West. "Being a bully is not the answer to the question,"
he told me. He knew what to expect of the vote, because the endless
human chain showed him "we had enough power" to make change.

Just days before the vote, Siavash made a prediction: "If Mousavi
does not win, it will cause big damage to society. You will see angry
people, it will be dangerous, and there will be a release of pressure.
People will be *angry*."

SO ARE TOOSKA AND Mahfouzian and Siavash—and all those
other tens of thousands of Iranians who voiced noisy support for
Mousavi during the presidential campaign—part of a Velvet Revolution to overthrow the regime in Iran, without even knowing it?

They are, if you are a ranking member of the Islamic Revolutionary Guard Corps, steeped in the ideology of "enemy," and your job is

to be obsessed with the "internal" threat to Iran. Obsessed with your own vulnerability to political change. And obsessed with the many examples of Velvet Revolutions that had, in the previous decade, brought a sudden end to inflexible authoritarian regimes like yours.

If you defined Velvet Revolution to include any change, then it was indeed happening. Analyst and editor Saeed Laylaz said his travels across Iran in the two months prior to the vote led him to believe that Mousavi could win outright with more than 50 percent of the votes. "If we have a free election, he may win at the first round," Laylaz predicted.[84] "What's happening in Iran now is a colorful Velvet Revolution." He suggested that hard-line efforts at securing victory at any cost were unraveling fast. "We can't run Iran like North Korea," he said.[85] "A group of militarists cannot stuff this civilization into a can and put it away. Iran cannot make up for its lack of economic might with nuclear technology, missiles and proxy threats in Lebanon and Palestine and elsewhere."

During the election campaign, the once-sacred *nezam* was subjected to unprecedented criticism, to charges of top-level corruption and lying amid the candidates' bruising campaigns. Constantly in attack mode, Ahmadinejad even fired corruption allegations at officials close to the Supreme Leader.

Iran's political elite was reeling, as it had from the first day Ahmadinejad came to power. "His questions undermined many things," Mehdi Karroubi, the reformist presidential candidate and former parliament speaker, told me.[86] "I don't say that's his intention, but because he wants to win he will say it to trick the people. He wants to say, 'My government is clean and pure.' " Karroubi said the Revolution's destructive political tendencies had to be checked: "Every movement should be toward moderation," the candidate told me. "We have seen much damage from every extreme."

Reaction was fierce to Ahmadinejad's charges against past governments during the freewheeling debates, because much more was at stake than just one political campaign. Suddenly the very institutions, people, and history that formed the sanctities and sinew of the Revo-

lution were being challenged—by the very man hard-liners were depending upon to preserve those sanctities.

"Hardly anyone else could have done so much damage," said
Nasser Hadian-Jazy, a political scientist at Tehran University who went
to school with Ahmadinejad.[87] "If this is a religious government and
it is corrupt, then what is the difference [versus secular rule]? It dam-
ages the whole notion of religious government." He drew for me on a
napkin a schematic of how dramatically Iranian politics had changed
in just a few weeks, and predicted that—if there was no cheating—
Ahmadinejad would lose in the first round.

Many more had reached that conclusion also, or were striving to
make it a reality. Describing how disparate elements were lining up
against Ahmadinejad, Borzou Daragahi of the *Los Angeles Times* noted
that the Guardian Council had squashed a hard-line effort to increase
the number of ballot boxes—which could have made fraud easier;
that conservative parliament speaker Ali Larijani "foiled" a presidential plan for yet more cash handouts; and that even the conservative
mayor of Tehran, Mohammad Baqer Qalibaf, "had loosened rules to
allow late-night campaigning and hung white banners in the capital as
spaces for political graffiti, benefiting Mousavi's young supporters."[88]

"The whole system of the government has come to the conclusion that Mousavi would be better," Reza Kaviani, an analyst at a
left-leaning Iranian think tank, told Daragahi. "With the way Ahmadinejad is going forward, he's threatening the whole system."

Regime stalwart Rafsanjani wrote an incendiary letter of complaint
to the Supreme Leader—and made it public before the vote. He was
infuriated by Ahmadinejad's accusation that he was the financial and
political puppeteer behind Mousavi, and that his family was corrupt—
all of which, at least regarding the Rafsanjanis, had more than a kernel
of truth.

"Tens of millions of people in the country and outside watched as
[Ahmadinejad] lied and violated laws against religion, morality, and
fairness, as he targeted the achievements of our Islamic system," Rafsanjani wrote.[89] He asked the Leader to take "serious action" to pre-

vent "this fire from flaring during and after the election." Ahmadinejad was attacking the icons of the Revolution, including the integrity of the Supreme Leader himself.

Iranians wanted the "truth that is directly linked with the legitimacy and prestige of our system and nation," Rafsanjani added, warning that otherwise "the volcanoes that are fueled by people's anger will form in society."

Ahmadinejad struck back with typical overkill. "No one has the right to insult the president, and they did it. And this is a crime. The person who insulted the president should be punished, and the punishment is jail," he told thousands of supporters.[90] "Such insults and accusations against the government are a return to Hitler's methods, to repeat lies and accusations . . . until everyone believes those lies."

FOR THE REVOLUTIONARY GUARD, the bloodthirsty state of politics on the eve of the election portended a far more ominous and strategic threat. Before their eyes, a viable opponent to Ahmadinejad had not only emerged, but his candidacy had caught fire, rekindling hope for reformists in just a few weeks, where there had been only burned-out despair for many years. And it had a color: green.

The reformist calculation, which I heard over and over again, was that the more people who went to the polls, the less chance hardliners could cheat and manipulate the results. Now all signs pointed to a huge turnout—and disaster for conservatives. Those were familiar ingredients, not unlike those seen before in Belgrade, and Georgia, and Ukraine, and . . . every previous Velvet Revolution. Still, in Iran there was little American "prodemocracy" money in evidence—Iranians at that point had largely been refusing such support. There were no civil society groups that were not under the strictest control. And conservatives held every level of power and virtual monopoly over every aspect of the vote, from the ballot box to broadcasting the result.

But had the Islamic Republic learned one of the most critical lessons of past Velvet Revolutions? That the most important key was in the government's hand? Had it learned, in all its studying of Velvet

Revolutions, that in every previous case a people power takeover was ultimately sparked by a government's own decision to fiddle with or steal an election?

Whether that lesson had sunk in was not yet clear. But this warning came loudly from the head of the Revolutionary Guard political office, on the eve of the vote: "Any move toward Velvet Revolution will be nipped in the bud through people's awareness," Brigadier General Yadollah Javani said. The opposition, through "heavy propaganda and a media-created atmosphere," intended to "thrill their supporters by early announcement of their victory, so that they will claim election fraud in case of their rival's victory."[91]

Unprecedented use of the color green in the run-up to the vote was a sure "sign of the Velvet Revolution project," Javani declared; but in Iran such an outcome was "impossible."

Yet perhaps it was already too late, judging by the scalding irreverence that Ahmadinejad had brought into his reelection campaign—indeed, that had marked his four years of divisive leadership. And also judging by the startling irreverence that Mousavi supporters aimed right back at their hated president.

Dressed in green and with their runaway expectations, Mousavi loyalists capped their campaign with an arresting image in the early hours, the day before the vote, near Vali Asr Square. It was a large canvas banner of the smiling president held upside down, the face crossed out with red ink and the words "Goodbye Dictator."[92]

I watched as two men wearing green face masks held the defaced portrait over a street that was packed with cheering people, motorcycles, and slow moving cars. Drivers wishing to express their desire for change could drive under and through the image of the upside-down Ahmadinejad. Many did so gladly, their horns blaring.

8

The Reckoning

2 + 2 = 5

—George Orwell, *Nineteen Eighty-four*

Freedom prevails absolutely in our country.

—President Mahmoud Ahmadinejad, June 14, 2009

Death to the Government that Fools People

—poster at Mir Hossein Mousavi rally, June 2009

*History tells us that repressive and cruel governments do
not survive.*

—Ahmadinejad letter to George W. Bush, May 2006

THE ELECTRICAL STORM CAME with the edge of darkness, the night before Iran's tumultuous election. The day had been stifling, all heat and no wind; a day legally free of campaigning, when Iran's exhausted politicians and political operatives caught their breath—and Iranians began to hold theirs.

As dusk began descending on Tehran, the last rays of the sun, its orb already below the horizon, caught spectacularly upon a growing bank of clouds to the west. They turned purple and brown as they bludgeoned their way across the sky, pushing before them a tempest of wind and electricity that drew me to the roof of my downtown hotel, the Karoon. From that roof in years past I had watched all manner of weather engulf the capital, and all manner of brightly lit national celebrations. On this night, a six-feet-tall white balloon with an image of Mir Hossein Mousavi, tethered to a sixty-foot-long cord on a neighboring building, was caught by the force of the wind and blown nearly horizontal in the dark shadow of the oncoming clouds.

From this roof looking west-northwest, I had a clear view of the top of Iran's hulking Ministry of Interior building, where the exterior lights had automatically turned on beneath the glowering ferocity.

Lightning erupted at 8:30 P.M., coinciding with the final call to prayer, which came plaintively from two minarets strung with lights at a nearby mosque. This lightning was no mere flash, but rather a burst that streaked dramatically—and lingered—across all the western horizon, above the ministry building. In a matter of hours this was where the results of Iran's much-anticipated presidential election would begin to be tabulated.

Each lightning strike was followed by explosions of thunder, which set off car alarms on the street, from where the hot dust of the day swirled upward into the churning skies, to meet the first big droplets of rain coming down. It was a cleansing downpour, reminiscent of the rainfall portrayed in a government get-out-the-vote television ad, which showed Iranians of all stripes reveling in life-giving rain, their arms held out in gratitude.

The storm didn't last long, but it was violent. And for any who might be looking for signs—particularly Iranian politicians who counted most on divine connections to sustain their leadership—it was a bad omen.

Creating an "Epic"

Voting day began on June 12, 2009, as it always had, with Iran's Supreme Leader stepping from behind a curtain—light brown this time—greeting poll workers and disciples and giving a smile as he cast the nation's first ballot. State TV then moved into position ahead of the phalanx of cameras to broadcast his words. Ayatollah Seyyed Ali Khamenei called on all Iranians to vote, to "have their share in governing the country and to choose who is best fit to govern for the next four years."[1] He thanked Iranians for their "enthusiastic presence" during the election campaigns, adding that "with their improved maturity, morality, and thought, [they] did not allow any sad scenes to be created amidst the enthusiasm."

The Leader warned cryptically, however, against believing rumors about him and the election, which had been passed along by those with "unsound minds." Khamenei turned, and as an aide drew back the curtain, God's (interim) Representative on Earth stepped through and disappeared from view.

FOR STUDENTS OF IRAN'S many elections, the casting of the Supreme Leader's ballot was the last "typical" event of that controversial 2009 vote, which in every other respect—from the broadcast of the results to the bloody aftermath—would write new history in the Islamic Republic. That history may one day show that the only semi-reliable government statistic to emerge was this remarkable gauge of enthusiasm: 85 percent turnout of the 46.2 million eligible voters—a regime record for an election.

That figure carried with it the clear expectation among Iranians that their vote would count, as it had in most previous elections. State television showed couples in their marriage finest, voting on the way to their wedding. "This election is as important as our wedlock; that's why we are doing both on the same day," said one beaming bride.[2]

Still, I was surprised to see how many voters carried their own pens to mark their ballots, after rumors circulated that operatives of President Mahmoud Ahmadinejad had imported two million pens with disappearing ink to be used at the polls—so that votes for Mir Hossein Mousavi would become invalid while they sat in the ballot boxes. A flicker of counterrumor held that it was in fact the opposition camp that had sneakily brought in such pens to invalidate a massive Ahmadinejad vote.

The divisions that had riven Iran during the raucous campaigns were easily seen in long lines to vote, even among families. I found housewife Zahra Khalili holding her seven-month-old baby outside one station in south Tehran, where she had voted for Ahmadinejad. "God willing," she said, he would be reelected. She clutched her black headpiece tight at her chin. "It's a day to decide our destiny and we hope many people vote."

But Khalili's arguments had not convinced her brother-in-law, a teacher who stood beside her. He took the baby while she got some wipes. "Mousavi is a correct thinker," Asghar Davoudi told me, rocking the infant in his arms. "We don't want a liar. Living simply [like Ahmadinejad] is not important. Doing good work, being active, is much better."

"Don't lie! You are going to vote for Ahmadinejad," replied the sister-in-law, mischievously. "The shadow of Imam Zaman [the Mahdi] is on this government."

"Each one of us has a free decision," argued Davoudi, handing back the baby. "As long as we have the Supreme Leader, we're good."

In that district of Shahr-e Rey, a southern suburb of Tehran with some very poor areas and copious Ahmadinejad graffiti and posters, a young banker called Nafiseh told me why she was voting for the incumbent. She wore a colorful headscarf and some makeup, and told me that the combative television debates and street demonstrations "showed democracy in our country, the honor of our country, because of the enthusiasm and because of the freedom of speech. No matter what they do, our *nezam* [system] will always be there. . . . A lot of people might say they don't believe in the *nezam,* but deep in their hearts they do."

Nafiseh accused the United States and the West of meddling in Iranian affairs, and said Ahmadinejad's aggressive and principled stands were correct: "We consider elections to be a war," she told me. "They say we have nuclear weapons, but the fact is we each are a nuclear bomb. The more they say against us, the stronger we become."

But even as she spoke, another woman dressed all in black, Fatemeh, stepped up and retorted in English: "Ahmadinejad is a big liar, one hundred percent! In four years [he] has lied to Iran, all our foreign policy is so bad. The oil of Iran goes to [Lebanese militants] Hezbollah, and not to us."

Babak the electrician from south Tehran wanted to change things, too. "This is very important for us, because we want to choose our own candidate—so we can choose our own destiny," he told me. "This is the first time that the campaign was marvelous. It was infinity!" He said Mousavi "will win one hundred percent."

THAT VIEW WOULD HAVE been music to candidate Mousavi, who himself voted in the mosque complex in Shahr-e Rey, where someone had spray-painted "Mousavi" on the wall in green. Officials at the polling station were uncertain how to handle their famous (or infamous) voter in this Ahmadinejad stronghold. As we photographers crammed in shoulder to shoulder, a podium was first set up a few yards away from the ballot box. Then it was moved much farther back and to the left. Finally, after a heated exchange between officials of the Ministry of Interior and Guardian Council—both pro-Ahmadinejad institutions that were jointly running Iran's elections, in a cumbersome dual system—the podium was moved all the way off to the side in a dark corner.

Pandemonium erupted when Mousavi arrived with his wife, Zahra Rahnavard, surrounded by a gaggle of cameras. Mousavi voted in businesslike fashion, like a man regularly described as uncharismatic. Then he moved to the out-of-the way podium, forcing all of us to scramble for new positions. He started to speak, but someone turned off the speaker system, just as someone had days before mysteriously shut down the speakers at Mousavi's final rally on the outskirts of Tehran.

Poking his finger, stained purple from the voting process, the candidate complained that some of his camp's election monitors had been refused access to polling stations. Early that morning Iran's text messaging service had also been cut off—a service that had been carrying ninety million messages a day, many of them pro-Mousavi notes to mobilize people.

"I thank all the people for their green presence which created a miracle," Mousavi told the crowd of heaving journalists. Iran's "unity and solidarity is an achievement of the Islamic Revolution. We should not be fearful about the free flow of information, and I urge officials to observe the law."

And where was Ahmadinejad? While Mousavi battled to have his voice heard in the scrum, the media-hungry president's office had kept uncharacteristically quiet about where he would vote. In fact, they kept it secret. He may have feared for his life after a man with a pistol—so the rumor went—tried to get into a recent rally. Some others suggested that his handlers did not want a repeat of popular discontent on election day, as Ahmadinejad had endured days earlier at another venue, when students chanted against him and rushed his convoy.

The president finally surfaced, but only a handful of enterprising photographers caught him flashing a victory sign while he held up his identity card, the pad of one finger inked with purple. "People's strong, revolutionary, and clear decision," he promised, "will bring a bright future for the nation."

But that future would not be with Ahmadinejad, if taxi driver Nasser had his way. He and his wife both had bachelor degrees; his kids were all engineers. He was a government worker but needed extra cash and drove the grimiest turquoise Paykan. I could see the road through the holes in the floor as he drove me to my next polling station.

"We don't decide with our heart, but with our brains," Nasser said. The usual stubble; trying to make ends meet. "All our family is for

Mousavi, because he is polite, he knows ethics and morality. It's the end of the line. People have never so easily expressed themselves. It's surprising, because for the last thirty years you could never say anything like this. Now people so easily say things against [the government]. It's nice."

And what about the turquoise color of his car? "It's the color of love."

THE ELECTION STARTED TO go haywire as dusk began to settle on voting day. Iranian TV had bathed its audience with a loop of platitudes, encouragement to vote, heroic scenes of mass turnouts in previous elections, and with updates on the huge turnout this time that prompted one, then two extensions of voting hours.

Yet some voting stations had inexplicably closed early; others ran out of ballots and were not resupplied.[3] Well before those polls closed, word spread that one Mousavi headquarters in a north Tehran district had been attacked by *basijis*. Video was immediately posted on the Internet of plainclothes militants breaking into the building with pepper spray and batons, smashing glass and office equipment. Mousavi activists locked the raiders into a single room until security police took them away. By the time I got there it was over, with police cars outside, flashing their lights, and the building cleared.

It was the first attack.

Eyewitnesses were also seeing fires set alight near other Mousavi offices, and menace began filtering onto the streets. Indications that much more serious trouble was on the way came during my ride back downtown. Voting stations in some places were still open, yet the Interior Ministry building was being fortified like I had never witnessed in any previous election. Already all foreign press and most Iranian journalists had been kicked out, leaving inside just the three main state-run media agencies—and outside more than a few surprised and alarmed Iranian journalists.

Policemen with radios directed cranes lowering concrete barriers to block access to the ministry—the huge monstrosity of a building where all votes nationwide were to be tallied and announced. In front of the concrete barriers were three rows of police cars, all with their lights flashing; behind them riot police were moving into formation. This was no spur-of-the-moment defense but clearly a measure carefully planned in advance.

Back at my hotel, the reason became obvious. The government was already putting out initial results, tabulating them far more quickly than during any previous election. They showed Ahmadinejad with a commanding two-to-one lead over Mousavi. That was a ratio that would remain precisely the same through the night as results were announced. Again, an oddity: in all previous elections the province-to-province returns affected the overall ratio as they came in.

It was time for celebration. In a statement late that night, Ahmadinejad's campaign declared that "a golden page in the glorious history of the Islamic Revolution has been witnessed."[4] It praised the Iranian people for proving that, while "reaching toward justice and fighting oppression, they will not stand down, and they will go against any darkness and filth."

Mousavi was appalled, and claimed that the true results were exactly the opposite, that it was he who had won an outright two-to-one victory. "In line with the information we have received, I am the winner of this election by a substantial margin," he said. He gave a warning: "People won't respect those who take power through fraud."[5] Mousavi's spokesman in Paris, the film director Mohsen Makhmalbaf, stated that the campaign had received a call from the Election Commission well before the first official results were announced, saying Mousavi had won. "Don't announce Mr. Mousavi's victory yet," they were told. "We will gradually prepare the public and then you can proceed."[6] At least three pro-Mousavi websites had been shut down that day—along with that of the candidate himself.

Mousavi complained of irregularities and sent the Supreme Leader an open letter about the risk of "illegal acts," asking that the ballot boxes be properly guarded and noting that his monitors had been barred from many polling stations.

As early as 6 P.M.—when polls were originally *meant* to close—the Fars News Agency, linked to the Revolutionary Guard, jumped the gun.[7] Their story said that Ahmadinejad had won with exactly that two-to-one ratio, but it was quickly taken off the Internet until many hours later, when it reflected the new "official" reality. Rumors spread that *Kayhan,* the mouthpiece of the archconservatives, had a banner headline ready for publication that declared Ahmadinejad the outright victor.

LATE THAT NIGHT ON voting day, I went out and watched hundreds of Mousavi supporters—frustrated, angry, some with tears in their eyes—as they gathered in front of the downtown campaign headquarters. They were in a state of shock.

"If there is rigging, Iran will be like judgment day!" they chanted.[8] "Mousavi: Congratulations on your presidency!"

One cleric among them stood up and spoke, his head barely higher than the rest in the poorly lit street. He reassured the crowd that so far only preliminary results had been announced. "The final vote is not in yet," the cleric said. The result could turn back in Mousavi's favor.

Those crowded around were mostly young Iranians, the same ones who had flooded the streets with such abandon and political boldness during Iran's electrifying three-week campaign. But now I watched as that hope turned to despair among those Mousavi supporters with green wristbands and headscarves. They had allowed their political hopes to rekindle, but their optimism for the future was about to be snuffed out by the police and other security forces. Already units hovered in the shadows just a few arm-lengths away, ready to pounce.

When the strike came, the police and state-sanctioned thugs tore into this group with batons, kicking and punching and blasting with pepper spray. The crowd tried to flee, shocked by the violence coming at them. I saw on one man's upper arm the imprint of the sole of a boot where he had been kicked. "This is robbery," he told me. "These people are not human."

One wisp of a young woman staggered away, sobbing and clutching her belly where she had been hit. She joined one cluster of people on the sidewalk that was burning pages of a newspaper, hoping the smoke would help dispel the choking gas. It was but a foretaste of the brutalities and bloodshed to come, as hundreds of thousands of Iranians took to the street against an election that they saw stolen outright by the regime to lock in hard-line rule in Iran for four more years—and perhaps forever.

"I think this is psychological warfare," one Mousavi supporter told me in the darkness while we hid behind scaffolding to avoid a police charge. "They want to scare us and give us the idea that we are losing."

THE MORNING AFTER, I watched as elderly women dressed in black celebrated Ahmadinejad's "victory" by handing out sweets to cars stalled in Tehran traffic. The president's local campaign offices were open, strung with lights and banners and in festive mood. Instead of waiting the usual three days to confirm the result—time in which irregularities would typically be investigated—Iran's Supreme Leader swiftly hailed the vote as a "divine assessment" and told the losing candidates to rein in "provocative behavior." [9] Ahmadinejad was the "chosen and respected president," Khamenei ruled, so every Iranian "must unanimously support and help him."

But such gentle scenes of joy and respect for divine writ would not last. Within hours, thousands of Iranians had taken to the streets of Tehran to protest the result, clashing with riot police and crying fraud. I watched as Mousavi supporters were forced out of their downtown headquarters by riot policemen with batons.

"The people's vote does not matter—it is all about Ahmadinejad winning," complained Majid as a line of some thirty motorcycles with two helmeted riot policemen on each roared past us to seal the headquarters building. [10] "These guys are serious—they don't care about anybody."

Tehran was erupting in violence as crowds gathered. Hundreds, then thousands, of riot police, *basiji* militiamen, and even vigilantes of Ansar-e Hezbollah sought to take control of the street. Motorcycles, a bus, and trash bins were torched, leaving columns of smoke rising thickly above the city. The sounds of ambulance sirens, car horns—many blaring in favor of Mousavi, as during the campaign—whistles, and screaming echoed throughout the day and long into the night. Protesters shouted, "Death to the Dictator!" and pelted police with stones.

It was difficult to avoid the violence. The friend I was meeting for lunch was nearly overrun by men racing away from a charge by riot police with Plexiglas shields, who had themselves been targeted by barrages of thrown stones. When the police charged, the protesters sought refuge at the front gate of the restaurant, their lungs heaving from the effort, while I hauled my friend in through the gate. When one lone cop caught someone on the street, people on their apartment balconies and in the street shouted, "Let him go!" and moved in for the rescue.

Mobile phone service was cut throughout the capital. But after the weeks of relatively good-natured street demonstrations and all-night political exuberance, it appeared that both sides were out of practice using violence or receiving it. Vigilantes, basijis, and police had not clashed violently with students or other protesters since 2003, and before that 1999, so these were largely inexperienced urban guerrillas. As political gatherings morphed into protests, as police and plainclothes thug infiltrators turned into club-wielding enforcers, no one had yet determined where the new red lines were, nor how far they could push their respective "enemy."

After nightfall on Vali Asr Avenue—that long boulevard where just a week before Pickup King Siavash had been inspired by the scale of the Green Movement's cross-city human chain; where I had ridden with Tooska at night into the pre-election street party—I watched as the riot police were supplemented by seventy-five vigilantes on motorbikes. They held aloft wooden sticks and clubs and chanted, "Hezbollah!" as they roared into a crowded intersection, their headlights flashing beams every which way on this urban front line.

Chaos ensued as the men of Ansar jumped off their bikes and started swinging. With long-sleeve shirts buttoned up to their beards and at their wrists, untucked, in light colors for *basijis* or darker hues favored by vigilantes, they were a force of menace. They were greeted by a rising chorus of complaint from the many Mousavi supporters on the street and the many more in their cars who leaned on their horns as the motorcycles had threaded their way through the traffic.

These were the same Ansar-e Hezbollah vigilantes who in 2001 had vowed future revenge and predicted, "This will be the decade of settling scores with the seditionists by the friends of the Revolution. And in this stage, the hands of the Hezbollah in repelling this sedition will not be tied." [11]

Now it was finally happening, as determined militants let loose in a cloud of motorcycle exhaust and revving engines. "The command was that we were to prevent any gathering of people taking shape," a *basiji* militiaman later told Lindsey Hilsum of Britain's Channel 4 News. He was a True Believer, from a household of front-line martyrs devoted to the Revolution:

> Any hint of protest was to be firmly suppressed. If anything occurred, to attack. Attacking people meant nothing. . . . Anyone who thought different to Ayatollah Khamenei and outside of the *velayat-e faqih* was considered an outsider. Therefore his protest has no place, therefore his opinion and protest is meaningless. It was simple. It was not for us to think anything of them—both voters and protesters. In our view, it was not a protest against the issue but a protest against Ayatollah Khamenei himself. And it's just not comprehensible to us that someone should want to question him. He is our guide. [12]

Iranians ran to escape the baton's bite, and so did I. Even faster than me getting away that first night was an older man, whose short gray hair and white beard I could just make out in the darkness as we hightailed it around a corner into an alley. He didn't slow up but looked back furtively to see if the club wielders were still at our heels. "Death to Imperialism!" he shouted. It looked to me like he had been here before, thirty years earlier—doing his bit to ensure a Revolution that would finally bring "freedom" to Iran.

Now those revolutionaries turned tyrants were themselves ordering the guns and billy clubs into the streets, just as the Shah had done. And once again Iranians were running from state-sanctioned violence as they struggled to restore their "freedom." This speedy old man, racing away in the darkness, his voice box full of bile, was showing me that Iranians were ready to fight.

AS UNREST SPREAD IN the following days, "defeated" candidate Mir Hossein Mousavi was defiant but not yet visible in public. "I'm warning that I won't surrender to this manipulation," he said on his resurrected website.[13] "The outcome of what we've seen from the performance of officials . . . is nothing but shaking the pillars of the Islamic Republic of Iran's sacred system of governance with lies and dictatorship."

Ahmadinejad fought back with a victory speech broadcast nationwide. The unrest was due to foreign media, of course. "All political and propaganda machines abroad and sections inside the country have been mobilized," he said.[14] "They have launched the heaviest propaganda and psychological war against the Iranian nation. Many global networks continuously worked, employing very complicated methods [in] a full-fledged battle against us."

Ahmadinejad declared that the vote had "awakened" Iran's pride and dignity. But it is difficult to describe the anger I heard that day, when Iranian reformists watched their dreams disappear and, worse, felt tricked into providing a mass turnout to suit the regime's own propaganda.

"I can't accept the results," one Iranian journalist told me. "When I left home yesterday I saw so many people line up. I've never seen that many, and many of those people came out for Mousavi." The accusations about Ahmadinejad manipulating the facts stuck in his mind; charges of government lying that were so prevalent that Mousavi rallies were populated with posters that read: "2 x 2 = 10," an Iranian version of Orwell's relative truth. "This guy is lying to the people every day. And if he has permission to lie, then he has the permission to change my vote."

I TRACKED DOWN TOOSKA, the law graduate, karate woman, painter of nudes, and music aficionado, who had been spurred to action by the promise of Mousavi's campaign. Like those of so many Iranians, the sky-high expectations created in her by the run-up to the election had been recorded by countless cell phones and video cameras. But were they now destined only to exist as useless memories?

"I was crying all the morning," Tooska told me while taking a break from the clashes.[15] She had been on the streets that night, protesting angrily alongside boyfriend, Mehdi, and mother, Leyla. Her eyes were red with emotion and tear gas, her heart broken. They had come off the streets long enough to talk. "Can you believe it? Do you think it could be true? How could it be possible?" Tooska asked me. "I will never vote again. Never. Never."

"I have something stuck in my throat," said Mehdi, who hadn't slept on election night, out of anger. "If you want to tell a lie, tell a big one."

The mother was angry, too, at herself for being suckered by Iranian politics one more time, and by Ahmadinejad's impossible win.

"You see this sadness in the eyes of the people," Leyla told me, pushing back her black headscarf. "They think we are foolish. Like a doll, they used us and then pushed us aside."

"That's why it hurts. It's shameless," added Tooska.

"One day they will push so hard, [Iran] will burst," said her mother.

"We're waiting for that day," said Tooska.

"Then we will vote," promised Leyla.

"That is the next political thing I will do," vowed Tooska. "Why do they think so many people voted? They *hated* [Ahmadinejad]. They came to vote him *out*."

"We won't be played with anymore," agreed Mehdi. "When I remember those nights [on the streets] and 'Ahmadi bye-bye!' even now I get goose bumps."

Sitting before me were two generations of Iranians, both beaten by the remnants of a Revolution that, to their minds, was far from fulfilling its promise of an Islamic *republic*. Yet Tooska's mother was an artist with a modest place up north, on the Caspian coast, and said that three of her workers had voted for Ahmadinejad, "because he is one of *them*." Leyla had last voted during Khatami's landslide elections in 1997 and 2001. But his failure to deliver looser restrictions and a kinder, gentler Revolution had turned her away from politics. Until this election.

"I promised I would never vote again," the mother said, the poison in her voice as thick as the black tar of her next cigarette. "That is why I am angry, because I was fooled again."

LATER THAT NIGHT, NOW the day after the election, from the balcony of my hotel room I could hear the back-and-forth of the street battles on Vali Asr Avenue. Armed with nothing but their rage, Mousavi supporters fought back with noise, whistles, hoots, horns, and chants. Leaving behind my cameras and notebooks and anything that would pinpoint me as a journalist—or even as a foreigner in the darkness—I would leave the hotel to dip into the running fights outside.

The resistance on the streets "was unprecedented," the former *ba-siji* militiaman told journalist Hilsum:

I had witnessed attacks before, but nothing at this level. People wouldn't stay back, they couldn't be suppressed and we were really in trouble. . . . The order came to attack everyone without restraint or mercy regardless of age. Anyone who was in disagreement. It was made clear, there was to be no difference between child or adult, men and women. Proper attack, without warning, or any discussion. This was very strange to me. Everything was surreal.

This was not trivial. We had permission to shoot. We were all to be armed.[16]

I hid behind my beard, plain button-up shirt, and black jeans, just enough cover to step into the action where police and vigilantes chased people down the sidewalks, and intelligence agents lingered in the shadows beyond the circles of streetlamp light, under trees, and at bus stops. Tehran's once-welcoming avenues, where the daily chaos of modern Persia played itself out in the boisterous capital, was transforming into a battleground.

Then, above it all, I began to hear the most powerful and incisive of calls, laden with meaning and resistance.

The first cry came and made my hair stand on end, a shiver shooting down my spine: *"Allah-o Akbar!"*—God is great. A statement of faith and of fact mouthed by every one of the world's 1.5 billion Muslims, but in Iran a phrase famous also as a tactic of nonviolent mass protest used during the 1979 Revolution to help bring down the Shah, as Iranians took to their balconies and rooftops to shout their defiant disdain. It was a religious phrase being used—like the choice of Islamic green as the color of the opposition—against the very Islamic Republic that should have had the monopoly on all such potent religious tools.

That one call that I heard—its vowels drawn out, by someone escaping an attack—was picked up from one set of lungs to another along Vali Asr Avenue. I began to hear *Allah-o Akbar!* spread, jumping from this apartment to the next, finding fertile voice everywhere it went.

The chorus continued for hours and leaped up in many other parts of Tehran. Whenever I view the video footage I shot from my balcony those nights, there is no denying the power behind these cries. The sense of shared resistance. Of angry hearts melded to common purpose. Of resolve not to give up again. Of the fact that women's voices often dominated.

Clashes and rioting continued into the night, blanketing entire districts in an acrid pall of black smoke. To see the scale of the damage, I called a taxi at 3 A.M. and went for a drive. A swath of destruction stretched from my downtown end of Vali Asr Avenue all the way north to Tajrish, and in numerous sections both east and west. Protesters were mostly gone, but roads were covered with shards of broken glass from state banks and wrecked bus stops, and the still-burning tires, garbage Dumpsters, and charred remains of motorcycles of security forces, their members caught and beaten.

Riot police dressed in camouflage suits and formfitting plastic armor, with chest, thigh, and shin guards, stood in tight clusters at the Parkway intersection, wreathed in foul-smelling smoke even as municipal workers began to sweep away the blackened mess. Streetlights had been pushed over and smashed. Heavy steel road dividers in front of the main offices of the state broadcaster IRIB had been ripped out and cast into the surging, rain-fed waters of the roadside drainage canals—in the same place where just a few nights before I had seen thousands of Mousavi supporters, whole families among them, ebullient with hope, mob a bus carrying their candidate from his last TV appearance before the vote.

That magical night I couldn't get close to the bus as Mousavi fans holding their mobile phones aloft to record the moment strained to get closer, sometimes literally swept off their feet in their bid for proximity. That night it took the bus an hour to painstakingly navigate the crowd. That night Mousavi bikers had revved their engines, clogging the roads and sidewalks alike while young Iranians bent my ear to tell me that they had never witnessed anything like this in their lives.

But the party had ended abruptly, and now on this lonely night the world was a different place, a stain of violence tattooed upon Tehran. As we passed two men on motorbikes, their shirts untucked and dirty work done, the driver complained. "They are *basiji*," he told me. "Mr. Ahmadinejad pays them a lot of money."

Iranians told me of security forces of all types—official and vigilante—beating Mousavi supporters, taking license plates, or breaking wing mirrors off cars that honked their horns for Mousavi, and even stepping into apartment parking lots where a single protester had sought sanctuary off the street, to smash headlights and car windows.

One *basiji* told a friend of mine: "We're still being soft on them. If we want to really crack down, this is very easy for us—it would take no time." [17] That *basiji*'s unit had used explosives to break into buildings where people had been raining stones down upon them; they arrested and beat twenty at a time.

After dawn, next to Mousavi's shuttered campaign headquarters, I found smears of dried blood along the wall and the sidewalk. Police denied that Mousavi was under house arrest.

The Sage was worried. "It's all spontaneous, and that's a negative [because] all things without a leader will go down," he told me. [18] Mousavi had not been seen in public for three days but issued a statement that encouraged "you, the Iranian nation, to continue your nationwide protests in a peaceful and legal way."

The fact that the Supreme Leader had anointed Ahmadinejad immediately meant the regime wanted to "wrap it up quickly," the Sage said. The defeated moderates Mousavi and Mehdi Karroubi—the cleric who as a presidential candidate in 2005 was denied a spot in the runoff by *basiji* and Revolutionary Guard fiddling—were not making a compelling case with their complaints. "There have been no documents, no details," the Sage lamented. "They said cancel the election, but based on what?"

His disenchantment was complete, as all the past examples of reformist failure informed his pessimism.

TO CONSOLIDATE "VICTORY" AND give the impression of business as usual, Ahmadinejad gathered all the foreign correspondents in Tehran for a press conference. Almost every journalist who applied had received a visa, so that we could verify the huge turnout. But now, until those visas expired, we turned to reporting on the most serious unrest in decades. Two days after the vote, the president-elect calmly took his seat onstage and proclaimed an unassailable result. Before him the usual mountain of fresh flowers; the backdrop a huge image of Iran's perfectly symmetrical Damavand mountain.

The True Believer began with a prayer for the speedy arrival of the

Twelfth Imam, then extolled the virtues of the vote. "Nearly forty million people took part in a totally free election," he said, calling it the "most glorious voting in recent history."[19] Liberal democracy as practiced in the West had manifestly failed, he said, while Iran had created a "new model of democracy" that "can be emulated" worldwide.

"We are noble people. We are smart people. We believe in truthfulness. The Iranian people hate lies," Ahmadinejad said, without a trace of irony. Iran wanted to "redress the political system around the world" and replace it with one based on "piety and justice for all," which did not rely on "bullying." The president dismissed the violence as "not important" and said the "government will be patient." He was the president of all Iranians and felt "love" for all citizens. "The situation in the country is very good now," he claimed. "[Iran] is one of the most stable countries in the world."

Ahmadinejad berated a British journalist who questioned the landslide result. "Don't worry about us," the president mocked. "Freedom prevails absolutely in our country—whatever they want, they say."

TO DEMONSTRATE HIS POPULARITY on the streets, Ahmadinejad invited journalists to join a rally he was holding immediately after the press conference at Vali Asr Square. The scene of burning barricades until early that very morning, the square had since been sealed off, cleared out, and carefully filled with regime loyalists.

We were taken to the rally in a couple of large vans but I was late and ended up standing in the last vehicle—a beaten-up open-backed truck that usually carried photographers during parades.[20] The view was excellent from this "official" car as we approached the first police cordons. The outer perimeter was patrolled by motorized riot squads, which had not been tipped off to the presence of journalists. We watched a phalanx of these menacing storm troopers in action as they rode two to a motorbike, with the passenger carrying a baton to savagely beat anyone trying to run away. The bikes chased down people in the street for no apparent reason, hurtling until contact, and then smashing backs and legs.

Another group of *basiji* and vigilante bikes, driven by men with beige shirts and truncheons and clubs—even lengths of wood—stuck into their handlebars, forced our "presidential" truck to stop and accused journalists of sneaking photographs of them. The thugs insisted that we all get out, but finally relented and let us pass.

Inside the security cordon at dusk, supporters of the hard-line president could demonstrate complete control. Many windows of state banks had already been repaired, the glass shards swept away. Waving Iranian flags and pictures of Ahmadinejad, the crowd crushed into the restraining bars, some of them shedding tears at the presence of their scruffily bearded hero. Most women were dressed all in conservative black, but there were a number of Western-looking women as well.

At the front and clutching a poster of Ahmadinejad to her chest, one woman sobbed uncontrollably. Creating a further barrier between the crowd and the crowned candidate were many officers of the Revolutionary Guard, which had already quietly taken charge of security in Tehran. Some stood at the precise spot where just days before I had witnessed motorists joyfully driving through the defaced portrait of the president.

Ever the pious populist, Ahmadinejad did not disappoint in his post-election rhetoric. High on a scaffolding stage hung with bunting, he eviscerated those Iranians who refused to accept the result. State-run TV showed footage of the rally throughout the evening, with heroic inspirational music and Ahmadinejad looking leaderlike, presiding over countless supporters in the heart of the capital. They gave the impression of determined adoration and of a huge turnout every bit as "epic" as the voter turnout had been. There were many thousands of people, and if framed a certain way they could look like tens of thousands. But that was not enough for the conservative trumpet *Kayhan*. The newspaper "Photoshopped" the most crowded elements of the image over and over, to create a front-page photo that portrayed an endless horizon of humanity, all turned out for the love of their president.[21]

· · ·

WHILE AHMADINEJAD WAS NOT able to muster hundreds of thousands—let alone a million or more—those numbers *did* in fact turn out the next day for Mir Hossein Mousavi, at Freedom Square. In defiance of an explicit government ban to hold a rally, the scale of the Green Movement support that stretched for miles across downtown Tehran shocked everyone who witnessed it. Since the first years of the Revolution, there had never been such a large march—a deliberate counterpoint to the stage-managed Ahmadinejad rally of the day before.

I had had to leave Tehran early that Monday morning, hours after my visa expired. The Islamic Guidance Ministry was ordered not to extend any journalist visas. I could not sleep, and overnight had been on the streets and on my balcony, where the chants of *"Allah-o Akbar!"* and "Death to the Dictator!" had begun again, with renewed fervor and more voices. It was raw defiance with blood-curdling effect. Still, when I left it was hard to see where the protest could go. Mousavi had yet to emerge. The Green Movement appeared leaderless. Ahmadinejad's rally had seemed to recapture the streets and the initiative.

That is what I was telling myself, sitting in the airport departure lounge and torn by my leaving, as dawn began to lighten the sky. "They can't change anything. It's done," a friend had told me of the opposition's bid to force a new election. From what I knew of the Islamic Republic, I expected that he was right. The Supreme Leader had spoken—a "divine" result could never be wrong, by definition, and would be enforced with all necessary violence. And the reformist camp had neither the tools nor, it appeared then, after years of intimidation and violence, the will to fight back.

Or so I thought. For it was just a few hours later, that very afternoon, day three after the election, a Monday, that the rally on Freedom Square reinvigorated the opposition's flagging confidence like nothing else. Mousavi made his first appearance in days, standing atop a car amid the ocean of people, many of them wearing green.

"God willing, we will take back our rights!" he shouted. "The vote of the people is more important than Mousavi or any other person." [22]

Marchers made fun of the aura that Ahmadinejad once claimed had surrounded him at the United Nations, chanting: "He saw the celestial halo, but he didn't see our votes."[23] One man on a balcony held a copy of the Quran over the heads of the protesters, in eerie echo of the send-off families once gave their sons, for blessings and for safety, as they departed for the Iran-Iraq front line.

Completely outnumbered, riot police were forced to stand by, helmets off and shields lowered. It was the first "silent" march in which there were deliberately few provocative chants. As demonstrators passed by one building that served as a *basiji* base, they surrounded it with a human chain and presented flowers, one witness told me.[24] But the calm was broken near dusk at another *basiji* base. News photographs showed a militiaman throwing a stone over the fence at protesters—one act that may have provoked the crowd to attack. Whatever the reason, the onslaught was fierce: Molotov cocktails set the building ablaze; stones were thrown, and people tried to climb the fence. Gunmen began shooting from the roof. There were shouts: "You killed our brothers, now we'll kill you!"[25]

"They shot three people in front of my eyes, while everything was going quietly and nicely," this witness told me, noting acidly that each victim had been shot in the chest or head. I had known him for years, and he was distraught, disbelieving. "Instead of tear gas, [they] started shooting in the air," he related. "That further agitated the people and they kept storming the building. Then they pointed without aiming [holding the rifles at hip level] and started to shoot."

This Iranian journalist described the gunmen as plainclothes *basijis* in riot helmets and body armor who fired an estimated three hundred bullets from the rooftop—roughly half into the air and the other half into the crowd, over the course of an hour. "The guy shooting from the roof was very calm, not like he was shooting at people," the witness told me. The gunmen fired as if "they were just trying to empty their guns into the ground, very cool, very relaxed."

The resulting images of protesters with green armbands carrying away their dead comrades—with looks of horror on their faces and shouts for help on their lips—evoked the prolonged bloody incidents that shook Iran before the 1979 Revolution. Back then, soldiers of the Shah had fired directly on student protesters, prompting a growing cycle of forty-day mourning protests, which produced yet more "martyrs" each round and eventually led to the fall of the government.

Anti-riot police on motorcycles rode in to reinforce the *basiji* militiamen but were knocked from their bikes by the crowd and beaten. The Iranian journalist was overwhelmed. "The taste in my mouth changed. I could not believe that [the regime] would be as stupid to do this. I felt angry. I felt that this was it. Blood cannot be ignored."

AND THIS IRANIAN WAS not alone, as news of the killings spread. "The idea of a *basiji* shooting a fellow Iranian!" exclaimed one war veteran quoted in the *New Yorker*.[26] "When I was a *basiji*, all we wanted to do was kill Iraqis. The idea of killing an Iranian wouldn't have entered my head!" The veteran related the reaction of his father, a retired bureaucrat who "adored Khomeini" and "would have given his life for the Iranian Revolution."

"You know what he said to me after he heard about the [eight] people who were shot last night? He said, 'I regret everything I've done in my life.'"

Hospital sources said eight bodies were collected by police at Rasoul Akram Hospital that Saturday, and another thirty-two at Imam Khomeini Hospital.[27] Many of the dead had multiple gunshot wounds, including one sixty-eight-year-old man shot twice in the back. Sweeping restrictions were imposed upon foreign journalists that prevented them from leaving their offices or hotels and banned all reporting on "illegal" demonstrations.

The regime's capitulation to a partial recount was "too little, too late," political scientist Sadegh Zibakalam said in Tehran.[28] "Nothing short of declaring the election result null and void would actually stop the protest of the people," he added. "The government is thinking all the time: 'If I stand tough, if I react violently, it will stop people from demonstrating.' What the government doesn't realize is that to react severely and try to suppress the people, it will only intensify people's anger."

Stealing the Vote

And there was no shortage of anger in Iran, as details of the election results pointed to a stolen election. Not just fiddled. Not just manipulated. Not just vote-rigged. All of which suggest tampering on the margins that made a slight difference. No. Many experts—and many Iranians themselves, who knew whom they had voted for, and why—saw that none of the numbers were adding up. The long-standing patterns of past elections were proving irrelevant. The only conclusion was that inside the Interior Ministry building—behind the concrete barriers, the rows of police cars, and ranks of riot police that had erected their ring of steel on election day even before polls closed—officials stole the election by simply making up the numbers. Period.

"We knew from both sides that Ahmadinejad was defeated," said Ebrahim Mehtari, a pro-Mousavi software engineer with access to mobile phone networks and polling results, who helped popularize the "Green" of the Green Movement.[29] "But we also saw them preparing from very early for Ahmadinejad's victory celebrations."

The "official" results from 39.2 million handwritten ballots gave Ahmadinejad 24.5 million votes, compared to Mousavi's 13.2 million, a ratio that Mousavi called a "dangerous charade."[30] But detailed local election data that in the past was always made public was not released for many days. And there were many discordant notes. Ahmadinejad made a surprisingly strong showing in wealthier cities and swept the countryside, and even more implausibly took the ethnic strongholds of his rivals.

Some key results were virtually impossible, in the context of Iran's social, ethnic, and political makeup. They showed Mousavi losing to Ahmadinejad in his hometown and ethnic Azeri heartland, for example. They showed reformist cleric Mehdi Karroubi, an ethnic Lor, getting hammered in his home province of Lorestan and scoring a minuscule number of votes nationwide. Official results showed him winning just 333,635 votes—a fraction of the five million he won in his 2005 bid, and a number even less than the number of campaign volunteers that Karroubi had painstakingly marshaled to his party over four years.

Mohsen Rezaei, a conservative candidate and former Revolutionary Guard commander, received almost as tiny a number of votes. The charade was complete when he actually *lost* votes over the course of four hours of the counting. Screen shots from Iranian IRINN television the day after the election clearly show that at 9:47 A.M., Rezaei had 633,048 votes; then at 1:53 P.M., with another five million votes counted nationwide, Rezaei's total actually *fell* to 587,913.[31]

And the tally showed Ahmadinejad winning Tehran province, where criticism has always been fiercest and the president, considering the capital a political write-off, had made little effort to campaign.

"I am convinced that they just pulled it out of their hats," said Farideh Farhi, an Iran expert who had studied Iran's election data for years.[32] "They certainly didn't pull it out of ballot [boxes] or even stuffed ballots; they just made up numbers and are putting it out. It just doesn't make sense. I do take the numbers of the Interior Ministry very seriously. I pore over them every election . . . to determine . . . what they mean. I always do that. In this election, I am not even going to spend time on this."

In fact, there *were* party monitors, many boxes were counted, and many records made, Farhi told me. "But at one point, immediately after the polls were closed, a very few people, without the presence of any monitoring mechanism, started giving out these numbers. And that's why I think this was brazen manipulation." She "simply cannot believe" that of the eleven million new Iranian voters, Ahmadinejad could have won eight million of them. "The history of the Islamic Republic is that they never vote for the status quo; they always vote for change."

According to the *New York Times,* it all took place inside that imposing Interior Ministry building—the one I had seen framed by dramatic lashes of lightning the night before the vote.

> One employee of the Interior Ministry, which carried out the vote count, said the government had been preparing its fraud for weeks, purging anyone of doubtful loyalty and importing pliable staff members from around the country.
>
> "They didn't rig the vote," claimed the man, who showed his ministry identification card but pleaded not to be named. "They didn't even look at the vote. They just wrote the name and put the number in front of it." [33]

The all-new results had a more strategic purpose than just putting Iran's archconservatives on top. It was the latest step in the plan to ensure that reformists—or moderates of any kind—would never again wield power in Iran. As Farhi told me:

> It wasn't that they only wanted Ahmadinejad to win. They also wanted to make a case that we can do anything we want to do. And they were, I argue, very much interested in demoralizing this twenty to thirty percent of extra voters that are coming in.
>
> They simply are not interested in these people [remaining] in politics in Iran. They want them to become demoralized and cynical, because their participation in the Iranian electoral process is extremely destructive for the *nezam*. . . .
>
> What they have not counted on, of course, is [that the] group of people that they essentially think of . . . as Westernized wishy-washy liberals, who never stand for anything, would actually be upset that this election was stolen in such a brazen way.
>
> They assumed: "Ah, you know, we go into the streets, we yell at them, and a couple of shots and they go home and close their doors."

There were plenty more anomalies. The Ministry of Interior put the number of eligible voters at 46 million, while Iran's Center of Statistics estimated 51 million.[34] Mousavi's newspaper reported that more than ten million votes were missing personal identification numbers, making them untraceable.

Because voters could also cast their ballots at any station, using only their birth certificates, there had been wide latitude in past elections for state charitable organizations to "rent" those documents from the poor.[35] Further, birth certificates are not always canceled upon a person's death, and duplicates for "lost" ones are easily obtained. Reformists claimed that in the 2005 presidential election, more than two million such "ghost" ballots were cast by *basijis* and others to rig the result.[36]

From the start, critics were also anxious that one-third of the forty-five thousand polling stations were mobile units impossible for party monitors to observe—ten times more numerous than in previous elections, and under the control of the Revolutionary Guard, not the police.

Almost three weeks before the vote, a group of Interior Ministry officials sent a letter to the president complaining that "more than 70 percent of the ministry's election experts . . . have been removed within the past three or four months."[37] They noted that "all the software production issues involving the coming presidential election" had been taken from the Interior Ministry and "handed over to one . . . from outside."

A letter from the Mousavi and Karroubi campaigns to the Guardian Council stated that 2.6 million more ballots were printed than those officially declared, and pointed out the "extremely dangerous and worrisome" fact that "the number of seals that will be used to stamp final tally reports is twice as high as the number of voting centers, without any plausible explanations."[38] The candidates further warned of rumors that "identification cards of soldiers at military stations have been collected"—so that their votes might be made for them. There was a highly unusual clandestine meeting with all provincial governors at the Interior Ministry, too: "What secretive and confidential issue was being discussed that only governors and the minister can know about, to the exclusion of the ministry's other officials and staff?" they asked.

Interior Ministry employees wrote a second letter five days before the vote, reinforcing concern that two seals had been allocated to each ballot box—instead of the usual one—and that 58 million ballot papers had been printed for 46.2 million eligible voters. The letter also declared the existence of a "religious decree to manipulate the results" by a cleric in Qom, with details that matched Ayatollah Mohammad Taghi Mesbah-Yazdi, one of the president's staunchest supporters.[39] The decree, according to the letter, said "everything is permitted to this end" to ensure an Ahmadinejad victory.

THE INCUMBENT WAS CLEARLY anointed for reelection long before voting day, according to one former *basiji*, who monitored ballot boxes and spoke to journalist Lindsey Hilsum:

> We had received orders a matter of months before . . . that Mr. Khamenei has Mr. Ahmadinejad in mind for the presidency and so he must be announced as the winner. It's he who is best suited to this Revolution, order and *velayat-e faqih*. . . .
>
> In the private meeting we had for those responsible for the ballot boxes, including my brother and me, it was made clear. The orders were announced as to how everything would be conducted on the day of the election. . . .
>
> For us who were responsible for the ballot boxes the order was this: that [Khamenei's] wish is for Ahmadinejad to win. For illiterate people and those not able to complete their ballots, you must do so for them and complete them accordingly [for Ahmadinejad], no matter who their vote was intended for. Same with blank votes. In the counting the blank votes wouldn't be announced as void.[40]

FOR ANECDOTAL EVIDENCE, CONSIDER the Zagros Mountains village of Bagh-e Iman, located near Shiraz. With 850 households, Bagh-e Iman featured in thirty years of research of Iranian villages by

Eric Hooglund.[41] According to "longtime, close friends" there, he reported, "residents were in shock" and "seething with moral outrage because at least two-thirds" of all adults there believed the election was stolen.

"The week before the vote had witnessed the most intense campaigning in the village's history, and it became evident that support for Mir Hossein Mousavi's candidacy was overwhelming," wrote Hooglund. "Supporters of Ahmadinejad were even booed and mocked when they attempted rallies and had to endure scolding lectures from relatives at family gatherings. 'No one would dare vote for that hypocrite,' insisted Mrs. Ehsani, an elected member of the village council."

Local election observers estimated that Ahmadinejed could not have won more than 20 or 25 percent of the vote. As Hooglund described:

Carloads of villagers actually drove to Shiraz to participate in the massive pro-Mousavi rallies that were held on the three nights prior to the balloting. And election day itself was like a party in Bagh-e Iman. Many people openly announced their intentions to vote for Mousavi as they cheerfully stood in line chatting with neighbors, and local election monitors estimated that at least 65 percent of them actually did so. . . .

By Saturday evening, the shock and disbelief had given way to anger that slowly turned to palpable moral outrage over what came to be believed as the theft of their election. The proof was right in the village. "Interior Ministry officials came from Shiraz, sealed the ballot boxes and took them away even before the end of voting at 9 p.m.," said [election monitor] Jalal. In all previous elections, a committee comprised of representatives from each political faction had counted and verified the results right in the village. The unexpected change in procedures caught village monitors off guard, as it had everywhere else in the country. . . .

People refused to believe that Ahmadinejad could have been reelected. Larger demonstrations [in Shiraz for three days] attracted carloads of supporters from Bagh-e Iman and other villages, including several that were sixty kilometers from Shiraz. . . .

Nevertheless, the Guardian Council unequivocally ruled out all chances of changing the result, even before investigating 646 complaints of irregularities. Accusations were overblown. "Statistics provided by the candidates, who claim more than 100 percent of those eligible have cast their ballot in 80 to 170 cities are not accurate," the Council spokesman said.[42] "The incident has happened in only 50 cities." Indeed, some of those cities registered as much as a 40 percent higher turnout than registered voters. Not to worry, the Council reported: that very unlikely anomaly affected *only* three million votes—just 7.5 percent of the total across all of Iran.

THE PROBLEM WASN'T IN Iran or with *real* Iranians, anyway, officials began to promulgate—it was coming from outside, from Velvet Revolutionaries unleashed by the election chaos who had planned to take to the streets, regardless of the outcome. Foreign Ministry spokesman Hassan Ghashghavi accused the BBC and CNN of setting up a "situation room and a psychological war room."[43] The BBC's permanent Tehran correspondent, Jon Leyne, was forced to leave the country after noting on air that the Supreme Leader had made the "biggest mistake of his life" in his mishandling of the vote, and that regime "thugs" had become the law. The Canadian-Iranian correspondent for *Newsweek*, Maziar Bahari, was arrested; so was Greek-British freelance writer-photographer Iason Athanasiadis.

Reports began to emerge of alternative and "true" results, such as one letter signed by dissident Interior Ministry employees, which registered Mousavi with 57 percent of the total, compared to Ahmadinejad with 28 percent.[44] In this scenario, the other two candidates had much more realistic returns (7.2 percent for Mehdi Karroubi, and 6 percent for Mohsen Rezaei), and turnout was slightly lower, at 81 percent.

Similar figures from an "informed source" at the Ministry of Interior also appeared on opposition websites. Further claims from insiders held that false statistics had been deliberately fed into the ministry's software programs to turn a doctored result into a plausible outcome. The truth of all these claims was difficult to establish. One trusted Iranian colleague told me he knew a Mousavi activist who had deliberately crafted a piece of disinformation—a letter purportedly from Ministry of Interior staff that put Mousavi in first, Karroubi in second, and Ahmadinejad in third in the final result.[45]

Actual incongruities were pinpointed by London's Chatham House think tank, which found that achieving the official election results would have required dramatic swings of political allegiance.[46]

For Ahmadinejad to have won all the votes attributed to him in one-third of Iran's provinces, for example, he would have needed to win "not only all former conservative voters, and all former centrist voters, and all new voters, but also up to 44 percent of former reformist voters, despite a decade of conflict between these two groups," the report noted. Official data showed that participation rates in several provinces increased by an extraordinary 75 percent, yet "regional variations in participation have suddenly disappeared."

Anomalies in the count of reformist cleric Mehdi Karroubi "suggest that they were created by a computer," the report found. Indeed, the official figures showed Karroubi's support plummeting in his home province from 55.5 percent in 2005 to just 4.6 percent—with the balance all swinging to the hard-line Ahmadinejad—Karroubi's political polar opposite. Concluded the report: "This, more than any other result, is highly implausible."

POWER, WEALTH, AND IDEOLOGY were all at stake as the new leadership troika—the Revolutionary Guard, the Supreme Leader, and Ahmadinejad and his neoconservative cabal—tried, once and for all, to attain political invincibility. But the increasingly bloody tug-of-war over votes was now exposing the so-called defenders of the Revolution as murderers and brutes. The protesters and their leaders were showing no signs of caving in, as they had every time in the past. And deep fissures were emerging among Iran's ruling elite as the power struggle commenced.

"Now we are entering the purge phase [of the Revolution]," a Western-educated Iranian analyst told me in Tehran.[47] "So the Leader wants to eliminate all the [other] first-generation revolutionaries."

Top of the hit list was rival and former president Ali Akbar Hashemi Rafsanjani, who had previously made no secret of his wish to curb the power of the Supreme Leader. As chair of the eighty-six-member Assembly of Experts, which in theory had the power to remove the Leader, Rafsanjani was often seen as a danger to Khamenei, and for weeks after the vote he tried unsuccessfully to lobby fellow assemblymen to censure the Leader.

It was Rafsanjani's letter, just days before that 2009 vote, that had warned of "fire . . . flaring during and after the election." But the fact that several members of Rafsanjani's family—including his daughter Faezeh—were arrested shortly after the vote signaled how the aging cleric's power had ebbed.

Mousavi was also a rival. When he was prime minister in the 1980s, Mousavi clashed frequently with Khamenei, who was then president. Ayatollah Khomeini would often have to intervene to end disputes, and sided frequently with Mousavi. Other titans being squeezed out included the still-popular Khatami and the defeated candidates Karroubi and Rezaei.

Still, in a bid to stanch the hemorrhaging of his power, the Supreme Leader met with representatives of all four candidates and the Guardian Council. "Their mentality is swollen with illusions about the enemy; they are trying to find the supposed leaders," one colleague told me in Tehran.[48] "This is what it takes for a new order to emerge, one shaped by the Supreme Leader, totally characterized by his own ambitions."

But senior clerics in Qom were also up in arms—many on the side of the "defeated" candidates. They were finally pushed too far by an authoritarian Supreme Leader they never considered very "supreme," who, they were convinced, was now endangering the Revolution by veering further from its most cherished ideals. Khamenei had for two decades been fighting a rearguard action against clerics of far more superior learning to establish his religious and political credentials. Disappointment was entrenched to the point that leading dissident Grand Ayatollah Hossein-Ali Montazeri, the once-chosen heir of Khomeini with tufted ears, had in 2007 warned that "people have changed and won't walk across minefields [as during the war] without asking questions." [49]

By mid-2009, the postelection chaos was proof of that change. "No one in their right mind can believe" the election results, Montazeri wrote, adding that "a government not respecting the people's vote has no religious or political legitimacy." [50] The grand ayatollahs had, by one count, voted three to one in favor of Mousavi. [51] One even advised Mousavi that he should consider his opponents to have an "erroneous and deviant type of thinking" that was the "enemy of God's religion." [52]

Those were the first of many attacks from senior clergymen, who began to wake from years of "quietist" slumber. Of course, not all clerics were unhappy. For hard-liners like Ayatollah Mesbah-Yazdi—Ahmadinejad's spiritual adviser, who approved shedding the blood of sinners—this was when the "corrupt on earth" were showing themselves.

Already, scores of senior reformists had been picked up, including in one day prominent strategist and 2000 assassination target Saeed Hajjarian, former vice president Ali Abtahi, former foreign minister and dissident Ebrahim Yazdi, and critic and economics editor Saeed Laylaz, all of whom I had interviewed many times. Khatami's brother, Mohammad Reza Khatami, was briefly arrested. The number of "untouchables" too important to arrest had shriveled to single digits. These were dramatic steps, all taken in the name of blocking Velvet Revolution in Iran. It was a dangerous gamble, one Iranian colleague told me: "Even if they get away with it, and Ahmadinejad survives, their legitimacy has taken a serious blow."

• • •

THE MOST VISCERAL EVIDENCE of that dissipating legitimacy
came at the hands of sinister men prowling the streets during the unrest: the armed intelligence agents and pro-government vigilantes
wearing everyday clothes. When clashes erupted, they would materialize from nowhere to take part in the fight, then disappear again.

Those violent phantoms of the regime were caught on film, their
images posted online in a name-and-shame campaign to stop them.

"We are now identifying them, one by one, [and] this really scares
them," an Iranian source in Tehran told me.[53] They were the ideological "pressure group" vigilantes so active during the Khatami era, who
were linked to senior hard-line clerics and the Leader's office. Mousavi
accused the government and those irregular forces of "appalling murder" carried out by "disciples of fraud and lies."[54]

Police often stood by as these anonymous elements worked. But
the Internet became indispensable in undermining them. "The pictures are coming from all over," the source told me. "People look at
them; some recognize them as their neighbors or someone they have
once known." The website emerged from Facebook, which, along
with Twitter, had become an important mobilizing tool for the opposition. Early in the protests, it began by showing nine images of
Iran's most shadowy forces at work. The top image was a close-up of
a helmeted man with an AK-47 assault rifle, a *basiji* who fired from the
rooftop at demonstrators, killing some of the eight who died during
the unforgettable mammoth rally the third day after the election.

Other images showed men beating protesters or engaging in thug-
gish behavior—all with their faces clearly visible. One man rode on
the back of a motorbike, tucking a pistol into his belt. Another held
a pistol in his left hand while he drove on the street. Yet another photograph showed a classic *chaghoo-kesh* street thug. But this was not a
young punk. It was a middle-aged man with a gray mustache and untucked short-sleeve white shirt, brandishing a long kitchen knife. It
was not long before details were volunteered about the thug, from his
name to rank in the Revolutionary Guard.

"We have his cell phone and home address," the source told me, gleefully. Some Mousavi supporters had paid a visit, but he was gone. "He has left town!"

"THIS IS THE ISLAMIC Republic's 'Twilight Zone.' People have not been here before," professor Anoush Ehteshami told me.[55] The *nezam* was following its "instinct" to clamp down and control information, to "behead the movement [and] get their people on the street." The U.K.-based Iran expert did not see a nonviolent way forward, but knew that the values once proclaimed by the Revolution—and enshrined in Iran's constitution—were under stress. "All the slogans are now having to be lived by: That the people have the right to express their opinion freely. Well, where is it? That they have the right to assembly. Well, where is it? That their vote is sacrosanct. Well, where is it?"

The Supreme Leader was steering Iran's Revolution far from the rich promise of April 1979, when Khomeini proclaimed the "first day of God's Government."[56] Iranians had created the Islamic Republic in a referendum "where the whole country rushed to the polls with ardor, enthusiasm, and love in order to cast their affirmative votes," Khomeini said in triumph back then. "God Almighty [turned Iranians into] exemplars for all the world's oppressed."

The first Leader of the Revolution made a vow: "Tyranny has been buried, and all forms of transgression will be buried along with it."

The Supreme Voice

But three decades later, the second Leader of the Revolution was trapped in a self-made labyrinth of tyranny. Ayatollah Ali Khamenei stepped to the Friday prayer podium precisely one week after the disputed 2009 election to deliver the most anticipated sermon in recent memory. Iran had not experienced such turmoil since the first years of the Revolution—the popular anger, the bloodshed, the depth of outright doubt about clerical and military rule.

Many Iranians were looking for a message of unity, expecting the Supreme Leader to unveil a compromise that would begin to heal the wounds of the previous week; that he might somehow find a way to give the Revolution back to *all* of them. But advancing age and two decades already as Iran's God-gifted Guide had left him rigid and inflexible. Khamenei wore the same black outer robe and turban that he always did, the *chafiyeh* scarf favored by the *basiji* a revolutionary totem around his neck. But the man who stepped to that podium—reaching for the barrel of the AK-47 (upright, on a permanent stand, and barely visible) with his good left hand, as he had so often done—was incapable of compromise.

He believed his post was infallible. Back in 2000, when some reformists had suggested that the man who occupied the Supreme Leader's position was not above the law, Khamenei said they were wrong. Iranian state radio had quoted him explaining that the "true meaning" of the concept of *velayat-e faqih,* or the authority of the Leader, is that "the person in charge of the Islamic government does not make mistakes and if he does he will not be the Supreme Leader from that moment."[57] He added: "This is an obvious point that must be understood well and spelled out properly."

SO IN JUNE 2009, with the air still acrid from the smell of burning tires, garbage, and tear gas, after one week of protest and beneath the weight of hundreds of thousands—perhaps as many as three million—fellow Iranians willing to step onto the streets to ask, "Where is my vote?" there could be no hint of error. No admission that the engineered stealing of the election, and its delegitimizing aftermath, might have been an imperfect process. Nor that the deployment of vicious ideological militiamen and riot police that had drawn so much blood from peaceful protesters—indeed, had attacked the *people*—was in any way a ruthless act of barbarism that belonged to a previous era. Nor that the Revolution, which was meant to bring "utopia" to Iran and serve as a model for all Muslims worldwide, had been derailed by a hard-line project to impose an undemocratic, repressive tyranny.

Instead Khamenei insisted it was all happening with divine sanction and godly insight. Those who did not embrace this sacred path were now the enemy—before God, and in the eyes of this middling cleric trying desperately to block further loss of his power. After thirty years of clear instruction, everyone in *this* congregation knew how to deal with enemies.

"If there is any [more] bloodshed, leaders of the protests will be held directly responsible," Khamenei told the overflowing crowd of tens of thousands that was bolstered by ranks of *basijis*.[58] The election was "God's blessing," and those who were defeated had better get used to it. He accused the protesters of aiming to overthrow the regime and of being used by the "espionage machines working for Zionists and the Americans." The British were the "most treacherous" in their involvement.

The Supreme Leader gave his imprimatur to a far fiercer crackdown. Khamenei warned the opposition that if they wanted to "break the law," they should "see the enemy working. They should see the hungry wolves. I suggest they open their eyes and see the enemy." Forty million Iranians voted, and "this might be considered as worship for many of these people," the Leader said, on his way to an especially Orwellian point. "People should know: the Islamic establishment will never manipulate people's votes and commit treason."

ACTIVISTS WERE ANGRY, AND not a little afraid. They had been labeled "enemy." The freedoms that were clearly defined by the constitution—to publicly gather, and to speak out—simply no longer existed. Even more than before, black was white. And white was black. Two plus two made five. Already the anger was broadening, turning the initial call for a rerun of the election into a new convulsion against the whole regime. Far from preserving the Revolution, the Leader's continued demand for total obedience was hastening its demise. More protests, he warned, would bring "blood, violence and chaos."

"*No room* for compromise. What are we going to do now? Go out and get killed?" one Tehran analyst asked me, deflated after hearing Khamenei's oration:

> He gave a clear green light to the thugs of the *basiji* to *kill,* and the responsibility is on *our* shoulders. There is no chance to *change* the system within the system. Not one iota. What the hell is he thinking? I, as an Iranian, can't figure this out. He is hanging himself. Shot himself in the *balls.*
>
> We have lost *trust* and *hope* in the *nezam.* [Khamenei] knows how dangerous that is. He said it in the sermon. Especially his last few words, when he became very emotional and talked about his disabled body, and whatever credit and dignity he has, he is ready to offer it to the Revolution and Islam—it's something like an unannounced war.[59]

BUT THIS UPRISING WOULD not be put down by mere words, no matter how high their provenance. Defiant protesters were on the streets the next day, despite the Supreme Leader's warning—or perhaps because of it. Police and "security" forces were waiting to crush them. Mir Hossein Mousavi rebutted every point made by Khamenei and said responsibility for the violence lay with "those who cannot tolerate non-violent actions."[60] He added, for his protesting supporters: "Rest assured that I will always be at your side."

In scenes of exceptional savagery, regime enforcers tore into the unarmed "terrorists" and "rioters"—the terms reserved on Iranian state TV for this "enemy"—across Tehran and other cities. Anti-riot police and religious militia used batons, clubs, water cannons, tear gas, and live rounds against civilians. Authorities cut off text messaging and cell phone use. Protesters fought back with bricks, stones, knives, and even screwdrivers.[61] On that day, *basijis* turned their fellow Iranian citizens into the equivalent of infidel enemies by rousing themselves up for battle with the chant: "Death to the opponents of *velayat-e faqih!*"[62]

As one *basiji* would later recall: "It was very hard. If there was an issue with killing, it was explained that the killing was for a cause and was a good deed. . . . Because the directive had been given, permission had been granted. It was intolerable. . . . I can't mentally and ideologically fathom what's happened." [63]

According to another *basiji:* "Islam had become a curtain for them, from behind which they could do whatever they wanted," the former militant told journalist Lindsey Hilsum. "Directives were presented as the Islamic directives. Everything we say is Islam. You mustn't question Islam. Disagreement with our directives is disagreement with Islam, in other words disagreement with God. We became like machines."

Iranians were feeling it. "There is a bloodbath on the streets of Tehran . . . It is fucking crazy!!" one Tehran observer told me of the fight.[64] Police were "more ruthless," he said, and he was hearing reports of forty dead, more than two hundred injured, and five hundred arrested. I suggested the level of carnage was "getting into Shah territory," referring to the year leading up to the Revolution when protesters were gunned down.

The observer was spitting: "Turning your gun on the people. *That* is already Shah's territory. Now they are working on beating his record, the bastards. And they may yet beat it. They may, but I promise: we shall prevail—this is a fact—when a government pulls its gun on its people, it is only steps away from its grave!!"

AMONG THE "TERRORISTS" THE day after Khamenei's ultimatum to stop or face bloodshed was an Iranian acquaintance of mine who had been at every protest and got within half a mile of Revolution Square before she had her biggest scare. Writing in an open letter, she estimated the crowd to be fifty thousand, though regime enforcers of all flavors were ready; water cannons were being used at the gates of Tehran University—site of some of the most important clashes in 1979.

> They kept breaking us up. . . . One young woman's head was broken in front of us. We all jumped in the gutter, and some of our men protected us from the batons. The girl was in a bad way. We

dragged her out and then the police just kept shouting. One of them had really red eyes and was screaming from the bottom of his lungs. Then the tear gas came and we kept running, but then we re-grouped. At some point the younger men among us started chasing them, chanting "Death to the Basij."

But then came more tear gas and batons.[65]

Speaking with me later, this protester said her clothes had been covered with blood during the rescue. She was not sure the girl with the broken head would live. But that was just the first round. Even trying to leave the area meant threading a gauntlet of riot police that had deployed across central Tehran. "At the cross section . . . the robocops were waiting, the ones in black with the rubberized gear," the witness recalled.[66] A friend of hers was hit on the knee, and another run over by a car. "She says the hospital was full of people coming in with broken heads and limbs."

Intelligence agents were now keeping hospitals under "severe surveillance."[67] Doctors had been ordered not to list any violence-related causes on death certificates. Bodies could only be retrieved by police, not families. The Revolutionary Guard sent an "urgent" memo marked "top secret" to the Ministry of Health, stating that "the disclosure of medical documents to all injured patients of recent events is strictly prohibited."[68]

And there was an important difference on that day of defiance to the Leader. This protester was struck by the diversity of the crowd, evidence that the dividing line in Iran's long-standing culture wars was shifting. "Today, there were all kinds of people there, not just rich Westernized Iranians," this protester wrote. Safe at home that night, she was frustrated and trying to steel herself for any future rallies. "We were scared, but we went. We don't know what will happen next, but if they organize it we have to go again, there's no other way," she wrote. "We can't let the extreme elements turn this into another Lebanon or Palestine. There is no way but to go out."

• • •

AMONG THE CASUALTIES THAT Saturday was Neda Agha Soltan, a twenty-six-year-old whose gory death after being shot in the chest by a *basiji* motorcyclist was caught on a cell phone video. The image captured the compelling human drama being played out across Iran, finally distilling in a single frame all the confusing, shaky cell phone video and chaos of seething street clashes, the burning motorcycles, the spurting blood, the hopeless asymmetry of opposing forces—and the tenacity of green-clad Iranians in taking on the charging brutes of the regime.

Here was the "Angel of Iran," icon of the epic battle between the powers of tyranny and torture, against those Iranian democrats willing to die for their cause of freedom, in the fourteen-century-long tradition of Shiite Muslim resistance.

None better understood the emotive global power of that iconic image of Neda's death than the Islamic Republic itself. The regime was among the most effective practitioners of visual propaganda—and of lionizing individual martyrs—of modern times. It was Ayatollah Khomeini, in fact, who reassured his followers at the start of the 1979 Revolution not to worry about their lack of weapons with the words: "Propaganda is explosive as a grenade." [69] Thirty years later, propaganda was just as potent, as Neda's new narrative punctured the bubble of divine perfection that the regime had long inflated around itself, replacing it with an irrefutable image of brutality. Of innocence crushed in the name of . . . what?

WHERE WERE THE IDEALS of God's gift to the modern world, the 1979 Revolution and its proclaimed "victory of light over darkness"? [70] The regime tried to wriggle away from responsibility for Neda's death. The hard-line newspaper *Javan* went so far as to declare that BBC correspondent Jon Leyne had staged the murder to spice up his television news report. [71]

But witnesses told a different and very damning story. Iranian doctor Arash Hejazi was standing close to Neda when she was shot and had tried to stop the bleeding, but the bullet had hit the young woman's aorta and lung, causing her blood to drain so fast that "in less than a minute . . . she couldn't survive," he told journalist Lindsey Hilsum.[72] As Dr. Hejazi tried to save Neda, he saw the crowd catch and grapple with a man who shouted, "I didn't want to kill her!" even as he was set upon and his Basij ID taken from him. Hejazi recalled: "All the people there had the impression he was the shooter or he wouldn't have shouted 'I didn't want to kill her.' "

The identity of the supposed killer, Abbas Kargar Javid, was swiftly posted on the Internet, along with copies of his Basij ID card, issued by the Interior Ministry, and details of his life. He was a member of the "Group of Fatemeh Zahra's Devotees—West Tehran Fighters," and on election day had been a Guardian Council monitor of ballot box 1218.[73] The West Tehran *basiji* force created this unit for "serious confrontation against the enemy's cultural encroachment" after a Khamenei speech along those lines in 1992.[74]

But it was all lies, according to the regime. No *basiji* could have killed an Iranian citizen. And regime enforcers weren't issued firearms. One *Kayhan* writer averred that "the bullet is not any of the calibers that are supplied to Iranian security forces. That at least we know. . . ."[75]

Neda's family was sternly instructed not to speak to the media nor to mourn. The doctor was forced to flee to the United Kingdom because his eyewitness testimony was so central to the Neda narrative, to its impact on public opinion. Later the regime would even accuse the doctor himself of killing Neda, and staged demonstrations by fist-pumping militants calling for Hejazi's extradition from England to face "justice" in Iran.

Neda's boyfriend, Caspian Makan, spoke out on BBC Persian TV and other Farsi-language satellite channels—until police came to bundle him off to Evin Prison, reportedly deploying snipers on nearby rooftops during the arrest.[76] Interrogators produced one false scenario after another that they wanted Makan to sign off on, for example, that Neda was a member of the anti-Iran Mojahedin-e Khalq (MKO/MEK), or she had been on a suicide mission. He denied them all during two months in prison, and so was charged with "conspiracy to overthrow the Islamic Republic of Iran." After release on bail he said he made daily dawn visits to Neda's simple dirt-covered grave, number 32, in a corner of the Behesht-e Zahra necropolis. He was under constant surveillance. Finally, for his own safety, he fled Iran—and Neda's grave.

"She joined the protesters from the beginning. She was very brave and strong," Makan said in an interview published after his overland escape to Turkey. The young couple had argued, with Neda devoted to the cause. She told him all Iranians were responsible now; it was her duty to go out. "Even if we had a child, I'd carry my child to these demos on my back," she told him.

Later a gravestone was laid there, but it was defaced—Neda's engraved black marble image chipped by a dozen bullets or by repeated blows from a blunt object. The grave was under twenty-four-hour guard to keep it from turning into a martyr's shrine.

"They didn't just shoot her once. They continue to shoot at Neda to this day by desecrating her grave," Makan said.[77] The government produced a new documentary that claimed Neda was a U.S. and British agent, and her death a hoax.

"This is about the very survival and legitimacy of the Islamic Republic," the U.S.-based political scientist Ahmad Sadri told me.[78] "The excuse is the [voting] irregularities, but the real complaints go very deep, to the very nature of the *nezam*." Candidate Mir Hossein Mousavi was taking care to distance himself from any attempt to overthrow the system, which he had done so much in his career to create and preserve. But he admitted, as the death toll climbed, that the protests were tapping deeper roots.

"These days and nights a turning point is being forged in the history of our nation," Mousavi said.[79] "We are not against the *nezam* and its laws [but] against the deviations and lies, and we want to reform them; a reformation that returns us to the pure principles of the Islamic Revolution."

Mousavi urged his followers to keep up the pressure—and take back ownership of Iran's most critical event. "The Revolution is your legacy. To protest against lies and fraud is your right. Be hopeful that you will get your right and do not allow others who want to provoke your anger [to] prevail." [80]

Mousavi was channeling sacred impulses that had first been voiced by Ayatollah Khomeini in the 1960s and 1970s, when the founder of the Revolution had bellowed, "A single word was enough once to cause a wave of enthusiasm among the people, because . . . [t]hey are living now in the shadow of the bayonet, and repression will let them say nothing. They want someone to stand up fearlessly and speak out." [81]

But in 2009, hope of change was fading as the regime fought back. Word spread of serious abuse and torture inside detention centers. Protesters were torn between their desire to challenge an election result they considered a fraud—relying on Article 27 of Iran's constitution, which says peaceful marches "may freely be held"—and their fear that yet more violence might not bring them closer to their goals.

The morning after the demonstration in which she had bloodied her clothes—when she vowed there was "no way but to go out" to future rallies—my marcher friend was having second thoughts. She had witnessed too much violence; she worried for her offspring if something were to happen to her.

"You know, today I'm feeling that it's something between them [rival clerics within the establishment], and we shouldn't get killed for it," this mother told me. [82] "I am wondering, what can be good? What can come of it? What are we going to get out of this? Giving up hope is probably the worst thing we could do. I'm telling you, as of an hour ago, I was gripped with a terrible sense of fear. And it keeps coming in waves, and going, because you just don't know what these people are going to do and what they are capable of. We're not violent, but they can be."

The violence had put this protester in "purgatory," she said, caught between making a pointless sacrifice and a desperate desire to act during these critical days, "because you feel you want to do something."

Taking Up Guns

The Basij, riot police, and vigilante forces were the regime's primary weapons to put down the protests. Within days of the vote, overall security for Tehran was given to the Revolutionary Guard; the Basij came under their command. The Sarallah IRGC headquarters in Tehran was the most important of the three Guard bases in the capital, and had been commanded for years by the man who now led the entire Guard force: Major General Mohammad Ali Jafari. His pedigree included intensive study of Velvet Revolutions and urban guerrilla warfare, which had been the focus of numerous IRGC and Basij exercises for years, to prepare for just this kind of "counterrevolutionary" street fight.

Now the Guard weighed in, calling on protesters to "end the sabotage and rioting" and ominously warning of a "revolutionary confrontation" if they dared to gather in public again.[83] The rising profile of the Guard showed what was at stake: the Revolution itself was in need of being preserved. Demonstrators were now burning banners of Khamenei that had been strung up on highway overpasses for the election. And they shouted for the Leader's death. Numbers on the streets were shrinking, but their target was more and more the system itself, not just the fraudulent vote.

Furious and frustrated, one pacifist in Tehran asked me, "When is it right to take up guns?"[84]

He had had enough. One of his brothers had been arrested, and a cousin was beaten and then disappeared. One of them had had pictures of demonstrations on his cell phone—something common to countless Iranians during the election period. The pacifist was hassled while trying to find his family members, pleading with intelligence and security agents in dark alleys. "The bastards were smiling, playing with me. The thought [of bullets for revenge] went through my head then," he told me. He had no idea when his family members could be released, or even where they were being held. "This is another of their sick mind games."

This man felt helpless and afraid that the surge of hope created by the demonstrations would dissipate beneath the boot of the regime's crushing counterattack. "We are emphasizing *silence* and *peaceful*. Is it wrong if I think about the violent way?" he asked me. This Iranian would not be put off, his rage already at high heat as he wrote to me:

> I think right now the aim is just to push them back and scare them enough to stop killing us, then we will think of what we want for the country. OK, I admit, I'm just looking for a way to disguise my thirst for revenge. But a few "killed by gunshot" would at least give them some panic, no? Or would it make them more aggressive?
>
> I'll get my revenge, but [when they kill more protesters in response] there will be more blood for me to avenge; vicious cycle.
>
> We never accused the police; we are after the Mother Fucking Basij [And, I asked, what if they believed they were doing God's work?] Then I shall help them in their journey to *Heaven*.
>
> I'm actually thinking how long it would take to put together a group of *armed* yet responsible people on our side. [A] few targeted killings. I think 60 percent of the Basij are very young guys, they have parents who have high hopes for their kids. If you make it dangerous for *basijis*, parents would keep their kids in, dealing a blow to their manpower.
>
> Getting guns, that is a different story. . . . I don't mean to be shooting at the *joojehs* [*basiji* foot soldiers derided as "chickens"], but shoot the big guys who have their hands dirty, scare the *joojehs*. I have even picked my targets. I've been seeing them every night, know their every move, know the right place, even know the right people to do the job.
>
> I just got to get them the guns . . .

He knew the dangers, knew that "this system has proven to have a long memory and a deep grudge against its enemies." That meant that for those in trouble "perhaps even their grandchildren won't be able to attend university or hold a government job."

But Khomeini himself thirty years before had sanctioned revenge against just such oppressors, stating as the Revolution peaked in early 1979 that "if club-wielding thugs and other troublemakers attack [revolutionaries on the streets], they can defend themselves, even if it results in the death of their attackers."[85] Likewise, when asked if it was permissible to kill soldiers, Khomeini said it was in three cases: self-defense, assassinating a major member of the Shah's regime, and "in punishing an officer who had been directly responsible for the slaughter of demonstrators."[86]

In Tehran in mid-2009, this pacifist turned guerrilla predicted that most protests would subside within another week, by the end of June. But he also predicted that the thoughts of revenge would smolder endlessly in angry Iranian hearts. "They will, and one day, one day [that revenge] shall burn the face of those who have fucked with my people."

THE FACE OF THOSE *basijis* was clear in the images of brutality that swept around the world on the Internet, feeding a voracious appetite for news from Tehran, even as most journalists were forced to keep away, or out of Iran altogether. I had met a number of these young pious militiamen over the years, part of a force conceived by Khomeini to be a twenty-million-man volunteer army. Estimated to be one million strong today—with the capacity to call upon millions more—a cardinal tenet for the *basijis* had been obedience and devotion, as exemplified best during the Iran-Iraq War.

These were the same zealous volunteers who served as cannon fodder at the front, the first to race across the minefields, to pave the way for the more experienced Revolutionary Guard forces. In peacetime they were ideological students and morality enforcers, even charity workers. On voting day I saw one gaggle of *basijis* at a mosque polling station in south Tehran. These ones were young innocents, watching voters line up and cast their ballots from inside their tiny bare room. None were physically strong, nor yet able to shave—if they had wanted to.

These were young *basiji* True Believers who, sitting on the carpets of their local mosque, had told documentary filmmakers, "We want to change the world, and save the world and its people from all tyranny and submit only to God."[87]

A prominent former *basiji* and member of Ansar-e Hezbollah provides a darker description of how these militiamen were prepared for the street fight. Amir Farshad Ebrahimi left Ansar in dramatic fashion during student protests in 1999, lived in exile in Germany for years, and wrote a well-known Persian-language blog. "I can genuinely say that it's a form of brainwashing," he told Jon Leyne of the BBC.[88] "It takes place every night or weekly in the mosques they attend, so much so that they really believe that the protesters and opposition supporters on the streets are standing against the Prophet's teachings and Islam; they are *mohareb* [enemies of God] and their blood can be spilt, they should be killed."

Ebrahimi battled back in his own way, by listing the names and phone numbers of a dozen vigilantes he recognized in photos and videos, as Borzou Daragahi relates in the *Los Angeles Times:* "One of them rang up in a tizzy. 'This is unethical,' his onetime friend told him. Ebrahimi was flabbergasted. 'You're killing people,' he said. 'Isn't that more unethical?' "[89]

The Basij were simply adjusting the same ideological template used during the Iran-Iraq War and turning it into a street crackdown to protect the sacred Revolution. They had been deployed in urban enforcement before, and in August 2005 were even deputized as police officers.[90] "There is no need at all to tell them what to do—when they hand them a baton or gun and tell them to go, it's clear what they have to do," Ebrahimi told Leyne. "It's like setting a wolf loose amongst a flock of sheep."

Those orders did not sit well with every *basiji*, according to one ranking member who made an issue of abuses, was detained for one hundred days and beaten hard by other *basijis*, and finally escaped to Britain. "I know that they took advantage of Islam," the former militiaman told Channel 4's Hilsum.[91] "I spent the best years of my life unaware. They used this. I was a tool for them to reach their objectives. I unwittingly got involved in their plans . . . Their slogan was that we were the force of the people, the eminent ones, that we must lead. We were unaware of what they brought on us. Our thoughts were not our own."

IT WAS THE HARD men of the Basij who gave every sinew of their being to the June 2009 battle to defend the Supreme Leader. A rare glimpse into that world came from Farnaz Fassihi in the *Wall Street Journal*.[92] She began getting to know a twenty-four-year-old *basiji* long before the election crisis and charted his actions throughout. Mehdi Moradani got his start at the age of nine, when he was enrolled in the Basij youth club, a "mix between the Boy Scouts and Bible school." From picnics to swimming lessons, to learning the qualities of martyrdom and field trips to shrines and war cemeteries, the youth graduate to become full *basijis* with jobs that range from helping law enforcement to organizing religious ceremonies.

So important is the indoctrination of young *basijis* and promotion of *"basiji* culture" that the task was solely conducted by the Revolutionary Guard.[93] The IRGC commander for Gilan, for example, listed 160 summer camps for that province alone, which in 2007 expected twenty thousand students between thirteen and fifteen years old.[94] From camping to chemistry, the young *basijis* also learned ways to organize anti-reformist student groups. The IRGC provided paramilitary training, too, for roughly six hundred thousand active *basijis*, with the aim of defending the homeland and combating the "soft threat."[95]

As Fassihi writes, Basij members, "both men and women, slip easily between roles, from social worker to community spy. In times of crisis, the Basij are tasked with restoring order and ferreting out dissidents." That is how Moradani began at the age of fourteen, when he was taken with a hundred other *basijis* in buses to Tehran University to beat up student organizers during the 1999 student uprising. He had already had weapons training and learned how to fight from trenches. He fought again in 2003, to quell more urban unrest.

"The Revolution and Islam need me. I will give my life in a heartbeat if the regime asks me," Moradani told Fassihi before the 2009 protests, in his small downtown shop where he sold religious and revolutionary materials, his shoes off in constant readiness for prayer. "Our society is now at the verge of sin and filled with anti-revolutionary people." This True Believer was training to become a singing religious storyteller. His mobile phone rang with a song about the Lord of Martyrs, Imam Hossein.

Moradani had campaigned for Ahmadinejad and was shocked at the protests afterward. On the first day he chased Mousavi supporters on his motorcycle, "shouting out the names of Shiite saints as he revved his engine," relates Fassihi. On the fourth day he was issued a thick wooden stick to beat demonstrators. On the eighth day—the day after Khamenei's uncompromising speech at Friday prayers—he mobilized a twelve-man motorcycle unit that used batons and tear gas to battle protesters, who fought back with rocks and bottles and even poured oil on roads to topple the motorcycles and beat their *basiji* riders. "Moradani says he handcuffed scores of demonstrators and dragged them away as they kicked and screamed," reports Fassihi.

"It wasn't about the elections anymore," the skinny *basiji* told the journalist. "I was defending my country and our Revolution and Islam. Everything was at risk."

But the price was high. Moradani's fiancée gave him back his engagement ring and left him because he would not leave the Basij. "She said to me, 'Go beat other people's children then' . . . and hung up on me," he told Fassihi. "The opposition has even fooled my fiancée."

ON THE STREETS, *BASIJIS* like Moradani and other regime enforcers were winning. The opposition was in despair. Mousavi had not been silenced, though his website stated that his access to people was now "completely restricted" and that he was under "pressure" to give up his challenge. He declared he would not keep quiet, exhibiting an unexpected boldness. Of all Iran's past politicians, he knew well the regime's ability to play with the facts, to redefine the truth.

"I cannot modify black as white and white as black. This is not the solution, to expect me to express something which I don't believe," Mousavi said.[96] "I am ready to show how the electoral wrongdoers, standing beside the main agitators that have caused the present disturbances, have spilled people's blood."

THE GUARDIAN COUNCIL PRONOUNCED that there had been "no major fraud" but agreed to recount 10 percent of the ballots. The recount was pointless, thanks to the opaque nature of Iran's "divine" election process. But it was not useless and revealed a rank amateurishness. Photographs of the recount showed officials in some cases "recounting" stacks of ballots that were marked in precisely the same way, on fresh and crisp ballots that had never been creased—unlike real ones, which had been handled by real voters and actually folded before being cast.[97]

More photographs showed that among the sealed ballot boxes piled up for recount was one clearly labeled from a previous election, for the city council. And who could explain the presence of four still-sealed ballot boxes, discovered during an opening ceremony of the Shiraz Central Library?[98] Or why the journalist who posted images was the subject of a formal complaint for "agitating public sentiment by publishing lies"? The discrepancies only reaffirmed how slipshod the process really was.

To prevent Iranians from watching the popular Farsi-language news reports on VOA or the BBC Persian service—which the Iranian leadership had accused, along with Western governments, of fomenting the protests—basijis began storming entire neighborhoods, ripping out illegal satellite dishes. They also arrested people for making the defiant call Allah-o Akbar! from their rooftops, a source of ironic mirth for many Iranians that such a thing—being arrested for shouting, "God is great!"—was even possible in a religious republic.

One protester freshly released from Evin said the prison facility was jammed with "thousands" of people, including every resident of one five-story apartment building, rounded up for chanting, "God is great!" "This shows the regime is not at all as unruffled as it would like to project," said journalist Tara Mahtafar, who told me the detainee's story.[99] "Their normal paranoia has gone haywire to include millions of internal dissidents."

It certainly extended to several thousand who protested at the end of June, taking advantage of an annual commemoration day—for the 1981 MKO/MEK bombing that killed more than seventy of Iran's top revolutionary leaders—to gather on the streets. Mousavi addressed the rally from his home, cleverly speaking through a mobile phone held up to a megaphone. The recommended slogan of the day was from Ayatollah Khomeini, about the prominent role of democracy: "The vote is the measure."[100]

Mahtafar was there: "The peace was short-lived. Initially the crowd tried to stand its ground, linking arms and chanting—'No fear, we're all together!'—but the Basij guards came down on us fast and hard. More gunshots, and in the space of a few seconds, the crowd began running the other way in panic," she wrote. "The sequence is one we are getting used to: Gather, disperse; march, run away; chant, get hurt; hide, tremble with others and share your common rage."

Mahtafar told me that among the crowd were conservative-looking older women dressed all in full chadors—who were the most abusive against the militants.[101] In this case, she said, the *basiji* were "goons with guns and knives on motorbikes with sloppy shirttails hanging out, burly and bearded and unwashed-looking."

"Savages!" shouted one woman in black. "God damn them!" and "Scum!" "How can an Iranian strike his Iranian brothers and sisters?"

"They've disgraced the regime," said another older woman. "Did we have a Revolution so they could spill our children's blood?"

The Military Coup

For the embattled commanders of the Islamic Revolutionary Guard Corps, the answer to that anguished question mattered less than their ability to keep control. As days, weeks, and months ensued of bloodshed, protests, incarceration, and political mayhem, from the streets to the highest levels of the regime, the extraordinary scale of the IRGC intervention—and how premeditated it truly was—became clearer.

To justify the military's injection into politics—in violation of the express orders of the revered Ayatollah Khomeini—the Guard finally acknowledged that the postelection violence and legitimacy crisis had inflicted serious damage to the Islamic system [*nezam*] and even jeopardized its existence.

The "riots took us to the edge of a downfall," IRGC commander Mohammad Ali Jafari told Basij university officials nearly four months after the vote.[102] Amazingly, Jafari declared that the "threat" to the Islamic Republic was even greater than that of the Iran-Iraq War of the 1980s. "The recent dispute which started about ten to twelve years ago in the country, is a dispute over the content of the *nezam*."

He was not done, in describing the impact. "The reputation of the regime has been tainted. . . . [T]hese events have compromised our internal unity and dealt a blow to the credibility of our regime," Jafari said. He added that the "negative effects" would take years to overcome. "The object of the enemy in the recent events was to destroy the Islamic aspect of the regime using the republic aspect as a tool. They wanted to secularize the religious system of Iran and weaken the place of *velayat-e faqih* by turning it into a ceremonial post."

That candid admission was part of a string of unprecedented political machinations that the Guard began to incrementally reveal. Less than one month after the vote, in early July 2009, IRGC commanders had described their takeover of Iran's security as nothing short of a "revival of the Revolution."

"Because the Revolutionary Guard was assigned the task of controlling the situation, [it] took the initiative to quell spiraling unrest," Jafari explained.[103] "This event pushed us into a new phase of the Revolution and political struggle and we have to understand all its dimensions." The chief of the IRGC political bureau who had warned about Velvet Revolution on the eve of the vote, Brigadier General Yadollah

Javani, was also explicit: "Today no one is impartial," Javani said.[104] "There are two currents—those who defend and support the Revolution and the establishment, and those who are trying to topple it."

But none of that added up, these generals claimed, to breaking the prohibitions against Iran's armed forces dabbling in politics. Suggested Javani: "The Revolutionary Guard is tasked with defending the Revolution and it has to play a determining role in protecting and eternalizing the Revolution. Such an attitude does by no means mean interfering in politics."

FEW IRANIANS WERE FOOLED. They had only to look back on their history to remember how the Guard had always placed itself at the confluence of political and military power. The IRGC was born from the armed groups that fought the Shah's army in the final stages of the Revolution. "[T]hey were men based on the mosques and revolutionary committees who, loyal to Imam Khomeini, went on to form the nucleus of the Revolutionary Guards," writes historian Hamid Algar.[105] The Guard would draw its ideological power from the same impulse that fed the Revolution itself, the "unshaken loyalty of the Iranian masses to Islam," which the 1960s ideologue Jalal Al-e Ahmad called "the secret government of religion."[106]

"The Guard . . . sees its involvement in politics as not only permissible, but as part of its mission to defend the Islamic Revolution," wrote analyst Kenneth Katzman years before the 2009 crisis.[107] As such, it had "clearly chosen to preserve its political role at the expense of military effectiveness [and] placed revolutionary purity ahead of military tactical efficacy and rationality." Added Katzman: "There are numerous examples in which the Guard teamed up with its political allies—or even acted alone—to undermine those political leaders whom the Guard leaders viewed as compromising the goals of the Islamic Revolution."[108]

So the Revolutionary Guard was no stranger to close combat with regime enemies. From mid-1981 to late 1982, a series of MKO/MEK bomb attacks and assassinations killed scores of revolutionary leaders and prompted a vicious response. While serving as the "protective shield standing between the clerics and those who would destroy them," writes historian Shaul Bakhash, the Guard was deeply involved in a wave of extremism, purges, and attacks that swept Iran and left between three thousand and eight thousand dead.[109]

"In the process, they secured once again freedom for the full expression of their lawless inclinations," Bakhash notes. "They entered homes at will, harassed members of households, and made unauthorized arrests. When they could not find the person they sought, they took away other members of the family. Believing guerrillas to lie behind every door, they attacked private homes and shot innocent people."

The reign of terror of the early 1980s left its mark, writes Bakhash: "Driven by fear, determined to crush the incipient rebellion, the authorities visited a terrible vengeance on their challengers. Executions of fifty a day became routine."[110] Back then, President Ali Khamenei—the man who would become Supreme Leader—finally admitted to deficiencies. He said a revolution "is a kind of surgery that at the beginning results in some blood being shed, but at the end it will bring some hope."[111] Yet the violence had instead caused public support to erode and reinforced extremists, notes Bakhash, and "enshrined terror as a legitimate tool of government."[112]

AYATOLLAH KHOMEINI HAD SOUGHT to soften the terror by late 1982, and applied its lessons for the future as he wrote his last will and testament. Khomeini praised all military forces as the "mighty arms of the Islamic Republic," but was explicit in this warning:

My emphatic counsel to the armed forces is to observe and abide by the military rule of noninvolvement in politics. Do not join any political party, group or faction. No military man or security policeman, no Revolutionary Guard or *basiji* is allowed to enter politics.

Stay away from politics and you will be able to preserve and maintain your military powers and thus be immune to internal division and dispute. . . .

Such involvement will surely corrupt and pervert them.[113]

Despite that direct order, Revolutionary Guard commanders have always found a way to justify their political presence, by citing Khomeini's also-famous dictum that preserving the *nezam* is even more important than prayer. Their catchall mandate is codified by Article 150 of the constitution, which gives the IRGC the perpetual "role of guarding the Revolution and its achievements."[114]

That mission kicked in for the hard-line leadership in 1997, with the election of President Mohammad Khatami. Back then, it was IRGC chief Yahya Rahim Safavi—later the senior military adviser to the Supreme Leader—who promised that the Revolutionary Guard would deal with reformists and "behead some and cut off the tongue of others."[115] He said the IRGC would be patient.

"The Guards . . . have identified many of the elements of these groups . . . but we will go after them when the time is right," Safavi said of reformists.[116] "The fruit has to be picked when it is ripe. That fruit is unripe now. We will pick it . . . when it turns ripe," he told a group of hard-line students. "We have thrown a stone inside the nest of snakes which have received blows from our Revolution, and are giving them time to stick their heads out."

As the battle against reform matured, Khomeini's last commandments against any military role in politics seemed to have vanished. During Basij Week in late 2007, for example, the Friday prayer leader of Mashhad said: "The idea that the Guards and the Basij as military forces should not intervene in politics . . . is the idea of the enemies of God, and of corrupt [political] movements who consider the Basij an obstacle in their path. . . . Non-intervention in politics equates to secularization of the Basij. The very essence of the Basij is one of religion, conviction, piety and belief in God."[117]

Not long after, as candidates were registering for a parliamentary vote, Khamenei's own representative to the IRGC encouraged "the chosen ones, such as the Guards and the Basij, [to] help the public to identify the correct values and the suitable candidates at times of election."[118] A local IRGC commander in Qazvin put that advice into practice when he claimed that a local reformist candidate "questions eight years of sacred defence on BBC radio."[119] He railed: "We should not allow dirty people to enter the parliament to fill the parliament with dirt. Those whose presence is religiously not permissible in the parliament should not enter it."

The growing influence of the Revolutionary Guard under Ahmadinejad was having a structural impact. "The IRGC is changing the nature of the Islamic Republic. While still ruled by the clergy, in practice [it] has begun to resemble other third world military regimes," wrote analyst Ali Alfoneh.[120]

Indoctrination materials such as *Political Questions and Answers* further entrenched the IRGC's political role.[121] Updated questions included, "Why do some IRGC commanders intervene in politics despite the statements of his holiness the Imam [Khomeini]?" The official answer justified a range of actions: "The activities of the Guards are of a different sort. For example, if a political group active in the country propagates the idea of separation between religion and politics, or . . . of providing a foreign government with certain privileges, the Revolutionary Guards considers itself obliged to protest . . . since ideals such as *velayat-e faqih* and the integrity of the country have been attacked."

Writing months before the stolen 2009 election, Alfoneh concluded: "Rather than protect Khomeini's vision of clerical rule, IRGC indoctrination has created a cycle of weakening civilian control over the military. . . ."[122] A "paranoid world view" and encouragement toward politics "reinforces the trend of militarization within the Islamic Republic, as the IRGC stages . . . a slow, creeping coup d'état in which it has become [Iran's] predominant power in reality, even if not in name."

• • •

SO WHY WAS AHMADINEJAD the chosen one, backed so consistently by the IRGC? This fierce ideologue and former soccer fanatic—who exposed the least muscled, most pale arms when he rolled up his sleeves prior to prayers to wash above his elbows—was the tool of choice of Iran's ultraconservative cabal. His years-long courtship with the Revolutionary Guard and the Basij made him a particularly suitable choice for them, and therefore also for the Supreme Leader.

Khamenei "realizes that the armed forces of the establishment are more supportive of Ahmadinejad than they would be of anyone else," Massoumeh Torfeh, an Iran specialist at the School of Oriental and African Studies in London, told me.[123] "Ahmadinejad came from them. . . . He's looked after them. . . . He's got the thugs. He's got the power behind him, and of course Khamenei has."

Ahmadinejad referred to his rapport with Khamenei as "like father and son," and the Supreme Leader repeated his blandishments that the embattled president was "brave and hardworking."[124] But that apparent intimacy did not ensure a trouble-free investiture on August 3, 2009. With unrest still seething below the surface, for the first time the ceremony was not carried live on television. And many of the Revolution's top figures, such as members of Khomeini's family, Mousavi, Karroubi, and former presidents Khatami and Rafsanjani, who traditionally would all be present at such an event, did not show up.[125]

The halting body language between the tainted president and the also-tainted Supreme Leader further betrayed the acute political uncertainty. In a scene of cringe-making awkwardness replayed around the world, Ayatollah Khamenei raised his left hand and stopped Mahmoud Ahmadinejad as the latter leaned over to kiss his cheek. The Leader only permitted a kiss to his robed shoulder—an icy touch after the warmth of their embrace four years earlier, which had been sealed with hand kisses.

ANY DOUBT ABOUT THE depth of Revolutionary Guard involvement in defeating Mousavi was dispelled by the IRGC itself. Commander Jafari acknowledged that the Guard had determined months before the presidential vote that a reformist victory would simply be too dangerous to be allowed—and had acted to prevent it. So it turned out that in February 2009, even as I had been stuck in a partly hostile crowd with then candidate Mohammad Khatami, the former president and other top reformists were already under close surveillance by the IRGC.

Jafari did not specify whether the Guard intelligence had used wiretaps, bugs in private homes and offices, or some other method to eavesdrop on the intimate conversations of top politicians. But he claimed that Khatami had said in February, "If in this election Ahmadinejad falls, then the Supreme Leader will be effectively eliminated; if at any cost reformists return to the executive branch, the Leader will have no authority in society. Through defeat of the principlists [hardliners], we must contain the power of the Leader." [126]

Jafari named a number of top reformists, and even quoted from unpublished Intelligence Ministry confessions. Among them, he claimed that Khatami's former vice president Mohammad Ali Abtahi had "confessed" that Khatami, along with Mousavi's campaign manager and a son of Rafsanjani, "had said that 'winning this election is very different from those in the past. [If we do win], the principlist camp and the Supreme Leader will not be able to keep their heads up, and this would mean finishing the job.' This implies greatly weakening the *velayat-e faqih*." [127]

In a scathing critique, analyst Farideh Farhi pointed out the significance of this "astounding public admission" by a military chief supposed to stay out of politics:

> If Jafari is to be taken at his words, even if in the official narrative the election had been won by Mir Hossein Mousavi, the IRGC would have had no choice but to enter the fray and overturn the results since such a victory would have brought to power people who wanted to undermine the Islamic Republic.
>
> Considering that in the minds of many Iranians doubtful of elec-

tion results this is precisely what the IRGC did, such an admission
was probably imprudent if not outright stupid.[128]

Jafari's words also revealed how, in the mind of Iran's most power-
ful military officer, the space for alternative views had been erased.
For him—and those legions at his command—any policy change in
Iran was now tantamount to regime change.

The Guard "are making sure they control all levers of state power,"
said Alireza Nader, an Iran analyst at the RAND Corporation.[129] "We
have a force now that is not only involved in politics, but is taking over
politics, and taking over the state."

The IRGC had long been the keeper of Iran's most important secrets, including its nuclear facilities and ballistic missile arsenal. Now
it was also becoming kingmaker in Iranian politics. Within months of
the 2009 election, the Guard bought a 50 percent, $7.8 billion stake in
the newly privatized telecommunications company—which put mobile and landline networks and Internet under IRGC purview. It added
a $2.5 billion rail contract to its bursting portfolio and announced the
creation of a new media conglomerate called Atlas.[130]

"From inside, Khamenei faces increased pressure from the opposition [and so] has chosen to rely upon the only center of power
which has remained loyal to him: the IRGC," Alfoneh told me.[131] "The
IRGC's support for Khamenei does not come cheap, and he has to
bribe the IRGC with economic monopolies."

The result was a "very deep and symbiotic relationship with the
Supreme Leader," Nader explained. The IRGC had "used the Ahmadinejad administration to not just solidify their hold on power, but to
enrich themselves at the same time."

The Abusers

As Iran's crisis dragged on, the true ferocity of the regime response
began to emerge, illustrating like nothing else the depth of its political
vulnerability—and its moral depravity. Khomeini had once admired

the Ministry of Intelligence, calling its agents the "anonymous foot soldiers of the Twelfth Imam." [132]

But now hundreds of reformists had been rounded up on national security charges. In the midst of Iran's near Velvet Revolution, the hard-line factions of the "coup government" saw fit to resurrect a practice that had been largely dormant—and largely discredited—for nearly twenty years: the public recantation. It had reemerged briefly during the 2007 incarceration of Iranian-American academics Haleh Esfandiari and Kian Tajbakhsh. But it was brought back in full in 2009 as some 140 top reformists, among them Ali Abtahi and other ranking officials and strategists from the Khatami era, stood trial.

It was a big leap backward for the Islamic Republic, which within a decade of the 1979 Revolution had realized that public confessions were counterproductive. As historian Ervand Abrahamian writes of those early years in *Tortured Confessions*: "Instead of focusing attention on the opposition, they reminded the public of the regime's own horrifying features. Instead of dividing the opposition, they helped bring it together." [133]

Twenty years later, the same advantages were accruing to the Green Movement as reformists appeared in Tehran "court" looking like damaged human beings, to describe their "crime" of pursuing political change. Wearing pale blue prison pajamas, the defendants looked dazed, wary, frightened, and resigned, besides unkempt and smoldering with contempt—if they had the energy to display it.

The once-jovial former vice president Ali Abtahi was markedly thinner and barely recognizable without his turban and clerical robes. His wife said he had lost forty pounds and been drugged with pills that "relieve him from this world's furore," and she said that "this Abtahi was not our Abtahi." [134] The wife of Karroubi adviser Ahmad Zeidabadi said her husband had been "driven to the point of insanity" by abuses in prison. [135]

Under the glare of television lights, lengthy indictments were read out. The election was the "golden page in religious democracy," and these reformists had tried to "sow sedition and blacken this great source of pride and undo society's order." [136] The indictment reflected deep regime paranoia. From "methods to destroy the Islamic Republic" to "statements by counter-revolutionaries," no ideological stone was left unturned in revealing what "might be named the West's Covert Action Manifesto."

The accused may have been stunned when they heard the scope of the conspiracy they were alleged to have been part of, in fomenting a "soft coup" against Islamic rule. Prosecutors claimed they were all working in tandem with entities as diverse as the BBC Persian channel (which established links with "domestic document forgers"); the London "intelligence-research" think tanks Chatham House and the International Institute for Strategic Studies; the Soros Foundation; elements of the MKO/MEK; and a German lawyer in Tehran who had "taken residence in a hotel . . . in a center of disturbances."

"Western spy agencies were not negligent in taking advantage of all domestic opportunities and resources afforded by the opposition," the group indictment read. It all aimed at "perpetuating insecurity and embroiling the *nezam* in strife and playing the role of pawns in the enemy's fifth column." U.S. efforts to bolster civil society were "making America out to be Iran's only savior." Foreign intelligence efforts sought to "prepare the ground" for domestic violence, rioting, and chaos and to engage in "psychological warfare against the Islamic Republic."

After the election, the indictment claimed, the top priority was to "weaken the *velayat-e faqih*'s status" by "dragging the . . . system's legitimacy into conflict." Prosecutors said they had disrupted a Velvet Revolution in the making. Did they believe it?

AMONG THE "CONFESSORS" WAS Maziar Bahari, the Canadian-Iranian filmmaker and *Newsweek* journalist who had in the past written about all the "Mr. Mohammadis" of the intelligence service who had questioned him, and reminded him at the conclusion of every meeting that they knew his address. His four-month incarceration at Evin Prison was a nightmare of mental games and constant beatings at the hands of his scented interrogator, whom Bahari named after the "rosewater perfume used by men who piously do their ablutions several times a day before prayers, but rarely shower." [137]

"Mr. Rosewater" accused Bahari of working for the CIA, Britain's MI6, Israel's Mossad, and *Newsweek*. Bahari was told he was "planning to eradicate the pure religion of Mohammad in this country and re-place it with 'American' Islam. A New Jersey Islam." He was told never to speak of his experience in jail, or he would be hunted down: "We can put people in a bag no matter where in the world they are. No one can escape from us." Bahari did not believe him, but noted this fact: "They are masters of uncertainty, instilling it among their enemies, their subjects, their friends, perhaps even themselves."

"Until my imprisonment I had never fully appreciated the corro-sive suspicion that is rotting the Islamic Republic from within," Bahari recalled. "The Guards see real enemies all around them—reformists within the country, hundreds of thousands of U.S. troops outside. Even worse are the shadows—supposed agents of Britain, the United States, and Israel—upon whom they impose their own fearful logic and their reinvented history."

Bahari was accused of having "masterminded" election coverage by agents of the Western media, of helping orchestrate Velvet Revolu-tion in Iran. "You are worse than any saboteur or killer," Mr. Rosewa-ter raged at Bahari. "Those criminals destroy an object or a person. You destroy minds and provoke people against the Leader."

The burly Mr. Rosewater had "meaty palms," which he applied to Bahari with force. "Move your hands, you little spy!" he shouted. As Bahari relates, "At one point he told me he beat me mainly because he was angry. 'What you have done, Mazi, makes my blood boil. I don't want to raise my hand against you, but what do you suggest I do with someone who has insulted the Leader?' "

HUMOROUS OPPOSITION SLOGANS SUGGESTED that Evin Prison was so choked with inmates that it had become a "university" for reformists. But as the scale and severity of abuses became clear,

Iranians began to ask how a regime that claimed divine sanction could be so brutal.

At Evin and an archipelago of secret detention facilities across Tehran—the one at Kahrizak so bad that Supreme Leader Khamenei shut it down—detainees were tortured, raped, and killed. Families of victims had known the truth, but were often intimidated or reportedly paid to keep silent.

Abuses at Kahrizak soared to prominence with the death in custody of Mohsen Rouholamini, the son of an adviser to Mohsen Rezaei, the defeated conservative presidential candidate. According to the coroner, the young man died from "physical stress, frequent beatings and hitting a solid object on his head."[138] Yet the official reason for death became "meningitis." Ayatollah Khamenei, speaking to a group of academics that included the father of Rouholamini, promised that the *nezam* "is not intending to have an attitude of ignorance or forgiveness toward those who did bad things or committed crimes."[139]

But the suspicious fate of a twenty-six-year-old conscript doctor assigned to Kahrizak to fulfill his military service—and the presence of a poisoned salad—was emblematic of the real forces at play. Dr. Ramin Pourandarjani witnessed the abuses of Iranians taken to Kahrizak during the postelection violence. He then testified to a parliamentary committee that Rouholamini was brought to him "in a dreadful state after being subject to extreme physical torture. He was in a critical state," according to opposition news reports.[140] When the detainee died, the doctor told the committee, "officials at Kahrizak threatened that if I disclosed the causes of the wounds of the injured at Kahrizak, I would not be able to live." Iranian opposition media reported that the doctor was forced to change the cause of death to meningitis.

Then, in early November 2009, the doctor himself died. Initially authorities called his father in Tabriz and told him his son had been in a car accident, had broken his leg, and they needed consent for surgery. Then the story changed to a heart attack in his sleep. A couple of weeks later, Iran's police commander said the doctor—facing previously unannounced charges over his Kahrizak duties—had killed himself in a courthouse lounge and had left a note on his body. The final version was that a salad brought to the doctor by a delivery man was laced with heart and blood pressure medicine. The Tehran public prosecutor stated the doctor died of "poisoning by drugs."

While prosecutors claimed not to know if the case was murder or suicide, the doctor's father was certain of murder. "Just the night before his death, my child talked to me on the phone, it was around eight or nine P.M. He sounded great, very dignified, displaying no sign of someone about to commit suicide," the father told the Associated Press.[141] "He was even full of hope," and making future plans.

Reformists were familiar with such nasty political violence. As President Mohammad Khatami had said a decade earlier, after the chain murders, "When we don't accept someone, we make of him a counter-revolutionary, a monarchist, corrupt, pro-Western, a threat to national security and an apostate. Then, if some ignoramus says this counter-revolutionary must be killed—well, they kill him."[142]

AS CHARGES OF POSTELECTION abuse multiplied, Mehdi Karroubi, the former parliament speaker and presidential candidate, wrote a letter to Hashemi Rafsanjani, head of the Expediency Council, stating that "severe and brutal beatings have been reported such that after forty days the victims are still not in stable condition."[143]

But far more explosive allegations involved prison rape and sodomy, acts religiously and culturally unacceptable in Iran. Citing sources who "have all held important official positions," and the victims themselves, Karroubi wrote that "something horrific has happened in the prisons. If only one case is true, it is a catastrophe for the Islamic Republic of Iran which has turned the bright, shining history of Shia clerics into an atrocious, shameful fate and has outdone many dictatorial regimes, including that of the tyrannical Shah."[144]

"Some of the detainees claim incarcerated girls were raped so harshly until their uteruses were torn apart, while young boys were sexually abused so savagely that they are suffering from serious depression as well as physical and mental traumas," Karroubi wrote.[145] Victims were "threatened with death if they disclose details."

Karroubi called for an investigation, so this "will remain a lesson for future generations, and will not serve as an opportunity for hooligans to humiliate the ruling system, the Imam and the Islamic Republic and to tarnish the thousand year contribution of the clerics." [146]

Already that was happening. The government denied all charges, and authorities shut down the opposition's committee to investigate detainee abuses—confiscating all records in the process and arresting Karroubi's representative, former Tehran mayor Morteza Alviri. Parliament speaker Ali Larijani claimed to have "personally" pursued the rape charges, that "parliament's fact-finding committee has denied that the detainees were sexually assaulted," and that "no evidence of sexual assault and rape was found." [147] A judiciary committee stated that the evidence of rape was fabricated; a police investigation at Kahrizak "proved that there was no rape." [148]

But not long after, a member of the Special Parliament Committee anonymously told the Iranian media: "It has definitely become evident to us that some of the post-election detainees have been raped with batons and bottles." [149] And the growing number of harrowing examples shook Iran's political establishment. One rape victim who spoke to Karroubi also made a video account, then was told he would be killed if he testified, as planned, before the parliament committee. He finally fled to Turkey. "I was ready to be tortured to death. But not ever to go through what happened to me there," twenty-four-year-old Ebrahim Sharifi told Nazila Fathi of the *New York Times*.[150] A student of computer engineering, Sharifi took part in daily rallies and was one day picked up on his way home. Handcuffed and blindfolded, he was beaten hard for four days.

"I don't know how long it lasted, but they kept beating me," Sharifi told Ivan Watson of CNN.[151] "The one who was beating us became very tired. And when he was beating us he was calling out '*Ya Hossein*' or '*Ya Zahra*.' One of those times that he was beating and calling for Hossein, somebody from the other side of the hall said 'Mir Hossein,' " to complete the pro-Mousavi slogan, "Ya Hossein, Mir Hossein." Beatings intensified after that. He was exhausted and lacerated, blood and urine on the floor, his tongue "hanging out on the floor. I could taste the piss."

Someone came in and asked, "What is it to you who becomes president? Why do you care who is elected?" Sharifi recalled to CNN. Later there was a mock execution with a noose tightened around his neck. "Somebody was constantly telling us you are the source of corruption on earth," that they had execution orders, but that the Supreme Leader "has forgiven you for the time being."

"I told the guard that he should go ahead and just kill me if he wanted to," Sharifi tearfully told the Times. "Then he called another guard and said 'Take this bastard and impregnate him.' " He was taken to another room, where the wall had handcuffs and two metal hooks to keep his legs open, and the guard raped him. "He laughed mockingly as he was doing it and said that I could not even defend myself so did I think that I could stage a revolution."

"In that moment, I couldn't think what was happening to me," Sharifi told CNN. "I couldn't accept what was happening, that in a regime which is called Islamic, such things can happen. My father served in the military. My father worked in law enforcement. Such a thing, for me, was unbelievable."

Sharifi feared for his life even in Turkey, until he eventually got to the United States. He said he was "relieved" that he was able to tell his story, to "break this taboo [and] take away their most efficient method of torture." Exposure of rape was devastating to its practitioners, who always claimed that rape charges were lies, Sharifi said. "What is the reason for that? Because the sanctity of the regime is gone. Which sacred system? Where is the sacred system?"

THOSE WERE THE UNVOICED questions in a Tehran hospital, where Mohammad K. lay beaten, raped, and dying in mid-July, according to a female witness who spoke to Borzou Daragahi of the

Los Angeles Times: "All but two of his upper teeth had been knocked out. His nails had been pulled out. His head had been bashed in. His kidneys had stopped working. But what most disturbed her, she said, were the stitches around his anus—a sign, the nurses told her, that he had been raped." [152] The victim was identified as Mohammad Kamrani in Persian-language reports. [153]

The witness, a secretary at a downtown company who supported the Green Movement, was visiting another patient. She "felt compelled to help empty the comatose man's urine container and change his bandages," but was so shocked that in the month afterward she had trouble sleeping and eating, and lost twenty pounds.

As Daragahi reported:

At 9:30 p.m. on July 16, a man described to her by nurses as the acting head of Kahrizak arrived at the hospital along with a group of soldiers and the young man's parents and uncle, who journalists later told the *Times* is a ranking official in the government.

The parent identified the young man, and the prison official signed a document declaring Mohammad K. "free," the secretary said. Outside, in the hospital courtyard, soldiers sipped fruit juice, she said.

"He is nearly dead and now you declare my son free," the weeping mother said. . . .

Hours later Mohammad Kamrani was lifeless. The official cause of the man's death was "meningitis," at Kahrizak. In an interview with the BBC Persian TV channel, the family described "their son as a martyr to the movement opposed to Ahmadinejad," the *Times* reported. At a memorial service—permitted only because of string pulling from the influential uncle—the cleric told sobbing relatives: "Death is our inevitable destiny. But the only death that is awful is . . . death in a society in which people are not allowed to think and explore the horizons of thought."

• • •

DEATH IN DETENTION WAS the fervent desire of "Ardeshir," the pseudonym for an engineering student who told his story to the *Times* of London in a Tehran park in mid-September 2009.[154] A hospital report confirmed anal damage, sustained during repeated rapes by *basiji* guards, he said, in the course of twenty-three days in detention. The *Times* spoke to the psychologist treating the student, who reported "extreme feelings of self-hatred resulting from a sense that he will never be clean again." His father said his son was a "broken boy."

Ardeshir was adamant: "When I first participated in the protests I was not demonstrating against the Leader or the Islamic Republic. I was protesting Ahmadinejad's cheating. But today, I say 'Death to Khamenei,' and having been raped by his henchmen I also say 'Death to the Dogs of Khamenei.' "

He had been picked up on June 20—the day after Khamenei gave his warning of "bloodshed" if protests continued—and thrown into a windowless van with more than a dozen other bloodied demonstrators. At an unofficial detention center they were stripped to their underwear and lined up. Two *basijis* "rubbed our genital areas with their batons, calling us 'scum' and saying 'Ah, yes, the balls of the foot soldiers of the heretic Mousavi,' " Ardeshir told the *Times*. "They then promised that we would confess to trying to overthrow the divine regime."

The next day, a seventeen-year-old student was called from the cell. They heard him screaming, then go silent. Ardeshir recalled:

A couple of minutes later two *basiji* grabbed me. . . . I felt faint and wanted to cry when faced with a scene I had never before in my life imagined. . . . The boy, completely naked, was seemingly unconscious on the mat, his face in a pile of vomit and with blood around his rectum.

A *basiji* called Mahmoud said, "Take a good look. That will happen to you if you resist, you faggot lover of Mousavi."

The *basiji* then said: "Now you." They threw me on my back on the ground. Mahmoud then urinated on my face, saying that this would teach me not to oppose the divine wishes of the [Supreme] Leader of the Revolution. "We have been sent to re-educate you, you spoilt Western piece of shit," he said.

That *basiji* raped him, and then another did. "All I could think of [was] when it was going to end, and was why these people who claim to be the most religious in our society can do such things?" Ardeshir told the *Times*. The third time they dragged him from his cell, he got away and ran into a corner. "I screamed, 'You say you are Muslim. How can you rape and humiliate us in this way?' They laughed and said they had religious sanction from the Leader to do so because we had gone against his word."

Before Ardeshir's release, he was taken to the commander and ordered to sign a confession that opposition leaders and foreign media had led him to challenge the regime. "Nothing illegal is taking place here," he was told. "Everything that has happened has been religiously sanctioned by the Leader in his battle against you, Mousavi and Karroubi scum. Now sign . . ."

BRUTAL BEATINGS AND RAPE with a baton are what drove Ebrahim Mehtari to flee Iran. "I don't have the mental strength to describe what happened to me," Mehtari told Anita McNaught of Al Jazeera English.[155] "This regime tries to portray itself as the most 'morally upright' in the whole world, but in our prisons . . . throughout the whole ruling system . . . it spreads only lies and immoralities."

Mehtari's medical report describes "blackness and swelling under the right eye" and burns on his hands, neck, head, and shoulders inflicted by cigarettes.[156] "Bruises are visible on both sides of the hips and the outer area of the anus caused by the hard object . . . and the hot object" that caused the other wounds, it reads. Mehtari was lucky his father made a copy, states a report by Amnesty International that detailed three rape cases.[157] "Once it became known that [Mehtari's] injuries were not the result of a criminal abduction but of torture by state officials, all the documents and evidence disappeared." Iranian officials, Amnesty continued, "have done their utmost to ensure that accounts of rape are discredited and not circulated."

Mehtari's job as a prodemocracy activist and software engineer was to deploy Iran's mobile phone networks as part of the legal pre-election campaign efforts, sending out millions of text messages in minutes and gaining a detailed understanding of candidate support across the country. In one instance, Mehtari sent out twenty-five million text messages and received nine million responses. Overall, Mir Hossein Mousavi was the "top-scorer" in his unscientific polling.[158]

After the vote, as street clashes intensified and text messaging was shut down, the twenty-seven-year-old Mehtari sent out mass pro-Mousavi e-mailings and leaflets and worked with fellow activists abroad to circumvent government restrictions. The first time he was arrested, interrogators were polite. The second time, for five days in late August, he was whipped with a metal flail and burned with cigarettes. He was sexually abused with a baton, which caused internal damage that could only be repaired after he escaped to Turkey.

But even there, Iranian intelligence agents tracked him down on a busy street in Turkey's capital, Ankara. They tapped him on the shoulder and warned him: "Shut your mouth, or we will shut it for you."

A large bear of a man with designer glasses, the young Mehtari told me that Turkey may have appeared safe but was "little different from Tehran."[159] Iranians could enter Turkey without a visa, so dissidents and whistle-blowers arrived there—along with many more Iranian agents. "Iran has many allies inside Turkey, but they can't do anything more than threaten," said Mehtari, a green cloth bracelet on his left wrist. "What they are doing now is the maximum they can do."

His example was but a footnote compared to the far deeper corrosion in Iran, he said. "The people shouting in the streets whose blood is spilled, who are tortured and raped in prisons or killed, or suffer other hardships at the hands of the system—everything they endure is the result of a disease called 'the lie,' and the loss of morality," Mehtari told McNaught. "When those men can sit in front of cameras and stand on platforms and say: 'We are all moralists, we are the sacred Islamic Republic system' . . . They should stop lying to themselves, and to the rest of the world."

"The enemy-paranoia which is gripping the ruling system [means] it tries its best to turn the whole world into an insecure place for its own people, its own nation," said Mehtari. "I profoundly believe . . . that this is a sign of weakness, of a ruling system which cannot turn its enemies into friends. Not only that, but it turns its friends like me into, if not enemies, then into the opposition."

PRESIDENTIAL CANDIDATE MEHDI KARROUBI came under fierce attack from regime hard-liners for pressing the rape charges. Instead of going after those who were responsible for the very acts that were destroying the Revolution's credibility, the chief purveyor of Orwellian "facts," *Kayhan,* charged Karroubi with "exaggerated" claims "revealed as lies."[160]

"Some of the reformists' senior figures who are still at large due to the unjustifiable negligence of the judicial branch believed that making a lot of noise over 'murder and torture of protesters' would give them even more protection," charged *Kayhan.*

Amnesty International reported that despite rigorous regime efforts "to suppress knowledge of the abuses and to further punish those victims and witnesses who courageously reported them, the massive scale of the violations is impossible to hide."[161] Amnesty's report notes that those charging rape by jailers were treated "as a further threat to the state simply for revealing the truth about the crimes they have suffered."[162] With typical bravado, protesters had begun to use a new slogan on the streets: "Rape and Torture do not scare us anymore."[163]

Eventually, in December, half a year after the reports of abuse first began to surface, Iranian authorities acknowledged that three jailed protesters had been beaten to death, and a military court charged twelve prison officials: three in the murders of Mohsen Rouholamini, Mohammad Kamrani, and Amir Javadifar, a musician and student of industrial management; the rest for other crimes.[164]

Yet those cases barely scratched the surface of a contradiction that

will always haunt the Islamic Republic—and belie its constant procla-
mations of piety. The *Times* of London had seen five hundred pages
of documents compiled by opposition investigators, a "small fraction
of the total" that included handwritten testimony and medical reports of postelection victims.[165] In the words of one investigator: "The
use of rape and torture was similar across prisons in Tehran and the
provinces. It is difficult not to conclude that the highest authorities
planned and ordered these actions. Local authorities would not dare
take such actions without word from above."

The contents gave the lie to what was then the official death toll of
thirty-six, according to the *Times:*

> The documents suggest that at least 200 demonstrators were killed
> in Tehran, with 56 others still unaccounted for, and that 173 were
> killed in other cities. . . . Just over half of the 200 were killed on
> the streets. They were beaten around the head or shot in the head
> or chest as part of an apparent shoot-to-kill policy—there are no
> reports of demonstrators being shot in the legs. . . .
>
> In Tehran alone, 37 young men and women claim to have been
> raped by their jailers. Doctors' reports say that two males, aged
> 17 and 22, died as a result of severe internal bleeding after being
> raped. . . .
>
> [The documents] cite instances of security forces storming hospi-
> tals and ordering doctors not to treat injured demonstrators, not to
> record deaths by gunshot and to suppress medical reports indicating
> rape or torture.

"These crimes are a source of shame for the Islamic Republic,"
presidential candidate Karroubi said. "I say to myself three decades
after the Revolution and two decades after the death of the Imam
[Khomeini]—what place have we reached?"[166]

THE ANSWER TO THAT question showed how the Revolution's
promise had dimmed. "The ideological fervor is not there," explained

historian Ervand Abrahamian.[167] "During the war, *basijis* were people willing to go and fight in the front, so there was an ideological commitment. Now there is no war; it's a completely different generation. What entices people to join is actually much more economic. You get better pay, maybe a motorbike—things like that."

War-era veterans of the officer corps today remain devout. "As soon as people join the Basij or the Guard, the whole ideology is that they are protectors of the republic and have that commitment, so they are given carte blanche to do whatever they want, as long as it is to protect the republic," Abrahamian told me.

Rape is not known to have featured in prisons during the first years of the Islamic Republic, because many of the wardens were devout Muslims. "They would be quite happy to hang people, but to actually rape—it would not fit into their psychology," said Abrahamian, author of a detailed study on the subject. But Iranian news reports indicated that thugs arrested in earlier social crackdowns like that of 2007 were being used and even employed to abuse and "torture the detainees."[168]

"Now it's no longer the ideologically committed people who are actually running these prisons," Abrahamian said. "These are people who have more likely joined the [Revolutionary Guard] because their career prospects are good, so ideology is less important, and you're more likely to get psychopaths [and] thugs who are quite happy to have their people do these things."

And such acts caused a loss of morale among even some of the most stalwart regime enforcers. "I've lost my world and religion," one former *basiji* told journalist Lindsey Hilsum, as he described the premeditated fixing of Ahmadinejad's victory and the orders to attack protesters "without restraint."[169] He says he and his brother tried to stop the rape of teenage protesters jammed into a number of shipping containers at one detention location, but they were refused entry and told by local commanders that the actions were code-named Fath al-Mobin—a religiously sanctioned "aid to victory." The same title, which means "Revelatory Victory," had also been the name of an important 1982 Iranian offensive of the Iran-Iraq War.

This *basiji* said his brother "was very angry. When we got there he said: 'What is this? Sexual abuse is a serious crime. Who gave the order? Who authorized this?'

"Haji calmly replied with a smile. 'This is Fath al-Mobin. It's a worthy deed. There's nothing wrong with it. Why are you complaining?' " recounted the *basiji*.

> I never thought that these matters could be contaminated like this. I thought that I was continuing the path of my uncles and our martyrs. All my interest and enthusiasm: to have the integrity for martyrdom. We really saw ourselves as upstanding and separate from others. We really believed that what we did was correct, that we were serving the people, that we were serving God and that our mission was nothing but worshipping God.
>
> But now I am ashamed in front of people . . . and I am ashamed in front of my religion. I committed crimes, knowingly and unknowingly.

Another *basiji* involved in the same incident—who was imprisoned for three months, beaten, and labeled a sellout and a spy by fellow *basijis*, his crime questioning the rape and violence—described to Hilsum how good religious intentions could lead to blind obedience.

"[Recruits] enter the organization of their own free will . . . driven by their own desire, out of love," the *basiji* told Hilsum:

> It's every young person's wish to enter university and continue his education to have a good life, to find a good job, to have [a] wife, a house, a car. These were all things that [the Basij] gave us with various methods.
>
> We felt good, we had a certain satisfaction. We noticed the differences. When I looked at my friends, they didn't have the car I had, the job I had, the further education I had, that had come to me

so easily. All through the Basij. That's not why I joined. It was out of interest and love, but these were a support. They gave us hope. They were bonuses that encouraged us.

I think these were things that they wanted to give us to trap us. So that we would be under their thumb. I think that's exactly it. We would do whatever they told us.

We grew up with this idea. I joined the Basij at an age that I was like putty that could be moulded.

THE VIOLENCE CAPTIVATED GLOBAL attention. After days of relative silence, President Barack Obama finally said he was "appalled and outraged" by events in Tehran. Those events deepened the dilemma for America in its new effort to reach out to Iran—and to convince it to stop its nuclear program.

Iranian hard-liners focused their first haranguing charges of foreign interference against the traditional whipping boy, Britain, and less on the United States. Yet the sudden need in Tehran for displays of international legitimacy meant that even as the regime was cracking down at home—and engaging in tit-for-tat expulsions of diplomats with London—the Supreme Leader's son Mojtaba was secretly sending very positive messages of engagement to Washington, I was told by American officials. That was exactly what the Americans had hoped for—*before* the election fiasco.

But Mojtaba was also the one believed to be orchestrating the brutal action on the streets, and the entire crisis raised doubts about whether Washington could or should engage. Even if Washington had once been willing to talk, with a more moderate president, the Iranian side was now preoccupied with political battles at home. Ahmadinejad barely attracted one-third of the members of parliament, 105 out of 290, to his official victory celebration.[170] Soon the focus on the British as the source of evil behind the Green Movement broadened to the Americans, restoring the Great Satan to its position as enemy incarnate.

The regime's vicious use of torture and rape made engagement an increasingly moral question—at least, one that could not easily be ignored. U.S. diplomacy began to move again to the default mode: more sanctions. At the same time, to justify its own actions, the Islamic Republic jacked up the threat from enemy agents, which it accused of leading Iran to capitulation and defeat, through Velvet Revolution. Ayatollah Khamenei spoke on the eve of the thirtieth anniversary of the U.S. Embassy takeover in November 2009. This had always been a day to revitalize anti-Americanism, to cheer what Imam Khomeini had called the "second Revolution, greater than the first." Khamenei slammed Obama as insincere.

"The new president of the U.S. he speaks nice words. He [sent me] messages repeatedly—verbal, written—[saying] come let us turn the page, come let us create a new situation," Khamenei said.[171] He reminded Iranians of his initial response the previous March, that he would not "prejudge" the American overtures, but be watchful in case the United States only "pulled a glove over an iron claw and extended [its] hand."

"Now eight months have passed [and] what we saw was opposite to what they have expressed in words," the Leader said. "The American government is a really arrogant power and the Iranian nation will not be deceived with its apparent reconciliatory behavior." It was business as usual for a Revolution under attack. Khamenei warned: "Americans should not lay hope on some post-election events in Iran because our [Islamic] system is more well-rooted than they think it is," he said. "Every time [U.S. officials] smile at the Iranian officials, it comes with a dagger hidden behind them. They have not stopped intimidating Iran."

Ahmadinejad too had kept to his theme of puffing Iran to superpower status while demeaning Iran's enemies. Iran had renewed talks with the West over its nuclear program but was negotiating from a position of strength. "While enemies have used all their capacities . . . the Iranian nation is standing powerfully and they are like a mosquito," he said.[172] "Given the negative record of Western powers, the Iranian government . . . looks at the talks with no trust. But realities dictate to them to interact with the Iranian nation."

WHILE THOSE LEADERS ADHERED to a decades-old script, the streets of Tehran told another story, of dramatic changes. The Revolutionary Guard and Basij militia called on Iranians to "exercise vigilance" in the face of likely "mischief and plots by the enemy's agents" on the anniversary of the U.S. Embassy seizure. Police warned that any "illegal" gatherings would be "strongly confronted."

Opposition protesters had also prepared for weeks for the November 4 showdown—as they would for every future calendar event—and published slogans in advance that included digs at the Obama administration for attempting to negotiate with the government, which many saw as a betrayal. "Obama, Obama, you are either with them or with us," was one slogan. Another: "Obama don't forget; Ahmadinejad is a killer."

Mir Hossein Mousavi issued a stirring statement in which he said the anniversary "reminds us that among us, it is the people who are the leaders."[173] Calling on Iranians to take to the streets, he said that on the "greenest days of the year" Iranians would "show the roots of their revolutionary spirit."

But more bloodshed would be a double-edged sword for the regime. "The tougher they appear, the more polarized Iranian society becomes, the more stubborn the opposition becomes, and the more persistent it becomes," historian Ali Ansari told me.[174] Likewise, "the longer the opposition exists, the more difficult it is for them. It's political guerrilla warfare, a war of attrition."

At the official rally along the outer wall of the old U.S. Embassy— that infamous "Den of Spies"—black- and camouflage-clad students chanted their standard dirge of death-to-America slogans and burned U.S. and Israeli flags. Prominent conservative Gholamali Haddad-Adel said opposition leaders could not consider themselves "disciples of

Imam Khomeini" because their statements were "making the enemies of the Revolution happy." [175]

One journalist at the rally told me that it *appeared* to be a typical pro-regime event: "Like usual, schoolkids busy with their mischievous fun—not even listening." [176] State TV kept its cameras firmly on the thousands at the rally, the largest turnout for years but not a sliver of the three million that the Basij had boasted would turn out.

Yet just beyond that sealed cordon, battle raged for the soul of Iran's Revolution. "Greens [won] by far. They proved that no longer can the government assemble people without any incident, and [the regime] has based everything since the beginning on [large] public assemblies," another witness told me. [177] They were creating a pattern of protest that would become as persistent in the future as it was effective. He saw *basiji*s "lead people into side streets [and] start hitting [them] right there and then."

The protests that had first begun in June and were limited to reversing Ahmadinejad's fraudulent victory, had now—energized by everything from the failing economy to prisoner abuse—clearly expanded to limit or remove the supremacy of Ayatollah Khamenei. The chant was heard: "Khamenei is a murderer; supreme religious rule is over." [178] Video showed protesters streaming across a huge portrait of Khamenei thrown down on the street, scuffing their feet on his face as they passed.

There were *basiji*s armed with electric stun guns; groups of twenty motorcycles, their black-armored menace armed with paintball guns spitting slugs of orange. "For the first time, people were actually sticking together and not running away, but saying, 'Let's hold out, let's hold out,' " one witness told me. [179] "Mostly it was women being hit because I saw a lot of the women pass me, tens of women pass me, all of which had been hit; older women who had taken paintball hits to the chest and legs were covered in orange paint," he said.

"I wouldn't say it's a victory, but it's not a loss. There was definitely a message put out there," the witness added. "It was important that everyday people in their cars [and] businesses got to see that women were being attacked by people with batons and [paint] guns. And they get to smell tear gas for the first time. It's horrible to call that a victory, but the ugliness is something" to behold.

The (New) Cultural Revolution

More needling control was coming: the postelection violence was used as pretext for a new Cultural Revolution. The "coup government," as critics called it, was preparing a more fundamental transformation of Iran, which harked back to the tectonic shifts of the first years of the Islamic Republic, when universities were closed for three years and Westoxicated learning was purged from the classroom.

A generation after Khomeini had demonstrated how to impose cultural upheaval on "miseducated" students, it was Supreme Leader Khamenei's turn to find "enemy plots" in the universities, where revolutionary standards had slipped again. Khamenei told college professors their primary duty was to prepare the minds of those who would defend against a "soft revolution." [180] In the months after the 2009 election, he took special aim at humanities and liberal arts, which accounted for two-thirds of student degrees and were un-Islamic. Such teaching led to "loss of belief" in God and Islam, Khamenei ruled, and "skepticism and doubt about religious principles."

"The more students and young people are religious, the less their thoughts and deeds would be spoiled," the Supreme Leader said. Students were the "young colonels in this front. . . . But university lecturers are the commanders of the soft war front. They should be aware . . . identify the enemy and discover its targets."

Reformists fought back. "Certain individuals reject liberalism, but their opposition is based on fascism and totalitarianism," said former president Khatami. [181] "Assailing an aspect of the Western experience by insisting on a more dangerous and worse view is doomed."

But professors in Iran, who had already watched their freedoms shrink during the Ahmadinejad era, felt even more pressure. They were instructed to notify university security departments before traveling abroad and told to report upon return about what they did and whom they met. One academic told me that intelligence agents tried to force his high school–age son to inform on him.

Even a purge of the Ministry of Intelligence was under way, with those who were not sufficiently suspicious of people like Haleh Esfandiari—the "Velvet Revolutionary" grandmother from the Wilson Center in Washington, who spent months in Evin Prison in 2007— on trial in closed court. Nearly two dozen intelligence officials were facing charges at the ministry, with opposition to Esfandiari's detention the number-one accusation. "These charges and allegations were there, but . . . the postelection crisis cleared the way for throwing out everybody who had the slightest sympathy with the reform camp, or who had misgivings about Ahmadinejad," one source in Tehran told me. "So they used the opportunity and the record of these people to impose harsh tactics against them."

The housecleaning reached far beyond the Intelligence Ministry, to especially include the Foreign, Petroleum, and Islamic Guidance ministries. "The purge is under way all over, but other places is more routine and less judicial," said the source. "Many retirements and similar tactics."

At the foreign ministry, at least twenty-eight diplomats abroad and inside Iran had resigned over the June 2009 election crisis and its aftermath, with two in Germany and one in London seeking asylum, according to Mohammad Reza Heydari, a veteran of the Iran-Iraq War and chief consular official at the Iran Embassy in Oslo until he defected in January 2010 and was given asylum in Norway.[182] In an interview with Meg Coker of the Wall Street Journal, Heydari charged that he was pressured by Iranian intelligence agents to change vote totals for Iranians living in Norway to favor Ahmadinejad and to identify opposition activists staging antigovernment rallies, which included his teenage son.

"My conscience couldn't stand it any longer. I couldn't serve a government turning its guns not on its enemies but on its own people," said Heydari. Iranian officials dismissed their former colleague as an "opportunist," and a Norwegian diplomat was expelled by Tehran in response. Heydari said he and his family received threats, and Norwegian police were providing a twenty-four-hour escort that included getting his two sons safely to school.

One of the diplomat's jobs had been to certify the results of expatriate voters. Of the 650 ballots cast at the embassy, 540 were for Mousavi—83 percent—a tally that he said was similar to the reporting of other Iranian embassies. "The will of the people was clear," Heydari told Coker. "I signed my name to the report saying it."

In Tehran, universities braced for special treatment after Khamenei announced the dangers of "liberal arts" programs. "This is coming close to a police state," one professor told me.[183] "We used to take pride in being very different than the rest of the countries in the region. We are fairly free in traveling, teaching, and the rest. But now, we are heading toward Iraq under Saddam Hussein."

The new measures were just the start, the professor said:

> We expect things to get even worse, way worse than this. This has been probably the darkest time of postrevolutionary Iran . . . they do not think rationally anymore. These are steps out of fear of losing control. The split at the top of the system is extremely serious. The anger below is unabating. It is not sustainable in the long run, but then that "long run" may take years.
>
> All sides have embarked on an irreversible path and the more the Supreme Leader relies on heavy-handed tactics, the more the population loses trust. Then the reaction of the public requires more repression, and the cycle keeps going on . . .

The universities were already "heavily depressed," and a purging Cultural Revolution would set them back years more, the professor told me. Officials had announced a plan to appoint a cleric in every school; clerics said that elementary schools in several provinces had already been transferred to control by Islamic seminaries.[184] " 'Gov-

ernment of God' is practically B.S. for most [people]. It is mostly survival. Some of course think that this is their God-given responsibility,"
he said. "These are a bunch of new kids on the block that have no
comprehension of what they were doing and have a very brutal and
tortured mentality."

The result was "absolutely corrosive," the professor said. His homeland was being destroyed by its self-declared defenders, his own arrest
imminent. I could hear his cry: "That is why Iran is incredibly hopeless, and happiness is gone."

Killing the Revolution

The Islamic Republic's arcing trajectory of faith—from its peak of
unquestioned belief and spirit, through to its self-doubt and self-
destructive violence—is captured in the story of one Iranian doctor.
"Farzad" is not his real name.[185]

Like Dr. Alireza Zakani, that frontline doctor I met during my earliest visits to Iran—the one who told me war stories, and stories about
the inspirational student pilgrimage visits to the former battlefields—
Dr. Farzad was a devoted Believer. He was convinced of the spirituality of Ayatollah Khomeini, of the power of the Revolution—and of
the will of so many Iranians to embrace it, as one family.

These two medical professionals started from the same place: both
volunteered their service during the Iran-Iraq War, in combat or in
combat hospitals. But since the late 1990s, Zakani had adhered to a
hard-line script that left little room for nonbelieving Iranians. A member of parliament who backed Ahmadinejad's faction, he directed the
hard-line website Jahan and fundamentalist weekly *Panjereh*. He was
quoted saying, "Anybody who goes out into the streets and gets assaulted has no right to object." [186] Zakani also praised the show trials
of reformists, which he said "promotes awareness among people over
the enemy's explicit and implicit measures." [187]

In contrast, Dr. Farzad took a different path. In his understanding,
the entire conservative project of stamping out reformists as traitors,

and then of stealing elections and murderously attacking fellow Iranians who protested, was rotting the Revolution from within.

"If they go like this, and really push to the end, this is going to make things worse and worse. I absolutely believe [it] will kill the Revolution," Farzad told me when we met outside Iran in late 2009. The doctor's trimmed goatee was white, his mustache gray; he switched glasses to a pair with rimless rectangular lenses when reading. This was a family man who, to me, seemed incapable of lying. And he was feeling the convulsions of his nation as if they afflicted his very body. Early in the Revolution, Farzad had meaningful contact with its top leaders, which taught him much about who they are—and how far, he believes, the Revolution had deviated from its original aims. Disgusted at the postelection violence in 2009, which had entangled his sons, he favored a family analogy.

"How can I hope that [by] killing this section of my family, that then the family will be OK?" asked Farzad. "This is a very, very deep wound. You can never recover from such an issue."

It was made more painful because of a special link he had with Ayatollah Khomeini, the Imam himself.

DURING THE IRAN-IRAQ WAR, Farzad's faith was total. "Somebody was calling us [to fight], who we could trust absolutely," he told me. "When Imam Khomeini spoke, we could absolutely trust him."

Years later, Farzad twice worked with Khomeini, as part of his medical team. He was there during the final weeks of the Imam's life, when the octogenarian preacher—the man who had pronounced fearlessly, who had shaken the world with *his* Revolution—was quickly losing strength. "He was semiconscious . . . very close to unconscious," Farzad recalled of Khomeini:

He was lying on the bed. The clock was above his head. There was no way he could see that—and he was not conscious enough to see that—but he was a sort of clock for me. When I had a feeling that now it is going to be prayer time, [he would] move his eyebrows or . . . shake a little bit a hand or a finger and somebody would come . . . and they would bring the water for him, and . . . wash his hands, face, and make him ready, and then again by some gestures, he would do the prayer.

That was important for me, because I could see that he really believes. You have some people [who pray only] as a religious duty. They do it. But he really believed. And when somebody believes, he is strong—whether he is correct or not. If it's correct, much better. But even if it's not correct and he believes, it gives him a strong sense. Especially in those times, I came to know why [Khomeini] is so strong and so independent. Because he absolutely, totally believed in what he was saying.

But something else convinced Farzad about the conviction of the emaciated man before him, whose imminent death would unfurl waves of emotion across Iran and the Shiite world. Gone were the thunderous sermons, the words and sharp tongue used to furious effect to captivate disciples and to crucify enemies. Missing too was the stern visage reproduced endlessly and iconically throughout the land. The man who redefined "resistance" for a generation of Believers was now resisting his last.

High in that old neighborhood of Jamaran, at the rocky foothills of the Alborz, where a few doors down from Khomeini's hallowed compound a used furniture salesman toiled, where a freelance electrician made repairs, and where the simple shop at the end of the narrow lane sold essentials like olives, cheese, and candy (how many blond hunks of soap from there had hand-washed the robes of the Imam?)—a lane where on the wall someone had, during the Revolution, spray-painted Khomeini's own words, "America cannot do a damn thing"—Khomeini showed Dr. Farzad gratitude in a most exquisite human way.

"He was not in a situation to express his thanks to me," Dr. Farzad recalled, his voice rich with the memory, two decades later:

He could never open his eyes within those two weeks when I was with him. But when I was touching him, doing some [medical] maneuvers, the moment my hand was somewhere that he could feel, and he *could* reach just by touch of finger, he was telling me: "Thank you." I have thought so many times, he really believed in people, and people mutually believed in him. . . . I will not say others do not believe in people. But I will very strongly say that *nobody* believes in people *that* way, with *that* strength.

BY CONTRAST, FARZAD HAD growing doubts about Khamenei, whom he had also come to know personally in the 1980s. When the cleric-president was elevated to Supreme Leader, Farzad was worried. "We believed that God would help, but everyone believed that [Khomeini] could not be replaced fully." His chief concern was how the less credentialed Khamenei would perform the role. "I [felt] that I couldn't have the same trust," Farzad told me. "But I think he was the best available."

The true test would really begin years later, in 1997, when, under Khamenei's leadership, Khatami and the nascent reform movement pulled off their stunning upset victory. It was an opportunity for the Revolution to regenerate itself, Farzad believed, but one that the Supreme Leader failed to utilize. "It was very clear what the people were saying . . . 'We *are* with the Revolution; we *are* with religion, we *are* with our beliefs. But still we need some more,' " Farzad told me. "This Revolution needs to be active, needs to be alive, [to] recover itself."

But instead of bridging the gap in a divided society and refortifying the Revolution, Khamenei increasingly favored the hard-liners and greater authoritarianism.

DR. FARZAD HAD WITNESSED fiddling of the 2005 presidential vote in his own village, at a mobile polling station. The "officials" wanted Ahmadinejad elected, told people to vote a certain way, and peered over voters' shoulders as they marked their ballots. One *basiji*, whom Farzad knew, tried to see which candidate he voted for. Ahmadinejad should never have made it to the second round, the doctor said. "You could see something was happening, this time very sharply, very clearly." The stakes were far higher by mid-2009, and so the steps taken to ensure Ahmadinejad's victory—and Farzad had no doubts that the vote had again been hijacked—were all the bolder.

"This is a very, very huge miscalculation," Farzad told me. "It is a spring. The more you push it, the more resistance you receive. If I have someone in my family killed, I am going to question that forever. I am not going to forget it." Arguments by hard-liners that they are the ones who survived the crucible of the Iran-Iraq War and can therefore rule society in the name of the martyrs and those lofty wartime ideals—and myths—hold little credence today.

"Nobody buys it," said this man who felt the Imam's human and spiritual touch. "Whatever I see [of Khamenei] now I cannot believe."

"He *was* a very humble man. He was *very* considerate," Farzad recalled. Khamenei encouraged his staff to get more and higher education, even paying for extra classes for them. Farzad noticed that Khamenei—who was already a big voice in the regime back in the 1980s, as Friday prayer leader and then president—used the same wartime system of coupons that every other Iranian had to use, to acquire goods like Danish feta cheese to eat with his bread for breakfast.

Khamenei in those days was considered a "pragmatist" who favored renewing ties with the West, including the United States.[188] Called the "poet president" for his passion for literature, some said he had also been partial to opium—a long-standing Persian pastime. When it was fashionable, Khamenei wore his shirt collar in the manner of those called "chic sheikhs."

"He was very open-minded. To be honest with you, some things I see from him now, I am afraid," said the doctor, speaking about Khamenei's tough 2009 postelection Friday prayer sermon: "I don't see that humble person in him anymore. When he goes there, talking with such a strong voice, talking about people as the enemy, I [was] surprised. . . . Believe me, if I could go to him now, I would ask him the same question: 'What has happened to you?'"

· · ·

AS THE 2009 CLASHES clouded Tehran streets with smoke and tear gas, Farzad did not join the protests himself. But he had bumped into a hard-liner near his home. Farzad berated him: "You are coming to the street and putting your gun on my head and saying, 'You think another way, I should kill you.' Just today when I was coming out of my house I did my prayer . . . and you did the same and we came out, and now you are the right and I'm the wrong? What's going on?"

The hard-liner replied: "I'm not talking about you, but some people are doing wrong."

Farzad asked: "How many people? One person? Two? Three? A thousand in the whole country of seventy million?"

It was a pointless argument, Farzad knew. Pointless because for these people—and that was how he described hard-liners, as *these people*—there was no room for argument. No room for doubt.

"Sometimes we sit together, my wife and my daughter, and talk together," Farzad confided. "And it's really sad; we see some opportunities that we [Iranians] are losing." Other families like his had been locked in argument, divided by politics, and certain that each was right, weakening the social fabric as the crisis continued.

"I would not say it's the beginning of the end, but it's the beginning of a new era that may be very much different from what we like, what we expect, and what we love," Farzad told me. "We are a family. We should be able to put this family back together again." He couldn't predict how or even if Iran's crisis could end. The problem was strategic and cut to the heart of the Islamic system: "I'm afraid. We can easily kill ourselves. If somebody believes, 'We will purify this family,' it is very stupid. This is not Islam. I believe our Prophet never started to throw some people away to purify the population."

Exit Stage Right

The model of resistance that has so defined the Islamic Republic emerged in the seventh century, on the blood-soaked plain of Karbala.

It is the example of Imam Hossein—who so defiantly chose to "let the swords encircle me," if his martyrdom would keep Islam alive. On the eve of the 1979 Revolution, Ayatollah Khomeini could not have spoken more powerfully of the need to resist the Shah—using that age-old example of Ashura, when "blood triumphed over the sword." [189] He said, "[Hossein] taught us how to struggle against all the tyrants of history, showed us how the clenched fists of those who seek freedom, desire independence, and proclaim the truth may triumph over tanks, machine guns, and the armies of Satan, how the word of truth may obliterate falsehood."

Three decades later, Iran's opposition leaders would use the same argument against the tyrannical excesses of the Islamic regime itself. So post–June 2009, resistance in Iran continued. Activists covered university classrooms and sidewalks with anti-regime graffiti. Banknotes were written over with Green Movement slogans or stamped with images of the dead icon Neda, blood pouring across her face, or the symbol of the IRIB state broadcaster with a Nazi swastika. [190] The central bank governor called defacing currency a "crime," and monitors were sent to popular moneychanging places, even bakeries and public toilets, in an attempt to stop their circulation. The tainted money was to be collected, burned, and replaced with new coins. [191]

Opposition leader Mir Hossein Mousavi—the once-uncharismatic, aged revolutionary who was resolved not to give one inch in confronting the regime—produced strong statements. He bolstered his loyalists and all Iranians who still felt the pull of the Revolution's earliest ideals—and saw them betrayed by the street violence and abuse of their compatriots.

"Today, is it conceivable that the flame of the people's movement may be extinguished, if a fellow countryman is kept silent?" Mousavi asked in late 2009. [192] "If such a thing happens, we will lose the fruit of forty-five years of our history and our struggle. And if it doesn't happen, this will show the roots of our revolutionary spirit. . . . These days, people are all asking of victory. When will we achieve it? How will we get there faster? And what will add to its perfection?"

Despite the regime threats of more bloodshed, despite having so few tools compared to the coercive capacity of the *nezam,* Mousavi remained as steadfast as Khomeini had, a generation earlier, when confronting the tyranny of the Shah.

DURING THE MASS TRIALS of reformists in August 2009, Iranian prosecutors singled out an obscure American political scientist in his eighties as a key figure behind the unrest. Gene Sharp, the retired Harvard researcher considered the godfather of nonviolent resistance, and whose work since the 1970s had served as the template for taking on authoritarian regimes from Burma to Belgrade, was fingered as the master of Velvet Revolution in Iran. He had compiled a list of 198 methods of nonviolent action, and his seminal book *From Dictatorship to Democracy: A Conceptual Framework for Liberation* was translated into two dozen languages, including Farsi.

Hailed as *the* manual by those who conducted people-power coups in Eastern Europe, its contents were no secret in Iran, where authorities had obsessed for years about their vulnerability to a Velvet Revolution. In fact, a few years earlier they had requested and were sent hard copies of Sharp's works. Officials saw the 2009 crisis as the fruit of those strategies.

The indictment of more than one hundred reformists read out by prosecutors was explicit: "According to the documents which we have obtained and the confirmed confessions of the accused, the occurrence of these events was completely planned in advance and proceeded according to a timetable and stages of a velvet coup in such a way that more than 100 of the 198 events were executed in accordance with the instructions of Gene Sharp for a velvet coup." [193]

The indictment said Velvet Revolution, with a timeline as long as a decade or more, was just as effective as a military coup at creating regime change.

"This technique of fomenting coups is so planned out that . . . it can stealthily and quietly complete the stages of the Velvet Revolution without attracting serious attention," the indictment read. "By the time the political systems come to their senses, the velvet coup has usually reached its final stage and the probability of its success has greatly increased."

Sharp does not take credit—nor accept blame—for the postelection crisis that senior IRGC commanders claimed brought the regime to the "edge of a downfall." Yet from "disclosing identities of secret agents" (Method No. 194), to "popular non-obedience" (No. 135), Sharp's ideas were clearly reflected in the political unrest.[194]

"We don't take charge of movements," Sharp told me, speaking from his Boston home, where he ran his nonprofit Albert Einstein Institute on a modest budget.[195] "We try to provide the materials to enable the people on the scene, who know the scene better than we do, by far, to make those decisions and do those things."

And that was exactly what Iranians did as postelection unrest swept across the Islamic Republic in June 2009. The number of free downloads of *From Dictatorship to Democracy* in Farsi spiked to 3,487 from just 79 the month before, on Sharp's website. Other sites hosting Sharp's work reported a similar boost in demand.

"The great irony is that people actually weren't focused on the Velvet Revolution option before the elections," Iran analyst Karim Sadjadpour told me.[196] "It's only after the elections, when Iranians have come to the realization that they can't change their political fate with the ballot box, that they've looked to more dramatic options."

Sharp, still largely unrecognized in the West, was becoming a celebrity in Iran—albeit notorious in some circles. A 2007 cartoon video created by Iranian intelligence portrayed Sharp as "the theoretician of civil disobedience and Velvet Revolutions" and "one of the CIA agents in charge of America's infiltration into other countries."[197]

But Iranians have their own history of "improvised struggles" that long predate his work, Sharp noted, including the 1979 Revolution, during which "protesters were even putting flowers in the guns of the Shah's followers."

"The notion that Iranians need to learn from Sharp on how to protest is absurd," wrote historian Ervand Abrahamian.[198] "Iranians have been taking to the streets to protest ever since the late nineteenth century—during the Tobacco Crisis, the Constitution Revolution (1905–1906), the 1911 Russian Ultimatum, the 1919 Anglo-Persian Agreement, the 1925 Anti-Republican Campaign, May Day Rallies in 1943–46, the 1951–53 Oil Nationalization, the 1963 Religious Demonstrations, and, of course, the 1977–1979 Revolution."

"Street protests are as Iranian as apple pie is American," wrote Abrahamian, adding that a number of Eastern Europeans involved in the 1989 events had told him they were impressed by reporting of the mass protests during Iran's Revolution a decade before. "Iranians don't need Western gurus."

While certainly true, such gurus and their ideas were having some impact. One Green Movement activist in Tehran confirmed that "Gene Sharp in Farsi was in fact being circulated widely in the summer, and likely helped boost civil disobedience efforts . . . such as writing on banknotes and a boycott on products advertised on IRIB [state TV]."[199]

In another case, student activist Sadegh Shojaii was arrested in Tehran less than ten days after the June election. When police raided his apartment, taking his computer, hard drives, and every scrap of paper along with them, Shojaii had already distributed about half his first print run of fifteen hundred pamphlets drawn from the book *Non-Violent Struggle—50 Crucial Points; A Strategic Approach to Everyday Tactics.*[200] Created by the Serbian founders of the Otpor (Resistance) student movement in Belgrade as a how-to guide to peaceful democratic change, and recently translated into Farsi, the material drew heavily on Gene Sharp's work.

The book says it "fills the gap between the tremendous theoretical insights about strategic non-violent conflict developed by scholars over the past several decades and the accumulated experience of front-line practitioners." Shojaii had stripped out the photographs and diagrams, condensed the text to fit onto one large sheet of paper, and folded it as a pamphlet. "I couldn't trust any professional printing house, so I printed them out with my own personal machine," Shojaii said, after his release and escape to Turkey, where he joined a growing exodus of activists leading resistance from outside Iran.

In practice some reformist actions were vintage Sharp, from Mousavi's refusal to negotiate or back down on demands about the election, to strict nonviolence on the streets. Sharp told me it was "quite amazing" that protests continued in Iran in the face of severe regime efforts to crack down that left scores dead and subjected detainees to torture and rape.

"If [protesters] learn a variety of nonviolent methods, they don't have to go out on the streets. The idea that you have to bring down a government with mass street protests is not true," counseled Sharp. "Just find out what are the sources of that regime's power, [stop them] and inevitably, no matter what their level of oppression is, it weakens the regime. If [activists] can hold out long enough, and do it skillfully enough—that's very important. Then the regime can do nothing but disappear."

Some tactics were obvious, such as marches (Sharp's Method No. 38) and "silence" (No. 52). Others were adjusted by Iranians to suit their case, such as the consumer boycott (No. 71) of Nokia and Siemens, which sold Tehran technology for deep spying on Internet users.[201] The use of "symbolic colors" (No. 18) gave the name to the opposition Green Movement. Slogan (No. 7), "paint as protest" (No. 26), "symbolic sounds"—the shouting of *Allah-o Akbar!* from the rooftops—and many other methods were used in Iran.

"These regimes always present themselves as all-powerful—absolutely omnipotent, so that resistance becomes futile," Sharp told me. "But if you learn this regime has these five, ten, fifteen, or twenty weaknesses—and you can deliberately aggravate those weaknesses—it weakens the regime. It helps it fall apart."

Sharp's ideas, adapted for Iran, were being circulated further by people such as Mohsen Sazegara—that founder of the Revolutionary Guard, turned reformist editor, turned "potential Yeltsin," turned Virginia-based anti-regime activist. After the June election, he produced a daily ten-minute video to encourage nonviolent action, which he claimed reached hundreds of thousands on the Internet in Iran. His website—where Sharp's books could be downloaded—was in late 2009 receiving two thousand e-mails a day, which often included new tactics that Sazegara beamed back into Iran in his videos.

"Iranians are an educated nation, especially the younger generation . . . and I'm sure that many of them study the experience of nonviolent movements in other countries," Sazegara told me.[202] "We think that if we make a mistake and go for violent actions, the regime [can be] more brutal than any violent opposition."

But it could still be a dangerous business, even thousands of miles away from Iran. Sazegara had received a number of death threats.

"If they kill me, so what? There will be thousands of Mohsen Sazegaras right now," he said. "Every one of the young generation has read these books, and know everything better than me."

FROM THE STREETS OF Tehran to the surprised doubt quietly expressed by Iran's allies, signs multiplied that the power of the Islamic Republic—which so recently had appeared to be on an invincible trajectory—was now tumbling dangerously like a missile that had run out of fuel.

"I think we've seen the peak of the Islamic Republic's power in its current configuration," historian Ali Ansari told me.[203] It was a crisis of legitimacy, and of authority. "They've lost control of the narrative, and the only way they can do it now is by force."

The regime had also lost the monopoly on violence. "The problem is that people are hitting back," said Ansari. He asked a friend in Tehran during the first week of the protests in June when people would react. The friend replied: "What do you mean *when*? A lot of the deaths they are keeping quiet are *basijis* butchered in the street."

Reform-minded Iranians were not backing down. Some displayed astounding courage. In a meeting with students transmitted live on Iranian TV, Ayatollah Khamenei declared that, months after the disputed vote, questioning the results had become the "greatest of all crimes."²⁰⁴ It was a forum usually full of praise for Khamenei, from a handpicked audience of Believers. But then Sharif University student Mahmoud Vahidnia—gold medalist in Iran's mathematics Olympiad in 2007—stepped up to the microphone. For twenty minutes he criticized the Leader, the bias in state-run broadcasting, and the fierce postelection crackdown.

News reports said the bespectacled Vahidnia "strongly criticized this matter of [Khamenei's] entourage turning him into a big idol."²⁰⁵ The math wiz complained about the "cycle of power" in Iran and how lack of criticism would "lead to discord and hatred."

As he spoke, Vahidnia was given a handwritten note saying his time was up, but he asked the Leader if he could continue. "From the very beginning the time was over, but I am in favor of you continuing your statements," Khamenei replied.²⁰⁶ State TV officials, in shock at what was happening, had already cut off live coverage. Undeterred, the student carried on, sometimes greeted with applause or cheers. Afterward, Khamenei told the gathering he was "absolutely not unhappy about saying such things," that he welcomed criticism and knew "there is a lot of it."

Nevertheless, instead of delivering the noon prayer as scheduled, Ayatollah Ali Khamenei—the second Leader of the Islamic Revolution—left the meeting early, disappearing from view as he stepped behind his curtain.

"The student said, 'They have turned you into an idol'—the word 'idol.' And that is exactly what is happening," historian Ansari told me.²⁰⁷ "There is a fight in Iran over this idea that a group, a cabal even, are setting up for themselves this holy, sacred state [in which] Khamenei and Ahmadinejad are representatives of the Hidden Imam." Use of the word "idol" recalled the term often applied to the Shah, who was *taghout*—an infidel or idol worshipper. Khomeini had ruled that "it is the duty of all of us to overthrow the *taghout;* i.e., the illegitimate political powers that now rule the entire Islamic world."²⁰⁸

"The Prophet [Mohammad] came and smashed the idol worshippers. It's a very loaded statement," explained Ansari. "So for a student to get up and say they are turning you into an idol—a *taghout*—that's shocking language. It goes to the heart of the issue."

Another bulwark of authority had been broken. And there would be others. The more IRGC commander Jafari and others talked about being "defenders of a sacred system," said Ansari, "the more the senior clerics in Qom and others are horrified by what's happening. It's like a return to the Middle Ages—the discussion is really about heresy and blasphemy. Both sides are accusing each other of blasphemy, saying, 'What the hell are you doing?' "

THE DEATH OF ONE of those clerics helped prompt more protest. Grand Ayatollah Hossein-Ali Montazeri—the tufted-eared senior theologian whom Khomeini had called the "fruit of my life," before he became an outspoken regime critic and finally spiritual mentor of the opposition—died in his sleep in December 2009, during the holy month of Moharram. Still feisty at eighty-seven, the opposition oracle could not have chosen a more propitious time to die—one week before the most sacred date on the Shiite calendar, Ashura, which commemorates the death in 680 A.D. of the "Lord of the Martyrs," Imam Hossein. No other Shiite event is more infused with religious symbolism and the glorification of Hossein's willingness to die for his beliefs.

"Moharram is very good for us, because Hossein's ideology stood against oppression," the activist software engineer who fled to Turkey, Ebrahim Mehtari, told me.[209] Since 1979, Iranian leaders had always cast themselves in the role of the religiously pure Hossein, facing off against the modern-day equivalents of the evil Yazid. That caliph claimed his state was Islamic but nevertheless killed Hossein, grandson of the Prophet Mohammad. The Green Movement now saw itself as the pure side of the Hossein saga, aided by the fact that Mousavi's second name was Hossein and that the opposition's Islamic green was waved constantly at such religious events.

"Now from our people's point of view, Khamenei is close to Yazid, and Mousavi and the Green Movement is the Hossein figure," Mehtari said. The regime "have all the tools of repression: the money, the guns. [But] it's impossible for the regime to stop people. If they slap one person in Tehran, they will be Yazid."

No one but Montazeri had both the theological gravitas and sheer political moxie to challenge the "Supreme" Leader Khamenei so openly, and to declare that Iran's Islamic republic was "neither Islamic nor republic." This was a man of courage, who had proven over the decades to be fearless in the face of power. His death at that moment (of natural causes) served to remind Iranians of the injustices of the Islamic regime, and the ultimately negative results for the *nezam* that for years he had predicted would come to pass. Montazeri was right, and if the regime rejoiced in his removal from the scene, it was short-lived—for in death in Iran you really *are* important.

Nobel Peace Prize laureate Shirin Ebadi called Montazeri "the father of human rights in Iran" and considered herself "one of the millions of his followers and students."[210]

Fifty buses full of Revolutionary Guard troops converged on Qom, sixty miles south of Tehran, as tens of thousands of mourners streamed to the Shiite holy city with quivers full of slogans: "Montazeri is not dead, it is the government which is dead," echoed one. And another: "Innocent Montazeri, your path will be continued even if the dictator should rain bullets on our heads."[211]

Hard-line vigilantes gathered by the hundreds with hard-line clerics outside Montazeri's house, where they attacked and tore up funeral banners.[212] One witness described to me how, early in the morning on the day of the funeral in Qom, Mir Hossein Mousavi, who had not been seen in public for months, had stepped out of the compound of the Grand Ayatollah Yusef Saanei, a fellow reformist, to cross the street to Montazeri's house.[213] At that moment a group of thirty bearded men, holding Montazeri pictures to blend in to the crowd, dropped the portraits and started lunging toward Mousavi with their fists raised and shouting, "Death to the hypocrite!" The former candidate had to be hustled to safety inside the Montazeri compound.

The same thing happened when cleric Mehdi Karroubi, whose public charges of rape of detainees still horrified Iran's political establishment, stepped into the street. This time groups of reformists were ready and pushed back the vigilantes so that Karroubi could pass.

One engineering student, his face covered with a surgical mask to hide his identity, said Montazeri's "demise, although very hard for us, is also a blessing—it brought people out [into the streets] again." [214] Mourners chanted: "Rape, atrocities, an unworthy government"; "This is the month of blood, Yazid will fall"; and "Montazeri's last wish, an end to this dictatorship."

A middle-aged cleric in the crowd said the timing and its religious significance would codify Montazeri's legacy of challenging authoritarian rule. Montazeri "was a critic. He started his criticism when he was powerful, not when he was weak. He could have remained silent and received benefits from that silence, but he didn't. He was always siding with the righteous and not the powerful."

AFTER THE FUNERAL, MOUSAVI'S convoy was attacked on its way back to Tehran by "plainclothes men riding motorcycles," who smashed the rear window of Mousavi's car, injured a member of his entourage, and forced the convoy to stop several times on the road. [215] Violence would erupt repeatedly in the following days, finally escalating to clashes across the country on Ashura that by one count left at least thirty-seven dead—the highest one-day toll in nearly seven months of protest.

By historical standards, that was a small price—and therefore easily paid—according to the Supreme Leader's representative to the Revolutionary Guard, who noted the far higher death toll of the first three wars of the Shiite Imams. "God had told his prophets to reach victory through soft power," said cleric Ali Saeedi. [216] "But when [Imam Ali] took control of the Islamic state, preserving the state was worth 75,000 people killed. What does resign mean? If this was the case, Imam Ali should have resigned when the elites . . . lined up against him. But he didn't give up, because preserving the Islamic state was absolutely mandatory."

In such an excruciating environment, Mir Hossein Mousavi knew what to expect: "I'm not afraid of being one of the martyrs who lost their lives in their fight for their rightful demands since the vote," he said in a statement.[217] "My blood is not redder than that of other martyrs."

Mousavi warned that no accusation of fomenting arrest or declaring opposition leaders "enemies of God" would work. "Let's assume that you silence people by arrests, acts of violence and threats," Mousavi said. "What solution do you have for the change in people's view of the regime? How can you make up for the lack of legitimacy?"

GONE WAS THE MODEL Islamic state that could preach from the moral high ground—to its neighbors in the Middle East and beyond— of a revolutionary, popular Islamic government; the one originally envisioned by Khomeini.

"Iran is more and more viewed as quite a fundamentalist, authoritarian Islamic regime, and not so much an Islamic state that wants to protect the rights of Muslims," Iran specialist Massoumeh Torfeh told me.[218] "After all, the people who are suffering in the prisons in Iran are also Muslims. The people who were killed in the demonstrations were also Muslims."

The result was a reputation in retreat, Torfeh said:

It's like killing the last drops of reformist blood. . . . The last drops of a softer approach to Islam. They are trying to kill it; they are trying to suffocate it. But when you do that, you are really suffocating the whole structure of the Islamic regime.

After thirty years, [the Revolution] is losing, it's getting tired, it's getting old. It no longer has any new ideas, any new strategy to offer. It's just fundamentalist heated speech, and nothing more than that. . . .

I think these are the final stages; it's going more and more to the right, as if it was exiting that way.

• • •

IN TEHRAN, THE SAGE was despondent, though surprised at how quickly the political tension was corroding even the families of insiders. Narges Kalhor, for example, the daughter of Ahmadinejad's culture adviser Mehdi Kalhor, had become a staunch supporter of the Green Movement. She had sought political asylum in Germany while at the Nuremberg Human Rights Film Festival in October 2009, after a screening of her new film, which condemned torture and totalitarianism.[219] She had received an anxious call from friends in Iran, who said spreading news of her film and her festival presence meant she "must" not return.[220]

It was the outspoken Mehdi Kalhor, with his short sleeves and oiled gray hair to his shoulders, who had said in 2005 that Ahmadinejad "wants everyone to be joyful" and promised to "prevent the government from interfering in private lives"—before being forced to eat his words. He once told me that "Westerners buy laughter" and that "cats live better than that." Iranians, by contrast, were "laughing heartily."

But not laughing now was Kalhor, who said he had divorced a year earlier because his wife was an "obstinate opponent" of Ahmadinejad.[221] The filmmaking daughter described how George Orwell had once featured in her father's open-minded worldview. Addressing a letter to her little brother, still in Iran, she wrote of a memorable irony:

> I recall vividly the first book that Father lent me. It was a short novel called *Animal Farm*. The prose was lucid and the arresting narrative told of the foment and the fall of a revolution. I was nine years old. I finished reading it in a day, but kept the book with me a few days longer. . . . Father gave me an interpretation of the story back then, and provided concrete examples in context. I was mesmerized by the author's ingenuity and Father's explanations.
>
> I doubt that when you learn to read and write, however, that he will lend you this valuable book. But I hope you will read it at the first chance. You can even ask him if he still has his copy; I

wonder how he'd respond. He may tell you, "I've never read that book." [222]

Narges Kalhor had clearly imbibed the message against tyranny. Her father, however, accused local political elements of playing a role in sending his daughter abroad. Kalhor fulminated against the opposition's "soft, complicated media war." [223]

To cap the family schism, the daughter wore a Mousavi-green scarf around her neck—and no head covering over brown ringlets—during an interview in Germany. "I believe that silence . . . was a wrong move," Narges Kalhor said.[224] "I felt like it was my duty to join these people; whether or not my family wants it." She encouraged her father and even Ahmadinejad to support the Green Movement: "Why not? People can change at any time. . . . We just need to open our eyes and see the right path; the one millions of people who went on the streets have chosen. What they want is freedom."

This was just one of many cases of severe discontent tearing at the families of insiders, the Sage told me. It demonstrated how "even people close to Ahmadinejad and hard-line power centers are increasingly losing their power to persuade and convince." [225]

"For the first time, many of the hard-core *hezbollahi*s and Revolutionary Guards and decision makers *saw* with their own eyes and heard firsthand that so many people are against them," the Sage told me, as the sound of his aquariumlike screen saver bubbled in the background. There was a "self-deception of many people in power, who thought that not only the whole Iranian population, but the whole Middle East and perhaps the world is supporting them. That perception was damaged very much, when people came to the street in the hundreds of thousands."

But instead of hard-liners recognizing any shortcomings of their own and making corrections, the Sage explained, they "closed the door and went with the other option: 'We are good, and if these people oppose us, there is something very wrong with them.' "

Yet any high ground was lost in the tussle to claim the legacy of the Revolution's most sacred icon, Ayatollah Khomeini. Said the Sage: "Of all these people in prison, most consider themselves followers of the Imam [Khomeini]. And all those who are torturing them *also* consider themselves followers of the Imam."

That struggle over Khomeini was playing itself out on the streets too as the protests expanded. Pictures of Supreme Leader Khamenei had for months been burned and trampled upon. But now state TV began repeatedly running footage of hands—their owners unseen—tearing up images of Khomeini. It was December 2009, and they blamed this sacrilege on student protesters, prompting a severe right-wing backlash. Prosecutors vowed "no mercy" toward those who had "insulted" the Imam.[226]

The students knew a provocation by hard-liners when they saw one, denied any involvement, and said it was concocted to discredit them and the Green Movement. Ahmadinejad duly predicted a "hurricane of the revolutionary anger of the nation."[227]

"Clearly Khamenei is [behind the photo insult] himself," an Iranian journalist in Tehran told me.[228] "[Khamenei] was very upset over the chants and burnings of his pictures, but he could not come out and say, 'You have to respect me'—he can't even imply that people don't love him. So he has to link it to Khomeini. Do you really think that the protesters would concern themselves with the dead first? We have a problem with the living first. We can later challenge the ideals and theories of the dead." The whole crisis had been stage-managed by the right wing, the journalist said. "[Iranian] intelligence is capable of anything. Look at the chants, look at the protests, look at the comments. They are all so fake, so staged and choreographed."

"They are scared shitless," this Iranian told me of the hard-liners. "These comments are not from a position of strength. They are clearly from a position of fear."

The flare-up told much about the state of mind of the regime six months after the election, and its frustration over an inability to smother dissent. "They are trying to make a big deal out of it," historian Ali Ansari told me.

But this idea that Khamenei can now rise the masses against the opposition on the basis of this one picture—this is exactly what [reformers] are arguing against. They are saying: "We have created idols of our clerical leaders." People are saying: "We don't *want* something sacred, we want to be able to criticize who we want."

Unfortunately, [the regime's] only reaction . . . is to continue getting more extreme themselves. When you say things like "obedience to Ahmadinejad is equivalent to obedience to God," it's complete nonsense.[229]

THE SUPREME LEADER WAS proving he was not so supreme, that he did not have the final word.

And yet, protesters also did not always have the last word. Both sides prepared for a showdown on the thirty-first anniversary of the Revolution, on February 11, 2010. Every opposition leader called for a huge turnout, and some Green activists confidently boasted regime collapse that very day. Ayatollah Khamenei promised that Iran's enemies would be "stupefied" by the regime's effective preemption—and he was right.

"It's going to be a big show of force, a big competition between the two sides over who can rule this day—and who can lay claim to the legacy of the Revolution," the Iran specialist Ahmad Sadri told me.[230] One list of tips for protesters on the Internet gave practical advice, such as carrying a napkin wet with vinegar to "fight the effects of tear gas," and requesting those with medical experience to carry small first aid kits. Don't carry weapons, it suggested, but those living along protest routes were asked to stash sacks of stones for throwing.

Yet in the run-up to the event, key student organizers were arrested, two people were executed on prodemocracy charges, nine protesters were put on death row, and checkpoints went up in Tehran a day before. Internet and cell phones were shut down.

"The basic agenda of the reform movement has been . . . to make the power of the Supreme Leader a ceremonial power, rather than a real source of power," Sadri told me. But that was sacrilege to those on

the right, as they fought for their political lives. "The trick for reformers is how to neutralize them," he said. "Even if the Green Movement
succeeds . . . if you don't include [the hard-line base], they can turn
into some kind of Baath Party and blow up things the way they are
doing in Iraq. Even if we win . . . they can shovel sand into the gears
of this democratic movement with obstructionism, with terrorism."

On the day itself, pro-regime turnout was hardly mammoth—
satellite imagery showed big gaps at Azadi (Freedom) Square, even as
President Ahmadinejad was about to ascend to the podium to decry
the "inhumane Western system," and to "officially" announce that
the "era of superpower bullying has come to an end in the world." [231]
Still, officials later crowed that tens of millions had turned out to support the Islamic system (nationwide, the figure was likely hundreds of
thousands). And they declared victory.

"They were really prepared to stop people gathering, and they did
it," the Sage told me, after he had come back from the streets that
day. [232] "It's easy if you have the numbers and guns and motivation, and
the other side is disorganized and leaderless and has no training."

Green activists were depressed by the result and felt defeated. Many
took advantage of a holiday judiciously extended by the regime to
leave town for Caspian resorts. "They say that it is becoming too dangerous," said one Iranian colleague who witnessed the heavily policed
official rally. He himself knew twenty hard-core opposition activists
who had left Tehran instead of protest. [233] "The slow process, the slow
progress, is taking its toll. People figured if this is going to be [violent,
it's] not worth it. They are waiting for the day when their participation
would finish the whole thing."

"I think the movement is dead. The regime pushed too hard,
the [Green] victim fell over the ledge. Now the Greens will go underground, they will lose their rationality, as the regime wanted all
along—it will become violent," the colleague predicted. He was expecting more underground action like vandalism, violence, and even
assassination of regime figures. "I've heard . . . that guns are more
readily available now."

The night before the showdown, some young Iranians had a gathering at the Sage's place, and they reflected the spectrum of opposition thinking. Among them was one "hotheaded radical who thought tomorrow is *the day* of victory," the Sage told me. Also there, a man "who has given up, who says this is leading us nowhere, it's a dead end."

Those views left room for sky-high expectations. "They had built it up so much by calling earlier [protest] days big victories, huge victories, giving the impression that it's only a few steps—c'mon, people!—it's just a few small steps and we are there. Given that mentality, of course it was disappointment," the Sage said. Those early victories sparked "too much optimism and wishful thinking," and confusion between "wishes and realities."

Yet for the disheartened opposition, the anniversary was a "great victory" for the Green Movement, calculated Shirin Ebadi, whose Nobel Peace Prize medal and diploma had been confiscated by Iranian government agents from a bank safe-deposit box in November 2009.[234] (Norway, which gives the Nobel prizes, formally protested the move—prompting a summons of the Norwegian ambassador in Tehran, who was told Norway had no right to criticize Iran. Weeks later the medal and diploma were returned.)

For Ebadi, the thirty-first birthday of the Revolution in February 2010 was a "demonstration of the weakness of the government," which had to deploy "all their financial and military resources to take over the streets and stop demonstrations."

TAPPING INTO THE THINKING of all stripes of Iranians had absorbed the Sage for years. As the fortunes of the opposition rose and fell, he had been asking young Iranians whether they saw themselves only as reformists, or as revolutionaries bent on toppling the *nezam*. More and more, he found, they wanted the Islamic system exorcised from their lives altogether. But they had no plan.

"One attractive young woman, after a few minutes of me questioning her, asked, 'How can we change the regime in a nice way? This is what we want, to change the regime but not with violence; in a *nice* way.' "[235] The Sage and I shared a laugh at this unlikely fantasy, of a *very* Velvet Revolution in Iran. We laughed more when I reminded him of his own words from years earlier, when he spoke of the run-away expectations of reformers. "They wish for a miracle," the Sage had told me.[236] "They expect to wake up and find Madonna giving a concert in the street, without getting a bloody nose. . . . They want improvement, but are not willing to do anything for it."

Speaking of the present, dreams of easy reform persisted. "I don't know what it takes to bring people to their senses," the Sage said, his heart heavy, despite the laughter. "[Talking about] change is OK, re-form is OK, but you also have to be careful about the regime in front of us—it can get really violent. There are still lots of people living in their dreams."

For many Iranians, those high expectations were first kindled in the buildup to the 1979 Revolution, with its stated determination to bring the freedom, social justice, and independence that only an Islamic state would provide. When Ayatollah Ruhollah Khomeini returned from exile to a tumultuous welcome in February 1979, he assured Iranians "we will cultivate your world; this world and the other world."[237] Sitting on a low platform with pine trees as a backdrop at Behesht-e Zahra cemetery, Khomeini gave voice to the promise of Iran's earth-shaking Revolution:

> In addition to providing you a rich satisfying life, we aim to improve the quality of your spiritual life as well. . . . Don't think it will be enough if we build a home for you. We will provide you water and electricity and bus rides free of charge. Don't be satisfied just by those. We will exalt your souls.

The Sage had once believed it, believed in the advent of a new age of spiritual enlightenment and freedom. But now Iran's Revolution was proving to be as corrupt, as power-hungry, and as inhumane as so many other upheavals of history. The Sage let out an exasperated sigh when I reminded him of the promises of utopia. Of how this regime specialized not just in finding enemies, but in making them—out of millions of its own citizens.

The hypocrisy. The collapse of idealism. The high-minded aspirations lost in the gap between all the soaring self-righteous rhetoric and the troubled, brutal reality of a regime that had simply failed to live up to the blood sacrifices made by its most devoted True Believers. This was a government of God, but with few divine attributes.

The Sage saw that tragic irony, and could but laugh as he told me, "There are too few exalted souls around."

Epilogue

The Pole of Cain, the Pole of Abel

Our future society will be a free society, and all the elements of oppression, cruelty, and force will be destroyed.

—Ayatollah Ruhollah Khomeini, November 1978

Truth has come and falsehood has vanished, verily falsehood is ever bound to vanish.

—Quran, on poster marking first anniversary of the Revolution, 1980

Elections are the pillars of our system. . . . A religious democracy cannot be established through words. A religious democracy is possible through the presence of people, by the will of the people. . . . Every single vote is important. . . .

—Ayatollah Seyyed Ali Khamenei, March 2009

THE DUST OF HISTORY has long been gathering at Tehran's cryptlike Martyrs' Museum, where the collected artifacts and legendary tales of the Iran-Iraq War are bathed in sad, reflective music.[1] I found the rooms devoid of visitors. Exhibits meant to inspire new Believers showed scraps of bullet-riddled uniforms, a beat-up pair of field binoculars, strings of prayer beads, and worn Qurans that had been carried into battle. But not many Iranians really rekindled radical flames here: just three or four sets of students each week, less frequent college and tourist groups, and only a daily handful of passersby like me, who stepped into the museum across the street from the former U.S. Embassy, where faded murals excoriated the United States and showed the Statue of Liberty with a freakish skull face.

Among the pantheon of Iran's immortalized war heroes, none is more exalted—and has a more unlikely pedigree—than Mostafa Chamran. With a Ph.D. in electrical engineering and plasma physics from the University of California, Berkeley, he was hired by Bell Laboratories and worked at NASA's Jet Propulsion Laboratory in the 1960s.[2] He later trained and fought alongside guerrillas in Egypt and Lebanon (where he helped found the Shiite Amal militia). Chamran returned to Iran after the Revolution, held a number of command positions—including military aide to Ayatollah Khomeini—and was named minister of defense.

But Chamran was no typical rear-echelon general. This former NASA-quality scientist and poet-warrior-devotee, a speaker of five languages credited with first designs of Iran's budding missile program and even a submarine, led boldly from the front lines. A picture from the time shows the man, a tinge of gray growing through his thick black beard and with trademark large square glasses, running along the front with an assault rifle in one hand and mud on his boots.

At the museum, the audio for the Chamran display set the tone. I pressed the button for English, and it began: "In the name of Allah. Dear visitor. Hello and welcome to this pleasant and purifying place where we respect the all-time martyrs of our history . . ."

Behind the glass was the bloodied right breast pocket and chest of the camouflage shirt that Chamran was wearing when he was killed, and a copy of a letter found in that pocket. Sensing his imminent martyrdom, Chamran had written a farewell elegy to his body:

"Oh life! I am going to separate from you, with all your beauty and greatness . . ."

Chamran told his legs: *"I know I have given you a lot of trouble, but you will be free of me in the next few minutes and have eternal rest."*

He begged of his heart: *"Withstand these last moments . . ."*

He promised them all peace, very soon. It was time to *"see the Lord, and these moments which I will dance in front of death will be stunning."*

While commanding an infantry unit, Chamran was twice struck in the left leg by shrapnel from a mortar shell. He refused to leave the war zone, to avoid, he said, sapping the "morale of the boys on the battlefront." Chamran died in June 1981, his passing remarked upon personally by Khomeini, who rarely praised anyone, by name, in public. Chamran was a "proud commander of Islam" who had "created epics on the fronts against falsehood," the Imam said. "He went with pride into the presence of the Great God."

The tour guide's voice was full of marvel when he told me: ". . . in spirituality, he reached such a high level."

In a city where every alley is named after another martyr—the memory of those glorified dead imposing the grid of their destinies upon the living—Chamran's name adorns the longest expressway in Tehran. And in addition to the Martyrs' Museum, he is also memorialized uptown, at Iran's military museum.[3] Alongside ancient Persian tools of war and a Safavid-period steel dagger with five blades, there were Chamran's distinctive square-lens glasses and the Kalashnikov he carried, still smeared with mud, from his moment of death. Pinned to the wall was the other half of the uniform: a pair of trousers with the lethal hole in the left thigh, and an eight-inch bloodstain.

But nowhere in these heroic displays is the other half of the story, that some in the regime harbored the belief—or even hope—that Chamran was too good to be true. There are no signs of rumors that Chamran's martyrdom may have been an inside job, orchestrated by the regime itself, or by opponents that infiltrated the ranks. Nor is there mention of the fact that, upon Chamran's death, top officials ordered a raid on his house and searched all his belongings, eager, according to one interpretation, to spitefully smear a man who had made them look bad because of his zealous insistence on actually practicing what they all preached: sacrifice in war, in time-honored Shiite tradition.

Chamran had all the privileges of high office, and the protections of power—if he wanted them—but "he left all of that to go to the front and died while leading a group of irregulars," a source in Tehran explained.[4] In Iran, this was the impossible equivalent of the U.S. secretary of defense dying from gunfire while leading a foot patrol in Fallujah, Iraq. Chamran's death "was much more an example of [Lord of the Martyrs] Hossein than all his turbaned brothers," the source told me. But the attempt to smear Chamran failed: "There was nothing to find. They found out he was real."

Also real was the devotion to this icon at the Behesht-e Zahra cemetery, where this martyr's resting place is unlike any other. Broad and rectangular like an aboveground sarcophagus, it had been encased in concrete—apparently someone had once tried to steal the remains—and lovingly painted over with an Iranian flag.[5]

I watched as every few minutes, in this maze of graves at Section 24, Row 71, No. 25, new pilgrims would come to Chamran's side. Iranian flags were strung up from wires overhead. Someone had left four potted plants. A father carried a toddler with a red hat, murmuring, "Imam, Imam . . . ," as if in a divine trance.

The official sanctity bestowed by the regime was echoing here. A woman wearing all black approached then delicately picked up a red rose that had been left by another visitor. Holding its stem, she brushed the petals through the scented water that had pooled across the top of the grave, back and forth, as if painting. Lost in her reverie, she gathered some other loose petals in her hand and wiped them through the water, too. When she walked away, she clutched close this crimson prize, beautiful new mementos invested with a *real* martyr's memory.

• • •

YET GROWING AND FUNDAMENTAL doubt about the war and its legacy for the Revolution could not be hidden, and some of the most strident voices of opposition came from those most engaged in propagating the primary myths. Reza Borji, for example, was a cameraman of *Revayat-e Fath,* the *Chronicles of Victory* television series that brought the war and its divine purpose into every Iranian household. He was a victim of chemical weapons attack, and years later made a documentary series called *Broken Medals.* Speaking of it, he called for a new dose of reality:

> Before we saw that the hero has to stand until the last moment. No, it is not like this. We were defeated. We retreated. . . .
>
> In our movies, we showed Iraqis as fools, and then a young person would say if this was the case, why did you fight for eight years and besides Fao and Halabja you couldn't capture any other place?
>
> . . . Everything was two sided. If we do not show these realities about the war, then we have wronged our own history. When the future generations want to read this history, they will realize it has been written in a one-sided and one-dimensional way. In [front-line battlefields] like Shalamche we gave a martyr every one-and-a-half meters; that is, the whole place was covered with [the bodies of] martyrs and this is the way we kept the place. . . . This war was sacred for us. Was it sacred for the Iraqis? We don't know. Even today when I remember Shalamche I begin to cry that I had to go over the corpses of friends with a motorcycle to get a job done.
>
> Now if many leaders want to say that the whole war was a victory for us, let them say it. They can offer whatever thesis they want, but the reality was something else. We were both victorious and defeated.[6]

WITH SUCH DOUBT EATING at the pillars of the Islamic Republic, how did revolutionary Iran survive for more than three decades? The *nezam* had successfully sought to win public loyalty with far-reaching charity. One of the clearest examples is the Imam Khomeini Relief Foundation, which has created a legion of lifetime supporters by mixing charity with ideology.

Among them is Massoumeh Delavar, a soft-spoken artist whose life was in ruins a decade before I met her. Getting an education was a distant dream, until she was rescued by the charity, known as Komiteh Emdad in Farsi. It was the largest in Iran, reaching 4.5 million of Iran's 70 million people, and by its own tally catering to 92 percent of Iran's poorest people in 52,800 towns and villages.

"My parents had died, and the rest of the family were drug addicts," Delavar told me in 2007, as she sat with a handful of young women with similar stories at a Tehran women's shelter run by the charity.[7] "This is the best thing that has ever happened to me." She planned to finish her university degree, find a job, and "be independent"—steps all paid for or heavily subsidized by Komiteh Emdad. "If I had stayed home, I would not have any of these opportunities."

The women's shelter was a faceless building in downtown Tehran, wedged among normal residential apartments, and reserved only for women from drug-broken homes. Inside it was tidy and spotless during my unannounced visit. There were ten or more bunks to each thickly carpeted room, with beds immaculately made. There was a courtyard garden. On the walls going up and down the stairs were ideological posters and slogans. One showed Hossein's shrine at Karbala, and read: "The Islamic Republic is the image of 'telling to do good, and advising not to do bad.' " Another proclaimed the Basij to be the "way of God."

From Komiteh Emdad's inception before 1979, when it had no name, and sustained the families of strikers who were challenging the rule of the Shah, the charity has grown along with the Islamic Republic. That first Iranian example—of translating into political power a range of good works from job creation and bank loans to orphan care and cheap housing—was later copied by Shiite Hezbollah in Lebanon, and then to a lesser degree by the Mahdi Army in Iraq, led by the anti-American cleric Moqtada al-Sadr.

In Iran, the charity was of critical use to the Revolution by "getting more people to be friendly with the clerics and the Imam," said Hamid-reza Taraghi, the conservative politician and one of the foundation's directors.[8] "Emdad emerged alongside the Revolution with Imam Khomeini, and helped with support and money. It was successful in aligning many of the poor behind the Revolution."

With a reach across society perhaps second only to Iran's military, Emdad still plays that role, blending outreach to the poor with doses of revolutionary thought. Official figures showed that 170,000 "good Samaritans" were sponsoring 270,000 orphans and children in poor families.[9] Once a year, on Benevolence Day, Emdad set up thirty donation centers across Tehran, and many others nationwide. When I visited one of these fund-raisers, women in black chadors were sitting at tables covered with cards, each with a photograph of a child. Sponsors pay roughly ten dollars per month, and usually two sign up for each orphan. Iranian TV carried live broadcasts from five of the donation sites.

Komiteh Emdad also insured 3.9 million Iranians, providing them free or cheap health care, and fielded nearly one hundred thousand volunteers. New housing fell under its purview, too; poor families often moved into new residential units in the capital. Since 1979, the charity had bankrolled 1.56 million loans. Such a scale was unimaginable in the early days.

"We started to help people who were striking against the former regime, to keep them strong," Taraghi told me. "We would give them money, food, and salaries so they could endure." Families of those who were jailed were also given support, and if a store or business was burned down during protests, the group would compensate the victims. After the Revolution, teams of volunteers sought out the poor in the remotest villages to assess their needs, and cared for families of martyrs.

At the beginning, there was little more than token cash to spread around. But public donations these days reach nearly $100 million per year—along with additional money from the government and the office of the Supreme Leader. Komiteh Emdad's "twenty-year vision" document describes it as "risen from the heart of the people, True Believers and allegiance [to] Islamic Revolution." It aims to create "a good Islamic life [for] the deprived who are the real shareholders of the *nezam*."

That welfare mission is shared more broadly in the Iranian constitution, which guarantees free education and commits the regime to end poverty, illiteracy, and unemployment. "In the three decades since the Revolution, the Islamic Republic—despite its poor image abroad—has taken significant steps toward fulfilling these promises," notes historian Ervand Abrahamian.[10] Illiteracy and fertility rates have dropped, while student enrollment and life expectancy have soared.

"The regime may not have eradicated poverty nor appreciatively narrowed the gap between rich and poor but it has provided the underclass with a safety net," writes Abrahamian. "Upcoming decades will test the regime's ability to juggle the competing demands of these populist programs with those of the educated middle class—especially the ever-expanding army of university graduates produced, ironically, by one of the Revolution's main achievements."

And those "upcoming decades" of regime life are a certainty for some beneficiaries. Officials estimate that Komiteh Emdad funds have launched 400,000 new jobs and assisted marriages of 50,000 people a year, avoiding a poverty trap that often follows. The charity has supported 800,000 students, of whom 70,000 were able to get university degrees. Among them was Marzieh Nazari, who had just completed her law degree after living for nine years at the women's shelter. She was the oldest I met, among others as young as nine.

"This has had a big effect on my life. . . . I would not have been able to go to school," said Nazari, who was looking for a job with Emdad's help. Her parents fought when she was a child, and then divorced; her brother was in a similar boys' home. "What I learned from living here is that I should give back whatever I have. If I can reach a point where I can help other people, I will always help."

Her gratitude was boundless, and for those like Nazari whose lives have been changed by Komiteh Emdad, that meant loyalty to the Islamic system. In the words of Taraghi, the conservative director, "The bond between people and the *nezam* becomes stronger, with the Islamic Revolution and its principles" of charity.

BUT ALSO BUILT INTO the DNA of the Islamic Republic was the constant tension of Iran's political and social divisions. Their foundations were laid down in the 1960s and '70s by the ideologue Ali Shariati—the thinker who inspired so many Iranians to take to the streets in Revolution. Shariati used the biblical story of Cain killing his brother Abel (the two sons of Adam and Eve, and the story of the first fratricide) to provide the framework for conflict.

As historian Hamid Algar explains, ". . . Shariati elevated to the position of universal paradigm the struggle of Cain and Abel, mentioned only elliptically in the Quran: everywhere in history and society he discerned a 'pole of Abel,' led by the prophets and their successors, and a 'pole of Cain,' composed of usurpers of power and wealth. . . ." [11]

A direct line can be drawn from those pre-Revolution ideas, through the three decades of vicious us-versus-them political war that has defined, corroded, and fractured the foundations of the Revolution, to the mid-2009 explosion of popular unrest that saw brother-on-brother battles in the streets.

SO IN IRAN, THE differences are extreme. There are those devotees who rise at dawn on Friday mornings, place a green flag on the gate of their modest apartment, and host neighbors for a Nodbeh prayer—a special extra prayer to call for the early return of the Hidden Twelfth Imam, the Mahdi.

I was invited to one Nodbeh session in a district on the edge of north Tehran.[12] The air was thick with respect, expectation, and "deep weeping from the heart" as the host sang the prayer from a small loudspeaker set up in the living room. Women were in the next room, praying too, separated from view by a curtain.

"Where is he who will end oppression? . . . Who will get rid of deviations? . . . Who will open the main pillars of religion [and] connect the ground to the sky?" the host sang. "Tell me where you [the Mahdi] are, and why you are away from me. . . . The promise on your face, on your smile, that I am in love for you, and I am going to give my life to you. . . . The flag of victory is visible."

"THERE MUST BE SOMETHING wrong with their minds," the karate-chopping nude painter Tooska told me, appalled when I described to her the Nodbeh prayer.[13] "To wait for someone to save the world. It's insane!"

And she was not alone in her irreverence. For at the opposite extreme of the social spectrum from devotees waiting for the Mahdi are those Westernized, barely God-fearing Iranian youth who relished turning their parents' home into a party venue where vodka was the drink of choice, as young men and women danced happily, tossing their long hair to the ebullient electronic sounds of Persian pop.

Until the doorbell rang, shortly after midnight.

The police were at the gate, and now anything—from a quiet warning and a bribe, to a raid inside the apartment *now*—became an immediate possibility.[14] I was surprised at how quickly the place was transformed, and how the danger had suddenly shot to hysterical levels. The music was unplugged; the lights switched on. Without missing a beat but with fear on their faces, the girls all quickly reached for headscarves and their long jackets, then raced through a side door and down the stairs to hide in a basement room.

I helped the boys pour opened beers down the drain, crush the cans, and put the bottles in sealed garbage bags that were then tucked far out of sight. Overflowing ashtrays that spoke of too many partygoers disappeared. Bottles of spirits were capped and then thrust into back bedroom closets, buried beneath clothes and sheets. Air freshener was sprayed, the windows opened to draw off the worst of the cigarette and alcohol fug that hung in the air. Spicy fixings and raw onions that had come with the takeout meal were chewed mechanically, to offset the worst booze breath.

The host stepped outside with a wad of cash in his pocket to negotiate with the cops. After sanitizing the best we could, we males settled down nervously on couches, to await the inevitable.

"Have you ever seen anything as stupid as this?" one young man asked me. Faces were long around that room; the party—and the girls' overreaction, they complained—was already a disappearing memory. The bribe worked, and the police left. The upstairs neighbor had called ten times to complain, the police said, so they finally had to take action, if only to stop his annoying calls.

But these party lads got their revenge. Hours later, at dawn, the capital awoke with its usual array of city workers with water hoses in parks, spraying until water ran down the sidewalks, creating a scent of green earth, of life from every green islet in the city.

Yet the man who had called the police repeatedly to shut down the party arose to another surprise. Several of those young and drunk Iranian boys had stepped outside at three o'clock that morning, unzipped their jeans, and pissed all over his car—taking special care to coat the windshield and door handles.

They couldn't stop laughing.

AS MANY DOUBTS AS those young men told me they had about the Islamic regime and its restrictions, there were no doubts at the Jamaran prayer hall where Ayatollah Ruhollah Khomeini once preached, as pupils piled in to mark the thirtieth anniversary of the Islamic Revolution in early 2009. In the dim light from high windows, the stream of schoolchildren never stopped. Class after class, herded by their teachers, made the pilgrimage to that nondescript north Tehran compound, where the decrepit neighborhood—the one with the electrician and used furniture salesman, and blond soap for the Imam's robes—gives way to steep rocky outcrops, the dark shoulder of the Alborz Mountains.

A banner spelled out the day's lesson: "This Revolution is not known anywhere in the world without the name Khomeini."[15] The ayatollah's defiant spirit still towered above all. From Iran's opposition to America as the Great Satan, to the spread of its ideology of resistance—as well as loving family moments—Khomeini's legacy was living on in fact and in myth.

"The Imam would enter through this door," religion teacher Alireza Boroujerdi told his group of twenty attentive boys sitting on the carpets. "From this closed and small place, he would move the world. He would say something and the backs of the world leaders would shake." Khomeini lived simply yet he inspired the "oppressed people" of Lebanon and the Palestinian territories to "stand up and resist" Israel, the portly teacher told his students. Every night Khomeini prayed, and cried so much that he needed a towel because "tissues were not enough to wipe his tears."

Such faith led inexorably to triumph for the Islamic Republic, the teacher lectured. The Omid (Hope) satellite launched by Iran the week before had "orbited around the earth sixty times already, all because of this leader. Our independence and reliance on God—all this is because of what happened here."

Another class. Another teacher. Another set of questions.

"People would come from all over the world for the honor of seeing the Imam for a few minutes," noted Amir Hossein Khosromadar, who told his group of seventy small boys how he had waited hours to catch his first glimpse of Khomeini. "He was not afraid of any power but the power of God. The Imam was once your age, and not an imam from the beginning . . . I ask you to pay close attention to all the things you see and hear, so [like him] we can all become the soldiers of Islam. . . ."

A boy raised his hand, then pointed to the chair that stood alone on the balcony, shrouded in a white sheet. He asked, "Is that the real chair of the Imam?"

No, the teacher explained. "When people first heard the Imam had passed away, the first group to arrive took pieces of it as sacred objects to remember him. So this is not the original chair."

• • •

"ON TV HE WAS a tough, stern person. But at home he was very soft, very warm, and very calm. He would never get angry with us," remembered Khomeini's granddaughter, Zahra Eshraghi.[16] "He would help me study. He insisted I go to university," Eshraghi told me, adding that he used to call her regularly to talk and to encourage more learning before she took a degree in Western philosophy. "He was much closer to us than a traditional grandfather."

Khomeini liked to play with his great-grandchildren games such as *maman-bazi*, the Persian equivalent of playing house. Her grandfather would "certainly" be disappointed with the level of social restrictions currently in force, complained Eshraghi, who was a strong advocate for women's rights and married to a prominent reformist politician, Mohammad Reza Khatami, the brother of the former president. "One of the main things in [Khomeini's] speeches was freedom."

DAWUD SALAHUDDIN, THE BLACK American convert to Islam who was born David Belfield and recruited to kill a Shah-era diplomat in Bethesda, Maryland, was by the spring of 1981 a fugitive in Iran. He met with Khomeini for twenty to twenty-five minutes. He also saw the ayatollah preach at Jamaran several times and was impressed.

"With Khomeini, you could swallow things and it would go down," Salahuddin told me over breakfast in Tehran. He had a welcoming face that did not fit the title of former assassin.[17] During their meeting, Khomeini "made reference to the gentleman in Bethesda [but] he wanted to talk of other things like my welfare. He asked: 'Anything I can do for you?' "

What struck the American most was Khomeini's evident spirituality.

"He was not interested in this world—he had no worldly ambition," recalled the soft-spoken Salahuddin, who wore a beard without a mustache and kept a low profile in Tehran, where he was increasingly critical of the regime. "For me, talk that he was a powermonger—it's nonsense. He lived in another dimension [and] when you deal with a person like that, normal criticism does not matter."

Still, preserving the Islamic system was the top priority. "I don't think *ruthless* is the wrong word," Salahuddin told me. "During the American Revolution, guess what the British must have called George Washington?"

SEYYED RAHIM MIRIAM WAS a servant of Khomeini who saw him several times a day for eight years. "It was because of his simplicity that he could tell what he did to the world. He would do nothing but for the happiness of God," he told me.[18] Miriam was a short man in soiled clothes and white sandals, his rough hands familiar with work. He rubbed them together and smiled, remembering how the aging Khomeini had advised him: "Pray when [you are] young, because when you are old you want to pray, but you can't."

JUST MONTHS AFTER PRESIDENT Mahmoud Ahmadinejad had declared that Iran was a superpower "real and true," the Islamic Republic was torn by a stolen election, by a persistent and courageous opposition not afraid to create martyrs for democracy, and by opponents willing to bleed on the streets for their rights. The great promise of the 1979 Islamic Revolution had been broken, finally, by those hardliners who spent so much time crowing about their adherence to its values.

But that didn't stop Ahmadinejad from adding two plus two differently than anyone else. His supreme overconfidence echoed the words of the Shah, who in 1978 declared: "Nobody can overthrow me. I have the support of 700,000 troops, all the workers and most of the people."[19]

Many Iranians now viewed as illegitimate usurpers the right-wing cabal of Ahmadinejad's neocon allies, the hard-line commanders of the Revolutionary Guard, and increasingly the Supreme Leader. Yet in December 2009, Ahmadinejad addressed Western governments during a speech in Shiraz and declared: "We do not welcome conflict with you, but you should know that today, [the] Iranian nation and government have become ten times stronger than in the past."[20]

It was another delusion, from a man who had proven himself a fantasist. Just days later, street battles would reach a crescendo on Ashura, the annual day of blood to commemorate the death of Imam Hossein those centuries ago. Police and vigilantes—fighting back with vengeance and live ammunition—were shocked at the scale and heat of popular rage, as they were overrun by stone-throwing protesters who were unafraid to show their faces.

But then weeks afterward, during the Revolution anniversary on February 11, 2010, that adrenaline rush for the opposition would turn to disappointment. The Green Movement's extravagant hopes for immediate "victory" dwindled with the meager turnout; the regime won that round, with an unprecedented deployment of security forces. Still, beneath the surface were abrasions to the social fabric that mattered, in places like the minds of some *basiji* militants.

"I didn't join the organization with bad intentions. Not just me, others too. Their intentions were good, to provide a service for people, rather than to get a bonus or perform their commander's orders," one former *basiji* told journalist Lindsey Hilsum.[21] "I believe that there are people who are now full of regret, who are not able to express this regret and they are not able to leave the organization. . . . I want to say that all those in the Basij are not bad people. We too are victims."

So a telling symbol of revolutionary Iran's true and irreversible decline was the fate of Haji Bakhshi, the bullet-draped regime cheerleader who had been at the fore of every pro-regime rally for decades, and nearly died in the front-line tank attack on his "morale" truck.

After the June 2009 election, cracking heads and drawing the blood of the reformist opposition—who were officially branded *mohareb,* or "enemy of God," and therefore punishable by death—would have been a natural for the grizzled veteran. He had once vowed: "As long as there is blood in our veins, not only us but our wives and children will be present for the Revolution, independence and the Islamic Republic of Iran."[22]

But Bakhshi and his totemic sniper rifle were barely visible as the regime fought for its life. This icon of resistance, this fearless bear of a man who was always ready to run barefoot to defend the *nezam,* had been fighting for his own life in a hospital at the end of 2008, struck down by a heart attack, and then lapsed into a coma.[23] Bakhshi revived long enough to attend a September 2009 pro-regime rally, but he was a fragile husk of his former self.

Like the regime he adored, the once all-powerful had become weak, and suddenly mortal. In the crowds the old warrior needed assistance to walk, even to stand.[24]

THE ISLAMIC REPUBLIC WAS still very capable of reaching beyond its borders, however, as it had done in the 1980s and '90s. A "Secret" (restricted to U.S. nationals) document produced by the U.S. Embassy in Abu Dhabi in 1997 had given this trenchant assessment: "This regime has shown that, if its survival is perceived to be in play, it will employ any available means, whether terrorism abroad or internal repression at home, to combat the supposed threat. . . . Another survival issue . . . is the use of assassinations as state policy. Over the years, the Tehran regime has been in the habit of killing its opponents, whether at home or abroad." [25]

That well-honed instinct kicked in after the June 2009 unrest, as Iran's intelligence apparatus abroad was bolstered with battalions of agents. They waged a sinister global campaign of intimidation, in which Iranians living throughout the diaspora, from Dubai to Sweden to Los Angeles, were threatened after attending opposition rallies abroad, or for anti-regime comments made on their Facebook and Twitter accounts.[26] An investigation by Farnaz Fassihi in the *Wall Street Journal* revealed dozens of cases in which parents still in Iran were arrested or questioned because of critical Internet postings by their children abroad. Visiting Iranians were forced upon arrival at Tehran's main airport to hand over account passwords there and then, and if criticism of the regime was found, their passports were confiscated.

The steps were in keeping with a November 2009 vow by the deputy armed forces commander, Brigadier General Masoud Jazayeri, that Iran, "if forced to, will even be able to seriously challenge the ex-

ternal elements of the coup based outside Iran."[27] He further warned
that a "wide spectrum of the sedition infantry is so far identified and
will be dealt with at the right time."

That was already happening in Germany, where a national intelligence report found that nine hundred regime critics were being monitored by Iranian intelligence operatives, and that agents were known
to be intimidating activists by videotaping protests, Fassihi reported.

The result of this mobilization of agents touched me in Turkey,
where many of the opposition activists most brutalized by the regime,
who had suffered rape and other tactics but survived, had come seeking sanctuary. Sometimes they came in harrowing cross-mountain
journeys guided by Kurdish people traffickers, to escape Iran unde-
tected and apply for asylum in America or Europe. As they registered
with the United Nations and waited weeks for their cases to be resolved, those refugees of reform in Iran were accosted on the streets,
sometimes beaten, and subject to late-night visits that sent the frightening message: "We are watching; you are not safe."

That *Spy vs. Spy* world seemed far from Istanbul's best-known pedestrian avenue, Istiklal Street, where in September 2009 I met the
U.S. government's top Iran watcher in Turkey, Geoff Odlum.[28] Coffee
shops are ubiquitous on Istiklal, but so are bars, and we sometimes
met in an especially dank bastion of seventies and eighties hard rock
and heavy metal called Old School—later renamed Köprüalti 6, or
K6—on a side street at the Taksim end of Istiklal. It was up a narrow
set of stairs and through a heavy, decibel-dampening door—which we
joked that no self-respecting Iranian agent would ever deign to pass
through. In the afternoon the small stage was empty—the whole place
was—and over ice-cold beers I opened my notebook for the interview.
The sound system made hearing each other difficult; being overheard
was impossible.

We were right that no Iranian operatives would linger in such a den
of iniquity; instead they were waiting for us outside. As we descended
the stairs and stepped out onto the street, I immediately noticed a
short and shifty-looking character directly across the narrow alley. He

looked too closely at me, took particular notice of the black pouch hanging from my belt, and made a subtle signal down the street.

We were turning left, toward Istiklal, and I whispered to Odlum, "I think we've just been tagged."

And sure enough, just as we approached the crowded pedestrian avenue, directly in front of us a man was holding up an iPhone, clearly filming us as we walked toward him. I could tell immediately he was Iranian, and not of a reformist bent: He wore a white shirt buttoned high and at the sleeves, with no tie, and Iranian-cut trousers worn with a belt slightly higher than necessary. He had a receding black hairline and several days of stubble, and continued capturing us on video for a moment even after we had taken notice, finally turning as if he were a tourist taking a panorama of the street.

The agent started trying to blend in and move away. We followed behind, then slowed up so as not to pass him, and from behind briefly engaged the agent by pointing at the phone, before he shifted quickly away to record . . . newspapers for sale on the street. It seemed more than a little odd that a "tourist" carrying a dirt-cheap faux-leather black shoulder bag—its crappy strap cracking from overuse—would also be using an exceptionally expensive iPhone to record his "vacation" videos.

I felt certain this was nothing less than Iranian intelligence agents at work, disconcertingly less than ten minutes' walk from where I was living. But I was also confident that the target was not me or even Odlum, but any Iranians he might be meeting—including those seeking refuge in America.

Were these men really Iranian operatives? The answer came several weeks later, when Ahmadinejad visited Istanbul. I went to the press conference at the Intercontinental Hotel, and while speaking to colleagues looked up and locked eyes with the man who had filmed me with the American diplomat. He also had not seen me until that moment, and we both recoiled at the simultaneous recognition. But with the agent's president about to appear, his job was to organize the press conference, and he couldn't hide.[29]

The tip-off man was there, too, in a lesser role. A colleague recognized him from the Iranian consulate, where he had appeared to be doing janitorial work in the waiting room.

SUCH PETTY GAMES SEEMED a distraction from the true and refined sensibilities of so many of the Persians I had come to know and respect. Heart, life, and love. Devotion. Belief. Resistance.

All of them were evidenced in the photograph once brought to me in Tehran by cameraman Ali Rajabi, who had so eloquently told me of his determination to get at the spirit of the Iran-Iraq War, to illustrate the beauty of the front-line ideology so he could share it with his fellow Iranians in the *Chronicles of Victory*.[30]

It was a deceptively simple image he set on the table. Shot in 1988, it showed a column of soldiers, heavily laden with weaponry and backpacks full of rifle-propelled grenade rounds and even a rolled-up stretcher, walking single file through a green field thick with red poppy flowers, against a dramatic backdrop of the northwestern mountains. In that lush expanse, the soldiers seemed already to be in paradise.

"It was Nowruz [the spring New Year day], when everyone wants to be with their family. But these are fighters," Rajabi explained to me, his fingertips touching the edge of what for him was a sacred image of a divine battlefield: "Although it was war, these people cared about the flowers. They loved nature, and all the things God gave them. This is a reminder of that time. These soldiers changed their steps, so they would not step on the flowers."

Acknowledgments

JOURNALISM RARELY HAPPENS IN a vacuum, and creating a book never does. So *Let the Swords Encircle Me* is the result of extraordinary generosity from many people—first among them the Iranians who shared so much of their lives, their friendship, and their confidences with me. Some are named in the book, but many others sadly cannot be. I have more close friends in Iran than in all the other dozens of countries I have reported upon, combined—a fact that has long driven deeper exploration. So let me thank the Sage, "Reza," "Samira," "Siavash," "Tooska," "Dr. Farzad," and so many other Iranians for their companionship, wisdom, and wit. I hope I have proven worthy of their ideas, their words, and their passions.

I have sought to give Iranians as much voice as possible, because they speak eloquently for themselves. It is for the rest of us to listen, to try to understand and divine meaning from this delicious mosaic—startling contradictions and all.

This book is full of devotions, and I hope it reads that way. Yet for me, few have played more important roles during some thirty visits to Iran than the translators whose jobs always require more than simply turning Farsi into English. They are the first interpreters of their complex society for a foreign journalist, so upon them rests the heaviest burden, and often the greatest risk from authorities.

These Iranian translators (who later became journalists, officials, and activists) have contributed immeasurably to my understanding of Iran. I thank Nazila Fathi, Nahid Hosseinpour, Alireza Shiravi, Saeed Kousha, Dariush Anvari, Dokhi Fassihian, and Dariush Sadeghi.

In more recent years, when intense reporting for this book was well underway, Abbas "Pedram" Khodadadi gamely kept by my side, sharing the laughter, aspirations, and sometimes despair of his fellow Iranians. Zuhair Khoeiniha translated for some key conservative war veterans and journalists. Naeim Karimi gave devoted attention—and his expert translations and analysis—to key religious texts and war-era films. A special nod also to Afshin Valinejad, who as an Associated Press writer in 1996 first took me to Behesht-e Zahra cemetery, introducing me early to the world of Iran's True Believers—and to its succulent dates.

Chief official facilitators since 1996 have out of necessity been those at the Ministry of Culture and Islamic Guidance (Ershad), who requested the permissions, wrote the letters for official interviews, and, perhaps most importantly, often recognized honest—if not palatable—reporting, and therefore at times stood in my corner during internal battles with Iran's foreign and intelligence ministries.

I would like to thank the directors general of foreign press Mohsen Moghadaszadeh, M. N. Haghighat, Mohammad Hossein Khoshvaght, and Hossein Nosrat. In the foreign media office, Ms. Efi Eghbali-Namin, Alireza Shiravi, and Gailareh Pardakhti deserve special praise for their patient, kind, and attentive work over many years—sometimes in the face of insurmountable bureaucratic obstacles. Farahnaz Abdi, Haji Karimi, Ms. Mahmoudi, and Mr. Zarikani have always been most courteous and helpful. At Ivan Sahar agency, price wrestling for fixing fees with director Masoud Mobasseri was a good-natured game, while Leily Lankarani and assistant Marzieh Kamali were efficient organizers.

THIS BOOK IS TESTAMENT to the freedom the *Christian Science Monitor* has given me over the years to report on Iran, among many other far-flung places. I did not cover the Islamic Revolution in 1979, or the Iran-Iraq War. But I was afforded the rare luxury among foreign correspondents of being able to cover Iran in depth during three separate postings for the *Monitor,* while based in Amman, Moscow, and Istanbul. The fluctuation of revolutionary politics in Iran—and their divisive, Manichean realities—requires understanding the slow-burn changes imposed by presidents as different as Mohammad Khatami and Mahmoud Ahmadinejad.

So I have great praise for my editors at the *Monitor,* who gave me free rein to explore the most delectable, vibrant, and surprising country in the region. Editors-in-Chief John Yemma, the late Richard Bergenheim, Paul Van Slambrouck, and Dave Cook have all been supportive as they steered a "writer's newspaper" of integrity that has found room for my reporting.

Foreign Editors David Clark Scott and before him Clay Jones approved journey after journey to the Islamic Republic. Deputy Foreign Editors Amelia Newcomb, Faye Bowers, Clay Collins, and Greg Lamb gave me uncommon encouragement and bonhomie. They also withstood painfully fastidious edits—"obsessive," I am sure they would say, imposed by me on all sensitive Iran reporting—along with the *Monitor*'s long-suffering Middle East editors. Most notable among them, in shaping my Iran coverage, have been Christa Case Bryant, Mike Farrell, Clay Collins, Jim Norton, Abe McLaughlin, Margaret Henry (Europe), and Kristen Broman-Worthington (Europe). In the *Monitor* library, Leigh Montgomery provided important research tools at a precipitous time.

No journalist could be more grateful for a newspaper that aspires to its noble mandate "to injure no man, but to bless all mankind."

At Getty Images in New York, I thank my longtime editor Sandy Ciric and Lauren Steel for their steady support of my photography over the years.

Among long-standing research tools for analysis, news archives, and translations, I credit Gary Sick's Gulf/2000 at Columbia University, and Nick Noe's MideastWire.com in Beirut.

I thank my excellent literary agent Kimberly Witherspoon at Ink-Well Management for first taking on my Africa book *Me Against My Brother* more than a decade ago. On Iran, Kim and David Forrer were instrumental in helping forge a book proposal that did much to sharpen my own thinking on the "Iran Project"—and appeal to just the right publisher.

Powerful praise is reserved for my editor at Simon & Schuster, the wonderfully indomitable Alice Mayhew, who has edited important Iran books in the past and brought her knowledgeable and incisive eye to *Let the Swords Encircle Me*. Alice and Roger Labrie encouraged, cajoled, and created a very effective chemistry that propelled me to produce a much better book. Early on, they saw the unique and comprehensive potential of such an Iran narrative, and exercised the patience of Job while I wrestled with the unwieldy text and endlessly recrafted. Gratitude also to Gypsy da Silva—who had fine experience of Iran in her youth—and copy editor Tom Pitoniak for the detailed care they gave the 1,100 manuscript pages and 1,300 endnotes. Thank you to designer Ruth Lee-Mui.

I am also deeply indebted to critical first readers. Farideh Farhi in Hawaii and Amelia Newcomb in Boston both graciously read early chapters and provided key feedback. Anita McNaught in Istanbul gave selflessly of her time and intelligence to help shape the manuscript, on issues large and small, and bolstered my spirit during dark moments on overwhelming days. Noushin Hoseiny in Istanbul for more than a year provided extensive and precise research, as well as Persian-language Web links, and ensured standardized and accurate Farsi usage throughout the text. Ali Ansari in Scotland kindly read the entire manuscript with a historian's eye for accuracy.

Any errors of judgment or fact that remain are my responsibility alone.

MY EXTENDED FAMILY IN Seattle have set the precedent for half a century, of traveling far afield and coming back to tell the rest of the tribe what they discovered. They have always supported my journeys abroad. Special thanks to my parents Ken and Merry Ann Peterson, sister Karin, and to my grandmother Rose Marie Crow and late grandfather Willard S. Crow. "Home," in their definition, will always remain a sanctuary of joyful return.

Thanks to Alex Peterson, who for many years kept our household in balance during my trips to Iran, across the Middle East, Russia, and the Balkans, and before that Africa.

Fundamental appreciation is given to my children, to whom—along with Iranians themselves—this volume is dedicated. The ambition and buoyant expectation that I see in the eyes of Olivia and Guy, Finn and Natasha, remains a revelatory reminder of goodness and love, and why we must always aim to achieve mutual understanding.

Notes

INTRODUCTION: "BECAUSE FOR US, THE WAR IS NOT OVER . . ."

1. Interview with Dr. Alireza Zakani, Tehran, September 21, 1998; see also Scott Peterson, "Iran Hears Echoes of a 'Sacred' War," *Christian Science Monitor*, October 2, 1998.
2. Visit to crossed swords monument, Baghdad, Iraq, April 30, 1997.
3. Mousavi statement on his *Kalemeh* website, as quoted in Jay Deshmukh, "Hundreds Arrested in Violent Clashes," Agence France-Presse, June 22, 2009.
4. Ayatollah Seyyed Ali Khamenei, sermon at Friday prayers, as translated live by PressTV, Tehran, June 19, 2009.
5. Ali Akbar Dareini and Lee Keath, "Clerical Discontent Challenges Iran Leader," Associated Press, July 8, 2009.
6. As described in Dominic Sandbrook, "After the Revolution," *New Statesman*, June 16, 2009.
7. Interview with schoolgirl, Tehran, March 10, 2008.
8. Meeting with Mahmoud Abdollahi, Tehran, September 15, 1996.
9. Multiple meetings with "Reza," a pseudonym, Tehran, beginning in fall 1999.
10. Student letters as provided by Dr. Alireza Zakani, Tehran, September 21, 1998.
11. See, for example, Patrick Cockburn, "The Botched US Raid That Led to the Hostage Crisis," *Independent*, April 3, 2007.
12. Seymour M. Hersh, "The Iran Plans" *New Yorker*, April 17, 2006; "The Redirection," *New Yorker*, March 5, 2007; and "Preparing the Battlefield," *New Yorker*, July 7, 2008. On U.S. support for Jundallah, see ABC News, "ABC News Exclusive: The Secret War Against Iran," April 3, 2007. Jundallah was never placed on the U.S. State Department list of Foreign Terrorist Organizations, yet would claim responsibility for a number of other operations, including a May 2009 blast at a mosque that left more than twenty dead, and an October 2009 suicide attack that killed forty-two. Iranian intelligence finally captured Jundal-

lah's young leader, Abdolmalek Rigi, when they forced down a commercial airline flying from Dubai to Bishkek, Kyrgyzstan, in February 2010.

Iranian officials released photographs they said showed Rigi at a U.S. military base in Afghanistan just days before his capture and claimed American support. In a videotaped confession aired on Iran's official English-language PressTV channel, Rigi claimed that "the Americans" promised "military equipment, arms, and machine guns," and a base along the Afghanistan border with Iran. U.S. officials dismissed the claims. Rigi was executed on June 20, 2010. (Scott Peterson, "Iran Arrests Top Sunni Militant Abdolmalek Rigi," *Christian Science Monitor*, February 23, 2010; see also Rigi confession transcript in "U.S. Offered Rigi 'Extensive Aid' for Iran Attacks," PressTV, February 25, 2010, at www.presstv.ir/detail.aspx?id=119481&sectionid=351020101.)

13. Louis Rene Beres, "The Case For Strikes Against Iran," *Christian Science Monitor*, May 8, 2007.
14. Scott Peterson, "Waiting for the Rapture in Iran," *Christian Science Monitor*, December 21, 2005.
15. Interview with Amir Mohebian, Tehran, December 10, 2005; see also Peterson, "Waiting for the Rapture in Iran."
16. See, for example, Daniel Pipes, "The Mystical Menace of Mahmoud Ahmadinejad," *New York Sun*, January 10, 2006, as reprinted at www.danielpipes.org.
17. Ed Blanche, "The Shark, the Crocodile and the 'Silent Coup,' " *Middle East*, February 2007.
18. Brigadier General Mir-Faisal Baqerzadeh, as quoted by Fars News Agency, March 12, 2007.
19. Morad Bakhtiyari, "Sending Correspondent, CIA Spy," *Siyasat-e Rooz*, March 15, 2007, as translated at BBC Monitoring Middle East—Political, March 26, 2007.
20. As described by Iranian friend, Tehran, November 25, 2007.
21. Visit by two Iranian intelligence agents, "Hosseini" and another, Ahvaz, Iran, March 13, 2007.

1. OLD GLORY, GREAT SATAN

1. Numbers as noted in Christopher de Bellaigue, "Stalled, May 2004," in *The Struggle for Iran* (New York: New York Review of Books, 2007), p. 72.
2. Interview with Javad Vaeidi, editor of *Diplomatic Hamshahri* newspaper and later senior official on Iran's National Security Council, Tehran, March 14, 2005; see also Scott Peterson, "Why the US and Iran Love to Hate Each Other," *Christian Science Monitor*, June 29, 2005.
3. Hooman Majd, *The Ayatollah Begs to Differ: The Paradox of Modern Iran* (New York: Doubleday, 2008), p. 237.
4. Reporting in Tehran, June 21, 1998; see also Paul Obejuerge, "World Cup: U.S. eliminated from Cup after 2-1 loss to Iran," Gannett News Service, June 21, 1998, and "1998 FIFA World Cup France—Match Report, USA-Iran," at www.fifa.com/worldcup/archive/edition=1013/results/matches/match=8754/report.html.
5. Reporting in Tehran, June 21, 1998; see also Scott Peterson, "Victory Over US Plays Into Iran's Big Debate," *Christian Science Monitor*, June 23, 1998.

6. Scott Peterson, "Driven by Oil and Spite for US, Iran Reaches for Dominance," *Christian Science Monitor*, April 8, 1997.

7. Ibid.

8. Franklin D. Roosevelt, "Acceptance Speech for the Renomination for the Presidency, Philadelphia, Pa.," June 27, 1936, document 82, in John T. Woolley and Gerhard Peters, *The American Presidency Project* [online], University of California at Santa Barbara (host), at www.presidency.ucsb.edu/ws/?pid=15314.

9. Interview with Shahriar Rouhani, Tehran, February 14, 2002.

10. Interview with Javad Vaeidi, Tehran, March 14, 2005; see also Peterson, "Why the US and Iran Love to Hate Each Other."

11. Communication with sources close to Vaeidi in Tehran, July 2005.

12. Peterson, "Driven by Oil."

13. Interview with Reza Alavi, Tehran, June 18, 2005.

14. Christiane Amanpour, "Transcript of Interview with Iranian President Mohammad Khatami," CNN, January 7, 1998.

15. Ayatollah Ruhollah Khomeini, "The First Day of God's Government," declaration from Qom, April 1, 1979, in *Islam and Revolution: Writings and Declarations of Imam Khomeini (1941–1980)*, translated and annotated by Hamid Algar (North Haledon, N.J.: Mizan, 1981), pp. 265–66.

16. Paul Johnson, *A History of the American People* (New York: HarperCollins, 1997), p. 28.

17. A. B. Forbes, ed., *The Winthrop Papers, 1598–1649*, 5 vols. (Boston, 1929–47), vol. 2, p. 293ff, as quoted in Johnson, *A History of the American People*, p. 33.

18. Harry S. Truman, "Radio Address to the American People After the Signing of the Terms of Unconditional Surrender by Japan," September 1, 1945, document 122, in Woolley and Peters, *The American Presidency Project*, at www.presidency.ucsb.edu/ws/?pid=12366.

19. Radio Tehran, quoted in *Foreign Broadcast Information Service*, March 10, 1982, as quoted by Robin Wright, *In the Name of God: The Khomeini Decade* (New York: Simon & Schuster, 1990), p. 82.

20. Interview with Hamid Reza Jalaeipour, Tehran, June 11, 2005.

21. George W. Bush, "Address Before a Joint Session of the Congress on the United States Response to the Terrorist Attacks of September 11," September 20, 2001, in Woolley and Peters, *The American Presidency Project*, at www.presidency.ucsb.edu/ws/?pid=64731.

22. Mahmoud Ahmadinejad, "Alternative Christmas Message," Channel 4 television, London, December 24, 2008; translation at www.channel4.com/programmes/alternative-christmas-message/articles/translation-of-the-alternative-christmas-message.

23. Interview with Amir Mohebian, Tehran, March 12, 2005.

24. Barbara Slavin, *Bitter Friends, Bosom Enemies: Iran, the US, and the Twisted Path to Confrontation* (New York: St. Martin's, 2007), p. 9.

25. William J. Clinton, "Excerpt of Videotape Remarks on the United States–Iran World Cup Game," June 18, 1998 (for broadcast June 21, 1998), in Woolley and Peters, *The American Presidency Project*, at www.presidency.ucsb.edu/ws/?pid=56159.

26. "US, Iran Gain Award for World Cup Gift Exchange," Reuters, January 22, 1999, as archived at www.farsinet.com/news/jan99.html.

27. "Radio 8am: President's message," as translated by *Akhbaar Ruz*, Tehran, June 22, 1998, vol. 19, no. 59, Morning Edition, p. 7.

28. "Radio 8am: Message by Esteemed Leader," as translated by *Akhbaar Ruz*, p. 6.

29. Interview with Ebrahim Yazdi, Tehran, November 8, 1999; see also Scott Peterson, "Iran Power Struggle Ignites New Round of Flag Burning," *Christian Science Monitor*, December 9, 1999.

30. Reporting and interviews in Tehran, November 4, 1999; see also Peterson, "Iran Power Struggle."

31. Interview with Cyrus Etemadi, Tehran, June 17, 1998; see also Scott Peterson, "For 'Trip of a Lifetime,' Americans Try Sunny . . . Iran?" *Christian Science Monitor*, June 29, 1998.

32. Interview with Trygve Inda, Tehran, June 25, 1998; see also Peterson, "For 'Trip of a Lifetime.' "

33. Reporting in Tehran, November 4, 2002; see also Scott Peterson, "U.S. Stirs Mixed Feelings in Iran," *Christian Science Monitor*, November 5, 2002.

34. As described in Trita Parsi, "Can Khatami Make a Comeback?" at Huffington Post.com, February 9, 2009.

35. Felix Belair, "Eden Bars U.S. Proposal on Iran; Role of Mossadegh Is Basic Issue," *New York Times*, November 8, 1951; and referenced in Stephen Kinzer, *All the Shah's Men: An American Coup and the Roots of Middle East Terror* (Hoboken, N.J.: Wiley, 2003).

36. "Stephen Kinzer on US-Iranian Relations, the 1953 CIA Coup in Iran and the Roots of Middle East Terror," interview with Amy Goodman on *Democracy Now!*, March 3, 2008. Britain's dependence on Iranian oil was complete, notes author/journalist Kinzer: "The standard of living that people in England enjoyed all during that period [1920s to 1940s] was due exclusively to Iranian oil. Britain has no colonies that have oil. Every factory in England, every car, every truck, every taxi was running on oil from Iran. The Royal Navy, which was projecting British power all over the world, was fueled one hundred percent by oil from Iran."

37. As quoted in Kinzer, *All the Shah's Men*, p. 95.

38. Interview with Reza Alavi, Tehran, November 16, 2007.

39. Interview with veteran revolutionary, March 22, 2000.

40. Dr. Akbar Etemad, the father of Iran's Shah-era nuclear program, interviewed by Maziar Bahari, " 'The Shah's Plan Was to Build Bombs,' " *New Statesman*, September 11, 2008.

41. United States Information Service, Tehran (Iran), dispatch from Edward C. Wells to the United States Information Agency, "USIS Program—Iran," October 2, 1953, document 110, as published in *U.S. Propaganda in the Middle East*, National Security Archive, December 13, 2002, at www.gwu.edu/~nsarchiv/NSAEBB/NSAEBB78/propaganda%20110.pdf.

42. Barry Rubin, *Paved with Good Intentions: The American Experience and Iran* (New York: Oxford University Press, 1980), p. 143.

43. Shah press conference of October 18, 1971, as quoted in Ali M. Ansari, *Modern Iran Since 1921: The Pahlavis and After* (London: Longman, 2003), pp. 172–73.

44. Christopher Xenopoulos Janus, "Persepolis and Alexander the Great Wonderfully Remembered," Hellenic Communication Service, at www.helleniccomserve.com/persepolis.html, on March 7, 2009.

45. As quoted in Geoffrey Wawro, "Letter from Iran: Our Special Correspondent," *Naval War College Review* 55, no. 1 (Winter 2002), pp. 115–16.

46. Ayatollah Ruhollah Khomeini, "The Incompatibility of Monarchy with Islam," declaration from Najaf, Iraq, October 31, 1971, in *Islam and Revolution*, pp. 202, 207.

47. Gary Sick, *All Fall Down: America's Tragic Encounter with Iran* (New York: Random House, 1985), p. 9, with quotation of the Shah from Mohammad Reza Pahlavi, *Answer to History* (New York: Stein & Day, 1980), p. 72.

48. Sick, *All Fall Down*, p. 8. Except where noted, details here of the U.S.-Iran military relationship, and especially the Nixon administration's efforts to lock a "blank check" for the Shah into the U.S. national security bureaucracy, are from Sick's excellent insider account, especially pp. 13–21.

49. As quoted in the Associated Press photo caption, published in Carroll Kilpatrick, "Nixon's Departure From Iran Marred by Terrorist Explosions," *Washington Post*, June 1, 1972. Plainclothes SAVAK agents at the party sponsored by Iran's Ministry of Information prevented the journalists there from photographing Kissinger's lap dance.

50. Details of explosions in Kilpatrick, "Nixon's Departure From Iran Marred by Terrorist Explosions." Details of the attack along the route to the airport are as described in William Shawcross, *The Shah's Last Ride: The Fate of an Ally* (New York: Touchstone, 1989), p. 164. Shawcross reports that after a second meeting with the Shah and lunch, "the motorcade set off for the airport. To avoid demonstrations, it skirted Tehran and went instead through unpopulated hills north of the town. But even there students were waiting; the limousines were pelted with stones. Hundreds of students were subsequently rounded up and imprisoned. . . ."

51. As quoted in Sick, *All Fall Down*, p. 15.

52. Anthony Sampson, *The Arms Bazaar: From Lebanon to Lockheed* (New York: Viking, 1977), p. 252, as cited in William A. Dorman and Mansour Farhang, *The U.S. Press and Iran: Foreign Policy and the Journalism of Deference* (Berkeley: University of California Press, 1987), p. 129.

53. Sick, *All Fall Down*, p. 15.

54. James A. Bill, *The Eagle and the Lion: The Tragedy of American-Iranian Relations* (New Haven: Yale University Press, 1988), pp. 381–82. Isfahan details are from Martie and Robin Sterling, *Last Flight from Iran* (New York: Bantam, 1981) as quoted and cited in Bill, *The Eagle and the Lion*.

55. Details at www.howardbaskerville.com; Bill, *The Eagle and the Lion*, p. 17; Wm. Scott Harrop and R. K. Ramazani, "Celebrating the Fourth and Cheering the Iranians," Agence Global, July 1, 2009.

56. As recounted in W. Morgan Shuster, *The Strangling of Persia: A Personal Narrative* (1912; rept. Washington, D.C.: Mage, 1987), dedication and pp. 331, 333.

57. Bill, *The Eagle and the Lion*, p. 17.

58. Ibid., p. 380.

59. According to Bill, *The Eagle and the Lion*, pp. 387–88, the U.S. Embassy com-

missary was the largest of its kind in the world, and members of the royal family were the only Iranians who could shop there. In one eighteen-month span to June 1970, American pets in Iran ate $35,703 worth of processed cat and dog food, their owners purchasing 125,178 packs and cans of the stuff that required American planes to airlift seventy-nine tons to Tehran, of everything from Gaines Dry Burger to sacks of dry food. Reports Bill: "Iranians quietly noted that there was hunger, and even famine, in the provinces of Baluchistan and Sistan in the east. But as one cynically noted, the American dogs are well fed."

That complaint echoed one of Ayatollah Khomeini's most severe criticisms of the Shah, leveled in 1964 at the monarch's agreement to provide legal immunity to Americans—and lodged ever since in Iran's collective memory as an example of national capitulation. ". . . I have barely slept," the cleric began, in a speech that would prompt his immediate expulsion from Iran.

> With sorrowful heart, I count the days until death shall come and deliver me. . . . They have sold us, they have sold our independence; but still they light up the city and dance. . . . They have reduced the Iranian people to a level lower than that of an American dog. If someone runs over a dog belonging to an American, he will be prosecuted. Even if the Shah himself were to run over a dog belonging to an American, he would be prosecuted. But if an American cook runs over the Shah, the head of state, no one will have the right to interfere with him.

(Ayatollah Ruhollah Khomeini, "The Granting of Capitulary Rights to the U.S.," October 27, 1964, in *Islam and Revolution*, pp. 181–82.)

60. Robert Fisk, *The Great War for Civilisation: The Conquest of the Middle East*, rev. ed. (London: Harper Perennial, 2006), p. 121. Most sources put the number of salaried SAVAK agents from 3,000 to 5,000. Fisk, who reported from Iran during the Revolution and before, even states: "At one point, it was believed that a third of the male population of Iran were in some way involved in SAVAK, either directly or as occasional paid or blackmailed informants." Rubin notes over 3,000 full-time SAVAK employees, "though the number of paid informers, including journalists, students, waiters, drivers, and businessmen, might have easily numbered twenty times as many"—or 60,000. Rubin, *Paved with Good Intentions*, p. 179.

61. Amnesty International Report 1974–75 (London, 1975), as quoted in Rubin, *Paved with Good Intentions*, p. 176.

62. Ervand Abrahamian, *Tortured Confessions: Prison and Public Recantations in Modern Iran* (Berkeley: University of California Press, 1999), p. 106. Abrahamian notes (p. 104) that SAVAK had more than five thousand full-time employees and "an unknown number of part-time informants."

63. Interviews and details drawn from visit to Ebrat (Lesson) Museum, the "SAVAK Anti-Sabotage Joint Committee Jail," Tehran, February 11, 2009.

64. Reza Baraheni, *The Crowned Cannibals: Writings on Repression in Iran* (New York: Vintage, 1977), pp. 133, 141.

65. "Biography," Office of the Supreme Leader Seyyed Ali Khamenei, at www .leader.ir/langs/EN/index.php?p=bio.

66. Sequences found on DVD *Morgh-e Del* (*Dove of the Heart*), produced by Ebrat Museum.

67. Abrahamian, *Tortured Confessions*, p. 169.

68. As described in Haleh Esfandiari, *My Prison, My Home: One Woman's Story of Captivity in Iran* (New York: Ecco/HarperCollins, 2009), p. 164.

69. The Shah and Carter quotations in "Jimmy Carter: Tehran, Iran, Toasts of the President and the Shah at a State Dinner," December 31, 1977, in Woolley and Peters, *The American Presidency Project*, at www.presidency.ucsb.edu/ws/ ?pid=7080.

70. Interview with Ebrahim Yazdi, Tehran, June 21, 1998.

71. Laingen story described by Kinzer on *Democracy Now!*

72. Introduction by A. M. Rosenthal, in Robert D. McFadden, Joseph B. Treaster, and Maurice Carroll, *No Hiding Place: The New York Times, Inside Report on the Hostage Crisis* (New York: Times Books, 1981), p. xvi.

73. Interview with Massoumeh Ebtekar, Tehran, November 17, 2007.

74. As described in Massoumeh Ebtekar, as told to Fred A. Reed, *Takeover in Tehran: The Inside Story of the 1979 US Embassy Capture* (Vancouver, British Columbia: Talonbooks, 2000), p. 61.

75. Ebtekar, *Takeover in Tehran*, p. 37.

76. As described in John W. Limbert, *Negotiating With Iran: Wrestling the Ghosts of History* (Washington, D.C.: United States Institute of Peace Press, 2009), p. 4.

77. As quoted in McFadden et al., *No Hiding Place*, p. 14.

78. As quoted in Tim Wells, *444 Days: The Hostages Remember* (New York: Harcourt Brace Jovanovich, 1985), p. 88.

79. As quoted in ibid., p. 70.

80. Visit to student offices of Daftar-e Tahkim-e Vahdat (Office of Fostering Unity), Tehran, July 5, 2000; see also David Clark Scott, "Reporters on the Job: 'File It Under Revolution,' " *Christian Science Monitor*, July 7, 2000.

81. Interview with Ebrahim Yazdi, Tehran, February 3, 1999.

82. As quoted in John Kifner, "How a Sit-In Turned Into a Siege," *New York Times*, May 17, 1981.

83. Cheaply bound paperback selections of the U.S. Embassy documents have been sold for years in the Revolutionary Guard shop at the corner of the U.S. Embassy grounds in Tehran. The continuing importance of these documents in Iran—as proof of superpower perfidy, and therefore as a tool to encourage permanent anti-American feeling—is evident in a recent complete translation and printing in ten hefty hardcover volumes. Published in 2008 by the Political Studies & Research Institute in Tehran, the *Documents from the US Espionage Den (American Embassy in Iran)* come with a set of ten DVDs. I have seen the complete set of books in such diverse places as the Tehran office of the hard-line editor of *Kayhan*, Hossein Shariatmadari, and alongside religious volumes at a mosque in the city of Birjand, eight hundred miles southeast of Tehran.

84. "Subject: Assistant Secretary Saunders' Statement," E.O.112065, Department of Defense, Joint Chiefs of Staff, Message Center, January 17, 1979, as printed in "Muslim Students Following the Line of the Imam," *Documents from the*

U.S. Espionage Den (63), *U.S. Interventions in Iran* (12) (Tehran: Center for the Publication of the U.S. Espionage Den's Documents, 1987), pp. 37–64.

85. Major Don Adamick, "Intelligence Appraisal: Iran: Renewal of Civil Disturbances (U)," Defense Intelligence Agency DIAIAPPR 195-78, August 16, 1978, as reproduced in *Documents from the U.S. Espionage Den* (63), pp. 1–9.

86. As described in Ebtekar, *Takeover in Tehran*, pp. 114–15.

87. As recounted in Mark Bowden, *Guests of the Ayatollah: The First Battle in America's War with Militant Islam* (New York: Atlantic Monthly Press, 2006), p. 176.

88. Interview with Abbas Abdi, Tehran, February 6, 1999; see also Scott Peterson, "Changes in Iran, Through the Eyes of a Hostage Taker," *Christian Science Monitor*, February 10, 1999. Abdi's role carrying the megaphone is described in Bowden, *Guests of the Ayatollah*, p. 14.

89. "Poll On US Ties Rocks Iran," BBC News, October 2, 2002, including poll results as published by Islamic Republic News Agency (IRNA) on September 22, 2002.

90. Nazila Fathi, "Iranian Pollster, a Top Reformist Politician, Goes on Trial," *New York Times*, December 26, 2002; see also Jim Muir, "Iran Tries Pollsters on Spying Charges," BBC News, December 3, 2002.

91. As quoted in De Bellaigue, "The Loneliness of the Supreme Leader, December 2002," in *The Struggle for Iran*, p. 41.

92. "Abbas Abdi's Disclosures from Inside Prison," letter of July 14, 2003, as reprinted by BBC Persian, July 15, 2003, at www.bbc.co.uk/persian/news/030714_a-mb-abdi.shtml.

93. Alan Friedman, *Spider's Web: The Secret History of How the White House Illegally Armed Iraq* (New York: Bantam, 1993), p. 27.

94. Bob Woodward, "CIA Paid Millions to Jordan's King Hussein," *Washington Post*, February 18, 1977.

95. Friedman, *Spider's Web*, pp. 32–33. Friedman recounts the decision of a White House interagency meeting on July 23, 1986, which explored ways of helping Iraq counter a new Iranian offensive. Vice President George H. W. Bush was sent to the Mideast to pass on the message of how to better bomb the Iranians. The State Department's Richard Murphy wrote a cable, labeled "Secret" and titled "USG Support for Iraq during the War," to the U.S. ambassador in Baghdad. "We have encouraged the Vice President to suggest to both King Hussein and President Mubarak that they sustain their efforts to convey our shared views to Saddam regarding Iraq's use of its air resources," wrote Murphy. "If Saddam does what he says he would do with the Air Force, that would be a major plus." Facsimile of document in Appendix B, pp. 310–311.

96. Friedman, *Spider's Web*, pp. 36, 38.

97. Descriptions of incidents and Lieutenant Colonel Roger Charles quotation in Friedman, *Spider's Web*, pp. 40–43.

98. One U.S. intelligence document stated that Iraq launched those offensives by firing some two thousand 122mm rockets full of mustard gas, sarin, and tear gas. A top Iraqi commander later claimed that Iraq had "won" and recaptured Fao because they used VX nerve gas. See "Scud Chemical Agent Coverage Patterns," August 1990 (FOIA-Gulflink), as quoted in Joost R. Hiltermann, *A Poisonous Affair: America, Iraq, and the Gassing of Halabja* (New York: Cambridge

University Press, 2007), p. 140; and *Independent* (London), July 3, 1998, as cited in Hiltermann, p. 141.

99. U.S. Central Intelligence Agency, "Issues (U)," DST-1620S-464-90, March 1, 1990 (FOIA-Gulflink), as quoted in Hiltermann, *A Poisonous Affair*, p. 145. The report continues: "The success of offensive operations in the southern sector in mid-1988 ultimately caused the Iranians to cease hostilities. The use of chemical weapons contributed to the success of these operations."

100. Anthony H. Cordesman and Adam C. Seitz, "Iranian Weapons of Mass Destruction: The Broader Strategic Context—Working Draft for Review and Comments," Center for Strategic & International Studies, December 5, 2008, p. 4. That analysis is drawn from "Iran-Iraq War (1980–1988)," Global Security, at www.globalsecurity.org/military/world/war/iran-iraq.htm, March 22, 2009, which states: "In the fall of 1988, the Iraqis displayed in Baghdad captured Iranian weapons amounting to more than three-quarters of the Iranian armor inventory and almost half of its artillery pieces and armored personnel carriers."

101. Ali Rahnema and Farhad Nomani, *The Secular Miracle*, p. 341, as quoted in Baqer Moin, *Khomeini: Life of the Ayatollah* (New York: Thomas Dunne, 2000), p. 268. See also Robin Wright, *In the Name of God: The Khomeini Decade* (New York: Simon & Schuster, 1989), p. 176.

A notable calculation about such "commerce" in martyrs comes from Global Security in "Iran-Iraq War," which notes: "Without diminishing the horror of either war, Iranian losses in the eight-year Iran-Iraq War appear modest compared with those of the European contestants in the four years of World War I, shedding some light on the limits of the Iranian tolerance of martyrdom." The analysis found that Germany's losses in the Great War, as a proportion of population, were "at least five times higher" than Iran's. It notes that the percentages of prewar population killed or wounded in World War I were 9 percent of Germany, 11 percent of France, and 8 percent of Great Britain.

102. Tehran Radio, July 20, 1988, as quoted by Moin, *Khomeini*, pp. 269–70.

103. Interview with Colonel Mohammad Akbari, Tehran, November 7, 2002; see also Scott Peterson, "Lessons from Iran on Facing Chemical War," *Christian Science Monitor*, November 19, 2002, pp. 1, 7.

104. Dr. Abbas Foroutan, who later became one of Iran's top experts on chemical exposures as medical director of the Medical Association for Victims of Chemical Warfare, as quoted in Hiltermann, *A Poisonous Affair*, p. 71.

105. "Report of the Secretary-General on the Activities of the Special Commission," United Nations S/1997/774, October 6, 1997.

106. Major General Maher Abd Al-Rashid, February 21, 1984, as widely quoted in news reports. A "Confidential" cable from U.S. diplomats in Baghdad to Washington pointedly warned that "a large scale Iranian offensive is imminent aimed at occupying Iraqi population centers." The cable says the Iraqi military spokesman said Iraq "would be compelled to strike deep inside Iranian territory," and then "gives a chilling warning that CW agents might be employed, stating that 'The invaders should know. . . .' " (U.S. Interest Section in Iraq Cable from William L. Eagleton to Department of State, "Iraqi Warning re

Iranian Offensive," February 22, 1984, in National Security Archive FOIA, at www.gwu.edu/~nsarchiv/NSAEBB/NSAEBB82/iraq41.pdf.)

107. Dr. Shahriar Khateri of Iran's Society for Chemical Weapons Victims Support, in "Press Release: New Information Necessitates Comprehensive Review of Chemical Weapons Use in Iraq-Iran War, Says NGO Representing Iran's CW Survivors," Tehran, April 5, 2008.

108. Interview with Brian Davey, head of OPCW's health and safety branch, by telephone to The Hague, November 5, 2002; see also Peterson, "Lessons from Iran on Facing Chemical War."

109. Central Intelligence Agency, "Iraqi Use of Chemical Weapons in the War with Iran," Washington, D.C., February 20, 1991 (FOIA-Gulflink); see also Peterson, "Lessons from Iran on Facing Chemical War." By late 1986, the CIA said, "chemical weapons were used effectively against staging areas to preempt Iranian offensives. Iraq also began to integrate CW into its successful battlefield tactics, using massed nerve agent strikes as an integral part of offensives."

Another CIA analysis noted that Iranian support troops sometimes sustained "large numbers of casualties" because they were the least ready: "In this regard, rear area chemical attacks may be a force multiplier for Iraq." (Director of Central Intelligence, "Impact and Implications of Chemical Weapons Use in the Iran-Iraq War," undated, late 1987 to early 1988 [FOIA-Gulflink]; and see Hiltermann, *A Poisonous Affair*, p. 13.)

110. For an exhaustive examination of claims and counterclaims that Iran used chemical weapons, see Hiltermann, *A Poisonous Affair*, esp. pp. 148–205. Among many other points, Hiltermann notes (p. 176) that "in eighteen metric tons (close to five million pages) of captured Iraqi secret police and intelligence documents, the Iraqis make not a single reference to any supposed Iranian chemical attacks at any point during the war, while repeatedly and unambiguously, if not always explicitly, acknowledging their own chemical weapons use."

As director of the Iraqi Documents Project for Human Rights Watch at the time, Hiltermann had unfettered access to those Iraqi state files, once they were airlifted to the United States after being captured by Kurdish *peshmerga* guerrillas during the March 1991 uprising in northern Iraq. The joint result of that three-year project was the detailed book, Human Rights Watch/Middle East, *Iraq's Crime of Genocide: The Anfal Campaign Against the Kurds* (New Haven: Yale University Press, 1995). Questions about the "illusion" of Iranian use of gas "fostered initially by reports from the US intelligence community strongly tilted toward Baghdad" are "false" (p. 19, and p. 316, n. 7).

111. Numerous reports from December 28, 1980, including "Reagan Rejects Paying Ransom to 'Barbarians,' " Associated Press, as printed in *Miami News*, December 29, 1980.

112. Ronald Reagan, "Address to the Nation on the Iran Arms and Contra Aid Controversy," November 13, 1986, in Woolley and Peters, *The American Presidency Project*, at www.presidency.ucsb.edu/ws/?pid=36728.

113. John Tower, Edmund Muskie, and Brent Scowcroft, *The Tower Commission Report: The Full Text of the President's Special Review Board* (New York: Random House/New York Times, 1987), p. 62.

114. As described in the chronology, August 18, 1982, in Peter Kornbluh and Mal-

colm Byrne, eds., *The Iran-Contra Scandal: The Declassified History; A National Security Archive Documents Reader* (New York: New Press, 1993), p. 380; and "Israel Reported Selling Iran Captured Arms," *Washington Post*, August 20, 1982.

115. Multiple references to Israeli officials and middlemen with ties to Prime Minister Shimon Peres, colluding with U.S. National Security Council and other senior officials, from early 1981, in *The Tower Commission Report* (see especially pp. 22–33), and *The Iran-Contra Scandal* (see especially pp. 379, 382, 386, 391–97).

A 1987 Senate Intelligence Committee report found: "Israel had a strong interest in promoting contacts with Iran and reportedly had permitted arms transfers to Iran as a means of furthering their interests. A series of intelligence studies written in 1984 and 1985 described Israeli shipments of non-US arms to Iran as well as the use of Israeli middlemen as early as 1982 to arrange private deals involving US arms." (*The Iran-Contra Scandal*, p. 382.)

The Tower Commission states (pp. 23–26) that much of Israel's military equipment came originally from the United States, so Israel "felt a need for US approval of, or at least acquiescence in, any arms sales to Iran. In addition, elements in Israel undoubtedly wanted the United States involved for its own sake so as to distance the United States from the Arab world and ultimately to establish Israel as the only real strategic partner of the United States in the region. Iran badly wanted what Israel could provide."

The Iranian arms dealer Manouchehr Ghorbanifar—who was discredited repeatedly by the CIA since 1980 as unreliable and a "fabricator" (*Fabricator Notice—Manucher* [sic] *Ghorbanifar; 7/25/84;* and *Ghorbanifar Polygraph—Date* [1985] *Incorrect*, as cited in the chronology, July 25, 1984 and January 11, 1986, *The Iran-Contra Scandal*, pp. 384, 396)—and Saudi Arabian businessman Adnan Khashoggi contacted private Israeli arms dealers, and then Peres's counterterrorism adviser. According to the Tower Commission, "These men believed that the United States, Israel, and Iran, though with different interests, were susceptible to a relationship of convenience involving arms, hostages, and the opening of a channel to Iran. The catalyst that brought this relationship into being was the proffering by Israel of a channel for the United States in establishing contacts with Iran."

116. As described by CIA Deputy Director John McMahon to Vice Admiral John Poindexter, January 24, 1986, in *The Tower Commission Report*, pp. 239–40.

117. As cited in *The Iran-Contra Scandal*, p. 215.

118. John Barry, "Sea of Lies," *Newsweek*, July 13, 1992.

119. Interview with Farideh Farhi, by telephone to Hawaii, June 29, 2006; see also Scott Peterson, "Pragmatism May Trump Zeal as Iran's Power Grows," *Christian Science Monitor*, July 6, 2006.

120. Statistics in this section found in Cordesman and Seitz, "Iranian Weapons of Mass Destruction," pp. 8–12, 15, which are in turn adaptations of data drawn from, among many other sources, annual editions of *The Military Balance* from the International Institute for Strategic Studies (London), U.S. Congressional Research Service, and various U.S. government agency reports.

121. Major General Mohsen Rezaei interview with English-language *Kayhan*, as quoted in "Iran Has No Intention to Start War with US," Reuters, June 29, 1997.

122. Center for Arms Control and Non-Proliferation, February 20, 2008. Comparison of Iranian and U.S. spending adapted from Cordesman and Seitz, "Iranian Weapons of Mass Destruction," p. 8; and Andrew J. Bacevich, *The Limits of Power: The End of American Exceptionalism* (New York: Metropolitan Books, 2008), p. 64.

123. Cordesman and Seitz, "Iranian Weapons of Mass Destruction," p. 13; see also Anthony H. Cordesman and Martin Kleiber, *Iran's Military Forces and Warfighting Capabilities: The Threat in the Northern Gulf* (Washington, D.C.: Center for Strategic and International Studies, 2007), pp. 29–30.

124. Patrick E. Tyler, "U.S. Strategy Plan Calls for Insuring No Rivals Develop," *New York Times*, March 8, 1992; see also "Excerpts From Pentagon's Plan: 'Prevent the Re-Emergence of a New Rival,' " *New York Times*, March 8, 1992, and Patrick E. Tyler, "Lone Superpower Plan: Ammunition for Critics," *New York Times*, March 10, 1992.

125. Secretary of Defense Dick Cheney, "Defense Strategy for the 1990s: The Regional Defense Strategy," January 1993. This and other documents related to the writing, leaking, rewriting, and declassification have been collected by the National Security Archive, at www.gwu.edu/~nsarchiv/nukevault/ebb245/.

126. Quotations from Patrick E. Tyler, "Pentagon Imagines New Enemies to Fight in Post–Cold War Era," and "7 Hypothetical Conflicts Foreseen by the Pentagon," both *New York Times*, February 17, 1992.

127. Trita Parsi, *Treacherous Alliance: The Secret Dealings of Israel, Iran, and the U.S.* (New Haven: Yale University Press, 2007), pp. 158–59.

128. Scott Peterson, "Iran's Prized, and Political, Nuts," *Christian Science Monitor*, December 2, 1999.

129. Clyde Haberman, "Israel Focuses on the Threat Beyond the Arabs—in Iran," *New York Times*, November 8, 1992.

130. Yitzhak Rabin, "Statement in the Knesset by Prime Minister Rabin—21 December 1992," Israel Ministry of Foreign Affairs, vols. 13–14: 1992–94, document 45, December 21, 1992, at www.mfa.gov.il; also quoted in David Hoffman, "Israel Seeking to Convince US that West is Threatened by Iran; Jewish Leaders Say Only Washington Capable of Restraining Tehran," *Washington Post*, March 13, 1993.

131. Rabin interview with *Davar* newspaper, as quoted in Hoffman, "Israel Seeking to Convince US that West is Threatened by Iran."

132. Israel Shahak, head of the Israeli League for Human and Civil Rights, and David Makovsky of the Washington Institute for Near East Policy, both quoted in Parsi, *Treacherous Alliance*, pp. 163–64.

133. As quoted in Parsi, *Treacherous Alliance*, pp. 163–64.

134. Hoffman, "Israel Seeking to Convince US that West Is Threatened by Iran."

135. Parsi, *Treacherous Alliance*, pp. 165–66.

136. Interview with Saeed Laylaz, Tehran, March 14, 2005.

137. Parsi, *Treacherous Alliance*, p. 167.

138. Interview with Mohsen Kadivar, Tehran, October 5, 2005.

139. Interview with Mohsen Aminzadeh, former deputy foreign minister in charge of Afghan affairs, Tehran, February 21, 2008. See also Hillary Mann, quoted in

John H. Richardson, "The Secret History of the Impending War with Iran That the White House Doesn't Want You to Know," *Esquire*, October 18, 2007.

140. Interview with Ambassador James Dobbins, Washington, D.C., April 9, 2008; for a detailed picture of Iran's positive role in these discussions see James Dobbins, *After the Taliban: Nation Building in Afghanistan* (Washington, D.C.: Potomac, 2008), esp. pp. 83–96.

141. Interview with Toby Dodge, by telephone to London, February 12, 2002.

142. Interview with Hadi Semati, Tehran, November 10, 2002.

143. "Iran's May 2003 Negotiation Proposal to the United States" and "Letter from Ambassador Guldimann to the US State Department," as reproduced in Parsi, *Treacherous Alliance*, Appendices A and C, pp. 341–42, 345–46.

144. Interview with Sadegh Kharazi, Tehran, November 19, 2007; see also Scott Peterson, "Iran's Reformers to US: Let's Talk," *Christian Science Monitor*, November 30, 2007.

145. Recounting based on interview with Lawrence Wilkerson, former chief of staff for then–Secretary of State Colin Powell, in Parsi, *Treacherous Alliance*, p. 248; and also quoted in Gordon Corera, "Iran's Gulf of Misunderstanding with US," BBC News online, September 25, 2006.

146. Interview with the Sage, Tehran, September 21, 2003.

147. George Orwell, *Nineteen Eighty-four* (1949; rept., New York: Harcourt Brace Jovanovich, 1983). As Orwell writes (pp. 176–77): "*Doublethink* means the power of holding two contradictory beliefs in one's mind simultaneously, and accepting both of them. . . . [B]y using the word one admits that one is tampering with reality; by a fresh act of *doublethink* one erases this knowledge; and so on indefinitely, with the lie always one leap ahead of the truth. Ultimately, it is by means of *doublethink* that the Party has been able—and may, for all we know, continue to be able for thousands of years—to arrest the course of history."

148. The Sage was paraphrasing Khomeini, who famously said that preserving the Islamic government "has priority over all other secondary injunctions, even prayers, fasting and *Hajj*. . . . The government is empowered unilaterally to revoke any religious law that it has conducted with people if those agreements are contrary to the interests of the country or of Islam." *Ettelaat*, January 8, 1988, as quoted in Mehdi Moslem, "Ayatollah Khomeini's role in the Rationalization of the Islamic Government," *Middle East Critique*, 8, no. 14 (Spring 1999), pp. 75–92.

149. Quoted in "Iranian President Mahmoud Ahmadinejad: The Countdown for the Decline of America's Demonic Power Has Begun. Zionist Germ of Corruption Will Be Wiped off the Face of the Earth," translated by Middle East Media Research Institute, June 2, 2008.

150. As quoted in Thomas P. M. Barnett, "The Man Between War and Peace," *Esquire*, April 23, 2008.

151. Henry Precht, recollection posted on Gulf/2000, June 23, 2009, used with permission.

152. Karim Sadjadpour, "Reading Khamenei: The World View of Iran's Most Powerful Leader," Carnegie Endowment for International Peace, March 11, 2008, pp. 14–15.

153. Interview with Hossein Shariatmadari, Tehran, February 21, 2004.

154. "Iran: Khamenei Addresses Students on Anniversary of US Embassy Seizure," transcript of *Vision of the Republic of Iran Network 1*, October 29, 2008.

155. Interviews during visit to Jamaran prayer hall, Tehran, March 10, 2008.

156. As recounted in Patrick Tyler, *A World of Trouble: The White House and the Middle East—from the Cold War to the War on Terror* (New York: Farrar Straus and Giroux, 2009), p. 554.

157. Among a number of examples, see Donald Rumsfeld on Fox News Sunday, June 26, 2005, as quoted in Voice of America, "Rumsfeld Criticizes Iran's President-elect as 'No Friend of Democracy' "; see also Peterson, "Why the US and Iran Love to Hate Each Other."

158. "Iran's Supreme Leader Says US 'Humiliated' by Election," Agence France-Presse, June 25, 2005.

159. Interviews in Tehran, December 15, 2006.

160. Boys shouting in Tehran, February 11, 2004; see also Amelia Newcomb, "Reporters on the Job: 'Unofficially, We Like You,' " *Christian Science Monitor*, February 13, 2004.

2. SCENT OF HEAVEN

Epigraph. Roxanne Varzi, *Warring Souls: Youth, Media, and Martyrdom in Post-Revolution Iran* (Durham, N.C.: Duke University Press, 2006), p. 62.

1. Ali Akbar Hashemi Rafsanjani, September 4, 1981, and April 23, 1983, as quoted in Haggay Ram, *Myth and Mobilization in Revolutionary Iran: The Use of the Friday Congregational Sermon* (Washington, D.C.: American University Press, 1994), p. 73.

2. Shahram Chubin and Charles Tripp, *Iran and Iraq at War* (1988; rept., Boulder, Colo.: Westview Press, 1991), p. 33.

3. Ibid., p. 34.

4. List as compiled and sourced in ibid., pp. 33, 36.

5. Mohammad Avini, brother of the late director Morteza Avini, as quoted in Varzi, *Warring Souls*, pp. 83–84.

6. Most news reports incorrectly ascribe one million "dead" to the Iran-Iraq War, when in fact there were roughly one million "casualties"—both dead and wounded. The best figures for Iran seem to be those of IRGC Commander General Rahim Safavi, who in 2001 said that 213,000 had died. The statistics office of the Martyr's Foundation in 2000 gave a figure of 204,795 Iranians (including civilians) killed. On the Iraq side, the former head of military intelligence Wafiq al-Samarrai said in 2002 that 180,000 Iraqis lost their lives. These and other key figures are detailed in Lawrence G. Potter and Gary G. Sick, eds., *Iran, Iraq, and the Legacies of War* (New York: Palgrave Macmillan, 2004), p. 8, n. 5.

7. Interview with Javad Vaeidi, Tehran, March 14, 2005.

8. Interview with Haj Khezeir Bavi, former grave keeper, in Ahvaz, March 14, 2007.

9. Details of Ahvaz cemetery and interviews with Gholamreza and Ali Akbar Khoshnazar, during visit to Ahvaz, southwest Iran, March 13, 2007; see also

Scott Peterson, "How Iran's True Believers Pass the Torch," *Christian Science Monitor*, March 27, 2007.

10. A term coined by Khamenei, May 9, 1980, as quoted in Ram, *Myth and Mobilization in Revolutionary Iran*, p. 72.

11. Khamenei, July 11, 1980, as quoted in ibid., p. 30.

12. Khamenei, January 9, 1981, as quoted in ibid., p. 75.

13. Khamenei, October 3, 1980, as quoted in ibid.

14. Saskia Gieling, *Religion and War in Revolutionary Iran* (London: I. B. Taurus, 1999), p. 44.

15. Khamenei, November 14, 1980, as quoted in Ram, *Myth and Mobilization in Revolutionary Iran*, p. 80.

16. Vali Nasr, *The Shia Revival: How Conflicts Within Islam Will Shape the Future* (New York: Norton, 2006), p. 50.

17. This version of Hossein's final words as recounted in manuscript by Abbas Qoli Khan Bin Mohammad Taghi Sepehr, *Nasekh ol Tawarikh* (Tehran: Mohammad Bin Ali Khansari, publisher, 1889 [AHS 1310]), vol. 3, p. 119, as referred to in "Analysis of the Dimensions of Imam Hossein's Uprising," November 11, 2009, at www.aftab.ir/articles/religion/religion/c7c1257941563 _imam_hossein_p1.php.

18. "Oh Army of the Master of Time," sung by Sadegh Ahangaran, Track K002, *Sounds of the Sacred Defense: Collection of Sounds of the War Time, Movie Soundtracks, Chorus of the Holy Defense and Revolution, and [Ashura-style] Mourning*, undated music CD, Tehran. The "Master of Time" is the Shiite Messiah, the Twelfth Imam Mahdi, who—like the Second Coming of Jesus for many Christians—is meant to one day return in triumph, to vanquish infidels and elevate Believers.

19. War-era footage of Khomeini speaking to soldiers and of *shahid* Mohammad Ebrahim Hemmat, broadcast on Islamic Republic of Iran News Network, IRINN, Tehran, November 23, 2007.

20. Gieling, *Religion and War in Revolutionary Iran*, p. 60.

21. Interviews, scenes, and narrative descriptions drawn from episode of documentary series, Morteza Avini, director, *Delbakhte (One Who Has Lost/Given His Heart to Love), Revayat-e Fath (Chronicles of Victory)*, produced by the Cultural Institute of *Revayat-e Fath*, 3rd program, 2nd collection, filmed in 1986.

22. Varzi, *Warring Souls*, pp. 24, 56.

23. Ibid., p. 230, n. 28.

24. The third volume, for example, was published on the fifth anniversary of the start of the war. It described the 1982 liberation of Khorramshahr after nineteen months in Iraqi hands—"Iraq's Stalingrad"—as a "God-ordained miracle" that filled Muslims with "happiness throughout the world." See War Information Headquarters, *The Imposed War: Defense vs. Aggression* (Tehran: Supreme Defense Council, 1985), vol. 3, pp. 7, 14. So far eight volumes in this series have been published. The most recent in 2008 is also the largest, and exclusively about the pivotal Khorramshahr battle.

25. Varzi, *Warring Souls*, p. 26.

26. Khomeini, as quoted in Peter Chelkowski and Hamid Dabashi, *Staging a Revo-*

lution: The Art of Persuasion in the Islamic Republic of Iran (New York: New York University Press, 1999), p. 264.

27. Farideh Farhi, "The Antinomies of Iran's War Generation," in Potter and Sick, eds., *Iran, Iraq, and the Legacies of War*, p. 104.

28. Visits to Martyrs Museum, Tehran, December 16, 2006, and February 3, 2009.

29. Writings of Morteza Avini, as rendered in Varzi, *Warring Souls*, p. 93.

30. Interview with Mehdi Homayoun-Fars, Tehran, November 25, 2007.

31. As described in Peter J. Chelkowski, "Ta'ziyeh: Indigenous Avant-Garde Theatre of Iran," in Peter J. Chelkowski, ed., *Ta'ziyeh: Ritual and Drama in Iran* (New York: New York University Press and Soroush Press, 1979), p. 3.

32. Interviews with Ali Ehsan Rajabi, Tehran, November 25, 2007, and February 18, 2008.

33. Details and Rafsanjani quotation in *Foreign Broadcast Information Service*, March 16, 1983, as quoted in Dilip Hiro, *The Longest War: The Iran-Iraq Military Conflict* (London: Paladin, 1990), p. 95.

34. Ayatollah Ruhollah Khomeini on March 7, 1988, as quoted in Joint Staff of the Army of Islamic Revolution, Operation Department, *Atlas of Iran and Iraq War: A Concise [sic] of Ground Battles 22 Sep. 1980 to 20 Aug. 1988* (Tehran: Center for War Studies and Research, 2001), p. 117.

35. Khomeini inscriptions in Chelkowski and Dabashi, *Staging a Revolution*, p. 286.

36. Seyyed Mahdi Fahimi, editor of *The Front's Culture: Placards*, and *The Battlefield's Cultural Lexicon: Signboards Inscriptions* (Tehran, 1990) in Persian, as quoted in ibid., p. 283.

37. Farhi, "The Antinomies of Iran's War Generation," p. 116, n. 13.

38. War postcard illustrated in Chelkowski and Dabashi, *Staging a Revolution*, pp. 287–88.

39. Rafsanjani, September 18, 1981, as quoted in Ram, *Myth and Mobilization in Revolutionary Iran*, p. 74.

40. As quoted in Sepehr Zabih, *The Iranian Military in Revolution and War* (London: Routledge, 1988), p. 220.

41. Details of classroom photographs, and story of children in minefield, cited as *Ettelaat*, May 7, 1982, both in Zabih, *The Iranian Military in Revolution and War*.

42. Elaine Sciolino, *Persian Mirrors: The Elusive Face of Iran* (New York: Free Press, 2000), pp. 178–79.

43. Iraqi officer Staff Colonel Abd-al-Wahhab al-Saeidy, as quoted in Hiltermann, *A Poisonous Affair*, p. 25.

44. Interview with Zabihollah "Haji" Bakhshi, Karaj, Iran, March 21, 2008; see also Scott Peterson, "Portrait of a Veteran Iranian Revolutionary," *Christian Science Monitor*, March 31, 2008.

45. Ervand Abrahamian, *Iran Between Two Revolutions* (Princeton, N.J.: Princeton University Press, 1982), p. 258.

46. Hamid Algar, "Religious Forces in Twentieth-Century Iran," chapter 20, in *The Cambridge History of Iran, Volume 7: From Nadir Shah to the Islamic Republic* (Cambridge, England: Cambridge University Press, 1991), p. 748.

47. Elaheh Hicks, "Iran, Power Versus Choice," Human Rights Watch, March 1996.

48. "IRNA's Staff, Majles Deputies Warned," *Jomhuri-e Eslami*, April 18, 1996, as reprinted in *News on Iran*, no. 73 (National Council of Resistance of Iran), April 22, 1996, at www.iran-e-azad.org/english/noi/noi-73.html.

49. Farhi, "The Antinomies of Iran's War Generation," pp. 104, 106.

50. "Our Leader: Mohammed Hossein Fahmideh," October 29, 2007, at www .tebyan.net/index.aspx?pid=52570.

51. Elham Gheytanchi, in posting on Gulf/2000, "Re: Shia Suicide Bombers," October 31, 2006, used with permission.

52. For example, see Robert Baer, "The Making of a Suicide Bomber," *Sunday Times* (London), September 3, 2006. The former CIA operative wrote that "the origins of suicide bombing lie among the Shiite in Iran," and then described Fahmideh's case. Making no reference to how similar acts of sacrifice have also been canonized as "heroic" in U.S. military history, Baer states: "Normally it is not easy to persuade anyone to kill themselves. . . . To create a willing martyr like Fahmideh or Hasib Hussein you need to overwhelm every natural instinct. Suicide bombers are not born but indoctrinated. And it helps to have a cult that glorifies those who have blown themselves up and so encourage fresh recruits."

[For one American example, see that of U.S. Army Specialist Fourth Class George Alan Ingalls, memorialized at the Vietnam War Memorial in Washington, D.C., panel 18E, line 35. (His Medal of Honor citation praises "the risk of his life above and beyond the call of duty." A grenade "landed directly between Sp4c. Ingalls and a nearby comrade. Although he could have jumped to a safe position, Sp4c. Ingalls, in a spontaneous act of great courage, threw himself on the grenade and absorbed its full blast. The explosion mortally wounded Sp4c. Ingalls, but his heroic action saved the lives of the remaining members of his squad. His gallantry and selfless devotion to his comrades are in keeping with the highest traditions of the military service and reflect great credit . . .") Vietnam War Medal of Honor Recipients [A–L], US Army, at www.history .army.mil/html/moh/vietnam-a-l.html.

Likewise the online Wikipedia entry for *Istishhad*, or "act of martyrdom," describes the "origin of modern *Istishhadi* attacks lie among the Shia in Iran" during the Iran-Iraq War, and lists Fahmideh as the "first Muslim to have participated in such an attack in contemporary history." In fact, others suggest that among Muslims, a much earlier case may have been the "first martyr" of the Iranian Mojahedin-e Khalq (MKO/MEK), senior ideologue Ahmad Rezai, who in 1972 killed himself with a grenade to avoid arrest while surrounded by SAVAK agents. (Iranian-American blogger Pedram Moallemian in posting on Gulf/2000, "Re: Shia Suicide Bombers," November 2, 2006; and Ervand Abrahamian, *The Iranian Mojahedin* [New Haven, Conn.: Yale University Press, 1989], pp. 90, 129.)

In another case in 1972, three members of the Japanese Red Army, acting on behalf of the Popular Front for the Liberation of Palestine, launched a suicide attack on the Lod Airport in Tel Aviv that left twenty-four dead. In Iran, the MKO/MEK later carried out high-profile political suicide attacks against leaders of the revolutionary regime in 1981 and 1982. Lebanese Shiite suicide bombers drove the truck bombs in Beirut in 1983 that destroyed the U.S. Marines and French Military barracks, as well as the U.S. Embassy.

Former CIA operative Baer notes: "There's not a single known instance of an Iranian suicide bomber since the end of the Iran-Iraq War in 1988. There's also no evidence that Iran has ordered any suicide bombing attacks by proxies since the Israelis left Lebanon in 2000." (Robert Baer, *The Devil We Know: Dealing with the New Iranian Superpower* [New York: Crown, 2008], p. 205.)

53. Interviews and details of Fahmideh grave drawn from visit to Behesht-e Zahra cemetery, Tehran, February 6, 2009.
54. Anonymous "G2K member in Iran," posting on Gulf/2000, "Re: Shia Suicide Bombers/Suicide Schools?" November 2, 2006.
55. Koroush Mozouni, as reported in Tehran, March 8, 2009.
56. Communication with source in Tehran, March 25, 2009.
57. Interview with north Tehrani, Tehran, December 5, 1997; see also Peterson, "Islamic Martyrdom Holds Iranians to Hard Line."
58. Ram, *Myth and Mobilization in Revolutionary Iran*, p. 76.
59. Farhi, "The Antinomies of Iran's War Generation," pp. 103, 110.
60. Ibid., p. 117, n. 21.
61. Ram, *Myth and Mobilization in Revolutionary Iran*, p. 32.
62. Gieling, *Religion and War in Revolutionary Iran*, p. 32.
63. "Further on Khomeyni April 4 Speech on War," broadcast April 4, 1985, FBIS-SAS-85-016, as quoted in Daniel Brumberg, *Reinventing Khomeini: The Struggle for Reform in Iran* (Chicago: University of Chicago Press, 2001), p. 133.
64. Grand Ayatollah Mehdi Haeri Yazdi, as quoted in Vali Nasr, *The Shia Revival*, p. 120.
65. As quoted in Gieling, *Religion and War in Revolutionary Iran*, p. 118.
66. Sciolino, *Persian Mirrors*, pp. 177, 180.
67. Interviews with a "Westernized" Iranian, Tehran, November 25, 2007, and March 11, 2008.
68. The term "instrumental use" has several variations in Iran; one of the clearest descriptions can be found in Farhi, "The Antinomies of Iran's War Generation," p. 103.
69. As quoted in Sciolino, *Persian Mirrors*, p. 252.

3. CULTURAL KHATAMI: "WESTOXICATION"

Epigraph. Unnamed blog posting at www.weblog.omila.com, February 13, 2004, in Nasrin Alavi, *We Are Iran: The Persian Blogs* (London: Portobello, 2005), p. 10.

1. Maurice Danby Copithorne, "1996 UN Commission on Human Rights Report on the Situation of Human Rights in Iran," October 11, 1996.
2. Interviews with "Samira," a pseudonym, Tehran, September 17, 1996, and March 23, 1997; see also Scott Peterson, "Iran's Revolution Competes with Hollywood, CNN," September 24, 1996, and "In 'Decadent' Tehran, Islam Cracks the Whip," March 28, 1997, both in *Christian Science Monitor*.
3. Pahlavi, *Answer to History*, p. 189.
4. Dress code guidelines from reporting in Tehran, March 1997; see also a similar

rendition issued by the Martyr Ghodousi Judicial Center, as quoted in Alavi, *We Are Iran*, p. 25.

5. Khomeini, broadcast by Radio Iran from Qom, August 20, 1979, as cited in Amir Taheri, *The Spirit of Allah: Khomeini and the Islamic Revolution* (London: Hutchinson, 1985), pp. 263–64.

6. Interview with the Sage, Tehran, February 3, 1999.

7. Interview with the Sage, Tehran, December 9, 2003; see also Scott Peterson, "Iran's Revolution at 25: Out of Gas," *Christian Science Monitor*, February 11, 2004.

8. Reporting in Tehran, February 2004; prayer statistics from Mohammad-Ali Zam, head of Tehran's cultural and artistic organization, and excerpts of official report, as published in *Entekhab* newspaper, in "Drugs and Prostitution Rampant Among Youth: Govt Report," Agence France-Presse, July 5, 2000.

9. Interview with Iranian professional, Tehran, November 29, 1997; see also Scott Peterson, "Ecstasy in Iran, Agony for Its Clerics," *Christian Science Monitor*, December 5, 1997.

10. Internet blog by "School Friend," May 23, 2003, as quoted in Alavi, *We Are Iran*, pp. 118–19.

11. Interview with Louise Firouz, Kordan, November 25, 2002.

12. Interview with Sadegh Zibakalam, Tehran, February 2, 1999.

13. Jalal Al-e Ahmad, *Occidentosis: A Plague From the West* (Berkeley, Calif.: Mizan, 1984), translated by R. Campbell, annotated by Hamid Algar, pp. 26–28, 43–44, 64. The title in Persian is *Gharbzadegi* and means infatuated, mesmerized, stricken, or stung by Western culture. It is clearly difficult to render accurately in English, and translations include *Westoxication, Occidentosis, West-stricken-ness, Euromania,* and even *Xenomania*. The translator Campbell writes that Al-e Ahmad makes clear "the force of the metaphor is clinical and focuses on the coercive and invasive qualities of Western influence" (p. 138, n. 2). A discussion of the meaning is found in Roy Mottahedeh, *The Mantle of the Prophet: Religion and Politics in Iran* (1985; rept., Oxford, England: Oneworld, 2005), p. 296.

14. Nasr, *The Shia Revival*, p. 128.

15. Abrahamian, *Iran Between Two Revolutions*, pp. 466–67.

16. Hamid Dabashi, *Theology of Discontent: The Ideological Foundation of the Islamic Revolution in Iran* (1993; rept., New Brunswick, N.J.: Transaction, 2006), pp. 106, 145.

17. Ayatollah Ruhollah Khomeini, *Islamic Government*, series of speeches in Najaf, Iraq, between January 21 and February 8, 1970, as published in *Islam and Revolution*, p. 38.

18. "Text of Speech of the Eminent Leadership Grand [*sic*] Ayatollah Seyyed Ali Khamenei at the Opening Ceremony of the 8th Organization of the Islamic Conference Summit Meeting, Tehran, 9 December 1997," p. 7, as published in bound edition of five languages at the OIC conference.

19. Ibid., p. 14.

20. Khatami speech at OIC summit, official transcript, Tehran, December 9, 1997.

21. Mohammad Khatami, "On the Virtues of the West," *Time*, January 19, 1998.

22. Details of Khatami's resignation in Scott MacLeod, "Iran's Big Shift," *Time*, June 2, 1997.

23. Mohammad Khatami, May 24, 1992, original as found in Farsi at www .fa.wikisource.org/wiki/. Portions also appear in English at www.drsoroush .com/English/On_DrSoroush/E-CMO-20010000-The_Paradoxes_of_Politics _in_Post-Revolutionary_Iran.html and www.iranchamber.com/society/ar ticles/coming_to_terms_with_modernity1.php.

24. As quoted in "Khatami visits Khomeini's Tomb as First Public Venue," Agence France-Presse, May 26, 1997.

25. As quoted in "Warning to Iran's New President," Agence France-Presse, May 30, 1997.

26. Ibid.

27. Khomeini's "Letter to the Clergy," February 22, 1989, as quoted in Baqer Moin, *Khomeini: Life of the Ayatollah* (London: I. B. Taurus, 1999), pp. 285–86.

28. Interviews with Alireza Mahfouzian and Golnar Akasheh, Dizin, February 19, 2000, and Tehran, February 21, 2000. See also Scott Peterson, "The Young Seek a Freer, Less Clerical Iran," *Christian Science Monitor*, February 22, 2000.

29. Interview with Sadegh Zibakalam, Tehran, February 2, 1999.

30. Interview with the Sage and young man, Tehran, November 4, 1999.

31. Jim Muir, "Condoms Help Check Iran Birth Rate," BBC, April 24, 2002.

32. Scott Peterson, "An Unlikely Model for Family Planning," *Christian Science Monitor*, November 19, 1999.

33. Interview with the Sage, Tehran, September 23, 2003.

34. Details of Khamenei voting from visit to Supreme Leader compound and taxi afterward, Tehran, February 18, 2000.

35. Interview with French diplomat, Tehran, February 20, 2000; see also Scott Peterson, "Large Voter Turnout in Iran Favors President," *Christian Science Monitor*, February 22, 2000.

36. Azadeh Moaveni, *Lipstick Jihad: A Memoir of Growing Up Iranian in America and American in Iran* (New York: PublicAffairs, 2005), p. 194.

37. Interview with Sadegh Larijani, Qom, February 23, 2000.

38. All details and quotes drawn from performance of *Romeo and Juliet*, Tehran, July 5, 2000; see also Scott Peterson, "Romeo and Juliet Back in Tehran. But No Kisses," *Christian Science Monitor*, July 18, 2000.

39. Richard Corliss, "Tehran Master," *Time*, April 27, 1998.

40. Hamid Reza Sadr, *Iranian Cinema: A Political History* (London: I. B. Taurus, 2006), pp. 237–38.

41. Ibid., p. 245.

42. Rana Dogar, "An Iranian Dynasty: A Young Director Claims Her Own Spotlight," *Newsweek*, October 26, 1998; and quoted in Sadr, *Iranian Cinema*, p. 246.

43. Richard Corliss and Richard Schickel, "All-Time 100 Movies," *Time*, at www .time.com/time/2005/100movies/.

44. Interview with Manijeh Mir-'Emadi, Tehran, July 5, 2000.

45. Interview with Mohammad Soltanifar, Tehran, July 4, 2000.

46. Interview with "Ali Sufi," a pseudonym for an illegal video dealer, Tehran, July 4, 2000.

47. Azadeh Farahmand, "Perspectives on Recent (International Acclaim for) Ira-

nian Cinema," chapter in Richard Tapper, ed., *The New Iranian Cinema: Politics, Representation and Identity* (London: I. B. Taurus, 2002), pp. 88–89.

48. Sadr, *Iranian Cinema*, pp. 239–40.
49. Khatami and Seifollah Dad in *Hamshahri*, as quoted in "Iranian New Cinema Chief Pledges to Ease Stifling Restrictions on Filmmaking," Agence France-Presse, October 24, 1997.
50. *Resalat* as quoted in ibid.
51. Sadr, *Iranian Cinema*, p. 217.
52. Viewing of *Snowman*, Tehran, December 6, 1997; see also Scott Peterson, "Reluctant Nod to Cultural Shift: Iran Eases Ban on Its Own Films," *Christian Science Monitor*, December 23, 1997.
53. As described in Douglas Jehl, "Iranian Film Rocks Hotbed of Tradition," *New York Times*, January 1, 1998.
54. *Salam* as quoted in "Iran Transvestite Film Draws Militant Fire," Reuters, December 14, 1997.
55. *Salam* as quoted in Jehl, "Iranian Film Rocks Hotbed of Tradition."
56. As quoted in ibid.
57. Viewing of *Test of Democracy*, Tehran, July 9, 2000; see also Scott Peterson, "Romeo, Juliet Back in Tehran"; using original real-time translation and film script, Makhmalbaf Film House, "Testing Democracy Dialogue List (English)," at www.makhmalbaf.com/articles.php?a=455.
58. Mohsen Makhmalbaf interviewed by Hamid Dabashi in New York, October 1996, as published in Hamid Dabashi, *Close Up: Iranian Cinema, Past, Present and Future* (London: Verso, 2001), pp. 165–77.
59. As quoted in "Iranian Leader Warns Women Against Copying Western Feminist Trends," Agence France-Presse, October 22, 1997.
60. Barbie details and interviews drawn from reporting in Tehran, February 5–6, 1999; see also Scott Peterson, "Barbie Struts Into an Islamic Stronghold," *Christian Science Monitor*, February 17, 1999. "Trojan horse" quote in "Iran's Answer to Barbie," Associated Press, October 23, 1996.
61. As recounted by the Sage, Tehran, February 3, 1999.
62. Interview with the Sage, Tehran, November 4, 1999.
63. Algar, "Religious Forces in Twentieth-Century Iran," in *The Cambridge History of Iran*, pp. 739, 742.
64. Abrahamian, *Iran Between Two Revolutions*, p. 143.
65. Algar, "Religious Forces in Twentieth-Century Iran," p. 741.
66. Christopher de Bellaigue, *In the Rose Garden of the Martyrs: A Memoir of Iran* (London: HarperCollins, 2004), p. 94.
67. John Limbert as quoted in Wells, *444 Days*, p. 5.
68. As quoted in "Iran to Export Sara and Dara, the Islamic Barbie and Kenny," Iran Press Service, July 20, 2002.
69. Poem 38, *The Hafez Poems of Gertrude Bell* (Bethesda, Md.: Ibex, 2007), p. 137.
70. Ayatollah Ruhollah Khomeini, "The Drunkenness of the Lover," as published in *The Wine of Love: Mystical Poetry of Imam Khomeini* (Tehran: Institute for Compilation and Publication of Imam Khomeini's Works, 2003), p. 50.
71. Ayatollah Ruhollah Khomeini, "The Assembly of the Rogues," as published in *The Wine of Love*, p. 51.

72. Interviews with nose job women and doctors, Tehran, February 20–21, 2000; see also Scott Peterson, "In Iran, Search for Beauty Leads to the Nose Job," *Christian Science Monitor*, March 9, 2000.

73. Helena Smith, "Iranian Police Raid Shops to End the Scourge of Barbie," *Guardian*, May 25, 2002.

74. Islamic Republic News Agency (IRNA), as quoted in "Iran to Export Sara and Dara."

75. Porochista Khakpour, "Islamic Revolution Barbie," op-ed, *New York Times*, March 8, 2009.

76. Scott Peterson, "In Iran, Barbie Seen as Cultural Invader," *Christian Science Monitor*, September 15, 2008.

77. Practice session with underground rock band Shanti, Tehran, September 23, 2003; see also Scott Peterson, "You Say You Want a Revolution? Iran Bands Rock On," *Christian Science Monitor*, October 1, 2003.

78. Khomeini, broadcast by Tehran Radio from Qom, July 11, 1979, as cited in Taheri, *The Spirit of Allah*, p. 263.

79. Interview with the Sage, Tehran, September 21, 2003.

80. Figures for 2007, as listed in United Nations Office on Drugs and Crime (UNODC), "World Drug Report 2009," p. 53.

81. Tehran statistics in Scott Peterson, "A Whodunit With Gray Eminences—And Red Faces," *Christian Science Monitor*, July 31, 2000; and Ramin quoted in Scott Peterson, "Heroin Still Grips 1 Million Inside Iran," *Christian Science Monitor*, July 2, 1998.

82. Karl Vick, "Opiates of the Iranian People," *Washington Post*, September 23, 2005.

83. Figures in UNODC, "World Drug Report 2009," pp. 49–50.

84. Figures from IRNA, as reported in "Iran Has 1.2 Million Drug Addicts," Agence France-Presse, May 8, 2009, and Nazila Fathi, "Iran Fights Scourge of Addiction in Plain View, Stressing Treatment," *New York Times*, June 27, 2008.

85. As quoted in Vick, "Opiates of the Iranian People."

86. Ibid.

87. Interview with Seyyed Alireza Assar, Tehran, September 25, 2003.

88. *Pasdar-e Islam* monthly, no. 86, January/February 1989, as quoted in Moin, *Khomeini*, pp. 281–82.

89. As quoted in Douglas Jehl, "Iranians Warily Await Reforms They Voted For," *New York Times*, October 11, 1997.

90. Interview with "Siavash," a pseudonym, Tehran, March 19, 2005; see also Scott Peterson, "Iran Eases Its Social Strictures," *Christian Science Monitor*, April 15, 2005.

91. Douglas Jehl, "Teheran Journal; Who Says There's No Fun in an Islamic Republic?" *New York Times*, October 13, 1997.

92. As quoted in John Daniszewski, "Iran Loosens up," *Los Angeles Times*, December 23, 1997.

93. Internet blog of "Borderline," June 16, 2003, as quoted in Alavi, *We Are Iran*, p. 14.

94. Moaveni, *Lipstick Jihad*, pp. ix, 81–83.

95. Interview with Saeed Laylaz, Tehran, March 14, 2005.

96. *Jomhuri-e Eslami,* as quoted in Paul Hughes, "Flirting Youths Outrage Iranian Hardliners," Reuters, February 3, 2005.

97. Interview with young woman, Tehran, March 24, 2005; see also Peterson, "Iran Eases Its Social Strictures."

98. Interview with "Siavash," Tehran, November 16, 2007; see also Scott Peterson, "Young Iranians, Once Avid Reformers, Leave Politics Behind," *Christian Science Monitor,* March 14, 2008.

99. Internet blog at www.younessa.com, January 30, 2005, as quoted in Alavi, *We Are Iran,* p. 333.

100. De Bellaigue, "Stalled, May 2004," in *The Struggle for Iran,* p. 67.

101. Interviews with Hossein and others at Golestan Mall, Tehran, February 13, 2004; see also Scott Peterson, "Many Iranians Flaunt Their Style," *Christian Science Monitor,* February 19, 2004.

102. As quoted in Brian Murphy, "In Show of Defiance, Iranian Lawmakers Take On Ayatollah," Associated Press, February 18, 2004.

103. Internet blog of "Water Lily," September 21, 2003, as quoted in Alavi, *We Are Iran,* p. 15.

104. Internet blog of Ebrahim Nabavi, February 3, 2004, as quoted in Alavi, *We Are Iran,* p. 123.

105. Interviews with Mohammad Hossein Azemi, Tehran, February 11, 2004; see also Scott Peterson, "Among Iran's Hard-liners, Little Respect for Reform-Minded," *Christian Science Monitor,* February 14, 2004.

106. Interviews with Yaghoub Ramazani and Safar Esfandiareh, Tehran, February 13, 2004.

107. Interview with Alireza Yazdanbash and Revolutionary Guard officer, Tehran, February 11, 2004; see also Peterson, "Among Iran's Hard-liners, Little Respect for Reform-Minded."

108. Interview with Alireza Mahfouzian, Tehran, March 23, 2005; see also Peterson, "Iran Eases Its Social Strictures."

109. Interview with Hamid Reza Jalaeipour, Tehran, December 11, 2003.

110. Interviews with Alireza Mahfouzian, Tehran, November 21, 2007; February 17, 2008; and March 13, 2008.

111. Interviews with Parvaneh E'temadi, Tehran, February 21, 2004; see also Scott Peterson, "Iranian Artists Fear Throwback to Days of Censorship," *Christian Science Monitor,* March 4, 2004.

112. Interview with Manijeh Mir-'Emadi, Tehran, February 21, 2004; see also Peterson, "Iranian Artists Fear Throwback to Days of Censorship."

113. Screening of *Marmoulak (The Lizard),* and interviews with Kamal Tabrizi and Mustafa Elahi, Tehran, February 20, 2004; see also Peterson, "Iranian Artists Fear Throwback to Days of Censorship."

114. Interview with Hossein Shariatmadari, Tehran, February 21, 2004.

115. Interview with Farzad Motamen, Tehran, February 21, 2004; see also Peterson, "Iranian Artists Fear Throwback to Days of Censorship."

4. POLITICAL KHATAMI: THE ENEMY WITHIN

Epigraph. Ayatollah Ruhollah Khomeini, Qom, August 30, 1979, from the original Farsi at www.porseshhayebipasokh.blogfa.com/8408.aspx, and quoted with slight correction from Jalal Matini, "The Most Truthful Individual in Recent History," *Iranshenasi* 14, no. 4 (Winter 2003), as translated by Farhad Mafie and republished as "Democracy? I Meant Theocracy," *Iranian,* August 5, 2003, at www.iranian.com/Opinion/2003/August/Khomeini, and www.iran-heritage.org, among others.

1. Interview with *basiji* Alireza Yazdanbash, Tehran, February 11, 2004; see also Peterson, "Among Iran's Hardliners, Little Respect for Reform-Minded."
2. Brumberg, *Reinventing Khomeini*, pp. 99–100.
3. "Khomeini Delivers Speech on Freedom, Plots," broadcast May 25, 1979, FBIS-MEA-79-103, as quoted and cited in Brumberg, *Reinventing Khomeini*, p. 103.
4. *Constitution of the Islamic Republic of Iran* (Berkeley, Calif.: Mizan, 1980), original as translated by Hamid Algar, Articles 5 and 107, pp. 29, 66.
5. Ayatollah Ruhollah Khomeini, "Formation of the Council of the Islamic Revolution," declaration issued at Neauphle-le-Château, France, January 12, 1979, in *Islam and Revolution*, p. 247.
6. Interview with Morad Veisi, editor of *Yas-e No*, Tehran, December 13, 2003.
7. As quoted in Said Amir Arjomand, *The Turban for the Crown: The Islamic Revolution in Iran* (New York: Oxford University Press, 1988), p. 182.
8. Geneive Abdo and Jonathan Lyons, *Answering Only to God: Faith and Freedom in Twenty-First-Century Iran* (New York: Henry Holt, 2003), pp. 111–12.
9. *Jomhuri-e Eslami*, January 22, 1988, as quoted in Arjomand, *The Turban for the Crown*, pp. 182–83.
10. De Bellaigue, *In the Rose Garden of the Martyrs*, p. 226.
11. Interview with Ebrahim Yazdi, Tehran, September 20, 1996; see also Peterson, "Iran's Revolution Competes with Hollywood, CNN."
12. Interview with Ebrahim Yazdi, Tehran, March 10, 1997; see also Scott Peterson, "Voters in Iran to Decide Islam's Political Clout," *Christian Science Monitor,* March 18, 1997.
13. Interview with Sadegh Zibakalam, Tehran, February 2, 1999.
14. As quoted in Moin, *Khomeini*, p. 280.
15. Reporting in Tehran, November 29, 1997; see also Daniszewski, "Iran Loosens Up"; and vodka detail in Christopher Dickey, "Iran's Soccer Diplomacy," *Newsweek*, April 27, 1998.
16. Interview with Canadian diplomat, Tehran, December 1, 1997; see also Scott Peterson, "Ecstasy in Iran, Agony for Its Clerics," *Christian Science Monitor*, December 5, 1997.
17. Montazeri interview published in *Kayhan Havai*, February 8, 1989, as quoted in Moin, *Khomeini*, p. 280.
18. Montazeri speech published in *Kayhan*, February 12, 1989, as quoted in Moin, *Khomeini*, p. 281.
19. Details and quotation in Moin, *Khomeini*, p. 290.
20. Letter to Montazeri, as quoted in Moin, *Khomeini*, pp. 287–89.
21. Khomeini, "Letter to the Clergy," February 22, 1989, as quoted in Moin, *Khomeini*, p. 276.
22. Ahmad Khomeini, *Yadegar-e Imam*, vol. 6, p. 468, as quoted in Moin, *Khomeini*, p. 270.

23. Khomeini, "Letter to the Clergy," February 22, 1989, as quoted in Moin, *Khomeini*, p. 285.

24. Montazeri speech about the role of the *velayat-e faqih*, November 14, 1997, at www.amontazeri.com/Farsi/Khaterat/html/1521.htm; see also Peterson, "Ecstasy in Iran, Agony for Its Clerics."

25. Khamenei speech broadcast on state television, as quoted in Douglas Jehl, "Iranian Clerics Hint at Treason Trial for Cleric," *New York Times*, December 16, 1997.

26. Khamenei speech on state broadcasters as quoted in "Focus—Iran Leader Blasts Critics, Urges Calm," Reuters, November 26, 1997.

27. As quoted in "Focus—Iran Leader Blasts Critics, Urges Calm."

28. "Debate Brews in Iran Over Legitimacy of Supreme Leader," Agence France-Presse, November 19, 1997.

29. Stephen Kinzer, "Iran's New Policies Face Conservative Backlash," *New York Times*, November 22, 1997.

30. Sciolino, *Persian Mirrors*, p. 86.

31. "The Continuation of the Practical Method of Imam Ruhollah [Spirit of Allah]," Episode 16 of documentary series based on Islamic Republic of Iran Broadcasting (IRIB) archives, "The Practical Method of Imam Ruhollah," IRIB, June 3, 2008.

32. A similar version was reported at the time, in which Khomeini was said to have told his inner circle: "[But] you have Mr. Khamenei who is eligible." See also *Payam-e Emruz*, no. 21, 1997, p. 15, as quoted in Moin, *Khomeini*, p. 287.

33. *Constitution of the Islamic Republic of Iran*, Articles 5, 107, and 109, pp. 29–30, 66–67.

34. For a deeper discussion of the significance of the 1989 changes to the Constitution, see Brumberg, *Reinventing Khomeini*, pp. 109–10.

35. See, for example, Maziar Behrooz, "The Islamic State and the Crisis of Marja'iyat in Iran," *Comparative Studies of South Asia, Africa and the Middle East* 16, no. 2 (1996), as published online in "Leadership & Legitimacy," *Iranian*, January 2, 1997, at www.iranian.com/Opinion/Jan98/Behrooz/. See also "Grand [sic] Ayatollah Ali Khamenei," at www.globalsecurity.org/military/world/iran/khamenei.htm; and Peterson, "Ecstasy in Iran, Agony for Its Clerics."

36. Shaul Bakhash, *The Reign of the Ayatollahs: Iran and the Islamic Revolution* (New York: Basic Books, 1984), p. 19.

37. Interview with Grand Ayatollah Nasser Makarem Shirazi, Qom, December 2, 1997; see also Peterson, "Ecstasy in Iran, Agony for Its Clerics."

38. Interview with Swiss diplomat, Tehran, December 1, 1997; see also Scott Peterson, "Elusive in Iran: Real Power," *Christian Science Monitor*, December 14, 1997.

39. "Ansar-e Hezbollah, Khamenei's Helpers," *Iran Brief*, June 3, 1996, as quoted in Michael Rubin, *Into the Shadows: Radical Vigilantes in Khatami's Iran*, Policy Papers No. 56 (Washington, D.C.: Washington Institute for Near East Policy, 2001), pp. 59–60.

40. Rubin, *Into the Shadows*, p. xiv.

41. Interview with Reza Alavi, Tehran, November 16, 2007.

42. As described in Hamid Algar, "Religious Forces in Eighteenth- and Nineteenth-

Century Iran," chapter 19, in *The Cambridge History of Iran, Volume 7: From Nadir Shah to the Islamic Republic*, p. 712.

43. Ibid., p. 713.
44. Ibid., p. 721.
45. As sourced and described in ibid., p. 726.
46. All three examples are as described from Iranian and foreign histories in ibid., p. 718.
47. For a description of these efforts, see ibid., pp. 736–38.
48. Algar, "Religious Forces in Twentieth-Century Iran," in *The Cambridge History of Iran*, pp. 748–49.
49. Abrahamian, *Iran Between Two Revolutions*, p. 499.
50. Ibid., p. 508.
51. Interview with political scientist, Tehran, November 12, 2007.
52. Interview with political historian, Tehran, September 20, 2003.
53. Interview with Grand Ayatollah Yusef Saanei, Qom, November 9, 2002.
54. Interview with Ebrahim Yazdi, Tehran, February 3, 1999.
55. Interview with Ebrahim Yazdi, Tehran, February 8, 2009; see also Scott Peterson, "Khomeini Revered as Iran's Revolution Hits 30," *Christian Science Monitor*, February 10, 2009. A similar recounting by Yazdi appears in "I Knew Khomeini," Al Jazeera English documentary, presented by Rageh Omaar, broadcast February 2009. Yazdi says: "Well, several people talked to him that this is not the way, but in one of his statements he told me that if you want the Revolution to succeed and remain, sometimes you need to kill."
56. As quoted in Abdo and Lyons, *Answering Only to God*, p. 207.
57. Khamenei remarks on September 3, 1998, as rendered in Rubin, *Into the Shadows*, p. 62. The official transcript of Khamenei's speech on that day, at the graduation ceremony of Tarbiat Modares University, September 3, 1998, at www .leader.ir/langs/fa/index.php?p=bayanat&id=1654, uses these words: "This very 'social freedom' which is so highly valued in Islam is harmful, if used to spoil a nation's spiritual or material fruits . . ." and "Of course if anybody takes action against the country's interest, his freedom would become restricted, which is logical."
58. As quoted in Afshin Valinejad, "Iran Leaders Assaulted by Militants," Associated Press, September 4, 1998. Ansar statement in "Political Group Says It Was Not Involved in Attack Against Officials," IRNA, September 5, 1998, as quoted and cited in Rubin, *Into the Shadows*, pp. 62–63.
59. Interview with the Sage, Tehran, September 23, 2003.
60. Abdo and Lyons, *Answering Only to God*, pp. 138–39.
61. Details and quotations from Montazeri's 1999 fatwa in ibid., pp. 140–43.
62. Montazeri had made a similar point a decade earlier, in his speech to mark the Revolution's tenth anniversary, as quoted in Moin, *Khomeini*, p. 280. In that 1989 speech, which prompted his censure by Khomeini, Montazeri said: "If they censor me what can others expect?"
63. Interview with Emadeddin Baghi, Tehran, November 6, 1999; see also Scott Peterson, "The Battle of the Pen in Iran," *Christian Science Monitor*, November 8, 1999.
64. Interview with Asian diplomat, Tehran, November 3, 1999.

65. Interview with Hamid Reza Jalaeipour, Tehran, June 23, 1998; see also Scott Peterson, "Iranian Revelations as Press Tests New Freedom," *Christian Science Monitor*, June 29, 1998.

66. Safavi and Mohajerani in *Jameah* and *Hamshahri* newspapers, as quoted in "Iran's Revolutionary Guards Chief Threatens to Crack Down on Liberal Dissent," Agence France-Presse, April 29, 1998.

67. "Khatami Cautions Against Narrow-Mindedness," *Iran Daily*, June 24, 1998.

68. As quoted in Scott MacLeod, "Testing the Tehran Spring," *Time*, May 18, 1998.

69. Peterson, "Iranian Revelations as Press Tests New Freedom," and Khamenei speech, variously quoted, at "Iranian Leader Orders Government to Restrict Liberal Press," Agence France-Presse, September 15, 1998.

70. As quoted in *Kayhan* (Farsi), September 27, 1998; see also Scott Peterson, "Power Struggle in Iran Clouds View for US Policymakers," *Christian Science Monitor*, October 16, 1998.

71. Interview with Akbar Ganji, Tehran, November 6, 1999; see also Scott Peterson, "The Battle of the Pen in Iran."

72. Events of late 1998, as described to me by the targeted journalist in Tehran, February 2009.

73. Abdolkarim Soroush explains his controversial role in this council in an interview, "Intellectual Autobiography," chapter 1, in Mahmoud Sadri and Ahmad Sadri, trans. and eds., *Reason, Freedom, & Democracy in Islam: Essential Writings of Abdolkarim Soroush* (New York: Oxford University Press, 2000), pp. xi, 11–13, 199–200, n. 6.

74. Ayatollah Ruhollah Khomeini, "The Meaning of the Cultural Revolution," address to students on April 26, 1980, in *Islam and Revolution*, pp. 295–98.

75. Abdolkarim Soroush, in *Tous*, December 1, 1997, as quoted in *Akhbaar Ruz* 18, no. 173, December 6, 1997.

76. Interview with Abdolkarim Soroush, Tehran, December 7, 1997; see also Peterson, "Elusive in Iran: Real Power."

77. Afshin Valinejad, "Iranian President Marks Year in Office," Associated Press, May 23, 1998.

78. "Excerpts from President Khatami's Anniversary Speech," BBC Monitoring, May 23, 1998.

79. As quoted in "Mass Iranian Turnout for Khatami Hailed as Endorsement of His Reforms," Agence France-Presse, May 24, 1998.

80. Afshin Valinejad, "Iran Pro-Democracy Rally Attacked," Associated Press, May 25, 1998.

81. As quoted in "Several Injured as Fundamentalists Attack Pro-Khatami Students," Agence France-Presse, May 25, 1998.

82. Valinejad, "Iran Pro-Democracy Rally Attacked."

83. Interview with the Sage, Tehran, June 21, 1998; see also Scott Peterson, "Victory Over US Plays Into Iran's Big Debate," *Christian Science Monitor*, June 23, 1998.

84. As reported by journalists for the *Guardian* and Reuters in a detailed account of the protests, in Abdo and Lyons, *Answering Only to God*, p. 197.

85. Interview with Shirzad Bozorgmehr, by telephone to Tehran, July 10, 1999;

see also Scott Peterson, "Struggle for Iran's Reins of Power," *Christian Science Monitor*, July 12, 1999.

86. Mehrdad Balali, "Angry Students Mount Pressure on Khamenei," Reuters, July 11, 1999; see also Abdo and Lyons, *Answering Only to God*, pp. 203–4.

87. Khomeini, "The Meaning of the Cultural Revolution," in *Islam and Revolution*, p. 298.

88. Khomeini, as quoted in Kifner, "How a Sit-In Turned Into a Siege."

89. Account of Kasrani from BBCPersian.com, as published in "Iran Student Protests: Five Years On," BBC News, July 9, 2004.

90. As quoted in Alavi, *We Are Iran*, pp. 317–18.

91. Judge as quoted in Scott Shane and Michael R. Gordon, "Dissident's Tale of Epic Escape From Iran's Vise," *New York Times*, July 13, 2008.

92. Letter as quoted in Abdo and Lyons, *Answering Only to God*, pp. 229–30.

93. Details of prison, mock hanging, and escape to northern Iraq and the United States in Shane and Gordon, "Dissident's Tale."

94. Interview with Ebrahim Yazdi, by telephone to Tehran, July 10, 1999.

95. "Statement in Support of the Spontaneous Movement of Tehran University Students and the Declaration of the Position of the United Student Front," July 10, 1999, as quoted in Robin Wright, *The Last Great Revolution: Turmoil and Transformation in Iran* (New York: Knopf, 2000), p. 265.

96. Details in Sciolino, *Persian Mirrors*, pp. 278–79.

97. As quoted in Ali Raiss-Tousi, "Police and Students Clash Again in Iran," Reuters, July 12, 1999.

98. "Full Text of Khatami's Speech" on national television, July 13, 1999, BBC Monitoring, July 15, 1999.

99. As quoted in Jonathan Lyons, "Analysis—Rules of the Game Change in Khatami's Iran," Reuters, July 12, 1999; and in Jim Muir, "Analysis: Khatami at the Crossroads," BBC News, July 14, 1999.

100. Interviews with student demonstrators, Tehran, November 7, 1999.

101. Details from wire reports and Sciolino, *Persian Mirrors*, pp. 277–78.

102. Rubin, *Into the Shadows*, p. 67.

103. Interview with government official, Tehran, November 3, 1999.

104. Interview with "Pejman," a pseudonym, and other students, Tehran, November 7, 1999; see also Scott Peterson, "A Look Inside Iran's Student Cause," *Christian Science Monitor*, November 22, 1999.

105. Interview with Hamid Reza Jalaeipour, Tehran, April 28, 2000.

106. Interview with the Sage, Tehran, April 29, 2000.

107. Abdo and Lyons, *Answering Only to God*, p. 204; and Ali Raiss-Tousi, "Iran Family at Last Buries Victim of July Unrest," Reuters, May 24, 2000.

108. Visit to student offices and interview with Ebrahim Sheikh, Tehran, July 5, 2000; see also Scott Peterson, "Iran Tries Peaceful Revolution," *Christian Science Monitor*, July 7, 2000.

109. As witnessed by author, Tehran, July 9, 2000; see also Scott Peterson, "Peace Rally in Iran Turns Wild," *Christian Science Monitor*, July 10, 2000.

110. Details from visit to Special Court for Clergy, Tehran, November 9, 1999; see also Scott Peterson, "Iran Power Struggle: Clerics Duel," *Christian Science Monitor*, November 10, 1999.

111. Peterson, "Victory Over US Plays Into Iran's Big Debate."

112. "Abdollah Nouri's Explanations in Court Have Convinced the Public of His Guilt," *Kayhan*, November 29, 1999, as quoted in Rubin, *Into the Shadows*, p. 71.

113. "Hezbollah Member Reveals Plots Against Reformists," *Sharq al-Awsat*, June 4, 2000, as quoted in Rubin, *Into the Shadows*, p. 73.

114. Interview with Abdollah Nouri, Tehran, November 12, 2007.

115. Details of SNSC report and court case drawn from Rubin, *Into the Shadows*, pp. 69–75.

116. As quoted in "July Unrest Police Trial, Second Session," IranMania, March 4, 2000.

117. "Student Anger at Police Acquittal," BBC News, July 11, 2000.

118. Interview with Gholam Hossein Karbaschi, Tehran, December 7, 1997; see also Scott Peterson, "Tehran's Mayor, Who Turned City Green, Draws Wrath of Hard-Line Clerics," *Christian Science Monitor*, December 15, 1997.

119. As quoted in "Tehran Mayor Denies Corruption Charges as Trial Opens," Agence France-Presse, June 7, 1998.

120. Interview with Saeed Hajjarian, Tehran, November 20, 2007; see also political reactions in Scott Peterson, "Are Hard-liners Taking Aim at Reformists?" *Christian Science Monitor*, March 13, 2000.

121. As described in Shirin Ebadi with Azadeh Moaveni, *Iran Awakening: A Memoir of Revolution and Hope* (New York: Random House, 2006), p. 137.

122. Ibid., pp. xiv–xv.

123. Official and hard-line reaction as quoted in Scott Peterson, "Iran's Arrests of Intelligence Officers May Be Watershed," *Christian Science Monitor*, January 8, 1999.

124. "No Safe Haven: Iran's Global Assassination Campaign," Iran Human Rights Documentation Center, May 2008, pp. 2–3, at www.iranhrdc.org.

125. Khomeini, as quoted in Sahifeh Nour, *The Complete Collection of Imam Khomeini's Guidelines*, vol. 5 (Center for Collection of the Culture Documents of the Islamic Revolution, 1983), p. 236, as cited in ibid., p. 5.

126. I met Salahuddin a number of times over several years in Tehran, where he worked in unhappy exile as a journalist and editor, and was frequently critical of manifest shortcomings of the Islamic Republic. Despite nearly three decades outside America, his accent had hardly changed, and he kept fully up to date on all U.S. and global news.

127. Thomas Sancton, "The Tehran Connection," *Time*, March 21, 1994.

128. Execution order signed by Mousavi Tabrizi, "Topic: Manouchehr Ganji, Ex-Minister," March 17, 1993, as reproduced as appendix in "No Safe Haven: Iran's Global Assassination Campaign," p. 56.

129. Statement published by IRNA, as quoted in Afshin Valinejad, "Iran Officials Arrested in Slayings," Associated Press, January 7, 1999.

130. As recounted in Ebadi, *Iran Awakening*, pp. 138–39.

131. Interview with Sadegh Zibakalam, Tehran, February 2, 1999.

132. Interview with Sadegh Zibakalam, by telephone to Tehran, January 7, 1999.

133. Ebadi, *Iran Awakening*, p. 141.

134. Visits to *Tarh-e No* offices, Tehran; see also Peterson, "A Whodunit With Gray Eminences—And Red Faces."

135. Interview with Reza Alavi, Tehran, July 4, 2000.

136. For a detailed account of the Mykonos killings, see "Murder at Mykonos: Anatomy of a Political Assassination," Iran Human Rights Documentation Center, March 2007, at www.iranhrdc.org.

137. Interview with Swiss diplomat, Tehran, July 4, 2000.

138. "Iran's Rafsanjani Says Reformers Behind Excesses," Reuters, January 26, 2000.

139. Interview with Hassan Ghafouri Fard, Tehran, July 8, 2000.

140. Interviews with Hossein Paya, Tehran, July 5 and 9, 2000.

141. Akbar Ganji, "Letter to the Free People of the World," June 29, 2005, as quoted in Akbar Ganji, *The Road to Democracy in Iran* (Cambridge, Mass.: MIT Press, 2008), pp. xvii, xx–xxii.

142. Interview with Iranian academic, Tehran, December 5, 2005.

143. Interview with Saeed Hajjarian, Tehran, November 20, 2007; see also Afshin Valinejad, "Iranians Urged to Pray for Gravely Wounded Reformer," Associated Press, March 13, 2000.

144. Interview with Ebrahim Yazdi, Tehran, February 3, 1999.

145. Peterson, "Are Hard-liners Taking Aim at Reformists?"

146. Visit to Saeed Hajjarian, Tehran, July 8, 2000; see also Peterson, "Peace Rally in Iran Turns Wild."

147. Interview with Saeed Hajjarian, Tehran, November 20, 2007.

148. Visit to reformist meeting to mark anniversary of Hajjarian shooting, Tehran, March 8, 2008.

149. Interview and campaign town hall meeting with Fatemeh Haghighatjou, February 15, 2000; see also Scott Peterson, "Women, Youth Key to Iran Vote," *Christian Science Monitor*, February 17, 2000.

150. Interview with Fatemeh Haghighatjou, Tehran, April 24, 2000; see also Scott Peterson, "Iran's Young 'Rookie' Lawmakers," *Christian Science Monitor*, April 27, 2000.

151. Graffiti on Tehran wall, April 27, 2000.

152. Interview with the Sage, Tehran, February 15, 2000.

153. Reporting at student sit-in, Tehran, April 24, 2000.

154. Interview with Zeinab Bolooki and Morteza Ahroon, Behesht-e Zahra cemetery, Tehran, November 8, 2002; see also Scott Peterson, "In Iran, a 'Second Revolution' Gathers Steam," *Christian Science Monitor*, November 29, 2002.

155. That figure of 84 percent IRGC support was several percentage points higher for Khatami than he received from the rest of the population, which in 2001 had given him a second-term landslide victory, with 79 percent of the voters from just a 67 percent turnout. A similarly significant IRGC endorsement had come in 1997, when Khatami was first elected, winning nearly 70 percent of the votes cast. Back then, the rank-and-file IRGC gave Khatami a 73 percent endorsement. Statistical evaluation of Ministry of Culture and Islamic Guidance, and senior officials, as cited in Wilfried Buchta, *Who Rules Iran? The Structure of Power in the Islamic Republic* (Washington, D.C.: Washington Institute for Near East Policy, 2000), p. 125.

156. Discussions with Iranian professional, Tehran, November 6 and 8, 2002.

157. Interview with British diplomat, Tehran, November 5, 2002.

158. Jim Muir, "Iran Press Gagged After Cleric's Attack," BBC News, July 11, 2002.

159. Taheri letter as quoted by Jim Muir, "Cleric Denounces Iran 'Chaos,' " BBC News, July 10, 2002.

160. Editorial and Montazeri quotes in Jim Muir, "Iran Death Sentence Angers Reformists," BBC News, November 9, 2002.

161. As quoted in Peterson, "In Iran, a 'Second Revolution' Gathers Steam."

162. Interview with Iranian professor, Tehran, November 8, 2002.

163. "Iran Hardliners Stage Show of Strength," BBC News, November 24, 2002.

164. Interview with the Sage, Tehran, November 5, 2002.

165. Khatami speaking to parliament, as quoted in "Khatami Rejects 'Dictatorship' Claims," BBC News, October 20, 2002; see also Scott Peterson, "In Iran, a Challenge to Hard-liners," *Christian Science Monitor*, November 14, 2002.

166. Interview with French diplomat, Tehran, November 6, 2002.

167. Reporting at student rally, Tehran University, November 12, 2002; see also Peterson, "In Iran, a Challenge to Hard-liners."

168. Visit to student rally, Amirkabir University, Tehran, November 13, 2003; see also Peterson, "In Iran, a Challenge to Hard-liners."

169. Rafsanjani at Friday prayers, Voice of Islamic Republic of Iran radio, as quoted by BBC News, November 1, 2002.

170. Interview with student Sassan, Tehran, December 9, 2003.

171. Interview with Shahriar Rouhani, by telephone to Tehran, June 14, 2003; see also Scott Peterson, "Iran's Angry Young Adults Erupt in Political Protest," *Christian Science Monitor*, June 16, 2003.

172. Interview with the Sage, by telephone to Tehran, June 14, 2003; see also Peterson, "Iran's Angry Young Adults."

173. Interview with Grand Ayatollah Yusef Saanei, Qom, December 14, 2003; see also Peterson, "Iran's Revolution at 25: Out of Gas."

174. Poll and details in Scott Peterson, "In Iran, Hopes for Democracy Dwindle," *Christian Science Monitor*, December 18, 2003.

175. Ahmad Jannati speaking at Friday prayers, as quoted in "Top Scholar Contradicts Khatami," Agence France-Presse, December 12, 2003; and in Peterson, "In Iran, Hopes for Democracy Dwindle."

176. Interview with Grand Ayatollah Saanei, Qom, December 14, 2003; see also Peterson, "In Iran, Hopes for Democracy Dwindle." The framed saying of Khomeini praising Saanei hangs on the senior cleric's wall and cites as its source "Imam's *Sahifeh Nour*, vol. 17, p. 231."

177. Interview with Grand Ayatollah Hossein-Ali Montazeri, Qom, December 14, 2003; see also Peterson, "In Iran, Hopes for Democracy Dwindle."

178. As quoted in "Iranian Dissident Says Hard-liners Should Submit to Elections," Associated Press, September 17, 2003; see also Scott Peterson, "Hard-liners in Iran Soften Their Edges," *Christian Science Monitor*, October 31, 2003.

179. Interview with Hossein Shariatmadari, Tehran, December 16, 2003; see also Peterson, "In Iran, Hopes for Democracy Dwindle."

180. As quoted in "Ms. Shirin Ebadi Interview by Radio Farda: Ganji Edging Closer to Death Each Day Due to His Brave Resistance," Radio Farda, July 7, 2005, at www.radiofarda.com/content/article/304628.html; and "Shirin Ebadi at Tehran Press Conference," Iranian Students News Agency (ISNA), October 15, 2003, at www.isna.ir/ISNA/NewsView.aspx?ID=News-296167.

181. Interview with Hamid Reza Jalaeipour, Tehran, December 11, 2003.
182. The hard-line *Jomhuri-e Eslami*, in a clear effort to show the scale of Ebadi's disrespect, was the only newspaper to run a full photograph of Ebadi accepting the Nobel—without a headscarf. See "The Nobel 21 Billion Toman Award Transferred to Shirin Ebadi's Account," *Jomhuri-e Eslami*, December 21, 2003, at www.jomhourieslami.com/1382/13820920/index.html; and Scott Peterson, "Iran's Nobel Winner Doesn't Make the News at Home," *Christian Science Monitor*, December 12, 2003.
183. As quoted in Scott Peterson, "Showdown Over Democracy's Boundaries in Iran," *Christian Science Monitor*, February 3, 2004.
184. Ibid.
185. Interview with Fatemeh Haghighatjou, Tehran, February 11, 2004; see also Scott Peterson, "Iran's Young Elite Face Trial by Fire," *Christian Science Monitor*, February 13, 2004.
186. As quoted in Peterson, "Hard-liners in Iran Soften Their Edges."
187. Khatami speech at Twenty-fifth Anniversary of Revolution, Tehran, February 11, 2004.
188. As quoted in Alavi, *We Are Iran*, p. 321.
189. Interview with Mohammad Reza Khatami, Tehran, September 23, 2003; see also Peterson, "Hard-liners in Iran Soften Their Edges."
190. Interview with Iranian analyst, Tehran, December 9, 2005.
191. Interview with the Sage, Tehran, February 14, 2002.
192. Interview with the Sage, Tehran, November 5, 2002.
193. Details and Khamenei as quoted in "Iran's Supreme Leader Quashes Press Reform Bid," Reuters, August 6, 2000.
194. Interview with professor, Tehran, September 2003.
195. Interview with Amir Mohebian, Tehran, September 16, 2003; see also Peterson, "Hard-liners in Iran Soften Their Edges."
196. Interview with Amir Mohebian, Tehran, February 19, 2004.
197. Interview with Ali Abtahi, Tehran, September 23, 2003.
198. Interviews with the Sage, Tehran, February 2 and 9, 2004; see also Peterson, "Iran's Revolution at 25: Out of Gas."
199. Interview with computer specialist "Samira," a pseudonym, Tehran, February 3, 1999.
200. Blogger "arareza," at www.dentist.blogspot.com, January 8, 2004, as quoted in Alavi, *We Are Iran*, p. 8.
201. Behzad Nabavi press conference, Tehran, June 13, 2005; see also Scott Peterson, "In Iran: Hope Battles Apathy," *Christian Science Monitor*, June 13, 2005.
202. Interview with Nasser Hadian-Jazy, Tehran, March 12, 2005.
203. Interviews with Western diplomats, Tehran, June 2005; see also Scott Peterson, "Familiar Face Emerges in Iran Vote," *Christian Science Monitor*, April 26, 2005.
204. Visit to Rafsanjani campaign meeting, Tehran, June 11, 2005.
205. *Jomhuri-e Eslami*, June 11, 2005.
206. "Khatami Defends His Government Achievements," June 11, 2005, official site of "Presidency of the Islamic Republic of Iran—News Archive," at www

.former.president.ir/khatami/eng/cronicnews/1384/8403/840321/index-e .htm#b2; see also Scott Peterson, "As Reformer Exits, Who Will Lead Iran?" *Christian Science Monitor*, June 17, 2005.

207. Rafsanjani campaign concert, Tehran, June 14, 2005; see also Scott Peterson, "Iran Politicians Woo the Young," and "Reporters on the Job: Follow the Music," both *Christian Science Monitor*, June 16, 2005.

208. Reporting at reformist election rally, Tehran, June 14, 2005; see also Peterson, "Iran Politicians Woo the Young."

209. Reporting at reformist election rally, Tehran, June 14, 2005; see also Peterson, "Iran Politicians Woo the Young."

5. AHMADINEJAD: THE MESSIAH HOTLINE

Epigraph. Ahmadinejad speaking to clerics at Imam Reza shrine, Mashhad, as broadcast on Iranian TV's Channel One, May 5, 2008, as translated in "Iranian President Says US President's Life 'Empty,' " BBC Monitoring, May 6, 2008.

1. Scott Peterson, "In Iran, a Campaign Ad Is High Art," *Christian Science Monitor*, June 24, 2005.

2. Reporting of the Ahmadinejad video, and also at www.dr-chamran.blogfa .com/8803.aspx.

3. Press conference with Mahmoud Ahmadinejad, Tehran, June 19, 2005; see also Scott Peterson, "Iran Votes Hard-liner Into Runoff," *Christian Science Monitor*, June 20, 2005.

4. Detail of second-round voting day and interviews, Tehran, June 24, 2005; see also Scott Peterson, "Rise of Hard-liner Baffles Iran's Political Elite," *Christian Science Monitor*, June 24, 2005.

5. Abbas Milani, "Pious Populist: Understanding the Rise of Iran's President," *Boston Review*, November/December 2007, at www.bostonreview.net/BR32.6/ milani.php.

6. Peterson, "Rise of Hard-liner Baffles Iran's Political Elite."

7. Scott Peterson, "Iran's New Hard-liner Maps Path," *Christian Science Monitor*, June 27, 2005.

8. Max Rodenbeck, "Correspondent's Diary: Splendid Isolation," *Economist*, March 14, 2008.

9. Voting-day interviews, Tehran, June 24, 2005; see also Peterson, "Rise of Hard-liner Baffles Iran's Political Elite."

10. As described in Kasra Naji, *Ahmadinejad: The Secret History of Iran's Radical Leader* (London: I. B. Tauris, 2008), p. 32.

11. Ibid., pp. 34–35.

12. Milani, "Pious Populist."

13. Ibid.

14. According to a "close associate of Ahmadinejad," as reported in Naji, *Ahmadinejad*, p. 46.

15. Jalal Yaghoubi, "Ahmadinejad and the Abadgaran," December 19, 2005, from the website of the Union of the Republicans of Iran, as quoted and cited in Naji, *Ahmadinejad*, p. 47, and at www.jomhouri.com/a/03art/005010.php.

16. Ali M. Ansari, *Iran Under Ahmadinejad: The Politics of Confrontation*, Adelphi Paper 393 (London: International Institute for Strategic Studies/Routledge, 2007), p. 23.

17. Ibid., pp. 23-24.

18. Ibid., pp. 16-17.

19. Naji, *Ahmadinejad*, p. 39.

20. Among numerous reports, see Pam O'Toole, "Two Reformers Face Quandary," BBC News, June 18, 2005; and "Iran Hard-liner Appeals For Votes," BBC News, June 22, 2005.

21. Letter of Moin's supporters to Ayatollah Khamenei, June 20, 2005, at www .mag.gooya.com/president84/archives/031508.php, as quoted in Naji, *Ahmadinejad*, pp. 74-75.

22. ISNA, June 20, 2005, as quoted in Naji, *Ahmadinejad*, p. 74.

23. Interview with the Sage, Tehran, June 25, 2005; see also Peterson, "Iran's New Hard-liner Maps Path."

24. Interview with Mohammad Atrianfar, Tehran, June 25, 2005; see also Peterson, "Iran's New Hard-liner Maps Path."

25. As described in Milani, "Pious Populist."

26. Naji, *Ahmadinejad*, pp. 76-77.

27. As detailed in Frederic Wehrey et al., *The Rise of the Pasdaran: Assessing the Domestic Roles of Iran's Revolutionary Guards Corps* (Santa Monica, Calif.: RAND National Defense Research Institute, 2009), esp. chapters 4 and 5; membership figures as detailed on p. 44.

28. Khomeini speech on occasion of anniversary of "Imposed War," *Tehran Times*, September 23, 1982, as quoted and cited in Zabih, *The Iranian Military in Revolution and War*, p. 157.

29. Khomeini quoted in Hamid Ansari, "Imam Khomeini's Direct Order And Testaments To The Armed Forces," 26 November 2007, as quoted and cited in Wehrey et al., *The Rise of the Pasdaran*, p. 78.

30. Zahra Ebrahimi, "It Must Work Much More Closely," *Shargh*, July 14, 2005, at www.iran.-emrooz.net/index.php?/news2/print/2829/, as quoted in Anoushiravan Ehteshami and Mahjoob Zweiri, *Iran and the Rise of Its Neoconservatives: The Politics of Tehran's Silent Revolution* (London: I. B. Tauris, 2007), p. 84.

31. Ibid.

32. Naji, *Ahmadinejad*, p. 78.

33. As described in ibid., p. 79.

34. As quoted in ibid.

35. Interview with city engineer, Tehran, March 19, 2005; see also Scott Peterson, "How Well Are Hard-liners Running Tehran?" *Christian Science Monitor*, April 11, 2005.

36. Interview with Hossein Shariatmadari, Tehran, December 16, 2003; see also Peterson, "In Iran, Hopes for Democracy Dwindle."

37. Naji, *Ahmadinejad*, p. 52.

38. Ansari, *Iran Under Ahmadinejad*, p. 29.

39. "Unveiling of the Graves for Unidentified Martyrs in the Imam Hossein University Dormitory: Brig. Gen. Baqerzadeh: 'Unidentified Martyrs Are Lying in

About 460 Commemoration Sites,' " *Kayhan*, April 28, 2007, at www.magiran .com/npview.asp?ID=1392800.

40. Details of clashes and activist Delbari quoted in Golnaz Esfandiari, "Iran: Students Protest Burials of War Dead on Tehran Campuses," Radio Free Europe/Radio Liberty/RFE/RL (Prague), March 15, 2006.
41. Interview with Amir Mohebian, Tehran, March 12, 2005.
42. Interview with Mostafa Tajzadeh, Tehran, March 16, 2005.
43. Naji, *Ahmadinejad*, p. 53.
44. Interview with Mohammad Atrianfar, Tehran, March 17, 2005.
45. Interview with Karim Sadjadpour, Tehran, June 14, 2005; see also Scott Peterson, "How Iran's Reformers Lost Their Political Way," *Christian Science Monitor*, July 1, 2005.
46. Mehdi Kalhor interview by Germany-based Mohajer satellite television network, transcript printed in *Etemaad*, June 29, 2005, as translated in "Iran Press: Ahmadinejad's Advisor Speaks About a Freer Society Under Him," BBC Monitoring, document BBCMEP0020050629e16t005sd, June 29, 2005; in Farsi at "Los Angeles Singers Come As Well," June 28, 2005, at www.topiranian .com/news/archives/003499.html. See also Peterson, "How Iran's Reformers Lost Their Political Way" and "Iran's Ahmadinejad to Go East on Fashion and Music: Aide," Agence France-Presse, June 28, 2005.
47. Reporting on debate in Parliament, Tehran, November 14, 2007; see also Scott Peterson, "In Iran, Ahmadinejad's Bold Gambits Boost Presidential Power," *Christian Science Monitor*, December 10, 2007.
48. Ehteshami and Zweiri, *Iran and the Rise of Its Neoconservatives*, pp. 90–91.
49. Mostafa Tajzadeh, deputy interior minister for political affairs, as quoted in "Iran: Ahmadinejad's Tumultuous Presidency," Middle East Briefing No. 21, International Crisis Group (Brussels), February 6, 2007, p. 4.
50. As tabulated in Wehrey et al., *The Rise of the Pasdaran*, p. 77.
51. Naji, *Ahmadinejad*, p. 212.
52. As recounted in ibid., p. 227.
53. Wehrey et al., *The Rise of the Pasdaran*, 77.
54. As quoted in Kim Murphy, "Iran's $12-Billion Enforcers—From Road-Building to Laser Eye Surgery, the Revolutionary Guard Dominates the Economy," *Los Angeles Times*, August 26, 2007.
55. Ehteshami and Zweiri, *Iran and the Rise of Its Neoconservatives*, p. 83.
56. Behrus Khlique, "The Position of the Guards and the Clergy in the Power Structure," www.falsafeh.com/sepah_khaligh.htm, as cited in Naji, *Ahmadinejad*, p. 258.
57. As detailed in Murphy, "Iran's $12-Billion Enforcers," and Wehrey et al., *The Rise of the Pasdaran*, p. 59.
58. Murphy, "Iran's $12-Billion Enforcers," and "Iran: Ahmadinejad's Tumultuous Presidency," p. 12.
59. Murphy, "Iran's $12-Billion Enforcers."
60. Interviews with clerics Seyyed Reza Boraei and Mojtaba Lotfi, Qom, December 6, 2005; see also Scott Peterson, "Iran's Leader Drawing Fire," *Christian Science Monitor*, December 12, 2005.
61. Interview with economist, Tehran, February 17, 2008.

62. Interview with Amir Mohebian, Tehran, December 10, 2005; see also Scott Peterson, "Waiting for the Rapture in Iran."

63. "Address by H.E. Dr. Mahmood Ahmadinejad, President of the Islamic Republic of Iran before the Sixtieth Session of the United Nations General Assembly, New York—17 September 2005," official transcript, Islamic Republic of Iran, Permanent Mission to the UN.

64. Video of Ahmadinejad speaking to Ayatollah Javadi Amoli, as seen in Tehran, December 2005; see among others Golnaz Esfandiari, "Iran: President Says Light Surrounded Him During UN Speech," RFE/RL, November 29, 2005.

65. As recounted in Naji, *Ahmadinejad*, p. 92.

66. Gieling, *Religion and War in Revolutionary Iran*, p. 121.

67. Khamenei, Iranian news source, 16/8/59 (1980), as quoted and cited in Gieling, *Religion and War in Revolutionary Iran*, p. 122.

68. Mehdi Khalaji, "Apocalyptic Politics: On the Rationality of Iranian Policy," Washington Institute for Near East Policy, Policy Focus No. 79, January 2008, p. vii.

69. Abbas Amanat, *Apocalyptic Islam and Iranian Shi'ism* (London: I. B. Tauris, 2009), pp. 226, 236.

70. Ibid., pp. 229–30.

71. Visit to Jamkaran mosque and prayer hall, December 6, 2005; see also Scott Peterson, "Worshippers Wail for Redemption Before Mahdi's Second Coming," *Christian Science Monitor*, December 21, 2005.

72. Khalaji, "Apocalyptic Politics," pp. viii, 14.

73. Quoted in Safinat ol Behar, vol. 1, p. 500, as cited in Ayatollah Seyyed Abdolhossein Dastgheib, *Gonahan-e Kabire (Cardinal Sins)* (Qom: Office of Islamic Publications, 2005), vol. 1, pp. 63–64.

74. The Toghi, or last letter of the Mahdi to his fourth and last ambassador, as quoted in Sheikh Sadough, *Kamal od-Din va Tamam on-Ne'ema (The State of Perfection of Religion and the End Limit of God's Blessings)*, vol. 2, ch. 45, hadith 45. See also "Falsehood of Seeing the Imam of Time," *Kayhan*, August 11, 2009, citing *Bahar Al-Anvar*, vol. 15, p. 163, at www.magiran.com/npview.asp?ID=1924071; similar quotations of *hadith* from *Kamal od-Din*, vol. 2, posted in "Questions About Contacting and Meeting With the Imam of Time," Rasekhoon, at www.rasekhoon.net/Article/Show-22344.aspx, March 4, 2009.

75. Interview with Grand Ayatollah Hossein-Ali Montazeri, Qom, December 6, 2005.

76. Ali Shariati, *Entezar Mazhab-e Eteraz* (Tehran: Hosseiniyeh-e Ershad, n.d.), as quoted and cited in Khalaji, "Apocalyptic Politics," p. 6.

77. Khomeini meeting members of parliament, September 7, 1981, as quoted and cited in Matini, "The Most Truthful Individual in Recent History."

78. Khomeini meeting Revolutionary Guard, January 24, 1982, as quoted and cited in Matini, "The Most Truthful Individual in Recent History."

79. ISNA, 22 Khordad 1383/13 June 2004, code 8303-09201, www.isna.ir, as cited in Ansari, *Iran Under Ahmadinejad*, pp. 86, 102, n. 19.

80. Khalaji, "Apocalyptic Politics," p. 17.

81. Amanat, *Apocalyptic Islam and Iranian Shi'ism*, p. 232.

82. Jamkaran website (www.jamkaran.info) "miraculous feats" (*karamat*) section, as quoted and cited in Amanat, *Apocalyptic Islam and Iranian Shi'ism*.

83. Interviews during visit to Jamkaran, December 6, 2005.

84. Interview with Mohammad Ali Ayazi, Qom, December 6, 2005.

85. Interview with Kurt Anders Richardson, Tehran, August 19, 2008; see also Scott Peterson, "What Drives Ahmadinejad's Combative Rhetoric?" *Christian Science Monitor*, September 23, 2008.

86. Interview with Seyyed Hadi Hashemi, Qom, December 6, 2005.

87. Interviews and visit to Bright Future Institute, Qom, December 6, 2005; see also Scott Peterson, "True Believers Dial Messiah Hotline in Iran," *Christian Science Monitor*, January 4, 2006.

88. Interview with Masoud Pourseyyed-Aghaei, Qom, December 6, 2005.

89. Interview with Seyyed Ali Pourtabatabaei, Qom, December 6, 2005.

90. "Rapture Index" at www.raptureready.com/rap2.html.

91. John Hagee, *Jerusalem Countdown* (Lake Mary, Fla.: FrontLine, 2007), p. 4.

92. *Harry Potter: Witchcraft Repackaged*, DVD, as sold on John Hagee Ministries, www.jhm.org/ME2/Default.asp.

93. Hagee, *Jerusalem Countdown*, p. 37.

94. Ibid.

95. Ibid., pp. 31–32.

96. John Hagee, *In Defense of Israel* (Lake Mary, Fla.: FrontLine, 2007), p. 75.

97. Mark Hitchcock, *The Apocalypse of Ahmadinejad: The Revelation of Iran's Nuclear Prophet* (Colorado Springs, Colo.: WaterBrook Multnomah, 2007).

98. Kenneth R. Timmerman, *Countdown to Crisis: The Coming Nuclear Showdown with Iran* (New York: Three Rivers, 2006), p. 320; see also "Hostage Roeder: 'Ahmadinejad Threatened to Kidnap My Son,'" Spiegel Online International, June 30, 2005, at www.spiegel.de/international/0,1518,363072,00.html, as quoted in Hitchcock, *The Apocalypse of Ahmadinejad*, p. 26. Timmerman, whose information on Iran and Lebanon has sometimes proven inaccurate, met with several former U.S. hostages about their supposed Ahmadinejad recollections. He adds in the endnotes (p. 392, n. 1) that one of them, "Kevin Hermening, who spoke with Roeder repeatedly, added the vivid details of Ahmadinejad's personal threat."

99. Hitchcock, *The Apocalypse of Ahmadinejad*, p. 5.

100. As quoted in ibid., p. 2.

101. Ibid., p. 141.

102. Walter Russell Mead, "God's Country?" *Foreign Affairs*, September/October 2006, pp. 27, 29, 33.

103. Revelation 6:8, 19:15, Holy Bible, King James Version.

104. Revelation 14:19–20, Holy Bible, King James Version. For one description of how such Messianic verses are used by American evangelicals, see Craig Unger, "American Rapture," *Vanity Fair*, December 2005.

105. As quoted in Unger, "American Rapture."

106. Khalaji, "Apocalyptic Politics," p. 4. Subsequent details of tradition and quotation from Sayed Sadral-Din Sadr, *Al-Mahdi*, ed. Sayed Baqir Khusroshani (Qom:

Daftar-e Tablighate Eslami, 2000 [AHS 1379]), pp. 195–96; Muhammad Baqer Majlisi, *Behar al-Anwar fi Dorrar-e Akhbar al-Aima al-Athar* (Tehran: Al-Maktabah al-Islamyah, 1993 [AHS 1372]), 52:283; and Dehsorkhi Isfahani Sayed Mahmoud Ibn Sayed Mehdi Moussavi, *Yati Ala al-Nas Zaman* (Qom: Entesharat-e Mir Fattah, 2004 [AHS 1383]), p. 659, all as quoted and cited in Khalaji, "Apocalyptic Politics."

107. Hadith of Jaber ibn Abdullah al-Ansari, as quoted in Ayatollah Seyyed Abdolhossein Dastgheib, *Gonahan-e Kabire (Cardinal Sins)*, vol. 1, p. 56.

108. Ansari, *Iran Under Ahmadinejad*, p. 75.

109. Reporting on election, Tehran, December 15, 2006; see also Scott Peterson, "Unexpectedly Large Turnout in Iran Vote," *Christian Science Monitor*, December 15, 2006.

110. As recounted in Naji, *Ahmadinejad*, p. 220.

111. Ansari, *Iran Under Ahmadinejad*, p. 79.

112. Interview with Iraj Jamshidi, Tehran, February 12, 2008. A figure of $270 billion earned during four years was reported on the eve of the June 2009 presidential election, in "Internal and International Implications of Iran's Economic Crisis," *Bulletin*, Polish Institute of International Affairs, no. 30, June 1, 2009. Figures of $250 billion have also been used in the Farsi press by, for example, journalist Bahman Amouee at www.amouee.net/spip.php?article297, and BBC Persian, which reports the figure "is more than double the revenue for the entire period before the Revolution," at www.bbc.co.uk/persian/iran/2009/01/090130_ir_economy.shtml. An Associated Press estimate puts the three-year total at $200 billion. See Ali Akbar Dareini, "Iran Feels Economic Pain as Oil Prices Fall," Associated Press, October 30, 2008.

113. Michael Rubin, "Iran's Economy Runs Out of Steam," *Forbes*, October 17, 2008.

114. Figures as reported in Laura Secor, "The Rationalist: A Dissident Economist's Attempts to Reform the Revolution," *New Yorker*, February 2, 2009.

115. Fars News Agency, June 15, 2007, as quoted and cited in Naji, *Ahmadinejad*, p. 229.

116. *Baztab*, January 24, 2007, as quoted in Naji, *Ahmadinejad*, p. 233.

117. Secor, "The Rationalist."

118. Hossein Askari, "Obama's Options On Iran," *Los Angeles Times*, December 13, 2008.

119. Naji, *Ahmadinejad*, p. 225.

120. These financial details as quoted and cited in Naji, *Ahmadinejad*, pp. 231–34.

121. Naji, *Ahmadinejad*, p. 233.

122. Interview with Saeed Laylaz by telephone to Tehran, July 11, 2007; see also Peterson, "Under Fire from US."

123. Press TV interview, as quoted in "One Billion Dollar Oil Money Still Missing: Iran's Auditor," February 26, 2009, Payvand, at www.payvand.com/news/09/feb/1323.html.

124. As quoted in "Ahmadinejad Under Fire Over Oil Money," PressTV, May 28, 2009, at www.presstv.ir/detail.aspx?id=96315&sectionid=35102101.

125. As described and quoted in Secor, "The Rationalist."

126. As quoted in Dareini, "Iran Feels Economic Pain as Oil Prices Fall."
127. Interview with Iranian journalist, Tehran, November 10, 2007; see also Peterson, "In Iran, Ahmadinejad's Bold Gambits Boost Presidential Power."
128. Ansari, *Iran Under Ahmadinejad*, p. 74.
129. Numbers provided by the President's Center of Public Complaints Examination are confirmed in this report: www.president.ir/fa/office/documents/files/48.pdf. It specifies that in the first thirty provincial trips alone, some 7,230,286 letters were collected, prompting the creation of a central headquarters and a system of making complaints by telephone, fax, text messaging, and a website, www.saamad.ir. The project was launched on December 22, 2008. RoozOnline reported that by June 19, 2008, the president's office had received more than ten million letters; at www.roozonline.com/persian/archive/news/news/article/2008/june/19//100-2.html.

   The total number of people who contacted Ahmadinejad by "letters or other forms of communication during his two rounds of provincial trips" came to nineteen million, according to Mashallah Saffar, deputy of the Public Complaints Center, in "19 Million Public Contacts with Ahmadinejad in Four Years," Ayande News, November 15, 2009, at www.ayandenews.com/news/15286/.
130. Hamid Reza Shokuhi, "The Provincial Trips and the Forgotten Principles," *Mardomsalari*, November 13, 2007, as translated at "Iran Paper Criticizes Provincial Trips by President, Ministers," BBC Monitoring, document BBCME-P0020071114e3be000b5, November 14, 2007.
131. Fars News Agency, June 22, 2005, as quoted in Naji, *Ahmadinejad*, p. 73.
132. As quoted in "Nuclear Report a Victory—Iran," BBC News, December 5, 2007; see also Scott Peterson, "Ahmadinejad: Rock Star in Rural Iran," *Christian Science Monitor*, December 7, 2007.
133. Reporting and interviews in Birjand and South Khorasan Province, November 7–8, 2007; see also Peterson, "Ahmadinejad: Rock Star in Rural Iran."
134. Interview with political scientist in Tehran, November 13, 2007; see also Peterson, "Ahmadinejad: Rock Star in Rural Iran."
135. Ali Akbar Dareini, "Ahmadinejad Calls His Critics 'Traitors,' " Associated Press, November 12, 2007.
136. Interview with Amir Mohebian, Tehran, November 15, 2007; see also Peterson, "In Iran, Ahmadinejad's Bold Gambits Boost Presidential Power."
137. Interview with the Sage, Tehran, February 2, 2009.
138. Interview, Sarayan, November 9, 2007.
139. Interview with Mehdi Kalhor, Birjand, November 8, 2007.
140. Interview with Mohsen Hedjazi, Bideskan, November 9, 2007.
141. Najmeh Bozorgmehr, "Picture Diary: 5 Days with Ahmadi-Nejad," *Financial Times*, April 22, 2007.
142. Orwell, *Nineteen Eighty-four*, pp. 176–77.
143. As quoted by ISNA, February 11, 2008, at www.isna.ir/ISNA/NewsView.aspx?ID=News-1084852.
144. Ahmadinejad speaking to clerics, May 5, 2008, as translated in "Iranian President Says US President's Life 'Empty,' " BBC Monitoring.

145. As quoted in Ali Akbar Dareini, "Ahmadinejad: Iran Won't Stop Enrichment," Associated Press, February 11, 2008; with further quotations at www.isna.ir/ISNA/NewsView.aspx?ID=News-1084852.

146. "Text—Ahmadinejad Letter to Bush," Reuters, May 9, 2006.

147. "Ahmadinejad's Letter to Americans," November 29, 2006; full text as at www.edition.cnn.com/2006/WORLD/meast/11/29/ahmadinejad.letter/.

148. *Death Sentences and Executions in 2008* (London: Amnesty International, 2009), pp. 15–16.

149. Ayatollah Ruhollah Khomeini, *A Call to Divine Unity: Letter of Imam Khomeini, The Great Leader of the Islamic Revolution and Founder of the Islamic Republic of Iran to President Mikhail Gorbachev, Leader of the Soviet Union* (Tehran: Institute for Compilation and Publication of Imam Khomeini's Works, 1993), pp. 7, 17. The letter itself is dated January 1, 1989.

150. Details and interviews from reporting in Tehran, February 11, 2008; see also Scott Peterson, "Many Iranians Say Revolutionary Ideals Still Unmet," *Christian Science Monitor*, February 12, 2008.

151. Interview with conservative government worker, Tehran, February 11, 2008; see also Scott Peterson, "Iran Reformers Hemmed In Ahead of Elections," *Christian Science Monitor*, March 4, 2008.

152. Interview with Iraj Jamshidi, Tehran, February 12, 2008; see also Scott Peterson, "Iran Debate: Who Owns the Revolution?" *Christian Science Monitor*, March 7, 2008.

153. Reporting in Lebanon, July–August 2006; see also especially Scott Peterson, "In Mideast, Cease-Fire Is a Start," August 14, 2006; "Lebanese Direct Growing Anger at US," August 10, 2006; "Unresolved: Disarming Hezbollah," August 15, 2006, all in *Christian Science Monitor*.

154. Khamenei at www.farsi.khamenei.ir/message-content?id=221; see also Scott Peterson, "Shiites Rising: Islam's Minority Reaches New Prominence," *Christian Science Monitor*, June 6, 2007.

155. Among many similar sources, see "Israel/Gaza: Operation 'Cast Lead': 22 Days of Death and Destruction," MBE 15/015/2009, Amnesty International, July 2009.

156. Visit to Jamaran, Tehran, March 10, 2008.

157. Interview with Hamidreza Taraghi, Tehran, December 17, 2006; see also Peterson, "Shiites Rising."

158. Interview with Amal Saad-Ghorayeb, Beirut, January 17, 2007; see also Peterson, "Shiites Rising."

159. As quoted in "Iran Says Anti-US Policy 'Bigger Than Hiroshima,' " Reuters, May 21, 2007.

160. As quoted in "Iran 'Number One World Power': Ahmadinejad," Agence France-Presse, February 28, 2008.

161. Interview with Iraj Jamshidi, Tehran, February 12, 2008; see also Peterson, "Iran Reformers Hemmed In Ahead of Elections."

162. Interview with Hamidreza Taraghi, Tehran, February 18, 2008; see also Peterson, "Iran Reformers Hemmed In Ahead of Elections."

163. Interview with political analyst, Tehran, February 2008; see also Peterson, "Iran Reformers Hemmed In Ahead of Elections."

164. Interview with Elyas Hazrati, Tehran, February 15, 2008; see also Peterson, "Iran Reformers Hemmed In Ahead of Elections."

165. Interview with Grand Ayatollah Yusef Saanei, Qom, February 16, 2008; see also Scott Peterson, "Iran Debate: Who Owns the Revolution?" *Christian Science Monitor*, March 7, 2008.

166. As quoted in "Revolutionary Guards Back Conservatives for Iran Poll," Agence France-Presse, February 9, 2008.

167. Hossein Shariatmadari, "The Mistake Should Be Admitted," *Kayhan*, February 13, 2008, at www.magiran.com/npview.asp?ID=1572270.

168. Hassan Khomeini interview in *Shahrvand* weekly, as quoted in "Khomeini's Grandson Speaks Out Ahead of Iran Vote," Agence France-Presse, February 10, 2008; and at www.shahrvandemroz.blogfa.com/post-495.aspx.

169. "The Secret of the Red Cheeks of Seyyed Hassan Khomeini," Nosazi website, February 9, 2008, before being taken down; then found at www.iranianuk.com/article.php?id=25217 and www.kamkendex.blogfa.com/post-1042.aspx. See also www.roozonline.com/persian/archive/news/article/2008/february/10//=58cd9c46db.html.

170. Shariatmadari, "The Mistake Should Be Admitted"; see also Peterson, "Iran Debate: Who Owns the Revolution?"

171. Interview with Grand Ayatollah Hossein-Ali Montazeri, Qom, February 16, 2008; see also Peterson, "Iran Debate: Who Owns the Revolution?"

172. *Kargozaran*, "Defending the Imam Until the Very Last Moment," with Rafsanjani brother quote also posted, February 17, 2008, at www.ebtekarnews.com/ebtekar/News.aspx?NID=28343.

173. All details and speeches drawn from reporting at the Fourth Annual Conference on Mahdaviat Doctrine, Tehran, August 14–15, 2009.

174. Sermon at Friday prayers, Tehran, September 28, 2007, in "Ahmad Jannati Referring to the President's Trip: Ahmadinejad Shone Like a Star at the United Nations," *Etemaad*, September 29, 2007, at www.magiran.com/npview.asp?ID=1491730.

175. Ahmadinejad speaking to clerics, May 5, 2008, as translated in "Iranian President Says US President's Life 'Empty,' " BBC Monitoring.

176. Ahmadinejad speaking to *basiji* students, November 13, 2007, at www.emruz.biz/ShowItem.aspx?ID=10989&p=1. See also "Iranian President Says 'The Dream of Your Martyrs . . . Is Rapidly Coming to Fruition,' " video clip posted by Fars News Agency, November 12, 2007, as translated by www.mideastwire.com, November 13, 2007.

177. "Iran: Crowning the Shadow of God," *Time*, November 3, 1967.

178. The Shah, quoted in Oriana Fallaci, *Interviews With History* (Boston: Houghton Mifflin, 1976), pp. 262–87, as quoted and cited in Abrahamian, *A History of Modern Iran*, p. 153.

179. Gholamhossein Elham, as quoted in Robert Tait, "Iran Accuses Hollywood of 'Psychological Warfare,' " *Guardian*, March 14, 2007.

180. Details and interviews drawn from visit to the Jamkaran mosque and the "Light of the Return" arts and cultural festival, Qom, August 16, 2008.

181. Story of Nasrallah meeting with Khamenei in Ayatollah Abbas Kaabi, *Exhibition of Water, Mirror and the Sun*, p. 11, as quoted and cited in *Mahdaviat and*

Complete Peace: Quotations from Dr. Ahmadinejad Regarding the Mahdi (Qom: Ayandeh Roshan, 2008), p. 51.

182. As quoted and referred to as "become a national joke," in Rasoul Montajabnia, "Some Questions for the President," *Etemaad-e Melli*, July 1, 2008, at www.magiran.com/ppdf/5061/p0506106820161.pdf and www.magiran.com/ppdf/5061/p0506106820021.pdf.

183. Montajabnia, "Some Questions for the President."

184. Gholamreza Mesbahi Moghaddam, as quoted in Yasameen Manteghi, "Suggestion to Establish 'Awaitance Ministry,' " August 26, 2008, at www.roozonline.com.

185. Ali M. Ansari, *Confronting Iran: The Failure of American Foreign Policy and the Next Great Crisis in the Middle East* (New York: Basic Books, 2006), pp. 229–30.

186. As quoted in Nazila Fathi, David E. Sanger, and William J. Broad, "Iran Says It Is Making Nuclear Fuel, Defying UN," *New York Times*, April 12, 2006.

187. Reporting in Tehran, February 3, 2009; see also Scott Peterson, "Iran Enters Space Race with Own Satellite and Rocket," *Christian Science Monitor*, February 4, 2009.

188. Interview with Mohammad Hazarian, Tehran, February 10, 2009.

189. Mahmoud Ahmadinejad, Thirtieth Anniversary speech, Tehran, February 10, 2009; see also Scott Peterson, "Iran's Ahmadinejad 'Ready' to Talk with America," *Christian Science Monitor*, February 11, 2009.

6. IN THE NAME OF DEMOCRACY

Epigraphs. Ayatollah Ruhollah Khomeini, speech on the political role of the clergy, in *Islamic Unity Against Imperialism: Eight Documents of the Islamic Revolution in Iran* (New York: Islamic Association of Iranian Professionals and Merchants in America, 1981), p. 8, as quoted and cited in Abrahamian, *Khomeinism*, p. 123; Hojjatoleslam Ali Khamenei, *Ettelaat*, March 5, 1981, as quoted and cited in Abrahamian, *Khomeinism*, p. 111.

1. Maria Rosa Menocal, *The Ornament of the World: How Muslims, Jews, and Christians Created a Culture of Tolerance in Medieval Spain* (New York: Little, Brown, 2002), pp. 11–12.

2. "Text of Speech of the Eminent Leadership Grand [*sic*] Ayatollah Seyed Ali Khamenei at the Opening Ceremony of the 8th Organization of the Islamic Conference Summit Meeting, Tehran, 9 December 1997."

3. Hugh Kennedy, *Muslim Spain and Portugal: A Political History of al-Andalus* (Harlow, England: Addison Wesley Longman, 1996), p. xv.

4. Soheila Pirooli Karharoodi, "Cultural Defense, Antibody for Andalusian Policies," *Resalat*, April 6, 2009, p. 17, and at www.magiran.com/npview.asp?ID=1828933.

5. Seyyed Hossein Alamdar, Preface (April 13, 1994) to *Discourse on Patience*, by Ayatollah Seyyed Ali Khamenei, as published in English at www.islam-pure.de/imam/books/patiance.htm [*sic*].

6. Hassan Ibrahimzadeh, "Freedom, a Phrase That Enchained Andalusia," *Ya Lesarat al-Hossein*, October 23, 2007, as reprinted from *Farhang-e Pouya*, no. 7.

7. Akbar Mozafarri, "Enemies and the Policy of Andalusiazation of Iran," *Ya Lesarat al-Hossein*, October 30, 2007, as reprinted from *Pouya*, no. 7.

8. Edward Gibbon, *Decline and Fall of the Roman Empire*, 5th ed., vol. 5 (London: Methuen, 1923), p. 482, as quoted and cited in Salah Zaimeche, "Toledo," Foundation for Science and Civilisation, Manchester, England, 2005, p. 3.

9. Menocal, *The Ornament of the World*, p. 11.

10. Chris Lowney, *A Vanished World: Muslims, Christians, and Jews in Medieval Spain* (New York: Oxford University Press, 2006), p. 14.

11. Menocal, *The Ornament of the World*, p. 36.

12. Kennedy, *Muslim Spain and Portugal*, pp. 128, 132.

13. Zaimeche, "Toledo," p. 14.

14. Ibn Bassam, *Dhakhir*, I, part ii, p. 430, in D. Wasserstein, *The Rise and Fall of the Party Kings* (Princeton, N.J.: Princeton University Press, 1985), p. 280, as quoted and cited in Zaimeche, "Toledo."

15. "Quoted by MacKay: Spain in the Middle Ages; 27 from M. Asin Palacios: Un Codice inexplorado del cordobes Ibn Hazm; *Al Andalus*; 2; 1934, p. 42; in D. Wasserstein, p. 280," as quoted and cited in Zaimeche, "Toledo," pp. 14–15.

16. Menocal, *The Ornament of the World*, p. 43.

17. Ibid., pp. 44–45.

18. Charles Julian Bishko, "The Spanish and Portuguese Reconquest, 1095–1492," from Harry W. Hazard, ed., *A History of the Crusades, Vol. 3: The Fourteenth and Fifteenth Centuries* (Madison: University of Wisconsin Press, 1975), p. 398.

19. Kennedy, *Muslim Spain and Portugal*, p. 308.

20. Details and quotes in Tim Weiner, "US Plan to Change Iran Leaders Is An Open Secret Before It Begins," *New York Times*, January 26, 1996.

21. As quoted in ibid.

22. Text of "Algiers Accords, January 19, 1981," at www.parstimes.com/history/algiers_accords.pdf; see also Gary Sick, "The Republic and the Rahbar," *National Interest* online, January 6, 2009.

23. Interview with Dr. Alireza Zakani, Tehran, September 21, 1998.

24. Interview with Mohsen Sazegara, Washington, D.C., April 10, 2008.

25. As noted in Sadjadpour, "Reading Khamenei," p. 18.

26. Ayatollah Ali Khamenei, "Reforms, Strategies, Challenges," July 10, 2000, as quoted and cited in Sadjadpour, "Reading Khamenei."

27. G. Curzon, *Persia and the Persian Question* (London: Longmans, 1892), vol. 2, p. 631, as quoted and cited in Abrahamian, *Khomeinism*, p. 113.

28. Abrahamian, *Khomeinism*, p. 127.

29. Pahlavi, *Answer to History*, pp. 145–46.

30. Ibid., p. 146.

31. Ibid., p. 73; see also Abrahamian, *Khomeinism*, p. 127.

32. Pahlavi, *Answer to History*, p. 59; see also Abrahamian, *Khomeinism*.

33. Pahlavi, *Answer to History*, p. 104.

34. Ibid., p. 155.

35. "The Iranian Revolution: An Oral History with Henry Precht, Then State Department Desk Officer," interview with Charles Stuart Kennedy, Oral Historian of the Association for Diplomatic Studies and Training, as published in *Middle East Journal* 58, no. 1 (Winter 2004), pp. 10–11.

36. Abrahamian, *Khomeinism*, p. 112.
37. Ibid., p. 122.
38. Reporting in Belgrade, January 7, 1997; see also Scott Peterson, "Serbia's Police Charmed As Protests Stay Peaceful," *Christian Science Monitor*, January 8, 1997.
39. As quoted in John Whitesides, "US Senators Push Alternatives on Kosovo," Reuters, March 25, 1999.
40. Fredrik Dahl, "Analysis—Balkan Stability May Depend on Milosevic," Reuters, July 31, 1999; see also Scott Peterson, "Serbia's Fracturing Opposition," *Christian Science Monitor*, August 23, 1999.
41. Interview with Zarko Korac, Belgrade, August 19, 1999; see also Peterson, "Serbia's Fracturing Opposition."
42. Details and quotes of Serbian town and Otpor in Roger Cohen, "Who Really Brought Down Milosevic?" *New York Times Magazine*, November 26, 2000.
43. Cohen, "Who Really Brought Down Milosevic?"
44. Gene Sharp, *From Dictatorship to Democracy: A Conceptual Framework for Liberation* (1993; rept., Boston: Albert Einstein Institution, 2002), pp. 16–17.
45. Interview with Alexander, Belgrade, October 8, 2000; see also Scott Peterson, "After Milosevic Exit, Time to Clean House in Yugoslavia," *Christian Science Monitor*, October 10, 2000.
46. As quoted in Cohen, "Who Really Brought Down Milosevic?"
47. Drawn from Vitali Silitski, "Preempting Democracy: The Case of Belarus," *Journal of Democracy* 16, no. 4 (October 2005), p. 89.
48. Interview with Anatoly Gulayev, Minsk, Belarus, September 7, 2001; see also Scott Peterson, "US Spends Millions to Bolster Belarus Opposition," *Christian Science Monitor*, September 10, 2001.
49. Peterson, "US Spends Millions to Bolster Belarus Opposition."
50. Silitski, "Preempting Democracy: The Case of Belarus," pp. 89–90.
51. Mark Almond, "Letter—For Nicaragua, Read Belarus," *Guardian*, August 21, 2001.
52. Interview with U.S. Ambassador Michael Kozak, Minsk, September 4, 2001; see also Peterson, "US Spends Millions to Bolster Belarus Opposition."
53. As quoted in Sergei Shargorodsky, "West Shuns Belarus Leader," Associated Press, September 5, 2001.
54. Silitski, "Preempting Democracy: The Case of Belarus," p. 84.
55. Interview with Giorgi Baramidze, Tbilisi, Georgia, November 25, 2003; see also Scott Peterson, "Georgia's Partner in Democracy: US," *Christian Science Monitor*, November 26, 2003.
56. Spending figures according to U.S. diplomats, background briefing, Tbilisi, Georgia, November 24, 2003; see also Peterson, "Georgia's Partner in Democracy: US."
57. According to "Alexander Lomaia—Minister of Education and Science (Georgia)," Organisation for Economic Co-operation and Development (OECD), at www.oecd.org/document/49/0,2340.en_21571361_36507471_37001521_1_1_1_1,00.html.
58. Interview with Mark Mullen and reporting, Tbilisi, Georgia, November 25, 2003; see also Peterson, "Georgia's Partner in Democracy: US."

59. Briefing to journalists by U.S. Ambassador Richard Miles, Tbilisi, Georgia, November 24, 2003.

60. See story, with images by Justyna Mielnikiewicz, "States in Caucasus, Central Asia Closely Monitor Development in Ukraine," *EurasiaNet-Eurasia Insight,* November 30, 2004.

61. Ian Traynor, "US Campaign Behind the Turmoil in Kiev," *Guardian,* November 26, 2004.

62. David T. Johnson, "Letters—What Uncle Sam Is Up To," *Guardian,* November 27, 2004.

63. Matt Kelley, "US Money Has Helped Opposition in Ukraine," Associated Press, December 11, 2004.

64. "How Yanukovich Forged the Elections. Headquarters' Telephone Talks Intercepted," *Ukrayinska Pravda,* November 24, 2004.

65. Pora activist Oleh Kyriyenko in interview with Margreet Strijbosch, "Ukraine: The Resistance Will Not Stop," Radio Nederland Worldwide, November 25, 2004.

66. As quoted in Strijbosch, "Ukraine: The Resistance Will Not Stop."

67. As described in Craig S. Smith, "US Helped to Prepare the Way for Kyrgyzstan's Uprising," *New York Times,* March 30, 2005.

68. Ben Barber, "Kyrgyzstan's Tulip Revolution," *Democracy Rising,* U.S. Agency for International Development, Bureau for Legislative and Public Affairs, September 2005, p. 14.

69. As quoted in "States in Caucasus, Central Asia Closely Monitor Developments in Ukraine."

70. As quoted in Fred Weir, "Russian Government Sets Sights on 'Subversion,'" *Christian Science Monitor,* June 1, 2005.

71. As quoted in Fred Weir, "Georgia Protests Revive Charges of Foreign Meddling," *Christian Science Monitor,* April 13, 2009.

72. George W. Bush, Inaugural Address, January 20, 2005, in Woolley and Peters, *The American Presidency Project,* at www.presidency.ucsb.edu/ws/?pid=58745.

73. Ben Barber, "Reaching for Democracy," *Democracy Rising,* pp. 1–2.

74. Silitski, "Preempting Democracy," p. 84.

75. Interviews with Amir Tehrani and band members, Tehran; see also Scott Peterson, "Iranian Musicians Try to Hit the Right Note," *Christian Science Monitor,* October 3, 2005.

76. Reporting in Tehran, translations of *Ya Lesarat al-Hossein* as they appeared in print, October 2005.

77. Concert at Vahdat Hall, Tehran, October 1, 2005; see also Peterson, "Iranian Musicians Try to Hit the Right Note."

78. Interview with Kambiz Roshanravan, Tehran, October 1, 2005.

79. "Ahmadinejad's Orders to Iran's Radio and TV," BBC Persian, December 19, 2005, at www.bbc.co.uk/persian/iran/story/2005/12/051219_fb_irib_guide.shtml.

80. "Iran: Ahmadinejad's Tumultuous Presidency," International Crisis Group (Brussels), p. 15.

81. "Music Is the Most Beautiful Sound in the World," Mehr News Agency, January 20, 2006, www.mehrnews.ir/NewsPrint.aspx?NewsID=279865.

82. "Prohibition of Broadcasting Pop Music by IRIB," *Etemaad*, March 3, 2008, at www.magiran.com/npview.asp?ID=1582565.

83. "Promoting Music Is Not Part of Iranian Values," Borna News Agency, August 28, 2008, at www.bornanews.ir/NSite/FullStory/?Id=185992.

84. Interview with Western-educated academic, Tehran, June 2005.

85. Interview with Reza Delbari, Tehran, September 29, 2005; see also Scott Peterson, "Iranian Leader Eyes Key Constituency: Young People," *Christian Science Monitor*, October 28, 2005.

86. Interview with Mehrdad Bazrpash, Tehran, October 3, 2005; see also Peterson, "Iranian Leader Eyes Key Constituency." For details on marriage training, see Alireza Ronaghi, "Iran Tackles Marriage Issues," Al Jazeera English, broadcast March 14, 2010. Unhappiness as reported at "Where is Bazrpash?" September 6, 2009, at www.khabaronline.ir/news/16464.aspx.

87. Interview with Mehdi Gomar, Tehran, June 24, 2005; see also Peterson, "Rise of Hard-liner Baffles Iran's Political Elite."

88. Interview with Mehdi Gomar, Tehran, October 3, 2005; see also Peterson, "Iranian Leader Eyes Key Constituency."

89. Reporting from Basij rally, Tehran, September 28, 2005; see also Scott Peterson, "Iran's Tough Stance a Hit at Home," *Christian Science Monitor*, September 29, 2005.

90. "An Hour with Mahmoud Ahmadinejad," *The Charlie Rose Show*, PBS, August 22, 2008, at www.charlierose.com/view/interview/9231.

91. Nazila Fathi, "Iran President Facing Revival of Students' Ire," *New York Times*, December 21, 2006.

92. Robert Tait, "Tyranny in Tehran," *Observer*, September 30, 2007.

93. As quoted in Fathi, "Iran President Facing Revival of Students' Ire."

94. Robert Tait, "Student Rebels in Iran Expelled and Earmarked for Army," *Guardian*, March 2, 2007.

95. As quoted in Tait, "Tyranny in Tehran."

96. As described by a student to Robert Tait, Tehran, August 2007, and shared in personal communication in Istanbul, September 13, 2009.

97. As described and quoted in ibid.

98. Farideh Farhi, "Iran's 'Security Outlook,' " *Middle East Report Online*, July 9, 2007.

99. Bill Samii, "Iran: Paramilitary Force Prepares For Urban Unrest," RFE/RL, September 30, 2005; see also Scott Peterson, "Iranians Wait for Change from Ahmadinejad," *Christian Science Monitor*, October 13, 2005.

100. "Ministers of Murder: Iran's New Security Cabinet," Human Rights Watch, December 15, 2005, pp. 11–12.

101. Ibid.

102. "Mohseni-Ejei bites Saharkhiz," BBC Persian, May 24, 2003, www.bbc.co.uk/persian/iran/story/2004/05/040524_mf_fight.shtml, and cited in "Ministers of Murder."

103. As quoted in Farhi, "Iran's 'Security Outlook.' "

104. "Official Apology to Mousavian; Ahmad Tavakoli: Accusations of Espionage Were Lies," September 17, 2008, RoozOnline, at www.roozonline.com/english/archives/2008/09/official_apology_to_mousavian.html.

105. As recounted in "Ministers of Murder," pp. 3–7.

106. Grand Ayatollah Hosein-Ali Montazeri, *Khaterat*, vol. 1, p. 635, at www.amon tazeri.com (accessed 2005), as quoted and cited in "Ministers of Murder," p. 4.

107. "A Brief History of the Serial Murders," ISNA, November 20, 2004, as quoted and cited in "Ministers of Murder," p. 9.

108. Human Rights Watch source, as quoted in "Ministers of Murder."

109. Ayatollah Mohammad Taghi Mesbah-Yazdi, "*Velayat-e Faqih*'s Legitimacy Is Divine and Is Not Conditioned on Others' Wishes," as published in Fars News Agency, August 4, 2009, at www.farsnews.net/newstext.php?nn=8805120937. This text drawn from "Rule and Legitimacy," part of a collection of Mesbah-Yazdi writings and opinions called *Questions and Answers*, vol. 3, 14th ed. (Qom: Imam Khomeini Education & Research Institute, 2001–2002), as described at www.mesbahyazdi.org/farsi/?../lib/Farsi_Abstract/book-6-3-1-3.htm.

110. Iranian Labor News Agency (ILNA), August 16, 2003, at www.akhbar.gooya .com/politics/archives/014798.php, as quoted and cited in Naji, *Ahmadinejad*, p. 99.

111. Iranian news reports as described in Naji, *Ahmadinejad*, pp. 102–3.

112. As detailed in Nazila Fathi, "Iran Exonerates Six Who Killed in Islam's Name," *New York Times*, April 19, 2007.

113. As quoted in "Kerman Murder Defendants: Mesbah-Yazdi Said That if One Repeats an Action After Three [*sic*] Times Warning Against Committing a Sin, His Blood May Be Freely Shed," Gooya News, October 12, 2004, at http://akhbar.gooya.com/politics/archives/017329.php; see also version in Naji, *Ahmadinejad*, p. 104.

114. As quoted in "Kerman Murder Defendants."

115. Naji, *Ahmadinejad*, p. 104.

116. Ibid., p. 103.

117. Ibid., p. 106.

118. Details of effort in Ewen MacAskill and Julian Borger, "Bush Plans Huge Propaganda Campaign in Iran," *Guardian*, February 16, 2006.

119. Among numerous examples, see "US Officials Raise Iran Specter to Justify Iraq War," Agence France-Presse, September 10, 2007; and Scott Peterson, "Are US and Iran Headed for War?" *Christian Science Monitor*, October 3, 2007.

120. As quoted in Borzou Daragahi, "Iran Tightens Screws on Internal Dissent," *Los Angeles Times*, June 10, 2007.

121. Seymour M. Hersh, "Preparing the Battlefield: The Bush Administration Steps Up Its Secret Moves Against Iran," *New Yorker*, July 7, 2008; see also Seymour M. Hersh, "Shifting Targets: The Administration's Plan for Iran," *New Yorker*, October 8, 2007.

122. Ayatollah Khamenei, speaking in Mashhad, March 21, 2007, as quoted by Fars News Agency, at www.farsnews.net/newstext.php?nn=8601020003.

123. "The Intelligence Minister in Ghazvin: England's Action in Politicizing the Invaders' Case Was Immature and Unwise," ISNA, April 10, 2007, at www.isna .ir/ISNA/NewsView.aspx?ID=News-902320.

124. "The Intelligence Minister: Shahram Jazayeri Still in Prison; Those Who Strike Against the Nezam, Whatever Titles They Hold, Will Be Confronted," ISNA, April 18, 2007, at www.isna.ir/ISNA/NewsView.aspx?ID=News=907055.

125. "Facts About Iran Government's Crackdown," Associated Press, June 22, 2007.
126. As quoted in Daragahi, "Iran Tightens Screws on Internal Dissent."
127. As quoted in Robin Wright, "Iran Curtails Freedom in Throwback to 1979," *Washington Post*, June 16, 2007.
128. As quoted in Neil MacFarquhar, "Iran Cracks Down on Dissent," *New York Times*, June 24, 2007.
129. Both officials as quoted in Stuart Williams, "Iran Crackdown on 'Thugs' Comes Under Fire," Agence France-Presse, May 20, 2007.
130. As quoted in Simon Tisdall, "Seized—For Showing Their Hair," *Guardian*, May 2, 2007.
131. Williams, "Iran Crackdown on 'Thugs' Comes Under Fire."
132. As described in Lara Marlowe, "Revolutionary Disintegration," *Time*, June 26, 1995.
133. Scott Peterson, "Regime-Change Fears Drive Iran's Vice Crackdown," *Christian Science Monitor*, December 20, 2007.
134. Interview with Iranian journalist, Tehran, November 10, 2007; see also Peterson, "Regime-Change Fears Drive Iran's Vice Crackdown."
135. Mark J. Gasiorowski, "The 1953 Coup d'État Against Mosaddeq," in *Mohammad Mosaddeq and the 1953 Coup in Iran*, ed. Mark J. Gasiorowski and Malcolm Byrne, eds. (Syracuse, N.Y.: Syracuse University Press, 2004), p. 235.
136. Donald N. Wilber, *Overthrow of Premier Mosaddeq of Iran: November 1952–August 1953*, Central Intelligence Agency, March 1954, as quoted and cited in Gasiorowski, "The 1953 Coup d'État Against Mosaddeq," p. 232.
137. Ibid., pp. 236–7.
138. Stephen Kinzer, *All the Shah's Men* (Hoboken, N.J.: Wiley, 2003), p. 172.
139. Gasiorowski, "The 1953 Coup d'État Against Mosaddeq," p. 252.
140. As quoted in Kinzer, *All the Shah's Men*, p. 177; see also Kennett Love, "Royalists Oust Mossadegh; Army Seizes Helm," *New York Times*, August 20, 1953.
141. As quoted in Kinzer, *All the Shah's Men*, p. 180.
142. As described in ibid., p. 187.
143. Michael A. Ledeen, *The Iranian Time Bomb: The Mullah Zealots' Quest for Destruction* (New York: St. Martin's, 2007), p. 226.
144. Ibid., p. 206.
145. Ibid., p. 226.
146. As quoted in "Lawbreakers Should Feel Insecure: Leader," *Tehran Times*, November 8, 2007.
147. Tait, "Tyranny in Tehran."
148. M. A. Jafari, "The Main Mission of the IRGC Is to Deal with the Internal Enemies," Mizan News, September 29, 2007, as quoted and cited in Wehrey et al., *The Rise of the Pasdaran*, p. 33.
149. As quoted in Golnaz Esfandiari, "Iran: Warnings Hint at Greater Role by Revolutionary Guard in Muzzling Critics," RFE/RL, October 5, 2007.
150. Peterson, "Regime-Change Fears Drive Iran's Vice Crackdown."
151. As quoted in Tait, "Tyranny in Tehran."
152. Interview with Seyyed Abolhassan Navvab, Tehran, November 14, 2007; see also Peterson, "Regime-Change Fears Drive Iran's Vice Crackdown."
153. Interview with political analyst, Tehran, November 13, 2007.

154. Frances Harrison, "Farewell to a Changed, Subtle Iran," *BBC News—From Our Own Correspondent*, July 7, 2007.

155. As quoted from ISNA in "Iran Sees 'Creeping Coup' in the Press—Report," *Reuters*, July 7, 2007.

156. Ayatollah Ruhollah Khomeini in *Iran Times*, November 21, 1980, as quoted and cited in Bakhash, *The Reign of the Ayatollahs*, p. 148.

157. Azadeh Moaveni, *Honeymoon in Tehran: Two Years of Love and Danger in Tehran* (New York: Random House, 2009), pp. 8–9.

158. Ibid., pp. 85–86.

159. Ibid., p. 251.

160. Ibid., pp. 206–8.

161. Maziar Bahari, "We Know Where You Live," *New Statesman*, November 8, 2007.

162. Interview with Saeed Laylaz, Tehran, July 11, 2007; see also Peterson, "Under Fire From US, Iran Reacts By Cracking Down at Home."

163. As quoted in Tait, "Tyranny in Tehran."

164. As described in Haleh Esfandiari, *My Prison, My Home: One Woman's Story of Captivity in Iran* (New York: Ecco/HarperCollins, 2009), p. 4.

165. Ibid., p. 74.

166. Ibid., p. 58.

167. Ibid., p. 62.

168. Ibid., pp. 63, 69.

169. Ibid., p. 71.

170. Ibid., pp. 76–77.

171. Ibid., p. 162.

172. Ibid., p. 138.

173. *Covert Terror: Iran's Parallel Intelligence Apparatus* (New Haven, Conn.: Iran Human Rights Documentation Center, 2009), p. 5.

174. Ibid., p. 10.

175. Ibid., p. 8.

176. Ibid., p. 3.

177. Interview with Ervand Abrahamian, by phone to New York, July 18, 2007; see also Scott Peterson, "Iran Uses Activists for Propaganda," *Christian Science Monitor*, July 20, 2007.

178. Haleh Esfandiari, as quoted in "confession" film *In the Name of Democracy*, in Peterson, "Iran Uses Activists for Propaganda."

179. Esfandiari, *My Prison, My Home*, p. 178.

180. Haleh Bakhash, "My Mother's Interrogators," *Washington Post*, July 18, 2007.

181. Interview with Iranian analyst, by phone to Tehran, July 19, 2007; see also Peterson, "Iran Uses Activists for Propaganda."

182. Ayatollah Ali Khamenei, Address to Cinema Directors, June 13, 2006, as quoted and cited in Sadjadpour, "Reading Khamenei," p. 10.

183. Interview with Nilufar, a housewife in Tehran who asked that her full name not be used when interviewed by a reporter in Tehran, July 19, 2007.

184. Interview with Karim Sadjadpour, by telephone to Washington, July 11, 2007; see also Peterson, "Iran Uses Activists for Propaganda."

185. Esfandiari, *My Prison, My Home*, pp. 211–12.

186. Ibid., p. 219.
187. "Speech of the Supreme Leader of the Islamic Revolution on the 16th Anniversary of Imam Khomeini's Departure," June 4, 2005, at www.farsi.khamenei .ir/speech-content?id=3295.
188. "Khatami Urges Iranians to Vote En Masse," Fars News Agency, March 12, 2008.
189. Multiple interviews with "Tooska," a pseudonym, Tehran, from March 10, 2008; see also Scott Peterson, "Young Iranians, Once Avid Reformers, Leave Politics Behind," *Christian Science Monitor*, March 14, 2008.
190. "Yes Boss," lyrics by Danish artist Mikkel Hess and Hess Is More, *Captain Europe* (album), (Copenhagen: Nublu Records/Music for Dreams, 2006).
191. Milani, "Pious Populist."
192. Interview with the Sage, Tehran, March 17, 2008.
193. Reporting at Friday prayers, Tehran, March 7, 2008.
194. Scott Peterson, "For Iran, Iraq Is a Two-Edged Sword," *Christian Science Monitor*, March 18, 2008.
195. Press conference with principlist faction, Tehran, March 11, 2008.
196. Interview with Dr. Alireza Zakani, Tehran, March 13, 2008.
197. Reporting on election day, Tehran, March 14, 2008; see also Scott Peterson, "In Iran Vote, Conservatives Set to Retain Power," *Christian Science Monitor*, March 15, 2008.
198. Interview with Ashraf Banoo Rahimikia, Tehran, March 14, 2008; see also Scott Peterson, "Iran Election: Hard-liners Hold On, Despite High Inflation," *Christian Science Monitor*, March 17, 2008.
199. As quoted in "Conservatives to Hold Power in Iranian Parliament," Fars News Agency, March 16, 2008; and Peterson, "Iran Election: Hard-liners Hold On, Despite High Inflation."
200. Reporting on election day, March 14, 2008.
201. Details and interview at Behesht-e Zahra cemetery, Tehran, March 20, 2008.

7. THE RISING

Epigraph. As quoted in Farnaz Fassihi, "In Iran, Campaigns Heat Up," *Wall Street Journal*, June 9, 2009.

1. Graffiti details and interview with Shirin Ebadi, Tehran, February 11, 2009; see also Scott Peterson, "Iran Turns Up Pressure on Rights Activists," *Christian Science Monitor*, March 3, 2009.
2. "They Are Laying the Groundwork for My Assassination: Shirin Ebadi Tells Rooz," RoozOnline, September 4, 2008.
3. Michael Theodoulou, "A Tough Place to Be a Woman with a Cause," *Christian Science Monitor*, October 15, 1999.
4. Interview with Shirin Ebadi, Tehran, February 11, 2009.
5. As quoted in Tait, "Tyranny in Tehran."
6. Interview with Seyed Mohammad Marandi, Tehran, January 31, 2009; see also Peterson, "Iran Turns Up Pressure on Rights Activists." After the June 2009 election, Marandi would become one of the few and most vocal defenders of that flawed election, and of Ahmadinejad's official "victory." This sta-

tus prompted Fareed Zakaria to ask him during a CNN interview: "Do you worry that you will be seen in history as a mouthpiece for a dying, repressive regime in its death throes? That twenty years from now you'll look back, and the world will look back at you, the way it did some of those smooth-talking, English-speaking, Soviet spokesmen who were telling us right in the middle of the 1980s, that the Soviet Union was all just fine and democratic and wonderful?" Marandi replied that he had "always been a critic" of Ahmadinejad's administration, though it was his "duty to be honest." He finished the interview with the words: "But if you think that I am somehow the Mouth of Sauron, I think you're mistaken." ("Iran's Power Struggle; Iranian Election Fallout; French Economy and Reforms," Fareed Zakaria, Global Public Square (GPS), CNN transcript, July 29, 2009, at www.transcripts.cnn.com/transcripts/0907/26/fzgps.01.html.)

7. "Situation of Human Rights in the Islamic Republic of Iran," UN General Assembly, Document A/C.3/63/L.40, October 30, 2008; resolution adopted December 18, 2008.

8. "Iran: Worsening Repression of Dissent as Election Approaches," Amnesty International, MDE 13/012/2009, February 2009.

9. Interview with Mohsen Sazegara, Washington, D.C., April 10, 2008.

10. Sazegara letter to Khamenei, as described in Abdo and Lyons, *Answering Only to God*, pp. 274–75.

11. Interview with Mohsen Sazegara, Washington, D.C., April 10, 2008.

12. Details and interview with Parvin Ardalan, Tehran, February 13, 2009; see also Peterson, "Iran Turns Up Pressure on Rights Activists."

13. As quoted in Michael Theodoulou, "Staying True to Khomeini," *Christian Science Monitor*, September 13, 1999.

14. As quoted in Ali Akbar Dareini, "Hard-line Unit Vows War with Reformers," Associated Press, December 5, 2002.

15. Interview with Masoud Dehnamaki, Tehran, August 17, 2008.

16. Nazila Fathi, "A Revolutionary Channels His Inner Michael Moore," *New York Times*, November 26, 2005.

17. As quoted in ibid.

18. Cinema screening of *Ekhrajiha* (*The Outcasts*), Tehran, March 17, 2007.

19. As quoted in Babak Dehghanpisheh, "The Laughing Radical," *Newsweek*, May 23, 2009.

20. Interviews with Masoud Dehnamaki, Tehran, November 20, 2007, and February 14, 2008; see also Scott Peterson, "Iranian Filmmaker Bridges Deep Political Divides with Irreverence," *Christian Science Monitor*, June 4, 2008.

21. Interviews with the Sage, Tehran, November 25, 2007.

22. Interviews with Masoud Dehnamaki, November 20, 2007, and February 14, 2008.

23. Interview with Dr. Shahriar Khateri, Tehran, November 11, 2007; see also Scott Peterson, "Iran's Peace Museum: The Reality vs. The Glories of War," *Christian Science Monitor*, December 24, 2007.

24. Interview with Lili Golestan, Tehran, June 11, 2009.

25. Naji, *Ahmadinejad*, p. 245, citing "When All the 180 Books of a Publisher Get Rejected," RoozOnline, May 7, 2004.

26. Ahmadinejad speech on Iranian Channel One, July 25, 2005, as translated at "Iran's New President Glorifies Martyrdom," Middle East Media Research Institute, July 29, 2005.

27. Interview with Ebrahim Mehtari, Ankara, Turkey, December 17, 2009.

28. Interview with Isa Saharkhiz, Tehran, February 12, 2009; see also Scott Peterson, "Iran's Reformers Put Hope in 'New Khatami,' " Christian Science Monitor, February 26, 2009.

29. As quoted at "Our Duty Is to Reform the Current Situation Through Election," Abrar, February 9, 2009, at www.abrarnews.com/politic/1387/871121/html/rooydad.htm#s338631; see also Peterson, "Iran's Reformers Put Hope in 'New Khatami.' "

30. "Iran: The Past, Present and Future of Reformism: Id=0835477," Restricted eGram No. 47582/08, British Embassy, Tehran, December 1, 2008.

31. All details and interviews of thirtieth Revolution anniversary and Khatami's "people power" walk are from reporting, Tehran, February 10, 2009; see also Scott Peterson, "Iran's Ahmadinejad 'Ready' to Talk with America," Christian Science Monitor, February 11, 2009.

32. As quoted in Esfandiar Saffari, "IRGC Preparing for Public Uprising," RoozOnline, March 3, 2009.

33. As quoted in ibid.

34. "An Hour with Mahmoud Ahmadinejad," The Charlie Rose Show, PBS, August 22, 2008, at www.charlierose.com/view/interview/9231.

35. Barack Obama interview with Al Arabiya, January 27, 2009, transcript, "Obama Tells Al Arabiya Peace Talks Should Resume," Al Arabiya, at www.alarabiya.net/articles/2009/01/27/65087.html.

36. Reporting in Tehran, February 5, 2009; see also Scott Peterson, "Is Iran Prepared to Undo 30 Years of Anti-Americanism?" Christian Science Monitor, February 6, 2009.

37. Interview with Amir Mohebian, Tehran, February 4, 2009; see also Peterson, "Is Iran Prepared to Undo 30 Years of Anti-Americanism?"

38. Interview with Hamidreza Taraghi, Tehran, February 1, 2009; see also Scott Peterson, "Iranians Wary of Obama's Approach," Christian Science Monitor, February 5, 2009.

39. Interview with Hossein Shariatmadari, Tehran, February 7, 2009; see also Scott Peterson, "From Iran's Hard-liners, Tough Talk—But Pragmatism As Well," Christian Science Monitor, February 18, 2009.

40. President Barack Obama, "Videotaped Remarks by the President in Celebration of Nowruz," White House, Office of the Press Secretary, transcript, March 20, 2009.

41. Ironically, President Jimmy Carter had quoted the same poem, but more fully and with a different translation, when he champagne-toasted his "irreplaceable" friend, the Shah, to usher in the year 1978—the Shah's last year in power. "Human beings are like parts of a body, created from the same essence," Carter said. "When one part is hurt and in pain, others cannot remain in peace and quiet. If the misery of others leaves you indifferent and with no feeling of sorrow, then you cannot be called a human being." ("Jimmy Carter: Tehran, Iran, Toasts of the President and the Shah at a State Dinner," December 31, 1977,

in Woolley and Peters, *The American Presidency Project*, at www.presidency.ucsb
.edu/ws/?pid=7080.)

42. Ayatollah Ali Khamenei speech in Mashhad, March 21, 2009, transcript of live
broadcast on *Tehran Vision*, IRINN.

43. President George W. Bush, "Statement on the Presidential Elections in Iran,"
June 16, 2005, in Woolley and Peters, *The American Presidency Project*, at www
.presidency.ucsb.edu/ws/?pid=73791.

44. Interview with Farideh Farhi, by telephone to Hawaii, March 25, 2009.

45. Among others, see "Iran Charges Detained US Reporter With Spying," Agence
France-Presse, April 7, 2009.

46. Among others, see "Obama Dismayed by Iran Sentence," BBC News, April 18,
2009; see also "Saberi 'On Hunger Strike' in Iran," BBC News, April 25, 2009;
and Scott Peterson, "Iran's President Makes Rare Intervention in US Reporter's
Case," *Christian Science Monitor*, April 19, 2009.

47. Interview with Karim Sadjadpour, by telephone to Washington, May 11, 2009;
see also Scott Peterson, "Iran Release of US Journalist Removes Obstacle to
US-Iran Dialogue," *Christian Science Monitor*, May 11, 2009.

48. "Roxana Saberi on Her Imprisonment in Iran," National Public Radio, May 29,
2009.

49. Mike Shuster, "Lawyer Discloses New Details In Saberi Case," *All Things Considered*, National Public Radio, May 13, 2009, at www.npr.org/templates/
story/story.php?storyId=104104552.

50. Saadollah Zarei, "To Participate or to Disrupt," editorial in *Kayhan*, February 13, 2009, at www.aftab.ir/articles/politics/iran/c1c1234470542_election
_iran_p1.php; see also Hossein Bastani, "Khatami Threatened to Death,"
RoozOnline, March 10, 2009; and Peterson, "Iran's Reformers Put Hope in
'New Khatami.' "

51. As quoted in Borzou Daragahi and Ramin Mostaghim, "Iran Urges Citizens to
Vote," *Los Angeles Times*, May 28, 2009.

52. As quoted in ibid.

53. As quoted in Thomas Erdbrink, "Relative Unknown Leads Challenge in Iran,"
Washington Post, June 8, 2009.

54. William E. Smith, Dean Fischer, and Johanna McGeary, "Iran: Meantime Back
in Tehran," *Time*, January 12, 1987.

55. As quoted in Erdbrink, "Relative Unknown Leads Challenge in Iran."

56. As quoted in Jay Deshmukh, "Iran's Ahmadinejad Kicks Off Combative Poll
Campaign," Agence France-Presse, May 22, 2009.

57. Watching Ahmadinejad and Mousavi debate, Tehran, June 3, 2009; see also
Scott Peterson, "Lincoln-Douglas Debates, Iranian Style," *Christian Science
Monitor*, June 3, 2009.

58. Comments by Tara Mahtafar, Tehran, June 3, 2009.

59. Mousavi as quoted in Erdbrink, "Relative Unknown Leads Challenge in Iran."

60. Interview with student Morovati, Tehran, June 3, 2009.

61. Details, interviews, and Khamenei speech from reporting at Khomeini shrine,
Tehran, June 4, 2009; see also Scott Peterson, "Iran: 20 Years After Ayatollah
Khomeini," *Christian Science Monitor*, June 4, 2009.

62. Ayatollah Khamenei, as quoted in "The US Misbehavior Would Endanger the

Region's Energy Security," Fars News Agency, June 4, 2006, at www.farsnews
.net/newstext.php?nn=8503140094; and Shirzad Bozorgmehr, "Iran Warns US
on Oil Shipments," CNN, June 4, 2006.

63. As quoted in "Khamenei Offers Implicit Support to Ahmadinejad," Agence
France-Presse, May 12, 2009.

64. As quoted in "Shun Pro-West Candidates, Says Iran's Khamenei," Agence
France-Presse, May 19, 2009.

65. Details and interviews from Mousavi visit, Birjand, June 6, 2009; see also Scott
Peterson, "In Iran, Ahmadinejad Opponent Sees Surge of Enthusiasm," *Christian Science Monitor*, June 6, 2009.

66. Details and interviews, Ahmadinejad campaign and Agha-Tehrani event,
Birjand, June 7, 2009; see also Scott Peterson, "Iran's Presidential Race Tightens," *Christian Science Monitor*, June 8, 2009.

67. As recounted in Najmeh Bozorgmehr, "President a Hostage to His Promises,"
Financial Times, February 28, 2008.

68. Poll results as described in Milani, "Pious Populist."

69. Milani, "Pious Populist."

70. Details and interviews with Hassan Shamshiri and other campaign volunteers
at Ahmadinejad headquarters, Birjand, June 6, 2009.

71. Interviews with Seyyed Mohammad Baqer Asadi and others at Hossein
mosque, Birjand, June 6, 2009.

72. Morteza Agha-Tehrani, *Sowday-e Rooy-e Doost* (Tehran: Ahmadiyeh, 2005 [AHS
1384]), as described and cited in Khalaji, "Apocalyptic Politics," pp. 23–24.

73. Video, "Morteza Agha-Tehrani in Zarand (1)," circa May 22, 2007, at www
.video.google.com/videoplay?docid=8640639692064592582#, and as reported
in *Etemad-e Melli*, July 9, 2007, at www.magiran.com/npview.asp?ID=1440165.

74. Details of Agha-Tehrani mosque "rally" and Ahmadinejad leaflets from reporting in Birjand, June 6, 2009.

75. Details and interviews from reporting in Tehran, June 6–11, 2009.

76. As witnessed by Nahid Siamdoust, Tehran, June 8, 2009.

77. Interview with the Sage, Tehran, June 7, 2009.

78. Scott Peterson, "Forecasting Iran's Vote," *Christian Science Monitor*, June 15,
2005.

79. Maziar Bahari, "Secret Poll Shows Voters Turn Against Ahmadinejad," *Newsweek*, June 15, 2009, posted online June 6, 2009, at www.newsweek.com/
id/200960. Clear understanding of Iranian political views before and after the
June 2009 elections has been muddied by a number of polls that purport to
show that the official Ahmadinejad landslide victory was no surprise, and in
keeping with widespread popular support for the president, for the government, and faith in the election process. Those polls exhibit a number of serious flaws; they extrapolate from suspect Iranian data—much of it conducted
by the University of Tehran—or by applying Western polling methods that
almost certainly would not yield accurate results in the Iranian political and
social context.

One example published by WorldPublicOpinion.org (a project managed by
the Program on International Policy Attitudes at the University of Maryland)
brings together ten tracking telephone surveys by the University of Tehran,

with eight of them conducted before the vote. The American authors ask if that data could have been manipulated, and state that "it is possible that the government stepped in and forced the researchers to put forward fabricated or falsified data. The same can be said for the GlobeScan poll that was conducted by a fielding agency in Iran through telephone interviews." The authors made "substantial efforts" to determine if such tampering took place, and note that it is "not easy to produce a credible dataset that includes multiple questions." The document states, however, that datasets can be acquired from Seyed Mohammad Marandi—the University of Tehran academic who has been one of the most unwavering supporters of the official line on Ahmadinejad's "victory." The link provided at www.fws.ut.ac.ir/ failed to work when accessed on May 20, 2010. (Steven Kull et al., "An Analysis of Multiple Polls of the Iranian Public," WorldPublicOpinion.org, February 3, 2010, at www.worldpublicopinion.org/pipa/pdf/feb10/IranElection_Feb10_rpt.pdf; see also "Analysis of Multiple Polls Finds Little Evidence Iranian Public Sees Government as Illegitimate," WorldPublicOpinion.org, February 3, 2010, at www.worldpublicopinion.org/pipa/articles/brmiddleeastnafricara/652.php?lb=brme&pnt=652&nid=&id=.)

Besides the university and GlobeScan data, the above analysis relied on one further survey carried out by WorldPublicOpinion.org itself from August 27 to September 10, 2009, more than two months after the election—and after the most serious street violence seen in Iran in three decades. The authors of the poll record a 52 percent refusal rate to answer, but state that they used an agency from outside Iran to call Iranians on computer-chosen telephone lines, with native Farsi speakers, so there would be "no political constraints on questions asked or speculation about the influence of Iranian authorities on the data collection process."

While such methods may be effective in an American or Western context, in Iran the apparent attempt at statistical due diligence simply can't overcome Iranian reluctance to share true political views with strangers—in almost any context, much less over the phone, and even less during a phone call from outside the country. Complicating the picture was the fact that, at the time of the polling, a fierce regime crackdown had left scores if not hundreds dead, details of rape and other horrific abuses in secret prisons were being made public, more than 4,000 activists had been arrested, more than 100 of those faced televised show trials during which they were accused—because of their opposition to the regime's election narrative—of acting against God, and Ayatollah Khamenei had declared that not accepting the "divine assessment" of Ahmadinejad's victory was the "greatest crime."

Despite this excruciating political context—during which any contact with people outside Iran was added to charge sheets of pro-Mousavi activists, and interrogators presented prisoners with e-mail and other transcripts of private communications—the poll authors stand by their results. Not surprisingly, they found that 48 percent of Iranians believed that the "degree of civil liberties" in Iran "have gotten better"—more than twice the number who said they had "gotten worse." The poll also found that 66 percent of Iranians believed the election was "completely free and fair," compared to the 5 percent who stated the opposite. Of course, Ahmadinejad was considered the "legitimate president of Iran" by 81 percent of respondents. ("Iranian Public on Current Issues—Questionnaire," WorldPublicOpinion.org, September 19, 2009, at www .worldpublicopinion.org/pipa/pdf/sep09/IranUS_Sep09_quaire.pdf.)

80. Source interviewed by Lindsey Hilsum in Tehran, June 12, 2009, and confirmed in communication with author to London, March 25, 2010.

81. Interview with "Tooska," a pseudonym, Tehran, June 7, 2009; see also Scott Peterson, "Once Apathetic, Young Iranians Now Say They'll Vote," *Christian Science Monitor*, June 10, 2009.

82. Interview with Alireza Mahfouzian, Tehran, June 8, 2009; see also Peterson, "Once Apathetic, Young Iranians Now Say They'll Vote."

83. Interview with "Siavash," a pseudonym, Tehran, June 10, 2009; see also Peterson, "Once Apathetic, Young Iranians Now Say They'll Vote."

84. As quoted in Parisa Hafezi and Dominic Evans, "Ahmadinejad Says Election Rivals Use Hitler Tactics," Reuters, June 10, 2009.

85. As quoted in Borzou Daragahi, "In Iran, Disparate, Powerful Forces Ally Against Ahmadinejad," *Los Angeles Times*, June 7, 2009.

86. Interview with Mehdi Karroubi, Tehran, June 11, 2009; see also Scott Peterson, "In Iran, Candidates Cap a Bitter Campaign," *Christian Science Monitor*, June 11, 2009.

87. Interview with Nasser Hadian-Jazy, Tehran, June 10, 2009.

88. Daragahi, "In Iran, Disparate, Powerful Forces Ally Against Ahmadinejad."

89. As translated by Muhammad Sahimi, "Rafsanjani's Letter to the Supreme Leader," Tehran Bureau, June 9, 2009.

90. As quoted in Hafezi and Evans, "Ahmadinejad Says Election Rivals Use Hitler Tactics."

91. General Yadollah Javani interview, "Any Moves Toward Velvet Revolution Will Be Nipped in the Bud by People's Awareness," in Revolutionary Guard weekly publication *Sobh-e Sadegh*, no. 402, p. 8, June 8, 2009, at www.sobhesadegh.ir/. For a less accurate translation see Dominic Evans and Fredrik Dahl, "Mousavi Camp Waging Velvet Revolution: Iran Guards," Reuters, June 10, 2009, which quotes Javani saying "supporters of Mir Hossein Mousavi on the streets is part of the Velvet Revolution."

92. Reporting in Tehran, June 11, 2009; see also Peterson, "In Iran, Candidates Cap a Bitter Campaign."

8. THE RECKONING
Epigraphs. Orwell, *Nineteen Eighty-four,* pp. 228, 239; "Text—Ahmadinejad Letter to Bush," Reuters, May 9, 2006.

1. IRIB News, June 12, 2009.

2. Details and interviews from reporting, Tehran, June 12, 2009; see also Scott Peterson, "Election: Iran's Decision to Oust Ahmadinejad—or Not," *Christian Science Monitor*, June 12, 2009.

3. According to the account of Abdofazl Fateh, editor of Ghalam News, who was close to Mousavi, as posted by Scott Lucas in "Iran: What Happened on Election Night? The Ghalam News Editor's Account," Enduring Amer-

ica, November 19, 2009, at www.enduringamerica.com/2009/11/19/iran-what-happened-on-election-night-the-ghalam-news-account/.

4. As quoted in "Nation of Iran Triumphed Again," Fars News Agency, June 13, 2009, at www1.farsnews.com/newstext.php?nn=8803230074; see also Scott Peterson, "In Iran First Results Give Ahmadinejad Commanding Lead," *Christian Science Monitor*, June 13, 2009.

5. As quoted in Anna Johnson and Brian Murphy, "Tehran in Turmoil: Anger Over Election Fraud Claims Boils Over into Violence," Associated Press, June 13, 2009.

6. "Makhmalbaf's Interview on Radio Farda," June 13, 2009, translated for Real News Network, at www.therealnews.com/t2/index.php?option=com_content&task=view&id=31&Itemid=74&jumival=3868.

7. Fars News Agency posted its first results declaring an Ahmadinejad victory at 6 P.M. on voting day, hours before many polling stations closed. The Fars story was quickly taken down, but had been picked up by the Asriran website, which posted an initial story at 6:40 P.M. ("The Early Report by Fars Over the Election Result," June 12, 2009, at www.asriran.com/fa/pages/?cid=75108.)

   Asriran quoted Fars's political reporter referring to "reports received from various sources" around the country to indicate that Ahmadinejad would win "60 percent of the votes in the first round," and that "one of the well-known candidates has been so far able to move ahead of the other three candidates and win the majority of votes." The Fars report—according to Asriran—estimated that Ahmadinejad won 85 percent of the vote in "villages and small towns," and with provincial capitals taken into account, "the average votes won by this candidate chanting anti-corruption slogans will exceed 60 percent."

   More details about the 6 P.M. posting by Fars and the reaction of Mousavi's Kaleme website are at "Did They Know?" Radio Farda, June 17, 2009, at www.radiofarda.com/content/RM_Ahmadinejad_Victory_in_News/1756572.html. Fars eventually posted its final results at 4:11 P.M. the next day, in "Ahmadinejad Winning 24 Million Votes Officially Becomes Iran's President," Fars News Agency, at www.farsnews.net/newstext.php?nn=8803231097.

8. Overnight reporting on streets and at downtown Mousavi election headquarters, June 12–13, 2009; see also Peterson, "In Iran, First Results Give Ahmadinejad Commanding Lead."

9. Khamenei speaks on state TV, as quoted in Johnson and Murphy, "Tehran in Turmoil."

10. Reporting in Tehran, June 13, 2009; see also Scott Peterson, "Ahmadinejad's Reelection Prompts Mass Protests in Iran," *Christian Science Monitor*, June 13, 2009.

11. An Ansar leader, "Brother Sadeghi," as quoted in Guy Dinmore, "Iran's Hardliners Dig In to Obstruct President's Reforms," *Financial Times*, July 10, 2001; also cited in Ray Takeyh, *Guardians of the Revolution: Iran and the World in the Age of the Ayatollahs* (New York: Oxford University Press, 2009), p. 225.

12. Defecting member of Basij militia, as interviewed in Lindsey Hilsum, "Iran: Basij Member Describes Election Abuse," Channel 4 News, London, December 16, 2009, at www.channel4.com/news/articles/politics/international_politics/iran+basij+member+describes+election+abuse/3466142. In private

communication with the author (January 25, 2010), veteran correspondent Hilsum said she had no doubt about the *basiji*'s account. She saw photographs of him in uniform and at his mosque Basij headquarters; he refused to shake hands with a woman and constantly used elaborate religious language. "More than anything he was very, very distressed," by making his revelations public, Hilsum recalled. "We had to stop the interview."

13. As quoted in Johnson and Murphy, "Tehran in Turmoil."
14. Ahmadinejad televised statement, as quoted in Ali Akbar Dareini and Anna Johnson, "Clashes Erupt in Iran over Disputed Election," Associated Press, June 13, 2009.
15. Interview with "Tooska," "Leyla," and "Mehdi," all pseudonyms, Tehran, June 13, 2009.
16. Hilsum, "Iran: Basij Member Describes Election Abuse."
17. As related in Tehran, June 14, 2009.
18. Interview with the Sage, June 14, 2009.
19. Ahmadinejad press conference and details of street clashes and rally, Tehran, June 14, 2009.
20. Details of street clashes and rally, reporting in Tehran, June 14, 2009.
21. *Kayhan* front page, June 15, 2009, with Photoshop adjustments visible, at www.gawker.com/5293988/someone-in-iran-probably-the-government-isnt -good-at-photoshop.
22. Among many reports, see "Shots Fired at Huge Iran Protest," BBC News, June 15, 2009; and Scott Peterson, "What Are Mousavi's Options Now?" *Christian Science Monitor*, June 15, 2009.
23. Halo and Quran details as reported in "Letter From Tehran: With the Marchers; A Resident Reports from the Streets and the Rooftops," *New Yorker*, June 29, 2009.
24. Communication with witness to killings, Tehran, June 15, 2009; see also Scott Peterson, "Eyewitness: Iranian Militiamen Shot 300 Rounds During Monday's Protest," *Christian Science Monitor*, June 16, 2009. Another eyewitness version of events is described in Maziar Bahari, "Blood in Tehran," *Newsweek*, June 15, 2009.
25. As quoted in Lindsey Hilsum, "A Day in Iran I Will Never Forget," June 16, 2009, Channel 4 News blog, at www.blogs.channel4.com/snowblog/2009/ 06/16/a-day-in-iran-i-will-never-forget/. See also Bahari, "Blood in Tehran," and footage of the clash shot by Bahari in "*Newsweek*'s Bahari Recalls Iran Detention," *60 Minutes*, CBS News, November 22, 2009.
26. As quoted in "Letter From Tehran: With the Marchers."
27. Communication with source in Tehran, June 16, 2009.
28. Sadegh Zibakalam interview with Al Jazeera English, June 16, 2009.
29. Interview transcripts of Ebrahim Mehtari with Anita McNaught of Al Jazeera English, Ankara, Turkey, December 1, 2009, as provided by McNaught.
30. Official results of elections, Ministry of Interior, Tehran, posted at www.moi .ir, June 14, 2009.
31. Screen shots of Rezaei vote loss in "Picture: Mohsen Rezaei's Votes Gradually Missing on the News Channel," June 13, 2009, originally at www.rezaee

.ir/fa/pages/?cid=8521 until taken down; then viewable at www.nasle2.com/post/404. News also at "The Final Results of the Tenth Round of the Presidential Election," June 13, 2009, at www.tabnak.ir/fa/pages/?cid=51716.

32. Interview with Farideh Farhi, by telephone to Hawaii, June 16, 2009; see also Scott Peterson, "Was Iran's Election Rigged? Here's What Is Known So Far," *Christian Science Monitor*, June 16, 2009.

33. As quoted in Bill Keller, "Memo From Tehran: Reverberations as Door Slams on Hope of Change," *New York Times*, June 13, 2009.

34. Mehdi Khalaji, "The Voting Manipulation Industry in Iran," PolicyWatch #1530, Washington Institute for Near East Policy, June 10, 2009.

35. Ibid.

36. Ibid.

37. "Mr. Ahmadinejad! Do You Know What Is Going On in the Interior Ministry's Election Headquarters?" May 23, 2009, originally at LahzehNews.com, then www.kamyabnews.com/fa/pages/?cid=7469.

38. Letter as quoted in Mojgan Modarres Oloom, "Mesbah-Yazdi's Decree to Rig Votes," RoozOnline, June 9, 2009.

39. Letter dated June 7, 2009, first at reformist Ghalamnews website, then "Warning By a Group of Interior Ministry Employees Toward Manipulations of Votes," at www.tabnak.ir/fa/pages/?cid=50992; also as quoted in Oloom, "Mesbah-Yazdi's Decree to Rig Votes."

40. Hilsum, "Iran: Basij Member Describes Election Abuse."

41. Eric Hooglund, "Iran's Rural Vote and Election Fraud," Agence Global, June 17, 2009, at www.agenceglobal.com/Article.asp?id=2034.

42. As quoted in "Guardian Council: Over 100% Voted in 50 Cities," PressTV, June 21, 2009, at www.presstv.ir/detail.aspx?id=98711&sectionid=351020101.

43. "Iran Accuses Western Media of Trying to Break Up Nation," Agence France-Presse, June 22, 2009.

44. Numbers as reported in Robert Tait and Julian Borger, "Analysis: Iran Election Statistics Muddy Waters Further," *Guardian*, June 15, 2009.

45. Correspondence with Iranian colleague, January 24, 2010.

46. Ali Ansari, ed., and Daniel Berman and Thomas Rintoul, "Preliminary Analysis of the Voting Figures in Iran's 2009 Presidential Election," Chatham House and the Institute of Iranian Studies, University of St. Andrews, June 21, 2009, at www.chathamhouse.org.uk/files/14234_iranelection0609.pdf.

47. Interview with analyst, Tehran, June 2009.

48. Interview with Iranian journalist, Tehran, June 13, 2009.

49. As quoted in "Dissident Cleric Warns Against US-Iran War," Agence France-Presse, November 6, 2007.

50. "The Grand Ayatollah Montazeri's Message Regarding the Presidential Election Results and the Following Incidents," June 16, 2009, at www.montazeri.com.

51. As reported in Christopher de Bellaigue, "Iran's Mullahs Divided," *Prospect*, no. 161, July 23, 2009.

52. Ayatollah Asadullah Bayat-Zanjani, as quoted in ibid.

53. Communication with source in Tehran, June 18, 2009, and site posted at the

time at www.lebasshakhsi.blogspot.com; see also Scott Peterson, "Who's Behind Iran Violence? Website Posts Video in Name-And-Shame Campaign," *Christian Science Monitor*, June 18, 2009.

54. As quoted in Thomas Erdbrink, "More Protests, Bitter Words as Iran Churns; Opponent Accuses Government of Lies, Murder," *Washington Post*, June 18, 2009.

55. Interview with Anoush Ehteshami, by telephone to Durham, England, September 18, 2009; see also Scott Peterson, "Can Iran's Top Clerics Defuse the Crisis?" *Christian Science Monitor*, June 18, 2009.

56. Khomeini, "The First Day of God's Government," in *Islam and Revolution*, pp. 265–66.

57. Khamenei on Iranian state radio, as quoted in "Iranian Leader Says His Authority Is Indisputable," Associated Press, January 26, 2000.

58. Khamenei speech, Friday prayers, June 19, 2009, translated as broadcast on PressTV.

59. Communication with opposition sympathizer in Tehran, June 19, 2009; see also Scott Peterson, "Iran's Khamenei Throws Down Hard Line with Protesters," *Christian Science Monitor*, June 19, 2009.

60. Mousavi statement, June 20, 2009, as quoted in Christopher de Bellaigue, "The Battle for Tehran," *Prospect*, no. 159, dated June 4, 2009 (incorporating events of June 20, 2009).

61. As detailed in De Bellaigue, "The Battle for Tehran."

62. As described in De Bellaigue, "Iran's Mullahs Divided."

63. As quoted in Hilsum, "Iran: Basij Member Describes Election Abuse." Second *basiji*, as quoted in Lindsey Hilsum, "Basij Militia Member's Story: Full Transcript," Channel 4 News, at www.channel4.com/news/articles/world/middle_east/basij+militia+memberaposs+story+full+transcript/3547452.

64. Communication with observer in Tehran, June 20, 2009.

65. Open letter, "We Went Today," received June 20, 2009; also published in Anonymous, "Dispatch From Tehran's Streets," *Washington Post*, June 20, 2009. See Scott Peterson, "At Stake in Iran Uprising: Trust in the Islamic Revolution," *Christian Science Monitor*, June 21, 2009.

66. Communications with author of open letter to Tehran, June 20–21, 2009.

67. Communication with source in Tehran, June 21, 2009.

68. Maysam Tavvab, "Hospitals Not to Disclose Medical Records of Victims," RoozOnline, September 22, 2009.

69. Khomeini, as quoted in Varzi, *Warring Souls*, p. 24.

70. Quotation from one-year anniversary of the Revolution, 1980, as reproduced in Chelkowski and Dabashi, *Staging a Revolution*, p. 263.

71. "BBC Documentary and Murdering a Person," *Javan*, June 24, 2009; and online at "BBC Correspondent in Tehran Hired Thugs to Kill Neda," June 24, 2009, at www.sarmayeh.net/ShowNews.php?49507.

72. According to transcript of interview with Lindsey Hilsum of Channel 4 News, London, July 30, 2009, as provided by Hilsum.

73. Among others, at www.goftaniha.org/2009/07/blog-post_19.html.

74. As described at www.valasr.ir/index.asp?cid=7&scid=10&code=5&action=5.

75. Interview with Nader Mokhtari for documentary *A Death in Tehran*, Frontline-BBC, PBS, November 17, 2009.

76. Details and Makan interview in Arash Sahami and Angus Macqueen, "Caspian Makan: 'I Cannot Believe It Yet. I Still Think I Will See Neda Again,' " *Observer*, November 15, 2009. Doubts about other aspects of Makan's story are found in Iason Athanasiadis, "Setting the Record Straight on Caspian Makan," Global-Post, April 4, 2010.

77. Detail of grave desecration and Makan quote in Martin Fletcher, "Neda Soltan's Grave Defaced as Iran Issues New Internet Restrictions," *Times* (London), January 8, 2010.

78. Interview with Ahmad Sadri, by telephone to Lake Forest, Ill., June 21, 2009; see also Peterson, "At Stake in Iran Uprising."

79. "Mousavi's Statement Number 5 to Iranian People," Kaleme, June 20, 2009, at www.kalemeh.ir/vdcf.cd1iw6dexgiaw.txt; and at www.elections.7rooz.com/englishnews/Mousavi%27s_statement_number_5_to_Iranian_people.

80. "Mousavi Says People Have Right to Protest Lies and Fraud," Agence France-Presse, June 21, 2009.

81. Khomeini, *Islamic Government*, in *Islam and Revolution*, pp. 131–32.

82. Communication with protester in Tehran, June 21, 2009.

83. As quoted in Ali Akbar Dareini and Jim Heintz, "Iran Revolutionary Guard Threatens Protesters," Associated Press, June 22, 2009.

84. Communication with Mousavi sympathizer in Tehran, June 23, 2009; see also Scott Peterson, "Iran's Supreme Strategy: Why Is Ahmadinejad the Chosen One?" *Christian Science Monitor*, June 23, 2009.

85. Ayatollah Ruhollah Khomeini, "Formation of the Council of the Islamic Revolution," January 12, 1979, in *Islam and Revolution*, p. 248.

86. Ayatollah Ruhollah Khomeini, speaking in Neauphle-le-Château in Paris, December 20, 1978, as paraphrased by Hamid Algar in *Islam and Revolution*, p. 314, n. 76.

87. As interviewed in documentary "Basijis: Iran's Culture Cops," by producer Kouross Esmaeli, posted August 28, 2007, as "Basijis: Iran's Culture Cops (VIDEO)—The Militia Backing Up Ahmadinejad," at www.current.com/items/76972552_basijis-irans-culture-cops.htm.

88. As quoted in Jon Leyne, "Will Iran's Basij Stay Loyal?" BBC News, August 13, 2009.

89. As quoted in Borzou Daragahi, "Iranian Exile Speaks Out Against Militia He Once Supported," *Los Angeles Times*, July 9, 2009.

90. "Paramilitaries to Get Police Powers," RFE/RL, *RFE/RL Iran Report* 8, no. 34, August 29, 2005, as cited in Wehrey et al., *The Rise of the Pasdaran*, p. 29.

91. As quoted in Hilsum, "Basij Militia Member's Story: Full Transcript."

92. All quotes and details of *basiji* Mehdi Moradani as reported in Farnaz Fassihi, "Inside the Iranian Crackdown," *Wall Street Journal*, July 11, 2009.

93. Wehrey et al., *The Rise of the Pasdaran*, pp. 37–38.

94. Colonel Sekhavatmand Davudi, "Rasht IRGC Commander Comments on Basij Goals in Misaq Program," *Rasht Mo'in*, FBIS IAP20070712011010, June 19, 2007, as quoted and cited in Wehrey et al., *The Rise of the Pasdaran*, p. 38.

95. As sourced in Wehrey et al., *The Rise of the Pasdaran*, pp. 44–45.

96. "Mousavi Says Pressure to Drop Challenge," Associated Press, June 25, 2009; see also Scott Peterson, "Ahmadinejad Fires Up the Anti-America Rhetoric Again," *Christian Science Monitor*, June 25, 2009.

97. See, for example, images published by the official IRNA News Agency at www .irna.ir/View/FullStory/Photo/?NewsId=567619, and at www.takseda1385 .blogspot.com/2009/06/blog-post_30.html. The amateurish recounting exercise further undermined the promise of Kamran Daneshjoo, the head of Iran's election commission, who said before the vote: "We consider guarding people's votes as a religious duty. We are not afraid of any supervision based on law because we have assured the people and the candidates we will guard the votes." (Farhad Pouladi, "475 Iranians Bid For Presidency," Agence France-Presse, May 10, 2009.)

98. Weblog of Mohammad Reza Nasab-Abdollahi shut down; see images at, among others, "Four Ballot Boxes Discovered in Shiraz," Parleman News, July 2, 2009, at www.parlemannews.ir/index.aspx?n=1520.

99. Communication with Tara Mahtafar, to Tehran, June 28, 2009; see also Scott Peterson, "After a Lull, Protests Revive in Iran," *Christian Science Monitor*, June 29, 2009.

100. Tara Mahtafar, "Beheshti's Ghost," Tehran Bureau, June 28, 2009, at www .tehranbureau.com/shahid-beheshti-calling/.

101. Communication with Tara Mahtafar, to Tehran, June 29, 2009; see also Peterson, "After a Lull, Protests Revive in Iran."

102. As quoted at "Head of Sepah: Basij [Must] Not Wait for the Superior's Order— [They Should] Take Action Directly," Aut News, October 3, 2009, at www .autnews.de//node/3303. Fear of the regime falling had eventually become so great, according to one young IRGC security logistics officer attached to the Supreme Leader's compound—who fled Iran in January 2010—that a jetliner had been put on standby for escape.

     "They were terrified. They'd prepared themselves to leave the country and flee to Syria, just in case the regime was to collapse. Khamenei's Airbus 330 was waiting, ready to get them out of Iran," Mohammad Hossein Torkaman told the *Guardian*. (Angus Stickler and Maggie O'Kane, "Iran's Revolutionary Guards Point to Fresh Dissent Within Oppressive Regime," *Guardian*, June 11, 2010, and a 16-minute film co-produced by the *Guardian* and The Bureau of Investigative Journalism [City University in London] during a three-month investigation, both at www.guardian.co.uk/world/2010/jun/11/iran -election-revolutionary-guard.)

103. As quoted in Borzou Daragahi, "Iran's Revolutionary Guard Acknowledges Taking a Bigger Role in Nation's Security," *Los Angeles Times*, July 6, 2009.

104. As quoted in ibid.

105. Algar, "Religious Forces in Twentieth-Century Iran," p. 762.

106. Jalal Al-e Ahmad, *Occidentosis*, p. 74; and as quoted in Algar, "Religious Forces in Twentieth-Century Iran," p. 763.

107. Katzman, *The Warriors of Islam*, pp. 1, 18–19, 80.

108. Ibid., p. 10.

109. Bakhash, *The Reign of the Ayatollahs*, p. 225.

110. Ibid., p. 220.

111. Khamenei, as quoted in R. W. Apple, "Khomeini's Grip Appears at Its Tightest," *New York Times*, November 21, 1982.

112. Bakhash, *The Reign of the Ayatollahs*, p. 222.

113. Ayatollah Ruhollah Khomeini, *The Last Message: The Political and Divine Will of His Holiness Imam Khomeini*, will dated February 15, 1983 (Tehran: Institute for Compilation and Publication of the Works of Imam Khomeini, 1992), pp. 68, 70–71.

114. Article 150, "Constitution of the Islamic Republic of Iran."

115. Safavi in *Jameah* newspaper, as quoted in "Iran's Revolutionary Guards Chief Threatens to Crack Down on Liberal Dissent," Agence France-Presse, April 29, 1998, and "Iran Guards Chief Blasts Liberalization, Critics," Reuters, April 29, 1998.

116. *Hamshahri* as quoted in "Iran Guards Commander Has More Tough Words," Reuters, June 4, 1998.

117. "Ayatollah Alam al-Hoda, Member of Assembly of Experts: The Claim That the Guards and the Basij as Military Forces Should Not Intervene in Politics [Are] the Words of the Enemies of God," *Ansar* (Tehran), at www.ansarnews .com/?usr=news/detail&nid=2426; see also "Friday Prayers Leader of Mashhad Demanded Basij and Revolutionary Guards Presence in Politics," *Mizan* (Tehran), November 21, 2007; both as quoted and cited in Ali Alfoneh, "Iran's Parliamentary Elections and the Revolutionary Guards' Creeping Coup d'Etat," American Enterprise Institute—Middle Eastern Outlook, February 21, 2008.

118. "Representative of the Supreme Jurist in the Guards: Strategic Voting Is a Political Jihad. It Is Among the Important Duties of the Elites, Such as the Guards and the Basijis to Introduce Values and Characteristics," ISNA, December 31, 2007, as quoted and cited in Alfoneh, "Iran's Parliamentary Elections and the Revolutionary Guards' Creeping Coup d'Etat."

119. "Revolutionary Guards Commander of Qazvin: Pay Attention So the Sixth Parliament Is Not Repeated," Noandish, January 3, 2008, at www.noandish .com/com.php?id=13287; as quoted and cited in Alfoneh, "Iran's Parliamentary Elections and the Revolutionary Guards' Creeping Coup d'Etat."

120. Alfoneh, "Iran's Parliamentary Elections and the Revolutionary Guards' Creeping Coup d'Etat."

121. *Political Questions and Answers*, published by the ideological-political unit of the Defense Ministry of Iran, at www.siyasi.ir/content/view/2973/1, as quoted and cited in Ali Alfoneh, "Indoctrination of the Revolutionary Guards," American Enterprise Institute—Middle Eastern Outlook, February 20, 2009.

122. Alfoneh, "Indoctrination of the Revolutionary Guards."

123. Interview with Massoumeh Torfeh, by telephone to London, June 21, 2009; see also Peterson, "Iran's Supreme Strategy," *Christian Science Monitor*, June 23, 2009.

124. As quoted in Ali Akbar Dareini, "Iran President Confirmed Without Symbolic Kiss," Associated Press, August 3, 2009.

125. Among reports see Iason Athanasiadis, "Opposition Skips Out on Ahmadinejad's Swearing-In," *Christian Science Monitor*, August 4, 2009.

126. Fars News Agency, as quoted in Farideh Farhi, "Is Commander Jafari Stupid?" at www.icga.blogspot.com/2009/09/is-commander-jafari-stupid.html.

127. Fars News Agency, as translated and quoted in Muhammad Sahimi, "IRGC's Deeply-Rooted Animosity for Reformists," Tehran Bureau, September 4, 2009, at www.pbs.org/wgbh/pages/frontline/tehranbureau/2009/09/irgcs-deeply -rooted-animosity-for-reformists.html.

128. Farhi, "Is Commander Jafari Stupid?"

129. Interview with Alireza Nader, by telephone to Washington, November 23, 2009; see also Scott Peterson, "Iran's Revolutionary Guard Tightens Grip," *Christian Science Monitor*, December 6, 2009.

130. Multiple sources, including "After Establishing a Bank, Iran's Revolution-ary Guards Purchase Telecom Company," RoozOnline, September 29, 2009; and Brian Murphy, "Iran Media Plan Stirs Talk of Elite Force at Helm," Associ-ated Press, November 16, 2009. See also Peterson, "Iran's Revolutionary Guard Tightens Grip."

131. Interview with Ali Alfoneh, communication to Copenhagen, Denmark, Novem-ber 24, 2009; see also Peterson, "Iran's Revolutionary Guard Tightens Grip."

132. As noted in De Bellaigue, *In the Rose Garden of the Martyrs*, p. 235.

133. Abrahamian, *Tortured Confessions*, p. 227.

134. Abtahi's wife as quoted by Mohammad Reza Tabesh, in "Tabesh: They Give Pills to Mohammad Ali Abtahi," Tabnak, August 1, 2009, at www.tabnak.ir/ fa/pages/?cid=57833; see also "Interviewing Fahimeh Mousavinejad, Abtahi's Wife: 'We Observed the Peak of Lack of Principle,'" Aut News, August 2, 2009, at www.autnews.de//node/1176.

135. "Zeidabadi Had Been Driven to Insanity," RoozOnline, August 19, 2009, at www.roozonline.com/persian/interview/interview-item/article/2009/august/ 19//-8c4e67e213.html; see also "Zeidabadi Seemed Insane Because of Pres-sure," RoozOnline, August 21, 2009.

136. Indictment of August 8, 2009, by Judge Abdol-Qasem Salavati, head of Sec-tion 15 of the Islamic Revolutionary Court, as quoted in Fereshteh Qazi, RoozOnline, August 9, 2009, as translated by Evan Siegel in "The Complete Text of the Indictment of the Second Group of Accused in the Project for a Velvet Coup," Iran Rises, August 18, 2009, at www.qlineorientalist.com/Iran Rises/the-complete-text-of-the-indictment-of-the-second-group-of-accused-in -the-project-for-a-velvet-coup/.

137. All details and quotations in Maziar Bahari, "118 Days, 12 Hours, 54 Minutes," *Newsweek*, November 21, 2009.

138. Fredrik Dahl and Reza Derakhshi, "Son of Iran Candidate Ally Died After Beating: Report," Reuters, August 31, 2009.

139. As quoted in ibid.

140. Scott Peterson, "In Iran, Death By Poison Salad and a Hair-Cream Overdose," *Christian Science Monitor*, December 3, 2009; details of salad death from Iranian opposition news sources, as reported in Lee Keath, "Iran Whistleblower Died From Drug-Laden Salad," Associated Press, December 2, 2009.

141. As quoted in Keath, "Iran Whistleblower Died From Drug-Laden Salad."

142. As quoted in De Bellaigue, *In the Rose Garden of the Martyrs*, p. 232.

143. As translated in "Iran: The Karroubi Letter to Rafsanjani on Abuse of De-tainees," dated July 31, 2009, Enduring America, August 10, 2009, at www

.enduringamerica.com/2009/08/10/iran-the-karroubi-letter-to-rafsanjani-on
-abuse-of-detainees/.

144. "Iran: The Karroubi Letter to Rafsanjani on Abuse of Detainees."
145. As translated in Borzou Daragahi, "Iran Roiled by Prison Abuse Claims," *Los Angeles Times*, August 12, 2009.
146. "Iran: The Karroubi Letter to Rafsanjani on Abuse of Detainees."
147. As quoted in Borzou Daragahi, "Iranian Official Denies Reports That Election Protesters Were Raped in Prison," *Los Angeles Times*, August 12, 2009.
148. "Iran Police Find No Evidence of Rape in Closed Jail," Agence France-Presse, October 7, 2009.
149. "Revealed by a Member of the Parliament's Special Committee: It Is Established That Some of the Detainees Are Raped with Batons and Bottles," Parleman News, August 26, 2009, at www.parlemannews.ir/index.aspx?n=2937; and as quoted in "Iran: Election Contested, Repression Compounded," Amnesty International (London), MDE 13/123/2009, released December 9, 2009, p. 51.
150. As quoted in Nazila Fathi, "Iranian Protester Flees After Telling of Torture," *New York Times*, September 26, 2009.
151. Transcript of interviews by Ivan Watson of CNN, Ankara, Turkey, September 28, 2009, as provided by Watson.
152. All details and quotes of Mohammad Kamrani in Daragahi, "Iran Roiled by Prison Abuse Claims." Victim is named "Mohammad K." in story to protect victim's family at the time, according to Daragahi communication with author (January 25, 2010).
153. See, for example, "Burial of Another Martyr of Iranian Green Movement: Martyr Mohammad Kamrani," July 18, 2009, at www.mowjcamp.com/article/id/924. After this opposition website was taken down, the story remained on the site of the Committee of Human Rights Reporters, at www.schrr.net/spip.php?article4627.
154. All details and quotes of "Ardeshir," a pseudonym, in Martin Fletcher, "Raped and Beaten for Daring to Question President Ahmadinejad's Election," *Times* (London), September 11, 2009.
155. Ebrahim Mehtari, interviewed by Anita McNaught in Ankara, Turkey, "Iranians Flee For Their Own Safety," Al Jazeera English, as broadcast December 10, 2009.
156. "Medical Report for Ebrahim Mehtari (Translation)," Appendix 1, "Iran: Election Contested, Repression Compounded."
157. Ibid., pp. 48–49.
158. Interview transcripts of Ebrahim Mehtari with Anita McNaught, Al Jazeera English, Ankara, Turkey, November 27, 2009, and December 1, 2009, as provided by McNaught; see also Anita McNaught, "Focus: Interview: 'My Torturers Deserve Pity,' " December 11, 2009, at www.english.aljazeera.net/focus/2009/12/2009121182756219661.html.
159. Interview with Ebrahim Mehtari, Ankara, Turkey, December 17, 2009.
160. Unattributed special report, "Karroubi: Do Not Request Documents from Me; *Kayhan*'s Special Report on the Liars' and Document Fabricators' Wave

of Scandal," *Kayhan*, September 12, 2009, at www.kayhannews.ir/880621/3 .htm#other304.

161. Elise Auerbach, Amnesty International Iran specialist, as quoted in "Amnesty International Says Iran Focused on Covering Up Horrific Abuses Committed During Post-Election Period," Amnesty International (London) press release, December 9, 2009; see also Scott Peterson, "Iran Protests: Amnesty International Details Abuse of Protesters," *Christian Science Monitor*, December 9, 2009.

162. "Iran: Election Contested, Repression Compounded," p. 59.

163. As heard at Jerusalem Day protests, noted among other sources in Jim Sciutto, "Anti-Israel Day Becomes Anti-Iran Day," ABC News, September 18, 2009.

164. Robert F. Worth, "Iran Charges 12 at Prison Over Death of Protesters," *New York Times*, December 19, 2009.

165. Investigation details in Martin Fletcher, " 'Torture, Murder and Rape'— Iran's Way of Breaking the Opposition," *Times* (London), September 18, 2009.

166. As quoted in ibid.

167. Interview with Ervand Abrahamian, by telephone to New York, December 9, 2009; see also Peterson, "Iran Protests: Amnesty International Details Abuse of Protesters."

168. See "Meeting Between One of Kahrizak Victims' Fathers and the Head of Judicial Branch," Ayande News, September 12, 2009, at www.ayandenews.com/news/12575; see also "Beheshti: They Have Deployed the Identified Thugs of the Social Security Plan in the Detention Centers," Parleman News, August 1, 2009, at www.parlemannews.ir/print.aspx?n=2338.

169. First *basiji* as quoted in Hilsum, "Iran: Basij Member Describes Election Abuse"; second *basiji,* as quoted in Hilsum, "Basij Militia Member's Story: Full Transcript."

170. "MPs 'Snub' Ahmadinejad Poll Party," BBC News, June 25, 2009.

171. As quoted in "Khamenei Says Iran Won't Be Deceived by US," Reuters, November 3, 2009; see also Scott Peterson, "Iran Warns Opposition on Eve of 30th Anniversary of US Embassy Seizure," *Christian Science Monitor*, November 4, 2009.

172. As quoted in Ali Akbar Dareini, "Ahmadinejad: Iran's Enemies a 'Mosquito,' " Associated Press, November 1, 2009.

173. "Iran: Full Translation of Mousavi Statement for 13 Aban Demonstrations," October 31, 2009, drawn from the Facebook site linked to Mousavi and translated by Enduring America, at www.enduringamerica.com/2009/10/31/iran-mousavi-statement-for-13-aban-demonstrations-31-october/.

174. Interview with Ali Ansari, by telephone to St. Andrews, Scotland, October 31, 2009; see also Peterson, "Iran Warns Opposition."

175. As translated by PressTV, live broadcast, November 4, 2009.

176. Communication with Iranian journalist in Tehran, November 4, 2009; see also Peterson, "Iran Warns Opposition."

177. Communication with witness along Karim Khan near Vali Asr, Tehran, November 4, 2009.

178. Communication with witness at Abbas Abad, Tehran, November 4, 2009.

179. Communication with witness north of Haft-e Tir, Tehran, November 4, 2009.

180. As quoted in "The Leader of the Revolution: University Professors Are the

Commanders at the Soft War Front," IRNA, August 30, 2009, at www.irna .ir/View/FullStory/?NewsId=658713; also at "Statements at the Meeting with the University Professors," August 30, 2009, at www.leader.ir/langs/fa/index .php?p=bayanat&id=5814.

181. As quoted in "Khatami's Criticism of Fascist Reaction Against Liberalism," September 6, 2009, at www.zamaaneh.com/news/2009/09/post_10374.html; see also Borzou Daragahi, "Iran Announces Plan to Purge Universities of Western Influence," *Los Angeles Times*, September 7, 2009.

182. Details of purges in communication with source in Tehran, September 2009. Iranian diplomat details as quoted and reported in Margaret Coker, "Inside Iran's Crackdown: Diplomat Alleges Vote-Rigging, Pressure to Spy," *Wall Street Journal*, March 19, 2010.

183. Communication with professor in Tehran, September 17, 2009.

184. "Iran Clerics Start Taking Control of Schools," Associated Press, November 25, 2009.

185. Interview with "Dr. Farzad," a pseudonym, outside Iran, September 2009.

186. Zakani on June 14, 2009, as quoted in "Announced at the Closed Session of MPs: Reading of the Report by the Parliament's Fact-Finding Committee," *Etemaad*, June 18, 2009, at www.magiran.com/npview.asp?ID=1883250.

187. As quoted in "Zakani: Karroubi's Correspondence Brings Propandistic Activities to Mind," Fars News Agency, August 15, 2009, at /www.jahannews .com/vdcj8tem.uqevozsffu.html.

188. Scott Peterson, "A Reformist in Conservative Clothing?" *Christian Science Monitor*, February 18, 2000.

189. Ayatollah Ruhollah Khomeini, "Muharram: The Triumph of Blood Over the Sword," November 23, 1978, in *Islam and Revolution*, p. 242.

190. Images as in Samnak Aghaei, "Coup Agents Confused by 'Bill-Writing,' " RoozOnline, October 28, 2009, at www.roozonline.com/english/news/news item/article/2009/october/28/coup-agents-confused-by-bill-writing.html.

191. Opposition websites, as described in "Green Banknotes Another Frustration for Authorities," October 13, 2009, at mowjcamp.com before site was shut down.

192. "Iran: Full Translation of Mousavi Statement for 13 Aban Demonstrations."

193. "Translated Text: The Indictment in the Tehran Trials," as translated by Evan Siegel in Iran Rises, as published at Fars News Agency and posted August 12, 2009, by Enduring America, at www.enduringamerica.com/2009/08/12/ translated-text-the-indictment-in-the-tehran-trials/#more-15121.

194. "198 Methods of Nonviolent Action," compiled by Gene Sharp and first published in *The Politics of Nonviolent Action, Vol. 2: The Methods of Nonviolent Action* (Boston: Porter Sargent, 1973), at www.aeinstein.org/organizations103a.html.

195. Interview with Gene Sharp, by telephone to Boston, December 11, 2009; see also Scott Peterson, "Iran Protesters: the Harvard Professor Behind Their Tactics," *Christian Science Monitor*, December 29, 2009.

196. Interview with Karim Sadjadpour, by telephone to Washington, D.C., December 16, 2009; see also Peterson, "Iran Protesters: the Harvard Professor Behind Their Tactics."

197. "Iranian Intelligence Ministry Broadcast Encouraging People to Snitch on

Spies Features 'John McCain' Masterminding a Velvet Revolution in Iran from the White House," Khuzestan TV (Iran), February 5, 2008, as translated by Middle East Media Research Institute, Video 1678, as posted at www.memritv.org/clip/en/1678.htm. Gene Sharp's video reply, posted as "A Conversation with Gene Sharp," at www.youtube.com/watch?y=54oUnvDPWFA.

198. Ervand Abrahamian, posting on Gulf/2000, "Re: Nonviolence in Iran," December 31, 2009, used with permission.

199. Anonymous Green Movement activist, posting on Gulf/2000, "Re: Nonviolence in Iran," December 31, 2009.

200. Details and quotes from Sadegh Shojaii, interviewed by telephone to Nevsehir, Turkey, by Noushin Hoseiny, January 25, 2010. See also Srdja Popovic, Andrej Milivojevic, and Slobodan Djinovic, *Non-Violent Struggle—50 Crucial Points; A Strategic Approach to Everyday Tactics,* Centre for Applied Non-Violent Action and Strategies, Belgrade, 2006; and Steve Stecklow and Farnaz Fassihi, "Thousands Flee Iran as Noose Tightens," *Wall Street Journal,* December 11, 2009.

201. Iranian Internet spying capabilities as described in Christopher Rhoads and Loretta Chao, "Iran's Web Spying Aided by Western Technology," *Wall Street Journal,* June 22, 2009, at www.online.wsj.com/article/SB124562668777335653.html.

202. Interview with Mohsen Sazegara, by telephone to Virginia, December 14, 2009; see also Peterson, "Iran Protesters: the Harvard Professor Behind Their Tactics." A number of Persian-language websites also made Sharp's books, excerpts, or videos available for download, including "The Green Revolution of the Iranian Nation," at www.doorandish.wordpress.com/2009/08/07/download-from-dictatorship-to-democrac/; "Democracy Through Violence, Yes or No?" on "One of Many Greens" blog at www.sabziazsabzha.blogspot.com/2009/11/blog-post_06.html; and "Who's Gene Sharp?" on Shabname (Night Letter) blog, August 2, 2009, at www.shabnameh.wordpress.com/2009/08/02/whoisgenesharp/.

203. Interview with Ali Ansari, by telephone to St. Andrews, Scotland, October 31, 2009.

204. "Questioning the Election is the Greatest Crime," October 28, 2009, at www.fararu.com/vdcgyq9w.ak9tz4prra.html and www.alef.ir/1388/content/view/56152; using translation in "Iran News Roundup," October 29, 2009, Iran Tracker, American Enterprise Institute, at www.irantracker.org/roundup/iran-news-roundup-oct-29-2009.

205. "Supreme Leader's Reaction to One of the Elites' Outspoken Criticism," Alef News Agency, October 29, 2009, at www.alef.ir/1388/content/view/56087/, as translated in "Iran News Roundup," October 30, 2009, Iran Tracker, American Enterprise Institute, at www.irantracker.org/roundup/iran-news-roundup-oct-30-2009.

206. Ibid.

207. Interview with Ali Ansari, by telephone to St. Andrews, Scotland, October 31, 2009.

208. Khomeini, *Islamic Government,* in *Islam and Revolution,* p. 147.

209. Interview with Ebrahim Mehtari, Ankara, Turkey, December 17, 2009.

210. Statement on reformist website Rahesabz.net, as quoted in Hiedeh Farmani,

"Iran Police, Mourners Clash After Montazeri Funeral: Website," Agence France-Presse, December 21, 2009.

211. Parisa Hafezi and Fredrik Dahl, "Grand Ayatollah Montazeri's Funeral Turns Into Protest," Reuters, December 21, 2009.

212. As reported by Rahesabz.net, in Farmani, "Iran Police, Mourners Clash After Montazeri Funeral: Website."

213. As described to me by Iranian journalist witness in Qom, December 21, 2009; see also Special Correspondent in Qom, and Scott Peterson (in Istanbul), "Iran Opposition Energized by Montazeri Funeral in Qom, Say Eyewitnesses," *Christian Science Monitor*, December 21, 2009.

214. All quotations and chants as described by witness in Qom, December 21, 2009; see also "Iran Opposition Energized."

215. As described on Kaleme, December 21, 2009, at www.kaleme.org/1388/09/30/ klm-6462; see also "Mousavi's Car 'Attacked' On Way Back From Funeral," Reuters, December 21, 2009. Ashura death toll at, for example, "Jaras Exclusive: Total of 37 Killed on Ashura," December 30, 2009, at www.rahesabz.net/ story/6669.

216. As quoted in "Hojjatoleslam Saeedi at the Conference of Defense Methods in the Soft War: Today Al-Samiris Try to Deceive the Nation and Deviate From the Revolution," Fars News Agency, January 12, 2010, at www.farsnews.com/ newstext.php?nn=8810220752.

217. Mousavi statement on Kaleme website, as quoted in Parisa Hafezi, "Opposition Head Mousavi: Iran in 'Serious Crisis,'" Reuters, January 1, 2010.

218. Interview with Massoumeh Torfeh, by telephone to London, October 30, 2009.

219. As described in Melissa Eddy and Lee Keath, "Daughter of Ahmadinejad Adviser Seeks Asylum," Associated Press, October 13, 2009.

220. As quoted in "They Said It Would Be Better if I Stayed Here," Local, October 14, 2009, at www.thelocal.de/society/20091014-22579.html.

221. As quoted in "It's More than a Year That I Don't Have Any Relations With My Daughter; Paternal Advice to Narges," October 13, 2009, Mehr News, at www .mehrnews.com/fa/NewsDetail.aspx?NewsID=964160.

222. Narges Kalhor, "Narges Kalhor: Little Brother," Tehran Bureau, November 20, 2009, at www.pbs.org/wgbh/pages/frontline/tehranbureau/2009/11/narges -kalhor-little-brother.html.

223. As quoted in " 'Medea' Is the Code Name of the Enemy's Soft Operation Over Iran," October 21, 2009, Fars News Agency, at www.farsnews.com/newstext .php?nn=8807290606.

224. Narges Kalhor interview with Hana Makhmalbaf, October 12, 2009, at www .youtube.com/watch?v=PR6shJzZ5Yw; as translated in "English Translation of Narges Kalhor Interview," October 14, 2009, Persian2English's Blog, at www/persian2english.wordpress.com/2009/10/14/english-translations-of -narges-kalhor-interview/.

225. Interview with the Sage, communication to Tehran, October 31, 2009.

226. Scott Peterson, "Iran Protesters Say Torn Khomeini Photos Were Staged," *Christian Science Monitor*, December 14, 2009.

227. As quoted in ibid.

228. Interview with Iranian journalist, in communication to Tehran, December 14, 2009.

229. Interview with Ali Ansari, by telephone to St. Andrews, Scotland, December 14, 2009; see also Peterson, "Iran Protesters Say Torn Khomeini Photos Were Staged."

230. Interview with Ahmad Sadri, by telephone to Lake Forest, Ill., February 9, 2010. Details and further quotations in Scott Peterson, "Iran Braces for Demonstration Showdown: Will the Future of Iran Be Changed?" *Christian Science Monitor*, February 10, 2010; and Scott Peterson, "Iran Opposition Protests Fizzle in Face of Overwhelming Security," *Christian Science Monitor*, February 11, 2010.

231. Satellite image of anniversary day rally at Azadi (Freedom) Square, with large gaps evident in the crowd, as published at www.rahesabz.info/story/10146. Video showing lines of buses used to bring pro-regime supporters at www.youtube.com/watch?v=Rua6TL4yzzE.

232. Interview with the Sage, communication to Tehran, February 11, 2009.

233. Communication with Green Movement sympathizer in Tehran, February 11, 2010.

234. Ebadi interview as quoted in Ian MacDougall, "AP Interview: Nobel Laureate Shirin Ebadi Says Iran Opposition Still Strong Despite Clampdown," Associated Press, February 14, 2010. Details of confiscation of the Nobel medal and diploma—the first time ever in the 108-year history of the prize—and its eventual return in Nasser Karimi and Ian MacDougall, "Shirin Ebadi: Nobel Laureate's Medal Confiscated by Iran," Associated Press, November 26, 2009, and Louise Nordstrom, "Sweden, Norway: Nobel Medal Returned to Ebadi," Associated Press, December 10, 2009.

235. Interview with the Sage, in communication to Tehran, October 31, 2009.

236. Interview with the Sage, Tehran, February 14, 2002.

237. Audio and videos of the February 1, 1979, speech, such as "Khomeini: We Will Provide You Free Electricity," and "Ahmadinejad: We Will Bring Oil To Your Table," October 18, 2009, at www.iranianuk.com/article.php?id=42828; also quoted in Khalaji, "Apocalyptic Politics," p. 27, n. 3; for context see Asaf Bayat, *Street Politics: Poor People's Movements in Iran* (New York: Columbia University Press, 1997), p. 99.

    Remarkably, this introductory portion of the well-known Behesht-e Zahra cemetery speech does not appear in the "complete" version published by the Islamic Revolution Documents Center at www.irdc.ir/fa/content/4958/default.aspx, or in another standard source of Khomeini's declarations, in this case "Address at Bihisht-i Zahra," February 1, 1979 (text incorrectly states date as February 2, 1979), in *Islam and Revolution*, pp. 254–60.

EPILOGUE: THE POLE OF CAIN, THE POLE OF ABEL

Epigraphs. Der Spiegel, Paris, November 9, 1978, as translated in Matini, "The Most Truthful Individual in Recent History"; Quran 17:81, as quoted on a first anniversary of the Revolution congratulations poster produced by the Embassy of the Islamic Republic of Iran in Washington, February 11, 1980, as reproduced in Shiva Balaghi and Lynn Gumpert, eds., *Picturing Iran: Art, Society and Revolution* (London: I. B. Taurus, 2002), p. 88; Ayatollah Seyyed Ali Khamenei, speech in Mashhad, March 21, 2009.

1. Visits to Martyrs' Museum, Tehran, December 16, 2006, and February 3, 2009; see also Scott Peterson, "In Tehran's Martyrs' Museum, Iran Courts New Believers," *Christian Science Monitor*, June 6, 2007.

2. Biographical details and Khomeini quotes from Martyr Dr. Mostafa Chamran, "Self-Construction and Development," booklet published by Martyr Chamran Foundation (Tehran, 2003), pp. 6–14.

3. Visit to national military museum, Saad Abad, Tehran, March 17, 2008.

4. Interview with source (with post-death raid details based on information from Chamran's wife), Tehran, August 17, 2008.

5. Chamran grave details and quotations drawn from visit to Behesht-e Zahra cemetery, Tehran, February 6, 2009. During my first visit to Chamran's grave on September 20, 1996, I was told by another visitor, "Do you know this tomb? He was one of the truest—I come to meet him once a week. The war was a conflict between truth and lies, and it continues. It will go on forever. I believe that—we believe that—Islam is the right way, the true way. And when comes the end of time, we will win. It will go on forever, this war."

6. Interview with Reza Borji, *Sorush*, July 7, 2001, as quoted and cited in Farhi, "The Antinomies of Iran's War Generation," p. 113.

7. Interview with Massoumeh Delavar, Tehran, March 8, 2007; see also Scott Peterson, "Iran's Successful Blend: Charity, Ideology," *Christian Science Monitor*, March 9, 2007.

8. Interview with Hamidreza Taraghi, Tehran, March 6, 2007.

9. Figures from Komiteh Emdad officials, and also drawn from www.emdad.ir/.

10. Ervand Abrahamian, "Why the Islamic Republic Has Survived," *Middle East Report*, no. 250 (Spring 2009).

11. Algar, "Religious Forces in Twentieth-Century Iran," pp. 757–58.

12. Visit to Nodbeh prayer session, Tehran, August 22, 2008.

13. Interview with "Tooska," a pseudonym, Tehran, February 11, 2009.

14. Party in Tehran, February 9, 2009.

15. Visit and interviews at Jamaran prayer hall, Tehran, February 7, 2009; see also Scott Peterson, "Khomeini Revered as Iran's Revolution Hits 30," *Christian Science Monitor*, February 10, 2009.

16. Interview with Zahra Eshraghi, Tehran, February 8, 2009; see also Peterson, "Khomeini Revered as Iran's Revolution Hits 30."

17. Interview with Dawud Salahuddin, aka David Belfield, Tehran, February 8, 2009.

18. Interview with Seyyed Rahim Miriam, Jamaran, Tehran, March 10, 2008.

19. The Shah in *U.S. News & World Report*, June 26, 1978, as quoted and cited in Fereydoun Hoveyda, *The Fall of the Shah: The Inside Story by the Shah's Former Ambassador to the United Nations* (London: Weidenfeld & Nicolson, 1980), p. 5.

20. As quoted in "President: Iranians 10 Times Stronger Than Before," IRNA, December 22, 2009.

21. As quoted in Hilsum, "Basij Militia Member's Story: Full Transcript."

22. As reported in *Iran* and *Nowrouz*, July 10, 2001, as quoted and cited in Farhi, "The Antinomies of Iran's War Generation," p. 118, n. 23.

23. "Haji Bakhshi at the Hospital in Bed," Fars News Agency, December 30, 2008, at www.farsnews.net/imgrep.php?nn=8710102090; and "Haji Bakhshi in Hospital," video at www.irannegah.com/Video.aspx?id=976.

24. As described in "Haji Bakhshi's Presence Among the Demonstrators on Qods Day," Fars News Agency, September 18, 2009, at www.farsnews.net/newstext .php?nn=8806270272.

25. "Thoughts on Iran—The Lion and the Cage," Secret/NoForn, Department of State Document 97 ABUDHABI3777, Ref: State 15528, Classified by David D. Pearce, Consul General, May 21, 1997.

26. Details of Iranian intelligence efforts abroad in Farnaz Fassihi, "Iranian Crackdown Goes Global," *Wall Street Journal*, December 3, 2009.

27. As quoted in "Brig. Gen. Masoud Jazayeri: Iranian Peoples' Cry of 'Death to America' Is Turned into an All-Embracing Global Model," *Kayhan*, November 4, 2009, at www.kayhannews.ir/880813/14.HTM#other1401.

28. Filmed by Iranian intelligence agents, Istanbul, September 29, 2009.

29. Two Iranian intelligence agents seen as members of Iranian consulate staff, during Ahmadinejad press conference, Istanbul, November 9, 2009.

30. As described in interview with Ali Rajabi, Tehran, November 25, 2007.

Index

About the Author

SCOTT PETERSON is the Istanbul Bureau Chief for *The Christian Science Monitor*. He has been the paper's Middle East correspondent, based in Amman, Jordan, and its Moscow Bureau Chief. He has journeyed to Iran more than thirty times since 1996 and won a Citation for Excellence from the Overseas Press Club of America for his reporting from Iraq. He is the author of the widely acclaimed *Me Against My Brother: At War in Somalia, Sudan, and Rwanda*, and a photographer for Getty Images.